Brendan Sweeney

Published by CQN Books, Scotland.
CQN Books is a trading name for CQN Publishing Ltd.

Copyright Brendan Sweeney. All rights reserved.

First published in the United Kingdom in 2015 by CQN Books.
ISBN 978-0-9934360-0-0

For further information please email david@cqnpublishing.co.uk

A catalogue for this book is available from the British Library.

Cover design by Ritchie Feenie

Internal design and typesetting by
Stephen Cameron
stephen@intocreative.co.uk

Printed and bound by CPI Group (UK) Ltd, Croydon CR0 4YY

Special thanks to Paul Brennan and David Faulds at CQN Books.
For more information please visit www.celticquicknews.co.uk

Acknowledgements

Writing this book has been a labour of love from start to finish and I hope you, the reader, share even a fraction of the excitement I felt in researching this work. You will notice that "we" and "us" are used in the description of our club over 125 years ago throughout this book. This is intentional. Of course we weren't there, but we ARE Celtic: past, present or future.

I would like to thank the authors of the many Celtic history books who have provided the benchmark and the inspiration for this humble tome.

The Celtic Graves Society are an organisation very close to my heart and they are due a very special mention for the work being done to cherish the memories of past Celtic players, staff and management. The Celtic Wikipedia website is another incredible resource on all things Celtic, put together by the hard toil and dedication of the Celtic support. Both of these Celtic fan initiatives have provided a huge inspiration to myself and many others.

I would like to thank in particular the following very special people:

Lisbon Lion Jim Craig for writing the foreword and for his sage-like words of advice: Paul McQuade for the onerous task of the proof reading as well as his timely advice and encouragement: Ritchie Feenie from Kinghorn Creative for the unique cover design: Stephen Cameron for the layout: and last but not least Paul Brennan and David Faulds from Celtic Quick News. All of the above gave of their time way above the call of duty, simply because it was Celtic.

I would also like to thank the staff at the Mitchell Library, Glasgow for their assistance during my research.

Any errors in the writing of this book are, of course, entirely my own.

Dedication

I would like to dedicate this work to my family who gave me the gift of Celtic.

My loving and devoted parents from dear old Donegal who are sadly no longer with us and are greatly missed: Thomas and Nora Sweeney, (nee McElhinney): my big brother Anthony and my younger sister Jacinta. I give special mention to my beloved younger brother Joseph after his second major brain injury in seven years, so soon after recovering from bowel cancer.

To Joe:

Let angels stand guard
Until it's time to rise
And softly sing Irish lullabies

Finally I would like to thank my wonderful wife Elaine, daughter Sinead and son Declan for putting up with me!

Foreword

by Jim Craig, Lisbon Lion

As a founding member of the Celtic Graves Society, Brendan Sweeney and his colleagues have performed an excellent job in both recognising and honouring the Celts of yesteryear. Now, In his new book, he has provided us with an impressive review of the first four years of Celtic's existence at the original Celtic Park , as well as the reasons behind our birth.

Brendan has obviously been busy doing an extensive amount of research and now relates the great moments – plus the trials and tribulations – of Celtic Football Club in those early years. It is an excellent read and I can thoroughly recommend the book to every Celtic fan.

INDEX OF ILLUSTRATIONS

20   Hugh Darroch

21   Joseph Francis McGroary

22   James Curtis

23   John Charles MacDonald

24   Joseph Shaughnessy

25   William McKillop

26   John O'Hara

27   Pat Welsh

28   David Meikleham

29   John Herbert McLaughlin

30   James McKay

31   Brother Dorotheus

32   Willie Maley

33   Tom Maley

34   The original Celtic Park adjacent to the north east corner of the current ground and sketched from the corner nearest to the current Celtic Park.

35   The original ground was bounded by Janefield Cemetery on the west, Springfield Road (then Dalmarnock St) on the east and Janefield St on the south.

36   The original footprint showing an overlay of the pitch running north/south, the pavillion on the eastern touchline and a stand on the cemetery side. Also marked with the main entrance on Springfield Rd and seven smaller entrances, as well as three entrances on Janefield St, one member's gate nearest to the current Celtic Park and two bigger gates for entrance/exit.

37   The same original footprint overlayed onto current google maps.

38   Hibernian v Cowlairs at the original Celtic Park on 8th May 1888. Celtic Park is open for business.

39   Dr John Conway's patron ticket, significantly for season 1887/88.

40   The original Celtic Cross from a 1920s share certificate.

41   The original Celtic Cross, as shown in Willie Maley's book, The Story of the Celtic, 1888 to 1938.

42   The final of the Glasgow Exhibition Cup. Celtic v Cowlairs at the Exhibition Grounds, Kelvinside Park on 6th September 1888. Celtic's first cup final was a controversial one, with the opponents strengthened by players from other teams on the day and the Celtic team given a torrid reception by the Glasgow public.

43   A young James Kelly of Renton. When he signed for Celtic, the rest followed. Such was the importance of the signing of the best player in Scotland, that the phrase No Kelly, No Keltic was born!

44   Not the original team, but this picture was taken at Millburn Park, Alexandria on 22nd December, 1888 in front of the pavillion that still stands to this day. Back row of committee men and trainer; Joseph Anderson (trainer), James Quillan, Dan Malloy, John Glass, John C MacDonald with John O'Hara and William McKillop in front. Players; Willie Groves, Tom Maley, Paddy Gallagher, Willie Dunning with the cap on to signify he was the goalkeeper, Willie Maley, Mick Dunbar and in the front row; Johnny Coleman, Jimmy McLaren, James Kelly, Neil McCallum and Mick McKeown. Celtic beat Vale of Leven 2-1. Interestingly one of our most iconic figures, Willie Maley, only just made it into our most iconic team photograph, as a late replacement for the lesser known Alex Collins.

45   The winners' medals went to Cowlairs on the day.

46   Janefield Cemetery looking south in 1850 from the Gallowgate. The original Celtic Park would be built bounding the top left section and the current ground built on the far side of the southern boundary.

47   Glasgow Cup tie. Rangers v Celtic at the first Ibrox Park on 27th October 1888. The first competitive match between Celtic and Rangers and our 6-1 win remains a record.

48   Scottish Cup tie. St Bernards v Celtic at Powderhall, Edinburgh on 3rd November 1888. The good old "football special", 1888 style. Significantly, the tickets were to be obtained at the three parishes we were set up to fund the Poor Childrens Dinner Tables at, or alternatively from a committee member.

49   Grand Charity Football Matches. Celtic v Mitchell St George at Celtic Park on 31st December 1888 and v Corinthians at Celtic Park on 3rd January 1889. The first big English teams arrive at Celtic Park with all funds donated to the St Vincent De Paul Society. Note members and season ticket holders are requested to pay.

50   Scottish Cup final. Celtic v Third Lanark on 2nd February 1889. The Celts' first Scottish Cup Final at our first attempt.

51   Johnny Madden in the green and white Celtic stripes which took over from the short lived original strip on the 10th November 1888 at home to Renton in a 1-0 win.

52   The Celtic line up in our first Scottish Cup Final v Third Lanark on 2nd February 1889, with the exception of John Kelly, who replaced Willie Dunning in goals.

53   Sketch from the match, "The Snow Final," as it became known, from the Scottish Referee on the 4th February, 1889.

54   Sketches of the action from the first match, which was replayed a week later due to the inclement weather. Celtic are in the lighter stripes, our green and white compared to Third Lanark's red and black.

55   Celtic fixture card and list of committee for the 1889/90 season

56   Celtic's first visit to London, on 16th February 1889, to take on the Corinthians again. Back row of trainer and committee men; Joseph Anderson, (trainer), Dan Malloy, John Glass, James Quillan and William McKillop. Middle row of Willie Maley with players; goalkeeper John Kelly, Mick Dunbar, Paddy Gallagher and Willie Groves. Seated in the front are Pat Dowling, Johnny Coleman, Jimmy McLaren, James Kelly, Neil McCallum, Mick McKeown and Phil Clarke..

57   Celtic v Blackburn on 3rd October 1889 at the original Celtic Park. Back row from left to right of committee men, referee and trainer; William McKillop, Tom Maley, referee J Robertson, John Glass, trainer Joseph Anderson, John O'Hara, Hugh Darroch, Joseph McGroary and Dan Malloy. Players from left to right at the back; Johnny Madden, John Coleman, goalkeeper James McLaughlin, Mick McKeown, Jerry Reynolds and Peter Dowds and John Cunningham. Front row; Paddy Gallagher, Mick Dunbar, captain James Kelly with the ball at his feet and Willie Groves. Celtic won the match 1-0.

58   Celtic 1890/91; Non playing staff from left to right of Paddy Gallagher, Mick Dunbar, Joe Anderson (trainer), James Boyle, John O'Hara, James Kelly and Tom Maley. Players in the back row; Jerry Reynolds, goalkeeper James Bell and Mick McKeown, middle row of Frank Dolan, Jimmy McGhee and Willie Maley and front row of Johnny Madden, Johnny Coleman, Peter Dowds, Sandy McMahon and Johnny Campbell.

59   The Celtic line up for the first five months of the 1891/92 season with Tom Duff in goals, before he was replaced by Joseph Cullen after a disastrous display in the New Years match of 1892. From the top; Jerry Reynolds, Tom Duff, Dan Doyle, Paddy Gallagher, James Kelly, Peter Dowds, Johnny Madden, Sandy McMahon, Neil McCallum, Alec Brady and Johnny Campbell.

60   The Glasgow North Eastern Cup, the first trophy won by Celtic on 11th May 1889, when we defeated Cowlairs 6-1 in the final. The trophy is now in the Hampden museum.

61   Celtic 1892 including big signings from Everton, Dan Doyle and Alec Brady. The picture is likely to have been taken in front of the pavillion at the original Celtic Park with James Kelly glancing over to the ongoing work to build Paradise, the current Celtic Park. Back row shows Johnny Coleman, Tom Maley and Alec Brady with Joseph Cullen and Jerry Reynolds circled. Front row shows Neil McCallum, Johnny Campbell, Dan Doyle, James Kelly, Sandy McMahon and Willie Maley.

62   The Celtic team on 28th May 1892 that beat 5th KRV 8-1 in a friendly at Palmerston Park, Dumfries; Back row; Alec Brady, Alex Collins, trainer Joseph Anderson, Hugh Clifford, Sandy McMahon and Joe Cullen, middle row; Paddy Gallagher, Dan Doyle, Johnny Madden and Johnny Campbell, front row of Neil McCallum and "Sparrow" Flannagan. Four days later we clinched our first treble.

63   Johnny Madden's prize of a pewter tea set in the 5 a sides at the Celtic Sports in August 1891. Celtic beat Kilmarnock in the final with a team consisting of Duff and McLeod guesting from Cowlairs and Dumbarton, alongside James Kelly, Sandy McMahon and Johnny Madden.

64   Scotland v Ireland at Celtic Park on 28th March, 1891. The only international match played at the original ground, but one which held a record crowd for the fixture.

65   The 2nd prize in the bicycle race at the 1891 Celtic Sports.

66   The first huddle? The Proud, Proud Celts dancing round the image of the three trophies, fittingly emblazoned on each leaf of the shamrock, in the Scottish Referee newspaper.

67   The first Celtic team to win the treble of the Scottish Cup, the Glasgow Cup and the Charity Cup in the 1891/92 season.

68   The Celtic team which beat Queens Park 1-0 in the Scottish Cup Final on 12th March 1892, but the match was replayed due to crowd encroachment.

69   The line up for same match.

70   The free supplement printed in every issue of the Catholic newspaper, the Glasgow Observer in February 1892 to mark our Scottish Cup Final appearance. Goalkeeper Joe Cullen is in the top row, then full backs Jerry Reynolds and Dan Doyle, President John Glass and Tom Maley are circled, then half backs Willie Maley, James Kelly and Peter Dowds, with the five man forward line of Neil McCallum, Alec Brady, Johnny Madden, Sandy McMahon and Johnny Campbell.

71   The victorious Celtic team which beat Queens Park 5-1 in the replayed Scottish Cup final on 9th April 1892. Johnny Madden was out injured and was replaced in the forward line by midfielder Peter Dowds, with Paddy Gallagher taking his slot in the middle of the park. From the top; Jerry Reynolds, Joe Cullen and Dan Doyle, with half backs Willie Maley, James Kelly and Paddy Gallagher, then forward line of Alec Brady, Sandy McMahon, Neil McCallum, Peter Dowds and Johnny Campbell.

72   The sketch plan of Celtic's new ground, from the Scottish Sport on 2nd October 1891.

Contents

CHAPTER THREE

CHAPTER FOUR

CHAPTER FIVE

CHAPTER SIX

CHAPTER ONE
LIFE BEFORE CELTIC

Close your eyes for a minute and try to envisage your life without Celtic.

Not just the Celtic you watch play football for ninety minutes, the Celtic you talk about every day in life, the Celtic you think about every other minute and the Celtic that pours out of every vein in your body, determines your mood swings, dictates your friendships, commands your social life and often attracts the person you marry to spend the rest of their life with you.

It shapes your life, your ethics, your morals, your principals and often your politics. It shapes your very existence. You cherish the days your father took you to your first games and you in turn gift the same devotion to your children and so it goes on.

For eternity.

Pause and imagine your life without Celtic. Take away everything that Celtic has given you in life. Who would you be?

More than a football club, a club like no other are catchy phrases in a modern world often burdened with their overuse, but on this occasion, they are truly apt. Celtic FC is not just a football club, we are a club like no other. Celtic are a phenomenon, an all consuming, roller coaster through life with no stops in between. You cannot leave Celtic, Celtic never leaves you. It takes you to the highest peak and in the very next breath can drop you to the lowest valley.

Above all, Celtic are an emotion which has carried us through the lean years, knowing that the good days will return, as they always do. It is not within our gift to ever leave Celtic. It is so intertwined into our very existence that the Celtic support has always stuck by the club throughout the bad times like no other.

Knowing our history and our humble origins is an integral part of what makes the Celtic support tick and before any history book on Celtic Football Club can begin looking at football, it's imperative that firstly we look at this very subject, life before Celtic. What were the reasons behind our formation, what were the social conditions, who made it happen and how did it all come together?

Today, we are able to look much deeper than ever before to analyse every step of the way and how it impacted on the birth of Celtic Football Club.

SAINT MARY'S CHAPEL IN GLASGOW'S EAST END

Celtic's formation was a complex matter brought together by a number of issues which created the circumstances over a number of decades, all of which we examine in detail, but for our first ingredient, we must look no further than the parish of St Mary's on Abercromby Street in the Calton, in Glasgow's East End.

St Mary's chapel became only the second Catholic chapel to be built in Scotland since the Reformation, in the year of our Lord, 1842. August 15th was the exact date on the Feast of the Assumption, (marking the assumption of the Virgin Mary into heaven), when the chapel opened and this was quite fitting, given the full title of the chapel is St Mary of the Assumption. The church was built under the instruction of Bishop Murdoch and it was Father Peter Forbes who made the parish his life work, taking over the running of the church for the next thirty years until he passed away in August 1872.

Initially, the parish boundaries went as far as to include Rutherglen in the south east, Busby in the south and to the outskirts of Coatbridge in the east and from the mother parish of St Mary's, missions were built in Rutherglen and Shettleston, with further missions built in Cambuslang and Baillieston.

In 1873, the mission of Sacred Heart was built in Bridgeton and in 1876 the mission of St Michael's in Parkhead was erected. Despite these missions being detached from the mother parish, St Mary's parish continued to grow and around the time of the foundation of Celtic, the Catholic population within its boundary was estimated at no less than 10,000. This compared to the previous century, when in 1790 there were 43 anti Catholic societies in Glasgow at a time when there were only 39 Catholics living in the city. Every Catholic living in Glasgow could have their own anti Catholic society named after them. The anti Catholic societies around the time of the birth of Celtic now had their work cut out to keep up.

The parish was central to the continued growth of the Catholic presence in the city in the 19th century, for example the cemetery attached to St Mary's was for a long time the only Catholic cemetery in Glasgow. Continuing its progress, a day school was built in 1850, followed by an Industrial School for the orphans of the parish and its surrounds. Not only did the parish continue to flourish, but so too did other organisations continue to blossom from within it. The Saint Vincent De Paul Society, the Catholic Union and the League of the Cross, to name just a few, were amongst those where the sharpest minds of the parish honed their debating and organisational skills, bringing to the fore in the late 1880s, many of the men who would go on to put their skills learned working together for the common good into the foundation of Celtic!

Indeed it was the structure of the mother parish of St Mary's in the Calton, alongside its satellite parishes that were to provide the platform for that birth.

In 1868, Pope Pius XI commissioned Celtic's future Patron, Charles Petre Eyre, to become the Apostolic Administrator of the Western District of Scotland in 1869. As an Englishman, he was chosen deliberately to unite the Catholic church in Scotland, which was divided into two main camps, that of the native Scots, who were in the minority, and the immigrant Irish.

The Western District covered a diverse area including Lanarkshire, Dunbartonshire, Argyllshire and Renfrewshire as well as Wigtownshire, Inverness-shire, the Western Isles, Bute and Arran. A hierarchy was established comprising two archdioceses, Glasgow and Edinburgh and four diocese, with Charles Eyre created as the Archbishop of Glasgow in 1878, which included around two thirds of the entire Roman Catholic population of Scotland; 250,000 compared to almost 400,000.

He was the first Roman Catholic Archbishop of Glasgow for over three centuries since the Reformation and he set about his task with great gusto to restore the Catholic hierarchy, to unite his flock, build chapels and schools for his people and a new seminary for aspiring priests. In short he revitalised the Catholic faith in Scotland and gave it the tools to expand and to re-establish itself. He gave us back our pride and without it, the Founding Fathers would not have been given the opportunity to reflect that diaspora in the sporting arena.

THE NEXT VITAL INGREDIENT
AN GORTA MOR - THE GREAT FAMINE

The Fields of Athenry by Pete St John

By a lonely prison wall
I heard a young girl calling
Michael they have taken you away
For you stole Trevelyan's corn
So the young might see the morn.
Now the prison ship lies waiting in the bay.

Low lie the Fields of Athenry
Where once we watched the small free birds fly.
Our love was on the wing, we had dreams and songs to sing
It's so lonely round the Fields of Athenry.

By a lonely prison wall
I heard a young man calling
Nothing matters Mary when you're free,
Against the famine and the crown
I rebelled they cut me down
Now you must raise our child with dignity.

Low lie the Fields of Athenry
Where once we watched the small free birds fly.
Our love was on the wing, we had dreams and songs to sing
It's so lonely round the Fields of Athenry.

By a lonely harbour wall
She watched the last star falling
As the prison ship sailed out against the sky
But she'll wait and hope and pray
For her love in Botany Bay
It's so lonely round the Fields of Athenry.

Low lie the Fields of Athenry
Where once we watched the small free birds fly.
Our love was on the wing, we had dreams and songs to sing
It's so lonely round the Fields of Athenry.

Although we were founded on November 6th, 1887 in St Mary's Hall, in the East End of Glasgow and played our first match on May 28th, 1888, we have to go back a further four decades to the famine in Ireland. An Gorta Mor caused the deaths of up to one million Irishmen, women and children and forced two million more to leave Ireland. It was the next vital ingredient in the birth of Celtic Football Club. Many fled to Scotland (the cheapest fare by boat), mainly to Glasgow and its surrounding areas, as well as to Edinburgh and Dundee and it's no coincidence that in every area where the Irish settled in numbers, they started a football team.

It was well documented that post-Reformation Scotland was a bleak place for the Irish to settle, especially Glasgow, which was the most hostile anti Irish city on planet earth, but the influx of Irish into the East End of Glasgow in particular over the next few decades were to provide the leadership and, more precisely, the founding father: Brother Walfrid. He was a child of the famine, born in 1840 in one of the worst hit areas of Ireland, in County Sligo, to set up the new football club in 1887, a club that was to rise from the ghettoes to become one of the biggest football clubs in the world.

The first seeds were being sown.

Pete St John's hauntingly beautiful ballad, The Fields of Athenry, sums up perfectly the despair of the famine and the deportation and emigration that was to deprive Ireland of so many of her young, ironically at the same time it did so much for the cities that hosted them. He tells the story of a young County Galway family, with Mary lamenting the cruel exile of her husband, Michael, banished to Australia on a prison ship for the heinous crime of stealing scraps of cheap Indian corn to feed his starving family. While Sir Charles Trevelyan, the Assistant Secretary to Her Majesty's Treasury in Ireland, sat back and did little to help.

The plight of the Irish was made worse by Trevelyan's inaction in directing government aid by way of food and finance to tackle the epidemic. His uncaring attitude was summed up in a private letter to an Irish Peer when he described the severe situation as an "effective mechanism for reducing surplus population," and as "the judgement of God".

Trevelyan's attitude was that the Irish should fix the problem themselves and if government aid was sent, then the Irish would become dependant on it, rather than dealing with the problem themselves. He tried to shift blame locally to the landlords but the inaction of the Conservative British Government was down largely to the influence Trevelyan had over them, which led to the severity of the problem being underestimated. He closed down the Relief Programmes that were in place to tackle the issue of the famine and he closed the food depots stacked with cheap Indian corn and stopped their transportation to Ireland as boat loads of home grown oats and grain left Ireland from the same harbours.

In short, he spent the bare minimum to feed the starving. Extremely controversial too, even by the standards of the first half of the 19th century, was the system of using prison ships to deport thousands of Irishmen for the most minor of offences to Botany Bay, Australia.

The Celtic support, almost two centuries later, remember the men, women and children of the famine, many of them were our forefathers, as we join Mary lamenting the loss of her husband to foreign lands in song on the seated slopes of Celtic Park. Similarly, many others contrasted the happy days before the famine, spent overlooking the low lying fields of Athenry alongside their loved ones, with their love, their hopes and aspirations metaphorically on the wings of the free birds overhead, to the aftermath of the famine, where they sat alone in sad lament.

Low lie the Fields of Athenry

Where once we watched the small free birds fly.

Our love was on the wing, we had dreams and songs to sing

It's so lonely round the Fields of Athenry.

Sing it loud and sing it proud and always pause for a moment to reflect on the lyrics and the emotion and meaning behind them. It should never be forgotten that it was these men, women and children and their descendants, who gave us the gift of Celtic Football Club.

THE MARIST ORDER COMES TO GLASGOW

In 1817, the Marist Order was founded by Saint Marcellin Champagnat, then a parish priest in France. The inspiration came when he was shocked to discover the number of Catholics who had no grasp of basic prayer.

Father Champagnat was a Marist priest, dedicated to the Virgin Mary, hence the name, and he set about establishing Marist Brother communities with the aim to educate young French men and women in religion through the work of Marist priests and teachers. "To make Jesus known and loved," and "To Jesus through Mary," was the message he wanted to spread and put to the fore.

The significance of the foundation of the Marist Order seventy years before Celtic's foundation cannot be underestimated as it gave us our founding father, it placed him in Glasgow's East End and it faced him with the challenges to feed the destitute children on his doorstep. The next ingredient is the arrival of the Marist Brothers to Glasgow. The Marist Order soon spread across Europe and in 1855 an invite was sent from a Mr Charles Thiebaut, a French linen merchant living in Dundee, who had mills in Lille and so had contact with the Marist Brothers there and at Beauchamps in northern France.

As a great admirer of their work, he invited the Marists to establish a novitiate, or a boarding school at his estate in Rockwell, County Tipperary. A delegation of two Marist Brothers were sent by their superior general, but they concluded that the time was not right and they returned via Glasgow, where Mr Thiebaut introduced them to Bishop Murdoch and Father Chisholm who had been transferred from St Alphonsus parish, near Glasgow Green, to establish the new parish of St Mungo's in Stanhope Street, Townhead in 1850.

Father Chisholm immediately requested three Marists to teach at the new boys school, but it was three years before this request could be fulfilled due to limited availability. Finally in July 1858, after letters from Bishop Murdoch stressing the need for their arrival, Brothers Procope, Tatianus and Faust were transferred from London to take over the teaching of St Mungo's school in Glebe Street. Father Chisholm had recently retired but Father Eugene Small took over and became the first man to welcome the Marist Brothers to Glasgow.

In a remarkable coincidence, in the same year that Brother Walfrid settled in Glasgow, the first seeds were being sown to bring the Marist Brothers to Glasgow too. To an impressionable young Sligo man, the new parish of St Mungo's would be his parish. It would be there that he would see at first hand the great work of Brothers Procope, Tatianus and Faust, who would become the inspiration for him to join the Marist Order himself. The first steps for him would be to impress the Brothers enough for him to be taken on as a Pupil Teacher in the early 1860s before travelling to Beauchamp in France in his next step of the journey.

The countdown was now on until the departure of Andrew Kerins and the arrival of Brother Walfrid...

BROTHER WALFRID - OUR FOUNDING FATHER

Brother Walfrid was born Andrew Kerins, in 1840 in Ballymote, Sligo, one of the worst affected areas of the Great Hunger in Ireland and it is said that he first came to Scotland in 1855 as a 15 year old boy, sailing on a coal ship from nearby Sligo Harbour to Glasgow's Broomielaw. To the young Irishman, escaping the after-effects of the famine was his immediate aim and an impoverished Glasgow in the 1850s seemed like heaven in comparison, where there were opportunities to work in the growing iron works in the north of the city or on the construction of the railways. Frustratingly, no proof exists of his early Glasgow days through any censuses that are carried out every 10 years. In the 1871, 1881 and 1891 census his address is given as 71 Charlotte Street, which was the address of St Joseph's Monastery, the Marist Brothers headquarters in Glasgow. Charlotte Street is between London Road and Glasgow Green, at the junction with, and south of, the Braemar Bar. If you walk down that street today heading to Glasgow Green, just before the end of the road on the left once stood the residence where Brother Walfrid lived, directly opposite from what is now the south car park of the Wise Group headquarters.

Many Celtic fans making their way to home games would pass this street, as well as many who enjoy a pre match refreshment in the Gallowgate, without knowing the significance of the area around the corner. It was from 71 Charlotte Street that Brother Walfrid would make his way along London Road through Bridgeton, which was at that time populated by a large number of Irish, towards the original Celtic Park. He would pass the current Celtic Park, then a free coup, before turning left at the bottom of Springfield Road, (then Dalmarnock Street) towards the original Celtic Park.

Residents at the Marist headquarters on 71 Charlotte Street in 1871 along with Brother Walfrid, aged 30 were: The Brother Superior, Brother Joseph; Dennis Dullen aged 30; Brother James; Thomas McCann who was the Assistant Superior aged 26, Brother Columba; Hugh O'Neill aged 29; Thomas Gilmartin aged 30;

Hector Cerf aged 27; Theophile A Lemaitre aged 24 and Philip Jeffrey aged 17.

Of the eight, only one was from Glasgow - Brother James - which showed the work the Marists had to do in attracting locals to the cause. Four were Irish: Brother Walfrid, Brother Joseph, Brother Columba and Thomas Gilmartin. Hector Cerf came from France, Theophile Lemaitre from Belgium and Philip Jeffrey was from England.

By 1881, 40 year old Brother Walfrid was promoted to Assistant Superior to the Belgian John Verbcere, aged 59, and the growth of the Marist Order in Glasgow is clearly evident with no less than 46 teachers accommodated, with more than half that number as pupil teachers learning their trade: Julias Annias, Dan Docherty, Henry Currie, Patrick Kelly, Mick McDermitt, Thomas Lynch, Thomas Hargeden, James Glancy, William Slevanth, Thomas Marshall, Peter Lambe, Patrick Mulroney, Patrick Wright, Stephen Moore, Timothy Leary, Peter Fitzgerald, John Keilty, James McMahon, John Walsh, George Brannan, Philip Sullivan, Bernard Rooney, Bartholomew Gillan, James Fitzgerald, Alan Griffiths, Pat McGovern, William Morris, Edward Reilly, James Donachie, William Marshall, Patrick Carroll, Thomas Jenkins, James Currie, John McGuire, Peter Hurt, Louis Greenwell, John Carrigan, Andrew Jordan, John Turley, Pat Gettigan, James Rogers, Thomas Jordan, Peter Connelly and Thomas Nolan.

Of the 46, which Brother Walfrid was second in command of, 20 were from Ireland, 12 were from Scotland, 10 were from England, 2 from Belgium, 1 from India and 1 from France. The numbers from Scotland were very encouraging but the country of birth of the pupil teachers is surprising with a mixture of Irish, Scots and English instead of a dominance of home-based Scots.

By the 1891 census, Brother Walfrid had been promoted to Brother Superior in 1886 and the numbers were cut back to 33 teachers, again including almost half who were pupil teachers:

Assistant Superior; Julias Annias aged 38, Edmond A Decoopman aged 35, Brother Dorotheus; Henry J Currie aged 34, Peter McLaren aged 39, James Bannon aged 41, William Flynn aged 33, Gairstave Nachbgaile aged 34, Timothy Calmont aged 24, Louis Greenwell aged 26, James Currie aged 24, John B Cubezolle aged 24, Jeremiah O'Connor aged 18, Patrick McAulay aged 19, Jeremiah Casey aged 25, Thomas Callaghan aged 18, John McAulay aged 18, John

Mulroney aged 17, Peter Cullan aged 16, Henry Walls aged 16, William Mulrooney aged 16, Joseph Cullan aged 16, Thomas Hanley aged 16, Thomas Igo aged 16, James Wright aged 14, Edward Barnet aged 16, James Colliston aged 15, Francis Jarvis aged 15, Arthur McIloney aged 15, Patrick O'Conner aged 16, Herbert Parish aged 15, Joseph Gallacher aged 15, Michael Gregan aged 15.

One name that is significant above is that of Henry J Currie, (Brother Dorotheus), then Headmaster of St Mary's who was also involved with Brother Walfrid in the birth of Celtic and who audited our first accounts.

Significantly, 13 were from Scotland, 10 were from Ireland, 6 were from England, 3 from France and 1 from Belgium. The large numbers of Scots teachers and pupil teachers was an unmistakable sign of the importance the Marists put on involving the community and ensuring its growth from within. This was the first year since the growth of the Marists in Glasgow that the majority of the staff attracted to the Order were home-based Scots, which was another huge sign of progress which would have delighted Brother Walfrid, with all of these teachers and pupil teachers under his supervision and his work in the city almost done.

When Brother Walfrid walked almost every day in life from 71 Charlotte Street, through Glasgow Green, past Templeton's carpet factory and along John Street, (now Tulis Street) and Muslin Street to Sacred Heart school in Bridgeton, it was with a spring in his step, a contented man who would leave Glasgow in a far, far better state than when he found it when he first arrived there as a 15 year old some 37 years earlier.

BROTHER WALFRID'S CURRICULUM VITAE

SAINT MUNGO'S

The name of Andrew Kerins first makes an appearance in the school log book of St Mungo's, Parson Street, to the north of the city centre, on the 12th April, 1869 on his arrival at the school, aged 28, stating simply:

"Andrew Kerins and Hugh O'Neill were entered as Assistants."

Andrew Kerins was of course to go on to be known as Brother Walfrid, with Hugh O'Neill taking up the name Brother Columba.

A month later, on the 18th May, 1869, on his 29th birthday, Andrew Kerins is mentioned again.

"Andrew Kerins may attend the next Christmas examination."

The importance of this news was that after four years training at Beauchamp, the next step was the final exams, usually three years later after gaining experience as an Assistant Teacher. The exams in Christmas 1869 would be Brother Walfrid's first in this process.

Daily log books were introduced to schools in 1864 as a legal requirement and they were checked as part of the annual school audit carried out by Government Inspectors who had the power to award grants. The logs were very formal, very matter of fact, with no flowery language. They didn't, therefore, give the full flavour of what it was like in a Catholic school run by the Marist Brothers in 1860s Glasgow, but what they did underline was the dedication, care, attention to detail and devotion that went into making the school a success - which was backed up by results that showed that in many aspects, Catholic schools were outshining state schools, in particular in greater discipline and efficiency.

Other examples of school life were given in the log book, for example on the 6th September 1869 school fees were paid for the poor by the Saint Vincent De Paul Society and two days later the Barony schoolboys were provoking the St Mary's kids and the police had to be called. A common occurrence back in the day it seems.

One example from before Brother Walfrid's arrival was on 23rd May 1864, when the kids were warned not to play with gunpowder as John McGrory had burned himself the previous year, which is always good advice. Not so long ago kids were warned not to play with matches, back in the day they were warned not to play with gunpowder.

The following grants for employees were received by the school:

Charles Daron; Brother Procope, Richard Sinott, John Gough, Thomas Hackett, William Sarsfield and Andrew Kerins (Night school), otherwise known as evening classes.

So we discover that Andrew Kerins was in charge of the evening classes at St Mungo's, which we learn from further additions to the log book, were pretty well attended. Significantly Brother Walfrid learned the importance of evening classes as it was the entry level for many children who had to work full time during the day and therefore it provided their only opportunity for education. This was something he carried throughout his teaching in Glasgow.

Indeed, it is very likely that Andrew Kerins first met the acquaintance of the Marist Brothers at St Mungo's after a day's hard graft, when he attended night classes. Frustratingly, as the log books were only introduced as a legal requirement in 1864, there is no record of him attending as he would have been a pupil before then. On showing promise, Andrew Kerins would have remained as a pupil teacher, which each school had for nominated kids aged from 14 to 19 years old. St Mungo's opened in 1857 but it was 1861 before the numbers rose significantly. It is very likely that Andrew Kerins was one of that number who joined the evening classes in 1861 before starting his novitiate in 1864 aged 24 years old.

Intriguingly in the St Mary's log book on 25th January, 1866 it states;

"B Walfrid from Saint Mungo's Academy"

This was during the time he would have spent training in Beauchamps, northern France. Did he come home during this spell to train at St Mungo's and visit St Mary's?

On the 8th March 1870, Andrew Kerins is mentioned again and it was good news;

"The two Assistant Teachers, A Kerins and H O'Neill, have passed a successful examination last Christmas."

It took over two months for the good news to arrive but it was worth the wait and Andrew Kerins was now looking forward to taking another step nearer to being known as Brother Walfrid.

In the meantime, he was added in the full list of staff by the HM Inspector who carried out his annual audit on the 3rd of May and shortly afterwards, another entry in the St Mungo's log book on 13th May, 1870 simply stated:

"Mr Andrew Kerins resigned today for Saint Mary's".

Although his time at St Mungo's was a short one, from 12th April, 1869 until 13th May a year later, an opportunity had arisen at the much larger parish of St Mary's in the Calton. It was one that he could not resist and it was another crucial step in the background to the formation of Celtic Football Club.

Although now gone, the name of Andrew Kerins lived on in the school log book, and two months later on the 15th July, 1870 he was amongst one of the prize winners announced at the end of term ceremony;

"Received results of the drawing exams - twelve children received prizes, the Pupil Teachers Hackett, McDermott and Wilson and Assistant Teacher Kerins also received prizes".

So Brother Walfrid was a mean artist. What price one of his drawings?

A fascinating article by former pupil, John McAdam, was printed in the Catholic newspaper, the *Glasgow Observer* in January 1893, describing his days at St Mungo's including his thoughts on Brother Walfrid. The author, a protégé of Brother Walfrid, was born in Glasgow in 1856 and after working as a "cub reporter" with the *Glasgow Herald*, he moved to Ballyshannon where he went on to establish and edit three newspapers in the north west of Ireland. His first newspaper, the *Donegal Vindicator* in 1889 took up the grievances of the Land Leaguers after they had specifically invited McAdam to Donegal, his mother's home county, to counter the *Donegal Independent* which represented the ascendancy class.

"Pa" McAdam from there on gave the Land Leaguers a voice from his first issue of the *Vindicator* on February 4th, 1889 and he certainly wasn't afraid of Samuel Trimble, the *Independent's* ascendancy mouthpiece, as they locked horns in their editorials with "Pa" giving as good as he got in favour of the Nationalist cause. In the end, Sam Trimble sold the *Independent* and it later came under McAdam's control and was merged with the Vindicator.

Bolstered by this turn of events, he then went on to found the *Derry Weekly News* and the *Tyrone Herald*, but thanks to his letter in the *Glasgow Observer*, we know he never forgot Brother Walfrid and his school days at St Mungo's. An accomplished artist, John McAdam also painted a popular stylised drawing of St Patrick with skills that were learned from Brother Walfrid.

REMINISCENCE OF SAINT MUNGO'S ACADEMY by John McAdam

"This Christmas Day, away in the wilds of Donegal, I sit looking out on the glorious Erne emptying itself over the falls of famed Assaroe, (near Ballyshannon), into the bosom of the ocean, when the Observer is handed to me.

Among the reports my eye first catches, is the annual presentation of prizes to the pupils of Saint Mungo's Academy, and thoughts of other years drift in upon my mind until half consciously I take up a few sheets of paper and the following little sketch grows rather than it is written, while a couple of dark haired girls and three laughing curly headed boys gambol round my chair.

I seemed to drift back to those days when we sat in front of the well polished desks under the tuition of dear, quick tempered, lovable Brother Walfrid and later, of the alas, too clever, Brother Austin.

Brother Procope was Superior in those days when the Academy was struggling to obtain adequate recognition among the high class educational establishments of Glasgow. The struggle is over long ago and the dear old Academy has been placed in the position to which it is entitled. Where are all my old school friends now? Scattered and strewn over the wide world - some at the pinnacle of fame, many in misery and want".

As Brother Walfrid taught at St Mungo's from 12th April, 1869 to 13th May, 1870 when he left to take up a teaching job at St Mary's and was replaced by Brother Austin, we know the article John McAdam reminisces about is dated to the thirteen months between April 1869 and May 1870.

Interestingly too he goes on to mention some school mates who, unknown to him, went on to become Founding Fathers of Celtic two decades later. The first was Joseph Nelis, captain of the opponents' "camp", which was the system introduced, whereby two groups were set up to oppose each other over the year and to introduce competition and encourage all pupils to give their all and not let their camp down. He mentions Cairns who was often his direct opponent in Joe Nelis's camp, but he doesn't mention if it was James or Michael Cairns, both of whom were involved at Celtic's foundation. However from Michael Cairns' obituary we learn that he studied at St Mungo's under Brother Walfrid so that clears this mystery up.

Joseph McGroary is mentioned, a founding father who went on to become a solicitor and a moving spirit of the Donegal Reunion each year. John McCreadie, another Celtic founding father and a son of Donegal and John Conway are others remembered. *"He's all right - and piling up the shekels, his brother now a friar",* was how Doctor John Conway was described, the man who was our first Honorary President and the man who kicked the first ball to open Celtic Park on Tuesday, 8th May 1888. He reminisced too about the clay pipe which half a dozen of them would get their hands on for a fly puff and take turns to be the custodian of, dreading the day they were discovered. The school fights with the local non denominational Barony and High schools were also a frequent appointment back in the day. Not much had changed a century later in Glasgow.

However he ends with great fondness, on an emotional note;

"Anyway bless them all and bless the good Brothers and their noble work. Some day I will go to see them and ask permission to sit at the desk and write upon an exercise.

Perhaps I could live it all over again, if only Brother Walfrid could be induced to come cautiously behind in the way I remember so well, and with an accompanying slap behind the ear, say "Hold your pen straight", might be eagerly welcomed. The years obliterated and the youthful pupil would sit there as he did - gracious, is it possible - yet those grey hairs tell the tale, only too truthfully, of the many years that have passed away since.

We were boys, happy, happy boys. Since we were boys together".

John McAdam's insight is invaluable as it paints a picture of the 29 year old Brother Walfrid in his first job, barely passed out as a Marist Brother, and it's done through the eyes of a 13 year old boy, as McAdam was in 1869.

It also tells us that Brother Walfrid taught Founding Fathers Joseph Nelis, Michael Cairns, Joseph McGroary, John McCreadie and Doctor John Conway and this created a strong bond with - and a great respect for - Brother Walfrid that would serve us in good stead at our foundation. Of Brother Walfrid's character it mentions him as dear, sometimes quick tempered and lovable and also not slow to give out a playful slap to the ear to follow through an instruction. Given that a newly founded Catholic school in the 1860s would have been a very strict establishment, with lessons taken very seriously, in this context, it is refreshing that Brother Walfrid is remembered with such fondness.

Prior to his first job at St Mungo's, Brother Walfrid took up his Marist teacher training in France which lasted around five years from 1864 to 1869, meaning that in 1869 he was one of the first Marist Brothers chosen to be sent to Glasgow to teach the children. In St Mungo's school which the Marists ran, they had two full time Marists, one who was Head Teacher, one Assistant and also four pupil teachers, who would be financed by the government. Many of the pupil teachers would go on to become Marist Brothers but for many too, it wasn't for them.

So we know where Brother Walfrid taught, but what did he teach? We know from Pa McAdam that he taught Art and we also know the subjects available at St Mungo's included Science, Geometry, Mathematics, Arithmetic, Music, English, Greek, Latin, French, German as well as Religious Studies, naturally.

SAINT MARY'S

Brother Walfrid honed his skills at St Mungo's under the very experienced Head Teacher, Brother Procope (Charles Daron) before being transferred to St Mary's on Abercromby Street on 13th May 1870, where he was promoted to Assistant.

The first entry at Saint Mary's on 13th May 1870 stated simply;

"Mister A Kerins began his duties as Assistant Teacher today".

On the same day, the school had a visit from Father Forbes from the parish instructing the Head Teacher that any children who could not pay their fees regularly were to be dealt with leniently. With hindsight the irony should have escaped no-one. It's uncanny that on the very first day Brother Walfrid set foot in St Mary's school, the parish priest visited and told the Head Master to go easy on the kids whose parents could not provide the fees.

On the 1st September 1870, Brother Walfrid used his experience at St Mungo's to introduce the camp system favoured by his former school and two opposing teams were set up, given classic titles, for example Greeks versus Romans, and a captain nominated for both. He had learned that this system of learning had proven to get the best out of pupils on both sides by introducing competition, which could be fierce, but it kept the pupils focussed.

A week later, the log book noted that the children had been fighting with the Protestant kids. Camp system still needing a bit of work, thought the Marist Brothers.

Between 14th November and 19th December 1870, Brother Walfrid was allowed to absent himself on afternoons to allow him to study for his Christmas exams, with the exception of the 17th November when as Assistant, he stood in for the Head Teacher, for the first time as Brother James (Thomas McCann) had to attend the drawing exams. On 7th March 1871, on the initiative of Glasgow-born Brother James and Sligo-born Brother Walfrid, a football was introduced into the St Mary's playground before school and at lunchtime to encourage the children to arrive at school early and to remain there during lunchtime and not to stray too near the non Catholic schools in the vicinity where trouble often flared between them.

Often a lack of mentions in the log book was a good thing as many of the comments concerned teachers or pupil teachers who were late, hadn't turned up at all or who weren't up to standard. In any regard nothing negative was ever written about our founding father. On 22nd August, 1871 Brother Walfrid must have been having an exasperating day as the log book noted:

"Remarked to my Assistant today that his tone of voice was high"

In comparison, just a few months later, on 11th January 1872, it was noted that one pupil teacher was strongly addicted to the pipe, but it had no effect on the annual audit by the Government Inspector, where comparison tables showed that St Mary's had a higher than average level of success. Punctuality was always a problem at the school, but on 25th September 1872, it was noted that it had improved by the introduction of a football however some children had to be cautioned a fortnight previous for playing in the graveyard, not with the ball it's hoped. Before Hibernian and most other clubs had ever been dreamt of, Brother Walfrid was well aware of the emerging popularity of the game of football but it was to be another fifteen years of his learning curve before he had the opportunity to use it to its maximum potential.

Intriguingly, on 13th March, 1873 the log book showed;

"Mister Kerins gave a lesson on coal and iron".

Where did Brother Walfrid learn about coal and iron? Was it from his personal experiences when he first arrived in Glasgow in 1855, at the height of the Industrial Revolution? We know from Pa McAdam's writings, that Brother Walfrid taught Art, therefore Brother Walfrid was part of the Science and Art Department at the school but there's no doubt he could also turn his hand to many topics. Backing this up on the 7th May 1873 a letter arrived from the Science and Art Department inquiring about Andrew Kerins' examination.

Indulge me if you will, but on the same day that Brother Walfrid gave his lesson in coal and iron it was noted that the name of one of the pupil teachers who worked with him at St Mary's was Thomas Sweeney, the same name as your author's father. It may be a trivial matter, but it gives great pride to know my father, the man who gave me Celtic, would be looking down and smiling at that little fact.

Brother Walfrid was again given some afternoons off in the build up to his Christmas exams and a strange incident happened the day before he returned to normal duties on the 20th December 1873, when a bull dashed into the playground, knocked a boy over and caused great consternation. Yes, you read that correctly.

The log book was again short and straight to the point on Monday, 22nd December, 1873 as it closed the book on Brother Walfrid's three and a half years at St Mary's with the following three words;

"Mister Kerin leaves".

SACRED HEART

After a thoroughly enjoyable spell at St Mary's, from 13th May 1870 to 23rd December 1873, where he made great friends with men he would rely on fourteen years later, Brother Walfrid was transferred the short distance to the new parish of Sacred Heart in Bridgeton where his talents were recognised and he took up the position as the first Head Teacher at the new school.

To our great misfortune, the school log book from Sacred Heart is not available or we would have been treated to the words of Brother Walfrid, in his own handwriting on a daily basis throughout his time at Sacred Heart, and during the formation of Celtic.

As an example of Brother Walfrid's generosity and the fact he never forgot a friend, Brother Christopher - who worked under Brother Walfrid at Sacred Heart - was transferred to St Mungo's to take up the position of Head Teacher unexpectedly in 1889 after the very strict Brother Mungo took unwell. His friendship with Brother Walfrid was never forgotten and he was given permission to use the facilities at Old Celtic Park frequently on Wednesday afternoons for the whole school to enjoy a programme of sports throughout his tenure at St Mungo's between 1889 and 1892. Brother Ezekiel, the cousin of Brother Procope, then stopped the practice when taking over from the more fun loving Brother in 1892.

Brother Dorotheus, who was also to become a great friend and ally of Brother Walfrid, later took over from him at St Mary's and both worked well together, in particular with the formation of the Poor Children's Dinner Tables. The boys school at Sacred Heart, fronting Dalmarnock Road, was built shortly before the mission of Sacred Heart was opened and Brother Walfrid was put in charge as its first Head Master. The girls school opened at the same time and were placed in the charge of the Franciscan Nuns.

IN THE WORDS OF BROTHER WALFRID

In the *Glasgow Observer* on 16th March 1895, Brother Walfrid kindly supplied the following piece on Sacred Heart:

"In 1872-73 the present school building was erected and a portion of Saint Mary's parish erected into a separate parish, with the late Father Noonan as its rector. It was intended to use the school as a chapel school, but when Father Noonan took the census of his mission, he found that the school would not accommodate the fourth of his people. He then, with the advice of his people and blessing of his Grace the Archbishop, resolved to erect the present temporary church.

The schools were opened on the 26th January 1874. The attendance of children was considered very good; boys 130, girls 120, infants 60. The worthy rector resolved on having his schools placed on a solid footing by having them placed in charge of religious and under Government, though many warned the good priest that he would not be able to meet the heavy expense; but his parishioners rallied around him and promised the necessary help to meet the expenses.

The staff consisted of - Boys School; 2 Marist Brothers and 3 pupil teachers. Girls and Infants; 2 Franciscan Nuns and 4 pupil teachers. The number of children increased annually up to the present, when the present numbers are - Boys 405; Girls 360, infants 320, Total 1085. In 1875 it was found necessary to provide a separate infant school; then the building that was situated at the end of the church was for sale, and in a short time was purchased and used for an Infant School and has done duty up to the present, when it has to give way to the noble structure that is being erected.

In 1884, the good Brothers of Saint Vincent De Paul opened the penny dinners for the school children, by which means the children were provided with a good warm meal for a penny. Should parents prefer they could send the bread and the children could get a large bowl of broth or soup for a halfpenny and those who were not able to pay got a substantial meal free. This has been a very great blessing to the poor children. The expenses for some time were met by subscriptions and collections, sermons etc, til the Celtic FC was started, the committee of which gave the good Brothers about 33 shillings a week up to a short time since.

In 1874, when the Sacred Heart schools were opened, the only Catholic school for the East End was Saint Mary's, Calton. Then the Board Schools were set a going, and in place of only 4 Presbyterian schools in the district, now there are no less than 9 Board schools. It is remarkable and well worth noting that there is hardly a Catholic child attending even the palatial Board Schools, this of itself speaks volumes for the zealous clergy and teachers. In 1876, there were 2 night schools opened for the working boys and girls, which have been well attended for years, the attendance being over 600, which may be seen in the blue books".

THE POOR CHILDRENS DINNER TABLES

Fittingly it was Brother Walfrid, along with the St Vincent De Paul Society, the charity which the Celtic Founding Fathers pledged to help maintain at our founding, who started the "Children's Free Dinner And Breakfast Tables" to give it its proper title, at the parish of Sacred Heart in the winter of 1884. The initiative was quickly followed by Brother Dorotheus at St Mary's, before St Michael's in Parkhead and St Andrew's on Clyde Street followed suit, but still not enough was being done to alleviate the problem.

With the debate raging in the Glasgow Observer just over a year later to try and raise awareness and to seek a solution to the problem, Archbishop Charles Eyre (Celtic's first Patron) took the debate a step further by preaching a Charity Sermon, fittingly at the chapel of Sacred Heart on Old Dalmarnock Road, Bridgeton, Brother Walfrid's parish, on 19th February, 1886.

Charity Sermons were regularly preached by priests and bishops and aside from raising serious issues of the day, they would also raise funds for a local charity from the collection taken. Despite the parishioners of Sacred Heart coming from a working class area, the funds raised on this occasion totalled £26, which translates into £2950 in today's money, (2015), and gives an idea of how many must have packed into the chapel and their generosity in such times of need.

The fact that the Archbishop of Glasgow was preaching this sermon and delivering an eloquent appeal showed how serious this issue was taken. In its first year, the average number of dinners provided every day (mostly soup and bread or stew) in this parish alone was as many as 200, with more than 60 breakfasts. Children whose parents were able to pay, paid a penny. Those who could not afford the penny were provided with dinner for a half penny as long as they could bring their own bit of bread. For those whose parents were unemployed and therefore unable to pay anything, a voucher for a free dinner was obtained from the Committee on request.

References are often mistakenly made that the dinner tables were for the children and the unemployed, however as stated above the dinner tables were set up for children. Those whose parents were unemployed were entitled to a free dinner as opposed to those whose parents could afford to pay a penny or a halfpenny. In that regard, no child from the parish was turned away. According to the Glasgow Observer on Saturday 20th February, 1886, in its first year alone, at Sacred Heart Parish, under Brother Walfrid and the Saint Vincent De Paul Society, the Poor Childrens Dinner And Breakfast Table provided over 48,500 dinners and 1150 breakfasts, at a total cost of £105, 10s, 6d.

The local Conference of the Saint Vincent De Paul Society had for some time rented a house at the back of Sacred Heart school on Savoy Street and it was from this perfect location that Mrs Murdoch dispensed a warm dinner to the children at mid-day. A breakfast table was also added in the winter of 1885 consisting of a large bowl of porridge and milk for the children. The logistics of such an undertaking were huge and required not only serious funding, business-like efficiency and organisation but heavy resources of volunteers on a daily basis to staff the scheme, source, deliver and store the food materials, before the meals were cooked.

Whilst dealing with hunger amongst the needy in the parish, which was the main problem on the face of it, a deeper and more sinister threat existed to the Catholics in the East End, that of proselytism: the act of attempting to convert someone to a different religion, on this occasion by offering free food to hungry children. From no less than the editorial of the Glasgow Observer on Saturday, 6th February 1886 and also preached from the pulpit at Sacred Heart in the sermon of Archbishop Eyre on Sunday 14th February, the gravely serious threat of proselytism was addressed head on and left no one in any doubt.

From the *Glasgow Observer* on the 6th February;

"The facts stand totally out before us that Catholic children are being every day proselytised before our eyes and we have the philanthropic intents of the proselytisers so far aggravated by the knowledge that they would and do pass over twenty Protestant outcasts for the sake of picking up one stray lamb out of the folds of "Popery".

Indeed there can be no question now as to the necessity of some action being taken and for the purpose of saving time we would like our numerous correspondents to make note of the fact that the only issue open for discussion is the means which the Catholic community of Glasgow should adopt as being the most effectual".

And on the 20th February;

"We fancy that no one who peruses the ample report of the Archbishop's sermon can remain in much doubt as to the gravity and urgency of the emergency which confronts us, or as to how deeply the honour of the Catholic population of Glasgow is concerned in the duty of counteracting the evil influence of the "Gospel Tents" and "Evangelical Halls" that are springing up, with such a vicious fecundity, (rate of reproduction), in every district of the city.

It is certainly a sufficiently serious and regrettable state of things when the Archbishop can stand up in one of the churches of the Archdiocese and inform us that, year by year, destitute children of the Catholic faith are falling victims to the snares and pitfalls that under the specious guise of charity, are so industriously prepared to decoy them from their religion. That institutions like the Free Dinner And Breakfast Table, in connection with the church of the Sacred Heart, do an immense amount of good there can be no doubt. But our columns have in recent weeks borne melancholy testimony to the fact that the provision made by the Catholic body for the wants of our destitute children is very far from being adequate to the pressing requirements of the situation".

And from the Archbishop's sermon;

It ought to be a prime object with the people of this parish to protect the children of the parish from the dangers and snares by which they were surrounded. They were aware that they had in their midst "Gospel Tents, as they were called, and "Evangelical Halls" and other places of that description where meat and food were given to the children and every inducement held out to draw Catholic children into these snares.

This was done, not for the love of God or of the children themselves, but in order to catch the souls of the poor Catholic children and to draw them away from their faith and their church. Now if the Catholic children were not provided by their Catholic people with what was necessary for their sustenance, the temptation offered by these Gospel Tents and Evangelical Halls might in many cases prove too great and Catholic children might be drawn into the snares placed in their way.

The food was not provided for the children through any feeling of charity, because if charity was at the bottom of it, these people would bring the money or the food to the priests and say "Here are meat and drink and clothing, give them to the poor children of your congregations. Charity however was not the object with which the children were provided for in those Gospel Tents and similar places - the real object was to decoy the Catholic children away from their religion."

And so there were the twin dangers of undernourished children going without food and also the perceived threat of the establishment church with the backing of wealthy philanthropists opportunistically tempting the Catholics of the city to forsake their religion to put food in their mouths and clothes on their backs.

On the 14th March, The Very Reverend Provost Munro went one step further in his charity sermon at St Mary's, Calton, entitled True and false charity:

"The case of the children whose faith was imperilled through the poverty of their parents was one that had lately stirred the Catholic community to it's depths and stirred the conscience of every right minded Catholic in the city - indeed there was hardly a Catholic, young or old, throughout the length and breadth of Glasgow that hadn't felt some part of the burden of rescuing and protecting these helpless children coming home to himself and presenting itself to his mind as a solemn and urgent duty.

Besides the sums already referred to, there were other vast sums in this city distinctly set apart for the perversion of the faith of destitute Catholics - both young and old - but more specifically the young. Were they aware that, in Glasgow alone, there were raised, year by year, sums of money amounting to more than £20,000 for the express and specific purpose of proselytising Catholic children? The proselytisers, he would point out, aimed expressly at destroying the Christian conscience in the hearts of parents and children as well. That was the first and greatest object, and once it was accomplished, the rest of the work of proselytism and demoralisation was an easy one."

The appeals of the Archbishop of Glasgow and others stressing that more must be done to alleviate the problem had a short term effect, as appeals tend to do, but one man was looking at ways of raising significant amounts of money to fund the Free Dinner And Breakfast Tables and at the same time provide entertainment for the masses, taking advantage of the huge up-turn in interest of the game of football.

That man was Brother Walfrid.

FOOTBALL AND CHARITY

1886 was a very busy year for Brother Walfrid. Since arriving at Sacred Heart as Head Teacher on Monday, 22nd December, 1873 from St Mary's, he had spent almost thirteen years in the parish which was given its separate mission and independence from the mother parish of St Mary's in the summer of 1873 when the Marist Brothers were given the responsibility of teaching the boys at the new school. The Franciscan Sisters of the Immaculate Conception, who came to Scotland in response to a plea from Father Peter Forbes of St Mary's in 1847, were given the responsibility of teaching the girls.

The parish priest from St Mary's appointed his assistant, Father Noonan to the parish of Sacred Heart in September 1873 and tasked him to set up the new church, school and presbytery and there was only one man Father Noonan wanted as the Head Teacher of the new school: Brother Walfrid who followed just three months later. Both men knew each other well from working together at St Mary's. Father Noonan was there from 1859, shortly after being ordained, and Brother Walfrid arrived at St Mary's from St Mungo's on 13th May, 1870. Walfrid was, no doubt, delighted to be working again with his fellow Irishman who was eight years his senior: the man from Ballymote, County Sligo and the man from Ballycallan, County Limerick setting up a new church and school in deepest Bridgeton.

Indeed the classic picture of Brother Walfrid, sat in his Marist robes with the large crucifix around his neck and a bible in his hands may well have been taken at the opening of Sacred Heart in 1873, with Brother Walfrid aged 33.

In 1874, just over 300 children attended the school, but by 1886 the numbers had risen remarkably to well over 1200 with no children in the parish attending any other school in the area such was its popularity. Indeed the Night School was one of the largest in the country and the school had almost reached its capacity. The congregation at the chapel had tripled between 1873 and 1886 from 2000 to 6000 and this success story was down, in no small measures, to the work of the two Irishmen: Father Noonan and Brother Walfrid.

By March 1886, with the rousing appeals for more funds for the maintenance of the Free Dinner And Breakfast Tables in the East End of Glasgow, along with the alarming warnings of starving children being tempted away from their religion in return for a warm meal, Brother Walfrid knew that he had to act and do so quickly.

Football was fast becoming a sport for the working classes and its popularity was reaching a height never seen before. The beauty was that all that was required to play the game was a home made ball of any description - which made it accessible to all walks of life - especially the poorest in society. Since introducing the football to the playground of St Mary's in March 1871, Brother Walfrid was well aware of the impact it had on the children. Now was the time to explore the game further as a ways of raising funds for the Dinner Tables.

On the back of the awareness raised by the Archbishop, there was no time to be lost and, with donations tailing off, Brother Walfrid organised a charity football match with the generous backing of Clyde Football Club who offered to host a match at their ground, Barrowfield Park, on French Street, off Dalmarnock Road, Bridgeton against a team of the Saint Vincent De Paul Society's choosing. To attract the largest audience possible to the match, a Catholic team would be the best attraction to provide the opposition, with the two largest in the country being Edinburgh Hibernian and Dundee Harp, in that order.

And so it was with Hibernian otherwise engaged that Dundee Harp, holders of the Forfarshire Cup and the Dundee Burns Club Charity Cup, faced Clyde at Barrowfield on Saturday, 8th May, 1886 at 4pm. Ironically it would be exactly two years later to the day that the opening of Celtic Park would take place. Dundee Harp were the club Brother Walfrid was to renew his acquaintance with to provide the opposition for Celtic's second match in June 1888, so this contact was to become a valuable one.

Adverts were placed in the Glasgow Observer and on every post in the surrounding areas of Bridgeton, stating boldly at the bottom in capitals:

PROCEEDS FOR THE PURPOSE OF SUPPLYING THE CHILDREN OF THE UNEMPLOYED CATHOLIC HOUSE HOLDERS OF SACRED HEART PARISH WITH FREE DINNERS AND BREAKFASTS.

The irony was not missed on one letter writer to the Glasgow Observer which gave an invaluable insight into the Bridgeton of the 1880s;

"Sir, time has changed and with them men and manners, for which God be thanked. Well do I remember the good old times of some four or five years ago in Brigton, ayont the toll, just barely known by its new high falutin' title of Bridgeton Cross, all dressed out in its finery of pagoda seats and all that, when it was scarcely safe for an Irish Roman Catholic to linger for a moment there unless at risk of grievous assault. Whilst today on passing by the toll and glancing at the many coloured and catching titles of the bills posted thereby, my eye alighted on the following;

Grand Charity Football Match for the purpose of providing free breakfasts and dinners for the poor children of the S.H. school.
(It wasn't brave enough to spell out Sacred Heart).

Albeit having had a peep or two behind the scenes and being more or less aware of what was about to happen, yet still when I saw the matter of the bill staring at me, I could only stare back in return, shake my head, and say to myself:

"Ah weel, weel, we are living under a new and improved dynasty in weaver toon, for in the days of long, long ago, (81/82), not only would it be impossible to have arranged a football, or almost any other match in Bridgeton, (excepting always a fighting match), between a Catholic and Protestant team of young men, but the very bills themselves that would have dared to announce such an event would have to put up with a very considerable amount of defacement"

And today, ah well events have marched rapidly, and we are thankful for what the gods have provided for us, and on Saturday 8th May, we hope to see the biggest crowd of this season in Barrowfield Park, to give a right loyal welcome to these masters in the art of football, the celebrated Harp of Dundee and the no less valiant and generous club, the Clyde, whose kindness in consenting to meet the Harp for the benefit of our poor little shivering, starving ones deserves the warmest and kindest feelings we can express towards them"

The placing of the adverts all around Bridgeton, boldly stating their purpose, was perfectly normal in a normal world, but to place the ads in such an area of sectarian tension as Bridgeton in the 1880s was a bold move which made it clear that nowhere was out of bounds when it came to spreading the word of charity. It was the first shot across the bows to any bigots that we were getting organised and would soon be off our knees. The Poor Children's Dinner Tables to feed the Catholic hungry were here to stay as long as they were required and we wouldn't be bullied or intimidated.

"A very large gathering of spectators was gathered," according to the match report in the Glasgow Observer on Saturday, May 15th, paying 6d each for admission and both teams were at full strength with one exception, with Clyde playing Leslie in place of Cherrie in defence. The match kicked off 15 minutes late at 16.15, hopefully to let the crowd in, and it was Clyde who were forced to play against the strong east wind, which blew into their faces.

For fully ten minutes, the Harp hemmed Clyde into their own half and the home team had defenders Leslie and Hart to thank for the game remaining goalless as *"the Dundee men surprised everyone by the cleverness of their play"*. Clyde however fought their way back into the game and *"several scrimmages took place in front of the Harp's goal"*. It was classic end to end stuff with chances falling to both teams but it was the home team who scored before half time when; *"Stephenson by a magnificent shot, sent the ball through between the posts"*.

Despite facing the wind at the start of the second half, the Harp, playing with a determination started the better, pressing Clyde back for the first ten minutes and this time however it was rewarded with the equaliser. The rest of the game was equal but it was the Harp who notched the winner to claim victory by 2 goals to 1. Both teams played well and it was deemed a good, close game fitting of the occasion with no rough play of any description.

Dundee Harp won the plaudits in the *Scottish Athletic Journal;*

"The Harp showed surprising combination and dash, and it is a pity we do not see them here oftener," as opposed to poor Clyde who; *"played fairly well, but should have done better".*

After the match, watched by a crowd described in the Scottish Athletic Journal as *"not large, but it was enthusiastic enough,"* Brother Walfrid presided over the luncheon which took place in the school house of Sacred Heart and was served by Mr McCarthy of the Regent Restaurant, no doubt as a favour to Brother Walfrid.

The usual toasts were proposed wishing each other well and responded to, before the gathering ended, with plenty of food for thought for Brother Walfrid. Excuse the pun.

What he learned that day was that football could assist him greatly in his mission to maintain the Free Dinner And Breakfast tables. Were the first seeds planted in his mind to start a football team of his own in May 1886?

A one-off charity match to take advantage of the goodwill in the area proved that this endeavour was certainly worthwhile and could and should be tried again, but did he have enough contacts in the area of a similar mind, was it proved beyond doubt that it could sustain itself long term and could it lead to success? All of the above were far from proven and Brother Walfrid had enough on his hands running a very busy school and trying to keep the Dinner Tables afloat along with the rest of the Committee.

FOOTBALL, CHARITY AND A PROMOTION

By August 1886, the healthy funds raised from the charity match between Clyde and Dundee Harp had dwindled, but Brother Walfrid decided to go to the well once more and he organised a match between Edinburgh Hibernians and St Peter's, from the parish of that name in Partick. The match was at Glengarry Park, adjacent to Clyde's ground in Bridgeton and at the time was the home ground of Eastern Rovers on Saturday, 18th September 1886. Around this time Brother Walfrid was promoted from Assistant to the position of Brother Superior of the Marist Order in Glasgow and he remained at his base at 71 Charlotte Street, but now his remit didn't just cover the well-being of Sacred Heart School but it took in all the schools in the city where the Marists taught.

The Head Teacher at St Mary's at the time was Brother Walfrid's friend Brother Dorotheus, (Henry Currie), and so on this occasion, the Dinner Tables at St Mary's, Calton were the recipients of the proceeds of the charity match. The same modus operandi existed with Brother Walfrid seeking the assistance of the Glasgow Observer to advertise the match and after the second biggest Catholic club, Dundee Harp, had provided the opposition the last time, he was delighted to get the approval from the biggest Catholic club in the country this time, Edinburgh Hibernian.

The winter of 1886 was forecast to be particularly harsh so raising enough funds for the maintenance of the Dinner Tables to see it through the coming months of dark, cold nights was a priority and so the entrance fee was set at sixpence for spectators. The only problem was that Hibernian were booked to play a friendly with Stoke at Easter Road on the same day, in return for a match hosted by Stoke the previous year.

This affected the attendance and limited it to around 1000 and it was also the cause of a huge shock when Hibs were beaten by five goals to nil. The first fifteen minutes had been tight but St Peter's then scored two goals in a couple of minutes to take charge of the game. No more goals were scored in the first half but at the start of the second, the Hibs XI came into the game and were unlucky not to score on a couple of occasions. Three more goals were scored but they were all at the other end as St Peter's took great credit in slaying the Hibs by five goals with no response.

Back at Easter Road, the Hibs first team beat Stoke 4-0, but that was no consolation to the St Mary's Dinner Tables Committee who, although grateful, were more than a little disappointed to book Hibernian, the top attraction, only to have to settle for their Second X1.

A NEW GLASGOW IRISH TEAM IS BORN

If Brother Walfrid had been tempted to start an Irish team in 1886, the idea was not a new one as there were numerous "smaller" Irish clubs in and around Glasgow, Lanarkshire and Dunbartonshire. The parish of St Andrews however, in particular their Catholic Temperance Society did just that in September, 1886 by founding the Glasgow Harp and announced it in the *Glasgow Observer;*

"Within the last few years the game of football has become exceedingly popular throughout Great Britain and particularly so in Scotland. The Edinburgh Hibernians having proved themselves pre eminent masters of this popular athletic sport, it is not surprising that youthful Hibs in Glasgow should desire to become proficient in this manly and healthy exercise. Presuming on your courtesy for the insertion of this letter, I have been requested to inform the Catholics of Glasgow, (through your valuable journal), that a Football Club, entitled the "Glasgow Harp", has been formed.

It consists at present of 30 active members who are connected with Saint Andrews Catholic Temperance Society, Glasgow. They have already strengthened in their enterprise by receiving the names of 150 honorary members. The active members of the club having been engaged in practice for some time past, hope on an early date, to show their ability in a creditable manner in athletic exercise.

With constant practice and fully equipped, the members hope not only to merit distinction, but also desire in course of time to prove a source of income to various Catholic charities. Meantime any application or communication relative to the Football club should be addressed to James Cairns, Treasurer, or to yours respectfully, James McGrory, Secretary, Glasgow Harp Football Club

Saint Andrew's Hall, Ropework Lane, Clyde Street, Glasgow"

If, and it's a big if, Brother Walfrid had any intentions of starting an Irish Catholic club in Glasgow in 1886, the foundation of another Irish Catholic club in Glasgow, and its announcement to *"inform the Catholics of Glasgow,"* would have been a blow, however it was too early for Brother

Walfrid to have his day and there were other ingredients still to be added before everything was in place. On the contrary this development could have been seen by Brother Walfrid as a positive, with someone else testing the waters, and if successful he would make contact with the club to follow up on their *"desire in course of time to prove a source of income to various Catholic charities"*.

For Brother Walfrid, the maintenance of the Dinner Tables was the complete focus, starting a football club to provide this maintenance was a means to an end. If Glasgow Harp were successful, earned the support of the Glasgow Irish and at the same time helped maintain the Dinner Tables, then he would have been more than satisfied. Today we would be following Glasgow Harp instead of Celtic.

Celtic Football Club, hence would never have been founded as there would have been no need. If Glasgow Harp were to be unsuccessful and fell by the wayside, then similarly, Brother Walfrid would learn valuable lessons, from the outside looking in, which would assist him greatly.

The name of James Cairns as Treasurer of Glasgow Harp is very interesting as there was a James Cairns involved in Celtic's foundation just over a year later. It would have been a wise move of Brother Walfrid's to involve James Cairns and to use his experience to advise against any mistakes that could be repeated. Significantly, James Cairns rose to become a member of the Celtic Committee from 1892 to 1894.

The name of the Secretary, James McGrory was no relation to our very own legendary Jimmy McGrory although the coincidence raises a smile. Neither was he a relation of one of our Founding Fathers Joseph McGroary, (note the spelling), who hailed from Mountcharles in dear old Donegal. In another quirk of fate Columba, one of the junior teams that Brother Walfrid founded, had as their Secretary - Jimmy Quinn. Incredibly, the coincidences don't end there as Eastern Rovers, who also played at Glengarry Park and who Brother Walfrid had renewed in 1885 after they had lapsed five years earlier, had a Jimmy McMenemy as Treasurer!

There is no truth in the rumour there was a Henrik Larsson kicking about the Calton in the background to our early history, but it's remarkable that the names of three of our greatest ever players - Jimmy McGrory, Jimmy McMenemy and Jimmy Quinn – were already known in the community.

The parish of St Andrews had also set up a Free Breakfast And Dinner Table and on November 16th, 1886, they held a Charity Ball in the City Hall, Albion Street to assist in its funding. Interestingly one of the names to contact to secure tickets was Timothy J Walls, who was well known for arranging large functions in Glasgow and another man who was to become an early Celtic member and committee man.

1886 CLOSES IN SADNESS FOR BROTHER WALFRID

Father Noonan, was born on the 21st December, 1832 in County Limerick and was one of the men crucial to the development of Brother Walfrid as a Marist Brother in Glasgow and it was he, who gave Brother Walfrid his first big opportunity by taking him to Sacred Heart in 1873 to set up the new school.

Both men had worked together at St Mary's from 1870 when Brother Walfrid arrived to teach at the school and the story of Sacred Heart parish in Bridgeton from its formative year in 1873 to 1886 was the story of the two men: Father Noonan and Brother Walfrid. They had a great respect for each other, gained through working together for 16 years, which encapsulated every year of Brother Walfrid's vocation as a Marist Brother with the exception of his first year at St Mungo's from 1869 to 1870. Therefore it is fair to assume that Brother Walfrid learned a great deal from the teachings and personality of Father Noonan.

What a tragic turn of events it was then on Saturday, 9th October 1886, shortly after Father Noonan had said his final early morning mass at 06.30 at his great friend's Marist HQ at 71 Charlotte Street. He took unwell around 11.30 after returning from a sick call to a nearby house half an hour earlier and just as he was about to leave Sacred Heart on another errand. Instead he felt weak and retired to his room requesting assistance.

By coincidence the Very Reverend Doctor Fox from Mossend was visiting the parish and gave last rites to the dying priest. Doctor John Conway, (a Celtic Founding Father just over a year later), was quickly summoned from his home on nearby Monteith Row and attended immediately but sadly Father Noonan, aged only 54, had fallen unconscious and nothing could be done. Doctor Conway remained there until the end and Brother Walfrid was called for as the point of death was nearing, *"as tears and prayers came alternatively from those in the room"*.

Having remained as Head Teacher at Sacred Heart whilst fulfilling his role as Brother Superior based at Saint Joseph's Monastery on Charlotte Street, it was Brother Walfrid's very sad duty on Tuesday, 12th October to attend the funeral of his great friend and colleague, Father Edward Noonan, at Sacred Heart chapel and to join every man, woman and child in the parish in mourning, before his remains were taken to Saint Mary's, Calton where he lies at rest in the vaults.

The *Catholic Herald* supplement on August 7th, 1909 summed both men up best;

"Of the immense good done by the highly esteemed Father Noonan, till his death in 1886, we need not speak. It may, however, be stated without exaggeration that, next to him, no one holds a higher place in the affection of the old parishioners of the Sacred Heart than dear old Brother Walfrid, whose work, especially among the young men of the parish, will not readily be forgotten."

A week later, Father Francis Joseph Hughes, a County Monaghan man who had previously worked with Father Noonan at St Mary's, was appointed in his place and would become another close colleague of Brother Walfrid.

THE FOCUS RETURNS TO THE DINNER TABLES AND THE THREAT OF PROSELYTISM

1886 ended with the 33rd Annual Concert of the Saint Vincent De Paul Society in the City Halls, Glasgow, on Tuesday, 9th November, presided over by His Grace, the Archbishop of Glasgow. Before the programme of events began, the Archbishop addressed those present and once more focussed on the main topic of the day: the maintenance of the Dinner Tables and the threat of proselytism, giving clear examples of its use.

Stressing the importance of funding the maintenance of the Dinner Tables, the Archbishop read from the six monthly written report from the Childrens Dinner Table at Saint Mary's. In the first six months of the year 26,421 dinners were given out to children. Of this total 1,032 were able to be paid for by the parents at one penny each; 7,682 were halfpenny dinners to those who could not afford more; and 17,707 were free dinners given to those who couldn't afford to pay. The problem was clear: demand far exceeded the income available as almost 70% could not afford to pay anything and less than 4% were able to pay the full penny. More had to be done and quickly.

The Archbishop then announced that the Sisters of Charity of Saint Vincent De Paul were undertaking the establishment of a Catholic Refuge for children at 21 Whitevale Street, (on the site where St Anne's Catholic chapel has stood since 1933), in an effort to counter the numerous proselytising agencies and societies. A house had been bought for the Refuge, which would not be an orphanage, it would be a temporary arrangement until the children could be provided for on a more permanent basis.

Brother Walfrid would have been in attendance at the concert, just like he was at the Charity Sermon at Sacred Heart on the 19th February when the Archbishop first spelled out and then tackled the problem of the twin threat to the Catholic children in the area. Brother Walfrid, as Brother Superior, would now feel more of a responsibility than he did nine months previously, when he was "merely" Head Teacher at Sacred Heart, but he would have been struck by the thought that in those nine long months, although a lot of good work had been done to tackle the issues, they were no closer to eradicating the problem.

THE FINAL INGREDIENT NEARS

Hibernian Football Club were founded in 1875 by Canon Hannan in Edinburgh's Cowgate, an area known as "Little Ireland." After his ordination as a priest in county Limerick in 1860 a month before his 24th birthday, he took up his first role as junior curate at St Patrick's, Cowgate after being persuaded by the bishop for that area whilst he holidayed in Scotland in 1860.

Quickly growing into the role he took on the social conditions in the area which affected the immigrant Irish and he opened a St Patrick's branch of the Young Men's Catholic Society four years after his arrival. Another four years later the foundation stone was laid in what would become the newly built chapel hall, known as St Mary's Street Hall, although its official title was the Catholic Institute.

Two years later his devotion was rewarded when he became the parish priest in charge of St Patrick's and his work with the community went from strength to strength. In 1875 he was approached by 21 year old CYMS member Michael Whelahan who proposed a football club should be started under the auspices of that organisation, which could provide training and changing rooms. In return Father Hannan was content that the youth could partake of healthy outdoor exercise through football instead of spending their hard earned money on drink and he ensured the project was under his control by becoming the first manager of the team.

Hibernian soon became the focus of support for the Irish throughout Scotland, although in those days with travel limited, that support was from a distance and Hibs would be dependant initially on local Catholic players until they spread their wings further afield into the west of Scotland where the vast majority of Catholic players lived. It is said that Hibs only played players who were members of the local CYMS and who were practising Catholics which sounds plausible at their foundation but less so as they competed with Hearts and other teams from the area for the Edinburgh Cup and East of Scotland Shield. It was less plausible still that a player would be dropped from the first team on a Scottish Cup winning run for not attending mass. Over the next dozen years, as Hibs continued to grow, new clubs popped up in many towns throughout Scotland with the name Hibernian in honour of the first Irish team to make it big.

Given the nature of Scottish football at this time, Hibs were not initially accepted into the local Edinburgh Football Association. The excuse given was that they would have to be accepted into the larger Scottish Football Association and so for the first two years of their existence, Hibs were barred on the grounds that they were not Scottish. Finally in 1877 after a petition signed by the leading players in Edinburgh, they were accepted into both organisations but were barred from participation in the Scottish Cup (which had started in the 1873/74 season) for another year. It's a competition that has not brought Hibs much luck since, but one that – on 12th February 1887 - provided a vital ingredient for the formation of Celtic Football Club. For it was on that day that Hibernian overcame Dumbarton to win the Scottish Cup – the greatest prize that Scottish football offered at that time.

Before Hibs lifted the Scottish Cup in season 1886/87, the previous thirteen finals had been won by only four teams: Queens Park on eight occasions; Vale of Leven three times; and Renton and Dumbarton once each. Hibs had reached the previous three semi finals in a row without ever getting to the final, but their big break eventually came on the 22nd January 1887 when they beat Vale of Leven 3-1 to reach the Scottish Cup final for the first time in the club's history. Exactly three weeks earlier they had lost at home to Aston Villa in a friendly on New Years Day by no less than 8 goals to 3 after trailing 4-1 by half time.

In the first three rounds of the Scottish Cup in those days the draw was regional, with up to 150 teams in the 1st round, although this changed for the 1891/92 season when qualifying rounds were set up and numbers cut to 32 for the 1st round, making things much more manageable. In one previous season, 1877, there were only three teams in the semi final due to brilliant mismanagement and Rangers were given a bye into the final - which they then lost to Vale of Leven. It would in fact be seventeen years before the Ibrox club won Scotland's premier trophy – which explains why their name isn't even on the cup itself.

Hibs' early record in the Scottish Cup from 1878 to 1883 was decent, usually getting through to the 5th round before losing out to one of the last 16. They were to suffer a massive blow in 1882 when they lost Willie Cox and James McKernan to Bolton and Frank Rourke, another early stalwart, emigrated to America. In 1883, Hibs played Lugar Boswell in Ayrshire in a friendly and returned east with Lugar's half-back line of Jimmy McGhee, Jimmy McLaren and Peter

McGinn. These players were to propel Hibs onto better things and from the 1883/84 season they reached the semi final of the Scottish Cup for the fourth season in succession, losing to the eventual winners in 84 and 85, Queens Park and Renton respectively.

Hibs were to return to Lugar in 1885 to sign Pat Lafferty and Willie Groves was a significant signing from Leith Harp in early 1886 as they continued to grow closer to their dream: getting their hands on the ultimate prize of the Scottish Cup.

VALE OF LEVEN PROTEST HIBERNIAN "PROFESSIONALISM"

The day they had been waiting on was due to arrive on Saturday February 12th 1887 after Vale of Leven were beaten 3-1 at Easter Road in the semi final, with Dumbarton causing a big shock in defeating Queens Park 2-1 at their own ground of Hampden in the other tie. This was Dumbarton's fourth Scottish Cup final and they were hoping for their second victory, whilst for Hibs of course, this was their first final.

However, in the build up to the final, Vale of Leven protested their semi final match with Hibernian on the following basis:

1. Coaching of his team by the Hibs umpire. (Each team would allocate a member of their staff to act as linesman, a role which meant they had to remain neutral).
2. Abusive language by the umpire.
3. Adverse attitude of spectators.
4. Professionalism.

On Monday 31st January the SFA met to hear Vale of Leven's appeal in front of the full committee which also included John McFadden, the Hibs Secretary, and Mr Campbell, representing Vale of Leven. Whilst the first three protests were faintly ludicrous, the fourth was deadly serious. Clubs in Scotland at the time were amateur and payments made to players were strictly forbidden under the threat of expulsion. Players could be compensated with "lost time," to make up for a day off work to enable them to play a match but that was as far as the rules went.

The matter was treated with the utmost seriousness and first up to put his club's case forward was Mr Campbell from Vale of Leven. His protest was based on an allegation that in the build-up to the semi final, Hibs players had not been at their place of work and had instead been training for the match. One player in particular, Montgomery, had allegedly arrived in Edinburgh the Tuesday before the match and stayed there until after matchday. It was hardly likely, Campbell added, that the Hibs players would lose their wages unless they were receiving an equivalent from Hibernian: in effect, he alleged, they were guilty of professionalism.

Hibernian denied all charges and the Chairman asked if the Vale of Leven had any proof. Crucially, they did not: they had been told of the allegations whilst in Edinburgh by a third party and based their whole argument of professionalism on this hearsay.

Mr McFadden then entered the room, having previously been told to stand outside during the questioning of the Vale of Leven representative, despite him claiming he should be allowed to remain as he was acting as a representative of the Edinburgh FA and not Hibernian. On his return, he then raised a laugh by stating he was now representing Hibernian. He was questioned by the Chairman and asked if there was any truth in this serious charge. McFadden responded in clear detail to every charge as he was probed, specifically by the Hearts representative Mr Spence, on how each player earned his living. Payments to Willie Groves in particular were the subject of scrutiny.

In return, McFadden's answers explained a number of plausible sounding reasons as to why many of the Hibs players were not at work in the build up to the semi final. He did let slip, however, that Mr McDonald, the club's Patron, had publicly promised the players a bonus if they won. Explaining away the Montgomery allegation, McFadden stated that the player was a cousin of the Hibs' Honorary Secretary and whilst in Edinburgh he stayed with family without payment as the family were well off.

Mr Spence, from Hearts, wasn't for giving up without a fight and proposed the sub committee on professionalism should be reformed to look into this issue, "and sift this case to the bottom." This received a seconder. Mr McCulloch, from Our Boys, nailed his colours to the Hibernian mast and moved that the protest be dismissed, stating correctly that it was up to the Vale of Leven to bring proof and they had brought none.

With sides being taken, Mr Dyer from Lanarkshire, in an effort to move things on and get them out of this tricky mess, responded that if the protest was dismissed, Vale of Leven could still bring forward proof of their charge at any time before the final.

Mr Carmichael from 5th KRV however wasn't content with that and hinted that possible inducements and even payments from the Hibs' Patron, Mr McDonald, needed looked into further. Mr Spence from Hearts (possibly betraying himself as knowing the source of the Vale of Leven's allegations that they were told "whilst in Edinburgh" of the charge of professionalism) pressed again for a sub committee to be reformed to look into allegations of professionalism at Hibs, adding that he had been told the alleged inducement promised by the Hibs Patron was £5 each and a gold medal.

This was a well-timed bombshell, designed to ensure the debate descended into uproar and Mr Crerar, from Third Lanark, pointed out that Mr McFadden had admitted that his players had been off work which was sufficient for them to inquire further into the matter.

Finally, Mr Nisbet from Cowlairs made a crucial point that settled any doubt over the question of Hibs' participation in the final, when he made everyone aware that if the protest was sustained, they would have to reinstate not only Vale of Leven, but every team Hibs had played in the tournament that season. This was something that was never going to happen in a month of Sundays, but what it did do was to focus minds on a solution without going round the houses any longer.

Immediately the protest was dismissed but the charge of professionalism against Hibs was left open for Vale of Leven to bring forward evidence within ten days.

This was a ground-breaking decision because if the SFA Committee had sustained the Vale of Leven's charge of professionalism, Hibs would not only have been thrown out of the Scottish Cup, but they would have faced expulsion from Scottish football as happened to St Bernards and also Renton (although both were subsequently reinstated). If this course of action had happened, it would have had serious repercussions for the founding of Celtic because it was on the 12th February in St Mary's Hall at the after match celebrations following Hibs' success that many of the ingredients were in the same room at the same time, with a challenge thrown down to the local Irish present just at the right time.

HIBERNIAN'S DATE WITH DESTINY ARRIVES

When the big day arrived, a lovely sunny day at that, it's true to say that Hibs were carrying the hopes and aspirations of the Irish throughout Scotland and this was backed up by the support they had on the day. Around 1,000 fans arrived from Edinburgh, a huge number of travelling supporters in those days, and the rest of the Hibs support that made up the majority of the 10,000 crowd were from the Glasgow area. At least as many again also took up every vantage point outside Hampden, as there were inside the ground.

The Hibs team travelled by train from Edinburgh Waverley, departing shortly before 13.00 and arrived into Queen Street station at 14.12, for the 15.30 kick off at the first Hampden at Crosshill (not far from the current Hampden). It is noted significantly in the *Glasgow Observer* on Saturday February 19th, that they were *"met by several of the more prominent Irishmen of the city"*.

Given that it was the Irishmen from the parish of St Mary's in the Calton that had organised the after match get-together at the chapel hall, it's fair to assume that they would have been among the prominent Irishmen of the city at Queen Street to welcome the Hibernian party.

Brother Walfrid, John Glass and Doctor John Conway would certainly have been amongst that number.

The Hibs team on their first ever visit to Hampden Park that famous day was: John Tobin in goals; full backs James Lundy and Barney Fagan; half-backs James McGhee, Peter McGinn and Jimmy McLaren: and a forward line of Paddy Lafferty and Willie Groves on the right, James Montgomery as centre forward and Phil Clarke and George Smith on the left. Interestingly half the team had comprised of former Lugar Boswell players: James Lundy, Jimmy McLaren, Jimmy McGhee, Peter McGinn and Paddy Lafferty. Is it likely that these individuals from Ayrshire would have moved to Edinburgh without some kind of inducement from Hibernian?

"Hibs made such havoc to their ranks," as the Scottish Athletic Journal stated in November, 1885.

Only two players, McLaren and Groves were to enjoy a successful career at Celtic.

James McGhee was the Hibs captain and James Montgomery replaced prolific goal-scorer Jerry Reynolds up front due to injury. This was the same Jerry Reynolds that Celtic "kidnapped" from

Carfin Shamrock on the eve of our Scottish Cup 1st round tie with Queens Park in September 1889 and converted to a defender, but more of that later. In the Dumbarton forward line, was another future Celtic connection in Johnny Madden, who was to play in the Scottish Cup Final for us in 1892 against Queens Park, which was protested and unfortunately he was out injured for the replay which we won.

The reality that was to be repeated many times over at future Celtic games, was that whilst the Dumbarton support represented a town in Dunbartonshire, to many in the west of Glasgow, the Hibs support represented a people and a cause.

The *Scottish Athletic Journal* painted a picture of those who attended the game:

"The scene on the way to the ground - say about half an hour from the start - was a most interesting one. There was one stream of cabs, hansoms and buses, all heavily laden for at least an hour before the game commenced. Pedestrians flooded the road in vast numbers and with eager feet as glibly talking tongues, they hurried towards the one centre - Hampden Park. As is usually the case at Hampden Park on big days, the entrances were inadequate to the requirements of the crowd, and in consequence, there was a good deal of pushing and scrambling.

On looking at the circle of faces around the ropes and on the stands, one could not but remark the predominance of the Irish cast of countenance. Sprinkled plentifully throughout the vast multitude were to be seen many enthusiastic followers of the Hibernians with knots of green upon their breasts, cards in their hats on which were inscribed the words 'Hurry Up Hibs', or with fanciful green sashes over their shoulders. Everywhere the Irishman was prominent, not only by his wearing the colour of his favourites, but the tones of the brogue, which were pitched in an extra high key to suit the occasion. The wrongs of country and all such kindred troubles were entirely forgotten in that short, sweet moment of triumph, and the wild impulses of the race found free vent in a wild "hurroo" of victory".

James McGhee led the Hibs team out a few minutes before half three "and were received by vociferous cheering again and again renewed." Hibs won the toss and played with the wind on the slippery pitch while Johnny Madden kicked off for Dumbarton. The pace was furious with lots of chances falling to both sides but Hibs would have been the happier of the two teams to hear the half time whistle with the match still goalless.

The *Glasgow Observer*, in its match report, stated;

"During the first half, the hopes of the Irishmen seemed crestfallen. McGhee knew what he was about. He allowed the Dumbartonians to assume the aggressive and he showed his own goal to be impregnable in the face of some really excellent play".

The second half resumed with Dumbarton again forcing the play but Hibs were far from out of it as they looked dangerous on occasion also, to the great excitement of the crowd.

"To say that the spectators were excited is using a mild expression, as every bit of play elicited vociferous cheering. When we have said this it will easily be conceived how intensely excited the multitude were, and how tremendous was the enthusiasm which greeted a smart piece of play by the Hibs".

And then Dumbarton scored in the 58th minute.

Ralph Aitken, it was, who opened the scoring, another surname which was to be synonymous with the fantastic fighting spirit of the Celtic team a century later.

Johnny Madden almost made it two, *"grazing the left upright,"* with a shot, but with fifteen minutes remaining, Hibs' attacking play was rewarded with the equaliser with Phil Clarke getting the credit for the goal, although the reporter from the *Glasgow Observer* credited it to Montgomery.

"A sharp shot was sent from the left wing by Clarke into the Dumbarton goal, and Macauley caught the ball, but let it slip from his hands, and Montgomery, (the Hibernian's centre), who was standing close beside, rushed in and sent the ball through, thus equalising the score".

"The cheer with which this performance was hailed was loud and long continued, and the entire crowd seemed waving hats, sticks and handkerchiefs in the most jubilant manner".

The Scottish Umpire described the goal as follows;

"A quarter of an hour from time, Clarke started a simple enough looking run up the left and to the surprise of all beat Macauley, who somehow missed an easy looking ball."

No mention of Montgomery is given in their account.

They then state that *"Dumbarton, who had previously looked all over the winner, and who unquestionably played the soundest game, seemed to lose their heads, became flurried and played erratically".*

Worse was to follow for Dumbarton and much, much better for Hibernian as recorded in the Scottish Umpire:

"Eight minutes from time, Hibs got up the centre, and passing out to Lafferty, who lay well up all by himself, that player, amidst cries of off-side, closed in unopposed upon the Dumbarton citadel, which he captured with a well directed shot. The Dumbarton players, trusting in their claim, very stupidly made little effort to save a perfectly saveable goal. Their appeal, however, was dismissed by both umpires, the referee not being called to interfere at all. No protest was made, though many think Lafferty was offside".

The *Glasgow Observer* had only two minutes remaining when they take up the story:

"A corner fell to Dumbarton, which was unproductive, and the ball was passed along. Groves got the leather at his toe and rushed on to Macauley's charge, while the Dumbarton were vigorously appealing for offside and put forth no effort to save their goal, the ball of course being sent through. Off-side was again claimed by the Dumbarton but the referee gave the goal - an intimation received with great enthusiasm by the Hibs supporters".

Despite the *Scottish Umpire's* less than subtle hint that Lafferty was in an offside position when gathering the ball from the breakaway and running up field to score the winner, the *Glasgow Observer* took up the story with the ball being passed to Groves. Both newspapers agree on the two main ingredients to the story: the claim for offside and the stupidity of the Dumbarton players in making no effort to stop the goal, so sure were they that it was offside.

At the end of the match, the Hibs supporters, containing thousands of Glasgow Irish, ran onto the Hampden turf and carried their favourites shoulder high to the pavillion.

The *Scottish Umpire* summed up the scene well;

"Probably never before was there such jubilation over a victory as that over the Hibs' success. The whole of Irish Scotland seemed to be in the merriest of merry moods and green was the prevailing colour, except in the Dumbarton ranks, where the blue seemed more to abound".

The records show that "Darlin" Willie Groves was credited with the winner and not Lafferty, and whilst Dumbarton's failure to play to the whistle cost them dear, it certainly helped complete the perfect celebratory atmosphere that filled St Mary's Hall, Calton shortly afterwards.

The Scottish Athletic Journal was less than generous at the start of their match report, but by the end they were smitten by the Hibernian support;

"The Hibernians have been very lucky all through the competition, and their good fortune extended even to the final tie. The Dumbarton, after having more of the game than their opponents and after giving as good an exhibition of combination as has been seen on Hampden Park this season, were actually beaten. Indeed, Dumbarton threw away the game if ever a game was thrown away. Jupiter nods occasionally and even that giant among goalkeepers, Macaulay, let through a goal in a most un-accountable way. The greasy state of the ball must be the reason for the great custodian letting it through his hands.

No goals were scored in the opening period during which Dumbarton had a dozen shies at the Hibernian fortress for every one the Irishmen had at theirs, but the shooting was not of the straightest, many splendid opportunities, being thrown away. Dumbarton drew first blood early in the second half, a grand shot by Aitken taking effect. Then about fifteen minutes from the finish a shot sent in from the left equalised the game, the ball going through Macaulay's hands, and five minutes later Groves ran the ball through, the Dumbarton team having stopped playing, claiming a foul. The goal, however was allowed and it proved the winning point, as nothing further was done, the Hibernians winning by two goals to one".

The language used could not hide the author's disappointment, but he was more graceful as he described the Hibernian celebrations;

"The Irish element was strong, but not until the close did their pent-up feelings find vent. The scene at the finish was something extraordinary, the enthusiasm being unbounded and the delight of the supporters of the Hibernians extravagant and truly characteristic of the warm hearted Irish race. The ambition of years had been gratified and those who witnessed the scene must have felt pleased that the Hibernians had been victorious."

Others at the *Scottish Athletic Journal* were more than pleased:

"A wild shriek of triumph went up from thousands of lusty Irish throats on Saturday at Hampden when the whistle blew and the Hibernians were loudly proclaimed the champion football team of the year 1886-1887.

The scene at the close was one of the most amusing we have ever witnessed at any football match. A good many of the Irishmen almost went mad with delight, while others, not so impressionable shook hands and congratulated each other warmly. Several of the players were carried shoulder high into the pavillion, round which the people flocked in vast numbers. Cheers were raised for the Hibs, and for the Dumbarton, and one or two irrepressible sons of Erin tried to do a bit of speech making but they were promptly silenced.

We are intensely Irish this week. There is no final in recent years which can vie with this one and point of interest. Never has such a wild exalted enthusiasm been shown in any game as was shown by the supporters of the Hibs on Saturday. Their yells were at times demoniacal and when it was seen that the Hibs had won their delight approached almost to madness. Truly the Irish are a warm hearted impulsive race and if winning the cup can give them so much delight, we need not grudge it them once in a while".

THE VITAL INGREDIENTS COME TOGETHER
- WAS DR. JOHN CONWAY'S SPEECH THE CATALYST?

The "prominent Irishmen of Glasgow" and its surrounds who welcomed Hibernian to the after-match dinner in the very hall where Celtic were to be founded nine months later, came from the various Irish political and religious organisations that thrived in the city and beyond at the time. It also came from the clergy and the Marist Brothers who were active in the city and it brought together the sharpest minds of the mother parish of St Mary's, Calton, amongst their number. It is no surprise that this most enterprising parish was the catalyst to host the celebrations where it can be said Celtic Football Club was conceived.

The list of political and religious organisations in the Glasgow area in 1887 was long and crucially the Founding Fathers of Celtic held prominent roles in many of them and they not only knew each other well through these organisations, they had experience of working on the same committees and knew each others' organisational strengths.

The local Catholic Union committees were led by John O'Hara and Thomas Flood and Joseph Nelis and Joseph Shaughnessy were founder members of the Saint Aloysius Association. The Irish National League, who campaigned for Home Rule in Ireland had one of their largest branches in Glasgow, which was given the title of the Home Government Branch and amongst their leading figures were Celtic Founding Fathers such as John Glass, William McKillop, James Quillan and brothers Arthur and Hugh Murphy.

The Irish National Foresters were also active in the area as a relief group set up to assist fellow Irishmen and by nature they were also pro Home Rule for Ireland.

Pat Welsh was a leading light in the Amnesty group which called for the release of Irish political prisoners and for good reason too. Pat and his brother were leading Fenian activists in troubled Ireland in the 1860s, they were both wanted men and to escape imminent capture, Pat decided to start out a new life and seek sanctuary in Glasgow in 1867. This involved a plan to embark upon a boat from Pigeon House Harbour in Ringsend, Dublin, but he was spotted by fellow Irishman, Sergeant Tom Maley - an Ennis, County Clare man - who was in his final years in the British Army and was stationed at the Pigeon House Fort, a heavily armed garrison to guard the nearby harbour.

On hearing the man's plight and his promise to make good a new life in Glasgow, the Sergeant sympathised and allowed the fellow Irishman, Welsh, to board the sailing from the harbour - and the rest as they say is history.

In Willie Maley's own words, in the Weekly News on 23rd May 1936, Pat Welsh *"told a pitiful tale to my father - a tale which so touched the old man's heart, that he helped him get out of the country and on his way to Glasgow."*

Welsh set up business as a master tailor on fashionable Buchanan Street in Glasgow city centre and then assisted Tom Maley Senior, just three few years later in 1870, after his discharge from the army, as he too settled his family, initially in the parish of St Mary's in the East End before moving to the village of Cathcart. When Brother Walfrid and John Glass travelled to Cathcart in 1887 to persuade Tom Maley to sign for Celtic, Pat Welsh was the ideal man to take with them as he knew the family well and knew that permission from the parents to talk to Tom - and Willie as it turned out - wouldn't be a problem.

And so the names of the Brother Superior at the Marist House at 71 Charlotte Street, Brother Walfrid and Brother Dorotheus, Head Teacher at St Mary's joined these other Celtic Founding Fathers named at the gathering on 12th February in St Mary's Hall: Doctor John Conway who read the congratulatory speech; William McKillop, John Glass, John O'Hara, James Quillan, Pat Welsh, James McKay, James Curtis and Michael Cairns; as well as subscribers to the original Celtic fundraising circular: John Higney, Pat Gaffney, John Brown and William Savage.

From the *Scottish Athletic Journal*;

THE HIBS ENTERTAINED IN GLASGOW

"A committee of Glasgow Irishmen entertained the teams after the match and much speech making and mutual congratulations were indulged in.

After the match the Hibernians, accompanied by several of their Edinburgh friends, were entertained to dinner in the hall of the Saint Mary's Young Men's Association, East Rose Street, which was tastefully decorated for the occasion. Doctor Conway presided and was supported amongst others by Messrs John Glass, Tim Walls, Michael Cairns, John Brown, William Savage, John McFadden and others.

The Chairman, in a few well chosen remarks, proposed the health of the Hibernians. He said that all Irishmen were delighted at their victory that day. Their success upon the football field was due to the untiring energy and determination of every member of the team. He strongly urged the necessity of emulating their example, not only in social but in political matters as well, so that the goal of every Irishman's ambition - the legislative independence of his country - would soon be attained. (Cheers).

The toast was received with the greatest enthusiasm. Mister McFadden, the energetic Secretary of the Hibs replied. In the course of a racy speech he said that on behalf of the team and himself, he thanked from his heart the people of Glasgow, and especially his Irish friends in the East End of the city, for the magnificent reception they had received at Hampden Park. All they wanted was a fair field and no favour. At Hampden Park they had a very fair field - (laughter) - and certainly no favour. (Cheers).

He said "There were warm receptions and warm receptions, but although they anticipated a warm reception from their Edinburgh friends when they reached home, it would be nothing in comparison to the warm reception they would have met with had they lost. (Laughter). They knew that the eyes not only of the immense crowd of spectators assembled at Hampden Park, but of every Irishman throughout the length and breadth of the country, were upon them today and they were determined to come off victorious. (Cheers).

Now however, having succeeded in winning the cup, they were going to keep it - (laughter) - and he hoped when the Hibernians came back to Hampden Park for the final next year that in the words of the poet "May I be there to see" - (laughter and cheers). The evening's entertainment which was of a most enjoyable character and reflects greatest credit upon the Committee and Brother Dorotheus, was enlivened by a selection of songs from the genial Chairman, the captain of the Hibernians and several others. Before breaking up, "God Save Ireland" was sung by the entire assembly, after which the team drove to the Queen Street Station, being loudly cheered by knots of people here and there on the way. They left for Edinburgh by the 8.20pm train amid the loud cheers of a large crowd".

From the *Glasgow Observer*;

"The team were afterwards entertained in Saint Mary's school, East Rose Street, Doctor John Conway presided and there were also present Fathers Nolan, Van Der Heyde and McColl, Messrs McFadden, Whelahan, Welsh and Hackett of Edinburgh, ex Councillor Walls, Mr Cairns, solicitor, Neilston, Messrs John Higney, Pat Gaffney, William Savage, James Quillan, John Brown, Edward Vallely, John O'Hara, James Curtis, James McKay, Daniel Blaney, John Horsburgh, Charles Crossan, William Toner, J Henigan, John Byrne, James Rodgers, W Flannigan, Patrick V McCulloch, Peter McAvoy and Michael Shannon.

After an excellent supper had been partaken of, the Chairman, (Doctor John Conway), who was received with great enthusiasm and applause, said:

Gentlemen my first duty is to congratulate our friends and countrymen, the guests of the evening, in whose honour we are gathered here tonight, upon the great success and widespread fame they have attained in the province of football, and more particularly to congratulate the Hibernians upon their grand exploit of today in defeating, after a hard struggle, the Dumbarton club, who once before held the cup.

This achievement we understand places them upon the very pinnacle of excellence amongst the football clubs of Scotland this year. By it they have added immensely in their already great renown, and they have reflected great credit on their friends and on their country. This conspicuous success today, was no doubt, mainly due to their own heroic exertions, but if the ardent hopes and fervent prayers of large numbers of their countrymen on the field and a multitude of them unable to be present had any efficiency, then they must be credited with helping towards the great result.

The performance of the Hibernian evidences that they must be possessed of the greatest pluck, skill and perseverance to have achieved such a glorious result amongst a host of competitors, animated not only by the rivalry which is the usual concomitant of the game but, I am sorry to say, in many cases by a bigotry so great as to be a much stronger incentive to exertion than any mere desire for victory could possibly be.

Now we all desire to give the Hibernians that high commendation which they have so well earned, and as it has become proverbial that imitation is the sincerest flattery, I think we could not please them better than by following their example each in our own department and seeking by the exercise of the same good qualities that have placed them so high among the football fraternity to place ourselves among the best men in our respective vocations.

The effect of this upon our own happiness will not be the only good result derived for each advance will increase vastly the weight of our influence and so enable us to render more efficient assistance towards obtaining for our country that which the united political sagacity of our trusted leaders has indicated as the first essential to her happiness - namely Home Government.

I have now, gentlemen, the greatest pleasure in proposing the health and continued success of the Hibernian". *(Loud cheering).*

In the reply from John McFadden, Secretary of Hibernian, he stated that;

"On behalf of the members of the club, he tendered the Irishmen of Glasgow his best thanks for the handsome reception they had met with and for the magnificent ovation they had received on Hampden Park. (Applause). The members of the team knew that day that the eyes not alone of the spectators that were present but the eyes of every Irishman in Scotland were upon them, and they were fully determined to show their opponents what Irishmen could do. (Applause).

The field was fair. Decidedly they received no favour. (Laughter). They felt proud that they had been the means of bringing such gladness to the hearts of their countrymen in Glasgow, and the very warm hearts of the Irishmen of the East End; and they only hoped that the club would go on upholding the high name they had all along strove to maintain. (Applause). Long windedness, he considered a good thing for a football player, but not for a speaker. (Laughter). From their hearts the members of the club thanked the Irishmen of Glasgow for the magnificent and warm reception they had given them that day. They would, indeed, have got a "warm" reception in Edinburgh if they had not been victorious. (Applause).

Songs were afterwards sung by the Hibs captain James McGhee, Doctor John Conway and Mr Shannon from Glasgow, Mr Smith from Edinburgh, and Mr Cairns. After a short address from William Savage the proceedings closed with the singing of "God Save Ireland".

Both reports of the festivities and significantly, the speeches, are similar from the *Scottish Athletic Journal* and the *Glasgow Observer*, but it's obvious who carried more weight with the organising committee, as it was the latter who had privy to the letter of Doctor Conway's oration and not just a summary.

Crucially, there is no mention in either report of John McFadden's short speech of him telling the packed hall of prominent Irishmen to "Go and do likewise," in the context of starting up an Irish team to represent the Catholics of the west of Scotland. Therefore, if we are to take the articles, in particular the *Glasgow Observer's* as gospel - excuse the pun - as an accurate reflection of the speech in full, then Tom Maley's assessment of McFadden's words, quoted on 15th July, 1916 in the *Weekly Mail* as "Go thou and do likewise", can only have been spoken in a private conversation rather than in his speech.

In fact more light is shed on analysing the very significant and very political speech of Doctor Conway, in particular to his reference, given as his exact words, *"imitation is the sincerest flattery,"* from the following in the *Glasgow Observer:*

*"Now we all desire to give the Hibernians that high commendation which they have so well earned, and **as it has become proverbial that imitation is the sincerest flattery, I think we could not please them better than by following their example** each in our own department and seeking by the exercise of the same good qualities that have placed them so high among the football fraternity to place ourselves among the best men in our respective vocations".*

Or in the summary from the *Scottish Athletic Journal;*

"The Chairman, in a few well chosen remarks, proposed the health of the Hibernians. He said that all Irishmen were delighted at their victory that day. Their success upon the football field was due to the untiring energy and

determination of every member of the team. He strongly urged the necessity of emulating their example, not only in social but in political matters as well, so that the goal of every Irishman's ambition - the legislative independence of his country - would soon be attained".

In the context of Dr Conway urging all Irishmen to strive for their best, in order to attain the ultimate goal of Home Rule, in doing so he appears to be referring strongly to the readiness of the Glasgow Irish for the ultimate imitation of Edinburgh Hibernian: an Irish football club in Glasgow. If not, it was quite a coincidence to use such a key phrase in such an important speech.

Was it the words of Doctor John Conway, recorded in their entirety in the newspapers of the day, and not those of John McFadden's spoken in private, "To go and do likewise," that were the true catalyst to the birth of Celtic? Certainly the Doctor's words would have caught the imagination of the prominent Irishmen present and if the words of John McFadden, "to go and do likewise," were in a private conversation after the speeches, it's very plausible to think that these words came in response to Doctor John Conway's quote in his speech, a consequence of which had set the ball rolling.

John McFadden was known to be of great assistance in assisting in the foundation of quite a number of other teams who sprouted up all over Scotland in the name of Hibernian and Glasgow was no different. It would have been perfectly natural for the Celtic Founding Fathers to be in touch with John McFadden during the discussions to start the club. It has to be remembered that our relationship with Hibs at the very start was excellent, with the Edinburgh club providing the attraction to open Celtic Park on 8th May 1888, in front of a large crowd against Cowlairs and also for John McFadden to referee the first ever Celtic match almost three weeks later on 28th May against Rangers. Indeed, if as claimed, Celtic were originally to be called Glasgow Hibernian right up until Brother Walfrid's interjection, then it would have been even more plausible for the Founding Fathers, very strong willed men, to keep John McFadden onside.

John McFadden, by the same token, was no-one's fool and must have realised from the very start that an Irish team in Glasgow would have serious repercussions for Hibs. Before our birth, Hibs had free reign over the huge pool of Catholic players in the west which they had often relied on. They had the backing of the Glasgow Irish in many away matches in the Glasgow area and they had no real competition for the Irish market. Crucially, Hibernian's dormant support was far larger in Glasgow than it was in their own city. An Irish team in Glasgow would change everything and it didn't take too much to figure that out.

From the *Scottish Umpire:*

"Their supporters in Glasgow and Edinburgh were justified in their celebrations of delight, and in both cities called in the requisition of bands and banners, coloured lights and stump orators, to fittingly celebrate their favourites' triumph.

The Hibs progress from Hampden Park, Glasgow to Saint Mary's Hall, Edinburgh, was one long triumphal procession. They were cheered from the field, feasted by their Glasgow admirers, (reference to the after match dinner at St Mary's Hall, Calton), escorted by a band and a cheering crowd to the station, met on arrival at the Waverley station by a tremendous crowd of all grades cheering vociferously, driven in a four in hand to their headquarters and there in presence of a crowded and harmonious company, lionised as the heroes of the hour. Nothing less than the passing of the Home Rule Bill could have evoked such an outburst of Hibernian delight. Their cup of joy is full and running over. Our wish is that it may not be soon drained".

From the Scottish Leader and adapted in the *Scottish Umpire* and the *Glasgow Observer;*

"The receipt of the news in Edinburgh was anxiously awaited. Early in the afternoon a bogus message had been received that the Dumbarton were two goals ahead at half time. On receipt of the final message however, the utmost enthusiasm prevailed, and long before the arrival of the victorious teams, a crowd numbering many thousands, the station being literally packed, were in waiting, headed by a couple of bands and a four in hand. The arrival of the train was the signal for an outburst of cheering, which was renewed again and again as the prominent members of the team took their place in the brake. (A small vehicle).

On the brake was a lantern shaped transparency, on which, surrounded with harps and shamrocks, were the following "Welcome, Hibernians, winners of the Scottish Cup, 1886/87". On the other side was the following inscription; "God Save Ireland. Hurrah for the green jerseys".

A procession was now formed. But the wagonette soon left the band far behind, and amid a scene of wild enthusiasm and cheering a move was made for Saint Mary's Street Hall, by way of Princes Street and North Bridge.

At the Tron an enormous crowd, headed by another band, was in waiting, and the cheers broke out afresh. In the High Street the crush and enthusiasm was simply enormous. In Saint Mary's Street red and green lime lights were burning. And the greatest excitement prevailed, and the appearance of the team at the street corner was hailed by a perfect salvo of cheering. The hall was packed by the members of the club and others, and on the team making their appearance on the platform they were again cheered. Mr Flannigan, President of the club, occupied the chair and congratulated the eleven on their splendid victory, when had placed them at the top of the tree among Scottish football players.

He was not a football player himself, but he was a great admirer of the game, and showed that it was by perseverance and courage that the Hibernian were at last successful. Mr Flannigan next paid a neat compliment to Mr McFadden, the Secretary, to whom not a little of the credit was due for the proud position in which the club was at present.

Mr McFadden, in reply, said he was amply repaid by the success of that day, as by their deeds they had proved that they were made of no mean stuff. He thanked the captain of the team, without whose aid he should not have been able to carry on the affairs of the club so successfully. Mr McGhee briefly replied, and the President counselling all present to get straight home, brought the day's proceedings to an end, the likes of which has never been witnessed in football annals"

GLASGOW RISES TO HIBERNIAN'S TRIUMPH

The reaction to Hibernians' Scottish Cup win amongst the Glasgow area's 250,000 strong Irish population, (which was ten times greater than the Irish population of Edinburgh), was intense and this was reflected in the numbers present at Hampden which outnumbered the "local" team. Also in the fact that Hibs were feted at St Mary's Hall, Glasgow, before heading home to Edinburgh. The thriving religious and political parties in Glasgow, boosted by the new found confidence that an Irish team winning the Scottish Cup brought, were not slow to pay tribute.

The St Mary's branch of the Young Men's Society passed a vote of congratulations to be sent to Hibernian and it was their President, James Curtis, who was soon to become a founding father of Celtic, committee member and reserve team coach, who did the needful.

In response, John McFadden wrote to James Curtis;

"I am directed by my committee to acknowledge the kindly expression of approval conferred on us by the Saint Mary's Young Men's Society through you, their President. We shall leave nothing undone to maintain the position we have attained, and trust that we shall always merit the encomiums (praise) of our fellow countrymen in the land of Gael."

At the branch of the Total Abstinence Society in the parish of St Michael's, Parkhead, a resolution was moved and seconded by Frank Havelin, (who was to become a founding father of Celtic), *"To the effect that the Secretary forward to the Edinburgh Hibernian FC, the hearty congratulations of the members of this society, for the glorious victory it achieved on Saturday last by carrying home to Edinburgh the Scottish Cup".*

But it was the Home Government Branch of the Irish National League in Glasgow that led the way at their first meeting after the cup final, with a proposal that a Testimonial should be held in Glasgow:

"Encouraging reports were given by various gentlemen of the interest manifested by all classes of Irishmen in the proposed testimonial. It was agreed that the presentation take the form of a public meeting, concert and ball in the Wellington Palace, Commercial Road, Glasgow on Monday 28th February".

One East End priest, Father Maginn, from the parish of St Alphonsus, wasn't happy with the circular sent round the parishes informing them of a Concert and a Ball that was arranged as part of the celebrations, which he felt were inappropriate during Lent. Speaking at a meeting of the Young Men's Guild in his parish, he explained he had no objections to Hibernian being honoured as he was glad, as Hibernians and as Catholics and members of the Catholic Young Men's Society, that they had succeeded in winning the cup, as no reasonable man could grudge them their well earned victory, but he hoped that the Hibernian team would decline to attend.

Good luck with that, as they say.

The Wellington Palace was a cinema in the heart of one of the most Irish parts of Glasgow, the famous Gorbals, and the *Glasgow Observer* gave a fascinating insight into the gathering:

"On Monday evening, the members of the Hibernian team, who won the Scottish Cup were each presented with a gold medal by the members of the Home Government branch of the National League, in the Wellington Palace, Commercial Road, south side Glasgow.

The hall was crowded, Mr John Ferguson presided, and was supported on the platform by a Mr William Simpson, Hillhead; Mr M Flannigan, Edinburgh; Mr James Sorden, Edinburgh; Mr McFadden, Secretary of the Hibernian Football Club; Messrs James McGhee, John Tobin, James Lundy, Barney Fagan, Jimmy McLaren, Peter McGinn, Paddy Lafferty, Willie Groves, James Montgomery, George Smith and Phil Clarke; the winners of the cup, Jerry Reynolds and Tom Maley; members of the Hibernian Football Club, Hugh Murphy, Edward Vallely, James Quillan, William McArdle, John Hopkins, Neil Mullen, James Tracy, John Carroll, Joseph Higgins, P and J McLaughlin and Joseph McGroary.

The Chairman, in opening the meeting, said it was not often that he had the honour or the pleasure of presiding on an occasion of that kind, generally it was more difficult, and less agreeable operations that were to be pursued. That night they had a very pleasant occupation.

They had a duty to perform towards their countrymen who had been fighting in a remarkable manner in a recent fight. (Applause). He remembered some years ago when an enthusiastic Irishman, talking in the House of Commons, about the policy of obstruction, said "Begorra, it's next best thing to fighting that I know." And he, (Mr Ferguson), thought that football contests sometimes look like fighting. (Hear. Hear).

Football, he considered, was a good and noble game, and could be played without ill temper, and they could be kindly and courteous to each other. Although he was not at Hampden Park on the day of the match, he had a report from one who takes a great interest in the game and who said that a more manly game he had not attended and one in which self reliance and self control of temper were displayed by the Hibernians to a man. (Applause). That was as it ought to be. He knew nothing of the rules of the game of football but he knew something of what moral power and moral conduct exercised over.

What a number of attempts had been made to take from their well earned glory. (Applause). Anonymous writers who knew nothing of the game were able to assure the public that wrong men had won. (Applause). Charges made and investigated before a fair tribunal are to be repeated. Surely this was undignified and unmanly? What would have been the condition of affairs had the other side won the cup under such circumstances? Why, manly men would not accept it. (Applause).

He was proud to think that there were among their opponents, men who declared the Hibernians won gallantly and fairly. (Applause). Was it not a most creditable thing to think that those young fellows should, after a day's work, go into the field and perform such prodigies of exertion and skill? They lived honestly by the sweat of their brows. They worked for their living and the charge of professionalism was an utter absurdity. (Loud applause). He understood by the word professional, a person who lived by some profession or occupation. (Hear, Hear). They lived by honest labour, and if they gave their leisure hour, their position did not permit them to pay their own expenses. (Hear, Hear).

Well they had assembled there that evening to honour those men because they were all Irish and because they gloried in the success of their countrymen in the fields of war, literature and morals. They did not exult in any vain glorious spirit and particularly in times like these when Scotland and Ireland were running side by side in the great struggle for their national rights, about which he did not intend to say anything that night. (Loud applause). They would not get him on that subject. (Renewed applause and laughter).

He regretted that he had to leave shortly and that he had to leave to another, that work which he would proudly and gladly do himself. (Loud applause).

A very enjoyable concert was then proceeded with and Mr Vallely took the chair vacated by Mr Ferguson. At an interval, the Chairman presented each of the members with a gold medal and addresses were afterwards delivered by Messrs Simpson, Sorden, Flannigan and McFadden".

The *Scottish Athletic Journal* reported on the same gathering on 15th March;

"On Monday evening, 28th February, the cup winners were presented with a handsome testimonial by the members of the Glasgow Home Government branch of the Irish National League in Wellington Palace, Commercial Road. The large hall was crowded with an enthusiastic body of admirers, and Mr John Ferguson, who presided, was supported on the platform by Messrs William Simpson, Hillhead; Michael Flannigan and J Sorden, Edinburgh; and Edward Vallely and James Quillan, Glasgow.

The full team - with the exception of Willie Groves, who had received a lovely black eye in the inter city match, (between Edinburgh and Glasgow), and was diffident about parading that tangible token of western regard on a public platform - were present under the baton of their indefatigable Secretary, and were accompanied by Jerry Reynolds and Tom Maley, and the club's Trainer J Martin of Halbeath.

The Chairman, in opening the proceedings, remarked that it was not often he had the honour or pleasure of presiding on an occasion of that kind - generally the operations to be pursued were of a graver and less agreeable character; but that night they had a very pleasant occupation. They had a duty to perform towards their countrymen, who had been fighting in a recent fight with native gallantry and persistence, and who carried off the blue riband of the Scottish Association from perhaps the strongest combinations in the football world. He remembered some years ago an enthusiastic countryman who, talking of the policy of obstruction in the House of Commons said "Begorra, it's the next best thing to fighting I know of".

Football contests sometimes did look like fighting, but football, he considered to be a noble and manly game, which could be played with courtesy and kindness, and without ill temper. He knew little of the rules of the game, but he knew something of what moral power and moral conduct exercised over society and the essence of these were to be found in self control of temper and kindly consideration for opponents - self reliance and fair play. These were qualities essential to the football player with whom football was to be made a pastime and not an occupation , and these qualities, he was glad to learn, were in the great match at Hampden displayed by the Hibernians to a man. He would advise his young friends to keep their tempers upon all occasions. Those who won could afford to laugh; and whether they won or not, if they controlled their tempers they came out of the contest as men who had acted a manly part, and whom defeat could not dishonour.

But some attempt had been made to rob the victors of their well earned glory. Anonymous writers had endeavoured to persuade the public that the wrong men had won. Charges made and investigated before a fair tribunal were to be repeated. Surely this was undignified and unmanly. What would have been the condition of affairs had the cup been awarded to the other side? Why manly men would decline to accept from a committee what they could not win from their opponents in the open field.

He was proud to think that there were men among their opponents men who declared that the Hibernians won justly and fairly. Was it not a most creditable thing that these young men, after a hard day's work, could go into the field and perform prodigies of exertion and skill? They worked honestly in the sweat of their brows; they worked for their living, and the charge of professionalism was an utter absurdity. He understood by the word professional, a person who lives by some occupation or profession. They gave their honest labour, and if they gave their leisure hour, their position did not permit of their paying the expenses necessitated by fulfilment of cup tie obligations.

Well, they had assembled there that evening to honour those men because they were Irishmen, and because they gloried in the success of their countrymen in the arena of manly pastimes as in the fields of war, morals and literature. They did not exult in any vain glorious spirit, particularly in times like these, when Scotland and Ireland were running side by side in the race for national rights. He regretted to have to leave early, and having to delegate to another that work which he would have proudly and gladly done himself.

A very enjoyable concert was then proceeded with, the programme being sustained by professional and amateur talent. At nine o' clock, very handsome shield shaped gold badges, of artistic design , having on one side, in relief, a harp surrounded by a wreath of shamrocks, and bearing an appropriate inscription on the reverse side, were presented by Mr Vallely to the cup winners, Mr McFadden's services being appropriately acknowledged by a similar token.

Mr Flannigan was next called upon and in the course of a short address interjected several humorous hits at the Hibs critics, which were well taken by the audience. He remarked that he had been greatly impressed by reading in a certain book of the wise men coming from the east bearing presents of gold, but he felt that the impression which the reading of that incident had made on his youthful mind would have to give way to that created by the new incident in which he as one of the wise men was about to take part in returning from the west garden as the ancients had been described .

An assembly, at which the greater number of the team took part followed, and dancing was kept up till an advanced hour. We are requested to state that the claims of Jerry Reynolds were overlooked by mistake, and that a badge similar in design to the others will be presented to him in recognition of his services in the cup ties preceding the final".

John Ferguson who addressed the hall, was the leader of the Home Government branch of the Irish National League. An Ulster Protestant, he settled in the Glasgow area in 1860 and followed in that great tradition of Protestant leaders of the Irish Nationalist cause.

Glasgow was awoken and had risen and the fact that Hibernian were being feted, again in Glasgow, and plain speaking was again the order of the day in the speech, spelled out once again that the mix between politics, religion and football were very much alive and well, at the time of our foundation.

At every celebration, you don't have to look far to see the involvement of many of our Founding Fathers. All it needed was one man to bring all these factions together from the political and religious circles, to give it a *raison d'être* namely working together in the name of charity and to provide the leadership and respect that every Catholic had for the work of the Marists in the city.

Brother Walfrid, being a religious man, did what was natural for him as Brother Superior at the Marist's headquarters, and so he sought the involvement of the nearby parishes of the East End including St Andrew's on Clyde Street, St Alphonsus on London Road and St Mary's, Calton, before later inviting St Michael's, Parkhead and Sacred Heart, Bridgeton, after some of the parishioners from St Andrews and St Alphonsus left the discussion, having felt sidelined.

St Mary's was the mother parish of the East End, built in 1842 before the chapel of St Alphonsus followed in 1846, Sacred Heart in 1873 and St Michael's in 1876. St Andrew's was the first chapel built in Glasgow in 1816 following the Reformation, after the number of Catholics in the city had risen from 450 in 1805 to over 3000 a decade later. Before the building of St Andrews, Catholics in the city, many of whom were Highlanders who settled and worked in the manufacturing business, celebrated mass in rented accommodation in Mitchell Street in the city centre in 1791, following the passing of the Roman Catholic Relief Act, which permitted Catholics to exercise our religion. Six years later, a larger building in Marshall's Lane off the Gallowgate in the Calton was rented, where Catholics could celebrate mass without fear of attack, as it was situated opposite the barracks, which were built in 1795. The barracks were located on the site of the current Morrisons supermarket on the north of the Gallowgate and so we can deduct that Marshall's Lane was off Marshall Street which once stood south of the Gallowgate and gives the location of the accommodation rented in 1797 for the Catholics of the city, many of whom were highlanders, to celebrate mass, as the lane behind the Hielan Jessie Bar!

The predecessor of the Roman Catholic Relief Act was the subtly named Papists Act of 1778, and before that the Penal Laws which basically excluded Catholics from public life.

Right from the very start, the Founding Fathers who sat around the table in the early months of 1887 knew that to succeed where many other Irish teams in the past had failed, they had to be successful on the pitch. They would be in the same market as Edinburgh Hibernian for players and support and we had to beat them, or at least be equal to them, to guarantee that the new club would take over their mantle as representing the Irish Catholics of the west.

If we failed to represent the Irish Catholics of the west, we would fail as a club. It was as simple as that.

Meanwhile, the task that awaited us was clear as Hibs went on to add to their fame on August 13th, at the start of the 1887/88 season, by beating the famous "Invincibles" of Preston North End, 2-1 at Easter Road in a challenge match. The game had been given the prestigious title of the "Association Football Championship of the World".

No pressure then.

As an aside the following Saturday, Preston North End, still licking their wounds, returned to Scotland to open Rangers' new ground at the first Ibrox Park (adjacent to the current one) after their lease at Kinning Park had expired. The result was an 8-1 win for Preston North End, with the match stopped before the end after the Rangers support invaded the pitch and attacked Preston's English International John Goodall.

You couldn't make it up.

HIBERNIAN FACE ANOTHER PROTEST

Hibernian, as the first Irish club to win the Scottish Cup, had enjoyed good fortune in the final with the winner coming from a goal so hotly disputed that the Dumbarton defence had stood back and allowed it to happen, so convinced where they that it was offside.

However, as they say, you make your own luck and Hibernian richly deserved the highest honour in the Scottish game. They now faced their toughest test and ironically it came off the field as the SFA waited just three days after the final to hear the Vale of Leven's protest against Hibs and their alleged professionalism on Tuesday 15th February 1887.

This was a charge that Hibs had to defeat or they would be stripped of the Scottish Cup and faced the ultimate sanction of being banned from Scottish football. There was no more serious a charge and it would, in turn, also have had serious consequences for the ongoing discussions to form what would become Celtic Football Club.

At the previous meeting, the Hibs Secretary John McFadden had been granted a 10 day period to respond to notice of the charge of professionalism. However when he raised this on the 15th February, the Vale of Leven representative, Mr Campbell dismissed the claim as he had actually been given notice of the charge at the original meeting on Monday 31st January and also at the Business sub Committee meeting of the SFA on Thursday 10th February, two days before the cup final when the Vale's witnesses were in attendance to give their evidence, the last day it was allowed to be received. He hadn't of course, but lets not allow the truth to get in the way of a good story.

The Hibs Secretary also complained that his club had not received a copy of the charge in detail but the Vale of Leven representative countered that it was not his job to put the evidence in the hands of the accused. The Chairman, Mr Richard Browne agreed on both counts with the Vale of Leven in an ominous start to the proceedings for Hibs.

The summary of events came from the Scottish Umpire on the 22nd February 1887:

The charges were read out:

1. That the Hibernians are alleged to have paid their players weekly for their services.

2. In particular, a member of the said club, named Willie Groves, who works with a Mr Joe Bizes, should have returned to his work, after the holidays on Monday, 10th January, 1887, but did not return until 17th January.

3. That the said member, Willie Groves, had informed certain parties that he was paid a sum weekly for his services as a member.

4. That the club met and had dinner daily at Wallace's Suburban Hotel, Cockburn Street, Edinburgh during the second week in January, 1887.

From the original four charges, the Vale of Leven had done their homework and now concentrated on proving the one serious charge of professionalism, by breaking it down into four examples, any one of which could point towards a guilty verdict.

Mr Campbell from the Vale of Leven called Mr Bizes, a workmate of Willie Groves and also offered to read two letters from witnesses who were unable to come forward, but this was ruled inadmissible by the Chairman.

Mr Bizes stated he worked alongside Groves for twelve months in a boot finishing factory. Groves was only 18 and worked as an apprentice on piece work (not full time) at the factory. Mr Bizes appeared a good witness, giving his evidence in an unshaken manner and he claimed of late that Groves had been off work a day or two now and then, and also between Christmas Day and January 22nd, the day of the semi final against Vale of Leven, a length of absence which was unusual for an apprentice.

Worse still for Hibs, he claimed that Groves had told him that he had been paid by Hibs, in the presence of a witness whilst having a drink in an Edinburgh pub.

Mr Bizes finished his evidence by stating that he had no animosity towards Groves or Hibs, he was not a supporter of any football club and merely wished to see fair play. He had not been prompted to come forward by anyone and had in fact wrote the letter voluntarily. He had in fact a lot to lose through his participation as he had been discharged by his foreman, who was a Hibs enthusiast.

The significance of Mr Bizes' evidence was that if Willie Groves was absent from his work for three weeks before the semi final, how was he earning his keep? Were Hibs in fact paying him?

Mr Walker from the Vale of Leven then called Mr Wallace, the proprietor of the Suburban Hotel, where the Hibs players dined.

The hotel was out of the way and could be entered without anyone noticing from the street. He stated that the entire Hibs team dined there during the week prior to the 15th January, the original date for the semi final. Also they dropped in, in twos and threes on occasion during the week. He was told the meals were sometimes paid by a member or two of the Hibernians. He also claimed that he knew several gentlemen who were willing to come forward with more evidence but they were unwilling to have their names made known. In finishing he also claimed that another gentleman had been told by Jerry Reynolds that he too was paid, £1 per week at Hibs.

The significance of the above evidence was the fact that even if Hibernian Football Club were paying for meals for their players in a hotel, this would be seen as a sign of professionalism.

Mr Wallace's evidence was then corroborated by a Mr Morton, a Private Detective who had been hired by Vale of Leven and who had provided evidence along with the hotel proprietor and a girl working at the bar that Hibs players had dined at the Suburban Hotel. Dined at the hotel, they may certainly have done, but who paid the bill was the big question.

Willie Groves was then called in.

Willie was one of Hibs rising stars on the pitch but he was still at a tender age: it was a daunting prospect to have to face the questioning of the SFA Committee and it showed, with question after question trying to ascertain how long he had been absent between Christmas Day and the 22nd January, the day of the Scottish Cup semi final tie.

In reply, Groves' answers varied and lacked clarity. He began by stating that he was on tour with Hibs in England for six days, and he was then off work for two weeks, one due to illness, then he was back at work for two weeks. Then on being asked if he was sure he was at work from the 10th to the 22nd January, he replied that he was at work the week after the Vale of Leven match, which related to the week after the 22nd, which wasn't the question. Then on being pressed that he was in fact off from the 27th December to the 22nd January, he replied weakly that he was only off during the frost and that the Vale of Leven game should have been played on the 15th January but was postponed. This went on for a few more questions to assist the young player's memory but to no avail and his performance was less than convincing.

Eventually and not before time, the questioning moved on directly probing him on whether he received any financial payments from Hibernian Football Club, to which he answered not for playing football, only for his expenses, or lost time as it was called, that is time away from his normal place of work.

How much expenses did he receive?
Groves: 10s, for three days in England came the reply.

What was the last amount of lost time he had claimed?
Groves: 3s, 6d, (17.5p), for the Vale of Leven match. His claims were always between 2s and 3s for lost time and would be paid directly by Mr McFadden, the Hibs Secretary and never by any of the committee men.

Finally his ordeal was at an end and Mr McFadden was called in, with Hibs' future hanging decidedly in the balance, to say the least. If truth be told, in football parlance by this stage they were a couple of goals down and in dire need of a comeback.

If Willie Groves was an inexperienced 18 year old out of his depth in front of the quick firing SFA Committee, Mr McFadden was in his element, well used to the work of committees and experienced in how to deal with their line of questioning.

On producing the club's cash book, Mr McFadden set the tone of the questioning, which was certainly high tempo and concentrated solely on payments to players with a selection as follows;

Is the cash book kept up to date?
McFadden: Yes, by the Treasurer each week.

Are you in the habit of paying money for lost time?
McFadden: Yes, where a man's wages come to 5s, 9d we give him 6s.

Do these payments appear in the cash book?
McFadden: I think you will find them all there.

What is the largest payment ever paid to Groves for a Saturday lost time?
McFadden: He only received payment once, 2s 6d, which is the same amount set by the Edinburgh Association.

Do you remember going to Dundee and giving the players money?
McFadden: I gave we gave them al the same, 3s, 6d.

Do you remember saying at the Business sub committee meeting that you had never paid Groves any money?
McFadden: Groves never asked for any money.

You said if he lost time you would pay him. There's an entry on 27th December with 15 men paid at 7s, 6d each.
McFadden: Ah yes, that was at Middlesboro but I think Groves was only paid 5s.

If Groves said he got 10s, would he be telling the truth?
McFadden: I distinctly remember paying him 5s myself.

Why does the entry say 15 players at 7s, 6 d each?
McFadden: As far as my memory goes, I am quite prepared to say Groves got 5s.

Can you tell us when the cash book was actually written up?
McFadden: It would be posted up week by week. I give you my word of honour it has not been written up for the occasion.

You told us at the Business sub committee meeting that Groves was off work because he was being kept and in training for a handicap, (a race).
McFadden: I stated he was training for a handicap but I did not say someone was keeping him, (paying him), for a handicap.

Each player was paid expenses and in addition 3s, 6d each for lost time, including Groves?
McFadden: Yes, I wanted Groves on one occasion to stay off work to catch a 12 noon train and he did so.

Did you incur any expense at Wallace's Hotel?
McFadden: No. Members of the club paid (not the club itself).

Would Groves receive payment for a practice match?
McFadden: Yes he would receive his wages. (The equivalent of).

In an entry from April for lost time it has 5 men at 35s, 9 at 25s and 2 at 20s. Who are those at 35s?
McFadden: Principally committee men.

Does it not seem curious that these men should get a certain sum, and Groves always got a special rate?
McFadden: We have complied with our portion of the order from this committee. Have the Vale supplied the parties who supplied them with the evidence? Either they are hidden in here, or they are not present. There has been nobody examined here except two members of the Vale of Leven club.

Chairman: The room has not been kept as a secret chamber. If you want to go in, it is at your disposal. We have done everything above board.

This concluded the examination of Mr McFadden and in the Chairman's closing remarks, he stated that we have heard the evidence of Groves and McFadden. The cash book seems to have been written all in one day as there is no variation in the writing, but we must accept Mr McFadden's word.

The committee then went on to discuss the matter in detail with the following given as a summary of the concerns raised:

Mr Crerar, (Third Lanark); Mr McFadden admitted they pay players well for lost time and he also admitted paying players for practice games.

Mr McCulloch, (Our Boys); This is nothing wonderful.

Mr Crerar, (Third Lanark); It is entirely against the spirit of amateurism in every shape and form and was the worst feature of the whole case.

Mr Carmichael, (5th KRV); Asked if the speeches of members would be reported in the athletic papers as had happened after the last meeting, with the result that one member had been threatened with violence.

Mr Mackay, (Northern); The Hibs have made certain admissions which virtually amount to professionalism.

Mr McCulloch, (Our Boys); If a man going on holiday tour in England should receive remuneration, there is nothing wonderful in that.

Mr Holms; There is one thing quite clear. Mr McCulloch is acting as counsel for the Hibs.

Mr Sneddon, (St Bernards); A club would be quite justified for paying players lost time if, for example, they played three or four matches on successive days in England.

Mr Mackay, (Northern); Any club is entitled to pay for lost time, but paying money for practice matches is handicapping any amateur team.

Mr Boag, (Partick Thistle); Is it fair for a man earning 10s to receive £1 for playing football?

Mr Sliman, (Battlefield); The first witness, a workmate of Groves stood a very close examination and stated Groves was paid by Hibs. Groves also told us he received certain sums from Hibs, and Mr McFadden contradicted the figures. The club paid players for practice matches.

Mr Haran, (Abercorn); We made a serious mistake allowing the cup final to be played. I beg to move the case be dismissed as not clearly proven.

Mr Harrison, (Ayr); Seconded. It would not have been advisable to delay the cup final, (at two days notice), As far as the case is concerned, the evidence is unsatisfactory.

Mr Dyer, (Lanarkshire); Groves admitted he earned between 8s and 10s per week yet he had been paid 3s, 6d for a match. On another occasion he received £1, is that in proportion to his weekly wage? It was openly admitted that Hibs pay players for practice matches. It was acceptable for players having to be paid lost time when they have to leave their work to play football but to give a club the power to get their players together and pay them for a practice match, was in his opinion, a clear case of professionalism. Amateur clubs in England did not have that power. I have no ill feeling towards the Hibs, merely in the pure amateur spirit I would like to see the game carried out - that the protest be sustained, and the Hibernians declared guilty of professionalism.

Mr Sliman, (Battlefield); We are an amateur association and we must put down our foot on professionalism. There is a strong feeling that professionalism has existed in some of our amateur clubs. It is unfortunate that the club implicated has just won the cup but that shouldn't alter our decision. If our premier club is guilty of professionalism, that is no reason why we shouldn't consider it. I second Mr Dyer's amendment that the Hibs be qualified.

Mr Nisbet (Cowlairs); At the General Meeting, the Vale of Leven did not back up their allegation with proof, therefore at the Business sub committee meeting two days before the final they were not justified in postponing the final, (on evidence not yet heard until today's meeting).

Mr Harrison, (Ayr); Is it not our duty to ask ourselves the question were the Hibernian club guilty alone. Are they not acting the same as other clubs in our midst?

Chairman; You are out of order.

The vote followed with Hibs' future as a top class football club hanging over the precipice. The thoughts expressed by the committee in discussion after the evidence was given would lead a betting man to gamble against Hibernian. But would representatives of clubs vote with the courage of their conviction or would they think long and hard on Mr Harrison's last point. Were Hibs acting the same as others in our midst, that is within the same SFA meeting?

If Hibs were found guilty of professionalism, could it lead to the finger of suspicion pointing at other clubs represented that day?

Did the SFA, as a body, want the scandal that would follow a guilty verdict on Hibernian, an acceptance that Scottish Football was guilty of professionalism and more importantly, that the Scottish Football Association had done nothing to stop it before it got to this stage? Although the charges were heard in four parts, the verdict was based on the one charge of professionalism. The first vote reflected the indecision with 6 in favour of a guilty verdict and 6 against, with 6 members not even brave enough to vote.

It was then put forward and seconded that the vote be taken by ballot. The original vote involved a show of hands, which is open to individuals being influenced by others with everyone wanting to be on the winning side. A ballot, in comparison, is done in secret with a simple yes or no ticked on a piece of paper but even on a vote on how to conduct the vote by a show of hands or by a ballot was close with the ballot winning the day by 9 votes to 6 - but incredibly 3 members didn't even vote on that!

To the inexperienced Chairman's horror, after the ballot was taken and every man present voted, the voting was again equal, 9 votes each. This put the Chairman of the SFA in the very awkward position of having the whole outcome in his hands with the use of his casting vote. He was up for re election at the end of the season, would he want to be remembered as the man who's decision brought Scottish Football into turmoil? He was a young man with a big future in the game and there was no way he was going to end it in controversy.

Was there?

Interestingly, his two biggest rivals for re-election were Vice President Mr Kennedy and Mr Crerar of Third Lanark, both of whom were pushing for Hibs' expulsion.

Would he go against Hibernian and rock Scottish Football to the core with a huge scandal that would lead to a purge on professionalism at the door of many of our leading clubs and an investigation into the suspension of the Scottish Cup for that season as every team who Hibs had knocked out would have a case to be reinstated, not just Vale of Leven?

Or would he give Hibs the benefit of the doubt and that would be the end of the matter?

The Chairman, Mr Richard Browne, President of Queens Park decided on the latter and Hibs drew a huge sigh of relief. In his summary however he chose his words carefully and made sure that Hibs knew just how close they had sailed to the wind.

"I need not tell you Mr McFadden, your club has had a very narrow escape. There is part of the evidence which condemned them to a very great extent. You have used a little freedom in the interpretation of the rule. You have given your players more than they were entitled to and we think you have seriously erred, but still do not feel inclined to find you guilty of professionalism".

Mr Campbell from the Vale of Leven responded by asking if they could carry the matter further to which the Chairman responded that they could and that indeed they were justified in the course they had taken and refunded them their 10s deposit.

Mr McFadden then hit back stating that the Vale of Leven had every chance to prove their case and asked was it fair that Hibs still carried this stigma over their heads. He considered now the Vale of Leven had nothing left to say.

In this aspect he was correct. Although a date was set for an appeal on Tuesday, 8th March, the Vale of Leven withdrew their charges at the very last moment by telegram, after John McFadden and James McGhee had already arrived in Glasgow for the hearing. They clearly felt that having put forward their best case and lost, they should now withdraw with their dignity intact rather than face another defeat.

Although Hibs were cleared, the charge of professionalism certainly hung over Scottish Football until it was introduced in 1893. If, and certainly it was a big if, Hibs were guilty, they certainly weren't the only ones.

BROTHER WALFRID LEAVES ANOTHER LASTING LEGACY IN GLASGOW

Not long before Brother Walfrid began the discussions which led to the foundation of Celtic, his life had taken on a series of big changes with the death of Father Peter Noonan on 9th October, 1886, parish priest of Sacred Heart since its inception in 1873 and his promotion to Brother Superior, head of the Marist Brothers in Glasgow, although he remained in his same base.

For fully 13 years before then, Father Noonan and Brother Walfrid had formed a formidable working relationship, with the priest and the Marist Brother tending to the religious and educational needs of the parishioners at Sacred Heart and even setting up the Poor Childrens Dinner Table in December 1884 to feed those who couldn't afford to put bread on the table.

When Father Noonan died, the parishioners decided that a suitable memorial to the man who built their parish should be undertaken and to this end a committee was set up in January 1887 which comprised of Brother Walfrid, James Quigley, Joseph Foy, Francis Mooney, Thomas Flood, Joseph Nelis and Father Hughes, who replaced Father Noonan at Sacred Heart.

From this seven man Committee, Brother Walfrid, Thomas Flood and Joseph Nelis were involved concurrently in the foundation of Celtic.

Father Hughes is mentioned in forthcoming AGMs when receiving a donation and Joseph Foy was on the sub committee set up by Celtic in 1892 to look at a suitable gift to Brother Walfrid on his departure to London in August of that year, in the end the committee proposed a gift of £10 which was accepted.

James Quigley, Thomas Flood, Joseph Foy and Father Hughes were also on the committee of the Catholic Union in the parish of Sacred Heart, and again we see an example of the close knit religious and political groups in the East End where Celtic's first committee men would initially get to know each other and work together, another reason why Celtic rose so quickly from our inception.

A subscription list was opened in April 1887 with all funds raised going towards the erection of a grand high altar at the original Sacred Heart chapel at 50 Old Dalmarnock Road, Bridgeton and Brother Walfrid was named on the list of committee men to send donations to, which would be gratefully acknowledged. It's interesting that just nine months later, Brother Walfrid would send out another fundraising circular to the parishes of the East End, this time for funds to assist in the foundation of Celtic. Wonder where he got that idea from?

Fundraising circulars around the parishes of the East End were a common way of appealing to other like minded Catholics in the same area to share the burden but although the initial circular had raised a fair amount, the committee were still short of the funds required to do Father Noonan justice. More than a year after the original appeal, in June 1888, work on the new grand high altar had not yet started and a fresh drive was made to reinvigorate the campaign.

This came not long after the opening of Whitevale Refuge, at 21 Whitevale Street, for destitute children in February 1887, just off the Gallowgate and also the opening of the original Celtic Park in May 1888. The building of Catholic refuges was a new initiative by the Archdiocese to combat proselytism by taking in and feeding destitute Catholic children on a temporary basis until a more permanent solution could be found. In response to the circular from the Archbishop, parish priests appealed for backing and committees were set up to organise door to door collections. Again the names of some of those involved in the formation of Celtic were not far away with Dominic McCreadie from the parish of Saint Andrew's donating £5 and David Meikleham, (soon to be Treasurer of the League of the Cross in the parish of Saint Alphonsus), part of the committee formed in the parish responsible for the collections.

So it was easy to see how difficult it was to raise funds for a football team, never mind a new altar, when competition for any spare pennies was from a refuge for destitute children.

A month later in July 1888, the Glasgow Observer was able to post an advert stating that the Father Noonan Memorial committee were now making final arrangements to erect the magnificent altar by the second anniversary of his death on 9th October. The committee was once again energetically at work promoting the object for which it was inaugurated over eighteen months previous. A large number of designs for the new altar were in the hands of the committee and it also took the opportunity to remind readers that the subscription list remained open.

Just after the second anniversary, the Glasgow Observer reported that the usual weekly committee meeting had been held in Sacred Heart school on Wednesday 17th October, with Joseph Nelis in the Chair. A large number of subscriptions had been handed in and several handsome designs submitted from eminent architects. Further it was decided that a sub committee should be formed to secure more information and the committee should continue to meet every Wednesday evening. The sub committee comprised of Brother Walfrid, Father Hughes, Joseph Nelis, Joseph Foy and William Savage.

In 1888, not only was Brother Walfrid involved in everything Celtic, he was also on the Father Noonan Memorial committee, a prime mover in the Poor Children's Dinner Tables under the auspices of the Saint Vincent De Paul Society, as well as his day job as Brother Superior, responsible for the Marist Brothers teaching in Glasgow's Catholic schools and also Headmaster at Sacred Heart.

Just before Christmas, 1888, the Father Noonan Memorial Committee announced that their labours were nearing completion and in a short time a beautiful new altar would be erected in Sacred Heart chapel in memory of Father Noonan, with mass celebrated by the Archbishop of Glasgow.

Finally progress was nearing a conclusion within the Father Noonan Memorial Committee and on 6th April, 1889 the *Glasgow Observer* was able to report;

"The erection of this altar is progressing rapidly, and it is expected that it will be ready for solemn dedication shortly after Easter. It is being built of caen stone. In its unfinished state it presents a very handsome appearance. Rising from the base on either side are two beautiful pillars of green marble, whilst the front is richly carved representing angelic figures and in the centre is represented the crown of thorns, surmounted by a coronet, the whole being surmounted by exquisitely formed laurel leaves. The site of the altar is behind that of the present one. It is expected that his Grace, the Archbishop will perform the opening ceremony".

On Sunday May 5th, 1889, the parishioners of Sacred Heart packed into their original chapel on Old Dalmarnock Road, Bridgeton to celebrate the inauguration of the new altar as High Mass was said at 11am in the presence of his Grace, the Archbishop of Glasgow (who delivered the sermon) and Father Maginn from St Alphonsus, Father McCulla from Sacred Heart, Father O'Connell, Monsignor Munro, Canon Maguire, Canon Caven, Canon McFarlane and Canon MacKintosh.

The Memorial Committee had taken over two years to raise awareness and more importantly raise funds and to study all the architects plans which were submitted for the design of the altar, since the committee was set up in January 1887, but when it was finally unveiled in May 1889, the results of their labour were breathtaking. They certainly achieved their objective and did the memory of the much loved Father Noonan proud.

A description of the altar is given in the *Glasgow Observer* as follows;

The altar is a magnificent erection, worthy in the fullest degree of one so beloved as he whose memory it perpetuates. The style is distinctly, but not decidedly, Gothic. Caen stone and coloured marble are the materials used in the building. The altar is flanked on either side by a stone turret, rising from the base of the steps and reaching the reredos, (decoration behind the altar). That on the epistle side contains hollowed in it a piscina, (shallow basin). The table rests on two pairs of pillars of Milan marble. Between these are three panels separated by a couple of buttresses showing two angelic figures bearing shields, on which are carved the implements of the passion - the pillar, scourge, sponge, spear, etc.

The central panel is however the chief point of beauty. This exhibits, carved in high relief, a more artistic representation of the Sacred Heart. A stream of blood flows into a chalice and the whole design is surrounded by a wreath of thorns and roses and surmounted by a crown. Along the top of each panel runs the legend Sanctus, Sanctus, Sanctus. The reredos is not yet finished because it is intended to transfer the high altar into a new and permanent church to be built at a future date. In its present state however it presents quite a finished appearance, Genoa marble being the material used for the shelves. Along it runs the inscription "Quam dilecta tabernacula tua Domine virtutum", (which means How lovely are thy tabernacles, O Lord of host").

Perhaps the most striking feature of the erection is the tabernacle. The designer has here given full scope to his genius. Octagonal in shape the pillars forming the doorway of the safe are of white stone, beautifully floriated. A door of burnished brass, studded with bulbs of crystal gives a richness and effect to the structure extremely pleasing. The throne is enclosed by a double colonnade of tall marble shafts, terminating in prettily carved capitals from which rises a canopy, pinnacled and tapering.

A coronal beautifully finished is enclosed and the structure as a whole is little short of dazzling. A rich curtain of deep marone plush is suspended at the rear of the erection, the arrangement being of course designed to last only so long as the altar stands in its present position. The sanctuary has been furnished with a tasteful carpeting, which adds considerably to the completeness of the ensemble. The church has, indeed, been totally renovated, the aisles laid with linoleum and the benches and walls being painted and decorated. The side altars have been in the hands of the brush wielders and they two make a brave attempt at looking as grand as possible.

The energetic and zealous, if somewhat retiring and self depreciatory pastor of the mission deserves a high meed, (share), of praise for his efforts, and to him and the committee who raised the funds necessary for the erection, the people owe a considerable debt."

It's a fascinating fact that this high altar was moved to the current chapel and re erected in 1910, when the chapel was rebuilt on the same site, and remains to this day in memory of Father Noonan - whilst at the same time is another visible and lasting legacy of Brother Walfrid's work in the East End.

THE EAST END CATHOLIC CHARITY CUP

The *Scottish Athletic Journal* were the first to break the news;

"It is said that the Renton and Hibs will visit the East End of Glasgow on the 26th to play a charity match for the benefit of the dinner table of a large number of poor children in the east and north east of the city. Rumour says that the committee have resolved to present the winning team with a silver cup - not a bad idea certainly. It is also said that the cup is a gift to the committee by a few kind friends".

Brother Walfrid, occupied with discussions to form Celtic Football Club amongst the parishes of the East End, turned his mind once again to charity, with the funding of the Poor Childrens Dinner Tables close to his heart. His previous fundraising efforts involving football matches had already provided desperately needed funds but on this occasion he set the bar even higher, inviting two of the leading clubs at the time, Hibernian, as Scottish Cup holders and Renton as newly crowned winners of the Charity Cup. To add to the occasion, he ensured a trophy was donated, and named the East End Catholic Charity Cup.

From the SFA Annual in 1892, we learn that after Hibernian's Scottish Cup final victory on 12th February 1887;

"The idea of forming a team to play for the specific purpose of charity dawned on a few, was circulated and as a result, a committee of enquiry was instituted. The result of the inquiry was very satisfactory and one fine morning the football world was made aware of the birth of a new club, weak, 'twas true at its birth, but subsequently it grew and thrived mightily".

Brother Walfrid's steering committee, set up to look at the possibilities of founding an Irish club in Glasgow came after 12th February and its first manifestation was the East End Catholic Charity Cup on 26th May, which had all the hallmarks of an embryonic committee at work that would grace Celtic Park with its marked level of organisation involved. It would be no surprise either if this same committee was made up of many of the men who organised the after match celebrations at St Mary's Hall on 12th February.

A mouth watering tie was set up between two of the top teams in the country, with a trophy organised for the winners. This was better than anything ever witnessed in the East End parishes and the funds raised would go to the Poor Childrens Dinner Tables. The success of this match, with 12,000 in attendance, underlined to the steering committee what could be achieved and started the clock ticking from that day forward, Thursday 26th May 1887 when there can be no shadow of doubt that the decision had been agreed that an Irish club in Glasgow would be formed and formal discussions between the parishes begun.

Meantime the steering committee would have its hands full to get a date arranged for the return match when both teams could play a rematch at the start of the new season. This would be the final test of their organising skills before the real planning started, which would culminate in the meeting on November 6th to finally formally constitute the new Irish club.

In Tom White's History of Celtic FC in his newspaper, the Glasgow Eastern Standard on the 3rd March 1923, he states;

"In the crowd at that match, (the 1887 Scottish Cup Final), were many from Saint Mary's, Abercromby Street and a discussion took place regarding the possibility of arranging a game with the Hibernians for the benefit of the Poor Childrens Dinner Tables. The matter was taken up enthusiastically by Mr John Glass, Mr John O'Hara and other East Enders and thanks to the kind offices of the later John D Graham of Bridgeton, the Clyde FC gave their ground free for a game which took place between the Hibs as Scottish Cup holders and the famous Renton at which a big crowd attended, to the great benefit of the charity concerned".

"The next step was to hold a meeting on the 6th of November, 1887 in East Rose Street, Glasgow at which it was agreed to form the Celtic club and to take over a field in Dalmarnock Street. The pioneers of the club were John Glass, John O'Hara, Doctor John Conway, Andrew Bryan, James McKay, John H McLaughlin, Pat Welsh, Hugh Darroch, William McKillop and James Quillan, Willie Maley was appointed as Match Secretary".

Again Clyde gave free use of their Barrowfield ground on French Street, Bridgeton and the date was set for the Thursday evening of 26th May 1887, with a 7pm kick off, and admission set at sixpence. Just six days earlier Renton had beaten Vale of Leven 1-0 in the final of the Charity Cup at Hampden Park, having beaten Hibs 3-2 in the first round on the 23rd April and then Rangers 2-1 in the semi final on the 18th May, after the first two matches were drawn.

The choice of teams was a master stroke by Brother Walfrid and his committee with Hibs, attracting the Irish Catholic support, and Renton providing mouth watering opposition intent on showing their worth as cup holders who had beaten Hibs en route. The previous meeting just a month earlier had been a controversial one with Renton storming into a two goal lead in the first half at Hampden, before Hibs clawed their way back into the game with a goal before half time, then an equaliser in the second half as the game reached a hugely exciting climax.

Hibs were on the front foot and were intent on completing a fantastic fightback when Renton broke up the park, and after Tobin saved the original shot, the ball was forced home after a goalmouth scramble. Despite the Hibs players' protests, the goal stood and Hibs were out the cup to the disappointment of their Glasgow based supporters.

The prospect of a return match, whilst the controversy was still fresh in the mind, helped fill Barrowfield to its capacity as an incredible crowd of 12,000 for a Charity match attended, a figure that was higher than the attendance at the Scottish Cup Final. Many more had of course climbed the barricades and gained entry for free at the cup final, but no one would dare do the same at a Charity match.

The *Scottish Umpire* gave the following glowing match report;

"The tail end of the season has furnished us with not a few surprising matches, and last Thursday's match at Barrowfield Park between the Hibernians and Renton will rank as one of the best exhibitions of the season. The match was remarkable for the hard nature of the play and the enormous attendance of spectators, and we believe the charity for whose benefit it was in aid of will reap a good sum. At the outset it looked as if the Hibs would walk round their opponents, but Renton soon settled down and at call of time, a pretty equal game ended in a draw - one goal each".

Mick Dunbar scored for Hibs and amongst his team mates who would also go on to make their name at Celtic were Jimmy McLaren, Paddy Gallagher and Willie Groves. The attendance figure of 12,000 provided Brother Walfrid with funding for the Dinner Tables that he could not have dreamt of and the result too, a draw, meant that he would have the chance in the new season to arrange a replay and do it all again.

If ever he had any doubts over the ongoing discussions to form an Irish club that Glasgow could call its own and which would enable it to fund the Dinner Tables, those doubts vanished into thin air on May 26th 1887.

The *Scottish Athletic Journal* stated;

"Football Bridgeton was on the qui vive last Thursday, for were not the winners of the Scottish and Charity cups to meet in the evening at Barrowfield Park in a charity match in aid of some local institution. Barrowfield is a pretty spacious ground, but it was not equal to holding the crowd of 12,000 people which turned out to see the game. Never was such a large gathering seen in Barrowfield. Both teams were up to their full strength and a warm game was confidently looked forward to. The game was indeed a very fast and very even one and it was voted by all who witnessed it one of the best struggles ever seen in the district. The men on both sides showed that they had not entirely lost their midseason form. A great many of the Catholic clergy were present. Something like £120 was drawn at the gate".

The season was nearing an end and so Brother Walfrid and his committee lost no time in arranging the replay for the very start of the following season. Barrowfield was again the location and the date was a good one, August 6th, the week after the opening Saturday of the football season with a 4pm kick off and admission again set at sixpence.

In a story that was to be repeated in the near future, Hibs suffered from a number of departures on the playing front which signalled the break up of the Scottish Cup team: Barney Fagan emigrated to America and fellow full back James Lundy signed for Grimsby Town, whilst George Smith and Willie Groves were talked out of moves south to Mitchell St George in Birmingham, after deals to take them away looked imminent.

In another blow to Hibs, Tom Maley, who had played occasionally for them during the previous season, decided to stay in Glasgow and along with his brother Willie, threw his lot in with Third Lanark for the 1887/88 season. He was soon to find himself at the centre of attention of both Brother Walfrid and John Glass who were seeking a man big enough to become the first captain of Celtic, until James Kelly too was enticed.

After losing in Dumfries to Queen of the South Wanderers by 8 goals to 2 the previous week, Hibs arrived at Barrowfield on Saturday, 6th August in the pouring rain and proceeded to be trounced 6-0 by an on form Renton, with five of the six goals coming from Neil McCallum, who was just breaking into the first team and who would score Celtic's first ever competitive goal before the season was finished.

The *Scottish Athletic Journal* spoke highly of McCallum;

"The hero of the afternoon was unquestionably McCallum. He is a tall, athletic looking fellow, who dashes off straight ahead, and generally overcomes all opposition. Out of the six goals scored, five have to be credited to McCallum, whose play all through was certainly of the highest class. This young player was tried at the back end of last season and his place in the team is now a certainty. I shall watch his future with some interest. It is of course premature to speak too laudatory after one game, especially when his opponents were not in the best condition. Still I think McCallum is a good man and will yet make his mark".

The same paper covered the match itself as a top attraction;

"The new season has commenced and the two champions of last season have ushered it in. The game between Hibernians and Renton, which was played at Barrowfield Park on Saturday, proved very conclusively that after ten weeks close time the football public are as enthusiastic as ever over this, their favourite pastime. The match under notice was a legacy left over from last season. Some friends of the Catholic charities presented a cup for competition between the Hibernians, (the Scottish Cup holders) and Renton, (the holders of the Glasgow Charity Cup).

When these teams met last June the game ended in a draw, the capacity of Barrowfield Park being taxed to the uttermost to contain the crowd. The season was then too far advanced to finally settle the destination of the cup and those who superintended the arrangements postponed the match until the new season was approaching. The Clyde FC have greatly improved their ground and a spacious grand stand has been erected. The crowd is variously estimated but there can be no doubt that 4000 were inside the gates and quite as many people occupied the points of vantage, of which there are a great number overlooking Barrowfield Park. Thus the funds which are to be assisted from the proceeds of this game - namely, St Mary's Hall and Edinburgh and Renton charities will receive substantial aid".

The heavy rain made the conditions unfavourable but they were the same for both teams and Renton adjusted better with a quick passing game that gave them a two goal lead by half time, despite having to play two young reserves in their team. Hibs drafted in Hearts forward Tommy Jenkinson and future Celts Paddy Gallagher, Mick Dunbar, Jimmy McLaren and Willie Groves also played as they made four changes to their usual eleven. The attendance was around the 4000 mark, with another 4000 outside looking in from whatever vantage points they could find. Although lower than the first match, the turn out was still a very good one and would help feed many hungry mouths in the East End. The fans stayed to the end in the downpour happy with the entertainment value, if not the score, as the majority were Glasgow Irishmen who followed Hibernian.

And so Renton became the holders of the East End Catholic Charity Cup, a trophy they never had to defend but it was a trophy that was another stepping stone in Brother Walfrid's learning curve towards the foundation of Celtic. If Hibernian had won the trophy undoubtedly it would still have pride of place in their boardroom.

Hibernian's decline had started, with fourteen goals lost in their first two matches of the new season as they failed miserably to build on their Scottish Cup win six months earlier. This was to set the tone for a disappointing season and more desertions from the playing squad, even before Celtic had kicked our first ball.

GLASGOW'S MAIN IRISH TEAMS BEFORE CELTIC

In 1887, the biggest Irish Catholic teams in Glasgow were St Mungo's (from the parish of that name in Townhead) and Glasgow Hibernian who played at Overnewton Park, in Yorkhill.

Both teams were described as juvenile, as were Glasgow Hibernian's local rivals, St Peter's Celtic, from Partick. The reason why no large Irish Catholic club had emerged in Glasgow before Celtic was that teams were often literally parochial, that is, many parishes had their own football team. Interestingly there was another Irish Catholic juvenile team in Glasgow in 1887, mentioned in the Scottish Umpire on 9th August under the name of Celtic, with contact details to arrange a match given as Hugh McCall, 20 Northburn Street, Maryhill.

When St Mungo's and Glasgow Hibernian amalgamated in 1887 it seemed that Glasgow may finally have a decent sized Irish Catholic club to call its own, but it didn't last long with a split emerging just a few months later and both clubs in dispute over who owned the title Glasgow Hibernian.

Glasgow Harp had failed to live up to its potential and the way was clear for a decent sized Irish club in Glasgow in late 1887, with all the ingredients coming together after Brother Walfrid's initiative to involve three of the parishes of the East End, then all five, to form a football club that would rise from the ghettos to become one of the biggest clubs in world football, with charity at its core and the greatest living manifestation of the Irish diaspora worldwide.

LIFE BEFORE CELTIC COMES TO AN END

In the summer of 1887, life before Celtic as we know it was coming to an end. Initially, three of the parishes of the East End were deep in discussions and were then joined by another two as some withdrew from the discussions. Willie Maley, in his book, "The Story of the Celtic, 1888-1938" takes up the story of the crucial meeting;

"St Mary's representatives, with the greatest enthusiasm, eventually forced matters to an issue, and at a big meeting held in St Mary's Hall it was decided to proceed with the formation of the club and to look for the necessary ground".

All the pieces of the jigsaw had come together: from the re-organisation of the Catholic Church in Scotland, to the Irish Famine and the ensuing immigration of large numbers of Irish into Scotland; the arrival of the Marist Order in Glasgow and in particular Brother Walfrid who was a prime mover in the creation of the Poor Childrens Dinner Tables; the threat of proselytism, the rise in popularity of football, (and Hibernian in particular among the Irish in the west of Scotland), and the social conditions of the Irish in the East End of Glasgow.

From all these ingredients, rose Celtic Football club.

6th November, 1887 was the day the club was formally constituted in St Mary's Hall after mid day mass but new evidence, which we look at in the next chapter, has shone light on a new date of significance: 1st September 1887, the date when memberships for season 1887/88 were started.

The final words on "life before Celtic" must be in honour of Brother Walfrid, the man responsible for gifting us Celtic Football Club. They come from a man who knew him very well: Joseph Foy was a member of the Sacred Heart parish who was on the Father Noonan Memorial Committee alongside Brother Walfrid and who became an original Celtic subscriber after the circular of January 1888, (donating the top rate of 20 shillings).

Joseph Foy told the story of the parish of Sacred Heart, written in the Glasgow Observer between 27th October, 1900 and 16th February, 1901, under the heading;

IN OLD BRIDGETON, REMINISCENCES OF THE SACRED HEART PARISH. MEMORIES OF THE OLD DAYS 1873-1900.

In it, Foy tells the story of Irishmen Felix Fahy and Ted O'Neil, who were great friends and neighbours in the Dublin land, in the parish of Sacred Heart, Bridgeton until Ted returned to Ireland after being left a bit of land and a house when his brother, Tim, died in Ballaghadereen, then in County Mayo. Ted then returns to visit his old parish in Bridgeton and bumps into his old friend where they reminisce about the old days. Foy wrote the Reminiscences in the form of dialogue between the two men, giving a true flavour of how the Glasgow Irish spoke at the time.

This particular sketch by Foy is of Celtic's founder is from the Glasgow Observer of Saturday, 24th November 1900;

SKETCH OF BROTHER WALFRID

"An' now in the name av evirything that's good, how's Brother Walfrid doin' at all, at all; or where is he now? You'll not be tellin' me he's dead too!"

"Indeed no, Ted, glory be to God, he's well, an' strong, an' is happy's the day's long.

Shure he's in London town, in a place they call St Annes, Spitalfields - an' they tell me that saw him this year, he's just as fresh lookin', an' the roguish look in his eye is jest as bright as 'twas whin he was in Brigton 15 years ago; only that the hair av his head is got white now, you wuld think that time had stud still wid him, an' left him as he used to be. But shure it's aisy to tell the raison av Brother Walfrid keepin' so fresh an' young.

It's jest because av the young hart av him, an' which same hart will nevir in this world grow ould; it'll always be young an' fresh, because he's always lookin' round to see what good thing he can do for eviry wan he comes anear, or comes anear him".

"Arrah Faylix, avick. D'ye mind how 'twas between Father Ned an' Brother Walfrid; shure they were more like two rale brothers, not like the parish priest an' the head masther av the school.

Did you evir see them, Faylix, together out in the counthry? T' wud do yer hart good t' see them - they wor jest like two big overgrown boys, (brothers maybe), who had come home fur their summer holidays - Father Ned's arm stuck thru Brother Walfrid's; an' the laffs uv them an' the fun av them. Shure, the sight av them would help t' liten the sorrows an' cobwebs of yer hart".

"D'ye remember, Ted, av the grate big lot av nice boys an' girls that Brother Walfrid used t' bring up t' the school afther their first Communion. An' shure then he had a feast that was good enuff fur a king an' this was all got up aforehand through Brother Walfrid askin' this wan an' that man for a little somethin' to help give the childhre a trate on the gratest day av their lives.

An' be my sowkens, but he did give them a trate an' no mistake an' wan that some av them can remember till this day. Indeed I do, for I was at two or three of them myself".

"Did you evir see the likes av him, Faylix, for lookin' afther the boys an' the girls too, for the matther av that?

We wud a'most think that Brother Walfrid had been marrid, an' that all the childhre that were under his care were his own; and sure so they were and it's him that wor under his care wor his own; an' shure so they wor, an' it's him that was mindful av them, eviry wan. T'wasn't even whilst they wor at school, but afther, long afther they had left, he was as mindful av them an' often more mindful than their rale fathers an' mothers. Shure there wasn't a place in Glasgow where he cud by hook or by crook get wan av his boys into, that he wudn't be huntin' late an' early. And shure, sines is an them, there's many a wan av them this day that's in good, respectable places, through Brother Walfrid. There was some av the big shops in the town that Brother Walfrid's boys got into sooner than any other wan, if there was room for them at all; an' it's a many a wan av them he got into the Granite Warehouse an' other big shops like that.

An' be the same token, shure the boys theirsel's began to have a betther notion av themsel's than many a other wans like them, an' it's telt av many av them t' this day they've lifted themsel's up above bein' common labourers".

"Ye won't mind, Ted, (because ye wor gone to Ballaghadereen), av the grand Literary Society that Brother Walfrid got up fur the boys that had left the school because he wanted to keep them round about him an' no t' let them be stragglin' away an' forgettin' their religious duties; because as he sed;

"T'was the most dangersome time for the young fellos, jest afther they had left school an' begun t' mix up wid Prodestand boys in the places where they wor workin'. An' so 'tis! So it is! The very most dangersome time for them."

Well, Brother Walfrid med a grand new Literary Society for them an' Father Hughes gev him two rooms, which he made int' wan in the ould buildin' alongside av the big school in Dalmarnock Road. An' there he put up a fine library av books an' he got the lads themsel's, wid his guidin', to draw up a fine set av rules in print, as grand as you like. Brother Walfrid was made Honorary President an' John Furey was made President an' Joe Girvan second President, with Hugh Munro Secrethary an' John McGee Treasurer an' a council av Johnny Gribbin, James Owen, Matt McHugh, Arthur McCourt and Charlie McAleese, an' among the other wans there was Ned and James Monaghan, James Burke, Alick McGregor, Pether Crolly, James Maxwell, John Ellis, Willie Gribbin, James Lavery, W. McFarlane, John Helferty, P. McAloon, P. McCabe, John Bolan, William Helferty, R. Geddes an' a whole lot more I can't remember.

An' I can tell you, Ted, t'was just a trate to get in there on a Sunday evenin' an' hear these young min, (indeed it's jest young gentlemen I shud call thim), giving lecthurs an' speeches, an' there was Brother Walfrid wid his face all wan great big smile av joy, at the way his boys wor comin' on.

An' I can tell you this, Ted, that a big lot av these same boys have turn'd out a credit t' themsel's an' Brother Walfrid an' indeed to the Sacred Heart parish.

But a few av them have gone t' their reward an' if 'tis any sign, their end was eviry wan av them as edifyin' as their life; an' among them wans that's gone are James and Ned Monaghan, Matt McHugh, James Queen an' a few others, (May Our Lord an' His Blessed Mother have mercy on their souls. Amen). An' while taking care av the boys' litherary education in that way, Brother Walfrid didn't forgot to have some fun an' amusement for them too; for he made a football club for them that was called the Columba; an' even there he had a fine fatherly care av his boys, for he rinted a park for them down at Glengarry, where they cud play 'ithout havin' to mix up wid the corner boys. An' the main prop an' support av the Columba an' wan that worked hard, very hard, for it undher Brother Walfrid an' kep the boys t'gether for many a long day, was Johnny Gribbin junior.

An' thin Brother Walfrid had magic lanthorns an' concerts besides – an' these same magic lanthorns an' many a wan besides that was gev in the schools to the schoolchildhre an' t' the grown up wans too, for many a year wor given by a man av the parish that deserves well av the Sacred Heart folks, as he has been always ready an' willin' to give his services for eviry purpose av the parish. An' I'm sure, Ted, you'll remember the wan I mane when I tell you his name".

"Indeed an' you don't need t' tell me for I mind him fine; 'tis Frank Kerrigan who lived in the Dalmarnock Road just beside where ould Tom Giblin – Tom's dead too – had his coal ree for many a year. An' shure he tuk a fotygraff av Bridget an' me afore we wint t' Ireland. An' i'm thinkin' 'twas just as good a pictur as I've seen these many a day. An' a good looking couple we wor".

"Yes Ted, that's just the wan, and he's still to the fore an makin' fotygraffs' an' givin' magic lanthorns till this day.

I'm thinkin' Ted, that the Free Poor Childhre's Dinner Table wasn't agoing afore ye wint away?"

"No, Faylix, an' what'na kind av table's that?"

"Ha ha! Throth avick, it's not any kind av table at all, only it's jist called that away, because the childhre sit down till it an' get their dinners an' because av a very hard winther which was here a dozen or so years agone, there was grate disthress an' many a poor wee boy an' girl wor comin' till the school wid their bare feet an' wid hungry bellies thro' the frost an' shnow.

An' Brother Walfrid, (who's hart was as big as his bosom), was jist mortial sarry for the little wans sufferin's, call'd a meetin' av a few av the men av the parish, mostly av the Saint Vincent av Paul Society an' he put the matther afore thim, an' he told thim he had a promise av a good dale av money from wans in the parish tae get up a somethin' t' help the little wans. The more betoken becase there was a whole lot av soup kitchens got up thro' the town by the Prodestands, because av the grate amount av sufferin' there was in the town; an' 'twas afeerd Brother Walfrid's was that some av his little wans wud be snared away an' get a thract for kitchen wid eviry plate av soup, the same as they used to do in Ireland long ago.

Well, shure enuff there was a little shop taken in Savoy Street an' 'tis there till this day, where eviry severe winther the poor little wans can get a good big bowl av warm broth an' a big slice av bread t' keep the life in thim".

"Ah thin Molly; I'm shure Our Lord will have a comfortable corner for Brother Walfrid because He loves all thim as is kind to His little wans".

"That's thrue for you, anyways, Ted".

"I was readin' a letther last week from one av Brother Walfrid's boys who is now a big man an' in a fine situashon. An' 'twud do your hart good t' read the words av affection an' gratitude there was in it about Brother Walfrid".

"I'm tellin' you, Faylix, 'twas like a'most another priest in the parish he was.

He was Father Noonan's right hand. I remember wan Sunday in the porch hearin' Father Ned a tellin' Brother Walfrid, an' Harry Kirk, an' Arthur Phillips a good story av wan you'll mind fine av - Denis McCaig. You'll mind he was a pass keeper for many a year along wid Jemmy Porteous who lived up by Garden-side in Dalmarnock Road; an' old Frank Reynolds an' Charlie Collins, who used to always kneel in the passage t' say his prayers t' Our Lady.

Well, Denis, you mind was an ould soldier, used to be very steady for a long whiles at a time, used t' take a dhrop too much once in a while; an' Mrs McCaig who was a very good, wise woman, used t' feel vexed at Denis; cam' for Father Noonan to see Denis. Whin he wint down to Dale Street, he tould Mrs McCaig;

"Have you fourteen pence on you!"

"Yis, your Reverence".

"Well go and get a half pint av the best an' giv Denis wan glass now, an' wan in three hours an' wan afore he goes t' bed an' thin give him wan in th' mornin".

"An' Denis, you'll come down an' see me tomorrow night".

An', Denis, he came, an' was right for many an' many a day afther. We should hear them all laffin at the long face av Mrs McCaig at Father Ned's cure".

CHAPTER TWO
THE HOLY GRAIL

At every home game Celtic play, thousands walk down Janefield Street, off Springfield Road, on their way to Celtic Park, but how many of us pause to think of the original Celtic Park which once stood there? How many take their kids to show them where our first goal was scored on 28th May, 1888? How many have stood where the pitch once was? Where Brother Walfrid once stood? How many dream of the first ever Treble won there in 1892? How many even know where the first Celtic Park stood?

Read on and discover the story of a forgotten Celtic, in a forgotten ground that the support helped to build, a community effort, the embryonic Celtic. The amateur Celtic, under Brother Walfrid, before his departure to London in August, 1892. This book tells of the growth of the club, our trials and tribulations, our successes and our failures and that's just in a short four year spell that was to whet the appetite before we moved to the current Celtic Park in 1892.

Every Celtic supporter has cried tears of joy and tears of heartbreak and this book tells our early history warts and all, just as we like it, with nothing covered up. No stone has been left unturned in the search for the complete story of Celtic Football Club, from 1887 to 1892 and as many direct quotes as possible are used in this book to give the reader the exact source of the information in the correct context, rather than having it paraphrased for you to come to my conclusion. I put forward my own analysis of the evidence shown but you, the reader, also have the opportunity, and are indeed invited to come to your own conclusion, taking into consideration all the facts presented in front of you.

On being asked to sum up the Celtic story during the Centenary season, Billy McNeill referred to the "fairytale" aspect of the club and no better analogy is possible to describe our magical journey. From a ghetto club, formed in the east end of Glasgow with humble charitable aims we have risen to our current status as one of the biggest clubs in world football.

Today we continue to live that dream but what sets us apart is the history, the Celtic story and it is our duty to cherish that history, the good days and the bad and to pass it on to future generations of Celtic supporters. They say that the more things change, the more they stay the same and never a truer word has been spoken in a Celtic context. Right from the outset, from our very first season, we were the victim of contentious refereeing decisions, fall outs with authorities and biased reporting in the Scottish press. To survive as an Irish club in the most anti Irish city on earth, we had to be strong, we had to be resolute and we had to be united. We had to give as good as we got, led by the men of vision on the Celtic Committee, and Brother

Walfrid, who with a steely determination, a will to win and a humble charitable objective, we wrote a new chapter in Scottish football.

This book tells the untold story of the early Celtic in great detail, of the men who established our club, of the original Celtic Park and of the fairytale that is...

CELTIC FOOTBALL CLUB

Felix Fahy and Ted O'Neil again take up the story, written by Joseph A Foy;

"IN OLD BRIDGETON, REMINISCENCES OF THE SACRED HEART PARISH 1873 - 1900"

From the *Glasgow Observer* on Saturday, 8th December 1900;

"Faylix, i'd like t' hear av you about the Celtic Football Club. My Patsey over in Ballaghadereen gets the Observer newspaper sint t' him eviry week, an' if ye wor t' hear him braggin' about the Celts, as the gommeral calls them, ye wud think 'twas in Glasgow he was eviry day".

"Well indeed thin, throth, Ted, they're gettin' on bravely, an' able t' hould their own wid the best in th' lan'. An' indeed, they're a credit t' the creed an' counthry the men all sprung from that used t' be in the ould Celtic Club. There wor Tom Maley an' Willie Maley, an' Mick Dunbar, an' Johnny Coleman, an' Willie Groves, an' J Smith, an' Phil Clarke, an' Jerry Reynolds, an' Dan Doyle, an' Sandy McMahon, an' Johnny Campbell, an Paddy Gallagher, an Johnny Madden, an' Jimmy Kelly, an' James McLaughlin, an' Neilly McCallum, an' Jimmy McLaren, an' a lot av other wans I cannot mind av.

Shure it's ourselves wor proud av thim boys; more betoken they wor eviry wan av thim Catholic boys. Shure i mind, Ted, wan Saturday mornin', in the Sacred Heart Chapel, wid Brother Walfrid there as large as life, an' eviry wan av thim goin' for'ad t' the rails an "Resavin" (receiving Communion), an' they wor to play the final cup tie that day at Hampden Park. But it's chang'd times now, Ted. There's no a very many av thim go t' the rails, be the token there's no very many av thim as that way av thinkin".

"Musha! Musha! You don't tell me Faylix".

"Troth i do. An' it's more the pity say I".

"Well! well! well! What way was the Celtic club first started, Faylix?"

"Well twas this away, Shure Brother Walfrid an' John Glass an' another wan av Brigton 'twas who first tuk the notion av havin' such a thing becase av the rayson, that afther a couple av games av football was play'd by the ould Harp av Dundee, an' a rale good ould Harp twas too. They cam there from Dundee an' played agin the Clyde in ould Barrowfield for the poor childhre's free dinner table I was tellin' you about, that was so much needed in thim hard times.

Well, as i was sayin' afther the Harp an' the Clyde played a game, shure didn't Brother Walfrid an' another wan, wid the grate help av Tom Maley, get the Renton an' the ould Hibs av Edinburgh to come to Barrowfield, an' play for the same rayson, an' be the same token, there was a grand cup give t' the winners. An' for shure there was a fine spread in the boy's school that same evenin' afther the game, wid songs an' speeches galore. 'Twas thin id cam t' the wans I spoke av twud be a grate thing t' get up a club av our own. An' shure no sooner sed than done. An' wid th' help of the two Misther Maleys, an' if id weren't for these same two, the sorra Celtic wud evir have been.

Thin 'twas all cut and dhry afore the club was med up, an' afore the players wor got t'gether, that the Celtic was t' be med up an' the wan object av the raisin av the club was to be for keepin' up av the poor childhre's free dinner table av the Sacred Heart, St Mary's an' St Michael's, Parkhead. An' shure enuff this was thrue, for 'twas put in prent, into the rules an' regulashons av the club.

Well, the club was med up an' wint on bravely, houldin' it's own again the best in the counthry, altho they wor howled at in the Exhibition Cup by a crowd of hooligans. But you wudn't hardly believe it, Ted. The sorra a single ha'penny have cum to these same poor childhre's dinner tables these a many a year back".

"You don't tell me, Faylix. An' whatna 'tall is the rayson?"

"Troth, Ted, the sorra a wan av me right knows; but, at any rate, 'tis as i'm tellin' you. An' you'd hardly beleeve me whin I tell you what in wan year the Celtic club drew more than ten thousan pounds".

"Oh, milia, murdher! Faylix is that thrue? £10,000!"

"Why faith shure. If they had only gev a wan tenth av that fur all these years there wud be a fine big chapel built av stone besides the poor childhre's dinners an' breakfasts, an suppers, too, fur the matther av that".

"Well, well! i'm shure 'tis little Brother Walfrid thought that wud be the way whin he started the Celtic Futbal' Club".

"An' do the St Vincent De Paul Society still keep up the childhre's dinners in the winther t'me?"

"They do indeed, an' the people are jest as ginerous as evir in helpin them. There was a fine young priest was here jist afther the Celtic was med up. An' oh my! What a mortial delite he tuk in seein the Celtic play. He was wan av the warm heartedest clergy evir you knew. An' he was so full av life an' mirth. 'Twas Father O'Connell they called him, and my, Ted, twud do yer hart good to see him goin' along the sthreet wid the jaunty step av him, an his umberel swingin' from side t' side. He was a grate man for the League av the Cross, and 'twas sore the membirs mis'd him whin he was taken away. He was only 27 or 28 years ould, an' ye wud take a lase av his life but, glory be t' God he died, a short time afther he was taken away - May the Lord have mercy on his soul!"

CELTIC AT OUR FOUNDATION

Celtic Football & Athletic Club were formally constituted in St Mary's Hall on Sunday, November 6th 1887 after mid-day mass, following lengthy discussions, originally between the leading parishioners of St Mary's, St Alphonsus and St Andrew's, brought together by Brother Walfrid, but which also included Sacred Heart and St Michael's, after the withdrawal of some, but not all, of the representatives of St Alphonsus and St Andrews parishes.

Interestingly the exact date given for the formation of Celtic in the early Celtic Handbooks, right up until 1925, is September 1887. Why it states September and not November, which is the obvious date, is not documented but will soon become clear to the reader.

As we have established, 12th February 1887 was a key date when all the ingredients came together in the one place, at the one time when Hibs were feted at St Mary's Hall immediately after they won the Scottish Cup for the first time. Discussions started some time after this date following Dr John Conway's "keynote" speech, deliberately primed to test the water of John McFadden, the Hibs Secretary with its reference to "emulating their example." McFadden's private reply to some of those in attendance, including the men who would go on to form Celtic, was to "Go and do likewise," ie, to build a team to represent the Catholics of the west as Hibs had done in the east. Crucially, it wasn't said in his speech as was originally thought, it was said in response to Dr John Conway's speech.

The very fact that Hibs were feted in the east end of Glasgow at St Mary's Hall, before they even thought of setting foot in Edinburgh underlined the importance that John McFadden put on his relationship with the Glasgow Irish and the man who was his contact in Glasgow and who he had brought his Hibs teams to the city to play in charity matches for.

That man, was of course, Brother Walfrid.

We have learned that after the 12th February date, a steering committee was formed to look at the possibility of forming an Irish team in Glasgow. No doubt it's findings were that for an Irish team to succeed in Glasgow, it would have to involve the finest minds of all the close knit parishes of the east end, surrounding St Mary's. The next date of significance was 26th May, when a mouth-watering tie was set up between Hibs and Renton and a trophy organised, the East End Catholic Charity Cup. This was a step up from the charity matches Brother Walfrid had previously organised for the Poor Children's Dinner Tables and the level of expertise involved had all the hallmarks of an early "Celtic" committee, if not in name.

The huge sums raised from a crowd of 12,000, bigger than that year's Scottish Cup final itself, ensured that an Irish team in Glasgow was no longer a pipe dream, no longer a possibility, it was now a certainty. What we do know is that the early meetings of the parishes were turbulent and that the dominant debaters from the mother parish of St Mary's held sway and pressed ahead with the plan with the parishes of St Alphonsus and St Andrew's feeling sidelined.

One interesting fact that has emerged is that the parishes of both St Andrew's and St Alphonsus had already formed parish football teams in the previous two years and as late as March 1887, St Michael's in Parkhead were discussing the formation of a parish football team under the auspices of their Total Abstinence Society. Did they feel part of Brother Walfrid's plan for another Irish Catholic club, one that would put their own in the shade or even force it to close down? If not, was this a crucial reason why two parishes decided to step away from the discussions?

Another factor was the characters involved. The parish of St Alphonsus was led by Irishman Father Michael Maginn and the parish of St Andrews was led by Scotsman, the Very Reverend Provost Alex Munro. Ironically, or not, both men were not taken by football, which they saw as a distraction from religious morals, which brought with it temptation. Did this play a part in their withdrawal? Very likely.

One other important date in our story was the 21st May 1887 when Renton beat Vale of Leven 1-0 at Cathkin and importantly east end parishes benefitted from the charitable donations distributed by the competition's organising committee. This, tied in with the match five days later at Barrowfield between Hibs and Renton, gave the parishes of the east end first hand experience of the good football can do, and the potential good an Irish club of our own could achieve in feeding the poor on our doorstep.

When we add the driving force behind Brother Walfrid's initiative, which was the maintenance of the Poor Children's Dinner Tables, to Archbishop Eyre's clearly expressed dismay at the amount of destitute children in the east end of Glasgow and his challenge for more work to be done to tackle this by maintaining the funding of our own Dinner Tables to stave off the danger of proselytism, and you quickly see a pattern developing where a dynamic force combining the right people with the right reasons at the right time all coming together in the name of charity.

Brother Walfrid was one step ahead of the game, having already founded the Dinner Tables at Sacred Heart and he saw the foundation of Celtic as the way to remain one step ahead of the game and to ensure the Dinner Tables were maintained. He had watched other Irish Catholic teams being formed in the Glasgow area, mostly parish football teams and many in imitation of Edinburgh Hibernian, who they took their name from.

What made Celtic different, however was two fold.

1. Brother Walfrid decided to involve the three biggest parishes of the east end, not just one, as others had done and this was the one pivotal decision, the brainwave, that brought together the most prominent minds of the three parishes to form a dynamic, energetic and enterprising Celtic Committee.

2. He wanted a club that was set up, not in imitation of Hibernian, but one that would not only stand on its own two feet, but would take on and defeat all others.

We were not formed to IMITATE the biggest Irish Catholic club in the country. We were formed to BECOME the biggest Irish Catholic club in the country.

Only then could our success be guaranteed and only then could the charitable aims of the club be fully maximised.

Brother Walfrid knew from experience, the difficulties involved in setting up and maintaining a junior parish team, when he founded Eastern Rovers in Bridgeton in the late 1870s when he was the Headmaster at Sacred Heart. The club played their home matches at Glengarry Park, which Brother Walfrid rented for their use, in an area of Bridgeton named after the Catholic Highlanders who settled there. It stood adjacent to Barrowfield, the home of Clyde FC and formerly Eastern FC up to 1884, before their move to Springfield Park.

Eastern Rovers reached the top of their game in the late 1870s but struggled to continue their momentum. The club lapsed from 1880 to 1885 but made a return after a meeting in the parish of Sacred Heart on 9th July 1885, with the purpose of reorganising the old parish football team. By 1887 there is no mention of them in the press of the day and a different club, Gordon Athletics, are named as playing their home matches at Glengarry Park.

Brother Walfrid also founded another juvenile club named Columba, who were formed in January 1885 and also rented the use of Bridgeton's Glengarry Park to play their home matches, after initially playing on public ground in Rutherglen. The football team were affiliated with the Sacred Heart Young Men's Literacy Society and were named after the Donegal abbot who is credited with spreading Christianity throughout Scotland after his self imposed exile from Ireland in 563 AD. Their Secretary was a Rutherglen man, Jeremiah Rearden, from the Main Street and he was succeeded by John Gribben from the parish of Sacred Heart in January 1888. Not surprisingly the team played in green uniforms. Another theory for their name could also have come from Hugh O'Neill, who was the Marist Brother who started at Saint Mungo's on the same day as Brother Walfrid on their first teaching post. His name was Brother Columba.

Interestingly, fellow Founding Father John Glass was one of the originators of Eastern Hibernian, a club who played their home matches in Parkhead and their secretary was local man, Edward McGuire, from 217 Westmuir St. The reserve teams of Eastern Hibs and Columba actually played on September 26th 1885 at the ground of the latter in a match that finished 1-1, penny for the thoughts of John Glass and Brother Walfrid as they stood watching their opposing sides that day.

The timing of Eastern Rovers' demise is very interesting. Brother Walfrid at this time was concentrating his efforts on establishing a larger Irish club, rather than a local one and he was taking the valuable lessons learned from Eastern Rovers that to succeed he would have to involve as many of the parishes of the East End as possible, not just his own. Ironically in the Scottish Junior Football annual of 1887/88, the name listed directly above Brother Walfrid's Columba, were Celtic, from Possilpark. Did that have an effect on Brother Walfrid's choice of name for his new Irish club?

WHO WERE THE FOUNDING FATHERS?

The story of Brother Walfrid, who was an honorary member of every Celtic committee, is one that every Celtic supporter cherishes with pride, but what is forgotten is that he was not only the prime mover in the birth of our club, he brought together key men from the parishes of the East End who ensured our club was sustainable and through that first committee's vibrancy and indefatigability, the success of our embryonic club was ensured.

JOHN GLASS

John Glass was born in 1851 in Glasgow, of Irish parents. He was a glazier by trade, but took up employment as General Manager of his brother Peter's successful wood merchants and builders business in the Gallowgate, which employed many of the city's Irish. A proud son of Donegal, he became a driving force behind the formation of our club as he met regularly with Brother Walfrid and Dr John Conway to discuss ways of tackling the poverty in the streets around them and he was at the heart of the decision-making process when the club was founded.

John Glass was Celtic's first President, Brother Walfrid's right-hand man, and the man who made things happen. His devotion to the club is best summed up by the fact that he never missed a single committee meeting from the club's inception in 1887 to his death in 1906.

In Willie Maley's words;

"John Glass is the man to whom the club owes its existence as he never shirked from that time till the day of his death to further the project which to him appealed as his life work. He was a great Irishman, ever ready to stand up for his rights and later did much politically for the cause so dear to him. These were not the days of written agreements and John Glass's word was always as good as any bond. For years he thought of nothing but Celtic. It was thanks to Glass that the organisation fulfilled the object which the first committee set out to make to make good; to prove that Irishmen could build as good a club as anyone".

Although he was a strong man with a big presence, it was his persuasive ability to charm the birds down from the trees that many found irresistible. Like many of Celtic's founders he was deeply involved in both political and religious circles and he honed his leadership skills as he led the local Catholic Union committee, a body set up to contest school board elections. He was also the President and Secretary of the St Mary's League of the Cross and the Treasurer of the Home Government Branch of the Irish National League. His list of prominent contacts was long. John Glass was THE politician around the table at the time of our formation.

DOCTOR JOHN CONWAY

John Conway was born in 1859 in Glasgow and became a leading member of the Irish community in Glasgow. His father, of the same name, was the first Catholic representative on the Parochial Board in Glasgow. John Junior excelled as a pupil at St Mungo's School, under the guidance of Brother Walfrid, before studying at St Aloysius College and then gaining entry to Glasgow University to study medicine, at a time when very few Catholics studied at this seat of learning. Although admitted to join the Royal College of Surgeons in London, he returned to work and live amongst his own people in the East End of Glasgow as a community doctor, helping to fight the battle against disease and poverty in one of the most under privileged areas in Europe at the time.

There he settled in Monteith Row, beside Glasgow Green with his wife, where he was prominent in the Conference of the Saint Vincent De Paul Society at his local parish of St Alphonsus, the Catholic Union, the Catholic Benefit Society, and the O'Connell branch of the Irish National Foresters. He was also the honorary physician to the Whitevale Refuge, and was one of the earliest members of the Catholic Literary Society.

When Hibernian were lauded by their Glasgow based Irish support at St Mary's Hall after their Scottish Cup triumph in 1887, it was Dr Conway who delivered the address in their honour. He was there when Celtic were officially launched in the same hall nine months later when he was made Celtic's first Honorary President and he was the man who kicked the first ball at the opening of Celtic Park on 8th May 1888.

JAMES QUILLAN

James Quillan was born in 1856 in Glasgow to Irish parents. He was a prominent member of St Mary's parish and also deeply involved with the Home Government branch of the Irish National League.

Ambitious in business he initially rented a premises on High St, and described himself as a barrel dealer, buying and selling solid oak casks. He then moved to larger premises, which he named East End Cooperage and which took up one side of Wilkie Street where he remained for 17 years. Wilkie Street ran parallel to the southern side of the railway line between Bluevale St and Millerston Street slightly north of where the two large tower blocks stood until 2015. He then further extended his business to premises on East Nelson Street, (now called Millerston Street), and also to Janefield Street, behind the Celtic end of the current Celtic Park, running at right angles to Janefield Street, which he named Caledonian Cooperage and which took up 380ft of frontage. By the height of his success he was a master cooper and owned the largest cooperage in Britain with 180,000 casks passing through it per annum.

James Quillan was an original subscriber to Celtic after the fundraising circular in January 1888 and he donated a generous 20 shillings. He was elected as the first Vice President on the original Celtic Committee but he was to become a controversial character, who lead the Quillanite malcontents at the 1889 AGM, which led to him forming a rival Irish club which he named Glasgow Hibernian.

JOHN H McLAUGHLIN

John Herbert McLaughlin was born in 1863 in Glasgow. Of Donegal stock and a parishioner at St Mary's Parish he was typical of many of the Founding Fathers. He received his early education in St Mungo's, Townhead, where Brother Walfrid taught, before going on to the famous Jesuit seminary of Stoneyhurst in Lancashire where he showed great intellect, carrying off the highest honours and was gold medallist for two successive years. On returning to Glasgow, he studied law, however instead of becoming a solicitor, he joined the commercial department of the Leather Manufacturers of John Tullis Ltd, of Bridgeton, working as a cashier.

At the young age of 19, he married Elizabeth Ann Shannon in 1882 in the Cathedral Lodge and they resided at 300 Duke Street, a short distance from the site where Celtic Park would be built and a large part of his life would be devoted. Five years later John H McLaughlin was central to the foundation of Celtic and at only 24 he was one of the youngest of the founding fathers. Although he was a shy man, he spoke with an authority that made people stand up and listen. He was without doubt the best football legislator in the land, a man who not only played a pivotal role at Celtic but also in bringing professionalism to Scottish football and the formation of the Scottish League. He also played piano at St Mary's and in the Rangers Glee Club which was formed in March 1888. A strange combination, it's granted.

JOHN O'HARA

John O'Hara was born in 1847, 10 miles from Derry, around Faughanvale, which is near Greysteel. He and his family left for Scotland when he was very young and they settled in the Bannockburn area. He became involved in the shoemaking business and quickly rose to be an organiser with the Boot and Shoe Operative's Union and Secretary of the Operative Shoemaker's Society.

He moved to the East End of Glasgow, finally settling at 77 East Rose Street, just a few doors down from St Mary's Hall and given his organisational ability, he became a prominent parishioner at St Mary's, where he was the Secretary of the local Catholic Union Committee. He was involved right from the very start with the organising committee who feted Hibernian at St Mary's Hall after their Scottish Cup triumph in February 1887 and he was instrumental in the founding of Celtic, where he was elected to become our first Secretary.

HUGH DARROCH

Hugh Darroch was born in 1859 in Glasgow of Irish parents, from County Antrim. Hugh's father, also called Hugh, was a miner and he died before his son's second birthday and so the family moved to Glasgow where they settled on London Road, Bridgeton, where his mother ran a clothes shop, before moving to the Gallowgate in the parish of St Mary's, where by this time he was a manager in a very successful Pawnbroker's. Hugh married Mary Walls in 1888 and they had one son, also named Hugh, following in the family tradition.

Like many of the Founding Fathers, Hugh Darroch was a mainstay of the parish of St Mary's and was also involved with the local Conference of the Saint Vincent De Paul before being central to the birth of Celtic, where his enthusiasm and energy made him a popular member of the first committee where he was elected as our first Treasurer in 1887.

Tragically, Hugh was diagnosed with cancer and became the first Founding Father to pass away, on the 11th September 1891, at the young age of 32. The flags at the original Celtic Park flew at half mast as the funeral cortege passed the ground on its way to Old Dalbeth.

WILLIAM McKILLOP

William McKillop was born in 1858 in Dalry of Irish parents from Glenarm in the Glens of Antrim. As a parishioner at St Mary's, William McKillop was a member of the Irish National League's Home Government branch in Glasgow and from there he fell into the company of John Glass, Pat Welsh and others who went on to become the Founding Fathers of Celtic.

Having come from a poor background and after working in various industrial jobs he and his brother John moved from Ayrshire to Glasgow where they set up a business as licensed grocers. Eventually they worked themselves up to become very successful and owned a chain of restaurants in Glasgow. His brother John, was also to become a future Celtic committee member. William McKillop went on to become the Nationalist MP for North Sligo and then South Armagh 8 years later.

In 1906, William McKillop donated a trophy, which was then named after him, and became a prestigious prize awarded to the winners of the Senior Gaelic Football Championship of County Armagh, where McKillop was the Nationalist MP.

JOSEPH SHAUGHNESSY

Joseph Shaughnessy was born in 1850 in Bridgeton to Irish parents and the family moved to Rutherglen when he was just 6 months old. He was taught by the Marist Brothers at St Mungo's and the Jesuits at St Aloysius College, before he attended Glasgow University and qualified as a legal practitioner in 1877. He quickly set up his own premises in Hope Street, Glasgow, where his reputation soon grew and he became the legal adviser to the largest Accident Assurance Society in the world. He took a keen interest in trades union affairs and was often consulted by the leaders of the Trades Union of Scotland and he took part in some very high profile cases.

A leading member of the Home Government branch of the Irish National League in Glasgow, he was a deeply religious man and was a member of his local conference of the Saint Vincent De Paul Society. Along with another founding father Joseph Nelis they were founding members of the St Aloysius Association. One of three lawyers involved in the establishment of Celtic, along with Michael Cairns and Joseph Francis McGroary, he was an important fixer for the new club, who knew his way around the corridors of local power and he also dealt with any legal issues which concerned the club.

JOSEPH MICHAEL NELIS

Joseph Michael Nelis was born in 1853 in Bridgeton, of Irish parents. He was the son of an Egg and Butter merchant and he went on to follow in his father's footsteps before establishing a Pawnbroker's shop in Nuneaton Street, near Celtic Park around 1877.

Joseph Nelis also followed the same path of many of the Founding Fathers in education, when he was taught at St Mungo's and then at St Aloysius College. As a local businessman, he was on the Parochial Board for Bridgeton in 1884 and as such was elected as a Manager of the poor by the Barony Parish a year later. He was also an early member of the Catholic Union of Glasgow and was a founding member, along with Dr John Conway and Joseph Shaughnessy of the St Aloysius Association which represented the small Glasgow Catholic professional class.

Joseph Nelis was the leaseholder of the original Celtic Park.

JOSEPH FRANCIS McGROARY

Joseph F McGroary was born in 1865 in Glasgow, the son of Irish parents from Mountcharles, in Donegal. Similar to many of the original Founding Fathers, Joseph received his education at St Mungo's under the Marists and at St Aloysius under the Jesuits. This would serve him well and on leaving school, he took up a law apprenticeship in the premises of Joseph Shaughnessy in 1880, and so his future Celtic connection began. He went on to study Law at Glasgow University before returning to Joseph Shaughnessy's practice in 1887 to finish his training as a fully fledged writer, (lawyer).

And so months later, in his involvement with Celtic, Joseph McGroary would find himself working with his boss, Joseph Shaughnessy. Both were present at the opening of Celtic Park on 8th May 1888.

Joseph McGroary had no immediate connection with the East End parishes and instead was a prominent member of the parish of St Joseph's on North Woodside Road, near St George's Cross.

MICHAEL CAIRNS

Michael Cairns was born in 1857 in Glasgow of Irish parents. He was educated at St Mungo's in Townhead around the time when Brother Walfrid taught there and he then qualified from Glasgow University with distinction as a law student and after finishing his training, he became one of the first Catholics in Glasgow to qualify for the practice after passing the final Law Agents examination. He went on to set up his own premises in Glasgow in 1889 as a lawyer at the age of 32, showing great promise in the profession, with a great career in front of him. His involvement with Celtic from our inception came through his friendship with fellow member of the Catholic Literary Society, Dr John Conway, although having been taught by Brother Walfrid, there's no doubt that he was drawn to the project by hearing of the Marist Brother's involvement. Along with fellow lawyers, Joseph Shaughnessy and Joseph F McGroary, they gave invaluable assistance to the club in our early years.

Tragically, Michael Cairns became the second founding father to be taken from us at an early age when he passed away on 18th February, 1892 at his home at Apsley Place, Glasgow at the young age of 35 and he is buried in the Conway family plot, in St Peter's cemetery, Dalbeth, just a mile along London Road from their beloved Celtic Park, as Michael Cairns' parents and relatives had predeceased him.

The *Glasgow Observer* paid this tribute;

"He never forgot his race or his religion, and as a Catholic and an Irishman, he was always on the alert, in his own quiet way, to spread the light."

PAT WELSH

Pat Welsh was born in 1848, and was a Fenian activist from Killargue in County Leitrim, just 37 miles from Brother Walfrid's home town of Ballymote. He first met the acquaintance of Sergeant Tom Maley, at Pigeon House docks in Dublin in 1867, as he tried to flee the country and board a boat to Glasgow. Taking pity on the fellow Irishman, Maley allowed Welsh to travel if he promised to stay away from trouble. Welsh agreed and eventually set up a successful master tailor's premises on plush Buchanan Street in Glasgow. Never forgetting the act of kindness which had given him a new lease of life, Welsh assisted the Maley's when they moved to Glasgow in 1869 and some 17 years later, he was to visit the home of the Maley's in Cathcart with Brother Walfrid and John Glass to try and tempt Tom Maley Junior to sign for the new Irish club, and ended up attracting Willie Maley too, with Brother Walfrid's famous words; "Why don't you come along too?"

Pat Welsh was a much loved and respected parishioner at St Mary's and was the Vice President of the Glasgow branch of the Irish National Amnesty Association, which called for the release of Irish prisoners. He was also a member of the League of the Cross, the local Conference of the Saint Vincent De Paul Society and the Home Government branch of the Irish National League as well as being a leading organiser of the Connaught Reunion in Glasgow.

JAMES CURTIS

James Curtis was born in 1864 in Glasgow to Irish parents and was another Founding Father who was taught at St Mungo's under Brother Walfrid. A school teacher, he taught at St Mary's under Brother Dorotheus and he lived locally at 3 Comelypark Place. When his first son was born, he was called William Dorotheus as a tribute to the Marist Brother

He was the Chairman of the Catholic Young Men's Society in the parish of St Mary's and in this role he wrote a letter of congratulations to the Hibernian Secretary, John McFadden, on their Scottish Cup victory in 1887. Months later, he was involved with Celtic at our inception, and became the Match Secretary of the Celtic Second XI, a team who broke all records in 1891, winning both trophies they competed in and playing football the Celtic way, with a team known for their attacking style. On one memorable occasion that season, they beat St Mirren 13-1 after losing the first goal, in the Scottish Second XI Cup final.

JAMES McKAY

James McKay was born in 1853 in the Calton to an Irish mother and a Scots father and they settled in Abercromby St, in the shadow of St Mary's chapel, the parish that was to become the birthplace of Celtic. James' father and namesake owned a hairdresser business on the Gallowgate, where the Bellgrove Hotel now stands, and James followed his father into the family business.

He married Margaret Malley in St Mary's chapel in 1884 and they had four sons and three daughters. Coincidentally, he had a brother in law by the name of Willie Malley, but there was no relation. James McKay would be elected to the post of Treasurer in the 1892 AGM.

He was the oversman in charge of the building of the current Celtic Park in 1892 when we relocated from the original ground and to him we shall be ever grateful for giving us "Paradise".

DANIEL MALLOY

Dan Malloy was born in 1862 in Bridgeton to second generation Irish parents and was a popular figure in the religious and political social circles that many of the Founding Fathers moved in, as a member of the Irish National Foresters, the Irish National League and the League of the Cross in the parish of St Mary's.

Dan was a very popular, jovial character in the parish and was never happier than when he played the fiddle at a good old fashioned Celtic social occasion, often to the background of John H McLaughlin on the piano or Neil McCallum on vocals singing a few Irish tunes. Described as an ironmonger's traveller, or sales representative, in 1887, he was one of the youngest members of the original Celtic Committee and such was his popularity, he was re-elected in 1889. A year later Dan emigrated to America with his family, before returning five years later and resuming his involvement with Celtic.

JOHN CHARLES MacDONALD

John Charles MacDonald was born in 1858 in Ireland and the family moved to Glasgow where they originally settled in the Irish ghetto of High Street, and later moved to Springburn, where John's father was employed as a labourer in the nearby St Rollox locomotive works. He and his uncle, also named John, were founder members of the Catholic Literary Society in Glasgow and through this initiative, he met the acquaintance of Dr John Conway, Hugh Darroch and Joseph McGroary. Through these contacts, John junior, a keen follower of professional foot running at Powderhall, became involved with Celtic at our inception. He was also a member of the League of the Cross at the parish of St John's in Portugal Street in the Gorbals, which was eventually replaced by St Luke's.

An engineer by trade, John C MacDonald had beaten all the odds to gain an apprenticeship in Glasgow, being a Catholic. He is listed as attending the opening match at Celtic Park and his first big task given him by the Celtic Committee was to travel to Renton with John O'Hara to persuade James Kelly, one of the hottest properties in football, to sign for the new Irish Club.

Although he had to call in the assistance of John Glass, it showed the faith the Celtic Committee had in John C MacDonald, to test him with such a task.

DAVID MEIKLEHAM

David Meikleham was born in 1850 in Rothesay before moving to Glasgow where he married Robina McLaughlin in the parish of St Alphonsus in 1873 and they would go on to have 13 children, 6 boys and 7 girls. A mainstay of the parish, he was a member of the local Catholic Union and was elected in 1887 to represent the parish on the Central Committee of that group.

His father owned a shoemaking business and so David followed in his footsteps, (excuse the pun). Through his hard work, he built up the business until he employed seven staff in 1881, and ironically he would come into contact with fellow committee man, John O'Hara on occasion as he led the Shoemaker's Union. David Meikleham was also a member of the Caledonian Catholic Association in Glasgow.

FRANCIS McERLEAN

Frank McErlean was born in 1845 in Belfast and moved to Glasgow where he married the daughter of an East End pawnbroker in 1869, before moving back to Belfast where he worked as a spirit merchant. The family returned to Glasgow before our foundation and Frank rented property on 735 Great Eastern Road, (the Gallowgate), where he ran a Pawnbroker's shop in the upper flat. The shop was severely damaged due to a fire caused by a defective chimney in March 1888, but thankfully he was insured.

A parishioner of St Michael's in Parkhead, Frank McErlean was a prominent member of that parish involved in the discussions to form Celtic in 1887 and he became Celtic's second Vice President in 1889 after James Quillan's departure. His eldest daughter Bridget married the Celtic captain James Kelly in January 1891 in the original St Michael's chapel, in Salamanca Street, Parkhead.

BROTHER DOROTHEUS

Brother Dorotheus was born Henry Currie in 1855 in Dundee and was Brother Walfrid's close friend and colleague at Celtic's foundation, as the Headmasters at St Mary's and Sacred Heart respectively.

Both men worked together on the setting up of the Poor Childrens Dinner Tables in their respective parishes and also in the charity matches played in Bridgeton, which was an important precursor to the birth of Celtic. Brother Dorotheus, who was 15 years younger than Brother Walfrid was one of the two named auditors appointed on Celtic's first published accounts in 1889.

TOM & WILLIE MALEY

No story on the Founders of Celtic could be complete without Tom and Willie Maley, who signed for Celtic in September 1887, after Brother Walfrid, John Glass and Pat Welsh turned up at their door in an effort to sign the older brother Tom, but in one of those magical twists of fate, with Tom out courting his future wife, Willie was invited along to have a word with the Founding Fathers too.

In this one example, it shows how circumstance came together that would guide the club through not only our early years but right up to our 50th year and beyond. One thing the Founding Fathers did not have was experience of running a football club, or even any great knowledge of the intricacies of the game itself. It was a means to an end to feed the poor of the parishes in the streets around them, but they needed someone who could instil in them a footballing brain and that man was the much respected Tom Maley.

Tom was born in 1864 in Portsmouth, all four sons in fact were born in different countries, due to the army career of their father, Sergeant Tom Maley, who was born in Ennis, County Clare, on 20th December 1830 and joined the Royal Scots Fusiliers in 1846 in Limerick. His father was Charles O'Malley, a land steward or agent on Lord Inchiquin's estate in County Clare. His duties included the running of the estate, but he also had the extremely unpopular job of collecting the rent from the tenants.

In 1887, Tom Maley was a much respected young footballer and athlete, who also had a sharp brain, as was proven by his "day job" as a trainee school teacher, having recently returned from St Mary's Catholic teacher training college in Hammersmith, London. Tom had already played for various clubs including Cathcart, Partick Thistle, Third Lanark and he was a member of the Hibernian party when they lifted the Scottish Cup. He was also a keen runner with Clydesdale Harriers and this turn of pace was evident when he terrorised full backs from his position at outside left. The Founding Fathers had done their homework and Tom Maley brought with him not only his speed, stamina and dash on the pitch which he described as his best assets, but also a list of contacts in the game that would be put to good use as he was asked to draw up a list of targets. Although it is said that when James Kelly signed for Celtic, others followed, Tom Maley's involvement should not be underestimated, as his name gave the club an instant kudos from the start and paved the way for many of the first XI to come along too.

Tom was suitably impressed with Brother Walfrid and John Glass to share their vision that at long last, Glasgow was to have its own Irish club worthy of the name. The biggest surprise was that it took so long to establish. Without a shadow of doubt, what made the difference was their charitable message, as Maley could have put pen to paper for any other club, with the exception of one obvious one, but he chose Celtic, who had yet to build a ground, select a team or elect a committee. We didn't even have a ball. One word; charity, was all that was needed to convince him to throw in his lot.

Tom's younger brother, Willie Maley, was born in 1868 in Newry in Ireland and the family moved to Glasgow a year later to settle originally in the parish of St Mary's when the now retired Sergeant Maley was appointed as an Instructor to the 3rd Renfrewshire Rifle Volunteers at Thornliebank, before making Cathcart their home three years later when the Sergeant was transferred to the same position there. Willie Maley left school at 13 and found a position in the offices of a calico printers, before moving onto a Telephone Company where he got his first big break after the manager was suitably impressed by his office work to offer him a position in his own private firm, training to become a Chartered Accountant.

It was Willie Maley's accountancy skills that appealed to the Founding Fathers, as well as his footballing and athletic skills and he was soon appointed as Match Secretary as well as being a decent half back. A tall, powerfully built young man, Willie had played a few games for Third Lanark, and along with his brother Tom, was tipped to play for them during that season. Similar to Tom, Willie was also a keen runner, who also represented Clydesdale Harriers on occasion.

Whilst training as a Chartered Accountant, Willie would have to combine his Celtic career by moonlighting under his mother's maiden name, Montgomery, so as not to arouse their suspicion. Thankfully Messrs Smith & Wilson didn't perchance upon a Celtic game and notice the young half back by the name of Montgomery was in fact their own trainee, Willie Maley!

Willie's athletic prowess and his love of the sport made him the driving force behind the original Celtic Sports and he finally became the Celtic Manager in 1897, a position he kept until the New Year of 1940. In short, Willie Maley, although he didn't give us Celtic, he can certainly lay claim to being one of the main men who made Celtic into the force we became on the field.

In summary, the Founding Fathers were Catholic to a man, born in Ireland or in Glasgow of Irish parents with only a couple of exceptions. Most were known to each other, working together in the various religious and political groups of the day in an overtly political era in Glasgow where Catholic and Irish National groups were many. Brother Walfrid, who was 47 at the time of our formation had brought together the smartest minds and the many of the prominent members of these committees, most of whom were based at the parish of St Mary's but certainly not all.

The age of the Founding Fathers ranged from the youngest, with Joseph McGroary only 22, James Curtis; 23, John H McLaughlin; 24 and Dr John Conway; 28 to the more experienced John Glass who was 36, Joseph Shaughnessy; 37, Pat Welsh; 39 and John O'Hara the oldest at 40.

All were successful in their own walks of life and none were involved in the spirit trade, which was frowned upon heavily within the Catholic hierarchy, although partaken of by many. We had a range of expertise on the first committee which grew to accommodate up to twenty members after our first season but was trimmed back to fifteen, which included office bearers as discussion was often long, time consuming and on occasion led to heated debate, such was the eagerness to succeed against all the odds.

The first committee included a doctor, two or three lawyers, the same number of pawnbrokers, a builder, a shoemaker, a secretary of a shoemaker's union, a master cooper, a master tailor who was a former Fenian on the run, a licensed grocer come restaurateur, a cashier, a salesman, a hairdresser, a teacher, a footballer come trainee teacher and a Chartered Accountant come footballer. No wonder there were fall outs but this group of men were to form a powerful, dynamic, enterprising and energetic committee that was to change the face of Scottish football for ever.

THE FIRST MENTION OF CELTIC IN THE PRESS

The *Scottish Umpire* on 29th November 1887 stated;

"We learn that the efforts which have lately been made to organise in Glasgow a first class Catholic football club have been successfully consumated by the formation of the Glasgow Celtic Football and Athletic Club, under influential auspices. They have secured a 6 acre ground in the east which they mean to put into fine order. We wish the Celts all the success".

Brother Walfrid and his organising committee had wasted no time in taking out a five year lease of six acres of land on 12th November 1887, just six days after they met in St Mary's Hall, 67 East Rose Street, Calton to formally constitute the club. We know the exact date of the signing of the lease as it's stated in one newspaper five years later that the expiry was due on Martinmas, the Feast of Saint Martin, which is on the 11th of November. The lease was signed by Joseph Michael Nelis.

The rent was fixed at £50 per annum, which compared well with Queens Park's annual rent for the first Hampden Park at Crosshill in 1882 of £80 per annum for the first two years and £100 per annum for the next three years and also the £60 per annum Rangers paid for their Kinning Park ground for their ten year lease between 1877 and 1887. The Oxford were a team known to have played on the new Celtic Park pitch in the 1870s until they were turfed out in 1881. Who knows, Brother Walfrid, aged 47 at our foundation, may even have watched them play there.

The second mention of Celtic in the press was in the Scottish Athletic Journal on 13th December, 1887;

"There had been some talk recently of starting a "Hibernian" football club in the east end of Glasgow, but now the thing is said to be an accomplished fact.

The ground is said to be near Dalmarnock Road, that Phil Clarke, of the Edinburgh Hibs is to be trainer and groundsman, that a cinder track is to be laid down, a grand stand erected and that the club will be set on foot next season with a team of players made up of the bhoys from the biggest clubs in the city".

This snippet given by a Celtic member to the press is accurate on most points. The ground bounded Dalmarnock Street, not Dalmarnock Road which was further south, there were plans for a cinder track and one grand stand and the club was set to be ready for the start of the season. Phil Clarke may well have been targeted as coach and groundsman as he had been a great servant to Hibs and although his best days were over, his experience would have been vital.

The last sentence is accurate too and again alludes to the make up of the team at our foundation. The team was to be made up of "the bhoys from the biggest clubs", that is the best Irish players available. We would be no different to any other Irish team of that era, in that we would be made up of Irish players, or those of Irish extraction and this was deemed perfectly normal in the press of the day.

In the Scottish Athletic Journal in 1887, there are mentions of Janefield Park, where different east end junior teams played their home matches at. On one occasion the address is given as Janefield Park, Springfield, which may well have been the same ground which was leased as the original Celtic Park.

In this area at the time of our foundation, football as well as other sports, had taken off and the following grounds were all within one mile of Celtic Park;

Dalmarnock Park was home to Eastern FC and before then the Cambridge, which was at the top of Dalmarnock Road near Springfield Road.

Beechwood Park was home to Thistle FC, which was further south east down Dalmarnock Road nearer to Dalmarnock Bridge.

Barrowfield Park was home to Clyde FC, which was south of Bridgeton Cross as far down as the Clydeside.

Glengarry Park was the home to Eastern Rovers and also Gordon Athletics, which was adjacent to and north of Barrowfield Park.

The Sheddens was an area that was home to Parkhead FC, which was on the north side of Shettleston Road at the junction with Westmuir Road.

Queens Recreation Ground was a race course which was on the south side of London Road, between Nuneaton Street and the present Clyde Gateway.

Why did the founders choose an area in Parkhead, to the east of the parishes of St Mary's and Sacred Heart, which were located in Calton and Bridgeton respectively? Albeit the ground would be situated near the parish of St Michael's, then in Salamanca Street, Parkhead, but Brother Walfrid and the founding fathers had less of a connection with that parish. Most of the founding fathers were from the parish of St Mary's and Brother Walfrid had taught at St Mary's and Sacred Heart schools for over 20 years.

One other option could have been Glengarry Park, where Brother Walfrid had arranged matches for the benefit of the Poor Childrens Dinner Tables in 1886 and 87, however Glengarry

Park was adjacent to Barrowfield, the home of Clyde FC and Brother Walfrid would have been well aware of the need to maintain good relations with neighbouring clubs and also the importance of having "our own patch".

Although Glengarry already had its own pitch, so too did the land Brother Walfrid leased. It was small and was bound on three sides, but it fitted our immediate needs, which were very humble according to the fundraising circular, almost certainly in the words of Brother Walfrid, sent in January 1888;

Celtic Football and Athletic Club
Celtic Park, Parkhead
(Corner of Dalmarnock and Janefield Streets)

Patrons

His grace, the Archbishop of Glasgow and the Clergy of St Mary's, Sacred Heart and St Michael's Missions, and the principal of Catholic layman of the East End.

"The above club was formed in November 1887 by a number of the Catholics of the east end of the city"

"The main object is to supply the east end conferences of the St Vincent de Paul Society, with funds for the maintenance of the "Dinner tables" of our needy children in the missions of St Mary's, Sacred Heart and St Michael's. Many cases of sheer poverty are left unaided through lack of means. It is therefore with this principal object that we have set afloat the Celtic and we invite you as one of our ever ready friends to assist in putting our new Park in proper working order for the coming football season.

We have already several of the leading Catholic football players of the west of Scotland on our membership list. They have most thoughtfully offered to assist in the good work.

We are fully aware that the elite of football players belong to this city and suburbs and we know that from there we can select a team which will be able to do credit to the Catholics of the west of Scotland as the Hibernians have been doing in the east. Again there is also the desire to have a large recreation ground where our Catholic young men will be able to enjoy the various sports which will build them up physically and we feel sure we will have many supporters with us in this laudable object.

CATHOLIC AND IRISH

In January 1888, it became clear that our main object was to simply feed the poor children on our doorsteps, in the three parishes in the east end.

The final paragraph reflects an ambition to match the efforts of Hibernian and to become a beacon of pride for the downtrodden Irish in the west, but it then goes back to basics in a simple desire to provide a ground where "our Catholic young men" can enjoy sport.

Forget about the mythical desire to forge links between the Scottish and the Irish, which is often quoted in regard to the club's foundation and the name chosen, There is no evidence of this whatsoever. In The Glory & The Dream by Tom Campbell and Pat Woods, the benchmark for all Celtic books, the claim is described as "fanciful" and the evidence three decades after that book was written backs this up. The current Social Statement reflects more of a need to placate an audience that historically has always been hostile to the club over a century later and in this it succeeds.

Glasgow in 1887 may well have been the place to forge links between the Scots and the Irish, but it certainly wasn't the time. Not just yet.

The fact that we were formed as an Irish Catholic club to raise funds for the Poor Childrens Dinner Tables of the three local Catholic parishes of the east end, by an Irish Marist Brother, who came to Scotland having suffered the ravages of the famine in his native Sligo, is absolutely nothing to be ashamed of and should never be subject to revisionism or rewriting.

In the newspapers of the day, Celtic on numerous occasions are referred to simply as "The Irishmen". Today anyone born in Scotland of Irish parents are referred to as Scottish and are even frowned upon if they assert a fondness for anything Irish. When Celtic were formed, Scottish society labelled anyone born in Scotland of Irish lineage as Irish, similar to America today where labels such as Irish, Italian or Hispanic are given to family descendants who came to America over a century ago.

Significantly there are no examples of any social integration policies or attempts made by the founding fathers to bring the Scottish and Irish together. The Celtic Committee clearly knew the benefits of keeping friends in the highest places in the media, and no doubt sufficient column inches would have been available to them for this gallant story. There are none.

It was simply never on the agenda, it's never mentioned in the press, in the minutes of any Annual General Meetings and it does not manifest itself at our foundation and early years in any way. In summary, it didn't happen.

THE NAME

The name Celtic is often said to have been an attempt to reflect both a Scottish and Irish identity, but again there are no quotes available to back this up. If there was such a grandiose plan in place there would be numerous examples. Again, there are none.

With no direct quotes available, the myth is impossible to prove so you have to take yourself back to the time and the place. As the founders of the club sat round the table in St Mary's Hall after mid-day mass on November 6th 1887, they were Catholic to a man, either born in Ireland or more predominantly, in Scotland of Irish extraction. The men who played for the club for the first two years were also Catholic to a man, either born in Ireland, or in Scotland of Irish extraction. Crucially this was the plan from the beginning, it didn't happen by accident and this is why, in your author's opinion, we were named Celtic.

The original pronunciation of the name was "Keltic," however this did not sit well with the Glasgow vernacular and the easier option with the softer sound of Celtic was taken up from the start.

The story goes that Brother Walfrid chose the name Celtic, but others preferred Glasgow Hibernian. The founders had a very good relationship with John McFadden, the Secretary of Edinburgh Hibernian, who was known to be very accommodating in assisting other Hibernian teams to be formed in Scotland. Numerous Hibernian clubs had sprouted up all over Scotland and Celtic would just be another, but this is the crucial point; Brother Walfrid didn't want a tribute act. He wanted the real thing.

The parish of St Mary's also had a football team and their name was Glasgow Hibernian. In the Scottish Athletic Journal on the 17th May 1887, an account is given of the Glasgow Harp versus Coatbridge Harp match on Glengarry Park. The Coatbridge team were running late, so with a crowd already gathered, Glasgow Hibernian, the team from the parish of St Mary's agreed to step in at the last minute and play an hour long match against Glasgow Harp. In the event the Harp won 5-1 and they then played the match with Coatbridge Harp when they arrived and also won that game, by 3 goals to 2.

It was therefore natural for the St Mary's contingent to favour this name, Glasgow Hibernian, at our founding.

Interestingly, at the time of our birth there was already a junior team called Celtic, who played in Possilpark in the north of the city and there was also another Glasgow Hibernian, a junior club who were formed in October 1884 and who played at Overnewton Park, near Partick, in the west of the city. Ironically Glasgow Hibernian would be local rivals to St Peter's, from the parish of the same name in Partick and we know from the Scottish Athletic Journal on the 4th March, 1885 that Partick Celtic played Glasgow Hibernian and beat them by three goals.

The parish football team originally went under the name Partick Celtic, then they amalgamated with Partick Hibs to become St Peter's, before oddly relocating from their home ground at Eastvale Park, Kelvin Haugh across the river to Copland Park, Govan in 1887.

Research has found the names of the committee and the club captain of Celtic, (sometimes referred to as Possil Celtic) and there is a surprise. At their AGM in July 1887, when electing their office bearers, none other than John McFadden of Edinburgh Hibernian is named as Honorary President. Club captain is named as J Graham and sub captain is J McGuire, Thomas Kelly is Treasurer, J O'Brien is Secretary and Hugh McCall of 20 Northburn Street is Match Secretary.

William McCorrikan of 219 Possil Road, Glasgow is named at a later date as Match Secretary.

John McFadden's role at the Celtic club from Possil would have been no more than honorary, but its interesting that he would have an influence over a juvenile team named Celtic in Glasgow and not named after Hibernian.

This shows that the name Celtic was increasing in popularity amongst Irish clubs in Glasgow in the years building up to our foundation. There was even a club named Celtic playing against Eastern as early as 1873 on Glasgow Green at Flesher's Haugh where many juvenile clubs without their own pitch played.

The juvenile game in Glasgow mushroomed in the 1880s with Associations springing up in the city to provide an organisational backbone to the game. By 1886 there was the Glasgow Junior Association, the Glasgow North East Junior Association and the Glasgow Catholic Association. The Glasgow Catholic Association even founded a cup competition at the start of 1886 with most matches played at Glengarry Park.

What is beyond doubt is that all the symbolisms of Celtic Football Club, including the club colours of green and white, the badges of the Celtic Cross, the harp, the three leafed shamrock, which was the official club badge until 1931, and the four leafed clover which has been used since, are all reflections of our Irish identity.

The headline in the newspaper describing the replayed Scottish Cup tie in 1889 between Queens Park, (who were then the Establishment team), and Celtic was "Scot v Celt" and almost took on the significance of an international match as opposed to a club match, with Celtic certainly not seen as a Scottish team, and were in fact described as Irish throughout the match report.

What is perfectly clear is that Celtic Football Club is a vehicle for good, a club born from charity, with charity remaining an integral part of the DNA of the club. Although social integration, or the conditions which would even allow it to thrive for Irish Catholics in the East End of Glasgow did not exist in the 1880s, Celtic Football Club HAS grown to become an institution that forges a positive link between Scotland and Ireland and enjoys an identity today that recognises BOTH our Scottish and Irish DNA.

1887 OR 1888?

Although 6th November 1887 is the date we were formally constituted, the official Celtic Handbooks gave the date of foundation as September 1887, right up until the 1925/26 "Wee Green Book". Why the date is given as September and not November 1887 as the recognised foundation has always been a mystery, as was the reason to change it almost fifty years later, with our jubilee upcoming.

These questions can now be answered.

It's widely recognised that 12th February 1887 when Hibs won the Scottish Cup and significantly were feted at the after match celebration at St Mary's Hall, Glasgow before they even thought of returning to Edinburgh, was the catalyst for the birth of Celtic. Brother Walfrid, Doctor

Conway and John Glass were amongst the founding fathers present that day, indeed Doctor Conway read the toast to the successful Hibernian team including the following;

"He strongly urged the necessity of emulating their example, not only in social but in political matters as well, so that the goal of every Irishman's ambition - the legislative independence of his country - would soon be attained."

Those within earshot listened intently to the answer given in private by the Hibs Secretary John McFadden that the Catholics of the west should "Go and do the same".

Indeed the trio of Brother Walfrid, John Glass and Doctor John Conway had met regularly to discuss initiatives to raise funds for the Poor Childrens Dinner Tables founded at St Mary's and Sacred Heart. There is no doubt that they would have rose to this challenge with a verve and a determination that manifested itself clearly in everything the new club did. Therefore there is no shadow of doubt that the work required to found Celtic Football Club, began possibly as early as March 1887 and certainly no later than the summer months. It has been suggested that the date of September 1887 signified the month when agreement was reached in the discussions between the parishes to finally commit to the plan and take up the challenge. However, it has never been recorded as such and therefore never proven.

It's clear then why there will always be the debate about what date should be recognised as the year Celtic were founded, 1887 when we were formally constituted, or 1888 when we played our first match. Indeed it was in 1908 that Celtic celebrated our 21st "birthday" not 1909, again signifying that 1887 was the date the founding fathers considered as our foundation.

Willie Maley finally clears up the mystery in the 1935/36 Celtic Handbook when he wrote;

"At the Annual General Meeting of the Company held on 23rd June, 1936, the Chairman announced that the Board had decided to celebrate the Club's Jubilee in January 1938. Although the Club was actually formed in September 1887, it did not really function until January 1888".

And so the mystery is over. The Board decided in 1936 that they should celebrate our half centenary in 1938 rather than 1937, citing the reason that although the Club was officially recognised as being formed in September 1887;

"It did not actually function until January 1888".

By functioning, Maley is referring to the first General Meeting of the club which took place on 19th January, 1888, however he doesn't mention the date of November 6th 1887 when the Club was formally constituted. Surely that is the first function of an elected Committee? Surely too, signing the five year lease on the ground on 12th November, 1887 is another function of the Committee as well as deciding on who should build it? Yet again when Brother Walfrid, John Glass and Pat Welsh travelled to Tom Maley's house in September 1887 in an effort to sign him?

The list of functions required by the new committee were long as well as the time spent in debating priorities and working to a plan and a budget. Yes, the first General Meeting was a sign of a functioning committee in January 1888, but the reports it gave were based on the progress made since the real date for the club's official formation, November 6th 1887 in St Mary's Hall.

If Chairman Tom White and his Board members Thomas Colgan, John Shaughnessy, John McKillop and Robert Kelly had deemed that the club's anniversary should be celebrated on 8th May, when Celtic Park was opened, or on 28th May, when we played our first match, both in 1888, then that would have been their prerogative but to quote January 1888, because it reflected when the committee started to function is historically inaccurate. The committee clearly functioned well before then.

There can be no complaint, however, about the credentials of the Celtic Board in 1936 to make such a decision;

Tom White joined the Board in 1906 when he was left the shares of one of the most hard working founding fathers John Glass on his death and he was to serve on the Celtic Board until his death on 4th March, 1947.

Thomas Colgan from Belfast also joined the Board in 1906 but had been involved with the club right from the very start. He was to serve on the Celtic Board until 1939 when he retired and went back to Ireland where he served on the Board of Belfast Celtic.

John Shaughnessy was the son of founding father and lawyer, Joseph Shaughnessy, whose skills helped the club out of many a murky water in the early days. He joined the Celtic Board in 1911 and was to serve on the Board until his death on 1952 and is to this day the longest serving Board member by a few months over Tom White.

John McKillop was the nephew of founding father William McKillop and joined the Celtic Board in 1921 after the death of Michael Dunbar. He was to serve on the Celtic Board until 1941 when he retired.

Robert Kelly was the son of James Kelly, Celtic's first captain, and he replaced his father on the Celtic Board on his death in 1932. He was to serve on the Celtic Board until his death in April 1971.

Including Willie Maley, who was Secretary and Manager, these men served Celtic in an official capacity for an incredible 41 years, 33 years, 41 years, 20 years, 39 years and 52 years respectively.

This didn't help them get the date correct on our foundation but it's too late to change things now. I prefer to recognise both dates of our foundation because 1888 was when we played our first match, but we were conceived almost 9 months earlier in 1887. So this clears up the mystery of when we were formed and why the date was changed as the Board prepared for the 50th year anniversary, but it doesn't explain why the original date is given as September and not November 6th when the club was formally constituted.

Until now

Sometimes we can over analyse things and look too deep for an answer when it's a lot simpler and has been staring us in the face. Again it is found in an early Celtic Handbook, for season 1937/38.

Willie Maley wrote;

"When I "took the shilling" for Celtic in September, 1887, I was 19 and a half years old and I played for them at the age of 20, and in the fifty years that have passed since, I have spent my life literally for the Club, which has now grown so dear to me."

Willie Maley was born on 28th April 1868, so in September 1887, Maley was correct in saying he was exactly 19 and a half. Although December 1887 is recorded as the date the Maley household were visited by Brother Walfrid, John Glass and Pat Welsh, Maley instead claims he "took the shilling" in September 1887. As Secretary, as well as Manager, it was Willie Maley's responsibility to write the annual Celtic Handbooks so naturally he would put September 1887, the month he joined Celtic as the date of our foundation because he couldn't join a club that didn't exist.

But finally, more significance to the month of September in our founding comes from the then Celtic Vice President, James Quillan in his letter to the Glasgow Evening News on 28th May 1889, when in protest at an increase in entry fees for the coming season he stated;

"I protested - and my protest was duly noted - against members who had joined the club previous to 1st September, 1888 being excluded from the meeting in direct violation of Rules 10 and 24".

The general meeting referred to was on the 2nd May 1889 to appoint auditors and adopt rules with the upcoming first ever Celtic Annual General Meeting set for June 18th 1889. By mentioning the date 1st September he implies that membership of the club was issued and expired on that date annually at our inception.

THE FIRST SUBSCRIPTION LIST

The subscription list sent in January 1888 resulted in the following list of subscribers who, along with the committee, were the first members of the club;

20s; His Grace the Archbishop, Very Reverend Canon Carmichael, Reverend Francis Joseph Hughes, Reverend Arthur Beyaert, Reverend Adrian Van Der Hyde, Doctor John Conway, John Higney, James Doyle, Arthur McHugh, Thomas McCormick, Henry Aylmer, Michael Aylmer, George Hughes, Daniel Hughes, James Quillan, James McQuillan, James McConnell, John McGallagley, John Clancey, Francis Henry, John Conway, James Conway, E. Williamson, Andrew Bryan, Joseph A. Foy, Mrs Flynn.

10s, 6d; The Granite House, John Brown, John Brien, Hugh Darroch, P. Donegan, Hugh Swan, Patrick Gaffney, James Hughes, James McCann, P. McCulloch, Owen Aylmer, Louis Mackenzie.

10s; John Blair, Edward Mooney, Charles Stewart, William Stewart, A Friend, A Friend, Mr Young.

There were numerous smaller donations sent to fund the club's launch but one look at the list of subscribers gives a good insight into our make up at the beginning, with Brother

Walfrid's influence on the clergy obvious. Once he had won over His Grace, Archbishop Charles Eyre and received his backing, other clergy in the area, who Brother Walfrid would have worked relentlessly with, quickly followed.

Dr John Conway, James Quillan and Hugh Darroch had been elected as prominent office bearers of the club at the original meeting to constitute the club on November 1887 in St Mary's Hall. The word "elected" gives a clue to the number of local prominent parishioners who were present and indeed vying for a place on the original committee for an election to have been necessary. Honorary positions were also offered to those who gave generously to the first circular.

Right from our very first meeting we were well organised with no shortage of volunteers willing to get the new club off the ground. This wasn't a meeting in St Mary's Hall attended by half a dozen people, more likely there were dozens there packed into the "mean little hall," ironically on "67" East Rose Street, with access to it gained from "Irish Wynd," off East Rose Street, now Forbes Street.

The exact location of St Mary's Hall today is within the grounds of Crownpoint Sports Complex, immediately to the left and behind the southern goal posts, directly in line with the second St Mary's Hall, which was built in 1892, a building which is still standing, on the other side of Henrietta Street, now Orr Street.

The coincidence that a football pitch now stands on the ground where Celtic were formally constituted, that the address of the original St Mary's Hall was number 67, our most successful year and the access lane from East Rose Street was called Irish Wynd are not lost on anyone.

Although we had the finest minds of the mother parish of St Mary's in attendance, along with other parishes, none of the original committee had any experience or involvement with football clubs and so to avoid Celtic becoming another one on the list of failed Irish clubs, a detailed plan would have to be devised to get the club up and running.

1. Elect a committee and sub committees to report back.
2. Lease a ground.
3. Organise a fundraising circular.
4. Attract new players to the club.
5. Liaise with other clubs to set up the opening of the ground and opposition.
6. Compile a fixture list for the 1888/89 season.

Brother Walfrid's hand would have been to the fore in much of the above, using his local contacts, and the tremendous respect he had in the east end to his great advantage. There would have to be a time scale for every stage of the plan to happen. The leasing and building of a basic ground would not be cheap and this could only partly be covered by the subscription circular in January 1888. Loans were taken from beneficiaries who would be paid back from the takings from the first games, hopefully.

Already in the month of November, the target for the opening of Celtic Park would have been no later than the following May, but ideally before that to build up a head of steam before the summer shut down in June and July. All that was required was a ground, financial backing, a support, some players, opposition to take us on and only six months to do it all in.

No pressure then.

19th JANUARY 1888 - THE FIRST MONTHLY GENERAL MEETING

The following from the Scottish Umpire on Tuesday, 24th January 1888 gives a great insight into how well organised the club were from our inception and how fast the committee were getting things in place;

"On Thursday last, the first general monthly meeting of the Celtic Football & Athletic club was held in the Hall, East Rose Street, Calton. There was a large turnout of members and patrons. The various committees submitted their reports, which were considered extremely satisfactory.

The Convenor of the Park Committee, Mr Bryan, said that if all went well, the ground would be ready for play in a few weeks. The pitch is finished, the paling well nigh up and the grandstand - capable of accommodating from 800 to 1000 - would be begun in the course of the ensuing week.

A good few members were enrolled; and several gentlemen, who were much interested in the welfare of the Celts, handed in their donations. The Committee meet every Thursday evening in the Hall, East Rose Street. Altogether, the Celtic bids fair to be a great success. It is expected that the Committee will put a first class team on the field for the coming season. The Secretary is Mr John O'Hara, 77 East Rose Street, Calton".

Since the initial meeting on November 6th 1887, when the first committee was elected and sub committees appointed, tremendous progress had been made in only two months for the committee to feel confident enough to call the first monthly General Meeting on Thursday, 19th January 1888. With the committee having met weekly on a Thursday evening in St Mary's Hall since 6th November it meant that the level of intensity for continued progress remained high and we had the ability at grass roots level to iron out problems immediately as soon as they arose.

In the same way the sub committees had to report to the full membership every month from January and this would keep them on their toes with everyone totally focussed on the task in hand. Similarly too with such frequent general meetings, the committee were keeping in touch with the man in the street who would go home from each meeting enthused and as word spread of the work being done by the parishioners of the east end, so membership would grow and donations increase.

Unfortunately, we are not graced with the minutes of the first general meetings but it is certain that a Finance sub committee led by the Treasurer would have been appointed as well as the Park sub committee as these were the two main tasks in hand, with one dependant on the other. The Secretary, John O'Hara, who would list all members' details, would also give his report at monthly meetings which would be chaired by the President, John Glass.

The first task of the Park sub committee, convened by Andrew Bryan, was to appoint a contractor to build Celtic Park, and local joiner Pat Gaffney, who would have been present at the original meeting, was given the task of building the original ground. Both men were subscribers to the original fundraising circular in January 1888.

In reality there was no decision to be made. Rangers, for example had just completed their new ground at Ibrox, adjacent to the current Ibrox Park in August 1887. They had the luxury of giving the contract to the well known construction company of Frederick Braby & Co Ltd. The difference was that Rangers had been in operation for fifteen years and although they had only won one trophy, without ever getting round to signing a Roman Catholic, they had built up a sizeable support in various parts of Glasgow where they had played.

Building a new ground in November 1887 with a very limited budget meant giving the job to one of our own men, Pat Gaffney, who owned a well established and successful local joiner's business based in Abercromby Street, yards from St Mary's chapel, where he was a parishioner. Pat, as a subscriber to the original circular in January, 1888, was a backer of the club from our formation. Although he owned a small company which advertised in the Glasgow Observer, this was his biggest job to date, thankfully this was a task like no other and there was no shortage of volunteers amongst the Irish community with experience in the building trade to lend a helping hand.

Not only did this good fortune save expenditure from the limited subscription funds available, it gave the Irish another reason to back the club, for Celtic played on a ground which they built, before a ball had been kicked.

The fact that the pitch was ready just two months after the lease was agreed during the height of the winter, points to the fact that a grass pitch was already there, and that remedial work only would have been required to roll the ground to ensure an even surface and most definitely drainage. A grass pitch could not have been grown in two months in the winter, and laying fresh turf was an expense we didn't need. What would have been required was the re positioning of the pitch already there to give enough space around the pitch for a stand potentially on both sides and terracing behind both goals.

From "Old International" in *25 Years Football* printed in 1896 and originally paraphrased in *The Glory and the Dream* by Tom Campbell and Pat Woods;

"It was only natural that, in choosing the district where the club should "pitch their tent," the East End of the city should most strongly commend itself to the promoters, and as the ground which they at first secured had, long anterior to their existence, served as a playing pitch for, i think, the Oxford - away back in the 70s - this fact also served as an inducement to open proceedings at Parkhead; and although the ground was a long way behind several of our model enclosures, so far as accommodation was concerned, yet this circumstance did not perceptibly militate against the growth of the club, but served rather to make the managers press on and seek all the more hastily for pastures new, wherein their huge following could be made comfortable while attending to cheer on their favourites".

The paling referred to was the perimeter wooden fence that surrounded the boundary, although this wouldn't have been required on the west boundary as the wall, marking the eastern boundary of Janefield Cemetery sufficed. Indeed it wasn't too long before the boundary wall was two deep with those without the 6d entrance money who were more than happy to take advantage of the excellent view of the pitch from the graveyard wall!

The grand stand, otherwise known as the Pavillion, was the open air stand built on the east side of the pitch, which ran north to south as opposed to east to west and this is confirmed in an answer to a question posed in the Scottish Referee newspaper on the 2nd May 1892.

From Andrew Bryan's Park sub committee report we learn that the pitch was ready in mid January, the boundary fence was almost complete and work would begin on constructing the grand stand in the following week, (late January). His assertion that all going well, the ground would be ready for play in a few weeks was optimistic, as can often be expected from sub committee reports.

Once the boundary fence was in place, the pitch level and the wooden grand stand constructed, work would have carried on moulding the basic terracing formed out of mounds of earth on the other three sides of the ground and covering them with cinder to avoid slippage. The primitive terracing was separated from the pitch by a basic running track which was only 6 foot wide but enabled the club to attract much needed finance at the Celtic Sports, which took place at the original Celtic Park in 1890 and 91.

Indeed the very name, Celtic Football & Athletic Club at our inception was a recognition that having the ability to attract hugely popular athletic meetings at the ground was financially rewarding and this is borne out by the fact that the Celtic Sports continued right up until the 1930s.

A total of seven entrance gates initially were built at the Dalmarnock Street, (now Springfield Road), side of the ground and with turnstiles not yet in place, the system employed required gatemen equipped with rolls of tickets which ensured the process of calculating crowd figures was a few years away from becoming an exact science. Indeed in the early days, gate receipts were announced rather than attendance figures and an estimate for the latter was gauged from the former.

Celtic Park was taking shape and although we didn't have the renowned engineering company of Fred Braby and Co building the ground, complete with the modern corrugated iron fencing around the boundary which they were building at Ibrox Park, and which was claimed at the time to be "unclimbable," it didn't specify whether its purpose was to stop supporters from climbing in or trying to climb out.

Being an Irish club in Glasgow, trouble was never far away from our door and the landlord, (and Chairman of Janefield cemetery), Andrew Waddell, originally from Upper Belvidere in Parkhead, but now living in Jedburgh, soon came knocking in the early stages of the build. His concern was that he had leased us a plain seven acres of grass land from 62 to 82 Dalmarnock Street, which we were now transforming into a football ground, complete with pavillion, paling, basic terracing and entrances. He wanted us out before we had kicked our first ball, but he had failed to take cognisance of who he was dealing with.

The 5 year contract signed on 12th November 1887 was a very simple one with few clauses inserted by the factor, Peter Young & Sons, therefore not only did the Celtic Committee refuse to budge on the issue, we refused any attempts at mediation by agreeing to return the land at the end of the lease in the state it was in when we signed it. Indeed we went a step further and turned the whole issue on its head by warning the landlord that any more interference would result in the club taking the fight to the highest court in the land.

This was the first sign of the confidence and the sheer determination of the Celtic Committee to let no man get in the way of our ambitions. We stuck to the letter of the contract which did not stipulate any restrictions on what we could build or could not build on the land or in what state it would be returned. If it did, we didn't have a leg to stand on. With his gas at a peep, the landlord was forced to withdraw his demands. The first victory, off the pitch, was ours and the word went out that we were not to be messed with.

We are here and we are here to stay.

As Walter Arnott, the then Queens Park captain stated over 25 years later, in an article on 7th March 1914 in the Evening Times;

"The institution of that club was only welcomed in the west of Scotland by those who had most to do with its formation. But, if ever a club confounded its enemies, surely that club is Celtic".

The Celtic Committee had a job to do and we could afford to let no man stand in our way, such was their focus. The Scottish Athletic Journal described this progress on 14th February 1888;

"A club composed exclusively of Irishmen and Scotchmen of Irish parentage has been started in the east end, somewhat similar to the Hibernians in Edinburgh. The name of the new club is to be "The Glasgow Celtic Athletics". A ground has already been secured in Dalmarnock Road, and it is to be called Dalmarnock Park. They have taken it on lease for five years at a rent of £30 a year.

It is a splendid field, with plenty of scope and includes a couple of pitches, one being for practices. There are to be two stands - now in course of erection. The club intend to draft the best players from the surrounding clubs. Of course the players must be Irish or of Irish extraction. They mean to have an eleven second to none. An effort will be made to open the ground at the end of the present month and if a fixture can possibly be arranged, between a Glasgow club and the Hibernians, these clubs will be the first to compete on the ground.

As the club has influential supporters and no lack of means, the necessary guarantee will be forthcoming. Failing a fixture with either of the above clubs, some other notable teams will be invited for the preliminary match. A cinder track, 12 feet broad, runs round the field. The Committee have held several meetings to discuss affairs in a hall on East Nile Street".

Although some of the facts stated turned out not to be the case, this is another valuable insight into the building of Celtic Park, slap bang in the middle of the process which started in November 1887 and ended in May 1888.

"A club composed exclusively of Irishmen and Scotchmen of Irish parentage has been started in the east end, somewhat similar to the Hibernians in Edinburgh".

The first sentence again nails the reason why the club was called Celtic. The first committee were made up of Irishmen or Scots of Irish extraction and so too were the players for the first two seasons. The fact the Journal knows this in the February of 1888 was because it would have been spelled out to them by a contact at Celtic, it wasn't a wild guess.

The article states that the original ground was to be named Dalmarnock Park and that the rent was £30 per annum but we know that the ground was named Celtic Park and the rent was £50 per annum. Was the article wrong or was this the case in February 1888? Had the Committee negotiated a lease of £30 and not the reported £50 or indeed had it risen? Was the original intention to name the ground Dalmarnock Park rather than Celtic Park or was this a sop to the landlord and a piece of misinformation thrown to the Journal so as not to arouse suspicion? I suspect the latter.

The rest of the article is fascinating. It states that there were to be two stands, now in the course of erection, but we know that there was only one stand built, the Pavillion on the eastern side of the pitch and that the second stand was built opposite in 1890. Again was the article wrong or was it the intention to build two stands in time for the opening of the ground? Was a lack of finances or time a factor in only one stand being built? Probably both.

Surprisingly it states that an effort will be made to open the ground by the end of that month, February, if a fixture could be arranged, which appears overly ambitious to say the least, but again it gives an indication of the speed in which progress was being made. Again, the article gives an exclusive, with the first details on the cinder track surrounding the pitch, which would allow the Celtic Sports to make their debut in 1890. All in the article is invaluable and paints a picture of a Celtic Committee man, or even Brother Walfrid himself, feeding snippets to the media to ensure a thoroughly positive Celtic story which would whet the appetite of our growing support, before a ball had even been kicked.

THE SEARCH FOR PLAYERS

Behind the scenes the founding fathers worked tirelessly to attract players to the club, and in this regard, Celtic were unique in world football. First we had a cause, then a committee, then a ground and a support before we had a single player or even a ball!

Tom and Willie Maley were amongst the first who agreed to come along and although they both had experience playing for Third Lanark, they were better known for their athletic prowess. The brothers were attracted to the venture by the persuasive tongues of Brother Walfrid, John Glass and Pat Welsh who would have sold them the charitable aims of the club as early as September 1887, when they travelled to Cathcart to meet Tom Maley only for his brother Willie to inform them that Tom was out courting his future wife. As the famous story goes, Brother Walfrid turned to Willie Maley on their way out and on confirming an invite for word to be passed to his brother Tom to get back to them, asked Willie to come along too, almost an afterthought that was to have a massive impact on the future of the club.

The date of September 1887, is important as it is cited by no less than Willie Maley himself in the 1937/38 Celtic Handbook and so a relationship between man and club that was to last until

January 1940 had begun, a relationship that was to become one of the most important decisions made by the founding fathers and one that was to mould the history of the club through not just our formative years, but throughout the whole of our first half century. Willie Maley was one of the first to commit to the club and the first stepping stone to success was in place.

Before a ball was kicked however, the charitable aims of the club had to be backed up with a business plan to make it succeed and the business types on the committee knew that the cause of charity would only keep the new club afloat if the club were successful on the pitch. For that to happen, big names had to be attracted to the cause.

And so the committee started at the top and worked their way down. The greatest player in the country at the time was James Kelly, from the great Renton team who self styled themselves "The Greatest Team in the World", after winning the Scottish Cup then going on to beat the English FA Cup winners, West Bromwich Albion at the second Hampden at Cathkin on 19th May 1888 by 4 goals to 1. Neil McCallum played for Renton in the same match and had to walk home to Renton in the heavy rain after missing his last train home. How football has changed.

Kelly was a local lad and played for Renton from 1881, but after a number of attempts to lure him to commit to Celtic, by John O'Hara and John MacDonald, it was the silver tongue of John Glass who finally persuaded Kelly to play in the first game, against Rangers on 28th May, with Hibernian also eager to lure him to Easter Road. In those days, players were signed on an annual basis for the one season and as the Scottish League had not yet been formed, a player only became the property of a club when he was registered to represent them in the Scottish Cup.

From the History of Celtic series in the *Evening Times* in 1931;

"Celts and Hibs took a hand. Both sat on Kelly's doorstep, but for a long time it was a cold seat. M'Callum, a light-hearted chap, was willing to play anywhere, but Kelly's heart was with Renton only, and he was determined to play for no other club. However, offers were being made by English clubs to Vale, Dumbarton and Renton players, so sensing the subsequent trek across the Border, Kelly resolved to preserve his amateur status, and making football a side-line, get into business in either Glasgow or Edinburgh.

Then followed a tug of war between east and west. West won; Kelly became a Celt for good, and the rest was easy for Parkhead. Once it was known that the famous centre half-back of the world-renowned Renton team had thrown in his lot with the new Glasgow club, other almost equally well-known players made haste to follow suit. What was good enough for Jimmy Kelly was good enough for them.

Down went another Celtic deputation to Renton, and the situation was fully explained to Kelly. If he would just play in the opening match against Rangers his name would help the game and his play would have a great deal to do with the result. Like the good sport he was, and is to this day, the Rentonian said he would be a Celt for the day. Further he would not promise. The great day came, and Kelly with it; by five goals to three Celts defeated Rangers".

With Kelly giving his word to turn out in the first match, although he wasn't committed beyond that, this made the committee's task easier to attract other top players. In fact, the fledgling

Celtic Committee were not short of offers from players who wanted to play for the new club, once James Kelly had shown an interest.

Indeed the phrase "No Kelly, no Keltic" was soon born, a phrase which underlined the importance to the new club of attracting the best player in the country.

An article in the Scottish Catholic Herald decades later gives an intriguing insight into James Kelly's signing by a man who claims to have been there and was his best friend. Bonhill man, William Doyle played for local side Vale of Leven Hibernian at the same time as James Kelly played for Renton and the story goes thus;

"Jimmy wouldn't make a move unless William approved and so it came about that he was asked to weigh up the pros and cons of an offer made to his chum.

Willie, Jimmy and two top-hatted figures sat around a table and one of the latter produced a document, at the top of which were the words Celtic Football & Athletic Club. Below that was the name of the first signing - Willie Maley. William nodded gleefully and down went the name of James Kelly".

William Doyle, then a riveter, as well as turning out for Vale of Leven Hibs remained friendly with the Kelly family and he actually became one of Celtic's first talent scouts. In a very interesting life, he then turned professional as a tenor singer working with Harry Lauder, before touring under the name WD Walker".

CELTIC PARK RAPIDLY APPROACHES COMPLETION

From the *Scottish Athletic Journal* on 27th March 1888;

"The grand stand in the new Celtic club's ground is about finished. The club house will be well fitted up. It is not definitely fixed re the opening match, but as the ground is ready, it may not be long".

From the *Scottish Umpire* on the same day;

"Our readers, especially those from the east end, will be pleased to hear that the Celtic FC's ground is rapidly approaching completion. We understand the Committee expect to have it ready in a few weeks.

The grand stand is almost complete, and will be a handsome one, capable of accommodating 1200 persons. The pavillion seems to be a bright idea, and fully realises the expectations of the Committee; it is large and commodious, 50ft by 14ft, and will be divided into three apartments. The necessary baths, lavatories, etc will complete it.

The park lies east of Janefield Cemetery, in Dalmarnock Street, within a few minutes walk of the Parkhead tramcar terminus. The London Road terminus is likewise convenient. The Committee will be glad to see visitors; the field is open daily until about 6pm. We wish the enterprising Celts every success and, no doubt, the Glasgow clubs will willingly insert their names in their fixture card for the forthcoming season".

This information would have come to the newspaper from Celtic's monthly General Meeting in March and gives another insight into the reason for the choice of the Parkhead area to host the new ground, with its close proximity to the tramcar termini at Parkhead Cross, and the railway station on London Road. It was also slap bang in between London

Road and the Gallowgate, (named Great Eastern Road back in the day), the two main thoroughfares from the city centre to the east of the city.

The grand stand, which the Park sub committee convenor Andrew Bryan stated would be started in the course of the ensuing week, (late January), was now being reported to be almost complete two months later. It was bigger than first envisaged too, with a capacity of 1200, compared to the original report of 800 to 1000. We are even given the size of the pavillion which was built under the grand stand and measured 50ft by 14ft. The three apartments housed the home and away teams either side of a reception/main meeting area and contained the mod cons of the day, including baths and toilets. There was also a referee's room, a trainer's room and an office for the committee to meet.

With the committee expecting the ground to be ready in a few weeks it meant it would be mid April before the opening match could be played but this date clashed with the start of the Charity Cup on the 14th April and therein lay a problem.

On April 10th, the *Scottish Umpire* reported;

"The Celtic Park is being pushed on very rapidly. It is expected to be ready early this week. We understand the date of opening will be fixed in a few days. In our next issue we hope to give our readers full particulars".

Again this information would have came from our April monthly General Meeting and the completion date remained true to the previous target, mid April. The aspiration to fix the date of the opening game in a few days was ambitious and was due to the start of the Charity Cup as previously stated and the uncertainties involved in which teams would make progress and who would be free to commit to opening Celtic Park. The full particulars of the opener would have to wait a few weeks until the results of the opening ties of the Charity Cup were known.

The building of the pavillion, complete with the facilities for the players underneath the stand was a departure from the traditional building of a separate "club house," as Rangers and Third Lanark had recently done. For a club with charitable aims, however, we had no need for airs and graces and no budget for the fancier trappings that some other grounds favoured.

THE OPENING OF THE GROUND - WHICH TEAMS WILL PLAY?

With the original ground taking final shape in mid April, the committee's next task was to ensure two top clubs would commit to provide a major attraction.

But who would those two clubs be?

The final of the Glasgow Cup was played in January and the Scottish Cup in February but the other main competition, the Charity Cup, was set to start on April 14th and finish with the final on May 12th. Just to complicate matters, eight teams were invited, instead of the usual four. The first round matches were to be played between April 14th and 26th, with the dates for the semi final on 4th and 8th May and the final on the 12th May. The 8 clubs competing were Queens Park, Hibs, Rangers, Dumbarton, Renton, Vale of Leven, Third Lanark and Cambuslang.

Dates had to be left open for replays and this happened on two occasions when Rangers and Vale of Leven replayed their 1st round match and Cambuslang and Dumbarton replayed their semi final after the tie was stopped short to allow Dumbarton to catch their last train home! Clubs filled the rest of the fixture list with friendlies before the formation of the League in 1890 but some of those friendlies could be lucrative, especially on Bank Holidays against the best English teams of the day.

This gave the committee a problem, because if we couldn't get the date set for May, we were into the close season and it would be August before the ground could be opened. A significant amount of money had been paid out in the building of the ground and the committee simply could not afford to have a heavy debt on their shoulders during the summer months awaiting the first ball to be kicked.

Hibernian were the obvious choice to open the ground and it was probably felt best not to put out an inexperienced Celtic team against them and risk a heavy defeat. Of course if we faced Hibs, it would have meant we couldn't have fielded half of their players, but more of that later. On the other hand it was a very wise move to get support along to the ground twice in the first few weeks, firstly to see the ground open, then to whet the appetite for supporters to return to see their new team, the Celtic play.

Immediately there was a complication in attracting the opposition to Hibs and it was a problem that was out of our hands. The Charity Cup semi finals were still to be played and on the date chosen for our opener, May 8th 1888, Rangers were playing Renton, who were the current Scottish Cup holders and therefore the top attraction, whilst Dumbarton were playing Cambuslang in a replay, just a day later. To further complicate matters Hibernian had been invited to play in the Charity Cup that season but to Celtic's huge relief, they were beaten in the first round by Cambuslang. If Hibernian had won that match they may well have been forced to pull out of the opening of Celtic Park, forcing the match to be put back, probably until after the date of the final on Saturday 12th May.

From the *Scottish Umpire* on the 17th April 1888;

"The Celtic club which has been formed in the east end of Glasgow had hoped to bring off their ceremony on the afternoon of Exhibition-day, May 8, but the arrangements have fallen through. It was expected that Renton and Hibs, would play the opening match, but evidently the date won't suit Renton. The management will require to requisition some other foemen worthy the Hibernians' steel. The Celts new field, pavilion, and stand are nearing completion, and the public will be surprised at the extent of the undertaking and the thoroughness with which it has been carried out".

It was a huge blow that Renton had to pull out of the opening of Celtic Park as a match between the Scottish Cup holders and Hibernian, the largest Irish team in the country would have brought a huge crowd, possibly around 10,000. Far from putting the date back, which would have guaranteed nothing, the Celtic Committee stuck to their task of delivering the opening of the ground on 8th May with another opponent sought to play Hibernian.

From the *Scottish Umpire* on 8th May 1888;

"The Rangers were asked to open the Celtic's new grounds at Parkhead tonight, but refused".

Willie Maley reminisced about this in the 1926/27 Celtic Handbook;

"Over the long years which have passed since the inception of the club, which took place in 1887, against the very stern opposition of the big clubs of that day, our lot has been, in the main, one of success and achievement. It is amusing to look back on our early days and think that at the beginning of the club the Rangers were asked to open the new Celtic Park, but refused to do so!

Time has taken ample revenge for that foolish act, but to their credit be it said that very soon after that action the Rangers, (always our good friends though sternest of foes), redeemed their blunder by playing at the new Celtic Park the first match played there by the now well organised Celtic Football Club, when the Celts won their first victory over their great rivals to be".

Queens Park would have been the obvious choice to oppose Hibs and they too were beaten in the first round of the Charity Cup but it was Cowlairs, from Springburn in the north of the city, not a big attraction and certainly not amongst our first choices but a club with no commitments for the final days of the season, who were chosen to play Hibs to open the new Celtic Park at 6pm on Tuesday, 8th May 1888, and adverts were quickly posted in the newspapers and around the new ground.

In an added complication to the already complicated matters, Cowlairs were playing Northern on Saturday 5th May at Barrowfield in the final of the Glasgow North Eastern Cup and the Celtic Committee must have been praying this match didn't end in a draw in case the re-arranged match was midweek and Cowlairs would have to pull out of our big opener at the last minute to give their replay their full attention. Thankfully Cowlairs won 1-0 in front of a large crowd of 5000 to claim the cup for the third year in a row, progress that would be halted the next two seasons ironically by the club whose ground they were to open three days later.

As an aside, Ayr United opened Somerset Park on 7th May 1888 with a 3-0 win over no less than Aston Villa.

Indeed it was a huge risk to set the opener for the 8th May, not only in direct competition with the Charity Cup semi final on the same day, but the opening of the Glasgow Exhibition in Kelvingrove by the Prince and Princess of Wales who arrived in Glasgow by train into Central station. Possibly it was felt that those likely to attend the opening of Celtic Park weren't too interested in Rangers playing or indeed in the visit of the royals to the city. Whatever the case was, the opener took place at 6pm prompt, 15 minutes after the Renton v Rangers match just a few miles away at the first Hampden Park, Crosshill, where Renton won 5-1.

In a lesson that we should never underestimate the ambition of the first Celtic Committee, it was on 17th April 1888 that the Scottish Athletic Journal revealed who our original target was to face Hibernian to open Celtic Park, before second choice Renton had to pull out;

"It is expected that the Renton and Hibernians will play the first match on the Glasgow Celtic Athletic FC's field, which is now almost finished. An attempt was made to bring down the Preston North End, but the guarantee asked for was too big".

The great Preston North End team of that era were nicknamed the "Invincibles" after they went through the 1888/89 season unbeaten in the League and FA Cup, to become the first English team to win the Double. They won the inaugural English League title by 11 points after winning 18 matches and drawing the other 4, whilst they won the FA Cup by winning all 5 cup ties without losing a goal.

Therefore opening Celtic Park with a match between Hibernian and Preston North End would have been a major coup, and a sign of intent, but with money extremely tight, the Invincibles would have to bide their time before they finally played at Celtic Park, as the cream of England all formed a queue.

THE OPENING OF CELTIC PARK

Finally in the *Scottish Umpire* on 1st May 1888 after the competing teams in the Charity Cup were confirmed, the committee were in a position to announce details of the opening of Celtic Park, it stated;

"We beg to refer our readers to an advertisement in an issue of today intimating the opening of the Celtic FC Park on the afternoon of the 8th. A day to be memorable in the annals of Glasgow owing to the opening of the Grand Exhibition. As will be seen, the match will not be played until the festive programme for the inauguration of the Exhibition will have gone through.

The popularity of the contending teams who have the honour of playing the first match on Celtic Park will doubtless secure a large attendance. A financially successful match would be particularly welcome as the Committee have been put to a great expense in the construction of their handsome park. No end of surprise has been created by the magnitude and extent of the undertaking and the marvellous vigour and resource of the committee who have spared neither time nor money to produce a field second to none and to place their chosen team on a footing of equality with our best and most experienced clubs".

Opening of Celtic Football & Athletic Park
Dalmarnock Street, Parkhead
Grand Opening Match - Exhibition Day, May 8th

Hibernians versus Cowlairs

Kick off at 6pm prompt. Admission 6d. Ladies free.
Grand Stand Sixpence extra each person
The Park is two minutes walk from the Parkhead and
London Road Tramcar and Railway Stations.

From the *Scottish Referee* on the 5th May 1888;

THE CELTIC FOOTBALL CLUB

"An advertisement in our issue of today announces the news of the opening of the above park in the afternoon of the 8th May, (the day of the opening of the Exhibition). As will be seen the match will not be played till after the

ceremony as the Exhibition is over. We are sure that there will be a very large attendance owing to the popularity of the teams who will have the honour of playing the first match on the Celtic Park; as well as the desire to give substantial aid to the Celtic exchequer, which certainly deserves the support of the admirers of the national sport.

The courage of the committee in venturing such a grand undertaking at the commencement is the surprise of many. Some idea may be formed of it, when we state that it is the opinion of competent judges that the Celtic Park is second to none in the country, and that is saying a great deal. The pitch is a perfect level; close on 110 yards long by 66 yards wide surrounded by a splendid track of 19 feet wide, which, we are sure, will be well patronised by our cycling friends. A magnificent Grand stand has also been erected which will accommodate persons, beneath the stand in a large pavilion divided into three rooms, a committee room 25 feet by 14 feet, and a dressing room at either side, 13 feet by 14 feet, with bath and lavatory accommodation attached to each.

There is plenty of light from front and back, with doors to admit the teams from the back and enter the field from the front. The gate, accommodation is excellent consisting of three large, and six small entrances, one of which is reserved for members. It is with unfeigned pleasure we offer our Celtic friends our congratulations on the great success that has crowned their labours so far and we wish them a long and a prosperous career".

On the day of the match, Tuesday 8th May, the Scottish Umpire gave the teams;

"The Celtic FC's fine new ground at Parkhead will be opened tonight with Hibs v Cowlairs, when a splendid game is sure to be witnessed.

Here are the teams - Hibs; Tobin, Doyle, McKeown, Gallagher, Kelly, McLaren, Naughton, McGhee, Groves, Dunbar and Coleman.

Cowlairs; Duff, McCartney, McLeod, Robertson, Sinclair, McPherson, Masterson, McKinnes, Carson, Scott and McPherson."

Of the Hibs team named, goalkeeper John Tobin would feature in a brief career at Celtic before becoming an agent, or scout, for English clubs enticing Scottish players south. Dan Doyle, Hibs new signing from East Stirling would join Celtic via Everton whilst Mick McKeown, Paddy Gallagher, James McLaren, Willie Groves, Mick Dunbar and Johnny Coleman would soon join Celtic and give the new team great service. Indeed Mick Dunbar played for Celtic in our very first match on May 28th May against Rangers, becoming the only player to have played in the first two matches at Celtic Park. Jimmy McGhee also joined Celtic but only after Hibs went bust in 1890. Willie Naughton played one game for Celtic in our first League match against Renton in 1890. In the event both goalkeepers named didn't play, with Docherty replacing Tobin for Hibs and Burnside, guesting from Northern, in goals for Cowlairs in place of Duff. Watch out for the name of Duff re-appearing in a couple of year's time in an infamous spell with Celtic.

Finally after just six months of toil, sweat and hard labour, Celtic Park was open. The underdogs had finally risen and we now had a collective home to call our own, a safe haven where we could express ourselves proudly without fear of retribution and a beacon of light shining out from the east end of Glasgow. It was to become the living embodiment of the Irish diaspora in Scotland, built by the community from which it sprang, an inspiration to the downtrodden, wherever they might be.

Writing in the *Weekly Mail and Record* in 1951 at the age of 81, no less a man than Willie Maley described it thus;

"The work of the club went on in great style and the new ground proceeded with great keanness. The enclosure was situated at the corner of Janefield Street and Dalmarnock Street bounded on one side by Janefield Cemetery. We had in addition to the playing pitch, a practice pitch. The old pavillion still lives on in my mind.

The dressing rooms were built under the stand which was built to hold around 500 people. In addition we had comfortable offices in the little erection. In the process of building the first team we used to have little practice games even before the ground was completed and I remember my first appearance on the famous pitch. With several other younger players who had been secured before the big catches had been made we stripped under the shadow of the stand in course of erection and wearing a shirt with a band of green across it from shoulder to shoulder the pioneers of the great Celtic trotted out before a handful of enthusiasts.

There was a level grassy playing field measuring 110 yards long and 66 yards wide. A basic earthern terracing around three sides of the ground and an open air stand with accommodation for a thousand that contained a pavillion, a referee's room, an office, dressing rooms and washing and toilet facilities. Terracing moulded from the earth around a narrow track was described as a garden path. Some watched on the cemetery wall on the west boundary. There were nine admission gates on the east side".

Milo, from the *Evening Times* on 9th April, 1904 described Celtic and Celtic Park;

"The Celtic club never knew what it was to have a suckling bottle - it had really no infancy. It sprang into being a full fledged "crack" all at once and commanded attention and gained honours from the very first. The ardent and enthusiastic, if somewhat novice, committee did it, and they did it in spite of difficulties - including a decided partisan prejudice - that would have appalled most veteran managements. I well remember the mild sensation caused right at the very start of the club's career by the threatened interdict of a disapproving landlord. His factor had let the ground without consultation for £50 per annum and at the expiry of the five years lease, he precipitated removal by demanding £500 per annum. Of course, he got his precious ground to keep.

I well remember when Celtic Park 1 was no bigger than a brilliant and beneficent idea on a little bit of paper. One fine day Brother Walfrid, a kindly, old, coaxing cleric, who with Mister John Glass, may be regarded as the fathers of the club, called upon me with a rough sketch plan of the projected ground and with a characteristic twinkle in his eye submitted it for inspection and suggestion.

It was almost the first definite information that had reached the outside with regard to the formation and especially the ambitious aspirations of the new east end club, organised chiefly in the interests of a poor children's charity. I am glad to remember that I did my little best to encourage the new venture.

There was nothing very remarkable about Celtic Park 1; it was certainly not an advance on anything that existed – merely a good sized level pitch surrounded by a narrow and almost unbanked cinder track, and flanked on the east by a somewhat provincial looking stand. Underneath the stand were the dimly lighted and sparingly furnished dressing rooms. By and by, (two years later), a second stand was run up on the western side and the gaps round the field were filled in by a modest attempt at mole hill terracing.

The success of the new venture - which by the way has had its unsuccessful imitators, in the Glasgow Hibs more particularly - was due to the successful organisation of a first rate team. That fact cannot be too strongly insisted upon. Had the promoters failed in that essential - and they were lucky to have begun their promotion so remote from those tied up registration times - all their enterprises would possibly have gone for nothing. It is the team more than anything that makes the club".

It's a very touching piece to read that Brother Walfrid and John Glass sought the opinion of certain men who they respected, carrying a small piece of paper with the original Holy Ground sketched on it. The well respected journalist was telling the truth in the article in his usual forthright manner, a trait that the founding fathers would have been drawn to, as although the original Celtic Park was functional and gave us the perfect platform in the heart of the east end, other longer standing clubs could afford to splash out more on the trimmings. Rangers had recently moved into the original Ibrox Park and their ground contained a grand stand 300 ft long with six rows of seating, with a separate pavillion in the north east corner, 36ft by 28ft in size with walls and roof made of corrugated iron sheeting and came complete with fancy ironwork. The pitch was 115 ft by 71 ft and was surrounded by a quarter mile running track with a 3.5 ft high white fence separating it from the 3ft wide ash terracing which rose to four terraces in parts. The perimeter of the ground was bounded by an 8ft high state of the art corrugated iron fence attached to wooden posts.

On top of the Ibrox pavillion were two flagpoles, one large and one small. On top of the large flagpole they flew a Rangers flag, (a white flag with the name Rangers on it), whilst on top of the smaller flagpole they flew the yellow and red Lion Rampant of Scotland. Flags and symbolism are very important to both Celtic and Rangers down the years and this is indicative of how Rangers saw themselves in the early years, before they morphed their image from a Scottish identity to a British identity, in reaction to our emergence as the Irish club.

Of the game itself from the *Scottish Umpire* on 15th May 1888;

"The ground of the Celtic FC was opened last Tuesday night, the Hibernians and Cowlairs doing the needful. From start to finish the game was of the hardest description, both teams experiencing the worst of luck in not scoring and time arriving without any points being scored.

Docherty of the Hibs is rapidly coming to the front as a goalkeeper which McKeown has scarcely been seen to better advantage. McLaren was quite a host at half. McGhee, Coleman and Groves in front showed good judgement in the passing line but the latter's shooting was a bit feeble. To a man Cowlairs played exceptionally well, young McPherson coming in for most favourable criticism. We would advise Cowlairs to keep Carson in the centre as he is seen to better advantage in that position".

Also in the same newspaper on the same day;

"The recently inaugurated Celtic Football Club, about which so much has been spoken, written and even feared in certain quarters "opened show" on Exhibition day - a most auspicious coincidence and must be congratulated upon the successful issue of the opening.

In the afternoon a match between the Hibernians and Cowlairs took place on their new and handsome grounds at Parkhead which, notwithstanding the strong counter attractions, was largely attended and in the evening a large and representative gathering of football notables assembled in the Royal Hotel who while doing full justice to an excellent supper did not omit to scatter profuse but simple compliments and desire a deserved success for the new and influential venture.

We heartily join in the one and endorse the other. The fear that Glasgow cannot support a purely Celtic club we believe to be a groundless one and are equally convinced that it can flourish without in the very slightest injuring the prospects of interfering with the success of their compatriots in the east, the Hibernians. We rather believe that the success of the one will be an incentive to the other and a result of the friendly rivalry - prosperity to both. Even so let it be".

"Burnside of the Northern kept goal for Cowlairs against the Hibs on the occasion of the opening ceremony for the Celtic FC. Considering the attractions of the Exhibition, royalty and the Charity Cup match at Hampden Park the attendance at this match was really good. It augurs well for Celtic Park yet becoming a popular rendezvous for east enders".

From the *Glasgow Evening News* on 9th May;

"Cowlairs v Hibernian - These teams met last night in a friendly match, and opened the beautiful ground situated on Dalmarnock Road, Glasgow, belonging to the newly organised Celtic Football and Athletic Club. There was a very large attendance. A few minutes from the start Hibs scored, but the point was disallowed for offside. The game continued to be exceedingly interesting, and visits to either goal were frequent. McGhee and McLaren, for the Hibs, made several good attempts at goal, while for Cowlairs MacPherson, on the left, very nearly scored from a fine shot, which landed on the bar. No scoring took place in the first half.

The second half was begun with much vigour on both sides, and Cowlairs had a fine run up by MacPherson nearly the whole length of the field, but the ball was allowed to run out of play a few yards from the goal line. The Hibs retaliated and commenced an exciting piece of play near Cowlairs' goal. A number of hot shots were sent in, but the defence was very fine - McLeod, Robertson and Burnside especially distinguishing themselves. A foul against the Hibs gave Cowlairs relief, and Docherty was called upon to save, which he did in fine style several times in succession.

The game, which had up until this time been mostly in Cowlairs' ground, was now carried on in Hibs quarters and much excitement was caused by sensational runs from Groves and McGhee, who twice raised the siege but the last visit to Burnside finished with an abortive stop from McLaren. The game, which was a very hard one throughout, finished in a draw, no legitimate points being scored. The members of the Celtic club, together with their friends, met after the match, and had supper in the Royal Hotel, where a very enjoyable evening was spent".

From the *Scotsman* on 9th May;

"Hibernians v Cowlairs - The beautiful ground of the Celtic was duly opened last night, the Hibernians and Cowlairs being the favoured clubs. Both teams were warmly received on stepping into the enclosure by the large crowd, fully 3000 spectators lining the ropes. The "Hibs" won the toss, and played with a strong wind in their favour, and scored in three minutes but the point was disallowed. Although playing against the wind, the Cowlairs gave their opponents much trouble and had many tries at goal but Docherty was ever on the alert and saved in splendid style.

Somehow or other the "wearers of the green," although having a little the best of the game, could not score, too much passing in front of the goal, spoiling their best chances. Half time arrived with no goals being scored on either side. The second half was started with great dash on both sides, the goalkeepers in both teams being taxed to the uttermost. Cowlairs scored after twenty minutes' play, but on appeal was disallowed. From this till the finish Cowlairs had, if anything, the best of the play, but time arrived with neither side in the ascendancy".

From the *Glasgow Observer* on 12th May;

OPENING OF THE CELTIC FOOTBALL CLUB'S PARK

"On Tuesday evening last, the new park and pavillion of Celtic Football and Athletic Club was formally opened. The park, which covers about 20 acres, is situated in Dalmarnock Street, Parkhead. Tram cars from the centre of the city convey visitors within a few seconds walk of the field, which is enclosed form the street by a wall of wood similar to that running round the other football parks in the neighbourhood.

The Grand Stand is an erection capable of accommodating in comfort a very large number of people. Underneath is the pavillion or clubroom, a large well lighted apartment, having dressing rooms at either side fitted up with all requisite toilet appliances.

On Tuesday evening the weather was all that could be desired. A trifle chilly, but bright and pleasant not withstanding.

In and around the pavillion were clusters of clergy and people. Among these were the reverend Messrs Father Beyeart, St Michael's, Parkhead; Father Hughes, Sacred Heart; Father McCulla, Sacred Heart; Father Van Der Heyde, St Mary's; Father Montgomery, St Alphonsus; and Father Foley, St Patrick's, Edinburgh. Brothers Walfrid and Dorotheus, Dr John Conway, Messrs Joseph Shaughnessy, William Toner, W McCaffrey, John McKillop, Joseph F McGroary, William McKillop, W P O'Brien, Charles Campbell etc etc.

Prompt to the advertised time, Doctor Conway and Mr Joseph Shaughnessy emerged from the pavillion and entered the field followed by the Hibernians and Cowlairs, James McLaren heading the procession of players. The Doctor placed the ball amid the cheers of the spectators who numbered fully 5,000.

The Hibs won the toss and played with the wind. About a minute after the kick off the Hibs with a good display of combination made a rush towards their opponents goal and attempted to score. They failed, but narrowly enough to evoke a round of cheering. Shortly after the resumption of play the Cowlairs had a look in, getting close to the Hibs' posts. McKeown made a vain effort to bar the way but a faulty shot on the part of Cowlairs spoiled their chance.

Play was now of a give and take nature, neither club having much advantage over the other. A couple of throw ins gave the Hibs a fair chance of scoring but the wind interfered with the kick and nothing came of the opportunity. A corner kick gave them a second chance but the leather on being started went through unopposed, so the point did not count. The Hibs seemed to press their opponent tightly at this period, but McLeod and McCartney were not to be passed. The Cowlairs now had the best of matters and quickly brought the ball to the goal of the ex champions. Docherty however was all there and fisted out safely.

Some unexciting play ensued until, at length, the Cowlairs broke away with a run that seemed threatening. On reaching McKeown however, that cool youngster quietly stepped in among a crowd of excited combatants and sent the leather to a safe distance. Half time was called without anything having being done. On changing sides some rapid play took place but neither side could manage to do much. The play until the call of time was uneventful and neither side could put on a point, so the first game played on the Celtic Park resulted in a draw. Mr McFadden was umpire for his team, the Cowlairs had their usual man and Mr McCulloch, (Our Boys) was the referee.

At the conclusion of the game, the players and Committee of the Celtic adjourned to the Royal Hotel, George Square, where a supper was served. Doctor Conway presided and was supported by Messrs Joseph Shaughnessy, Joseph F McGroary, McGallagly, James Mackay, Charles Campbell, (Queens Park Committee member and ex player), W P O'Brien, Pat Gaffney, John Glass, James Quillan, Hugh Darroch, John O'Hara, Tom E Maley, Willie Maley, Vaughan, John McFadyen, Connoll, Peter Glass, Green, McHugh, Mick Rodgers, James Rodgers, Kilpatrick, Pat Welsh, McKillop, Michael Shannon, James Curtis, Dan Blayney, Hugh Blayney, John McDonald, Dan Molloy and players; Dolan, Doyle, Pearson and McLaughlin.

Representatives of Queens Park, Rangers, Renton, Third Lanark, Clyde, Thistle, Shettleston, Cambuslang, Airdrieonians, Cambuslang Hibs, St Mirren, Dykebar, Abercorn, Port Glasgow Athletic, Greenock Morton, Dumbarton Athletic and Dumbarton clubs were also present. When the viands, (dishes of food), had been done justice to, Doctor Conway who was received with cheers rose and formally proposed the toast of "The Hibernians", which was warmly honoured.

Mr McFadden who was called upon to reply, thanked the company for the hearty manner in which the toast had been responded to. The Hibs were only too glad to have an opportunity of showing their friendship for their compatriots in Glasgow. They had never forgotten the great encouragement which had been shown to them on past occasions in which they visited the city. (Cheers).

It would be a sorry day indeed for the Irish in Scotland when the Irish residents of one city should act in an unfriendly way towards those of another. They all sprung from one spot and with God's help they would from first to last be friends with one another. (Cheers).

In meeting the Cowlairs they knew they were meeting a club who could give as much as they got. If the Celts went on as they had begun and made friends with their neighbours, he had no doubt they should be meeting in a year or two to witness the presentation of the Scottish Cup and badges to the team to whom the Hibs would least grudge them, the Celtic Football Club. (Cheers).

Doctor Conway proposed the health of the Cowlairs, coupling it with the name of Mr Henderson, the Secretary. Mr Henderson suitably replied, and on behalf of his club wished the Celts every success.

The next toast was that of "The Celtic" proposed by Mr McCulloch, Dundee Harp. Mr Thomas E Maley replied and in doing so remarked that there was no reason why the Celtic should not obtain a good position among the clubs of Glasgow. He felt sure that the enthusiasm of the members would bring the team to the front rank (Cheers).

The next toast was that of "Kindred Clubs," proposed by the Chairman and responded to by Mr Charles Campbell, (SFA Committee member), who confessed his astonishment at seeing the field and the pavillion so well prepared. In conclusion, he proposed the health of "The umpires and referee", whose task was always arduous. The toast was heartily pledged.

Mr Joseph Shaughnessy, proposed the toast of "The Press," which was replied to by Mr Stewart Mackay. The concluding toast was that of "The Chairman", which was spoken to by Mr Collins of the Clyde Football Club. Doctor Conway appropriately replied and the proceedings were brought to a close with the singing of Auld Lang Syne.

During the course of the evening, songs were given by Mr Thomas Robertson, Mr Good, Mr Bishop and Mr Shannon. Mr Thomas E Maley recited George R Sims' "Lifeboat," in a most artistic and sympathetic style and was warmly applauded as were the other gentlemen who contributed to the entertainment of the company. Taken all through, the opening was most successful and with so auspicious an inauguration, great things may be looked for from the Celtic Football and Athletic Club".

The above lengthy report in the official Catholic newspaper of the day for a football match was unheard of at the time and pointed towards Celtic having contacts inside the paper. The only time a previous edition had given so much attention to a game of football was when Hibs won the Scottish Cup the previous year.

The first thing that stands out is the list of clergy present at the opening of Celtic Park, with the east end parishes of St Mary's, St Michael's and Sacred Heart naturally represented, but also St Alphonsus, who had pulled out the talks to form Celtic, along with St Andrews. The latter parish was the only one not represented, which may give an insight into the relations between the parishes at the time. It must be said though, that although the parishes left the discussions, many good men from those parishes stayed in the discussions to form the club, men such as David Meikleham from St Alphonsus and the McCreadie brothers from St Andrews, amongst others.

It was evident right from the start that the enthusiasm of the Celtic Committee meant that we never did anything by halves and the opening of Celtic Park was done on an impressive scale to ensure those who visited, including every top club in the land, would want to return. The potential was there right from the very start. From the match reports, the original Celtic Park was described as handsome and even beautiful, but in truth this was down more to its fresh and tidy appearance rather than for its groundbreaking design as Milo stated in the *Evening Times,*

"There was nothing very remarkable about Celtic Part 1; it was certainly not an advance on anything that existed – merely a good sized level pitch surrounded by a narrow and almost unbanked cinder track, and flanked on the east by a somewhat provincial looking stand".

Most grounds in those days contained a separate pavillion, almost akin to a detached house and also a covered main stand. The Celtic Committee were to follow this exact formula when building the current Celtic Park in 1892 but four years earlier, with funding at a premium, a stand with no roof and changing rooms and facilities housed underneath showed the strict budget under which we worked at our formation.

The first appearance of the names of the initial Celtic Committee who adjourned to the Royal Hotel, George Square, for the after match supper is invaluable with Office Bearers such as Honorary President Doctor John Conway, Vice President James Quillan, President John Glass, Secretary John O'Hara, Treasurer Hugh Darroch and the builder of the original Celtic Park, Pat Gaffney, all mentioned.

Others who would have been on or close to the committee were Joseph Shaughnessy, Joseph Francis McGroary, William McKillop, Pat Welsh, James Curtis, John McDonald, Dan Malloy, James Mackay, players Tom and Willie Maley all mentioned right from the start along with less prominent names such as Mick Rodgers, James Rodgers, Michael Shannon, Peter Glass, (brother of John), Dan Blayney and Hugh Blayney as well as Vaughan, McFadyen, Connoll, Green, McHugh, Kilpatrick and McGallagly, some of whom would compete in future elections for places on the Celtic Committee.

WILLIE MALEY SETS THE SCENE FOR OUR FIRST MATCH

From the *Celtic Handbook 1935/36*;

"I often think of the first day I wore Celtic colours. The Old Stand or Pavillion had not been finished, and the then Committee were anxious to see the new Team in the fine white shirts, with green collars and Celtic badge, that had been presented to us by Mr Penman, of Bridgeton.

So one night a practice game was announced and we stripped under the temporary roofing of the stand and trotted on to the field in the famous Green and White which was to make football history. The crowd, not too big, gave us a great cheer and so the die was cast and the Celts who have caused so much discussion all over the world came into being".

OUR FIRST EVER CELTIC MATCH

With the opening match a tremendous success and a decent turn out on a Tuesday evening, the founding fathers were given tremendous heart that this was indeed a viable prospect and the endless unpaid hours that they had put in at the end of their own working day could pay off. All they now had to do was to get a Celtic team on the pitch that would capture the hearts of the downtrodden Irish.

They had no time to relax because once again, time was running out on the 1887/88 football season and it was essential to follow up the success of the opening match with the unveiling of the Celtic team to their eagerly awaiting audience. Due to the restrictions on finances available, the first ever Celtic team was made up of players loaned to the club for the day, as often happened in friendly matches, but there was a mixture of big names amongst the not so well known too.

James Kelly and Neil McCallum from Renton were the biggest attractions, as well as Johnny Madden from Dumbarton, Mick Dunbar from Hibs and the Maley brothers from Third Lanark all of whom went on to become popular first team players. Michael Dolan, Eddie Pearson, James McLaughlin, Phil Murray and Charlie Gorevin enjoyed varied careers at Celtic but these eleven names should always be remembered as the first to pull on a Celtic jersey on Monday, 28th May 1888, long before the names of Quinn, McGrory, Gallagher, Tully, McNeil, Johnstone, Dalglish or Larsson had ever been dreamt of.

Having pulled out all the stops to get James Kelly to play, the Celtic Committee had to endure nine days of anxiety when he played for Renton against West Bromwich Albion, the respective winners of the Scottish and English cups on Saturday, 19th May at Hampden.

On the 24th May, the Western Hibernians, a team comprised of the best "Hibernian" players from both the west and the east of Scotland, (as it turned out), and who were put together to play charity matches, played against Cowlairs at Saracen Park, home of Carrick FC. Amongst those in the Western Hibernian team that day who would play for Celtic in our first ever match, just four days later, were James Kelly, Neil McCallum and Johnny Madden. 2000 attended the match with all funds raised going towards the St Mungo's Poor Childrens Dinner Table in Townhead. Of the eleven Western Hibernians select, nine would go on to play for Celtic; Hugh Clifford, James Kelly, Neil McCallum, Johnny Madden, Phil Clarke, Jimmy McLaren, James McLaughlin, and James Coleman, as well as the better known Johnny Coleman.

Thankfully none of the Celtic players chosen to play in our first ever match were injured in the build up, especially James Kelly who also played for a Scoto/Anglo select against a Scoto/Welsh team on Saturday, 26th May as part of the Glasgow International Exhibition, meaning his debut for Celtic was his fourth match in eight days.

From the *Scottish Umpire* on the 5th June 1888;

"It would appear as if the newly formed Glasgow club, the Celtic FC has a bright future before it. At any rate if the committee can place the same eleven on the field as opposed the Rangers last Monday evening or an equally strong one, the Celtic will not lack for patronage and support.

A good team is essential to success and this fact the committee have not lost sight of. It will be interesting to many of our readers to know the composition of the team which represented the new organisation in its first club match.

Here it is; Goal, Michael Dolan (Drumpellier); Backs, Eddie Pearson (Carfin Shamrock) and James McLaughlin (Whitefield); Half backs, Willie Maley (Third Lanark), James Kelly (Renton) and Phil Murray (Cambuslang Hibs); Forwards, Neil McCallum (Renton), Tom Maley (Third Lanark), Johnny Madden (Dumbarton), Mick Dunbar (Hibs) and Charlie Gorevin (Whitefield), a pretty good eleven.

The Rangers were without D Gow, JR Gow, Hotson, Peacock, Allan and Aird but had Soutar, (Partick Thistle) doing duty - the remainder being drawn from the Swifts.

The match was a capital one, fast and friendly - the home organisation playing with a combination which could scarcely have been expected for an opening display. The Celtic retired victors by 5 goals to 2, a result which must be indeed gratifying to their supporters.

After the match over 70 gentlemen sat down to supper in St Mary's hall, East Rose Street where a pleasant evening was spent. Doctor Conway occupied the chair and on the platform were also Messrs McFadden, (Hibs), McCulloch, (Our Boys), Grant, (Rangers) and Brother Walfrid. The latter gentleman who took a deep interest in the origin of the club has every reason to flatter himself as to the success of the Celtic. Long may it flourish in our midst".

Attendances at the two opening matches of 5000 and 2000 may not sound very impressive but it doesn't tell half the story. With Saturday afternoon dates not available to the committee, Monday and Tuesday evening matches were not the most popular as many men worked until late in the day. Hibs were always going to be a big attraction no matter what and a crowd of 5000 to see the opener is actually a very decent crowd back in the day.

The 2000 who attended Celtic's first match would have represented a good percentage of the men and women of the east end parishes, with much of the rest of Glasgow caught up in the Exhibition taking place in the west end, well before our fame had spread further afield. Many tickets were bought direct from the Saint Vincent De Paul Society who handled Celtic tickets and were guaranteed a percentage, so everyone was a winner, both Celtic and at the same time, charity.

Rangers around this time were floundering as Milo from the *Evening Times* remarked in September, 1888;

"The Rangers, I am afraid, have been living in a fool's paradise during the last few months, imagining they were strong when everybody outside of them was telling them they were weak".

Ironically, whilst the mainstream newspapers of the day concentrated fully on page after page of coverage of the Glasgow Exhibition attended by hundreds of thousands as well as the royals, an event that was happening just a few miles away in the east end of Glasgow was to have much more significance to the city and would resonate for much longer, for ever in fact. The birth of Celtic Football Club.

By 29th May, Celtic were confident enough to state that we were now arranging fixtures for next season, with the match secretary named as Willie Maley, Argyle Place, Cathcart.

Far from taking a well earned rest during the close season and looking forward to concentrating on fixing up as many teams as possible for the following season, the committee had no intention of resting on their laurels. We were heavily in debt and so a further three friendly matches were arranged throughout the month of June, which was rare to say the least back in the day. From the *Scottish Umpire* on 5th June;

Grand Football Match - Saturday First, 9th June.

Celtic v Harp (Dundee)

Celtic Park, Dalmarnock Street, Parkhead.
Kick-off at 4.30pm. Admission 3d. Ladies Free. Stand, 3d. each person.

Dundee Harp, who had obliged Brother Walfrid on 8th May 1886 to play in a charity match in aid of the Poor Childrens Dinner Tables against Clyde at Barrowfield, again obliged Brother Walfrid and became the second visitors to play the hosts at Celtic Park in our first Saturday match on 9th June. In front of a fantastic crowd of 6000, triple that of our first match thanks to the Saturday billing, the Celts won 1-0 with a late goal from Johnny Coleman as the names of Boyle, Hughes and Coogan made their debuts for the Celts.

From the *Scottish Umpire* on 12th June;

"The Celtic, who seemingly are bent on playing throughout the summer, had a visit from the Dundee Harp on Saturday. Both Kelly and McCallum, of Renton, were expected to play in the home ranks, but at the last minute the services of Boyle and Hughes had to be called into requisition.

The play throughout was stoutly contested, but it was close on time ere any scoring took place—Coleman, after a piece of manoeuvring, notching the first, and what proved to be, the only point of the match. The strongest point of the Celtic's team on Saturday was the back division, Phil Murray at half being particularly noticeable.

The forwards did not pass well to one another, a fault which time will remedy. O'Kane for the Harp was in grand style, and treated the spectators to a fine display of long kicking. The halves worked well, but, like their opponents, the forwards were poor at close quarters".

A week later on Saturday, 16th June, Mossend Swifts were the visitors with the Celtic team bolstered by James Kelly and Neil McCallum of Renton.

Reid from Mossend scored the opener after five minutes to become the first player to put his team a goal up against Celtic, but Jimmy McLaren equalised twenty minutes later with a high shot which beat the keeper easily. Not be outdone, Reid became the second player to put his team a goal up against Celtic, before Charlie Gorevin scored just before half time.

In a spirited second half, Boyd from the Swifts became the third player to put his team a goal up against the Celts and it looked like it would prove to be the winner until Neil McCallum, after a dashing run, scored a late leveller with just a few minutes remaining to earn the plucky Celts a 3-3 draw with the crowd given as 4000.

The *Scottish Umpire* summed it up thus;

"The Celtic exhibited an improvement in combination towards the close. A few such games and they will prove a hard nut to crack".

On 16th June the *Glasgow Observer* stated;

THE CELTIC FOOTBALL CLUB

"More than once for the last few months, we have informed our readers of the progress made by the Celtic Club. Today we are able to state that the park and stand are in a complete state, nor has the team, the essential part, been forgotten.

It is considered that next season, the Celts will have a team equal to any in the city. Twice already they have entered the arena and came off victorious. The first time they had the Rangers, a first class club all will admit, and who had to lower their colours on leaving the field as the Celtic beat them by five goals to two, not a bad start.

The second match was played with the Dundee Harp, who placed their best team on the field, and with some hesitation, the Celtic, with a weak team, (some of the best being engaged in a charity match), to the surprise of many gained a victory by one goal to nil.

Judging by the turnout of spectators, and the counter attractions over the Hampden way, the two teams have very good prospects. We are safe in saying fully 6000 persons were present. We understand that the redoubtable Mossend Swifts, the holders of the Edinburgh Shield, have consented to play today, (Saturday), a benefit match for the Celtic. We are sure if the clerk of the weather is in good humour that the gate will be a bumper one, and we hope a victorious match for the plucky Celts, who we understand will place their best team on the park.

We should very much like to see a friendly match with their neighbours, the Clyde, who have walked off with the Graham Cup last week against the Thistle. We are sure that the east enders would turn out in big numbers to witness the first contest between the two teams".

The *Scottish Umpire* on June 19th stated;

"The Celtic are enjoying great patronage in their summer matches, a fact partly attributable to the excellence and reputation of the players who do duty for them.

It goes without saying if they can play such a team on the field next season as they did on Saturday they will not lack support. Their match with Mossend Swifts attracted close upon 4000 spectators, the stand being packed. Celtic Park looks better every visit and the playing pitch shows signs of consolidation. The Edinburgh Shield holders had a good team and despite the warmth of the atmosphere a capital game was witnessed".

Finally on Saturday, 23rd June, nearby neighbours Clyde came to Celtic Park and became the first team to beat us, returning to nearby Bridgeton with a 4-3 win. They were without four first team players but Britton still managed to score a hat trick, the first against Celtic and so two records were achieved by Clyde that day which could never be broken.

Of our future stars, James Kelly, Jimmy McLaren, Johnny Coleman and Mick Dunbar played against Clyde, with Neil McCallum failing to show. Johnny Madden from Dumbarton was still guesting for the club but it would be another season before he agreed to sign for the bhoys and instead he returned to Dumbarton for the 1888/89 season.

As season 1887/88 came to a close, Brother Walfrid and the founding fathers had much to be proud of and so much more to look forward to. The game of football was increasing in popularity and the parishes of the east end had rose almost to a man to welcome their new football club. By the last week in June, James Kelly and Neil McCallum from Renton had signalled their intention to play for Celtic in season 1888/89, as had James McLaren, Paddy Gallagher, Mick Dunbar and Johnny Coleman from Hibs. Before a fortnight was out, Willie Groves from Hibs had applied to play for Celtic and his wish was granted, giving us a team with a nucleus of four Scottish Cup winners, McLaren and Groves with Hibs and James Kelly and Neil McCallum with Renton and a team that would explode onto the Scottish scene. Season 87/88 saw Renton win the Scottish Cup and the Charity Cup and Cambuslang won the Glasgow Cup, but very soon there was to be a new name challenging for the trophies and changing the game forever.

The game against Clyde was the last of five matches played at Celtic Park since we opened the ground on 8th May, but the fact we played three matches in June, normally seen as close season, reflected the financial state we were in at the beginning with huge amounts laid out to put the ground in order and every penny coming in a prisoner.

The committee still met weekly during the close season and referring to the weekly meeting on 9th July, 1888, John H McLaughlin reflected on the club's serious financial position in the *Glasgow Evening News* on 30th May 1889;

"That meeting, did not pass a resolution to make the entry money 10s, but simply resolved that no new members should be admitted on account of the precarious condition the club then stood in, and this was done on the advice of our law agent".

Things must have been serious if we had been advised by a law agent not to take on any more memberships, a key indication that there was no guarantee we could carry out our fixtures. Thankfully, we weathered the storm and crucially made a good start to the 1888/89 season which had the Celtic support rallying to the ground to see their favourites.

As Alec Maley, brother of Tom and Willie and also the former manager of Clyde, Clydebank and Hibs was to reminisce in the *Glasgow Eastern Standard*, (owned by Celtic Chairman Tom White), on 5th August 1933;

"Attendances at the game had gradually increased since 1888, the year of the birth of the club. It may be argued that other clubs must take a certain amount of credit from this, but in the minds of those whose memory can carry them so far back there can be no doubt that the coming of Celts created a boom in football.

Make no mistake. This was not owing to the popularity of the new club; quite the reverse. There is no doubt that in the early days the crowds were attracted in the hope that the green and white brigade would be beaten".

FIXTURE LIST FULL

Willie Maley, in his role as Match Secretary, certainly didn't rest and one of the best and biggest fixture lists yet received, as described by the Scottish Umpire, was released in that newspaper with an incredible list of 40 matches, not including any of the Cup matches yet to be drawn and a New Years tour from December 31st to 3rd January, which it stated;

"Should keep the fine combination, which the club has got together, hard at it with full steam on".

The first name on the fixture list, a home game with Hibernian, (minus six of their players now in our ranks), was a very clever move and would whet the appetite of the Celtic support and the media throughout the summer.

THE FIRST TROPHY WON AT CELTIC PARK

The first trophy won at Celtic Park also occurred at the end of June, on Wednesday the 27th, when Royal Albert from Larkhall beat Cambuslang Hibs 5-3 in the final of the Motherwell Charity Cup, after no less than three draws. 1500 attended the match, with the majority being Celtic members who were supporting Cambuslang Hibs.

The princely sum of £10, 7s, 8d was taken at the gate but this only just covered the travelling expenses of both teams, policemen, groundsmen, referee, bills, advertising, refreshments and committee's expenses etc. Celtic may not have been involved on the pitch, but it was a compliment that Celtic Park, just a month after its opening, was chosen to host a cup final. No doubt, the Celtic Committee, always looking at ways of getting a return on our investment, were more than happy to offer the use of the ground in return for a small fee and the exposure that went with it, a nice bonus during the close season which helped keep the wolves from the door.

CHAPTER THREE
OUR FIRST SEASON - 1888/89

"Let them scoff and jeer. Celtic will yet win to our proper position by our own merits and those who scoff today will one day have to applaud".

The Celtic Founding Fathers had no experience of Scottish football at the top level, but they were certainly not slow in making a name for themselves as they blew away the cobwebs of the stuffy old men running Scottish football at the time. They quickly realised that if the new Irish club were to succeed, where many others had failed, we would need to give the public what they wanted. The first few months of the season were crucial if we were to get onto a secure financial footing, and we had to make hay whilst the sun was shining, before the bleak winter followed which would affect attendances in our uncovered ground.

THE REASONS BEHIND THE HIBS' DEMISE

The date of Saturday, 4th August 1888 when Hibernian played the first game of the season at Celtic Park, (with half of the Celtic team made up of former Hibs players), certainly lived up to its billing and showed that for pure theatre there was no other show in town.

Hibs were reeling from the departure of some of their players and it was to be a while before the bad feeling that emanated from Easter Road towards Celtic Park was to simmer down. In truth however most of the Hibs players were from the west and knew they had better chances of picking up a job in the larger city of Glasgow to supplement their amateur status. They had originally been snapped up almost en masse from Lugar Boswell in Ayrshire so it was a case of the kettle calling the pot black. Indeed, Hibs carried on their usual modus operandi of returning to many of the smaller Irish teams in the west of Scotland to look for replacements and came back with Hugh Clifford, Paddy Naughton and James Whyte from Carfin Shamrock, Paddy McKenna and Paddy McGovern from Whifflet Shamrock, as well as Paddy McVey from Durhamtown Rangers, who merged with four other teams to form Bathgate FC in 1893.

As far back as 17th April, 1888, it was noted in the Scottish Athletic Journal that Hibernian were on the decline, well before the arrival of Celtic;

"St Patrick's Day and Easter time is one of the seasons at which the Irishman lets himself loose from all worldly cares. Perhaps this is the reason of the very poor football that the Hibernians are treating their friends to. Certainly, whatever the cause, they could not give much poorer exhibitions than they have given lately if they tried. This year has been quite disastrous enough, so that if they want to redeem themselves it is time some move were made.

The shifting policy, and the introduction of new men week after week, has had its natural and only effect, and those responsible have the happiness of seeing the club about as far down the hill as ever it has been. If any more shifting is to be made, some of those who have been the favoured ones to the victimising of others require removal."

Questions were already being asked about the ability of the Hibernian Committee, but the Celtic Committee had shown they were true to their word in attracting the best Irish players to the club and in setting up the opener with Hibs they knew that their was no such thing as bad publicity.

The *Glasgow Evening News* on the 4th August gave the following prospects for our inaugural season;

"THE CELTIC gives promise of becoming one of the best teams in the country. Its management certainly means business, as will be seen from one glance at the names of those who compose their team today. Every man of them has a reputation as a player, but it would be interesting to know by what means they were gathered together from all parts of the country. Their secretary, Mr Maley, who is a very genial fellow, has had no difficulty in arranging a splendid list of fixtures".

5000 packed into Celtic Park, a large crowd in those days, as the following former Hibs players; Mick Dunbar, Willie Groves, Johnny Coleman, Jimmy McLaren and Paddy Gallagher took to the field in their new strips with the white top and green collar, topped off by the green Celtic Cross on a patch of red leather to replace the harp of the Hibs.

Mick McKeown was the other signing from Hibs, but he didn't play in what was a very tough game as Hibs fought for their honour right to the death. In fact Hibs took the lead twice only for Coleman and McCallum to equalise, before "Darling" Willie Groves scored the winner for the Celts late on after Jimmy McGhee was forced to come off injured with an ankle knock, reducing the Hibs men to ten. James Kelly was named as the first Celtic captain with Paddy Gallagher, known for his no nonsense, battling style of play, named as his assistant.

Interestingly in the *Scottish Umpire* on 5th July, a few weeks before the game, it doesn't speak of the Celtic Committee chasing after Willie Groves' signature, instead, it stated;

"Groves has applied for membership of Celtic FC."

Who was wooing who? Certainly Hibs players ticked every box for the Celtic Committee, but at the same time they were more than happy to return homewards. This was the same Willie Groves who was courting suitors from down south, in particular Mitchell Saint George from Birmingham, regarding a move the season before he joined Celtic, so any notion that these players were "stolen away" from Hibs is more than a little exaggerated.

The same Willie Groves, too, that after only eleven months at Celtic, travelled south and signed professional terms with Everton, before a change of mind brought him home. The very next year, Groves was on the move again, and signed for West Bromwich Albion. A fantastic player for both Hibs and Celtic, Willie Groves was a player who knew his value and he certainly didn't need to be stolen away from anyone. In fact, any team who had him, knew just how difficult it was to keep him.

Also from the *Scottish Umpire* on 24th July;

"We should say that the Hibs will not be able to regard the Celtic with the warmest feelings, or to entirely disassociate their break up with its rise. We do not know the precise reasons which have induced so many of the Hibs to change their club, but we were not entirely unprepared for the exodus.

First of all the majority of them were western men, who had been got together by the Hibs, because the club held an enviable prestige, and for that reason the men were not fixed with an unbreakable bond. Then Glasgow, as a centre, will always be able to command first choice when clubs go to the trouble of providing work for likely players.

The crowd, also, is in the western city, and where the crowd is, the money is there also. We do not of course insinuate that the money has anything to do with the transference of players - although even that has been hinted - but money makes not only the mare to go, but has a wonderful facility for oiling the wheels of a club, and players indirectly feel the benefit in a large share of comfort".

In an "Open Letter to the Hibernian Football Cub," in the Scottish Umpire on 7th August, a Hibs supporter, (possibly a member of the committee), was given carte blanche to issue support to the Hibernian Committee whilst having more than a swipe at the Celtic Committee at the same time. The veracity of the account has to be weighed up considering the bitterness of its author but some of it has historical value, especially its account of the original Celtic Park and it's a worthy example of the bitterness that enraged the Hibs support.

"You were no doubt struck when you entered the grounds at the manner in which the formation of the new club has been taken in hand, and at the evidence of wealth with which the appearance of everything impressed the beholder. It certainly made a brave show; the spacious grounds commodious stand and the white flag with green crossbar flying triumphantly above. (Club flags back in the day were of a simple design and usually spelled out the club's name on a white background, which was likely to have been the case here).

Put eleven green (Hibs) shirts on the field, I said, and the Celts will never put the ball past them. This was perhaps overdrawn a little, but the feeling which I had was that the Hibernians did not pretend to be anything else than true Irishmen; who are not ashamed, but proud to wear the green, and who don't wear a white shirt and edge the collar with green so that it requires a microscope to detect the colour at all".

The author of the letter has a very short memory as his own team, Hibs, started off just 13 years earlier with a white shirt with no green on it whatsoever, Hibs' white top with a Harp as the badge compared to our white top with green collar and a green Celtic Cross upon a piece of red leather. Our famous strip only lasted until the 19th November when we changed to the green and white stripes. He talks of Celtic Park and its evidence of wealth. There was no evidence of wealth. It was built by the bare hands of the Irish community and it was functional, but not ornamental in any way. The vitriol of the outburst is best summed up by some of the sentiments at the end of the piece where the author tells us;

"Evil deeds never prosper, the duplicity of the founders of the Celtic club will defeat its purpose. Irishmen in Glasgow and throughout Scotland, show what you think of the effort to ruin the Hibernians, whose headquarters are Easter Road".

The final irony in the piece was that one of the names Hibernian had considered at their foundation was, yes, Celtic.

The hugely respected Milo, from the *Evening Times* stated on 9th April 1904;

"The astute organisers of the Celtic Club had a shrewd notion where they might find the men for their team, and when their calculations materialised, the battle was much more than half won. They were accused of plundering other clubs, and notably the Hibs, in order to raise themselves to the big boy's bench all at once. And I will confess that there was apparent justification for the accusation; but the Celts' version of the story puts a different face upon it. The men, in the majority of instances, I am assured, sought them - not they the men".

The biggest irony for Hibs was that whilst the poisoned letter was being penned to the Scottish Umpire, they were already in dire straits off the pitch and they couldn't blame Celtic for the real reason they were in crisis, an issue which left many of their best committee men resigning. Hibernian were based at the Catholic Young Men's Society Hall and they had been founded as an integral part of that organisation. The Young Men's Society were founded in 1849 in Limerick by Dean Richard O'Brien who later became a Monsignor. One of the rules of the society was the exclusion of party politics, in order to guard against the Society becoming a tool of any political party.

Therefore, although Hibs flourished from that foothold within the Catholic community of Edinburgh that the CYMS gave them, they had to abide by the rules of that organisation, which were non political. Indeed, that organisation had also to abide by its own rules. Home Rule in Ireland was the main topic at the time and things hotted up when the Plan of Campaign was launched in October 1886, whereby tenants attempted to secure a reduction in rent, in cases of hardship, by offering to pay the landlord a discounted rent, and if it was refused they would instead pay no rent at all. The discounted rent would then be collected by campaigners, banked and then used to assist evicted tenants.

The tenants were taking ownership of their own problem and fighting back, however the reaction from the authorities was heavy handed and the issue threatened to split political and religious views right down the middle. The British Prime Minister, the Conservative Lord Salisbury, declared the campaign an unlawful and criminal conspiracy in December 1886 and the situation often descended into violence as the Coercion Act was introduced which led to hundreds of innocents being imprisoned, amongst them many MPs. (James Hozier, the original landlord of the current Celtic Park in 1892 was Lord Salisbury's Private Secretary and Foreign Secretary in 1886 before he sat for the South Lanarkshire seat).

The Catholic Church could stand back no longer and had to act and so it did in July 1887, when it sent Archbishop Persico to consult with prominent members of the hierarchy in Ireland over the next six months before returning to the Vatican. On 20th April 1888, a Papal Rescript was issued which condemned the Plan of Campaign and any involvement by the clergy, and just two months later on 24th June, it was followed up with the Papal encyclical, (circular to Bishops), "Saepe Nos," (translates as "Often have we", which was the first few words of the text in Latin).

It was a lengthy document, which contained the following instruction to all Irish bishops, who had no choice but to act on it;

"We cannot disguise that tidings which have recently come to Us from Ireland have deeply pained and grieved Us. We have learned that an untoward excitement has suddenly arisen because the Sacred Congregation, whose office it is to vindicate the authority of the Church against those who resist it, has decreed that those methods of warfare known as Boycotting and the Plan of Campaign, which had begun to be employed by many, may not lawfully be used. And what is more to be deplored, there are not a few who have come forward and summoned the people to excited meetings, where inconsiderate and dangerous opinions are set in circulation, the authority of the Decree not being spared. For not only is the real scope of this Decree grievously perverted by means of forced interpretations, but, furthermore, it is even denied that obedience is due to the Decree, as if it were not the true and proper office of the Church to decide what is right and what is wrong in human actions.

Such a manner of acting is but little in harmony with the profession of the Christian religion, which assuredly brings in its train the virtues of moderation, respect, and obedience to legitimate authority. Besides, in a good cause, it is not fitting to seem in some sense to imitate those who in the pursuit of an unlawful end seek to attain it by disorderly effort".

There was no real surprise that the Vatican didn't come out and back the Plan of Campaign and Boycott, however labelling it as a "method of warfare," caused deep resentment. The reaction to the edict, as far as Hibernian were concerned, was a follow up letter from Archbishop Smith, whose remit included the CYMS in Edinburgh, to Canon Hannan, informing him that the President of the St Patrick's branch of the CYMS, Michael Flannigan, had been deposed from his office.

This caused uproar and many of the CYMS committee resigned in sympathy at his treatment as a scapegoat and Hibernian, with many of their committee overlapping with the CYMS, lost more than a few good committee men. Flannigan's crime was that he presided over and spoke at CYMS meetings in support of the Plan of Campaign and he had not taken the opportunity to apologise for his actions. Far from apologising, Flannigan resigned from his post to save any embarrassment and carried on where he left off in support of the Plan of Campaign.

A few more CYMS meetings followed which only led to more resignations, before Hibernian called an emergency meeting on Friday, 17th August. By the third week of the new season in August, Hibs were already in crisis, which showed how desperate the malaise at the club was and how the loss of six players to Celtic was only one of a list of problems at the club.

From the *Glasgow Evening News* on 24th August;

HIBERNIAN FOOTBALL CLUB

"A crowded meeting of friends and supporters of this club, from which, it is said, several members of the first eleven recently seceded and became connected with a Glasgow club, was held last night in St Mary Street, (Upper) Hall, Edinburgh - Mr Michael Regan presiding. The chairman said the object of the meeting was to take steps towards the maintenance of the club. All present knew its record for a good many years, and the difficulties at the present time. It depended greatly on the honorary members whether the club would cease to exist or go on. The club were willing, he understood, to do all they possibly could, to maintain their position in the eastern district of Scotland, (Hear, hear), if supported financially, they would bring together the best team they could get.

1 Brother Walfrid

THE
FATHER NOONAN MEMORIAL.

It has been decided that the MEMORIAL about to be raised to the Memory of FATHER NOONAN will take the form of a

GRAND HIGH ALTAR,

To be Erected in the

SACRED HEART CHURCH,
DALMARNOCK ROAD,
BRIDGETON, GLASGOW,

And the Subscription List is forthwith Opened. Subscriptions sent to any of the following gentlemen will be gratefully acknowledged :—

JAMES QUIGLEY, Chairman,
3 Dalmarnock Road.

JOSEPH A. FOY, Treasurer,
78 Muslin Street.

FRANCIS MOONEY, Financial Secretary,
266 Dalmarnock Road.

THOMAS FLOOD, General Secretary,
172 Dalmarnock Road,
Bridgeton, Glasgow.

Rev. F. J. HUGHES, P.P.,
50 Old Dalmarnock Rd.

Brother WALFRED,
71 Charlotte Street.

GRAND CHARITY

FOOTBALL MATCH.

CLYDE v. HARP OF DUNDEE

(Holders of the Forfarshire County and the
Dundee Burns Club Charity Cups)

IN

BARROWFIELD PARK,

FRENCH STREET, OFF DALMARNOCK
ROAD, BRIDGETON,

ON

TO-DAY (SATURDAY), MAY 8th,

KICK-OFF AT 4 P.M.

PROCEEDS FOR THE PURPOSE OF SUP-
PLYING THE CHILDREN OF THE
UNEMPLOYED CATHOLIC HOUSE-
HOLDERS OF SACRED HEART PARISH
WITH

FREE DINNERS & RREAKFASTS.

6

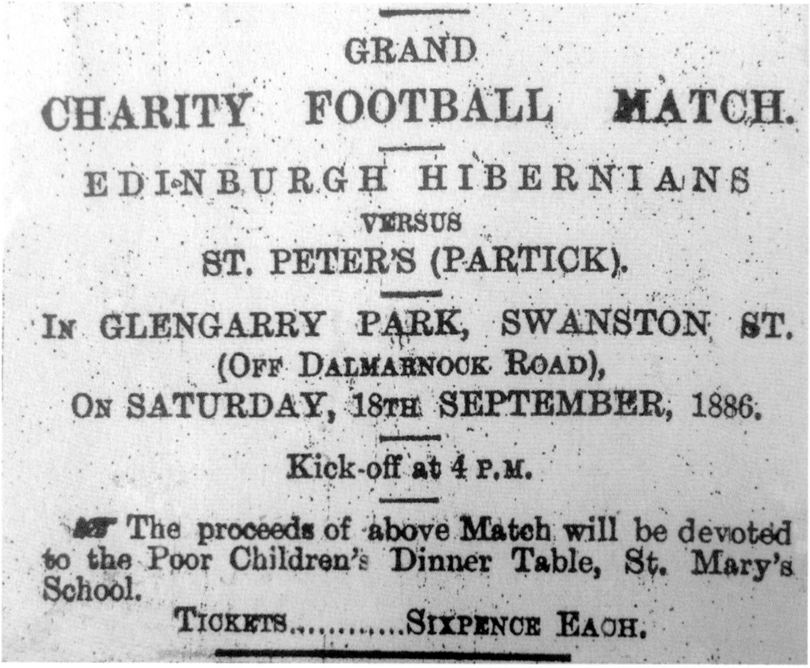

GRAND

CHARITY FOOTBALL MATCH.

EDINBURGH HIBERNIANS

VERSUS

ST. PETER'S (PARTICK).

IN GLENGARRY PARK, SWANSTON ST.

(OFF DALMARNOCK ROAD),

ON SATURDAY, 18TH SEPTEMBER, 1886.

Kick-off at 4 P.M.

☞ The proceeds of above Match will be devoted
to the Poor Children's Dinner Table, St. Mary's
School.

TICKETS..........SIXPENCE EACH.

7

GRAND CHARITY FOOT-
BALL MATCH.
RENTON
(Holders of the Charity Cup, &c.)
V.
HIBERNIANS
(Holders of the Scottish Cup, &c.),
IN BARROWFIELD PARK, FRENCH
STREET
(Off Main Street, Bridgeton),
On THURSDAY EVENING, MAY 26.
Kick-off at Seven prompt.
Admission Sixpence.

8

GREAT FOOTBALL MATCH.
UNDECIDED
EAST-END CHARITY CUP TIE,
SATURDAY, 6TH AUGUST,
RENTON
(Holders of Glasgow Charity Cup, &c.)
Versus
HIBERNIANS
(Holders of Scottish Cup, &c.),
BARROWFIELD PARK,
FRENCH STREET, off MAIN STREET,
BRIDGETON.
Kick-off at 4 P.M. prompt.
Admission, 6d.   Ladies Free.
'Buses will be run by the Tramway Company
from foot of Queen Street to Ground.

9

10

11

SCOTTISH FOOTBALL ASSOCIATION.
FINAL CUP TIE.—Saturday First, 12th February.

DUMBARTON

VERSUS

HIBERNIAN

HAMPDEN PARK, Crosshill.   Kick-off at 3.30 p.m.
Admission One Shilling.   Ladies Free.
Grand Stands One Shilling extra each person.

Dr John Conway

Celtic Football Club.

J. M. NELIS, HON. PRES.

James Quillan

Celtic F.C., 1889,
Photo taken before a match in London against the Corinthians

19 Dan Malloy

20 Hugh Darroch

21 Joseph F McGroary

James Curtis

22 Celtic Reserve team 1891

John C MacDonald **23**

25 William McKillop

Joseph Shaughnessy **24**

26 John O'Hara

Pat Welsh

DAVID MEIKLEHAM SENIOR

  John H McLaughlin

James McKay

31 Brother Dorotheus

32 Willie Maley

33 Tom Maley

Of course, they could not guarantee a team that would give the same satisfaction as formally - (A voice, "They will do their best") - but, as had been observed, they would do their best, and as long as the club put forth their best efforts, he was sure that among those who took tickets for the season there would be no grumbling should the club go down. (Voices, "No, no" and applause).

A meeting of the club committee was held during the week, and a deputation from the committee of honorary members met them. A desire was expressed on the part of the deputation that some representatives of the honorary member's committee should be added to the club committee. (Hear, hear). The club committee were quite willing that this should be done, which was very satisfactory. (Applause). It was also proposed that, in order to keep down expense, the honorary members committee should continue throughout the season rendering assistance on the occasion of matches. (Hear, hear). He invited the giving in of names for tickets, which cost 5s each, so as to substantially help the club, who in the meantime, he said, were not in the position to say who the players would be.

It was resolved that in future a quarterly meeting of honorary members should be held. Some discussion ensued as to whether a new committee of honorary members should be appointed or not. It was agreed that three of their number, twelve in all, should be added to the club committee, and five names were submitted; but in the end it was resolved that the twelve should meet and select three from among themselves. Tickets were afterwards taken out for the season".

Herein lay the root cause of Hibernian's alarming slump in fortunes. Whilst those fortunes were not helped by the departure of six Hibs players to Celtic, it was the off the field events that were to have such a devastating effect on the pitch at Easter Road. With many of their committee departed, questions were being raised over the quality of the replacements who were thrown in at the deep end in the middle of a crisis with the huge problem of securing a long term lease on Hibs' ground hanging precariously over their head and remaining unsolved.

On the 7th August, the *Scottish Athletic Journal* had this to say about the contrasting fortunes of Celtic and Hibernian;

"We have never yet met a team collected from the four winds that was capable of great things before time had done its work in moulding them together. They have a good example of this in their brethren, the Hibs career.

McLaren going over to the Celts has been a great surprise in Edinburgh, more especially as he has beforehand had many temptations to leave the Hibs. He will never raise himself to such favour or have such friends in Glasgow as he did in Edinburgh. There is nobody to shed tears over Groves. He played good football a couple of years ago, but gave lots of trouble last season and only kept his place in the team, but no more".

OUR FIRST COMPETITIVE MATCH

Our first ever competitive match was played in the Glasgow International Exhibition against Abercorn on the 1st August and we soon realised that an Irish Catholic team in Glasgow wasn't going to be welcomed with open arms.

The *Scottish Umpire* on 7th August stated;

"The Celtic could hardly be well pleased with their reception at the Exhibition on Wednesday. It was anything but gratifying towards the close of the game".

The tournament was part of the Glasgow International Exhibition in Kelvingrove Park to promote Glasgow and its industry and commerce and matches were to be played at Glasgow University's Recreation Grounds in Kelvinside, (roughly where the tennis courts now stand in Kelvingrove Park), during the month of August. Sixteen "lesser" teams were invited as follows; Celtic, Airdrie, Dykebar, St Mirren, Abercorn, Albion Rovers, Clyde, Northern, Morton, Dumbarton Athletic, Partick Thistle, East Stirling, Cowlairs, Glasgow Thistle, Kilbirnie and Kilmarnock.

The draw was given as follows in the Scottish Umpire on 11th July but appears to have some errors;

Celtic v Dykebar
Clyde v Northern
St Mirren v Abercorn
Cowlairs v Glasgow Thistle
Morton v Dumbarton Athletic
Kilbirnie v Kilmarnock
Partick Thistle v East Stirling
Albion Rovers v Airdrie

In actual fact, the matches played and results shown were as follows;

Celtic 1 Abercorn 1
Dykebar 2 St Mirren 4
Dumbarton Thistle 2 Morton 1
Cowlairs 9 Glasgow Thistle 1
Kilbirnie 1 Kilmarnock 0, (replayed after a 1-1 draw),
Airdrie 2 Partick Thistle 5
Albion Rovers 4 East Stirling 3
Clyde beat Northern, (no details of score available)

Note we played Abercorn and not Dykebar, St Mirren played Dykebar and not Abercorn, Partick Thistle played Airdrie and not East Stirling and Albion Rovers played East Stirling and not Airdrie. Apart from that, the draw advertised in the Scottish Umpire was spot on!

Although our 1st round match with Abercorn was drawn 1-1, there is no record of a replay. In actual fact, we offered to play the match on Monday, 13th August, but Abercorn didn't agree and with Dumbarton Athletic awaiting the victors in the next round the following Tuesday, 21st August, Celtic were awarded the tie, after Abercorn scratched, (withdrew). At the same venue on the 21st, the Celts raced into a three goal lead early on against Dumbarton Athletic and won 3-1, although we had to battle to stem a second half comeback, with former Hibs player Tobin kept very busy in the Celtic goals, as we qualified for our first semi final. John Tobin was a spectator at the Clyde v Celtic match just three days earlier, giving notice of his availability, and so he was given his debut for Celtic as we tried to settle on a worthy first choice goalkeeper, a position that was to prove a problem for the first three years of the club's existence.

The full list of quarter final scores was as follows;

Celtic 3 Dumbarton Athletic 1
Clyde 0 Cowlairs 5
Kilbirnie 1 Partick Thistle 2
Albion Rovers 0 St Mirren 4, (replayed after a 1-1 draw)

We then faced Partick Thistle in the semi final on the 29th August and scored the only goal with one of the last kicks of the ball. In the other semi final, Cowlairs also beat St Mirren 1-0 and this set up a final in our first competition entered, on Thursday, 6th September. Interestingly we had intended to pull out of the Thistle match on the Wednesday evening as we had our 1st round match of the Scottish Cup against Shettleston on the Saturday, it was a weak excuse as all four semi finalists were in the same position and thankfully wiser counsel prevailed. It did show however, the importance of the Scottish Cup to the Celtic Committee as it was this match that our new players would prove their commitment to the club for the season and be considered "signed". West Bromwich Albion, in particular, were keen on signing James Kelly and Neil McCallum and so the Celtic Committee hence were very nervous, until both bhoys waved their advances away. West Brom, fresh from their defeat against Renton in the "Champions of the World" match at Hampden just a few months earlier, were also courting two other players from Renton, Andrew Hannah and Bob Kelso. Hannah lasted a very short while in the Midlands, before returning to Renton and then going on to play for both Everton and Liverpool, whilst Kelso also enjoyed a successful career down south with Newcastle, Everton and Preston North End, before returning to play for Dundee.

Our Renton pairing of James Kelly and Neil McCallum, meanwhile, were cool as you like taking in Renton's home match at Tontine Park on the 28th August on a free day, amongst all the transfer speculation. Very likely too, they were sounding out Kelso and Hannah's views on events.

Meanwhile, the Celtic support continued to grow and 10,000 packed into Barrowfield in Bridgeton's Clydeside as the Celts showed once again our incredible drawing power, even this early, as we beat Clyde 5-1. Whilst our recruitment drive was fast and furious for first team players, our reserve team still needed strengthened significantly and this was shown when we lost to Rangers Swifts at Celtic Park on the 4th August by nine goals to one, on the same day our first team won 6-0 at Airdrie. It was no wonder that the "Rangers Swifts" lived up to their name as they were strengthened by the use of five first team players, Nicol in goal, McFarlane in defence, Cameron at half back and Aird and Pringle up front.

O'Kane from Dundee Harp, O'Connor from Vale of Leven Hibs, Pat Coogan from Port Glasgow as well as Pat Lafferty's younger brother were signed as back up but our work wasn't yet done. Pat Lafferty himself wasn't targeted as he was deemed to have only one more season left in him before retiring.

THE CELTS ACCEPTED INTO THE GLASGOW FOOTBALL ASSOCIATION

On Tuesday, 14th August, Celtic were accepted along with the following other teams; Kelvinside Athletic, Cambuslang Hibs, Pollokshaws, Pollokshaws Harp, Rutherglen, Temperance Athletic, Govan Athletic and Maryhill. St Andrews and Westburn were struck off for non payment of subscriptions.

In the 1st round of the Glasgow Cup we were rewarded with a bye, as the odd number in 25 entrants.

A LIMERICK TO McKEOWN

The *Scottish Athletic Journal*, on the 14th August, penned this little poem about Mick McKeown's penchant for elaborate celebrations by way of turning somersaults and standing on his head, which don't always go according to plan;

"There was a young man named McKeown
Who thought he could stand on his crown
He did so once or twice
But, trying it thrice
He flopped on his sit-me-down"

THE PRESS POINT THE FINGER

Celtic's rise was never going to be allowed to happen without raising the ire of sections of the press and "Viator" from the *Glasgow Evening News* was at the front of the queue to cast the first stone on 17th August;

"It so happens that i occasionally am forced to ask ugly questions, which bring pain and concern to those who have the right of answer. The question which I am about to ask may or may not be an ugly one, but its answer - if it be answered at all - will be read with interest. It is this.

Can anyone tell me how the Celtic FC managed to secure players from all parts of Scotland to form their first season's team? I do not insinuate anything; I am merely anxious to find a solution of what is to me a mystery. I am not so credulous as to believe that a man will sever the ties which bind him to the club in which he was bred and go to one a hundred miles away out of pure love for the sport. It may be that the club to which the player migrates resorts to the lawful, but nonetheless sinful, policy of getting the man they want a good job, and by this means secure his services. This getting of jobs is a most pernicious thing and if it were possible to legislate against it, I would lead a crusade at once. It is really a species of professionalism and an instrument for the evasion of the law. A man for whom a club procures a situation knows well enough that he is practically entering into a contract whereby he gives in return for the situation his services as a football player.

He also knows that the moment he fails in his part of the contract he will lose his situation. This, I hold, is nothing more nor less than paying a man for his services as a football player, and is therefore, professionalism pure and simple. It may be argued that to legislate against this evil would interfere with a man's freedom of action, in as much as it would prevent him bettering himself in a business sense. Such an argument will not hold water. The "bettering of himself" is a minor consideration with a player who leaves his home and home ties and perhaps a good enough situation and goes to a distant town, say Glasgow, where he can get a slightly increased wage.

There must be other benefits than those derived from a good situation to make a man do all this. What these benefits are I cannot say, but I know they are most decidedly contrary to the law and the pure spirit of amateurism. It is quite evident that Scotch footballers are not possessed of the natural instance of amateurism and if they can find a way - and this situation business is a grand loop-hole - to evade the law, they will do it. The question is - is it politic for the Association to enforce amateurism, when three fourths of the football playing public are professional by tendency? No doubt the legislation of professionalism would do a good deal of harm in many ways, but we would have the consolation that we were acting honestly and not hoodwinking ourselves that all Scotchmen play for the pure love of the sport alone. It would stifle, too, such weeds as migrate from one club to another, shading their demoralising influence wherever they go. Their true value would be written large upon them and they would be taught to forget the art of shuffling. They would also learn the very useful lesson of knowing their own place and how to keep it.

Until the class of players I speak of is securely muzzled, we will be continually in hot water. If we are to remain amateur let us be thoroughly amateur. As a beginning let the Association put its veto on this pernicious habit of alluring players by offers of good situations. This dissertation is perhaps a little removed from the question I put concerning the Celtic, but its bearing on my query will, no doubt, be apparent. Again I repeat, I insinuate nothing. I assert nothing. I simply want to know what influence, attraction, inducement, or power succeeded in securing the services of the men at present in the Celtic team. Perhaps someone will be good enough to satisfy my curiosity".

The same hack, in an article further down the same page "exclusively revealed";

"A novel football match, I am informed, will take place in the Celtic Football ground early in September when eleven priests of Irish extraction will play a match with an eleven of their Scottish brethren. The Archbishop will be referee. Father McGinnis keeps goal for the Irish and likely Monsignor Munro will do the same for the Scotch. The gate goes to the poor".

In all likelihood, the Celtic Committee had got wind of his attack and decided to pull the wind out of his sails with a spoof story that he fell for hook, line and sinker. Certainly if ever such a charity match was dreamt up, there's no evidence it ever took place.

A week later, the hack was despondent that the Celtic Committee hadn't risen to his bait and he complained;

"Apparently i am not good at drawing the badger, as the query I put in last week's notes concerning Celtic has gone unanswered. I am rather pleased than otherwise at this. It shows that there is a dubiety on the part of the Celts about entering the lists and having a fair tilt for the honour and purity of their name I said last week, and I repeat it here, that if the Celts have gained the services of the men presently in their team by giving them employment they are doing a wrong, and that they are morally although not nominally, a professional club.

I have no desire to harm anyone; I simply wish to see the game kept pure and unsullied. Since last week i have sounded several well known gentlemen who have seats on the SFA Committee, and they all agree with me that providing a player with a business is contrary to the pure spirit of amateurism, of which, i am afraid, there is not much left in Scotland. None of them will move to have the evil redressed. Some of them are afraid that legalisation on the point might hit pretty near home; others fear a re-opening of the vexed question of professionalism.

It is this spirit of timidity in its legislators which has been the bugbear of Scottish football. Why not tackle the evil boldly, without regard of consequences? Surely an honest, open-handed professionalism, if it does send a few clubs which ought really to have existed to the wall, is highly preferable to the present sneaking burlesque of amateurism".

Once again, the Celtic Committee were one step ahead of the baying sections of the press. The only point that really mattered was that Celtic, just like many other clubs, may have been acting "contrary to the pure spirit of amateurism," however they were not acting contrary to any legislation within the laws of the game. Although Viator took his frustrations out on the easy target that was Celtic, his gripe was in fact with the shamateurism that enveloped the Scottish game and which was ignored by those in authority.

OUR FIRST SCOTTISH CUP TIE

Our first full month of the season had saw us compete in a total of nine matches, but only one was at home, the lucrative friendly with Hibs which attracted 5000 to Celtic Park. Our visit to Clyde brought a fantastic crowd of 10,000, of which we would have received a generous return on the gate.

The *Scottish Athletic Journal* on the 21st August opined;

"Celtic are the champions of the East End of Glasgow, they will not be content, however, until they are champions of the world".

The Exhibition Cup gave us three ties and a good run to the final, but what we needed for September was a good cup run in the big cup, the blue riband of Scottish football, the Scottish Cup, to give us the exposure we needed, to get the support behind us and to keep the Treasurer happy.

On 1st September, the day after Jack the Ripper's first victim in London, Celtic Park saw its first ever Scottish Cup tie as nearby Shettleston took the short trip down the road, only to receive a 5-1 battering for their troubles. The fellow East Enders were delighted with the very gentlemanly way in which they were welcomed by the crowd on their first visit to Celtic Park, on a wet and windy day, but that was where their enjoyment ended. By half time the bhoys were two goals to the good and we kept up the pressure in the second half and piled on another three goals to the visitors solitary one.

Another sign of our progress met the fans before they entered the ground, with new pay boxes erected, which were deemed a great improvement as the Celtic Committee had to make alterations to the ground after only five home games.

The day was also momentous in that by playing for Celtic in the Scottish Cup, James Kelly and Neil McCallum of Renton, Mick McKeown, Mick Dunbar, James McLaren, Paddy Gallagher, Willie Groves and Johnny Coleman of Hibs as well as James Coleman from Dumbarton, John

O'Connor from Greenock and Willie Dunning from Johnstone in goals, all committed their future to the Celts, and couldn't play for any other team that season. Hibernian were hurting at the loss of six of their men especially their most experienced man James McLaren, nicknamed "The GOM" at Hibs, short for the "Grand Old Man," after the British Prime Minister William Gladstone, but now renamed "The Ould Giniral" by the Celtic support.

THE PRESS POINT THE FINGER AGAIN

With West Bromwich Albion trying and failing to capture both James Kelly and Neil McCallum on professional terms, there was a huge sigh of relief when both men committed to Celtic for the season, but this reaction wasn't shared by all. Viator from the *Glasgow Evening News* sniped;

"Surely there is an attraction in the Celtic that ordinary men want not of when players not only are so eager to join it, but equally averse to leaving it. It cannot be the considerations of religion that draw such men together, although some would have us believe that such is the case".

An anonymous letter followed rising to the bait from "Black and Gold," before the end of August;

THE CELTIC FOOTBALL CLUB

"With your permission I would like to call attention to a matter which is of the utmost importance to the purity of football in Scotland - I mean the recent formation of the Celtic Football Club in the east end of Glasgow. The able critic who signs himself "Viator" in Friday's News has done an eminent service to the noble game of football in bringing the fierce glare of public opinion to bear upon the doings of this remarkable combination and i only wish to supplement his comments and strictures.

In the first place, the principle of organising a club of which the membership shall be confined to Roman Catholics is not one agreeable to common sense or religious tolerance. If the object were to elevate football and its associations by wedding it to religion we should be silent, but no one can pretend that this will be the effect that will flow from the motley crowd that compose the Celtic team.

But perhaps, the greatest objection to the Celtic club is the manner in which its prominent players have been gathered from all parts of Scotland by the most barefaced and detestable tactics yet practiced by a Scotch club. Was it their Irish patriotism that induced Kelly and McCallum to desert the strongest football combination of modern times, the present champions of the world? And here I should like to put an arithmetical question to the SFA legislators. How is it that by his daily work a player in Dunbartonshire makes say fifteen shillings a week and on being taken under the patronage of a club such as the Celtic makes double that amount? If that workman had not been a clever player would he have got the same wages?

Certainly not; and is, say, his employer so zealous for the success of Catholic football as to be fifteen shillings per week out of pocket for the sake of retaining the services of this able player? I don't think so. The whole business is a disgrace to Scotch football. This system of wholesale poaching is degrading a noble pastime; it makes men divert their best thought and energy from the real business of life to what should only be a sport, a recreation. The sooner our football legislators deal with such clubs as the Celtic, and that sharply, the sooner will Scottish football be cleared of the mists of corruption that at present envelope it".

I am &c.,
Black And Gold.

The following week, on 7th September, Viator recoiled in mock outrage at the letter and implored further correspondents on the subject.

"I am very sorry to observe that my remarks regarding the Celtic FC have raised a discussion into which the religion of the members of the club has been dragged. Such, I need hardly assure my readers, was not my intention. I merely wished to point out that the peculiar circumstances under which the club has been formed and if those who are inclined to plunge deeper into the argument will waive their religious contentions and stick to the true point of the case, they will do me a favour".

How anyone could accuse the hack of bringing religion into the debate, God only knows, (excuse the pun), so just to underline his point, the following quote has of course, nothing to do with religion;

"It cannot be the considerations of religion that draw such men together, although some would have us believe that such is the case".

The hack used the age old tactic employed by some knights of the pencil and in particular the self appointed modern day talk show experts who light the fuse of a debate on a quiet day then retreat safely as naive callers queue up to take the bait. The usual accusations of professionalism followed, with Celtic singled out despite the fact that almost every other club in Scotland were already well versed in the policy of shamatuerism, (players being given inducements), which was alive in the Scottish game before professionalism became legal in 1893. The players Celtic signed from Hibernian had all made their names and were available at the end of the 1887/88 season, why did no other top Glasgow club do as we did and sign them en masse?

Was it their religion that wasn't to some clubs' liking? Rangers had been founded in 1872 but it took them another 19 years to get round to signing a Catholic, Tom Dunbar, ironically from Celtic and he only lasted one season before returning.

Hibs' Pat Lafferty and a certain Neil McCallum from Renton, who went on to score our first ever goal, were a rare breed, Catholics who guested for Rangers, but even then it was only when Rangers were desperate. In Lafferty's case when they were bolstering their team to play in their 1886 English FA Cup run and in McCallum's case in February 1888 in a friendly at Aston Villa when they were in danger of not having enough players to travel south after committing to play.

Celtic's rise to prominence in the Scottish game was described as "mushroom like", thanks to the dynamics of the committee who were well aware of the many Irish clubs in the Scottish game who had floundered due to lack of success. If this Irish club was to make an impact, we had to attract the finest Catholic players of Irish extraction in order to build up a support amongst the dormant Catholic support in the city and surrounding areas.

Before Celtic's foundation, most of our support would have followed Hibernian as they were the major Irish club before our arrival on the scene, but they would have also been spoiled for choice amongst the many smaller Irish clubs in Glasgow and around. However limited travel in those days meant that although many would have had a preference for Hibs, for example, it was only when Celtic were on their doorstep, did the Irish have a team to support in the true sense of the word and to call our own.

OUR FIRST CUP FINAL

Thursday, 6th September 1888, was the date of our first ever cup final, in the Glasgow International Exhibition and the Celts played our usual eleven, whilst Cowlairs were strengthened by the inclusion of two internationals, half back, Allan Stewart from Queens Park and Jamie McCall, the ace Renton forward. After Cowlairs opened the scoring from a free kick which came from a perfectly good challenge on the edge of the box from Jimmy McLaren, the Celts' heads went down in front of the hostile crowd and we lost another goal before the end of the match which lasted two halves of 35 minutes. Despite competing in an even match throughout, where we were very unfortunate to lose the first goal, our first cup final was lost by two goals to nil.

It was a disappointment on the pitch, but off it the lasting memory was one of the players being spat on and treated disgracefully by a large section of those present as they made their way out of the pavillion to play a team who had been unfairly bolstered in order to beat the new Irish team - at any cost. Right from our very first season it was clear there was a large section of Scottish society who did not welcome us and who would go to extreme lengths to stop us succeeding.

At the after match function, Celtic President John Glass stood up to the bigots by referring to the unsportsmanlike reception the new club received in a famous speech;

"Let them scoff and jeer. Celtic will yet win to our proper position by our own merits and those who scoff today will one day have to applaud".

WHO INTRODUCED THE RELIGIOUS ELEMENT?

The *Scottish Umpire* on 11th September, 1888 took umbrage at a writer in the Sporting Chronicle who described Celtic thus;

"The Glasgow Irish Roman Catholic combination recently created under the designation of the Celtic club met Glasgow Cowlairs in the final tie for the Exhibition Cup in the Exhibition Grounds, Glasgow last night before 6000 spectators".

"Why introduce the religious element? It is very bad taste," asked the Umpire.

The religious element had been introduced into the Scottish game long before the birth of Celtic, the problem was that it was ignored, until it was used as a stick to beat Irish teams. Rangers being the classic example having yet to sign a Catholic player since their inception in 1872.

On the same day, a contributor to the *Scottish Athletic Journal* asked the question;

"Why are the Celts so unpopular is a parallel to the great question "Is marriage a failure," and the shorthand battle. Many have undertaken to answer it on both sides. Still the answer seems a simple one".

A simple one indeed, but it was one of the biggest struggles Celtic faced at our inception, and often to this day; anti Celtic feeling.

LINGERING SUSPICIONS REMAIN FROM SECTIONS OF THE PRESS

Lingering suspicions still hung over the club, with much of it coming from those who simply couldn't handle the early success of the new Irish combination in a fiercely anti Catholic city.

The *Scottish Umpire* on 11th September, faced the issue head on;

"Much has been asserted of late and more insinuated, regarding the mala fide of the Celtic club which, like a mushroom, has risen to a front position amongst the leading clubs of the country in an incredibly short space of time. Now we are not in a position to affirm or deny these charges and innuendoes, but we are not so un-English as to cry down a club until the accusers have justified their accusations. Let those who so loudly assert the professionalism of the east end organisation come boldly forward like men and prove their assertions, or be forever silent.

It is mean and contemptible to persistently traduce the Celts and yet shirk the responsibility of producing evidence. The Celts may be all they are accused of, but we at any rate are bound to regard them as innocent until they are proved guilty. If they are guilty and that fact is made abundantly evident after a fair trial, then we will be the first to launch the denunciations of indignant public opinion against them until they renounce or amend their ways. In the meantime, however, neither the charge, nor the evidence is forthcoming in the proper quarter and in consequence, we are entitled to infer that neither can be tabled. We therefore challenge those who have anything to say vitally affecting the status of the Celts to say it, or cease their envious carping. We venture to think that with some, the Celts' only fault is being strong".

It was a critical moment for the embryonic Celtic, but as it turned out the silence from our critics was golden. Just a week previous, in the same newspaper, the name of Celtic was brought into the debate regarding the break up of the famous Renton team;

"It has recently become common to sneer at the Celtic and to accuse it indirectly of a variety of mal-practices, but the fact is, so many of our clubs are more or less guilty of similar conduct that very few of them indeed are in a position to throw stones".

Never a truer word has been written.

THE CELTS GO MARCHING ON IN THE SCOTTISH CUP

After our victory over Shettleston in the 1st round of the Scottish Cup, the next round brought Cowlairs to Celtic Park and the dark green jerseys we wore that day brought us luck as the bhoys got revenge for the Exhibition Cup defeat. The Springburn team were thrashed 8-0 with four goals in each half, in a match where it was said that the Celtic way of playing fast, flowing, attacking football was invented. Neil McCallum opened the scoring after 20 minutes, *"and a shout arose sufficient to wake the sleepers in the adjacent cemetery,"* before Mick Dunbar headed the second and Groves scored the third with a thunderous shot.

With the nature of our Exhibition Final defeat at the hands of Cowlairs still on our minds, the Celts kept up the pressure right until the closing minutes on a day when it was accepted that no defence in the country could live with our attacking play.

The *Glasgow Observer* was suitably impressed by the match and it opined;

"The Celtic Football Club have by one decisive battle placed themselves in the very forefront of first class clubs. Their fixture last Saturday was the cause of unbounded gratification".

The *Scottish Athletic Journal* added;

"Revenge is sweet, but when it is got by legitimate means it must be all the sweeter. The Celtic with their own team wiped off the Exhibition defeat in a handsome manner by 8 goals to 0."

Take note of the Cowlairs keeper, Tom Duff, whose brother was also a goalkeeper. The result, it was said would have been more crushing if not for Duff in goals, who never faulted, but little over three years later he was to feature in another 8-0 defeat at Celtic Park, this time in his last game FOR Celtic, when it was said that his performance was that bad that if he had played in goal for the opponents, Dumbarton, the result would have been reversed!

But more of that later.

A favourable home draw followed with the visit of Albion Rovers to Celtic Park on 13th October, but the Coatbridge team shocked everyone by taking a first half lead. Thankfully it brought the Celts to their senses and we quickly hit back with two goals before half time. The match was turned in our favour, but we couldn't break down the stubborn Rovers defence who were playing out of their skin. Finally, late on, just as the visitors were starting to contemplate an equaliser, the bhoys put the game to bed with two more counters before the final whistle went to finish the scoring at 4-1.

Our run of four consecutive home ties had to come to an end sooner or later and so it did in the last 32 when we were drawn to play Saint Bernard's at their ground in Powderhall, Edinburgh. Despite the wet conditions, a large crowd was in attendance, as there always was when we played in the capital. Large adverts had been placed by the Celtic Committee for our first ever "fitba specials", the special trains leaving Bellgrove at 13.30 and Parkhead at 13.35, and returning from Edinburgh Waverley at 19.30, with return tickets costing 2s, 6d, Tickets were available between 8pm and 9pm on Tuesday to Friday from the "usual outlets" at St Mary's League of the Cross Hall, 67 East Rose Street, St Michael's, Great Eastern Road and Sacred Heart, Howard Street, or from any member of the Celtic Committee.

Two first half goals by Neil McCallum and Tom Maley gave us one foot in the last 16 and the Celts' superior passing game was the story of the second half as Willie Groves notched two more goals for the bhoys with the Saints notching a goal in between. That was to be the last of the excitement for one day with the final score; Saint Bernards 1 Celtic 4.

The *Scottish Referee* on 5th November started its match report well with its opening line; *"Bould by name and bould by nature are my friends the Celts,"* but by the end of the article, the writer became the first to describe the Celtic support as "Mickies", a slang name for Irishmen, in his match report;

"Grand old man Jimmy McLaren played one of his real old Hibernian games on Saturday, and didn't the "Mickies" praise him highly for it too?"

The phrase was of course taken up eagerly by Rangers supporters many years later, many of whom delighted in referring to us as mickies, fenians, bead rattlers or papists, or even all four, depending on the circumstance.

We awaited the draw for the last 16 with bated breath.

Everywhere we played, we were attracting huge crowds by the standards of the day and it was soon being mentioned that if things continued, Celtic would soon be the richest club in Scotland, having taken £300 at the gate for the match against Renton, estimates of up to £400 for the Glasgow Cup tie against Queens Park and another £300 against Clyde in the Scottish Cup, albeit the gate for cup matches were halved between the two teams. Over a thousand pounds in takings within a few weeks was business not heard of, even down south where the biggest clubs of the day were Preston, Aston Villa, Blackburn Rovers, Wolves, Everton and West Bromwich Albion.

OUR FIRST VISIT TO IBROX AS THE GLASGOW CUP BECKONS

Our first ever Glasgow Cup tie was played on the 6th October, as Shettleston again took the short trip down the road to Celtic Park, just five weeks after their 5-1 mauling in the first round of the Scottish Cup. This was the last draw Shettleston wanted and this time they fared no better, in fact it was much worse, as they departed the scene nursing their wounds after an 11-2 seeing to. It could have been so much worse still as the half time score stood at 8-0, (a record), with abacuses at the ready to calculate the final count. As the reporters sharpened their pencils for the expected onslaught, the bhoys eased up not wishing to rub their neighbours noses into it too much and the scoring in the second half was a much more modest three goals to Celtic and two for Shettleston.

We then made our first visit to the original Ibrox Park, which stood adjacent to where the current ground stands today, for our quarter final tie of the Glasgow Cup. It is often claimed that the first ever Celtic v Rangers game on 28th May 1888 featured a weakened Rangers side, missing half their players. Therefore the date of 27th October 1888 in the 3rd round of the Glasgow Cup, deserves significant recognition in the story of the early Celtic, as a barometer of the merits of the two teams.

The Celts left no room for doubt as we recorded an emphatic 6-1 win, our biggest victory at Ibrox to this day and the Celtic support, who were in the majority of the 4000 crowd, were described thus;

"With all anxiety gone, the Celtic followers gave vent to their hitherto restrained wit and didn't they make it hot for the home supporters?"

The Celts kicked off playing into a strong wind and it was the home team who scored the first goal after 20 minutes. Straight from the kick off we levelled through Willie Groves and Mick Dunbar put us ahead shortly after. The bhoys started to turn on the style but half time arrived with no more goals scored. Playing with the wind in the second half, the Celts turned the screw and first John Coleman, then Tom Maley with a header and then

Mick Dunbar made it three goals for the Celts in five minutes as the score stood at 5-1. We weren't finished yet and Neil McCallum, after some very good work by James Kelly, made the final score; Rangers 1 Celtic 6. A record at Ibrox to this day.

The *Scottish Athletic Journal* summed it up on the 30th October;

"Rangers were beaten by the Celts on Saturday in the Glasgow ties in the easiest manner possible".

Both the Glasgow Cup and the Scottish Cup were reaching a climax with two matches in seven days at Celtic Park which were our first huge tests. In the Scottish Cup we were rewarded with a very attractive draw at home to Clyde in the last 16 on Saturday, 24th November, but it was in the Glasgow Cup that the plum draw was made that was to propel the meteoric rise of the club into another orbit. A home draw with Queens Park a week before, on Saturday 17th November, 1888 was the only show in town and brought together the Establishment Team, who had enjoyed unrivalled success since their foundation in 1867, with the new kids on the block, who were taking the game by storm.

OUR FIRST VISIT TO EASTER ROAD

From the *Scottish Umpire* on 23rd October;

"The Celtic made their bow to the Edinburgh public on Saturday. They were hissed and groaned at, mobbed at one stage, and on the whole "warmly" received. A good deal of feeling was expected. Everybody was quiet until the game started and then the fiery tongues began. The Easter Road spectators were in form, if the players were not.

Abuse - that is a mild word - was showered on the Celtic players. We will descend to the vulgar, and quote one or two remarks. The Celtic were dubbed everything objectionable-from "mouchers" to professionals. Let us go over the team. Of Dunning nothing was known. McKeown was styled "three bunches a penny;" McLachlan, "bow-wow;" on Gallacher a vocabulary was extended; Kelly and McCallum were reminded of Renton; Groves was called "a spoilt snob," etc. We are tired of more.

The injunctions to the home team were numberless. A sweep or coal heaver frequently found his way on the field. When the crowd broke in he made his way to Gallacher; when the crowd went out Gallacher's white shirt resembled the colour of mother earth. The Celtic umpire wanted to give up the game with thirty minutes to go. It was given up before time, at any rate. It must be said that the crowd were most bitter against the players the Hibs had "brought out" themselves; all the adjectives applied against the Irish Secretary were trotted out.

There was no serious injury, however after all, and the Celtic, in all fairness, won by 3 goals. They are as far as can be seen a fine combination. What they could do was not apparent at Easter Road".

In a match that had been agreed since the start of the season when Celtic published our fixture list, we travelled to Easter Road to take on Hibs on the 20th October in a friendly match that was never going to fit that bill. The former Hibs captain, Jimmy McLaren wisely missed the trip as well as Tom Maley and they were replaced by Willie Maley and John O'Connor in a Celtic team that contained five players who had just left Hibs; Willie Dunning, James McLaughlin, Mick McKeown, Paddy Gallagher, James Kelly, Willie Maley, Neil McCallum, Johnny Coleman, Willie Groves, Mick Dunbar and John O'Connor.

Mick McKeown, Paddy Gallagher, Johnny Coleman, Willie Groves and Mick Dunbar were the former Hibs players and the Hibs support made their feelings well known as they gave each one a level of abuse that they wouldn't forget in a long time.

The Celts rose above it and let our feet do the talking in a hard fought 3-0 win, with all three goals coming in the first half, ironically from former Hibs players Johnny Coleman and Mick Dunbar. This tormented the Hibs support even more and the bad atmosphere threatened to boil over when hundreds of fans spilled onto the pitch when Hibs forced two corners in a row in the second half.

The referee, Mr Muirhead, made a mad dash for the safety of the pavillion, where he had to be cajoled to return, as the Celtic players stood their ground and remained on the pitch intent on playing on. To their credit, the Hibs players helped to protect the Celtic players from the hordes and fortunately the pitch was cleared and the match restarted.

The *Scottish Umpire* also stated;

"It must be said that the crowd were most bitter against the players the Hibs had brought out themselves".

With both sets of players getting dog's abuse from the Hibs support and with the match finished as a contest by half time, the cowering referee finally put a stop to the poisonous atmosphere in the "friendly," with ten minutes left on the clock.

HIBS IN TURMOIL AS SECRETARY STANDS DOWN

Just a month later there was more turmoil over at Hibs, when as another fall out from Michael Flannigan's resignation as the head of the St Patrick's branch of the CYMS, John McFadden stood down from his role as Secretary of Hibernian, to replace him. Hibs fans were stunned by the news, but thankful at the same time that McFadden wasn't following half their team to Celtic Park. Instead he had accepted the position of Secretary of the Catholic Young Men's Society in Edinburgh, as that organisation tried to weather the storm, but with serious repercussions for its "sporting wing".

Whilst Hibs were imploding, the Celts were going from strength to strength with Fred Dewhurst of Preston North End, the highest profile Catholic player down south linked, unsuccessfully, with a move to Celtic and a post as Headmaster at a school in Glasgow. We were of course still an amateur club at this time, like every other club in Scotland although professionalism in England had been introduced in 1885. How then could an amateur club entice a professional player to give up his wages and play for free?

Shamatuerism was the well used phrase of the day to explain the well used process of "skimming off" the size of an attendance in order to give inducements to players, a tactic used by the majority. Celtic were fortunate too in that we had some generous supporters, and one practice included the lease of a public house to a big name signing to ease his passage to Celtic Park.

At the home match against Renton it was reported in the *Scottish Sport* that a supporter quipped;

"No wonder the Celtic team are good players, they are all professionals," to which a deep hibernian voice from behind replied, "They are not sur, they are all Roman Catholics!"

OUR FIRST CHANGE OF STRIP

The 10th of November 1888 saw a historical day at Celtic Park, not only because the friendly match between Celtic and Renton was watched by our biggest ever crowd to date, around 10,000, but it was the day the green and white stripes replaced the white top with the green collar and the Celtic Cross badge on it as the Celts showed off our new strip for the first time. Jimmy McLaren headed the ball home from a Tom Maley corner in the second half to score the only goal of the game and the Celts would go on to wear the green and white stripes for the next fifteen years, until 29th August 1903 when they were replaced by the green and white hoops, which have become synonymous with Celtic the world over ever since.

Celtic had trialled a dark green jersey in the home match with Cowlairs in the 2nd round of the Scottish Cup on the 22nd of September but it may have been considered to be too similar to the dark green of Hibs and it was the green and white stripes that were to be synonymous with the early Celtic teams. Between May 1888 and January 1889, we had played in four different strips, firstly the original white top with green collar and Celtic Cross, secondly a dark green jersey, thirdly the green and white stripes, then finally a pea green top and white shorts. Both the dark green and the pea green jerseys were used as alternative strips if there was a clash.

From the *Scottish Sport* on the 13th of November 1888;

"Celtic v Renton

Over 10,000 at Celtic Park. A more enthusiastic and exciting match has not hitherto been witnessed at Parkhead and when the brave Celts returned with another victory to register, their fans cheered lustily. The team again appeared in new uniforms, this time green and white striped. Lucky to have such patrons".

A YEAR ON FROM THE CLUB'S FORMAL CONSTITUTION

From the *Scottish Sport* on 20th November 1888;

"It is worthy of note that it is just a year ago this week since the first meeting connected with the inception and formation of the now formidable Celtic F.C. was held. Only a year, and yet in that short time what a substantial fabric has been erected; what a reputation reared. The success which has attended the efforts of the founders of the club has been most marked, and are the blossoms which, we may fairly presume, indicate still riper fruit yet to come.

They have a strong team, which may be expected to become yet more formidable as success is added to success; all that is wanted to consummate a great triumph is wise and judicious management, and the pursuance of a high-principled policy. There is only one way to become at once popular and powerful, and that is by acting zealously and judiciously, and always on the square. See to it, gentlemen of the Celtic".

OUR FIRST CUP "SHOCK" AT CELTIC PARK

For the much awaited Glasgow Cup semi final tie with Queens Park on 17th November, a match in which we were considered favourites, the Committee raised the entry price into the Pavillion stand to a shilling. Normally the entrance fee was sixpence to the ground and an extra sixpence would be taken at the grandstand, once inside the ground to transfer to an uncovered seat.

Much of the season in the very early days before the introduction of the League in 1890, was taken up by friendlies, so the Scottish Cup and the Glasgow Cup matches were the highlight of the season. The hype around the match increased as the game neared and the media, as usual, played their part. This was the game of the infamous "Scot v Celt" article in the Scottish Sport, setting the scene thus;

"Hundreds who went to Parkhead attracted quite as much by the fact that an international battle was to be fought, as that the issue was a semi final tie for the Glasgow Cup. The clubs engaged were the premier club of Scotland, the famous, the redoubtable, and popular Queens Park, and the best combination of Irishmen that has ever been raised in Scotland, knitted by an unquenchable desire to do honour to the Emerald Isle, from which they spring".

The Celtic club has attracted to our football enclosures a class of spectators who hitherto ignored the game and found no excitement, because they had nothing to interest them. It is strange that in Glasgow, where such a large population of Irish is centred, many hundreds of whom pursued the favourite winter pastime in the ranks of other clubs - a club on similar lines to that which flourished in Edinburgh under the name of the Hibernians - was not organised hitherto.

The founders of the Celtic have done their work well, though they may not have shown veneration for vested interests when collecting players of Irish extraction from other clubs. The main object appears to have been to get together a strong team and leave time to do the rest. Short as the season has been during which the Celts have stood before the public, they have made a reputation and enjoy a respect which any club might envy and while they have secured many friends, their very success has also brought them enemies.

They can afford now to ignore the spiteful remarks made by ignorant and prejudiced scribes when they first started, writers who could not understand that football players, usually so greedy of gain, could entertain such a lofty sense of patriotism as to sever old associations in the desire to do honour to the Old Country. The Celts have lived down all that and now have the satisfaction of knowing that their merit and ability and as a playing combination are acknowledged on every hand and must feel proud that they hold a position in the football world second to none.

The Scot is no less patriotic than the Celt and knowing a certain political significance was attached to this great cup tie, the supporters of the Queens Park were drawn from a much larger constituency than usual. It would not be wrong to say the majority of the crowd, however, were Irish and no one could for a moment doubt their enthusiasm. That spoke for itself."

The *Scottish Sport* also had a strange comparison between the players and the inhabitants of the graveyard over the boundary wall;

"The quick and the dead" - the thousands of excited footballers on Celtic Park and the thousands who sleep their last sleep over the boundary wall in Janefield Cemetery".

As it turned out, thunderstorms and heavy rain spoiled the game as a spectacle and limited the number who attended a ground with no shelter from the elements. Still 8,000 attended, but the heavy state of the quagmire pitch didn't suit Celtic's quick passing game, described as "scientific," and thanks to an early goal for the visitors from a long shot which slipped inside the post, we went in at half time a goal down with the referee feeling the wrath of the Celtic support, desperate for our first major cup final, as he was booed relentlessly. The Celts later claimed we had received the worst of the refereeing decisions.

Worse was to follow when Queens Park added a second goal and Johnny Coleman was forced to stay on the pitch despite a heavy injury. In those days substitutions had not been introduced and it was common practice to leave an injured player on the pitch as no more than nuisance value to the opposition. Giving a clear indication of our rise to prominence in the Scottish game in just six months, it says it all that the result was seen as a shock.

Although defeated, two of the fabrics of our DNA were evident as we fought right to the end and continued to play our attractive fast passing game throughout. Unfortunately, another fabric of the DNA of the Scottish game was evident, as the *Scottish Sport* couldn't hide their glee at Celtic's defeat;

"Joy, unspeakable joy, was apparent on the physiognomies of the Hampden Park habitués so long as evening held out on the last day of the byegone week. There was evidence abroad, too, that a very large constituency found gratification in the overthrow of the Celts, rather than in the ascendancy for a time of the black-and-white brigade"

OUR FIRST CROWD TROUBLE

One negative, that is not part of the club's DNA, was the reaction at the end of the game when Celtic Park witnessed its first scenes of crowd trouble. One of the umpires, Daniel Gillies, who was the Convenor of the Grounds Committee, a sub committee of the Rangers Committee, was on his way off the pitch at the end of the game when he was set upon by a couple of ruffians at the entrance to the Pavillion, who also lashed out and kicked the Queens Park defender, Smellie, (real name).

It was shameful behaviour and something that the Celtic Committee could not tolerate. There had been no police presence inside the ground, but there were plenty of priests as the press kept up their fixation;

"The clergy give not only their support but their countenance to the Celtic. The cloth was conspicuous on the grand stand and within the pavillion enclosure."

Men of the cloth were allowed free entry into Celtic Park right from our inception in a popular tradition that lasted right up until the Revolution of 1994 when they were happy to change with tradition to assist the club through our next stage of rebirth.

Newspapers of the day called for a police presence inside football grounds in the aftermath of the original "shame game". Unlike the "shame game," almost 125 years later when three Rangers players were sent off at Celtic Park as they lost the plot and reverted to type with the outcome that Neil Lennon received a three match ban, followed by no less than a government inquiry, Celtic, in the actions of a small section of our support on this occasion, were guilty and the press weren't going to let us forget it.

The *Scottish Sport* on November 23rd led the condemnation;

"The Celtic Club, like many of its neighbours, is not blessed with a quiet and unassuming following. In fact from what we saw and heard on Saturday last, we should say that at least a section of its support are far more ardent than discreet. They have, in a sense, the welfare of the club at heart, but they take about the very worst means possible to show their devotion. Instead of their support of the Celtic standard steadying it, it is only calculated to shiver it in contempt. The assistance of their throats may act as a spur and an incentive to the players, although we doubt it, but assuredly the assistance of their violent hands is a serious hindrance".

CONTROVERSY IN THE SCOTTISH CUP

The following week Clyde visited Celtic Park to play in the 5th round of the Scottish Cup and with a police presence inside the ground, there was an even bigger shock than the previous week as Clyde came away with a 1-0 victory thanks to a thirty yarder just before half time which left John Tobin in the Celtic goal, another former Hibs player, with no chance.

The match was played in similar conditions as the Queens Park match with heavy rain and thunderstorms resulting in the ground being heavy with the Celts failing to adapt to the conditions, Near the end of the match in front of the large crowd of 7000, there was a small pitch invasion, the first one seen at Celtic Park during a game, but it was more out of over enthusiasm than an attempt to halt the match and the police presence on duty quickly had the game restarted. The Clyde keeper, Chalmers was the busiest man on the pitch and no matter how much we tried, we couldn't get the ball past him as Clyde held on for another cup shock.

The Scottish Referee on 26th November summed up the mood of the Celtic support;

"Be me sowl", said a burly Irishman at Celtic Park on Saturday, *"The Clyde might as well have built a brick wall in their goal as put Chalmers there."*

Both teams enjoyed the after match dinner at Pinkerton's restaurant on Main Street, Bridgeton where the make up of the Celtic party, was remarked again upon in the Scottish Referee on November 26th; "Several of the clergy were present". However the clouds hung over Celtic Park for the first time and there was a fear that with two home cup defeats in the two main competitions in the one week, our bubble had finally burst.

OUR FIRST PROTEST

Far from the bubble bursting, the Celtic Committee again made its mark on the Scottish game, using the common practice of protesting the Clyde result on the basis that the pitch was unplayable due to heavy rain and that the game had been finished in darkness due to the late start caused by three Clyde players who had to remove illegal bars from their boots.

The facts showed that the match started at 14.57 and ended at 16.33, ninety six minutes later. In the referee's opinion the last 8 minutes were played in darkness. The timings given for the length of the game are interesting as it alludes to only 6 minutes being taken up for injury time and indeed half time.

Celtic won the protest by 7 votes to 4, with 9 abstaining and the match was ordered to be replayed at Celtic Park. In a very interesting case, the enquiry revealed the following in the *Scottish Sport*;

"Clyde stated; *The ground was gone over by a member of the Clyde Committee, accompanied by several Celtic Committee men, some time before the gates were opened to the general public and was found to be quite playable.*

Celtic responded; *No member of the Celtic Committee and, so far as we know, no member of the Clyde Committee went over the ground before the gates were opened. About fifteen minutes before the game was started, however, the President of the Clyde, accompanied by the President of the Celtic, went over the ground and the result of their deliberation was that both asked the referee to declare the tie off.*

Clyde stated; *The referee found no fault with the ground and both captains agreed to play the cup tie.*

Celtic responded; *The referee was not asked his opinion of the ground and did not express any. The Celts captain all along strenuously objected to a cup tie being played, but had to submit, of course, when the captain of the Clyde insisted.*

Clyde stated; *Tom Maley of the Celtic was the last player to go on to the field previous to the kick off, so that any delay that took place was occasioned by him.*

Celtic responded; *As the Celtic started play with eleven men and Clyde ten, Tom Maley could not possibly have been the last player to go on the field. Moreover, the Celtic intimated at 14.45 that we would start then with ten men.*

Clyde stated; *No protests of any kind were intimated, either on the field or in the club house before or after the match.*

Celtic responded; *The protest was intimated to the referee in the pavillion after the match and to the captain of the Clyde after the supper.*

Clyde stated; *In his speech at the tea after the match, the referee declared that the Clyde had won the tie "fairly and squarely."*

Celtic responded; *The referee said the Clyde had "won the game", not the tie. Mister Young forgets to mention that he also said, "I cannot say the better team won."*

Clyde stated; *The only intimation we got that Celtic intended to protest on the plea of darkness was from the secretary of the SFA on the Wednesday night, following the match. This is against Rule 17, Cup Competition Rules, which states that protests and appeals must be formally intimated to the referee and the competing club at the time the violation takes place.*

Celtic responded; *Both grounds of protest were fully intimated to the Clyde. The part of Rule 17 which Mister Young quotes has no bearing on the case. It falls under the second part of Rule 17, which says "any objection relative to ground etc must be lodged with the referee on the day of the match."*

Clyde were incensed and appealed the decision, losing by only one vote, 8 votes to 7, with 2 abstentions. They made their displeasure known in the replayed match at Celtic Park, not by beating the Celts on the pitch, but by refusing to use the Celtic Park changing rooms and instead they turned up already stripped for action. Unfortunately for them, Celtic Park was jam packed in the unusually autumnal weather that contrasted with the thunderstorms at the previous match and significantly it reflected the good fortune that had returned to Celtic Park as the Celts strolled out easy 9-2 victors in our second biggest win to date.

Although the final score is convincing to say the least, the first half was anything but, with headers from Tom Maley and Jimmy McLaren in the first ten minutes getting the Celts off to a flyer only to see Clyde respond with two goals in a couple of minutes midway through the first half, before Tom Maley regained our lead a few minutes later. Maley added another for his hat trick at the start of the second spell and shortly after, Clyde were reduced to ten men, with Hart forced to retire injured.

At 4-2 down and reduced to 10 men, Clyde threw in the towel and Neil McCallum headed a fifth before Willie Groves scored a sixth, the best goal of the match, as we started to get things totally our own way. Groves scored again to make it seven and two more goals were added in the final ten minutes, but by this time the reporters' pencils were blunt.

Chalmers in the Clyde goal, far from having a nightmare, was actually Clyde's best player and but for him, the scoring could have been well into double figures as the Celts passing game surpassed even our own expectations.

CELTIC AND CHARITY

From the **Scottish Referee** on the 26th November;

"It is not generally known that the object which the promoters of the Celtic F.C. had in view when they organised the club was "charity." This is a laudable fact, and one worthy of all credence. In regard to this a few may be rather sceptical, after the manner in which the new combination was brought together. However, one has only to go and see for himself that the priesthood have as much say in the matter as anyone else. They take a hearty interest in the welfare of the club. The new enterprise has had enough and to spare of outward opposition but that by good and judicious management they may outlive such and become as charitable as they are prosperous".

BROTHER WALFRID IN THE COMMUNITY

As well as his involvement with Celtic, the Father Noonan Memorial Committee and his day jobs as Brother Superior of the Marist Order in Glasgow, and Headmaster at Sacred Heart school, Brother Walfrid accompanied the children of the school, on Friday, 12th October 1888, along with the children of all the east end parishes on a special day out, driven in brakes to the Exhibition at Kelvingrove. The children from Sacred Heart were under the supervision of both Father O'Connell from the parish and Brother Walfrid and a great day was had by all.

In mid November 1888, Brother Walfrid commenced that winter season's dinners to the poor in the parish of Sacred Heart and opened a subscription list towards its funding, which would be thankfully received by himself and Father Hughes. The difference now, thanks to the commitment given at Celtic's inception and written in our first constitution, was that Brother Walfrid could rely on our support.

CELTIC AND PROGRESS

From the *Scottish Referee* on the 3rd December 1888;

"THE CELTIC is a club which, by reason of its peculiar constitution and position, has had its brief but brilliant history traced again and again, and I need not therefore go into details. The club had a phoenix-like origin - it arose from the fading ashes of many another organisation, but even though its talent is of the purest stuff, it has not been without its reverses. These are of recent date, and need not be mentioned. The men of the Celtic team know the value of science and practise it persistently.

Science, however, has its drawbacks. Bad weather and soft grounds dont agree with it, and this the Celts are fully aware of, I am sure. Having successfully crossed the Clyde - and the crossing operation was not pleasant to the Clyde - the Celts mean to have a say in the final, and I have no doubt they will, as they are a playing combination I have a very healthy respect for".

The above article is very interesting as it gives a very early view on our progress, little more than six months after our first match. It covers our charitable status, the attention we have attracted, how we "rose from the ashes" of the many failed Irish teams before us and our new "scientific" style of play, the quick passing game that overtook many of the long ball experts of the day. The fact too that our chances of reaching the Scottish Cup final in our first season was being discussed openly underlined our "phoenix like origin".

ANOTHER SCOTTISH CUP SHOCK - NEARLY!

The bhoys were back in the Scottish Cup and in the next round we were drawn away to East Stirling, a match which almost resulted in a shock result that would still be spoken of to this day.

As the *Scottish Sport* wrote on the 18th December;

"The greatest event ever chronicled in the football history of the old town of Falkirk".

"If ever the new Irish combination had a narrow squeak, it was certainly on Saturday."

With only two and a half minutes to go, the Celts were a goal down and attacking the East Stirling goal relentlessly as if our lives depended on it. Finally, the sighs of relief could be heard back at Celtic Park as Neil McCallum notched the equaliser in the 88th minute before grabbing the winner a minute later as the home team's defence crumbled.

We had marked our arrival on to the scene with entry to the semi final stages of the Scottish club, the blue riband trophy and the rest of Scottish football had to sit up and take notice of the Irish team from the east end of Glasgow, a club like no other, who in our very first constitution pledged to give a £5 monthly donation to the Saint Vincent De Paul Society in order to fund the maintenance of the Poor Children's Dinner Tables in the parishes of St Mary's, Sacred Heart and St Michaels. This was no lame gesture, it was written in stone in our first constitution.

Alongside Celtic in the semi final draw stood Dumbarton, (winners of the Scottish Cup in 1883), Renton, (winners in 1885) and Third Lanark, who had yet to make the final despite some close encounters. The draw wasn't kind and we faced a trip in the new year to "Fatal Boghead" as it was then known, to play Dumbarton, who stood in our way of a place in the final.

OUR FIRST TEAM PHOTOGRAPH

December 22nd 1888 is another historical day in the history of Celtic that seemed at the time to be no more than a friendly visit to Alexandria, by train to Renton, to take on the local Vale of Leven team and beating them 2-1, with a performance that delighted everyone who attended. However what was significant about this day was that both teams were photographed before the match in front of the newly built Millburn Park ground's pavillion. The ground still stands to this day, as does the pavillion, although its appearance has changed over the years.

The original team photograph of the Celtic players in the white jerseys and green collars with the Celtic Cross on the right breast taken that day is the only one that has survived the test of time. The iconic image is not of the very first Celtic team on 28th May 1888 as many think, it's the team who beat Vale of Leven at their ground on 22nd December, 1888. In fact the strip was seldom, if ever used by December as the green and white stripes replaced it a month previously.

It's noted that at the Vale of Leven match the Celtic team changed their jerseys at half time, which is unusual. It doesn't stipulate why we did this or if we changed into the new striped jersey, very possibly only wearing the original classic top for the photograph. Vale of Leven wore all blue so there was no clash of colours with either Celtic strip and no report of bad weather which may have forced the players to change their jerseys. Whatever the reason, whoever had to carry the hamper with the team strips on the train got his money's worth that day!

The fact that the original classic photograph was taken at Vale of Leven's ground in Alexandria on the date given above is confirmed by Tom Maley in an article in the *Glasgow Observer* on Saturday, 29th April 1911;

"I have vivid recollection of the Celts' first visit to Millburn Park. Many of the older school will no doubt remember, aye even have in their possession, the "first proof" of the first Celts. It was on the pavillion front at Millburn that the Celts were first "tuk." We had a grand game that afternoon, a single goal victory being ours after a hard, fast and free going match. The Leven lads were then a power, but since when, alas and alack, the old order has changed".

FISTICUFFS AT IBROX ENDS UP IN COURT APPEARANCE

Many of us still remember the events on the 17th October 1987, when Frank McAvennie, Chris Woods and Terry Butcher were sent off in Celtic's turbulent trip to Ibrox, and Graeme Roberts joined the trio in the courts charged with conduct likely to provoke a breach of the peace. Not many will be familiar with the events in the same ground on the 22nd December 1888, almost a century earlier when Abercorn played Third Lanark and a player from each side "were asked to leave the field," after firstly a boot was swung then an exchange of fisticuffs was partaken of.

There's nothing too unusual about that in the grand scheme of things, but what was different was the charge of breach of the peace which followed against a player from each side, Robert Buchanan of Abercorn and Alexander Lochhead of Third Lanark. Unusual too, was Lochhead's defence that the man who started the fight should be punished and that the Third Lanark player only "vindicated his position as a man and struck back".

In reply to theories as to what could have been the consequence of crowd trouble in reaction to the fisticuffs, the Abercorn man's brief correctly insisted that the men should not be punished based on what might have happened but on what did occur. Both men or neither should be punished, but in his opinion the court's time had been wasted as the men had already been punished enough by the football authorities after being suspended for a month. The judge obliged in punishing both men, Buchanan who started the brawl, was fined two guineas with the option of 30 days imprisonment and Lochhead, who retaliated, was fined 30s, with the option of 20 days in the slammer.

A century later, Woods and Butcher were let off lightly after being found guilty. Woods was given a fine of £500 and Butcher was fined £250. There was no option of serving up to a month in Barlinnie, but it's highly unlikely this would have been considered the favourable option in any circumstance.

THE FIRST ENGLISH TEAMS VISIT AS CHARITY IS THE BIG WINNER

On 29th December, the Glasgow Observer ran an advert for our double bill festive season matches at Celtic Park and at the same time promoted the matches with the proceeds going directly to the Childrens Dinner Tables at St Mary's, Sacred Heart and St Michael's.

From the *Glasgow Observer*;

CELTIC FOOTBALL CLUB

"Many of our readers will, we are sure, be surprised to learn that the Celtic Club, which is not yet twelve months formed, has resolved to give some tangible proof of its existence and the object the promoters had in view in establishing the club. Though there is still a heavy debt on the club, the Committee feel that they can have a few matches for the charities which so far have received nothing from the other charity matches played last year.

We beg to refer our readers to an advertisement in our columns of today where the Celtic have a nice bill of fare for the new year holiday week in the shape of two matches, the first with the Mitchell St George of Birmingham - a team with no small repute - who will try the strength of the Celtic on Monday next. This being their first visit to Glasgow we hope they will get a good reception especially from the east end people as the proceeds will be handed over for the Childrens Dinner Table of St Mary's, Sacred Heart and St Michael's parishes.

On Thursday, 3rd January, the famous Corinthians of London will visit the Celtic Park when we are sure there will be a large turn out of spectators to see a very fine exhibition of the game. This match will probably be more popular as a number of the city conferences of St Vincent De Paul are to receive the whole of the drawings. This should secure a large attendance and to the generous Celts the encouragement due them for so early endeavouring to attain the end for which they came in to existence".

Once again the committee's ingenuity gave the Celtic support a couple of massive attractions to look forward to over the festive period when Mitchell Saint George, (an amalgamation of Birmingham teams Mitchell and St George, not surprisingly), and the great Corinthians team travelled to Celtic Park on the 31st December and 3rd January respectively, to become the first English teams to do so. Reputations, we are told count for nothing and the Englishmen were seen off to the tune of 7 goals to 1 in the case of Mitchell Saint George and 6-2 in the case of the Corinthians as the Celts' stock grew considerably.

Mitchell Saint George turned up late for the 2pm kick off which eventually started 25 minutes later, but it was the visitors who kept no one waiting for the first goal after they took the lead in only the second minute. After a good passing movement from Mick Dunbar and Neil McCallum, Tom Maley scored following a cross from the former Renton man. Both sides had chances in an open match but it was Willie Groves who added two goals before half time as the bhoys' quick passing game, as we kept the ball moving quickly on the ground bemused the visitors who had a couple of players suffering knocks.

The Celts added a fourth goal just after the start of the second half and for long spells the visitors were seldom able to mount an attack. We were playing with the wind at our backs and although the Englishmen replaced their goalkeeper with an outfield player, we could not be contained, with our passing described as "simply perfection" as we knocked in three more goals, two of which came from McCallum and Dunbar as we finished the scoring at a resounding 7 goals to 1.

It gives great pleasure to note that the funds raised from both matches were donated to the Poor Childrens Dinner Tables Fund. Even the visiting clubs' guarantees were paid out of club funds. The attendance for the Corinthians match, "The flower of English football," is described as anywhere between 20,000 and 30,000, which is incredible given the size of our ground, but the game was spoiled by the state of the pitch in the inclement weather, which was described as a quagmire.

Corinthians had bucked the trend in England and remained amateur when all others went professional but astonishingly, in 1889, they had still supplied more players to the English national team than any other. To play for Corinthians, you had to either be a member of Oxford or Cambridge University Association clubs, or you had to have been capped by England.

On their tour, the Corinthians played Queens Park at Hampden on New Years Day and lost 3-2 but at Celtic Park they found the going even tougher, as the visitors struggled to adapt to the conditions on the heavy ground which seemed to be less of a problem for the Celts, who were more agile. Whilst the Englishmen tried to dribble their way forward on the mud, the Celts played a passing game, as described by the Scottish Referee;

"The Celts forwards played some of the most scientific football it has been my pleasure to look at for a long time. Their passing was simply a treat and it is still a mystery to me how they did it, when their opponents could not get the ball to move at all".

Ironically the visitors started better but it was Neil McCallum who scored the opener in five minutes after a great run by Willie Groves. Johnny Coleman added a second five minutes later, but Fred Dewhurst scored from a header to close the gap to a single goal. However, it only lasted a minute as the Celts went straight up the park, and after a fist by the goalkeeper to clear his lines, Mick Dunbar "chested" the ball home to restore the bhoys' two goal lead. The Celts piled on the pressure and Tom Maley made it 4-1 before half time, following "a scrimmage".

The bhoys added a fifth after a fantastic run by Willie Groves to set up Neil McCallum, but the goal was disallowed for a foul and shortly after the start of the second half, the Corinthians scored a second goal in hotly disputed circumstances from a free kick but the goal stood. This only spurred the Celts on to greater things and Neil McCallum added a fifth, before Johnny Coleman finished the scoring at Celtic 6 Corinthians 2, a score which sent shockwaves throughout English football, as the bhoys, usually best suited to dry ground, adapted brilliantly in three inches of mud.

The *Scottish Referee*, as was its wont, got the final word on the match with its fixation with the clergy at Celtic matches with the following;

"The clergy at Celtic Park on Thursday were all eager to shake hands with Fred Dewhurst. Fred, we have no doubt, would have been much better pleased had they asked the Celtic players not to be so kindly attentive to him".

THE REFEREE WANTS TO KNOW DETAILS OF CHARITY DONATIONS

On 7th January 1889, the *Scottish Referee* printed the following swipe at Celtic, hiding behind a so called crusade of convenience, ie, the public wanting to know;

"When the public support any charitable movement, they generally like to know all about the affair to which they subscribe. We understand that the proceeds of last Thursday's match between the Celtic and Corinthians were devoted to the cause of charity, but we scarcely think such an explanation enough.

The public would like to know to what good cause or causes the money is to be devoted, and how much there is to devote. The Celts may consider that this is purely their affair, but we beg respectfully to differ with them. The club has a perfect right to do with the money as it likes, but so also has the public a perfect right to accord its support where it chooses.

For instance, there are many who, if they thought the money was to be devoted only to Catholic charities, would at once withdraw their support from the club. Charity is far beyond the touch of either sect or creed and if the Celtic club are to live with but this great and glorious act of charity in view, it can only do so by infusing its help without condition or consideration of any sort".

THE GLASGOW OBSERVER (THE CATHOLIC ORGAN FOR SCOTLAND) RESPONDS

No doubt taken aback at the mean response to such a generous charitable act, the club, through the *Glasgow Observer*, gave the full details at length of the donations received from these matches on the 26th January 1889 and also detailed the fact that the Saint Vincent De Paul Society had actively sold an astonishing 16,700 tickets, through their conferences, for the Corinthians match. Less than eight months since our first match, the club had to deal with scurrilous scandal mongering in sections of the press but responded well without being dragged down to their level;

"It has become quite the fashion now for first class Scottish football clubs to pay periodical visits to England and the north of Scotland. Ostensibly, they arranged these fixtures to exhibit football and carry out certain profitable engagements - the real object is to afford a specious pretext for indulgence in a round of dissipation. It does not require a strong or very fervid imagination to picture to oneself the unpleasant consequences that frequently attend these football ventures.

Disastrous defeats, loss of players and distressing physical injuries are a few amongst the many evils that dog the steps of football enthusiasts exhibiting and sporting abroad. The Celtic, an Irish club in Glasgow, being thoroughly aware of all this, wisely resolved to remain at home and assist the many wretched ones whose extreme poverty may make the festivities of Christmas a social farce and a heart-rending mockery.

The Match Secretary of the Celts opened up a correspondence with some of the leading English clubs, with the result that the valuable services of the Mitchell Saint George and the celebrated Corinthians were secured. On the 31st December, the Mitchell Saint George made their first appearance in Glasgow, before an enthusiastic crowd in the Celtic Park. The Celts somewhat astonished the sturdy southerners by presenting them with the substantial defeat of 7-1. This important match placed £51 at the disposal at the committee to alleviate the sufferings of those in abject want. The money was dispersed amongst the three east end parishes of Glasgow - St Mary's, Sacred Heart and St Michael's, for the purpose of replenishing the Poor Childrens Dinner Table.

On the 3rd January, the memorable match with the Corinthians was played. The splendid reputation of the strangers and the brilliant form lately developed by the Celts, drew an immense crowd. The spectators were treated to a magnificent game, which ended in favour of the Celts by 6-2. This match was played with a view to replenish the funds of the various conferences of the Saint Vincent De Paul Society. Some weeks previous to the match, 16,700 tickets were distributed amongst different conferences. Four conferences declined to accept any tickets, for reasons best known to themselves. The handsome sum of £160 was realised by the sale of these tickets and thus a powerful means of effecting much good was generously placed in the hands of devoted men, who make it a duty and a pleasure to seek out the poor and destitute that they may alleviate their distress and help them out of the difficulties inseparable from extreme poverty.

The money actually received at the gate left a large surplus of £55, of which £50 was sent to the Glasgow Children's Refuge and £5 was devoted to procuring altar requirements for the Barony Poorhouse, Barnhill. The committee of the Celtic are to be highly complimented on their extraordinary generosity. Their career in this respect is quite a unique one and must command admiration; while the public will doubtless heartily accord their support to a club whose prosperous existence promises to become a boon to many impoverished persons. The committee, it is believed, intend to assist other institutions as soon as they can play the matches arranged for this purpose. This is all the more creditable, as the large debt contracted in starting the club has not yet been cleared off".

THE REFEREE OFFERS ADVICE TO THE CATHOLIC CHURCH

With sections of the press taking advantage of the opportunity to attack the Celtic support after our isolated misbehaviour against Queens Park in the Glasgow Cup semi final tie at Celtic Park, the Scottish Referee went a step further and poked fun at the "new breed of fan," otherwise known as Catholics, that Celtic had brought to the game in another petty and indeed, bizarre article on the 7th January, 1889, building up to their demand to know which charities were benefiting and to how much from Celtic, the *Scottish Referee* stated in their lead article;

"The Celtic club has perhaps a greater circle of friends than any other in the country. People who imagine that these friends are football enthusiasts by education are very far wide of the mark. Three fourths of the support is accorded to the Celts because of the coincidence of national and religious feelings. There is certainly no harm in a man admiring anything Scotch because he is a Scotchman, or pinning his faith to a body because its members hold the same religious views as himself; but it is always extremely desirable that a man who has formed a connection on these grounds should keep the mouth closed in order to hide his ignorance.

For instance, a stalwart Celt, who stood near a prominent Third Lanark player on Thursday wanted to know why the Celts didn't also get a corner when they got a goal, as the ball went over the line all the same. A gentleman who had a seat in front of the pavillion and who wore a well to do air, was quite angry because the referee dared to say that one of the Celts was offside. It is out of this sort of gross ignorance that most evil to the game is to be feared. When men will follow a club blindly, not knowing even the first principles of the game, it is not to be wondered at that their actions are sometimes wild and rowdy.

If the Catholic clergy are anxious that this game should flourish for charity's sake, don't they think it would be as big an act of charity as they could perform if they were to teach their flock what it all means, so that they may enjoy the games from the standpoint of critics, not as ignoramuses?"

As journalistic claptrap goes, this buffoonery deserves special credit, with this line surely an early contender for the Pulitzer Prize of 1889, an award for achievements in journalism, if only it had existed in Glasgow at the time;

"It is out of this sort of gross ignorance that most evil to the game is to be feared."

And the winner of the greatest advice to the Catholic church in the year of our Lord, 1889, goes to the writer of the Note Book column in the *Scottish Referee* for the suggestion that Catholic priests should lecture from the pulpit on the nuances of offside.

Ignoramus indeed.

CELTIC AND HIBS TO BURY THE HATCHET?

In the new year, relationships between Hibs and Celtic had cooled enough for John McFadden to be seen at Celtic Park to fix up a friendly match between the two teams at Celtic Park in the near future with a date set for 9th March. The Celtic Committee, with their usual generosity agreed that the funds raised from the match would be donated to Hibs to help them out of their financial difficulties.

On the fixture card Celtic released at the start of the season, we were due to play Hibs at home two weeks later on the 23rd March, but the friendly was brought forward to assist Hibs in their financial embarrassment. It also allowed Celtic to travel to Newcastle on the 23rd to play Newcastle West End at Saint James Park, a train journey that also accommodated the Rangers team who were playing at Sunderland. For the record, the Celts beat Newcastle 4-3.

In 1892, Newcastle West End merged with Newcastle East End to form Newcastle United.

The *Scottish Sport* on 8th January, 1889 told the story;

"We have remarked upon the frequent appearances of Mr McFadden of the Hibernians at Celtic Park of late and were at a loss to account for them, but the cat is out the bag and a mild and amiable creature it proves to be. We understand that, as a result of Mr McFadden's exertions, there is likely to exist from henceforth a much better feeling between the Celtic and Hibs.

The hatchet is to be buried and the pipe of peace is to take its place. We congratulate both clubs on the issue. The Celtic, with their usual and commendable generosity, have promised to play the Hibs in Glasgow at an early date and to give the entire proceeds to their Edinburgh brethren, not merely as a peace offering, but also as an earnest gesture of their desire to establish a better understanding between the clubs. Such a game will be particularly attractive, and the gate, in consequence, should be such as set the good old Hibs on their feet again".

CELTIC IN THE COMMUNITY

The *Glasgow Observer* frequently carried snippets involving Brother Walfrid and other founding fathers which painted a picture of their tremendous work in the community around the turn of the year. Brother Walfrid was invited to the end of year prize giving at St Mungo's Academy as a former teacher and on an inclement December evening, he shared the platform with His Grace, Archbishop Eyre, (Patron of Celtic), Father Hughes from Sacred Heart, who was also the secretary of the diocese and Father Maginn from St Alphonsus, amongst others.

Around the same time the parish of St Andrews held their Charity Ball in aid of the poor children of the parish and again the list of attendees included many of Celtic's founders, socialising in the same circles; William and John McKillop, Joseph McGroary, Timothy Walls, John McCreadie, James Quillan, Hugh Darroch and Doctor Scanlan. To complete the who's who of Celtic, Belfast man Francis McErlean, (who would become the Vice President of Celtic in the AGM of June 1889 by a large majority over James Quillan), was the Vice President of the League of the Cross at St Michael's, Parkhead and chaired their last meeting of the year.

On New Year's day 1889, the parishes of the East End, under the auspices of the conferences of the Saint Vincent De Paul Society treated the children of the parishes to dinner, with 230 in attendance at St Mary's. After the dinner, songs and entertainment were provided with Doctor John Conway on the piano, with John Glass and James McKay also in attendance. After the children's entertainment, the Saint Vincent De Paul Society held a little party at which the members of Celtic Football Club were present, with Father Van Der Hyde presiding over "an hour of mirth and pleasure".

This was a fitting gesture by the Saint Vincent De Paul to show their appreciation towards Celtic and it underlined their thanks in particular for the funds raised by the club towards the Society in order to maintain the Dinner Tables, in particularly at the two matches over the New Year.

A day later, Brother Walfrid was amongst the Celtic party present at the O'Connell Branch of the Irish National Foresters' first annual supper, as explained by the *Glasgow Observer* on 12th January 1889;

"The first annual supper of this branch was held in Pinkerton's Hall Main Street, Bridgeton, on Wednesday 2nd January, Reverend Father Van Der Heyde occupied the chair. Amongst those present were Reverend Brother Walfrid, Doctor John Conway, John Glass, John H McLaughlin, Dan Malloy and several other well known gentlemen in the East End. After some very appropriate remarks from the reverend chairman, the toast of the evening, the INF, was proposed by Dr John Conway and responded to by Brother Lafferty.

Various other toasts having been proposed, among then the Celtic FC, which was proposed by Brother O'Kane and responded to on behalf of the Celts by John H McLaughlin, numerous songs followed, which were principally supplied by members of the Celtic, Neil McCallum's songs being one the features of the evening; time after time they hauled him back up again. Selections on the violin, were rendered by Mr Dan Malloy, Mr John H McLaughlin presiding at the piano.

A very enjoyable evening was brought to a conclusion by all present singing "God Save Ireland".

Just two days later, on Friday, 4th January, at the Children of Mary's social gathering in the parish of Sacred Heart, Brother Walfrid presided over a limelight show, known as a magic lantern, giving views of a visit around Ireland, which was said to be an excellent one. Limelight shows were a popular form of entertainment at such gatherings and were no more than the use of photographic images projected and enlarged onto a wall with accompanying commentary, akin to slide shows of the next century.

At last, "Pastimes" of the *Scottish Athletic Journal* gave credit where credit was due for Celtic's huge charitable donation over the festive season, without looking for fault;

"The Celtic club is mainly composed of Roman Catholics, and the local priests take great interest in the results of the matches. The committee decided to devote the whole of the proceeds of the match with the Corinthians to charitable purposes, and, with the object in view, the visitors agreed to forego a share of the gate and receive a lump sum for their expenses. This sum the Celtic paid from its own funds, and generously handed the whole of the receipts, nearly £400 to the charities".

THE SONS OF THE ROCK v THE SONS OF THE SHAMROCK

The semi final of the Scottish Cup at Dumbarton on 12th January, 1889 gives another great insight into how Celtic were seen not just as a football team but as an identity. Again we are referred to only in terms of the club's Irishness, with the game billed as "The Sons of the Rock versus The Sons of the Shamrock."

The team travelled by steam train from Queen Street, at 12.57 and the carriages were jam packed with over 500 Celtic fans from the east end. Many more couldn't get on board and had to pile onto the next special services from Bellgrove at 13.35 and 13.45 calling at Queen St, Partick and Kilbowie enroute to Dumbarton for the 14.30 kick off.

In one of life's great ironies, the Celtic team made their way to the ground led by a two man Italian band playing "Marching Through Georgia." Yes, the same "Marching Through

CELTIC: THE EARLY YEARS

Georgia," which the Rangers support took up as their unofficial sectarian anthem decades later. Of course the original lyrics weren't good enough and had to be adapted to suit the sectarian mentality of the singer.

Hurrah! Hurrah! We bring the jubilee!
Hurrah! Hurrah! The flag that makes you free!
So we sang the chorus from Atlanta to the sea
While we were marching through Georgia.

Changed to;

Hello Hello we are the Billy Boys
Hello Hello you'll know us by our noise
We're up to our knees in fenian blood. Surrender or you'll die
For we are the Brigton Derry Boys

Back to the football and still more fans came from Dumbarton and the Vale of Leven and they were not there to support the home team, as it was noted in the Scottish Sport;

"The Vale is thick with sons of the Emerald Isle and Dumbarton even more so".

The attendance was the biggest ever seen at Boghead and the Celtic fans were in the majority. Many of the fans had cards in their hats with the legend "Hurry Up Celts" in green lettering and it was not just the size of our support that set us apart, but the enthusiasm shown as we were given half of the home team's grandstand. This was of course a massive boost to the Scottish game with our arrival on the scene and many clubs shared in the financial benefits of the large Celtic support. Previously Clyde had attracted a crowd of 10,000 to Barrowfield, unheard of in those days at their ground and thanks mainly to the Celtic support, and although the home team were beaten 5-1 by Celtic, the Treasurer had a busier day than the Clyde keeper!

To the Dumbarton match itself, the green and white blew away the orange and black of the home team by a hefty 4 goals to 1 as we became the first team to beat the four ace Dunbartonshire teams in one season; Dumbarton, Dumbarton Athletic, Renton and Vale of Leven. Scottish football was shaken to its boots as we reached the Scottish Cup final at our first attempt.

The recently established *Scottish Referee* weekly, with its first issue on November 5th 1888, gave its match report under the headline of *"Thistle v Shamrock,"* and described the *"trial of strength between the Scot and the Celt for the blue riband of Scottish football,"* in which the Celtic supporters urged their team to *"Hurry up"*, whilst the Dumbarton fans encouraged their team to "Ho away". It considered the main reasons for *"the shamrock beating the thistle"*, as the hard pitch which suited the Celts' fast passing game and also *"the cool, calculating, easy going manner in which the Celts wrought the ball which must have been a revelation to the Dumbarton people"*.

The match report in the *Scottish Referee* finally concluded;

"The sword is away from the Castle, (Dumbarton), and the cup from "The Rantin", (Renton), whilst the dear little, sweet little, shamrock blooms verdant and more power to it, say I".

The *Glasgow Evening News* added;

"The victory was received with immense satisfaction in some parts of Glasgow, and those of the Celts' supporters who accompanied the team on their mission of conquest made the Rock town resound with their enthusiastic cries".

THE DIFFERENCE BETWEEN THE CELTIC AND THE HIBS?

In the build up to the Scottish Cup final between Celtic and Third Lanark, the *Scottish Sport* printed an article on the 15th January on the make up of both supports;

"The Volunteers, (Third Lanark), have a very large and enthusiastic following, which has been greatly increased because of the treatment meted out to the club by those in authority. The Celtic have even a larger, and certainly more enthusiastic crowd of supporters. It is extraordinary the amount of interest taken in the Celts and their doings by the Irish population of Glasgow and the west of Scotland. The difference between the Celtic and the Hibernians is that the latter was both a religious and a political organisation.

The majority of the members of the Celtic, it is true, belong to one religion, but adherents of other religions are not debarred from joining the club and playing in the team. Irishmen who have hitherto taken no interest in football are now quite as enthusiastic as the maddest of us all, and none more so than the Roman Catholic clergy, who, by taking a practical interest in the amusements of the people, set a worthy example to ministers of other denominations".

A week later they had to print a retort from a Hibernian friend of the newspaper;

"A valued friend of ours sends me the following, which we have great pleasure in making public; Permit me, as one of the Patrons and founders of Hibernian Football Club to correct an error into which you have fallen in your issue of Tuesday last. Neither the club nor the team are confined to the members of any religious persuasion. Apart from the fact that I am a Protestant myself, men like Brogan of Bolton, and Higgins of Kilmarnock were Protestants and members of the team.

No inquiry as to religion was ever made, but the fact of the club getting the use of the Catholic Institute, in Saint Mary's Street, Edinburgh for their meetings, no doubt gave rise to the belief that only Catholics were admitted as members of the club".

The fact that the letter came from a valued friend of the newspaper gave it credence as the source was known and it backed up his points as genuine.

What he didn't mention was that James Brogan was a Catholic, albeit not a practising one. He was signed in October 1883, scored 6 goals in his debut against Edina in the Scottish Cup but lasted only ten weeks after it was discovered he was not a practising Catholic. He joined Hearts but didn't last long there either and two months later the Beith man was on his way to Bolton where he played for eight seasons before giving up the game for a job on the shipyards.

Hibs had been founded under the auspices of the Catholic Young Men's Society and were, if you will, the sporting wing of that society. To take up the social activities of the society, that is to play for Hibs, you had to be a member of the society. Therefore you had to be, by the nature of the whole set up, a practising Catholic and a tee totaller. The author of the letter, claiming to be a founder and patron of Hibs and known to the Scottish Sport newspaper as a Protestant was never publicly identified.

In the original piece, printed on the 15th January, it stated;

"The majority of the members of the Celtic, it is true, belong to one religion, but adherents of other religions are not debarred from joining the club and playing in the team".

The crucial point here is that although at that time and for another 20 months, no non Catholic players had signed for Celtic as yet, there was, as the article states, no bar on non Catholics playing for Celtic, as there was at Hibs. The article concluded that;

The difference between the Celtic and the Hibernians is that the latter was both a religious and a political organisation.

This is the case in that Hibs, as part of the CYMS, were a part of a religious organisation who had become embroiled in the politics of Ireland, but at the same time, individual members of the Celtic Committee, by their dual membership of branches of the Irish National League, particularly the Home Government branch in Glasgow, which was the largest outside Ireland, had more freedom outside the confines of any other organisation to be more politically active than their Hibernian brethren, as they so wished.

OUR FIRST RECORD BREAKING ACHIEVEMENT

Celtic became the first team to play in a national cup final in our inaugural season and with Third Lanark beating the favourites Renton in the other semi final, the Celts, incredibly, were given a great chance of getting our hands on the national trophy at our first ever attempt. Rangers 2012, it should be noted, did manage to reach the semi final of the Scottish Cup Final in 2014 in only their second season after beating Airdrie, Falkirk, Dunfermline and Albion Rovers after a replay, before eventually losing 3-1 at home to Dundee United.

2nd February 1889 was the date set and the venue was the original Hampden Park at Crosshill, which was just west of the current ground at Hampden Park, on ground now covered by the railway line at Crosshill station, which the ground was demolished to make way for. The current Hampden Park is actually the third Hampden. The second Hampden Park was at Cathkin, which was slightly north of the current ground and was the ground Third Lanark played on until they went out of business in 1967.

The team named for the biggest day of our short history was as follows;

John Kelly in goals, Paddy Gallagher and Mick McKeown at full-back, Willie Maley, James Kelly, and James McLaren as half backs and Neil McCallum, Mick Dunbar, Willie Groves, Johnny Coleman and Tom Maley as forwards in the usual 2-3-5 formation of the day. Thankfully Neil McCallum had recovered from a recent severe illness, and despite being weak, was able to play.

The *Scottish Referee* stated;

"The supporters of the Celtic were out in strong force and of the wearing of the green, there was galore. The Bould, Bould Celts too, as they stepped on the field had it in appearance, their green and white stripes looking guy pretty".

The big day was noted for two things. Firstly, the highest ever attendance at a Scottish Cup Final with 17,000 crammed into the ground, three quarters of whom, it was said, were Irish or had Irish sympathies and secondly, the worst weather ever at a cup final. The downside of holding the final of the main competition in February had come home to roost as a snowstorm covered Glasgow the night before the match and continued throughout the day of the game. Ironically, the winter of 1888/89 had been hitherto mild.

It was decided just over two hours before the 15.15 kick off time that the pitch was still playable, however both teams protested the decision before the match, the Presidents going as far as drawing up a legal document and to that effect the game was played as a protested cup tie as it couldn't be deemed a friendly without the word of the referee, which wasn't asked for or given, bizarrely.

With both sets of players pelting each other with snowballs as they entered the field before the start of the match, the crowd may well have taken the hint and suspected that the game was being protested, which often happened in those days. Instead of calling a game off with late notice and no way of stopping fans travelling to the game, a friendly match was often played. However no announcement was made and it was only after the game finished that word came out that the replayed match would be played on the following Saturday at 15.30, again at Hampden. This was of course welcome news to Celtic as the poor underfoot conditions again didn't suit our game and we lost 3-0.

An ode from the *Scottish Sport*;

The Scottish Cup Final

From Parkhead's classic precinct came a whale of discontent
The air was filled with sounds of woe with lamentations rent
Right gallantly the Celts did fight; alas it was all in vain
Old Erin's heroes bit the dust, they never smiled again

Swift as the haunted dear when pressed, the bold McCallum flew
His fearless eye like lightening flashed as near the goal he drew
Too long he lingered on the ball, Lochhead was on his train
They met - bang bang! alas! poor Mac - he never smiled again

Brave Johnny Marshall down the right did then attempt to fly
And to relieve him of the ball, young Mick McKeown did try
In the snow they found a resting place - the parting gave them pain
For til the whistle sounded time, they never smiled again

The noble "Punt" McFarlane now appeared in dire distress
As to his nose Jim Kelly, his two fists began to press
For the honour of his club poor Punt a martyr did remain
A tear rolled down his manly cheek - he never smiled again

At last when all could see the gallant 3rd were sure to win
The Sons of Erin made their voices heard above the din
"Oh Celts asthore! For god sake score!" was yelled with might and main
Alas! twas not to be - poor souls, they never smiled again

Long will that fight remembered be and ages hence will stand
In bold relief the victory gained by Cathkin's warrior band
The Celts although defeated, still their prestige did maintain
But til the Scottish Cup they win - they will never smile again

Brilliant poem but after all that effort from the well versed and quick witted poet, the match was replayed a week later.

You guessed it. He never smiled again!!

On the day of the replayed match there was, once more, a pitch inspection before the game and the gates were opened as the pitch deemed playable. 65 policemen were on duty as the Celtic support was again in the majority, but again it was Third Lanark who scored the first goal. The Celts got back into the game when Neil McCallum equalised, described in the Scottish Sport thus;

"When the Celtic equalised, it looked as if two thirds of the crowd were in paroxysms of delight. And they did hum out their joy. It lasted for nearly five minutes".

But it just wasn't to be and the Thirds came back to score the winner, a disputed goal which gave them their first Scottish Cup after a number of close calls.

At the after match dinner and presentation in the Alexandria Hotel, John Glass in his speech refused to accept that Third were the better team and instead gave an impassioned delivery recognising that although we had lost to the Thirds for the third time, he insisted that the boot would be on the other "fut" in the next meeting of the two clubs. When that meeting came on 30th March, 1889 at Celtic Park, his prophecy was true as the Celts got their revenge in front of an "enormous and enthusiastic" crowd of 10,000 with a 4-1 win, with all our goals coming in the first half.

It had no outcome on the destination of the Scottish Cup, but that particular trophy was yet to give us many of our greatest days.

THE INTRODUCTION OF THE RELIGIOUS ELEMENT?

"Viator," from the Glasgow Evening News again returned to his favourite subject of religion in the aftermath of the Scottish Cup Final. In an article on the 15th February on a subject which he had managed to ignore before our foundation despite many opportunities to take even a cursory glance at some of the teams not very far away, he stated;

"In the extensive discussion which has followed the train of our best-on-record final, there is one feature which I cannot allow to pass unnoticed. That is the introduction of the religious element. The idea prevalent in the minds

of not a few writers to the press and of many followers of football seems to amount to this, that because a club hold certain religious views they ought to be boycotted from taking part in the competition for the Scottish Cup. At first sight, I feel disposed to treat the matter lightly and not seriously; but from the persistency with which the subject has been trotted out before the public, I have every reason to believe that those who approve of such a course are in earnest, so much so that I hear we are, as an off-set to the Celtic FC, to have a team of Orangemen, with no doubt, a title suggestive of their creed and country.

Now, what I wish to impress on all interested in football is, that the game knows of no such distinctions, nor can those who are responsible for the conduct of the game acknowledge them in the slightest degree. There is surely enough of excitement in the sport, regarded purely as a sport, calculated to incite strong enthusiasm, without adding the bitter partisanship of religious bigotry. Football knows nothing of creed. All that she concerns itself about is the ability, honesty and conduct of those who follow the game as a means of physical recreation.

The football field must not be made an arena for championing the cause of any sect; the church is the place for that. Spiritual, not physical, are the weapons for the war of creeds. Those who legislate for the game should endeavour by all means to discourage the introduction of the discordant element, which, if allowed to creep in, will do much to spoil our noble game, and rob it of the power it undoubtedly possesses of breaking down class and creed distinctions. It ought to be on the football field as it is on the curling pond and bowling green - all should meet on equal terms with one common aim, to follow the sport without regard to matters which are quite foreign to it as a pastime."

All very noble words by Viator, but the fact they came less than 9 months after our first match and almost 17 years after the birth of Rangers, and with it their sectarian policy, lessens its impact and its impartiality.

THE CELTS HEAD TO LONDON

On 16th February, the Celts were invited to play Corinthians in a return match at the Kennington Oval, just south of the Thames in central London. The ground had held the first FA Cup Final in 1872 and the first international match between England and Scotland in 1876 and it was to hold Celtic's first ever match outside Scotland.

The home team were keen to avenge their 6-2 defeat at Celtic Park on the 3rd January and they were boosted by the news that both Maley brothers were unable to play. They were replaced by Pat Dowling and Phil Clarke, guesting from Hibs, which was another example of the improved relations between the two main Irish teams. The crowd was limited to 3000 due to the nearby rugby international between England and New Zealand at Blackheath and also the heavy rain which didn't suit Celtic's fast attacking style and played a large part in the reason we lost by three goals to one.

President John Glass, Vice President James Quillan and committee men Dan Malloy and William McKillop, as well as trainer Joe Anderson and Willie Maley travelled south by train with the eleven players in a party of seventeen which left St Enoch station, (on the ground where St Enoch Shopping Centre now stands), at 21.15 on the Thursday evening, for the Saturday match. Interestingly the cost of the trip was £73, with only £40 given as a guarantee pledged by the home club, which caused some unrest in the camp, especially when the guarantee still wasn't forthcoming by the arrival of the AGM.

The Celts had ordered new pea green jerseys and white shorts for the trip, as Corinthians played in white tops and black shorts and socks, however we are photographed outside the pavillion wearing our green and white stripes.

There was controversy around this match as the Scottish "Trials" were set for the same date and five Celtic players had been invited to play in the match that would determine who would be selected for the Scotland team to play England, (ironically at the Kennington Oval), Wales and Ireland. The Celtic Committee were stuck between a rock and a hard place and after the issue was raised at a committee meeting it was decided to honour the agreement with Corinthians as no other date was available.

The decision was not the players' making and although they honoured the decision reached by the committee, they felt they had a case for inclusion in the Scotland team on merit. In the event James Kelly and Jimmy McLaren were picked to play against England in a famous 3-2 victory and Willie Groves and Mick McKeown were selected to play against Ireland at Ibrox in a 7-0 victory, in which Willie Groves scored a hat trick.

CELTIC TAKE ON THE CLYDESDALE HARRIERS

On 23rd February 1889, Celtic played a team from the Clydesdale Harriers athletic club in an attraction that incorporated a Cross Country Championship, with no less than 50 athletes running around the pitch during half time, before setting off on a 10 mile cross country race before re-entering Celtic Park to cross the finishing line.

The football match itself looked a formality, but the Harriers had already beaten the famous Invincibles of Preston North End and they were up against a "scratch" Celtic team, far from full strength, with Mick McKeown and Neil McCallum playing for Glasgow against Edinburgh in an inter city match, and Jimmy McLaren out injured.

Jerry Reynolds, guesting from Carfin Shamrock, and Phil Clarke, guesting from Hibs played for Celtic whilst Chalmers, of Clyde played in goals for the Harriers and was man of the match, as he managed to keep the Celts out for the full ninety minutes. The Celts had the better of the first half but couldn't beat Chalmers. In return the visitors scored three times in the second half to win convincingly in front of the crowd of 4000.

The Glasgow Herald on 25th February takes up the Cross Country race, which gives some detail of the lay out of the original ground;

"At seven minutes past four, half time, the Harriers, numbering about 50, entered the enclosure and the batch were sent on their journey. After going twice round the enclosure, the competitors left the ground on the north side of the stand and went off into the country. The trail, which was clearly defined, led over grass parks and hedges, and northwards past Shettleston, along the banks of the canal, then onto Springboig to near Ellesmere, where a turn for home was made to Woodend and Fullerton.

During the run, four water jumps had to be negotiated and the competitors re-entered the enclosure at the south west corner and finished at the south east corner of the grand stand, running nearly once round. The race being won by JW McWilliams, of Ayrshire, in 77 minutes and 40 seconds".

Unusually, the Cross Country Championship was the main attraction, with the football thrown in as an after thought to keep the crowd amused, but the sight of 50 athletes running twice round the track at half time was a stirring one before departing through an exit to the north of the grand stand, which would have lay between Celtic Park and Ivy Cottage on Dalmarnock Street.

Half an hour after the second half of the football finished, the patient souls who remained to witness the finale of the race were rewarded when Clydesdale's own AG Colquhoun entered the ground within yards of JW McWilliams of Ayrshire. The entrance chosen to re-enter Celtic Park would need to be the biggest one to stop bunching and so the members gate at the south west corner of the ground, nearest Celtic Park was used. Unfortunately for the Harriers, McWilliams increased his lead as he ran round the running track to complete the race, fittingly in front of the packed grand stand.

GREEK MEETS GREEK

"Greek meets Greek," was often the description used when Celtic met Hibs in the early years, a term to describe two like minded people brought together in a "distant" land. The Celts played Hibs at Celtic Park on 9th March 1889, in a friendly match with all proceeds going to Hibernian to help ease their financial plight, a generous gesture by the Celtic Committee to reach out to their fellow Irishman.

Hibernian in turn, had approached Celtic knowing that in their hour of need, their only hope of a significant financial boost came from their countrymen. Interestingly, in the *1923/24 Celtic Handbook*, Willie Maley still referred to Hibs as our fellow countrymen, ie Irish, almost thirty five years later, when describing our 1-0 win in the Scottish Cup final on 31st March, 1923, on a day when Hibs were managed by his brother, Alec Maley;

"Starting the ties as almost rank outsiders, the team, by real good Celtic football, worthily regained the title of cup holders, although finally at the expense of our fellow countrymen, the Hibs, after a very hard struggle at Hampden".

And so it turned out with a large crowd welcoming Hibs back to Celtic Park for the second time this season, even though they arrived 30 minutes late on this occasion. Former Hibees, Mick McKeown and Willie Groves were on international duty playing for Scotland against Ireland and they were replaced by Mick Dunbar's brother Tom and also James Quigley who was guesting from Campsie FC.

There was none of the unpleasantness at this match that marred the meeting at Easter Road in October, and the Celts were again too good for Hibs, but it wasn't until the second half before we built up a good lead and even then we almost threw it away. Tom Maley scored the opener for the Celts in the fifth minute, but the Hibs equalised fifteen minutes later, before two goals from Neil McCallum put us 3-1 up. The free scoring first half continued when Hibs got one back before Mick Dunbar made it 4-2 before half time.

The second half was only just started when the Celts scored a fifth and the rest of the match was open, with both teams having their chances to add to the scoring but were thwarted by the performance of both goalkeepers. Late on, Hibs regained some pride with two late goals to put a respectable slant on the final score line of Celtic 5 Hibs 4. A certain young Sandy McMahon shone for the visitors. No prizes for guessing which club he would go on to become a legend for.

LADIES GAIN FREE ENTRANCE INTO CELTIC PARK

Throughout the 1880s it was popular to allow ladies free admittance into football matches, not just at Celtic Park, but all over Scotland and England. The policy however was a victim of its own success and its downfall began in 1889 when Everton calculated that no less than 2000 female Evertonians were gaining free access to their ground.

At the original Celtic Park, there was a ladies bench in the stand where females would yell their appreciation at their favourite players and the initiative remained in place throughout the four years of the original ground, giving enough time to encourage the ghirls to follow the famous bhoys in green.

CELTIC CELEBRATE SAINT PATRICK'S DAY 1889

Founding fathers Brother Walfrid, John Glass and Joseph Nelis celebrated St Patrick's Day as the Children of Mary held their annual re-union in honour of the patron saint of Ireland at Sacred Heart schoolhouse in Bridgeton, with fully 600 in attendance for a dinner in the boy's schoolhouse and then a concert in the girl's schoolhouse. The Children of Mary are a Marian group, not too dissimilar to the Marist Brothers in their devotion to Mary and in their work. The original Children of Mary were young women, but in the 1830s it was agreed they could set up a separate sodality to carry on their work throughout adulthood.

The address given before the concert in Bridgeton by Father McCulla of Sacred Heart, gives an insight into the interchangeable nature of Catholic and/or Irish gatherings in that era;

"We should hail with joy on this eve, the glorious deeds of our suffering people at home, and repudiate which scorn the power that binds us in the slavery of oppression. He asked them to earnestly hope and pray that Ireland's fatal destiny of centuries might soon be reversed and their country a restored nation, wisely governed and ruled by her present great leaders, and flourishing again with that prosperity and peace which was the constant struggle of Saint Patrick to obtain it".

Around the same time, March 1889, St Alphonsus Young Men's Guild held an election for a vacancy in their 23rd ward and with Father Maginn sharing the platform, Celtic founding father, David Meikleham was elected after a question and answer session with the three candidates. This was another example of St Alphonsus men, as well as those from St Andrews still working in the parish as well as on the Celtic Committee, despite those parishes pulling out of the original discussions to found Celtic. Some may have pulled out, but evidently not all of them.

CELTIC: OUR FIRST SEASON - 1888/89

THE SHOE IS ON THE OTHER "FUT"

The visit of Third Lanark to Celtic Park on 30th March gave the Celts the perfect opportunity to carry out John Glass's prophecy at the after match social when Third Lanark were presented with the Scottish Cup just seven weeks earlier that on the next time they met, he hoped the shoe would be on the other "fut."

This was the fourth time the clubs met, with Third Lanark winning all three, 4-3 at home in a friendly at Cathkin in August, 3-0 in the original Scottish Cup Final match that was played out as a friendly due to the heavy snowfall and 2-1 in the replayed match. A fourth defeat in a row was unthinkable for the Celtic Committee and so the Celtic support turned out in their numbers to cheer on the bhoys in the glorious sunshine. They were rewarded too with a fantastic first half performance with four goals scored to no reply. First Johnny Coleman scored after only five minutes, then Willie Groves added a second in 12 minutes. Neil McCallum got in on the act in 35 minutes before Mick Dunbar scored the fourth just before half time.

In the second half the visitors raised their game and notched one goal back but they couldn't get back into a game that went from end to end with chances missed for both teams. The whistle blew with the Celts well on top and John Glass the happiest man at Celtic Park, with the cup holders well beaten.

The *Glasgow Evening News* opined;

"It goes without saying that the Irish element in the crowd were highly delighted at the victory".

The "Irish element" in the crowd being the Celtic support.

The *Scottish Referee* on 1st April reported;

REVENGE AT LAST

"Ireland has no further cause to grumble. Have not the Celts righted her wrongs by humbling the proud Saxon in the shape of Third Lanark in the dust?

The game at Celtic Park on Saturday was not a pretty one and considering that I had been nearly squeezed to death in my endeavour to get through the 9 inch entrance way which does duty for a gate at Celtic Park, I was not pleased at what I saw. The crowd was a very large one, and composed for the most part of east enders, whose enthusiasm, if not quite of the first quality, is none the less genuine".

Looking at it now, the political comment in a match report seems oddly out of place, but in our formative years this kind of language was not unusual when the Scottish press discussed Celtic or Hibernian.

In the same issue, the *Scottish Referee* commented;

"The Fiery Cross had evidently been sent round and in response the people turned out ten thousand strong".

The use of the term "Fiery Cross" is an interesting one. The modern perception of this phraseology would portray the extremist Ku Klux Klan, in their long white robes and pointy hats in a threatening pose complete with a burning cross. It certainly didn't fit in with the language used to describe the gathering of the Celtic support.

However, the imagery of the burning cross wasn't taken up in America by the KKK until the mid 1920s. The origins of the "fiery cross" is actually in Scandinavia and also across Scotland where it was used during the Jacobite Rising, (rebellions with the aim of restoring the deposed Catholic King James to the throne), when a wooden cross, set alight, would be passed from town to town to summon clans to arms in times of impending danger.

The club's first badge was the Celtic Cross in green, said to have been on a red background. Why the red background? Was it simply the colour of the leather patch stitched onto the strip or was there a significance? Did it signify a fiery cross used to spread the word? Was there a religious significance or was the use of the term "fiery cross" in early Celtic match reports a coincidence?

The only picture of the first strip that remains today does not help in clearing up the mystery as not only is the badge not clear, the background to the green cross does not appear to be a dark colour, which would make it difficult for a green cross to stand out. It's more likely for me that the background to the green cross was simply the colour of the leather patch used.

The Third Lanark match on 30th March 1889 was actually the second time in our inaugural season that the fiery cross terminology was used to describe the gathering of the Celtic support. It was also used in the match report when we played at Dumbarton on the 12th January in the Scottish Cup semi final;

"The fiery cross, though, had evidently been sent round and from hill and dale, town and village, the people came pouring into Dumbarton".

OUR FIRST EVER TOUR

The prime movers of professionalism in the English game were the northern teams, with the southern teams clinging on to the romance of amateurism. For this reason it was teams like Preston North End, Everton, Bolton Wanderers and Blackburn Rovers who were prominent at the time of Celtic's foundation and so it was no surprise that our first ever tour would take us to the north of England at the Easter break. The Celts travelled south by train to take on Bolton and despite our quick passing and speed on the ball, which was greatly admired by the 7000 crowd in the first match, we couldn't get the ball between the posts and lost 2-0. The very next day we travelled to Burnley where scoring wasn't a problem with Willie Groves getting the opener in the first minute and we went in at half time three goals up. The home team replied in the second forty five and the game finished a comfortable 3-1 win for the Celts at Turf Moor.

The Celts were firm favourites with the Lancashire crowds who turned up in big numbers to see what the fuss was about the team, who despite being less than a season old, were already being described as famous.

OUR FIRST TOUR OF IRELAND

Following our two games in the north of England on consecutive days, the Celts travelled to the north of Ireland and after just one day off, we played our first match on Irish soil against Distillery at Broadway in Belfast, on 22nd April 1889. A massive crowd back in the day of 6000 welcomed the Celts as Jimmy McLaren scored the only goal of the game. The next day we returned to the same ground and beat United Belfast 5-2 after going in at half time 2-1 down in front of another huge crowd.

It was our fourth game in five days with three wins and one defeat and the Celts were grateful to head back to Glasgow for a well deserved rest.

ANOTHER VOLLEY IS FIRED FROM THE EAST

Whilst we were away spreading the word, another volley came from Easter Road directed at the Celtic Committee with a letter from the Hibs Secretary to the *Scottish Sport* complaining;

"I am sorry to trouble you again with another of our grievances. I hear on good authority that the Celts are tampering with one of our players. The first batch they took away we only ventured on a gentle remonstration; the second consisting of Willie Naughton and Willie McCallum, we allowed to go without a word; but we are determined to lose no more men.

After all their professions of friendship and good wishes for our success in the east of Scotland, they are doing their best to kill the Hibernian club. Do they imagine our Committee are so many children, because they have been so forbearing? Their existence depends on us. If we come down, they will have to take the consequences".

The tone of the letter sounds very much cloaked in the same language as the previous one they delivered after the opening match of the season which Hibs lost 3-2 at Celtic Park in August 1888. However the most interesting part of the letter is the following;

"The first batch they took away we only ventured on a gentle remonstration, the second consisting of Naughton and McCallum, we allowed to go without a word."

This flies in the face of the story passed down the generations that the Hibernian Committee were outraged and again points towards an acceptance that the Hibs players wanted to come to Celtic, rather than having to be enticed to Glasgow. They were all originally from the west, (except Sandy McMahon who came later), and they were keen to move to the bigger city where work could be more easily gained. Certainly the Hibs support were outraged, but that is understandable as they lost half their team.

There had been ongoing talks between the two clubs led by the former Hibs Secretary John McFadden resulting in Hibs being given the fundraising match at Celtic Park but unless the Celtic Committee pledged not to target any more Hibs players during McFadden's visits, then Celtic were perfectly entitled to pursue more Hibs players when we saw fit. Quite simply, it was the nature of the game, and Hibs, once at the top of the food chain, were now further down the stream and cut off from the plentiful supplies of Irish talent in the west of Scotland, that had sustained them.

Indeed the *Scottish Referee* reported that when Celtic played Third Lanark at Celtic Park at the end of March;

"Several of the Hibernians were at Celtic Park on Saturday ready to assist the ground team against the Cup holders".

The Celts were at full strength and had no injury worries therefore there was no need to request any assistance from Hibs players. Again, who was wooing who?

SCOTLAND'S TWO MAIN IRISH CLUBS AT LOGGERHEADS

Much is made of the fact that Celtic signed many of the Hibs team and indeed played six of them at the opening game of the 1888/89 season at Celtic Park between Celtic and Hibs.

This story deserves closer scrutiny because, although it's true that Celtic included Easter Road in their search for the best Catholic players of the day, of the Celtic team that played against Hibs on the 4th August 1888; James Kelly had only played a handful of guest matches for Hibs and Mick McKeown, Paddy Gallagher and John Coleman had only joined Hibs in 1887, they were hardly experienced Hibees and only Willie Groves, who had been at Hibs for two years and Jimmy McLaren, the Auld Giniral, who had been there since 1883 were first team regulars over a long spell.

Indeed only two players from Hibs' famous Scottish Cup win in 1887, Jimmy McLaren and Willie Groves were signed in our first season by Celtic and enjoyed illustrious careers at Celtic Park. John Tobin, Jimmy McGhee and Phil Clarke signed later but played only fleetingly.

The less than convenient truth for Hibs was that their decline started even before the political controversy involving the CYMS at the start of the 1888/89 season. It began during the 1887/88 season when they were knocked out of the Scottish Cup by Hearts, 3-1 in the 3rd round, the Edinburgh Cup, the Edinburgh Shield by Mossend Swifts 1-0 and the Glasgow Charity Cup by Cambuslang, 3-0 in the 1st round, (which they were invited to participate in), and none of this had anything to do with Celtic. Hibs got revenge on Mossend Swifts for their shock defeat in the Edinburgh Shield, to win the Roseberry Charity Cup, but it was to be Hibs' last Roseberry Charity Cup until 1893/94. They wouldn't see the Edinburgh Shield again until the turn of the century and although the Scottish Cup was to return to Easter Road in 1902, it hasn't been seen at Easter Road since, which is an incredible statistic.

Hibs in fact have never won the Scottish Cup at the present Hampden since it was opened in 1903, having won their first cup in 1887 at the original Hampden at Crosshill and their second cup in 1902 at Celtic Park, after the venue had to be changed at the last minute, following the original Ibrox Disaster shortly before the final was due to be played.

Five players from Hibs' famous victory in 1887 had been taken from Lugar Boswell; Jimmy McGhee, Jimmy McLaren, Peter McGinn and Paddy Lafferty, as well as Mick McKeown. Therefore it begs the question. Is it perfectly au fait for Hibs to take five players from Lugar

Boswell but not au fait for Celtic to do likewise to Hibs? Lugar, in darkest Ayrshire near Cumnock, is a tiny village, built to house the workers from the newly opened ironworks in 1845 and had a population of around 1300 in the 1880s. Their football team, Lugar Boswell was founded in 1878 and they came to Hibs attention when they reached the 5th round of the Scottish Cup in the 1882/83 season and in March of the same season, when they beat Hearts 10-2, a score which remains Hearts' record defeat to this day.

After Hibs' decline, following their magnificent Scottish Cup win, it was perfectly natural at Celtic's formation, that the Hibs men, originally from the west, would want to return to the west of Scotland. Too much is made of Celtic's attempts to take the players and not enough emphasis on the Hibs players, who were only too happy to return nearer home. Just as Hibs had acted perfectly legally and above board in 1883 and the following years when they turned to Lugar Boswell for new talent, so too did Celtic in 1888 and the following years.

The greatest irony is that it was Hibernian, not Celtic, who avoided a charge of professionalism only by the casting vote of the SFA Chairman, who held the whole future of the club within his hands and gave them the benefit of the doubt in 1887.

Mick Dunbar signed for Celtic from Hibernian and played from our first match on 28th May but again, he had only signed for Hibs in 1887 from Cowlairs and was from Busby, on the southern edge of Glasgow.

Tom Maley joined up with Celtic after Brother Walfrid came to his house in September 1887, but again Maley had only guested for Hibs on a handful of occasions. Jerry Reynolds and Dan Doyle were former Hibees who were to make their names with Celtic, but only after they had already left Hibs for pastures new. Reynolds, who only missed out on the 1887 cup final through injury was signed from Carfin Shamrock on the eve of our big cup match with Queens Park in the first round of the 1889 Scottish Cup and Dan Doyle, who made his debut for Hibs in the match after their cup final, was brought to Celtic from Everton after he left Hibs to join Grimsby Town.

A lot of water had run under the bridge since John McFadden refereed the first ever Celtic match and managed at the same time to disallow a sixth goal for us, but the writing was on the wall not just for Hibs, but for McFadden himself.

Mismanagement in the face of the new rivals in the west meant that Hibs had no decent reserve team to call on and therefore no back up of Catholic players to step into the places vacated by those who departed west. Celtic on the other hand were not only building a strong first team, but a reserve team too was registered which would provide many a promising younger player over the next few years. Off the pitch, Hibs were in turmoil when Michael Flannigan stood down from his role as President of the Edinburgh branch of the Catholic Young Men's Society after their and his public political support of the Plan of Campaign and Boycott in Ireland.

Celtic's founders were under no such censure and openly gathered at, or indeed chaired, Irish National League and Irish Foresters meetings in the east end of Glasgow in support of Irish Home Rule, which was the major focus at that time, thoughts of rebellion were a long way away.

On the pitch too, Hibs were in turmoil in the first two months of the season, being knocked out of the Scottish Cup in the 1st round by Mossend Swifts and by Leith Athletic in the East of Scotland Shield. By the end of September they were struggling to get enough players off work to fulfil fixtures and when they did play, they suffered humiliation. losing 7-1 at home to Queens Park.

JOHN McFADDEN ABSCONDS WITH CYMS FUNDS

Worse was to follow for Hibs when Secretary John McFadden resigned his position in October 1888 to take over full control of the St Patrick's branch of the Catholic Young Men's Society, taking up much of the work of Michael Flannigan.

The fortunes of Hibs continued to slump throughout the 1888/89 season but no-one expected the news that arrived in February 1889 when John McFadden absconded to America, taking with him an incredible £400 of the CYMS funds, around £24,000 in today's money.

The *Glasgow Observer* reported the story;

THE YOUNG MEN'S SOCIETY AND FRIENDLY SOCIETY

"The secretaryship of the Edinburgh Young Men's Society has been confered on Mr Thomas Cairns, in place of J McFadden. The Friendly Society books have been examined since the disappearance of the late secretary, and it is now officially stated that the defalcations on that account reach the sum of £400. This large sum is being met by Canon Hannan, and on Sunday last claims to the value of £298 were paid. Mr D Donworth has accepted the secretaryship of the Friendly Society".

A letter was received by his shamed family shortly afterwards promising he would pay back the funds if spared, but this never happened and a man who had done so much to promote and assist the birth of numerous Irish clubs in Scotland left in the dark of night with his reputation ruined. How long had he planned this? Were his peacemaking attempts in early 1889 with the Celtic Committee a possible ruse to bring forward the fundraising match organised in March between Celtic and Hibs at Celtic Park so as he could make off with the funds raised? Or was it to an attempt to replenish the funds which he had already planned to abscond with? From the sums of money involved, it can only be surmised that the deception had gone on for a significant length of time to accrue such an amount. Was John McFadden siphoning off money from Hibs when they won the Scottish Cup two years previously and were charged with professionalism? Did John McFadden have anything to do with the accusation that Hibernian's financial records had been written up on the day in the same handwriting, despite different members being responsible for their upkeep?

On Sunday 27th January, just weeks before his departure, John McFadden was present at the annual general meeting of the Edinburgh Young Men's Society, where he was happy to remain on the committee for the coming year after reports that following a difficult twelve months when the President of the society was forced to stand down, memberships had decreased by around 15%.

Income for the past year was given as £485 and expenditure as £488, reflecting a very tight ship being ran, but that ship was about to face a crisis that no-one could have predicted.

Having left in such circumstances it would have been prudent for him to lie low in America but it seems this was not his style and he continued his interest in football, according to the match report in the Scottish Sport on 4th September 1891 concerning the high profile football match between New York Thistle and the runners up in the America Cup the previous season, Longfellows, on 15th August at Ridgewood Park, Brooklyn with a trophy at stake in the final of the Foresters Sports.

The match was a rough house, with Thistle emerging 4-3 winners and the best player on the pitch was Patrick, formerly of Kilmarnock, who now played at the back for Thistle as well as Stewart, formerly of Dunfermline Athletic and Masterton, formerly of Hearts, both of whom played in the Longfellows side. The article also mentioned Charlie Gorevin, who played in Celtic's first ever match, playing for Brooklyn against New York Thistle at Ridgewood Park on 2nd August, 1891.

The article finished as follows;

"PS - Perhaps it might interest your readers to know that the referee at the match referred to above between New York Thistle and Longfellows was Mr John McFadden, formerly of the Edinburgh Hibernians".

One thing that must be said however, is that Celtic Football Club owe Hibernian Football Club a debt of gratitude for laying the foundations for the birth of Celtic. If there had been no Hibs, there would be no Celtic as we know it today.

OUR FIRST GAME IN THE CHARITY CUP

Back to matters on the pitch and the Celts had two pressing issues in the form of the Charity Cup semi final against Renton on 4th May at Hampden Park and the North Eastern Cup Final a week later against Cowlairs at Barrowfield, as our first season reached a climax. Renton, as holders of the Charity Cup for three seasons in a row, were the favourites to see off the new upstarts and so it proved as they were too much for the Celts, minus Neil McCallum and we went down 5-2 to an admittedly brilliant Renton performance as they made it four finals in a row in front of a huge crowd of 18,000 which was more akin to a Scottish Cup final.

Renton's trainer, Peter Campbell had come up trumps again with his infamous training regime which involved feeding the players daily on "chicken bree," which was in fact a cocktail of port and eggs!

The *Scottish Sport* described the setting thus;

"Long before the kick off the masses swarmed into the enclosure and when the Renton and Celtic stepped into the arena there could not have been less than 18,000 spectators present and the romantic appearance and interest of the whole, was enlivened by the barricades all round, despite the iron spikes being lined with a living mass, like so many crows on a fence".

The fact that the other Charity Cup semi final was held between Queens Park and Third Lanark and that Rangers were not one of the four teams invited to the annual competition shows how low their stock was in 1889, having won only one trophy in their 17 years of existence. The Celts were knocked out of the three main trophies, the Scottish Cup, the Glasgow Cup and the Charity Cup by the eventual winners but it was no consolation for a club with the ambitions we shared, even at this early stage of our development.

OUR FIRST EVER TROPHY

If justice was to be served on a brilliant opening season, unknown in the annals of Scottish Football, then surely the Celts would get our reward in the North Eastern trophy, the lesser of the four trophies which we entered at the start of the season and as the name suggests, was contested only by teams based in the north and the east of Glasgow, namely Clyde, Thistle, Cowlairs, Celtic, Northern, Shettleston and Clydesdale.

The Celts had made easy work of our path to the final, beating Clydesdale 5-1 at Southcroft Park, Glasgow Road, Rutherglen on 29th December, before making light work of Northern by 4 goals to 1 at Celtic Park on 16th March. This match gave the club the first chance to celebrate St Patrick's Day at Celtic Park and as the *Scottish Referee* stated;

"Socks, pawn tickets and shamrocks were kicking about the Celtic's pavillion on Saturday in commemoration of Pat Gallagher's Day".

Paddy Gallagher was of course a Celtic player and a favourite with the fans so the play on words was clear.

Our opponents, Cowlairs, had a tougher run to the final and it took them three games to oust the Thistle before beating Shettleston 7-1 in the semi final. Both the Charity Cup semi final and the North Eastern Cup final kicked off at the exact same time, 4pm on Saturday, 11th May just under two miles apart, but this didn't stop a capacity crowd packing Clyde's ground, with the huge Celtic support, as usual, in the majority.

This was the fourth meeting of the clubs in our first season, with Cowlairs 2-0 victors in the Glasgow International Exhibition final in September 1888, after fielding a strengthened team, the Celts avenging it with a crushing 8-0 victory at Celtic Park just a couple of weeks later in the 2nd round of the Scottish Cup and a third match, a friendly, at Cowlairs' Gourlay Park in April 1889 which resulted in a 1-0 win for the bhoys.

The Celtic team on this momentous day was James McLaughlin in goals, Mick McKeown and Pat Dowling at full back, Willie Maley, James Kelly and James McLaren at half backs and a forward five of Paddy Gallagher, Willie Groves, Johnny Coleman, Mick Dunbar and Tom Maley.

The Celts started the stronger and opened the scoring in the 15th minute when the ball was bundled over from a corner from Paddy Gallagher and this was followed up three minutes later by Willie Groves. We were well in command now and Willie Maley added a third before Cowlairs grabbed one back before half time.

Cowlairs' tails were up as they tried to get back into the game at the start of the second half but the match was finished as a contest when Peter Dowds scored a fourth, before Johnny Coleman and Willie Groves put the outcome well beyond doubt with a fifth and a sixth, almost a year to the day Celtic Park was opened.

It was the perfect end to an almost perfect inaugural season but it wasn't finished yet. The Celtic Committee, as enterprising as ever, arranged for the top two teams in England to play at Celtic Park and so Preston North End and Bolton Wanderers travelled north for glamour matches with every penny raised going towards the Home For the Aged at Garngad Hill, which was ran by the Little Sisters of the Poor and took care of over 400 senior citizens.

THE CREAM OF ENGLAND SENT HOME TO THINK AGAIN - AGAIN!

Thursday, 23rd May was the date of the Bolton Wanderers match and the Celts were eager to gain revenge for our 2-0 defeat at Bolton on Good Friday, just five weeks previous. Dan Doyle played for Bolton and he may well have shown an initial interest in the Celts as he visited Celtic Park again just days later to watch the Preston North End match. Doyle would have left the ground more than impressed by this Celtic team who blew away Bolton by 5 goals to 1 in front of a large crowd delighted with the score and contented too that the funds raised went to the Little Sisters of the Poor, a charity close to the hearts of east enders.

The Celts started on the front foot and only the performance of the Bolton keeper kept his goal intact, however after we had a goal disallowed, Johnny Coleman and Mick Dunbar scored two goals in quick succession. Bolton were pinned back into their own half for much of the first 45, but on one foray forward, they scored with a low shot after some clever passing. Shortly after the start of the second half, Peter Dowds scored a third and Bolton were pressed back for the full ninety minutes, happy to get out of Celtic Park with the loss of only two more goals.

The Evening Times reporter at the match claimed that a commissionaire at the pay boxes had told him that there had been 300 reporters in attendance at the game. His tongue must have been planted firmly in his cheek as he revealed the ingenious method, that many Celtic supporters without the 6d in hand, had thought up to see their favourites. You can just imagine the line of "reporters," Murphy; Daily Bugle, McGillicudy; Carfin Advertiser, Kelly; Coatbridge erm Chancer.

Two days later on Saturday, 25th May, the English Cup holders Preston North End arrived at Celtic Park. The Celtic Committee had shown their usual expertise by attracting the top English team with a guarantee of £80 on condition that they did not appear in Glasgow against any other club in the four weeks preceding the match from the 27th April.

The match started a few minutes late due to the brake carrying the Preston team getting lost on the way to the ground but fortunately the players were already stripped and ready to go. They weren't quite ready enough though, as the Celts stormed into a two goal lead within the first seven minutes in front of another crowd of just under 10,000. Willie Groves got the first after only two minutes with a beautiful shot and Mick Dunbar headed in from a cross just five minutes later. The visitors playing with nine Scots in their team were struggling but they did manage to get one goal back when Ross beat James McLaughlin with a soft shot which the goalkeeper didn't see. No more goals were forthcoming and the Celts reputation soared once more amongst English teams who were being taken on and beaten regularly by the "new Irish combination".

ONE YEAR TO THE DAY

On May 28th 1889, on the first anniversary of our first ever match, Celtic Park again played host to a big match, with the ground being chosen to host the final of the Glasgow North East Association's Second XI final between Clyde and Thistle.

OUR FIRST ANNUAL GENERAL MEETING

The Annual General Meeting on Tuesday, 18th June 1889 in the Mechanics Hall, Canning St, Bridgeton at 7.30pm was packed with all members requiring to show their membership cards to gain entry, such was its popularity. Honorary President, Doctor John Conway opened the meeting from the chair, then passed on to John O'Hara to read the Secretary's report.

Of 60 matches played in our first season, we won 43, drew 5 and lost 12, scoring 204 goals and conceding 92. Of the four trophies entered we won one, reached one cup final and two semi finals. More importantly, given the reasons for our birth, we raised a total of £421, 16s and 9d for charity, the equivalent of around £25,000 in today's money.

In the former Celtic Chairman, Robert Kelly's book, simply titled *"CELTIC"* and published in 1971, he printed the first ever balance sheet which covered the period from 1st December 1887 to 31st May 1889. This gives us a precious insight into the early working of the club, laid out in full detail and audited by Brother Walfrid's fellow Marist, Brother Dorotheus.

Under incomings, it lists Members and Patrons fees as £99, 7s and under Season Tickets we took in £37, 2s and 6d. Back in the day a season ticket gained you access to all games played in the ground for that season of any description. Each game is listed with the takings at the Stand and Gate separated as well as away matches where we secured a half share of the gate.

The first match ever played at Celtic Park, between Hibs and Cowlairs was said to have been watched by a crowd of 5000 and the balance sheet shows £14, 11s and 6d taken from the stand and £58, 2s and 6d taken from the gate. This compares almost identically to the match between Celtic and Hibs in August 1888 when £13 and £57 were taken in at the stand and gate in a match where the crowd was also given as 5000.

The first ever Celtic match attracted a crowd of 2000 and this was reflected in the gate of £16, 5s and 6d with £5, 8s and 3d taken at the stand. Ironically only two matches attracted a lower crowd in the accounts, both against Airdrie when only 1000 turned up for each friendly match, one of which was only set for two periods of 35 minutes, instead of the regulation 45 minutes.

Guarantees were a good earner and the Celts committed to play the following teams for the accompanying fee; Dundee Harp £15, Newcastle West End £40, Bolton £25, Burnley £25, Distillery £28 and United Belfast £28. In return, Celtic had to return the favour and pay out guarantees to attract some of the top teams to Celtic Park as follows; Mitchell Saint George £25, Corinthians £45, Bolton £25 and Preston North End a whopping £80.

Loans received by backers was a vital part of the accounts and it names those who provided the funds to get the club off the ground, before the subscription list had been sent, in order to fund, for example, the lease of the ground and the materials to build it.

Charles McGallagly is named as the biggest lender, backing the club to the tune of £50, closely followed by Doctor John Conway with £40, John Brien with £30, John Higney with £20 and two other members known to Doctor Conway with a total of £20, Hugh Darroch with £15 and James Quillan and James Doyle with £10 each. Of these lenders, Doctor John Conway was the club's first Honorary President, Hugh Darroch was Joint Treasurer with John H McLaughlin and James Quillan was named as the first Vice President.

Outlay on the ground was listed amongst expenditures as;
Material (Soil, Ashes, Seed, Manure etc); £47, 7s and 6d.
Labourers wages; £257, 6s.
Stand, Pay Boxes, Barricade and various erections on ground; £514, 6s, 6d.
Rent etc; £75.
Committee Rooms; £5.
Taxes; £8, 4s, 6d.

Whilst the rent is given as £75 it should be remembered that this balance sheet covered 18 months so the historical fact that the rent was £50 per annum is correct. The outlay on the pitch, ie soil, manure and seed showed that work had to be done in this regard too, it wasn't just a matter of throwing up a stand, a boundary fence, some pay boxes and some ashes for grip on the makeshift terracing around a pitch that was already there.

The pitch had to be brought up to the standard required. There was two pitches on the original piece of land so work had to be carried out on both to give us a decent playing pitch and also a smaller one to train on.

Other outgoings were very interesting and included;

Balls; £17, 7s, 10d.
Uniforms etc; £64, 11s, 5d.
Police, Groundsmen and Referee; £97, 3s, 4d.
Commissionaires and Cash Collectors; £67, 1s.
Entertainments to teams; £115, 7s, 6d.
Refreshments; £102, 7s, 9d.
Brakes, cabs etc; £27, 10s, 7d.

This shows that although the players were restricted by amateurism; the groundsman, the doorman, the cash collectors and the referee were paid a wage. Back in the day a football match was a social occasion with the home team footing the bill for the after match dinner at a local restaurant where speeches would be made and toasts given and responded to, adding to the drinks bill as they did.

Given the expenditure on balls over the 18 month period, it seems the design of the original Celtic Park, open on four sides, had a lot to do with a good few exiting the ground during a match or practice to the great joy of the street urchins outside who would have had no desire in rushing to return them.

Travelling expenses and lost time to players gives an insight into the funds spent to spread the name of Celtic on tours of England and Ireland;

£143, 18s, 6d was spent on local matches.
£73, 3s, 8d was spent on the London trip to play Corinthians, from which we received a £40 guarantee.
£26, 19s, 5d was spent on the trip to Newcastle against a £40 guarantee.
£123, 10s, 11d was spent on the Easter Tour against guarantees from Bolton, Burnley, Distillery and United Belfast which totalled £106.

Half gates paid out to visiting clubs were listed next and without a shadow of doubt this was a bug bear with the first Committee as the figures in both columns show the money going out to visiting teams was rarely reciprocated at their ground when we visited.

The balance sheet also breaks down every charitable donation given by the club over the 18 months which totalled £421, 16s, 9d, not including charity matches, which added a good deal more to the total on top of this.

The full list of donations in our first balance sheet is as follows;

Edinburgh Hibernian; £45.

Saint Vincent De Paul Society; £164, 16s.

Home for Children; £50.

Father Dyer, for vestments for the Poor House; £5.

Saint Mary's Poor Childrens Dinner Table; £27.

Sacred Heart Poor Childrens Dinner Tables; £15.

Saint Michael's Poor Childrens Dinner Tables; £9.

Hand-loom weavers of Bridgeton; £10.

Shettleston FC Subscription sale; £2, 10s.

Father Bird, for Barlinnie Chapel; £5.

Edinburgh Hibernian; £18, 10s, 9d.

Father McFadden Defence Fund; £10.

Sisters of Mercy, Lanark; £10.

Little Sisters of the Poor; £50.

From the donations given, it is clear that although we were set up to fund the maintenance of the Dinner Tables in the parishes of St Mary's, Sacred Heart and St Michael's, there were many other just causes in the local area deserving of our attention that were not missed.

Very prominent in the list are two large donations to Hibernian FC. Much is made of the fact that many of the Hibs players returned to the west of Scotland and signed for Celtic but not very much is heard about these two large donations and also the match between the clubs a week before St Patrick's Day, 1889 at Celtic Park when all the proceeds were given to Hibernian to boost their finances. The former Hibs Secretary, John McFadden, may not have been slow in making up with the Celtic Committee during the 1888/89 season, but the Hibs support were in no mood to move on just yet.

Political, as well as religious causes were not ignored and a prime example of this was the £10 donated to the Father McFadden Defence Fund. Father James McFadden was the parish priest in Gweedore, Donegal at a time when evictions were rife when families could not afford exorbitant rental increases from absentee landlords. Lord George Hill was the landlord for Gweedore and his attitude towards the Irish was probably best summed up by the following quote attributed to him;

"The Irish people have profited much by the Famine, the lesson was severe; but so were they rooted in old prejudices and old ways, that no teacher could have induced them to make the changes which this Visitation of Divine Providence has brought about, both in their habits of life and in their mode of agriculture."

In late January, 1889 a warrant was issued for the arrest of Father McFadden after he had stood in the doorway of a house within his parish as the bailiffs tried to evict a young Catholic family onto the street. The date carried out for the arrest was Sunday, 3rd February as he said mass in the chapel, which was insensitive to say the least and naturally inflamed the passions of the parishioners who saw Father McFadden not only as their spiritual leader, but as their shining light in the fight against the evils of landlordism and its effects on the local population.

After Father McFadden celebrated mass, he was approached by three policeman outside the chapel, one of whom, allegedly brandished a sword before an arrest warrant was finally shown. This incensed the locals and as the party headed for the Parochial House, stones were thrown and Inspector Martin was struck on the head and tragically died from his injuries.

The reaction was swift from the authorities and no less than 43 arrests were made, including that of Father McFadden. This caused uproar and branches of the Father McFadden Defence Fund were set up all over Ireland and further afield, with one based in Glasgow naturally. Celtic Committee man, Joseph Francis McGroary, was elected as the Secretary as Glasgow and the surrounding areas threw their support right behind the people of Gweedore as demonstrations and concerts were organised to highlight their plight.

At one public meeting in the National Halls, Glasgow, in late April 1889, over 3000 attended with a side hall having to be opened to accommodate the overflow of 1200. The Committee had hoped to attract Father McFadden himself to attend but he was out on bail from his Derry prison cell and therefore could not possibly leave Ireland.

At the meeting the following resolution was agreed;

"That this meeting of Irishmen and Scotsman condemn in the strongest terms the actions of the Irish landlords in laying desolate the homes of the peasants of Gweedore and that we pledge ourselves to support them in their struggle in defence of hearth and home".

Joseph McGroary, the Secretary of the Glasgow Donegal Reunion Committee, as well as the Glasgow branch of the Father McFadden Defence Fund received the following letter from Father McFadden himself after his release from imprisonment;

"My dear Mr McGroary,

I owe yourself and my dear friends of the Donegal Committee an apology for the delay in acknowledging your warm letter of congratulations on my discharge from gaol on 20th April.

Kindly convey my deepest thanks to your colleagues and assure them that I am always gratefully sensible of their unfailing devotion to the cause of Ireland and their ever ready and valued service to Donegal and their undeserved respect and esteem for myself. In have no doubt suffered in mind and body at the baseless iniquity heaped upon me, but I am rewarded by the valued admiration of my friends in Glasgow and elsewhere.

I feel personally honoured by your magnanimous and successful efforts in aid of the Evicted Tenants and Fair Trial Fund. I heartily thank all the donors and wishing upon yourself and your colleagues every manner of blessing. I remain, yours always, truly.

James McFadden P.P.
Gweedore, County Donegal
17th May 1889".

When the case finally came to court in October 1889, sentences ranged from 5 to 10 years penal servitude for manslaughter, whilst others were given 2 to 6 months for rioting. Father McFadden was declared guilty of obstructing the police and bound over to keep the peace.

Back to the Celtic balance sheet and even the sundries list provokes interest;

Printing; £134, 12s, 2d.

Advertising; £12, 18s, 2d.

Secretarial expenses, books, stationary, telegrams etc; £46, 7s, 5d.

Entrance fees to various Associations; £2, 11s.

Furnishings, Tolls etc; £23, 3s, 8d.

Repairs, washing etc; £22, 16s, 10d.

Trainer's wages and expenses; £69, 18s, 10d.

Allowances for players for lost time through injuries; £9, 7s, 6d.

Insurance for Stand; £2, 12s, 6d.

Insurance for 1st Team; £7, 16s.

Marriage present to John Coleman; £10.

Marriage present to Mick McKeown; £10.

Mr James Quillan, Proportion of expenses on London trip; £2, 4s, 4d.

Mr James Quillan, Season Tickets sold; £1, 5s.

Sundries; £37, 7s, 7d.

Interestingly, allowances for lost time through injuries was calculated separately from lost time playing matches and it would have been no comfort to players that the trainer also received a wage and was not bound by amateur rules.

Marriage gifts were very generous and were no doubt given as a boost to offset any quarrels from the new matrimonial quarters where the good lady would be justified to ask how well rewarded her beloved was for his football skills compared to professional players down south.

Balance, cash in bank; £160, 15s, 11 d.

Balance, cash in hand; £14, 1 s.

Total turnover; £3807, 17s, 8d.

Outstanding income was listed as follows;

£40 was still to be received from Corinthians for our guarantee on our visit to London, a half gate of approx £25 was outstanding from Cowlairs FC and our share of the North Eastern Association Cup Final tie amounting to £31 was still to be received.

THE ORIGINAL MALCONTENTS - THE QUILLANITES

Everything in the garden appeared rosy but there were strong seeds of doubt in the background with declarations from the "malcontents," led by Celtic Vice President, James Quillan which was a clear indication of a split in the camp. Ironically this word was to be introduced again to the Celtic support a century later when the great nephew of James Kelly, Kevin Kelly used it to describe the rebel camp of the Celtic support of the 1990s, who were to end the families dynasty at Celtic Park.

A great deal of sensationalism was being banded about in the Scottish press with the following allegation used here as a prime example, from the Scottish Sport, on the 24th May 1889;

"Last Wednesday evening a few malcontents connected with the Celtic Club, tried to hold a hole and corner meeting in a certain well known public house in Main Street, Bridgeton. It was intended that it should be a success, as an office bearer and a few Committee men took part in it.

The matter under consideration was;

1. The present Committee's mismanagement and the advisability of those present taking charge of the club.

2. Should they sever connection with the Celts and take in hand with the Benburb and raise it to a senior team.

After some discussion, the "Ould Giniral" who was invited, made a speech of some length and did not seem afraid to lay round him - not on the absent, but on the present - and did he not squelch them in style. After his oration the meeting broke up in confusion. Moral - these pubs are not suitable places in which to hold meetings of young man and still less of old men.

Oh ye Celtic, what a narrow escape you have had from these - friends of the club. How a prominent member of Committee in Bridgeton must have looked aghast when he heard of this secret conclave. When the next meeting of these sages is held, we would suggest that they keep the door closed, or have some official report sent to the press".

There was no smoke without fire with some of the rumblings true and others not so true. The allegations had risen from the general meeting on 2nd May 1889, organised to appoint auditors and adopt rules and led to recriminations in private and public, which lasted right up until the AGM on the 18th June.

Both the *Scottish Sport* and the *Scottish Referee* gave the right of reply to one of those present at the so called hole and corner gathering in a public house in Bridgeton.

The *Scottish Sport* reported;

"Sir I was astonished on looking over your bill of the contents of the Scottish Sport to observe the rather sensational item "Intrigue in the Celtic camp".

As one of the parties referred to, allow me respectfully, but emphatically, to state that the whole paragraph is a pure fabrication, and contains several mis-statements of fact, not to use a harsher term.

In the first place there was no meeting held, "hole and corner" or otherwise. Returning citywards from the athletic meeting at Barrowfield, one or two Celtic members called into a public house kept by a strong supporter of the club. As their doing so was purely accidental and unpremeditated and their number in all reached five, the spiteful remark that it was intended that it should be a success is, you will perceive, as uncalled for as it is, to put it mildly, in bad taste. The advisability of those present taking charge of the club was never mooted.

Should they sever their connection with the Celtic and take in hand with the Benburb and raise it to a senior team and the invitation and speech of the Ould Giniral, (Jimmy McLaren), are simply pure inventions of the distorted imagination of your correspondent. Those five who met must plead guilty to having arrived at the age of maturity and understanding which it is hoped the writer of the sensational paragraph may in time attain.

In regard to the final advice as to having some official report sent to the press, we are quite at one with the writer and feel sure that you, sir, have been entirely mislead or the paragraph would never have appeared. The matter is probably beneath contempt in one way, but when it is considered how great and noble a factor for good the national game is and how much such puerile effusions are calculated to nullify its efficiency, reluctantly, Mr editor, we are constrained to ask your kind insertion of this letter in the hope that it may partly, at least, show the public out of how little much is made and at the sensational statements must be accepted "cum grano salis", (with a pinch of salt).

Apologising for troubling you and thanking you in prospect for your courteous insertion,

I am, Sir, yours, etc.
"ONE OF THE SO CALLED MALCONTENTS"
Glasgow, 27th May 1889"

From the *Scottish Referee*;

THE CELTIC AND THEIR COMMITTEE

"Sir

I was astonished to see in last Friday's issue of Sport a report of a supposed hole and corner meeting of Celtic members held last Wednesday in a spirit shop in Main Street, Bridgeton, where an official and several members of committee took park in considering the advisability of severing their connection with the Celtic and raising the Benburb to a senior team, also the mismanagement of the Celtic team and the necessity of appointing a new committee.

Having been at the Clydesdale Harriers Sports in the Clyde's park, I called at the shop under notice on my way home, like the others who were there, and remained until the last. I can testify that no matter how badly the Celtic club may be managed or how great may be the necessity for appointing a new committee, there was no meeting held there, nor anything submitted for the consideration of those present, nor any speech made by McLaren, our famous half back, or anyone present - not even the issue of Celtic or its committee was ever mentioned.

When the attention of the GOM, (Jimmy McLaren), was called to the article, he seemed utterly disgusted at the members of the party who made such a statement. One is at a loss to know the object of such despicable conduct, whether it is an electioneering dodge on the part of some of the "dear friends" of the present committee seeing the annual general meeting is about to be held.

Be that as it may, the members of the club will no doubt be able to judge such conduct in the proper light and appoint those only to office who will look after the real interests of the club".

I am, etc.,
FAIRPLAY

A fortnight before the AGM, the *Scottish Referee*, on 27th May, warned of unrest in the camp when it opined;

"Since being organised, the Celtic Club has went through many trials and has endured many hardships. Its most recent affliction is by way of a covert attack upon several highly prominent members - playing and non playing. The rather enigmatical insinuations used were the chief weapons of this attack today pointedly and emphatically denied and which will be found in our letters columns. Unfortunately the author of the letter, for reasons which he has satisfactorily explained to us, cannot in the meantime give his name. He does not err on the side of rashness in doing this, as the attack came from an anonymous source, and deserves therefore to be answered anonymously.

While being neither desirous nor able to discuss the affairs of the Celtic, we cannot refrain from putting on record our opinion that the scandals which have been too frequently raised about the club and out of which other people have been making capital, tend to show up its management in a very bad light. While we are not inclined to believe all that has been said, we are in the opinion that in the great mass of damaging gossip which has been put in circulation, there is bound to be some modicum of truth. Truth, like murder, will out and so we live in hopes of learning within a few weeks the true state of affairs in the Celtic camp.

That dissatisfaction exists and has existed for some time back among certain members of the Celtic is proved by the fact that a short time ago arrangements were all but completed for the formation of another Hibernian club in the east end of the city. A ground had been secured and over £500 had been raised in order to give the new organisation a fair start, when it was resolved to abandon the idea temporarily and await certain developments in the Celtic camp. These developments are expected within the next three weeks so that the lapse of that space in time will see the settlement of the question as to whether we are to have a new club in Glasgow next season.

Should the new club be formed its objects will be the public distribution of aid to charitable institutions, to widen the resources of recreation of the working classes and to popularise the game generally.

The prime object of the club - the public distribution of aid to charitable institutions strikes at being a hit at (an attack on), the Celtic. That club holds the position it does towards charity and as we have always held, have made known the dealings with the various funds to which they contribute. If Celtic showed the distribution in a public rather than a private way the present dissatisfaction might never have arisen.

The annual general meeting of the Celtic will take place in a fortnight, when there will no doubt be some fun over the election of office bearers. Almost all last season's officials will be put up again and as there are several prominent outsiders anxious for posts, the competition is likely to be keen. Some of the players are, we believe, so strongly in favour of the re-election of Mr Glass to the President's chair that they have in private declared that they will leave the club should he happen to be ousted. This says much for Mister Glass's popularity with the playing section. In the general membership he has not got so many friends and no doubt he will have to fight for the honour".

The Celtic Committee were well aware of the malcontents and how deep the malaise had reached as they had already secured a ground and funding for a new club in the city to rival our own. All that was holding the malcontents back from making their move was the upcoming Celtic AGM were they wanted to test the water in regards to their level of support by nominating some of their number for election onto the committee.

It's worth examining the objects of the new club, obviously leaked to the Scottish Referee in more detail as they are very similar to our own. The only word that stands out is the *"public"* distribution of aid to charitable institutions. Why did the malcontents want more transparency in Celtic's charitable donations? Certainly details of every donation made was already included in the Treasurer's report at the AGM and in print in the balance sheet.

The club had donated the entire takings from the three biggest matches of the season at Celtic Park to the Saint Vincent De Paul Society and the Little Sisters of the Poor, we had fulfilled our pledge in the original constitution to donate £5 per week to the Poor Childrens Dinner Tables Fund and we had donated a total of £421 to charity.

What exactly was he getting at regarding entrance fees and subscription money? There's no doubt whatsoever that the club, before professionalism was introduced in 1893, could not have attracted the players we did without the assistance of supporters in the licensing trade, as practiced by other clubs with the exception of Queens Park, who remain amateur to this day. Some were given proprietorship of public houses, with Peter Dowds and Neil McCallum said to be the latest and so this was their means to an end, how they earned a living. This would have benefited Celtic too as it didn't involve physical labour and the committee knew exactly where to find their players, who would be easily contactable at any time. The owner of the public house in turn would see a rise in his profits from the patronage of the Celtic support hoping to sup in the company of one of their heroes.

Was Quillan's argument that more money should be donated to charity and less paid to attract top players? Was he originally in the pro Glasgow Hibernian camp at our formation and therefore strongly against the signing of Hibernian players, which admittedly damaged the Irishmen of the east? If so, why didn't he come out and say exactly that? The committee were all volunteers and didn't take a penny so they were above suspicion. Why did he want the original ruling omitted rather than amended regarding entrance fees and subscription money? Why did the battle he chose to fight concern a relatively minor matter, rather than an issue that may well have split the camp more evenly? What was his game plan?

In the Celtic Handbook of 1935/36, written by Willie Maley, he quotes the first set of Rules, Constitution and Bye laws of the Celtic Football & Athletic Club which was issued in 1888. It states that entry money and annual subscription was 5s each. The entrance fee into an individual Celtic match was sixpence, which is self explanatory, with a further sixpence added for admission to the grandstand. Therefore a season ticket would cost 5 shillings, as well as the annual subscription which would gain you membership of the club and the right to attend AGMs and be nominated for a place on the committee. Season tickets would allow you entry into every match played at Celtic Park, therefore they would be very good value, albeit you would be required to pay up front at the start of the season, money which the vast majority did not have.

Significantly in the report on the AGM, it stated that;

"Few, very few could understand the position adopted by Mr Quillan, for as fast as one portion of his contention was cleared away, hydra like another raised its head".

This was all in regard to the same item, the Secretary's report read out by John O'Hara. No questions were raised during the Treasurer's report and it was adopted unanimously, therefore Mr Quillan's issues were not in regard to funds given to charity or it would have been asked during that report.

Was there enough evidence to state beyond doubt that it was the beginning of the battle for the club's soul, with the charitable and the professional ideals coming to a head? Certainly it was the first public spat and it had serious repercussions that was to become clear before the new season had begun.

THE INCREDIBLE CORRESPONDENCE AS BOTH PARTIES BATTLE IN PUBLIC

Finally, during the research for this book, the answers to all of the above were found, not in the sports pages where you would expect to find them, but in the Letters pages of the Glasgow Evening News, where James Quillan, the chief malcontent, spelled out his case precisely and incredibly, in return, no less than John H McLaughlin, from the Celtic Committee responded in a public correspondence that carried on from the 28th May throughout 11 issues, right up to the eve of the AGM on the 18th June. Talk about washing your dirty linen in public?

The first mud was slung by James Quillan on the 28th May;

THE CELTIC CLUB AND THEIR COMMITTEE

"SIR - As there have been various rumours circulated in regard to the working of this club, will you kindly grant me space for the following remarks; - On the 2nd inst., (May), a general meeting of the club was held to appoint auditors and adopt rules. I moved that old members should be admitted on payment of 5s, which was seconded by Mr Howie, and carried by 59 against 42 votes. By the rule as read - This majority, (including of course, myself), understood that new members were to be admitted on payment of 7s, 6d. On seeing the new rules when published we were surprised to find that instead of 7s, 6d, the sum of 12s, 6d was stipulated.

I protested - and my protest was duly noted - against members who had joined the club previous to 1st September, 1888 being excluded from the meeting in direct violation of Rules 10 and 24. On the 9th of July, 1888 a meeting was alleged to have been held, notice of which was not given to me, although I then held and still hold the office of Vice President, at which another violation of the rules occurred, a resolution being passed making the entry money 10s instead of 5s. Without acting in any way the part of "the captious critic," it seems to me that twelve out of the twenty four rules have been disregarded. As a sincere well wisher of the club and in its best interests looking to the good it has accomplished and in the hope that a bright and useful future is still in store for it, I take this opportunity of laying those facts before its many friends".

I am, &c.,
JAMES QUILLAN
Vice-President, Celtic FC

For an office bearer, never mind a committee member, to write to the letter pages of a Glasgow evening newspaper to express his concerns over the internal workings of that committee was highly unusual to say the least and would be ruled out of order and would almost certainly lead to that member having a vote of no confidence called upon him.

From a historian's point of view, its very fortunate that he did take this course of action as the ensuing mudfight has revealed a great deal about the early workings of the formative club which we would never have known.

For Quillan to take the unprecedented approach of corresponding publicly in a newspaper, he must either have felt totally undermined in his position as Vice Chairman where he could have called an office bearer's meeting to put his points across, or he was undermining the committee, and electioneering for support at the upcoming AGM, knowing that as things stood, he didn't have the numbers to win the debate.

He had to choose his battle carefully, a battle he could win, but he was on shaky ground. Subscription and entry fees were two distinctly different payments. Any supporter, similar to today, can pay entry fees up front, ie, a season ticket and in 1888 the cost was 5 shillings. A subscription, ie, membership of the club which gained you access to meetings and to stand for election was also 5 shillings in 1888. A year later, entry fees, ie, season tickets were raised from 5s to 7s, 6d for new members, giving a total expenditure of 12s, 6d instead of 10s for both.

There was no doubt that there was bad feeling amongst the first Celtic Committee and this issue was one of others which were to raise its ugly head in public. Unfortunately for James Quillan, on this occasion, the Celtic Committee responded with one of our big hitters, John H McLaughlin, a man who didn't mince his words, as his lofty replies showed.

Two days later, on the 30th May, the reply came from John H McLaughlin;

THE CELTIC AND THEIR COMMITTEE

"SIR - I read with great pain, but with no surprise, the extraordinary effusion our Vice President treats your readers to in your issue of last night. As the person directly responsible for the drafting and printing of the rules perhaps you will allow me space to reply to his misrepresentations. I will refrain from commenting on the indecency of an official in his position, who so loudly proclaims himself "a sincere well wisher of the Club" &c, vide the incoherent conclusion of his letter dragging into print, matters which ought never to have been discussed outside of the club, but will confine myself to a bare statement of the facts. The rule which Mr Quillan calls in question reads as follows; -

"The annual subscription shall be 5s. New members, besides their subscription shall pay an entry money of 7s, 6d".

Now this rule was read over at the meeting on 2nd May no less than five times, and was moreover, discussed clause by clause, and this last clause adopted unanimously. If Mr Quillan didn't understand the rule at that time, it can only be attributed to his inability - which was quite apparent - to grasp the difference between the terms "entry money" and "subscription' - a difference he has since seemingly mastered. Through the rest of his rambling letter I do not care to follow him. His alleged grievances have been discussed at many committee meetings, and he has again and again been proved to be totally and hopelessly wrong.

Arguments and facts, however, seem to be thrown away on him, and I shall, therefore not recapitulate what has been explained to him a dozen times over; but for the benefit of those of the Celtic members who do no know Mr Quillan, and might therefore be inclined to attach some weight to his vapourings; allow me to state - firstly that the alleged meeting on 9th July was the usual weekly meeting of the committee, and that if Mr Quillan was absent from it, it was entirely his own fault; and secondly, that that meeting did not pass a resolution to make the entry money 10s, but simply resolved that no new members should be admitted on account of the precarious condition the club then stood in, and this was done on the advice of our law agent, a fact which Mr Quillan is perfectly well aware.

What he means when he says that 12 out of 24 rules have been disregarded, I don't know - probably he does not himself - and until he explains it I shall take the liberty of regarding it as unintelligible nonsense; a fitting ending indeed for a tirade of misstatements, which, in common with the other ebullitions of himself and his friends in print lately, I can only designate as electioneering dodges of the flimsiest character. I leave the members of the Celtic to judge whether it is a disinterested regard for the welfare of the club, or a desire to advertise himself, and to pose as "the poor man's friend," (a role he seems to have a special liking for), that has inspired his precious epistle".

I am, &c.,
JOHN H McLAUGHLIN
Glasgow, 29th May 1889

Although John H McLaughlin lacked somewhat in subtlety, James Quillan certainly knew where he stood after this contretemps, the first recorded version of the "hair dryer" treatment, which Alex Ferguson was to make famous over a century later as McLaughlin pointed out the error of Quillan's allegation.

A day later, Viator, in his Athletic Jottings in the *Glasgow Evening News* opined;

"Out east matters are not moving very smoothly with the Celtic. There are two factions in the club, and it is not improbable that these will become separate and distinct organisations in the course of time. As has been very truly remarked elsewhere, the Celtic Club has undergone many hardships during its short but brilliant career. The club has instituted more on account of the good it would do to charity than anything else.

Some of the members are, amongst other things, anything but pleased at the way in which this charity has been administered. I am half inclined to agree with them in one particular. The hand that gives silently is most appreciated. The Celtic, however, should not have spread their benevolence anonymously. This is one of the sore points with some of the members. It appears too, that a great many of them have got into a fog over some of the rules. I trust that the breach will not be widened, and that at the annual meeting, which is to be held in a few days, all differences will be amicably settled".

In commenting, Viator pointed out what was already common knowledge, although it had not yet raised its ugly head in the debate, that by the end of May, James Quillan had already decided to start up a rival club. This crucial point meant that his electioneering was more than simply that. He was not trying to gain support for re-election to the Celtic Committee, he was canvassing support for a rival club, from within the Celtic membership.

James Quillan responded;

CELTIC CLUB AND THEIR COMMITTEE

"SIR - With reference to your issue of 30th inst. you publish a letter from J H McLaughlin purporting to be a reply to mine of 28th inst, which I consider is far from it. I have no wish to bring myself before the public in any way but honesty, and decline to follow his personalities. The rule that has been referred to, (No 15 of the new issue), is said to have read over five times and discussed clause by clause. This I deny. I admit that the first portion of the rule was read over twice and discussed, with the following result, From my amendment:- that instead of old members being charged 12s, 6d per annum as the rule then read for adoption, that the charge should only be 5s, and that they should enjoy all the privileges of ordinary members. In opposition to my proposition a member stated that no working men would grudge to pay 12s, 6d annually to be a member. When I was again accosted from another source, of patting the working man too much.

My opinion of the Celtic FC is and has been all along, that it is entirely for charitable purposes and my sympathy follows it. By exacting the figure of 12s, 6d prevents many of the working class from joining as members. Far be it from me overlooking the interest of the working class; my objections are entirely against the excessive charge, which looks as if they were not wanted as members, although in my opinion they are being the bone and sinew of the Celtic. The grievances to which reference has been made were not mine, but were of a general nature. With reference to my letter of 28th May regarding the violation of the rules, I have only to refer your correspondent to rules number 2, 4, 5, 7, 9, 10, 15, 17, 18, 19, 20 and 24, (of the old issue), and ask him to show wherein they have been strictly adhered to.

I fail to trace any rule relative to weekly meetings and do not understand what your correspondent refers to when he says that 9th July was the usual weekly meeting of committee. From information a number of members of committee have been placed in a similar position to myself and are ignorant of what transpired at said meeting. Should any ignorance be displayed in the interpretation of these rules I shall be glad to enlighten them on the subject".

I am, &c.,
JAMES QUILLAN
Vice President
31st May 1889

In his comeback letter, Quillan again showed an ignorance of the structures of payment, but to his credit, he highlighted an issue which seemed to have not afflicted himself alone, this misunderstanding being the responsibility of the committee to ensure everyone came to a clear understanding before agreement was reached.

He went on to list the 12 rules which he believed hadn't been strictly adhered to and although we have no original constitution and rule book to check back on, his inference is clear, that the committee had been less than scrupulous in sticking to the letter of the rules and had forged on without the full co-operation of the membership.

John H McLaughlin responded;

THE CELTIC AND THEIR COMMITTEE

"SIR - I had hoped that Mr Quillan would have had the good taste and sense to drop the discussion of matters which, as he well understands cannot be settled in the columns of a newspaper. But as I have already suggested, these letters of his are written with an eye to the impending election and may be looked on as his "address to the electors". I fear I cannot congratulate him on his success. It is too much to ask the members of the Celtic, (including the working men, whose friend he poses as, or in other words, whose vote he is seeking), to believe that he is deeply interested in the welfare of the club, while at the same time he persists in dragging on a controversy that cannot possibly do the club the least good, and will in all probability do it a great deal of harm.

As to this latest effusion of his, I must confess I don't understand it. It seems to me a lot of drivelling nonsense, without cohesion, point, or argument. His first letter was in reference to the subscription of new members - this one, so far as I can fathom it, to the subscription of old members - his next, if there is to be a next, will probably wander to some other subject. As usual with Mr Quillan's literary productions, the present bristles with inaccuracies, which, however, with one exception, I shall leave to be fully dealt with and explained in the proper place - the annual general meeting.

The exception I refer to is with regard to the annual subscription. Mr Quillan asserts that it was proposed to raise this to 12s, 6d. This I most emphatically contradict. Such a proposition was never even dreamt of, far less laid before the meeting. What was proposed was that the subscription be raised to 7s, 6d. This may be taken as a sample of Mr Quillan's facts, and your readers will be able to gauge from it the true value of his utterances. In conclusion, I would advise Mr Quillan if he feels that he must "stump the constituency", to adopt some other means than writing to the newspapers, as neither the matter nor the construction of his letters are likely to raise him in the opinion in the members of the Celtic, or induce them to entrust him with the management of its affairs".

I am, &c.,
JOHN H McLAUGHLIN
Glasgow, 1st June 1889

In this letter, John H McLaughlin got personal and lowered the debate which can often ostracise opinion that was already in your favour by the tone taken. All that was required to be re-iterated in a short response was the fact that the alleged proposal to raise the annual subscription from 5s to 12s, 6d was totally untrue, as he stated, a proposition that was never even dreamt of.

THE CELTIC AND THEIR COMMITTEE

"SIR - Although an admirer of the Celtic Club since its inauguration, I may state that the last letter of Mr McLaughlin staggered me. Having copied as much American slang as his fertile brain contains, he makes an attack upon an Irishman who through weal and through woe has stuck to "Ireland's a nation". I would not trouble you with my letter in connection with the above did your correspondence stick to the arguments raised by Mr Quillan. But in as much as he charges him with "stumping the constituency" and issuing an "address to the electors", I may tell him that Mr Quillan has had in the past - and, indeed, at the present time - more honourable positions assigned to him than any position the Celtic place him in. But I am happy to know he declines any position in that club in future, not from any objection to the members, but to the contemptible gang who, with two exceptions, have never identified themselves with any Irish movement, and who may discover before long, if they do not alter their tactics, that their game is played out".

I am, &c.,
HUGH MURPHY
167 East Nelson Street
3rd June, 1889

Hugh Murphy was a major player in the Irish National League where he was a close colleague of the Celtic President, John Glass. His introduction into the debate was one of moral support of James Quillan as a friend in Irish political circles against John H McLaughlin, whose social circles were more of a religious nature in the parish of St Mary's, without dabbling in politics.

What Murphy did add to the debate was his reference that James Quillan was not electioneering, as he would not accept any position in the Celtic Committee at the upcoming AGM. This backs up the point that Quillan was canvassing support for a rival club by exposing and undermining the Celtic Committee and its so called "disregard" for the working man.

In the same day's edition;

"SIR - In reference to the above correspondence now appearing in your columns, would Mr J H McLaughlin kindly descend for a few moments from his lofty altitude in the heavens and explain -

1. How was it that the majority of the five shilling members never received any notice of the general meeting of the club, whilst those who were thought safe were post carded?

2. Why the committee were so chary, (reluctant), in supplying a copy of the rules to every member upon joining?

3. Why the wholesale revision of the rules was not submitted to members, as it should have been, before the frustrated packed public meeting?

Of course there is no use asking him why he leaves his place amongst the angelic choir to reply to Mr Quillan, if he thinks the discussion can't be settled in the columns of a newspaper; nor why he thinks that Quillan will be re-elected, when he knows that this wont be the case so long as the present committee have a blank membership card at their disposal".

I am, &c.,
THOMAS MOORE
10 Duke Street
3rd June, 1889

Thomas Moore made many good points although his sarcastic tone, (responding in kind to same, on occasion, by John H McLaughlin), failed to give a true reflection of his candour. What he underlined was the committee's alleged modus operandi whereby the membership weren't always consulted, nor were they kept up to date with the basic working of that committee. A lack of communication and administration skills may seem minor failings, but overlooking details where members are concerned can often lead to recrimination and ill feeling and this is allegedly what happened on this occasion.

And again on the same day's edition;

"Sir - Re Mr J H McLaughlin's bilious attack of 1st inst, if I needed any lessons, either in good taste or sense, I am very much afraid I would not employ "J H McL," aristocratic though he may be. Your readers can see his ideas of good taste in nearly every line of his effusion and can judge for themselves his claim to set up, as an "apostle of culchaw". As for his sense, he shows it by asserting that "discussion will hurt the club". That I deny. It cannot hurt the club but it may hurt the committee.

What I asserted in my first and last letters I assert still - namely, that the meeting carried by a majority a resolution that members should be admitted by paying 5s and that not one in a dozen knew that 12s, 6d was to be the charge for new members. This was owing to the manner in which J H McLaughlin read the rule, reading in a low tone, portions that no discussion was wanted on. Again I would like to know why when the committee require 14 days notice to be given if a member desires a change in any of the rules, they should spring a series of new rules upon the club without any notice whatever.

In the generality of clubs I believe it is customary for a copy of the additions or alterations in rules to be several days before the members, so that they may have time to weigh them and see their full bearing. This as it should be, and being so it is not surprising that the Celtic committee should have none of it. As for Mr McLaughlin's sneers about the "address to the electors", he knows perfectly well that I will not on any consideration again occupy an official position on the Celtic. That there are some electioneering dodges being played at the present time I haven't the least doubt, and am glad that upon that point, and on that point only, I can agree with the figurehead of the present committee.

I am, &c.,
JAMES QUILLAN
Vice President, Celtic Club
3rd June, 1889

Carrying on the less than convivial tone, James Quillan ridiculously claims that less than one in twelve members understood the proposed alteration to the charges because John H McLaughlin's spoke of them in such hushed tones. Surely one of that dozen could have spoke up and requested that John H McLaughlin stated his points in a clearer fashion?

More pertinent was his point regarding the committee's actions in pushing through amendments to articles without the required 14 days notice which again pointed to an extent to issues of poor housekeeping within the committee. Suffice to say, the mechanisms available to members to raise these points through the proper channels by writing to the committee, rather than to the evening papers would have elicited a better chance of a successful outcome.

THE CELTIC COMMITTEE

"SIR - As a Celt I am proud of our football team, but with many others, share the distrust in our present committee. I have observed Mr McLaughlin's replies to our Vice President's statements, and without going into the merits of the case I should like to know why he has arrogated to himself the duties of Honorary Secretary. Is Mr O'Hara incompetent that he cannot take charge of the rules &c., but must needs be over-ridden by Mr McLaughlin?

It is well known that Mr McLaughlin is a fair weather friend of the Celtic Club, and while its affairs were in a "precarious" state he held aloof from it. Now success is assured, he is only too anxious to identify himself with it, in committees and newspapers. It is manifest from his letters that there is a deficiency of business capacity and system in the committee. They have tried the experiment of finding "wisdom in the multitude of counsellors," and during the season have added to their numbers friend after friend, until the committee now comprises 20 members, the majority of whom were selected with the view of forming a clique. If they had desired to act with fairness, why were the members of the club not served with notice of the proposed increase of yearly subscription and its amount? This is the regular course in such matters, and if followed, any subsequent disputes as to the sum - 7s, 6d or 12s, 6d - &c., would have been avoided.

The fact is the committee imagined they could dictate anything to the members, and because their pretensions have been overthrown, they and Mr McLaughlin have nothing but sneers for the working men who are the chief supporters of the club. I trust the Celtic Club will, at its general meeting, make a clean sweep of this committee clique, and that under capable gentlemen the team will next season win the laurels they so nearly secured this year".

I am, &c.,
A CELT
4th June 1889

"A CELT" correctly raised the point that the committee should have notified the membership of the proposed increases in writing and therefore part of the blame for the ensuing misunderstanding lay at the door of the committee. Unfortunately he cloaked his point in the sarcasm and petty name calling that marred this public spar.

His opening question, however, with regards to why John H McLaughlin was answering on behalf of John O'Hara is flawed as McLaughlin had made the point in his opening letter that he was directly responsible for the drafting and printing of the rules.

THE CELTIC AND THEIR COMMITTEE

"SIRS -Mr Quillan is to be congratulated on the vast improvement in the style of his last letter - indeed were it not that his signature is appended to it no one would recognise it as emanating from the same source as the previous letters. To add to the dissimilarity, I may point out that in his undated last letter that appeared in your issue of 1st inst, he announced his intention of "declining to follow my personalities," a resolution that has evidently been forgotten in the concoction of his last contribution.

The point at I sue between us is a very simple one, but one that, as I have already told him, cannot be settled in the columns of a newspaper. He asserts that the vast majority of the meeting - eleven out of every twelve are numbers he gives - understood that new members were to be admitted on payment of 7s, 6d. Well, he has a very easy way of finding out whether he is right or wrong. Let him bring up the question at the annual general meeting, when it will be definitely settled. I am quite willing to abide by the result. Is he?

Besides reiterating his previous statement, Mr Quillan, as I predicted in my last, raises a new complaint. I am not, however, going to play his little game and enter into an interminable correspondence with him, and I shall therefore refer him again to the annual general meeting, where the explanation, of which, however, he is already perfectly cognisant, will be given if he has the courage to ask for it. The letters of your other correspondents, I do not feel called upon to answer as Mr Murphy is not a member of the club, and has therefore, no locus standi on the matter, while the slanderous imputations contained in the other, render it beneath contempt.

I have entered this discussion with reluctance and I take leave of it now with the utmost pleasure. It is, I suppose, the fate of every club or association, no matter of what nature it may be, to be blessed - or the reverse with a select coterie, who are always in opposition, and whose sole aim is to find fault and criticise. As a rule, however they have wisdom on life to hide their bickerings and jealousies from the public eyes. Unfortunately it has been quite the reverse with the Celtic. I should have imagined that its unparalleled success would have had the effect of inducing everyone, even the most cross grained and ill conditioned, to join in a genuine chorus of felicitation.

Apparently, it has only caused the "cave" to try by every means in their power - legitimate or otherwise - to publicly discredit the management who have so successfully steered the club through the shoals and quicksands of the past season. I have every confidence, however that the members of the Celtic will be able to judge between those to whose work the prosperity of the club is due, and those who seem prepared to sacrifice everything - even the club itself - to their inane desire for publicity and power".

I am, etc.,
JOHN H McLAUGHLIN
7th June, 1889

Finally good sense prevailed in the mudslinging that did no-one any good and John H McLaughlin withdrew from the debate, whilst at the same time stuck to his point and challenged James Quillan, to raise the issue at the AGM where it would be debated face to face. He ignored, at the same time, the allegations of a headstrong committee not keeping the membership up to speed with developments and railroading alterations without proper consultation.

In the same day's edition;

"SIR - My attention has been drawn to a letter which appeared in the News from J Quillan, and the rules as to membership charges, &c. I was at the meeting, where it was distinctly agreed, after considerable discussion, that the annual subscriptions for present members be 5s and for those now joining an additional 2s, 6d is required, as entry money, making 7s, 6d for first year".

I am, &c.,
A MEMBER
7th June, 1889

"A MEMBER" joined the debate to challenge James Quillan's version of events, which is well within his right, as he was, as his name implied, a member.

THE CELTIC AND THEIR COMMITTEE

"SIR - I am truly grateful that such an eminent authority on classic literature as Mr J H McLaughlin has designed to notice the style of my letters, and has condescended to express his approval of same. Though the recognition has been tardy enough, coming four days after my last, still, I suppose I ought to feel grateful and undoubtedly would have been so had he attempted to answer my contention. What I pointed out is that the committee are doing their level best to get rid of their 5s members, who were the bone and sinew of the club.

During the time of the bungled lease these men were the only ones who were in any way liable for the debts of the club - any member paying anything above the sum being made "an honorary," and therefore a non liable member. The working men were at the time the saviours of the club when certain gentlemen were calmly looking on as outsiders at the trouble they had helped to create. Of course, its now convenient to forget these things and its perhaps pardonable in Mr J H McLaughlin and a few others to have such short memories. That does not excuse them, however, in attacking by false and malicious anonymous statements, both in private and public, those whose memories are not so treacherous.

Had it not been for these slanderous attacks I would never have penned a line, and Mr McLaughlin would not have needed to "reluctantly" withdraw from a correspondence which he entered upon with such a light heart. The threat of personal violence taking place at the general meeting I treat with the contempt it deserves. In conclusion I may say that I agree with Mr J H McLaughlin about the select coterie in every club - only, unfortunately, in ours the select coterie are in power. But if the members are only true to themselves they will relegate them to their original obscurity. The Celtic prospered before these parties crushed themselves in, has prospered in spite of their bungling mismanagement and will flourish better than ever once they are turned out".

I am, &c.,
JAMES QUILLAN
7th June, 1889

James Quillan again reverted to type and just couldn't help himself in his final contribution to John H McLaughlin, with accusations and allegations cast left, right and centre without backing them up with hardened facts.

What evidence did he have for the ridiculous allegation that the Celtic Committee were trying to get rid of the working class, "5 shilling subscriber?"

What was bungled about the 5 year lease on the original Celtic Park?

Finally he tried to defend the indefensible, his outrageous behaviour in opening a correspondence through an evening newspaper instead of through the proper channels.

He certainly didn't cover himself in glory.

THE CELTIC COMMITTEE

"SIR - I do not wish to interfere in either side of the contest, but Mr Quillan, in his last letter, talks about "the bungled lease." Will Mr Quillan explain what he means by this expression; and why he refused to sign the lease for Celtic Park and allowed an outsider, (Mr Joseph Nelis I understand), to do so? His reply will satisfy more"

ANTI HUMBUG
13th June, 1889

This is a question we'd all love answered. What was bungled about the lease on Celtic Park? At £50 per annum over 5 years it was less than Rangers had paid for Kinning Park, which was £60 over a 10 year fixture of tenure between 1877 and 1887 and was deemed to be very cheap at the time, and less still for the original Hampden which Queens Park paid £80 per annum, rising to £100.

THE CELTIC COMMITTEE

"SIR - Your correspondent, "Anti Humbug," has, I doubt, none of the "anti" about him, but is a humbug pure and simple. He should know by this time that it is not usual for people to answer anonymous attacks and I would not answer his did I not know that others were making the same statements. The reason why I did not sign the lease was that I wanted other persons in the club of financial standing to join me and not men of straw, who had nothing to lose.

The lease was signed by the gentleman named in "Anti Humbug's" letter, but I understand that the rent of the ground for the number of years the lease has to run had meanwhile been lodged in the bank".

I am, &c.,
JAMES QUILLAN
14th June, 1889

James Quillan answered one question fairly but totally ignored the main question, therefore the mystery remains. There has never been any evidence or even hearsay from any source to suggest the lease for the original Celtic Park was bungled. Judging by the lack of any supportive evidence, and the fact that Quillan immediately dropped the claim when challenged, this was more likely to have been more mudslinging in the hope that some of it would stick.

It was an affliction that only "muddied the waters" of his allegations, some of which appeared genuine, but others appeared to be an attempt to disassociate Celtic's working class grass roots support and take them with him to his rival club. Quillan alleged too that the rent for the ground for the next four years of the lease had already been lodged in the bank and therefore there was no risk attached to being a leasee, who was responsible for the terms of the agreement. This was nonsense, as these figures do not appear in the balance sheet in Robert Kelly's book and neither is it mentioned at the AGM.

THE CELTIC COMMITTEE

"SIR - From the correspondence which has taken place in your columns it is easy to see that an attempt has been made, and will likely be again repeated to exclude working men from the club. If the present committee are successful, it will be the fault of the working men themselves in not paying their subscriptions, and therefore, not having the right to vote.

Is it then too much to ask my fellow members to get their subscriptions paid by hook or by crook on or before Tuesday 1st, so that they may send the "mashers," (the men about town) and the admirers to the rightabout. If they don't help themselves now, they may never be able to do so again for by the new rules the committee may add whom they like to their number, and so swamp the votes of the elected. Arise, then fellow workmen, and make the club what it is not, but what it should be, a national club - not a star chamber institution. By voting straight a blow will be struck at the miniature castle from which it will never recover".

I am, &c.,
SHAN VAN VOCHT.
16th June, 1889

The last throw of the dice was made in the debate with the use of a pseudonym, which although sounding peculiarly German, was actually the phonetic version of "An tSeanbhean Bhocht," which translates as "Poor Old Woman," a traditional name for Ireland, and the name of a book by James Murphy on the Irish Rebellion of 1798.

The pseudonym was no coincidence and the rallying of the troops was a noble one, but the cause was flawed as it was based on a false premise. It was in no-one's interest to exclude the working men from the club. The club needed every penny it could raise and it was not within the committee's gift to turn it away from our biggest source, ie, our large working class support. The committee were simply raising the price of a season ticket from 5 shillings to 7 shillings and 6d to attract more finance to the club as we faced a constant battle to stay one step ahead with a far from secure future. We were certainly debarring no-one. Far from it.

Our friend, Viator from the *Glasgow Evening News*, remaining in the background of the debate, commented on Friday, 7th June;

"Where the disturbance in the Celtic camp is likely to end, it is hard to tell. The belligerents whose effusions have appeared in the papers are agreed upon one point - namely, that the rules have not been acted up to. I have never had a great fondness for newspaper correspondence, and I am sorry to see the members of the Celtic indulge in it. The club has certainly done a great deal of good, and if only capably managed, may do a great deal more.

Where the difference arises it is hard to say. It is evident that party jealousy has crept into the club. A very strong endeavour should be made at the annual general meeting to expunge it. The Celtic are very well aware that a house divided against itself shall fall, and the sooner they begin to set theirs in order the better. The idea of starting a new club in Glasgow is scarcely feasible. We have already too many clubs in the east end".

Meanwhile, the *Scottish Sport* stuck it's oar in with a comment on 4th June, which even by 1889 standards was far from politically correct, tarring the whole Irish race with the same brush and comparing a Celtic AGM to Donnybrook Fair in Dublin, an event allegedly so notorious for drunkenness and violent disorder, that it was banned in 1855;

"A great many Irishmen are looking with interest to the General Meeting of the Celts, as if they expected a sprinkle of Donnybrook. There is not much unnatural in that, for it stands recorded against the race that they are never at peace except when they are fighting".

Viator's comments lacked the Scottish Sport's schadenfreude, the art of taking pleasure from other's suffering and were instead concise and straight to the point, summing up the state of play perfectly, prophetically stating that starting a new club in Glasgow was scarcely feasible and that there were already too many clubs in the east end of Glasgow. If only James Quillan had listened he would have saved himself a whole lot of wasted time and expense.

The Celtic Committee had no previous experience of running a football club, their organisational skills were honed from their experience in political and religious groups in the east end of Glasgow. They were dynamic, potent, enterprising, energetic and full of drive, with a deep passion to succeed, they had the original will to win, which propelled many Celtic teams down the decades to pull off feats of greatness when the cards were down and the clock ticking.

What they lacked was first hand experience in the job at hand and almost certainly they would have been overwhelmed with the workload, an unpaid workload, as the club grew "mushroom like" in our early years. What the committee learned from our first year was that they would have to hone their communication skills and involve the members in decision making. Once the rule book and constitution had been written, they had to follow it, to the letter of the law. They were headstrong, in a rush to get things done, but this was a lesson that if things weren't done correctly, a backlash could follow.

The club had enough enemies in the most anti Irish city on the planet without getting the backs up of some of our own. Petty jealousies, cliques and ill feeling are the scourge of many committees and memberships, where, if left to ferment, can lead to serious division and self destruction. For the Celtic Committee, this was a warning shot, they were getting the big decisions correct and the club was prospering beyond anyone's wildest dreams, with a Scottish Cup final appearance in our first season, but they had to make more effort to take everyone, or nearly everyone, with them.

In the event, the debate was a damp squib when James Quillan rose to John H McLaughlin's challenge and made his point at the AGM with the result that he only mustered 17 votes, compared to Joseph Shaughnessy's amendment, which gained 104. Enforcing the point of an orderly meeting, with over 85% of the members present of the same mind, when it came to the election of the under fire office-bearers; Doctor Conway, John Glass, John O'Hara, Willie Maley and Hugh Darroch were all returned unopposed. James Quillan was opposed as Vice President and lost the vote to Belfast man Francis McErlean.

Twenty three names were nominated for the remaining nine places on the committee, a very healthy sign, and the following were elected; Tom Maley, William McKillop, John H McLaughlin, Joseph Shaughnessy, John MacDonald, Dan Malloy, Michael Cairns, James Curtis and Pat Shannon.

Although the correspondent, "A CELT", had complained that the committee had "Tried the experiment of finding "wisdom in the multitude of counsellers" and during the season had added friend after friend until the committee comprised 20 members, the majority of whom were selected with the view of forming a clique," every committee member co-opted had to stand for election at the Annual General Meeting, just like everyone else nominated.

It was noted that the "malcontents" were not in the number elected onto the committee at the 1889 AGM, which told its own story. They were soon to make their next move.

Viator, again commented on Friday, 21st June, after the AGM;

"At one time the storm in a tea cup in the camp of the Celtic promised to develop into something more formidable. The annual meeting held on Tuesday evening, 18th June, proved however, that the elements of discord were not strong enough to raise a disturbance of dimensions worth noticing. The Quillanites were severely sat upon, and it will be some time ere they come up smiling to the same attack.

I rather dislike the autocratic manner in which the chairman refused to listen to the malcontents, and it is questionable if in doing so he did not do more harm than good. According to the financial statement, the Celtic Club must be a very rich concern. The majority of the members of the club are for unity and progress, and I trust that those who were so discontented at the annual meeting have now joined in the good cause. There can be no doubt that were the Celtic Club properly managed and rationally supported, it would become one of our greatest football institutions".

The final word on the subject is left to the *Scottish Referee* on 24th June;

"At last all is peace and quietness in the camp of the Celtic. The Quillanites have been squashed and the original leaders of the club now go on their way rejoicing. The doings in the legislative chambers of the Celtic are kept so quiet that it is hard to say what the row was about. The objects of the club are praiseworthy, and it is hoped that the new offices and committee will work towards this end as one man".

Argument and hostility, or so the press would have you believe, went hand in hand with the running of an Irish club, but they forget one of the greatest characteristics of both the Irish and the Scots, the ability to laugh at our own expense.

Amongst all the rancour and name calling of the Quillan saga, one "inhabitant" of Janefield cemetery, identifying himself only as Lair 0, 014, joined in the letter writing craze and put pen to paper for the benefit on the Glasgow Evening News readers on 10th June, comparing the committee with a soldier in battle about to meet his fate, in the words of an old Irish song, A Soldier and a Man;

"SIR - Being a permanent resident in Janefield, and having been so this number of years, you will, no doubt, pardon me for putting in a few words of complaint now that the Celtic Committee's misdoings are coming before

the public. I believe that I am as reasonable as any other well behaved corpse should be, and though I did complain bitterly at the first on account of my rest being disturbed on the Saturdays, through time I got used to it and did not grudge the people on the other side of the wall the one and a half hour's enjoyment.

But what I complain of now, and my complaint is shared in by the occupants of the lairs surrounding me, is that our rest is being disturbed on the Sundays also by people using the pavillion. Of course the song, "A soldier and a man," is a very good one, especially when given with popping cork accompaniment, but in my time here we preferred to sing it on the Saturday night, and have more solemn tunes for the day of rest. In fact, Sir, a deputation of our number were about to make complaint to the committee, only we deferred on hearing that perhaps in a few days they would be on our side of the wall".

I am, &c.,
Lair 0, 014
10th June, 1889

The minutes of the 1889 AGM in full as reported in the Scottish Sport on 21st June;

CELTIC FC's ANNUAL MEETING

"The general meeting of the Celtic Club was held on Tuesday evening in Mechanics' Hall, Bridgeton. There was a very large turn out of members, only those showing membership tickets being admitted to the meeting. Dr Conway, Honorary President, occupied the chair and in a brief address opened the preceding by calling on Mr John O'Hara to read his report of the year's precedings. The report was listened to with great interest by all the members, as it was really a very interesting and detailed account of the formation, early struggles and latter-day successes of the "green and white" brigade. The report included a portion of what is usually dealt with by the match secretary, viz - the record of the club's performances. The Celts have played in all 60 matches - won 43, lost 12 and drawn 5; scored 204 goals, as against 92. Notable performances also received a share in the worthy secretary's report, such as defeating the English cupholders and Scottish cupholders and also defeating the Dunbartonshire teams. The report was unanimously adopted by the meeting.

The secretary was then called upon to read the minutes of the last general meeting. On these being read, Mr James Quillan said he would move the adoption of the minutes if a certain rule, (pertaining to entrance fees and subscription money), were omitted, as said rule was not the rule as passed by meeting. (Mr Quillan read his motion). A seconder being found, the chairman received the motion. Mr Joseph Shaughnessy then rose, and moved as an amendment that the minutes be held as a correct reflex of general meeting and be passed as such. About a dozen gentlemen sprang to their feet to second Mr Shaughnessy's amendment. A short discussion followed. Few, very few, could understand the position adopted by Mr Quillan, for as fast as one portion of his contention was cleared away, hydra-like another raised its head.

The amendment and motion being placed before the meeting and a vote taken, showed that for Mr Shaughnessy's amendment 104 votes were given; whilst Mr Quillan's could only total 17. This early presage of the feeling of the meeting caused jubilation and dismay to reign in each of the opposing parties. The next business before the meeting was the treasurer's report. As each member had been supplied with a balance -sheet, the treasurer was spared the trouble of reading that clear and excellent, though lengthy, report. The meeting found no fault and the report was accordingly unanimously adopted.

During the incidents above mentioned, a person named Maloney questioned the right of Messrs Tom and Willie Maley, Neil McCallum, etc, etc, to vote. As was to be expected, his question was answered in a sharp and summary manner. Loud cries of "withdraw", "put him out", "apologise", let this individual know that his partisanship had evidently overcame his discretion.

Reports having been satisfactorily disposed of, votes of thanks were accorded to the various officials for their services. Mr Cortey moved a special vote of thanks to the team, which was heartily accorded to by the meeting; and on Tom Maley responding, the meeting rose en masse and sang out lustily "He's a jolly good fellow".

The election of office bearers then took place, prior to which Mr Joseph Shaughnessy moved that Michael Davitt Esq., be made Honorary Patron of club, this was received with acclamation. Dr Conway was proposed as Honorary President for the ensuing season and on no opposition being given, was re-elected in a similar way. Mr John Glass was re-elected President - this giving eminent satisfaction to the team. For Vice President, three nominations were made, but on a vote being taken Mr Francis McErlean was returned by a large majority. Messrs John O'Hara, Willie Maley, and Hugh Darroch were installed in their former offices unanimously - contrary to rumour. Twenty three nominations were made for nine places on committee. Tom Maley was elected unanimously. The remaining twenty two were then put before the "electors", with the result that the following eight were chosen:- Mr William McKillop (100), John H McLaughlin (95), Joseph Shaughnessy (92), John McDonald (91), Dan Molloy (88), Michael Cairns (87), James Curtis (78), Michael Shannon (78). It may be interesting to note that none of the "malcontents" are in above number, for which the CFC have every reason to be thankful. Mr Tom Maley was appointed representative to SFA and Mr John O'Hara to Glasgow Football Association. Votes of thanks to chairmen, etc, brought the meeting to a close.

Reviewing the three and a half hours' work of the meeting, an unbiased person present would perforce have to confess that the meeting was an orderly, well-conducted affair. Once only had the chairman to exercise his authority, causing a speaker to desist. Personalities were not indulged in and such a thing as recriminatory remarks passing between speakers entirely absent. How the sensational headings insert in publications can be accounted for is a mystery no one cares to solve."

FOOTBALL AND POLITICS

It is at this juncture that it would be interesting to raise the mantra that "Football and politics should not mix". The Celtic Committee, since the club's foundation was well aware of the target audience we had to attract if we were to be successful and as the original fundraising circular makes clear, no concession was made to ecumenism.

We were, from birth, an Irish Catholic club. Our original Patron was Archbishop Eyre, which gave us a nod of approval from the Catholic church without forming any formal ties or coming under the jurisdiction of the church. The committee at the 1889 AGM were well aware that the motion to invite a convicted felon, namely Michael Davitt to accept the post of Honorary Patron, was a move that would raise a few eyebrows. To put it into perspective it's the equivalent of the present Celtic Board inviting Gerry Adams or Martin McGuinness to become the Patron of the club.

In short and without beating about the bush, when we were formed, it wasn't about what should or shouldn't mix; football, religion and politics were all central to the mix at our formation.

Similarly on the field, the only position we had trouble in filling with a Catholic player good enough for a long term place in the team was the position of goalkeeper. Michael Dolan, Willie Dunning, James McLaughlin, John Kelly, John Tobin, even James McLaren were tried in goals before goalkeeper Jamie Bell was signed in 1890, to become the first non Catholic Celtic player. This is backed up in Willie Maley's book, *The Celtic Story*, written in 1938;

"We have always been a cosmopolitan club since our second year, and we have included in our list of players a Swede, a Jew and a Mohammedan. Much has been made in certain quarters about our religion, but for forty eight years we have played a mixed team, and some of the greatest Celts we have had did not agree with us in our religious beliefs, although we have never at any time hidden what these are. Men of the type of McNair, Hay, Lyon, Buchan, Cringan, the Thomsons, or Paterson soon found out that broadmindedness which is the real stamp of the good Christian existed to its fullest at Celtic Park, where a man was judged by his football alone."

At the beginning, we were a club filling a gap in society and signing players who many others ignored simply because of their religion.

The "country clubs" as they were known, such as Renton and Vale of Leven all signed Catholics but the city clubs, for example Rangers and Queens Park weren't as forthcoming although early Celtic Committee man David Meikleham was one exception as he was an ex Queens Park member, as stated in the Daily Record's report of our 1895 Glasgow Cup final win over Queens Park by 6 goals to 3 in November of that year.

The opportunities weren't always there for Catholic players to progress. Celtic filled this gap and once again, it was common practice for the Irish clubs to sign players of Irish Catholic stock and we were simply a continuation of the norm. We certainly didn't introduce sectarianism into the Scottish game, it was alive and well long before 1888. The backbone of the original Celts were signed from Hibernian and not Queens Park for example, for a reason. We had a distinct identity from the beginning and although Queens Park were the biggest and most successful club in the land at the time, providing the national team with most of their players, none of those players were targeted by Celtic.

The election of office bearers then took place and the first motion should leave no one in any doubt whatsoever of the make up of the Celtic Committee and the membership of the club in 1889. Michael Davitt was a hero of the Irish working class immigrants in Britain and it was his name which was put forward by Joseph Shaughnessy at the 1889 AGM to become the joint Honorary Patron of Celtic FC, alongside Archbishop Eyre of Glasgow. It is noted in the report of the AGM that the motion was received "with acclamation".

Michael Davitt was born in Straide, County Mayo in 1846 during the height of the famine and having been evicted from their home in 1850 due to rent arrears, the family fled to England and settled in Haslingden, Lancashire in the search for a better life. At the age of nine, he left school to take up work in a local cotton mill and just two years later he lost his right arm as it got tangled in a cogwheel of a spinning machine.

In 1865 he joined the Irish Republican Brotherhood and soon rose to become the Secretary of the North of England and Scotland area, responsible for arms smuggling using his cover as a "hawker" or travelling salesman and he played a role in the Fenian Rising of 1867. He evaded capture until 1870 when he was arrested and sentenced to 15 years for "treason felony". Seven years later he was released after furore over his treatment in Dartmoor and he rejoined the IRB, rising to become a member of the Supreme Council. In 1879 he was a founder member of the Land League in Mayo, a democratic organisation set up to organise resistance to evictions, assist in the reduction of rent and to implement the three F's ; Fair Rent, Fixity of Tenure and Free Sale, in other words ownership of the land for those who could afford it. The movement grew and the Irish National Land League was formed.

It was this work that introduced the term "boycott" into our language in 1880 after the Land League's campaign of ostracism of land agent Captain Charles Boycott, who was eventually forced to leave Ireland. A year later, Davitt was imprisoned again, for making outspoken speeches and the Irish members of parliament protested so loudly they were ejected from the House of Commons. In 1882, whilst in Portland Jail, he was elected as MP for County Meath, but was disqualified as he was in prison.

Having already spent seven years in Dartmoor from the young age of 24, Davitt was back inside aged 35. Throughout his year long incarceration, Davitt had time to think through his strategy of land nationalism and redistribution, and on his release from jail, he travelled to America where he raised funds for the Land League and he also got back to the grass roots and campaigned throughout Scotland, England and Ireland for land nationalism. In 1883, he was imprisoned again for his support of the Irish National League but on his release he toured far and near, including Australia, South America, South Africa, Russia and all across Europe to lecture on humanitarian rights. It was an extensive and exhaustive tour, even by today's standards of modern flights, compared to weeks on end sailing through choppy seas in the 1880s to spread the word.

In 1886, he finally married and settled down in Dublin, his health having suffered from his highly demanding schedule, although he continued his fight against the injustice of the land system in Ireland where tenants were being evicted onto the street. He kept up his campaign throughout Scotland, England and Ireland and was elected to the seat of North Meath in 1892 before it was overturned on petition. Just a few months later in February 1893 he was elected unopposed for the North East Cork seat but resigned from the House of Commons just three months later. He returned in 1895, elected to represent South Mayo and lasted four years before again resigning, this time in protest at the Boer War and he went on to visit South Africa in support of the Boers.

A year earlier in 1898, Davitt set up the United Irish League in Mayo. Finally, after the 1902 Land Conference, Davitt's ambition was finally realised when an amicable solution to the land issue was agreed, and ownership of the land finally transferred from the landlords to the tenants through the Land Act of 1903.

Michael Davitt died just three years later, ages 60, on 30th May 1906 and is buried in the grounds of Straide Abbey, County Mayo, near his birthplace. He is remembered as a leading member of the struggle against landlordism in Ireland but also as an active supporter of the underprivileged wherever they may be.

FIRST HAND ACCOUNTS - BY THOSE WHO WERE THERE

Every effort has been made to quote and date all sources in full and the following are first hand accounts by some of the most prominent men in a position to talk with authority on our foundation.

BYGONE DEEDS IN CELTIC HISTORY OLD TALES RE-TOLD in the *Glasgow Observer* from 15th October 1898;

"Ten years are but a short period in a man's life, but in the history of a football club they constitute an era. Players come and go so rapidly; cup tie succeeds cup tie; and League matches follow each other in such bewildering profusion that one is apt to forget the stirring contests of a few seasons ago. To the younger generation especially the early deeds of the now famous Celtic are almost unknown and it is only from the imperfect reminiscences of their seniors that they learn anything about the doings of the club which on its inception, proved such a sensation and which, by its brilliant achievements has completely altered and improved association football in this country.

ORIGIN OF THE CELTIC

Founded in a very humble way at a meeting held in the St Vincent De Paul rooms, East Rose Street, on November 6th 1887, it was not until May 28th in the following year that the Celts played their first match, though the ground had previously been opened on May 8th, the contestants being Hibernians and Cowlairs. Considering the prominent part which Celtic and Rangers have since played, it is remarkable that the very first match the Celts every played was against the Ibrox Club. The game took place on May 28th, as stated above and the Celts made a good beginning, for they won by 5 goals to 2, thus commencing a long series of victories over the light blues. The names of the Celtic team which took part in this match are not at hand, but in a game played a few days later against Dundee Harp, we find the following; Michael Dolan, James McLaughlin and William McLaughlin; Phil Murray, Willie Maley and Hughes; Tom Dunbar, Coogan, Charlie Gorevin, Mick Dunbar and Johnny Coleman.

Maley, Coleman and the Dunbar afterwards acquired prominence, but to the average readers many of the others are practically unknown. Willie McLaughlin and Charlie Gorevin came from Govan, the latter afterwards going out to the States. James McLaughlin is better known as a referee now, and Mick Dolan, who belonged to Drumpellier, has long since retired. All together five matches were played in the latter end of the season of 1888 and it almost makes one smile when they read that the first defeat administered to the new Irish combination came from the "puir wee Clyde", who won by the narrow score of 4 goals to 3. These games were the means of bringing the Celts under favourable notice and stimulated the energetic committee to further exertion. Accordingly no time was lost in getting together a first class 11 and to this end emissaries were sent out to survey the land and obtain capable Irish players.

From the first, the eyes of the Celts, were turned to Edinburgh, where the Hibs had built up an excellent team and before the new season began, Mick McKeown, Paddy Gallagher, Jimmy McLaren and Willie Groves were brought to the west. Considering that the Hibs had given the new club every encouragement and actually opened their new ground, the eastern club was naturally wild with indignation and it is extremely unlikely that this feeling of resentment against the Celts will ever die out in Edinburgh while one of the old stock remains. Johnny Coleman, who first rose to fame in the Vale of Leven team, was also an ex Hib, but he had previously gone over to the Celts in company with his chum, Mick Dunbar.

Renton too was visited and Jim Kelly and Neilly McCallum left the village. An act which was even more bitterly resented by their club mates than the secession of Willie Groves and his pals by the Hibs. Tom Maley had already come over from Third Lanark, and in company with his brother Willie, then a tall, lanky young customer, promised to still further strengthen the new club. How these stars were drawn to the east end, what alluring promises were made, and what glorious prospects were held out to the newcomers - all these things would require reams of paper to chronicle. Suffice it to say that in Reverend Brother Walfrid and Mr John Glass, the club had a pair of silver tongued advocates, who were able, by their pleadings, to gather together the above brilliant collection. These were before the days of signing on, transfer money, and all the attendant tramellings of professionalism; a player was free to go to any club he pleased, and so successful were the Celts in inducing players to do the green and white jersey that Mr Glass can truthfully boast that he never failed to secure any player on whom he set his heart.

Chiefly through his efforts, the Celts began their first season - 1888-89 - with the following team - a team, perhaps, the best balanced and certainly one of the most successful that ever carried Celtic colours:- Willie Dunning; Paddy Gallagher and Mick McKeown; Willie Maley, James Kelly and Jimmy McLaren; Neil McCallum, Mick Dunbar, Willie Groves, Johnny Coleman and Tom Maley.

No time was lost by the Celtic in beginning the season of 1888-89 which they did by competing for the Phantom Cup on the Exhibition grounds. Abercorn, Dumbarton and Partick Thistle were in turn met and overcome, but Cowlairs, by bringing in outsiders, managed to defeat the Celts 2 goals to 0. These engagements, which went a long way towards consolidating the new eleven, also gave the Glasgow crowds an opportunity of showing their anti-Celtic feeling.

No words of abuse were too strong to hurl at them and even the athletic press of that period attacked the new club in the vilest manner. The bitter feeling is still present, as witness the disgraceful reception given the Celts in the Anglo Scots trial match at Ibrox a couple of seasons ago; but the press of today, with perhaps one exception, treat the Parkhead club fairly. The Celts were soon destined to avenge their Exhibition defeat, for meeting Cowlairs in the second round of the Scottish Cup they simply pulverised them to the extent of 8 goals to 0. How strangely does history repeat itself! Ten years almost to a day, the Celts went to Ibrox to meet the Rangers in the Glasgow Cup. Despite their defeat a few weeks before the Light Blues were unusually confident, but took the precaution of selecting their very best team, which was as follows:- Nicol; A Vallance and D Gow; Hotson, McIntyre and Muir; Whyte, Wylie, Wilson, Pringle and McKenzie. Of these the best known are Alec Vallance, (lately deceased). Donald Gow, Tuck McIntyre, Johnny Muir, (now linesman for the Rangers), and Alec McKenzie, who several times afterwards kept goal for his team with success. The Celts also had out their best team, viz:- Willie Dunning; Paddy Gallagher and Mick McKeown; Willie Maley, James Kelly and Jimmy McLaren; Neil McCallum, Mick Dunbar, Willie Groves, Tom Maley and Johnny Coleman. The attendance was reckoned a splendid one, the crowd numbering over 2,000.

What a change to the 45,000 seen at Parkhead a few weeks ago and how much credit is due the Celts for thus developing interest in the game. Starting early in the match the Rangers looked upon the tie as being their own, but the goals from Willie Groves (2), Johnny Coleman and Willie Maley put an end to this idea. Towards the finish the Ibrox team was quite demoralised, as proved by Mick Dunbar, of all men, scoring and James Kelly following with a 6th.

How often did Mick Dunbar score for his side afterwards? Lack of goals to a forward's credit is usually a sign of weakness, but in Dunbar's case it was almost a proof of merit, for never had the Celts an inside player who sacrificed himself for his mates as did the Cartvale man. Neil McCallum and Willie Groves came in for praise afterwards, which they only partially deserved, for while they were playing to the gallery, Mick Dunbar was putting in the donkey work for both, and woe betide the half-back who chance to get a shoulder charge from that bony individual. It was just as if a stone wall had been built and players soon learned to give him a wide berth rather than risk getting an elbowing in the short rib. Thus did the Celts win their first cup tie as well as their first friendly over the Rangers, and as will be seen, it was long ere they were forced to acknowledge defeat from the Light Blues.

The overwhelming defeats of Cowlairs and Rangers in the Scottish and Glasgow Cups respectively were now followed up by several equally clever victories of the Parkhead club. St Bernard's were beaten away and Renton at home, and a number of fairly good clubs made to look second raters. The semi final, (Glasgow Cup), draw brought the Celts and Queens Park together and it was felt on all sides that Scotland's leading and oldest club would at last find its match in the youngest. Celtic players and supporters alike looked upon the game as good as won, especially when Arnott refused to turn out.

With this exception both teams were at their strongest and a great game was looked for. True to their reputation the Queens fairly rose to the occasion, and showed that the fame of the Celts had not frightened them in the least and how often since that day have we seen the Hampden players rouse themselves and achieve victory against the Celts when the odds were vastly against them? Probably no team has so often baulked the Celts when victory was almost within the Irishman's grasp. Always slow in starting, the Celts were caught napping in the very first minute and "Poem" Berry scored for his side. This was a rude awakening for the Celts, who now crowded on all sail, but again and again were they baffled by Gillespie, the Queen's custodian. Smellie, too, was in great form, and as time wore on the Celtic made frantic but unavailing efforts to score. Once Groves seemed to have the ball through, but Gillespie saved miraculously, and half time found the Queens leading by 1 goal to 0.

Still the Celts did not lose heart. Tom Robinson headed a second goal from a corner and to make matters worse, Johnny Coleman was hurt and rendered useless and McKeown knocked out of time. This double disaster turned the tide and from being attacked, the Queens became the attackers. For the last fifteen minutes they laid siege to the Celtic goal, but Willie Dunning was now as clever as was Gillespie in the first half and managed to avert further scoring. The result was therefore, an unexpected but thoroughly deserved victory for Queens Park, who as will be seen later on, followed up this victory over the Celts by several others scarcely less meritorious. For the Queens; Gillespie, Smellie, Robertson, J Lambie, and Berry excelled, and for the Celts; Willie Dunning, Jimmy McLaren, Willie Groves and Neil McCallum. Partick Thistle had qualified for the final, but the Queens vanquished them by 8 goals to 0, a record score for either Glasgow or Scottish Cup.

A FAMOUS PROTESTED CUP TIE

A stranger strolling through Bridgeton on a certain Saturday night in November, exactly 10 years ago, would have been struck speechless at the behaviour of nine tenths of the male inhabitants from six to sixty years. Such handshaking, such cheering and general jubilation, such drinking and mad speechifying. And why this rioting and noisy rejoicing? Because the "Bonnie wee Clyde" had swamped the crack Celtic team, and that on the ground of the Irishmen. Even at this interval of 10 years, one can remember the joy - not confirmed to Bridgeton either - which was evinced when the news went forth that the Celts were knocked out of the Scottish Cup by the Clyde, who it will be remembered, were the first to lower the Celtic colours a few months previously. But the Celts recked little of their friendly defeat, and looked upon the cup tie as a virtual walkover.

Unfortunately, Johnny Coleman had not recovered from the injury sustained in the Queens Park match, and Connor, a player of average merit, filled the position. Willie Dunning too, stood down to make way for the famous John Tobin, a player who in his day, was one of the best custodians in the country. In those days Greenock Morton were a right good lot, and included some splendid amateurs in the Coats, Nugent, Joyce, Barrie and Fleming. But Tobin was the bright particular star, as he was afterwards in the old Hibernian team, where Tobin, Lundie and Fagan were a trio that took some beating. But clever as he was, Tobin was to see in the match under notice of one of the most brilliant displays of goalkeeping ever given in Glasgow. To sum up the play of that day, it may be at once said that the Celts beat the Clyde, but Chalmers beat the Celts. How he kept out some of the shots was a marvel, and coming so soon after Gillespie's display, it was hard lines on the Celts to find themselves baffled at every turn. To add to their discomfiture, "Fisty" Britton scored what proved to be the only goal of the match. The ground cut up as the game proceeded, until at the finish it resembled a quagmire. This of course, was all against the Celts, who had to retire without a goal to their credit.

But the joy of the Clyde was short lived, for the Celts at once lodged a protest on the state of the ground and on the darkness which prevailed at the finish. The first part of the protest was dismissed, but on it being proved that the Celts were kept waiting on the field on account of 2 or 3 dilatory members of the Clyde, it was settled by 10 votes to 7 to replay the tie. The Clyde were furious at this unexpected turn of affairs, and they first had serious thoughts of refusing to play. Better counsel prevailed, and in beautiful weather the teams met once more. The Celts scored thrice early on, but the Clyde followed suit with a couple, and a most exciting first half ended in favour of the Celts by 3 goals to 2. But what a change on resuming; goal after goal was piled on by the Celts, though Chalmers was as plucky, though not so lucky, as ever. Hart, one of the Clyde backs, was injured and this upset the others, who towards the finish were completely outplayed. Six goals were scored by the Celts in this half and the result, 9 goals to 2, was in strange contrast to the defeat by 1 goal to 0.

So badly did the Clyde take the protest and defeat that they cancelled a friendly fixture with the Celts, and even now it is not safe to refer to this same defeat in the presence of a Bridgetonian. Now however, there is complete harmony between the clubs, both of whom have passed through stormy and troublesome times since their meeting of 10 years ago. Not one of the 22 players of that day now take part in the game, a point that a footballer's career is short, if merry.

THE MEMORABLE TIE WITH EAST STIRLINGSHIRE WHEN THE CELTS GOT A TERRIBLE FRIGHT

The Celts will never forget their first year's battles for the Scottish Cup, but of all their experiences that year their miraculous escape at Falkirk in the 5th round was certainly the most exciting. Having measured their strength with the leading city clubs, and with one exception, came out victorious, it was almost with a pan of regret that they received the draw with East Stirlingshire. Fancy having to waste an afternoon on a lot of country yokes. The match was looked upon as of the picnic variety, and at one time there was an idea of engaging a special for the club's supporters. This arrangement fell through, but a big crowd accompanied the Celts, who luckily as the sequel proved, took through their full team.

The game was begun quietly by the Celts, who of course thought it a matter of goals. Even when the locals had the audacity to put 2 goals to their own credit, there was not the slighted anxiety. Why should a team that had scored 6 times against the Rangers, 9 times against the Clyde, and 8 against Cowlairs, care for a paltry brace of goals. But they were now to learn what putting up the shutters meant. The ground, like most country grounds, was very narrow, and this allowed the locals to crowd round their goal and actually shut it out from the view, much less the aim of the Celtic sharp shooters. It need scarcely be said that the fusillade upon the East Stirlingshire goal was something to be remembered. Backs, half backs, and forwards alike tried their luck, but without success.

A panic laterally set in and as time drew near all hope was gone. One prominent player, who afterwards secured international honours of all kinds, is reported to have divided his time between prayer and work, but McLaren set all minds at rest by gaining a corner just three minutes from time. This was so accurately placed that the Celts drew level at last, The Falkirk men were now compelled to line up for the kick off from centre, and thus for the first time were forced to leave the goal they had packed so well. The result was that the Celts put on their second and winning goal, and thus pulled off the most exciting match they have ever taken part in. The East Stirlingshire earned unstinted praise for their bold show, but only one of the team afterwards rose to prominence. This was Danny Kirkwood, who afterwards took service with Everton, where in conjunction with Latta, Brady, Chadwick and Millward, he made up the best set of forwards ever put on the field by the Liverpool club. Many thrilling contests have the Celts been engaged in since that December day, 10 years ago, but it is safe to say that never have they won on the post so cleverly as on that memorable occasion.

CELTS AND CORINTHIANS - THE STORY OF A MEMORABLE GAME

Having now tested themselves against all the leading Scottish clubs, the Celts, like Alexander, sighed for more worlds to conquer and lost no time in tackling two English organisations, the now defunct Mitchell St George and the better known Corinthians. The former like so many English clubs owed its position to the munificence of a wealthy patron, and Mr Mitchell of Birmingham was a thorough sportsman. The teams met on December 31st, the Celts winning easily by 7 goals to 1. The centre that day was none other than Jack Devey, the present Villa skipper, and it is pleasant indeed to see this popular player hold his own on the cricket and football field after ten years hard work. But this match only paved the way for the meeting with the Corinthians which took place three days later on January 3rd.

Both games were on behalf of the Poor Children's Dinner Fund, a deserving object, which the Celts did much to secure in the old days. The desire to do good to the poor has not deserted Parkhead, but with a wage list of £70 or £80 a week, it is felt that charity must begin at home, though no opportunity is lost of doing a little for the good cause as occasion permits. But to the game. Quite 16,000 thronged old Celtic Park to see the Corinthians first - and last - encounter with the Celts in Glasgow. The customary New Year's Day match had been played at Hampden and several of the Queen's players lent the amateurs a helping hand.

The teams for this great match were therefore:-

Celtic - John Kelly; Pat Dowling and Mick McKeown; Paddy Gallagher, James Kelly and Jimmy McLaren; Neil McCallum, Mick Dunbar, Willie Groves, Johnny Coleman and Tom Maley.

Corinthians - Cooper; A.M and P.M Walters; Alan, Stewart, Wreford-Brown and Holden-White; J Lambie, Cotterill, Fred Dewhurst, Farrant and Currie. The writer can still remember the amused expressions of the massive Englishmen when they saw the natty little Celts indulge in a preliminary kick at goal. That such pigmies could even stand up to them, much less beat them, seemed absurd, but two hours later their opinions had undergone a complete change. The ground was fearfully heavy and altogether unsuited to the strangers, who could do nothing against the wonderful skill of the home forwards. Many a good game have the same quintet played, but never were they seen to such advantage as on this occasion.

Tom Maley especially had a day out and the brothers Walters are not likely ever to forget that afternoon's chasing of the flying Celt who beat them at their own game. Goal after goal was rattled on, until the score stood at 6 to 2, when the Celts eased up. The Corinthians' big forwards got an awful showing up and the team all round such a thorough dressing that never since have they ventured to meet the Celts at home, though a few weeks afterwards they met a weak Celtic team at the Oval and beat them rather easily. The Dewhurst mentioned above was Fred Dewhurst of North End fame. A master of the Preston Catholic Grammar School, Dewhurst early found his way into the famous team and those who ever saw Gordon, Ross, Goodall, Dewhurst and Drummond play one of their best games witnessed the finest forward play the world has ever seen. Poor Fred is now alas gone from us and better for him had he never had any connection with the national game. Both he and the brothers Walters appeared afterwards against Scotland, but a fatal accident to a younger brother was the cause of these two backs giving up the game. Wreford-Brown like Devey has lasted well, for he will be remembered as England's centre half this year at Parkhead.

Over £400 was drawn at these two matches so that the Catholic charities benefited considerably and there it may be mentioned that one who did good work in those days is now lying dangerously ill, We refer of course to Paddy Gallagher than whom a pluckier player never donned the green and white jersey. Better players may have succeeded him, but never one who had his heart in the team as Gallagher had, and whose enthusiasm for the jersey he wore is now a thing of the past in these days when players are spoken of as triers or non triers.

CELTIC VICTORY

Fatal Boghead! What visions of bygone struggles do these two words bring forth! Well might the club tremble which was drawn against the famous Dumbarton at Levenside. Not one could scarce hope to escape without disastrous defect in those days, and when the semi-final ballot decided that the Celts were to visit that fated field it was felt that they were asked to take something almost beyond their ability. At Parkhead and on the various city grounds they were certainly very good, but to think of going down to Dumbarton and vanquish the Sons of the Rock as they proudly styled themselves, was preposterous indeed. But the Celtic team of that day had a pretty high opinion of themselves, and viewed the coming conflict with complacency.

Only once change was made in the usual team, Willie Maley coming permanently into the eleven. He had been rather young hitherto to take his place, and he could hardly have entered into a stiffer contest than the one under notice. Dumbarton had the greatest difficulty in sinking off St Mirren in the previous round, for it was not until a third trial of strength that they overcame the Saints by three goals to one, the match taking place at Ibrox. Even after a lapse of nine years, one can remember and almost feel the thrill of enthusiasm which pervaded the large Celtic following that day. Many an exciting struggle has the team taken part in since, but not once has the enthusiasm risen to such a pitch. Hundreds stopped off work and made the day a holiday; round the ropes the old war cry - now alas, forgotten - "Hurry up Celts" was displayed on thousands of hats and the quiet burgh roused as it had seldom been before.

Both teams were at their strongest, and both were confident of success. The Celtic team: John Kelly; Willie Maley and Mick McKeown; Paddy Gallagher, James Kelly, Jimmy McLaren; Neil McCallum, Mick Dunbar, Willie Groves, Johnny Coleman and Tom Maley. Dumbarton were represented by Jamie Bell; Stewart and Hannah; McMillan, Dewar, Keir; Lapsley, Johnny Madden, Jack Bell, Chapman and Aitken. Against such a grand trio of halves, the Celts were perfectly aware that individual efforts would profit little and shaped their plans accordingly. From the very start they settled down beautifully, and nothing could be finer than the manner which they came down on Jamie Bell time after time, all in a line like a perfect machine. The Dumbarton defence was splendid, but nothing could withstand the terrible Celtic attack. "For heaven's sake break up that combination," yelled Joe Lindsay from the stand, as the Celts swept over Boghead in irresistible fashion. Easier said than done; but yet Dumbarton stuck to their guns, though half time found them two goals down. Both scored from combined rushes.

The only regrettable incident was the rough treatment accorded Johnny Madden. Four free kicks in succession were given against the Celts for rough work against the Dumbarton Irishman, and surprise was felt on all sides that the Celts should single out one of their own kith and kin. It was rumoured at the time that Madden had disappointed the Celts by refusing to don the green and white jersey after having promised to do so, and if this be the case, it seems the players thought they were paying off an old debt. The second half saw the Celts maintain their form and seventeen minutes from the resumption the finest individual run ever seen on the ground was put in by Willie Groves. Getting possession of the ball well up the field, and closely pursued by George Dewar, Groves threaded the ball through the entire defence, finishing up with a shot which gave Jamie Bell no earthly chance. It will be long ere Groves' achievement be forgotten, for even yet when one sees a fine bit of dribbling on new Celtic Park we hear some old stager refer with kindling eye to this single handed effort of the old Celtic centre. This brilliant run fairly settled Dumbarton, as may be judged by Mick Dunbar, of all men scoring a fourth goal.

Just before the finish Johnny Madden had revenge by scoring the only goal for his side and thus one of the finest games ever seen on Boghead ended in the defeat of the home team by 4 goals to one. Time works wonders in football as in most other things, hence it is scarcely surprising to find three of the Dumbarton team of that day afterwards wearing a Celtic jersey. These were of course the two Bells and Madden. The Celts decisive victory was looked upon as sensational and paved the way for their famous finals against Third Lanark when the Parkhead team first experienced that slice of bad luck which has since so often fallen to them.

THE SNOW FINAL - A FOOTBALL FIASCO

The Snow Final? Who will ever forget this brilliant fiasco? Certainly not one who made the journey to Hampden that wintry afternoon and braved the blinding snow storm will ever allow the stirring incidents to escape his memory. The final tie to be fought out by Celtic and Third Lanark excited more interest than any in the previous history of the cup. The reason for this unwanted interest were not far to seek; first because only twice before had two city teams met in the final, then the severe struggles which each team encountered ere reaching the final stage, and lastly the enormous following which the Irish club had brought into the game. The Celts' victories in the earlier ties have been already noticed, but the Third had performed quite as brilliantly.

They defeated Queens Park who protested on the ground that Love of Thornliebank had already played in a senior tie and a replay took place, when the Third again won. It will be remembered that it was only at the third attempt that Dumbarton got rid of St Mirren and strange to say another Paisley club almost bowled over Third Lanark in the next round, for it was only after four games that Cathkin qualified, and strange coincidence - Ibrox was the venue of each decider. Having overcome all opposition, the Celtic and Third Lanark at last stood face to face. Unfortunately snow had fallen early on the day of the great contest, but referee Campbell inspected the ground at 11 o'clock in the forenoon and declared it playable. The snow continued to fall slightly until one o'clock, when the gates were opened, but between 2 and 3 o'clock a regular blizzard set in, which promised to veto the proceedings. To play a cup tie with snow a foot deep was farcical, but how to appease the 20,000 spectators was a problem. At last the committees of both teams met in Hampden pavillion and signed a joint agreement to play a match, but protesting against it being reckoned a cup tie. So both teams entered the snow covered pitch to the cheers of their frenzied supporters. The rumour had gone abroad that the Celts had secured Wilson of the Vale of Leven, to keep goal for them and despite letters to the evening papers from that player and several Celts denying this, the crowd fondly hoped to see the Vale custodian guard the Celtic uprights.

The Parkhead team turned out exactly as published, viz:- John Kelly; Paddy Gallagher and Mick McKeown, James Kelly and Jimmy McLaren; Neil McCallum, Mick Dunbar, Willie Groves, Johnny Coleman and Tom Maley. The Thirds were represented by - Downie, Thomson and Rae; McFarlane, Auld and Lochead, Oswald Junior, Marshall, Oswald Senior, Hannah and Johnstone. It was at once seen that the players were in a frisky mood, for the team started snowballing each other, not in the manner of two elevens about to engage in a terrific struggle for supremacy. However both sides did their best to make the game as interesting as possible; but the Celts were once again to find themselves beaten by a goalkeeper, for try as they might they could not once get the better of Downie, while the Third beat Kelly three times with comparative ease and so a game which was utterly spoiled by the weather ended in favour of the Volunteers by 3 goals to 0.

From the protege of John Glass, Brother Walfrid's right hand man...
Celtic Chairman, Tom White in the Glasgow Eastern Standard on 10th March 1923;

HISTORY OF CELTIC FC.

"The history of the Celtic club inevitably brings in the name of the Edinburgh Hibernians as it was an emulation of the doughty deeds of the Edinburgh country men that the Celtic were formed. The Hibernians were established in 1875, the team playing on a public pitch on the East Meadows and from that time onwards they strove mightily

to attain honours in the east which they ultimately gained, although in their early days they had to fight against all sorts of difficulties and objections. The Hibs lived this down and made a name for themselves in Scottish football by winning the Scottish Cup in 1887 on Hampden Park, Glasgow.

In the crowd at that match were many from St Mary's, Abercromby Street and a discussion took place regarding the possibility of arranging a game with the Hibernian for the benefit for the Poor Childrens Dinner Tables. The matter was taken up enthusiastically by Mr John Glass, Mr John O'Hara and other east enders and thanks to the kind offices of the late Mr John D Graham of Bridgeton, the Clyde FC gave their ground free for a game which took place between the Hibs, as Scottish Cup holders and the famous Renton, at which a big crowd attended to the great benefit of the charity concerned.

The next step was to hold a meeting on the 6th November, 1887, in East Rose Street, Glasgow, at which it was agreed to form the Celtic Club and to take over a field in Dalmarnock Street. The pioneers of the club were John Glass, John O'Hara, Dr Conway, Andrew Bryan, James McKay, John H McLaughlin, Pat Welsh, Hugh Darroch, William McKillop and James Quillan. Mr William Maley was appointed Match Secretary. The committee wrought hard and the new ground was opened on the 8th May, 1888, by a match between Hibs and Cowlairs at which a very good crowd attended. Thereafter Celtic joined the Scottish and Glasgow Associations and the new club was from that point in the making.

The first players of any note to assist the new club were the brothers Maley, Tom, at the time a teacher and playing occasionally for 3rd LRV and Hibs, and Willie, a young raw stripling, playing for his village team, Cathcart, and occasionally for 3rd LRV. The prospects of the Glasgow club attracted several of the Hibs players who belonged to the west of Scotland, and Groves, McLaren, McKeown, Dunbar, Gallagher and Coleman took the plunge and joined the Celtic. These, together with James Kelly and Neilly McCallum formed the nucleus of a first class team. Celtic's first team in the opening game with Rangers at Celtic Park was; - Michael Dolan, Eddie Pearson. and James McLaughlin, Willie Maley, James Kelly and Phil Murray; Neil McCallum and Tom E Maley, Johnny Madden, Charlie Gorevin and Mick Dunbar. Celtic won that game by 5 goals to 2 and it is interesting to note that Rangers did not beat Celtic in any game from that date, 28th May, 1888, until the 18th February, 1893.

That season Celtic played 56 games, won 42, lost 3, and drew 11, scoring 109 goals and losing 81. Surely a wonderful record for the first year of a club in first class competitions. The first cup won by the Celts was in 1889 when they won the North Eastern Cup in which they defeated Clyde, Thistle, Northern and Cowlairs, all at that time leading Glasgow clubs.

Then that same season they played into the final tie of the Glasgow Exhibition Cup, being defeated by a Scottish Select team gathered together by Cowlairs for the final. Revenge came swift and sure, however, to the now rapidly rising Celts, as being drawn against Cowlairs in the Scottish Cup they wiped out the Exhibition Cup fiasco by beating their opponents by 8-0 and displaying to the Glasgow public the finest exhibition of the short passing game that had been seen in Scotland. The "men who did" that day deserve mention. They were:-Willie Dunning; Paddy Gallagher and Mick McKeown; Willie Maley, James Kelly, and James McLaren; Neil McCallum and Johnny Coleman, Willie Groves, Mick Dunbar and Tom E. Maley.

It might be mentioned here at a dinner given after the Exhibition Final, in responding to the toast of the losers, Mr John Glass referred to the very unsportsmanlike reception the new club had received from the spectators, he in conclusion, said;

"Let them scoff and jeer. Celtic will yet win to our proper position by our merits and those who scoff today will one day have to applaud".

His words have been amply fulfilled as all will see.

The Scottish Cup that season found the Celts in rampant form and they played right into the final after brilliant victories in the various rounds. Against the 3rd LRV in the famous "Snow Final," with luck entirely against them, they went under to the Cathkinites after a fierce struggle. It was a terrible disappointment to the thousands of Celtic supporters all over the country and to the faithful hard-working committee who had set their hearts on the blue riband of Scottish football. It was however, like all great disappointments, ultimately for the best and when the first sorrow of the day was over, it was felt by all that it would have been too much to expect such great success in a first attempt and that it was all for the best and only stimulated everyone to fresh efforts to make the team stronger and fitter for the future trials.

Before leaving this glorious year of the Celts, I would like to point out what a wonderful thing it was for this committee to form a club, build a ground, and place on the field a first class team all within nine months, especially when we realise that with one or two exceptions they had no knowledge whatever of the game and its management. Enthusiasm, however, surmounts all difficulties and it was this in boundless force, which carried the good ship Celtic on the high seas of Scottish football with such a dash.

The old ground, now built over, was for a time in serious trouble, as the landlord wanted to break his contract, but when told the club would take him to the House of Lords if need be, he relented, although latterly he raised the rent from £50 per year to £500 which was the reason for constructing the present Celtic Park.

As the club grew and prospered the desire to get on the committee, became strong throughout the city and various names were added in turn to the list. The late John McKillop devoted more time now to the club, as also did the late Hugh Murphy. The only time any serious trouble arose in our ranks was in 1897, when, with a heavy expenditure on the field looming overhead, the men who had signed for a big bank overdraft asked that they should have some fixity of tenure in office with their responsibility, but not getting that, moved for limited liability and so the present company came into existence and from that date the company has never looked back and is equal of any club in Britain in every sense of the word. The Celts are almost the first club in Scotland to purchase their own ground and no club in Britain has donated anything approaching the money that the club has given to charities of every description.

The founders of the club, as you will have seen, were all east enders although it has been stated that the club did originate in St Andrews parish. I might state that the late Monsignor Munro, with that stern religion which characterised him, disapproved entirely of the club and its doings. I might also state a form and point a moral from the early days of the club. In these days Brake Clubs were originated, but they were men and lads whose conduct and baring were as orderly in defeat as in victory and a credit to the club, a sad comparison to some of the men who call themselves football followers today and disgrace our clubs and our game".

EARLY DAYS OF CELTIC HISTORY

By Man In The Know in the *Glasgow Observer* on 25th June 1927;

THE VERY BEGINNING

"The first steps in connection with the foundation of Celtic Football Club were taken in the year 1887 and in the beginning of 1888 the following circular was addressed to the leading Catholics of Glasgow:-

The main object of the club is to supply the east end conferences of the St Vincent De Paul Society in Glasgow with funds for the maintenance of the "dinner tables" of the needy children in the missions of St Mary's, Sacred Heart and St Michaels, Parkhead. Many cases of sheer poverty are left unaided through lack of means. It is therefore with this principle object that we have set afloat the "Celtic" and we invite you to assist us in putting our new field in proper working order for the coming football season. In these projects we have the assistance, sanction and good wishes of his Grace, the Archbishop of Glasgow and the clergy of the missions mentioned above.

EARLY CELTIC FIGURES

From the above it will be seen that the primary object of the Celtic club was to assist the Poor Childrens Dinner Table. The connection between football and charity may not be at once obvious to everybody and it might be interesting to indicate how this connection was brought about. For many years the members of the St Vincent De Paul Society in the east end had worked quietly and steadily to relieve the poverty and suffering in the district, but the claims upon the society far exceeded the slender sums at its disposal, and the members began to look around for some source of income yet undiscovered. The Edinburgh Hibs, who that year had won the Scottish Cup, were asked to play a charity match against Clyde at old Barrowfield Park, Bridgeton.

The move was pleasingly successful and the then wonderful sum of £50 was realised after all expenses had been paid. This happy windfall placed football in a new light and some of the farseeing members of the St Vincent De Paul said "If £50 can be raised by a single game between strange teams, why should we not have a team of our own, and the surplus profits divided among local charities?" Thus it came about that on 6th November, 1887 the Celtic F.C. was formally constituted at a meeting in St Mary's Hall, East Rose Street, Glasgow. Having put their hands to the plough, the promoters lost no time in getting to work and a week later - November 13th - ground was leased in Dalmarnock Street, Parkhead. Of course, this meant money and subscriptions were asked for and ready response was made. The first subscriber being Reverend Father Van Der Hyde, a Dutch curate in St Mary's under the late Canon Carmichael.

Of course, it should be understood that the originator of the club and the mainstay of its early days was the late Reverend Brother Walfrid, the then head of the Marist Brothers of Glasgow. Brother Walfrid did more to start the club and set it on its feet than any other man and among the old guard who still survive, the name of the popular Marist is held in affection and his memory is evergreen. It seems that the choice of club colours gave food for argument and much discussion, and it was only after long discussion that the present colours, green and white, were chosen. On 1st May, 1888 the first officials and committee were appointed and in view of the many changes that have since taken place it may be interesting to give the list in full. Here it is:- Honorary President Dr John Conway; President, Mr John Glass; Vice President Mr James Quillan; Treasurer, Mr Hugh Darroch; Match Secretary, Mr Willie Maley; Honorary Secretary, Mr John O'Hara. The committee included, among others, Messrs James Rogers, Mick Rogers, Michael Shannon, John McDonald, James Curtis and Dan Molloy.

CELTIC v RANGERS

On the threshold of their career, the club was confronted with an unfortunate hitch. The proprietor of the field took offence at the way in which the ground was being laid out and threatened to interdict the opening game which had been arranged. The outlook was black. The club prepared to carry the case to the court of session and finally the landlord withdrew his opposition. On the 8th May, 1888 the first match was played on Celtic Park, not by the Celts, but by two invited teams, Hibernians and Cowlairs, both at that time at the height of their fame. The Celts first game took place soon after, when a side composed of young Irish players met and defeated Rangers by 5 goals to 2. This was a glorious send off for the new club, who followed up their victory by beating Dundee Harp, drawing with Mossend Swifts and suffering their first reverse from Clyde, who won by the narrow margin of 4 goals to 3. It is remarkable that the Celts' first victory was over Rangers and that their first defeat was inflicted by near neighbours, the Clyde. What ups and downs have taken place in the football world since those early days! Celtic immediately joined the Glasgow and Scottish Associations and the new club was definitely launched on its new career".

"Veteran," of the *Evening Times* was known to be a man who Brother Walfrid confided in;

THE HISTORY OF CELTIC By Veteran in the Evening Times

FIRST ARTICLE, 16th May, 1931

"There is a striking similarity in the history in nearly every football club as far as its origin and early struggles are concerned. We nearly always read of a handful of youths putting their pennies together towards the purchase of a football betaking themselves to some open space and their knocking the ball and each other about just for the fun of the thing.

Challenges from one side to another followed the public, or at least a small section of it, began to take notice and after a time the clubs began to take money. The open spaces were deserted, grounds rented and railed off and admission charges made.

From such lonely beginnings, all but one of our first grade clubs have arisen. The Celtic F.C. is as unique in its origin as it has been outstanding in its achievements. While other clubs were instituted to give exercise to its members, without thought of the subsequent mercenary developments which have made a business of a pastime, the promoters of the Celtic club were out for money right from the beginning. But not for themselves.

Writing as one who was in close touch with the club and its creators from its first days of its existence, I can testify to the integrity and enthusiasm of its founders who gave freely of their time, labour and money without hope of fee or reward, their only recompense, the inward satisfaction of being associated in an enterprise it would, it was hoped, help towards relieving the distress of their less fortunate brethren.

IN THE EAST END

In the east end of Glasgow individual charity attempted to do what state aid is doing today. The "Poor Childrens Dinner Table," was the forerunner of the state kitchen and to provide daily dinners for hundreds of poor east end kiddies, money was required. The job was too big for any individual or committee to tackle; donations dwindled and still the children went hungry. Something big had to be done, some organisation must be set up if the pot were to be kept boiling.

Living and moving among the poor of the east end were Mr John Glass, Brother Walfrid, head master of St Mary's schools and Dr Conway. Often did they confer as to the question of ways and means. Interviews with others interested in the welfare of the poor followed and eventually someone pointed out that the charitable organisation with which he was connected had only recently received a donation from the committee of the Glasgow Merchants football cup competition. Renton and Cambuslang were the finalists and £1,050 the amount garnered by that season's competition.

At once the question of football and charity was eagerly discussed, "If only we could have a club of our own, one that could earn a little towards feeding our children". A committee was formed and a suitable pitch secured in Dalmarnock Street. These were comparatively easy tasks. Much more difficult was it to build up a first class eleven, a team that would play itself into popularity, the club into affluence right away. Second rate "haund-me-doon" players were of no account; only the very best talent could fill the bill.

ANOTHER STORY

How these players were secured is another story that will hear telling. How successful were the efforts of players and officials in achieving the object of the promoters is indicated by the third annual report of the club, which stated that, in addition to giving £5 per week to the dinner fund, no less than £1,400 had been allocated to other charities. Good going this for a new club after fitting up a ground, held on a three years lease only and faced with a costly fitting to the present enclosure, now the property of the club for all time.

It has been said that the creation of Celtic FC was due to the success of the Hibernian team in the Scottish Cup final of 1886-87; that, what an eastern Irish club could do was possible for one in the west. Nothing could be further from the truth. No doubt ambition was responsible for the founding of the new club, but it was ambition of a laudable nature, a determination to have a team just good enough to raise sufficient funds to keep the kiddies' pot boiling.

The early Celtic team builders were content to leave it at that. The most far sighted of them never glimpsed the possibilities of present day football. There's money in the cup had no meaning for them. Pot filling not pot hunting was their sole aim; to feed the hungry their one ambition. And after 40 years and more the same spirit exists at Parkhead. True the game has become a business proposition but the old philanthropy is still there. A Celtic balance sheet is a marvel of mystery and one thing it does not disclose is the handsome donations that bring good cheers to many deserving institutions at Christmas time.

Founded for charity, the Celtic club, more perhaps than any other, has lived up to the ideals of its promoters, now nearly all passed away.

ON JIMMY KELLY'S DOORSTEP - SECOND ARTICLE, 23rd May 1931

As already stated, the early Celtic officials began as no other club ever did; they built a ground first and then cast round for players. Voluntary labour and a little cash made the first task comparatively easy to build up a team in keeping with the ground and the promoters' ambition was another and a much more difficult undertaking.

"Hitch your wagon to a star," wrote the poet, and this is just what the Celtic pioneers did. They reckoned that if they could secure one outstanding player, one whose football ability and personal character marked him out as a leader among men, others would be found to follow that leader.

To those who remember the part played by the Renton team at this period - they had just done the hat trick in the Glasgow charity club competition and beaten Cambuslang by six goals to one in the final of the Scottish Cup - it will not come as a surprise to learn that James Kelly, the centre half back of the village team, was the bright particular star to which the Parkhead committee desired to be yoked. But to connect with this star seemed as futile as to cry for the moon. Kelly was very happy and comfortable in the village he was born and bred. He had a good trade on his hands, ambition to launch out as a builder, and desired nothing better than a quiet life on Leven side.

NOTHING DOING

The first Celts to broach him on the question of playing for another club than Renton were Messrs O'Hara and McDonald. There was nothing doing. The elastic laws of that period allowed a player to assist any other club in any match, save a Scottish Cup tie. So a half promise was given by the Renton man that if Celts had a really important game on hand he might assist them for the day and for that day only. As it happened, Celts had no game on hand, important or otherwise, for the simple reason that they had a ground but no players.

Now, in the previous year, Hibernian had made history by defeating Dumbarton 2-0 in the final of the Scottish Cup. Unfortunately, in the words of a long forgotten song, "They had never done anything since," except to play second fiddle to their rivals of Tynecastle. In every game, cup and friendly, Hearts simply "ate the cupholders," and to make sure of further success they brought in Hull, Sneddon and Reid, an Airdrieonian contingent, for the Hibs special benefit in the semi-final of the Roseberry Cup. Two could play at this game, so the Hibs astute Secretary, Mr. John McFadyen, thought.

Down went John to Renton and told his tail of woe - told Kelly that, bent on rubbing it in, Hearts had assembled a picked eleven to wipe the floor with the already well-beaten Easter Road boys. As one would expect from such a chivalrous nature, the appeal was not lost on the Renton lad. He would assist Hibs for that one occasion and further, would bring his clubmate too, Neilly McCallum.

A PACKED TEAM

The bold McFadyen was delighted, for well he knew that where Kelly led, others would follow. They did, with the result that a picked Hibs team thrashed a picked Hearts eleven on the Stockbridge ground and then went on to win the final with their own players.

By this time a team of a sort had been gathered together at Parkhead, not just the committee's idea of what a team should be, but the best that could be obtained. At any rate, it was deemed good enough to justify the Celtic officials taking on Rangers in a friendly match. This in itself was asking for trouble as the Ibrox team had just run into the final of the Glasgow Cup, which they lost to Cambuslang by 3-1. Along came Renton, and as already mentioned, they did for Cambuslang in the Scottish final, what the latter club did for Rangers in the city event.

To mention Renton at once suggested Kelly, but that player had been already approached and no business done. There was just the chance that he might do for Celtic what he had done only a few weeks previously of Hibernian - lend a hand for one day only. It was a big day too, even though only a friendly affair, since it was the Celts' very first match and success or failure in this, the all important opening game of the new club, would possibly make or mar it for all time.

FOR ONE DAY

Down went another Celtic deputation to Renton and the situation was fully explained to Kelly. If he would just play in the opening match against Rangers, his name would help the gate and his play would have a great deal to do with the result. Like the good sport he was, and is to this day, the Rentonian said he would be a Celt for the day. Further he would not promise. The great day came, and Kelly with it; by 5-2, Celts defeated the Rangers, and it is quite unnecessary to state that this was the fore runner of many arduous battles between clubs that have developed into monopolists.

The first meeting of Celts and Rangers on May 28th 1888 was not the first match on new Parkhead. Cowlairs and Hibernian had the honour of opening a ground, which subsequently witnessed many stirring encounters before it was vacated nearly 4 years later. It was not a great Celtic team that inflicted first defeat on Rangers, but it served. The players were:- Michael Dolan (Drumpellier), goal; Eddie Pearson (Carfin Shamrock) and James McLaughlin (Govan Whitefield); Willie Maley (Cathcart), James Kelly (Renton) and Phil Murray (Blantyre); Neil McCallum (Renton) and Tom E Maley (Third Lanark); Johnny Madden (Dumbarton); Mick Dunbar (Busby Cartvale) and Charlie Gorevin (Govan Hibernians).

EXODUS

Though very young at the game, the Celtic officials were old enough to realise that this eleven would not carry the club very far, even if all the players were inclined to continue as Celtic players, which some were not - Madden for one.

It could hardly be expected, that two members of the "Champions of the World" team would think of leaving Renton, but soon there was an awakening in the Leven Valley, where wages were small and inducements from England as specious as they were secret. Things began to happen. Everton, Sunderland, Newcastle, and others were calling - in the double sense.

Celts and Hibs took a hand. Both sat on Kelly's doorstep, but for a long time it was a cold seat, McCallum a light hearted chap, was willing to play anywhere, but Kelly's heart was with Renton only and he determined to play for no other club. However offers were being made by English clubs to Vale, Dumbarton and Renton players, so sensing the subsequent trek across the border, Kelly resolved to preserve his amateur status and making football a sideline, get into business either in Glasgow or Edinburgh.

TUG OF WAR

Then followed a tug of war between east and west. West won; Kelly became a Celt for good, and the rest was easy for Parkhead. Once it was known that the famous centre half-back of the world renowned Renton team had thrown in his lot with the new Glasgow club, other almost equally well known players made haste to follow suit. What was good enough for Jimmy Kelly was good enough for them.

CELTIC'S FIRST GAME IN 1888

A CUP TIE WON AT KELVINGROVE - THIRD ARTICLE, 30th May 1931

When Celtic opened their first season on the 1st of August, 1888, Johnny Madden was still thinking it over in Dumbarton. Without him there were all the elements of a grand eleven:- Willie Dunning; Paddy Gallagher; Mick McKeown; Willie Maley, James Kelly, Jimmy McLaren; Neil McCallum, Mick Dunbar, Willie Groves, Johnny Coleman and Tom E Maley.

This was the eleven that faced the starter. Would they face the music? In other words, would they hang together until September 3rd when Shettleston were due in the first round of the Scottish Cup? For in those days there was no signing players on or off. Until one played in a Scottish tie he was a free agent. He could play for Celtic today, for Hibs, Renton, or Cowlairs tomorrow.

It was an anxious time for a new club like Celtic since there was no knowing when, for example, Secretary McFadyen might induce one or all of the Hibernian contingent to retrace their way east. But no, they had given their word to Kelly that if he stayed, they did likewise. Hence the centre half was more than a pivot and a mainspring. Had he gone back to Renton at the last minute, the majority of the others would have disappeared from Parkhead. A team of a sort would have been fielded, something akin to the Govan Hibs of that day, or the Glasgow Hibs of a later date.

It is a certainty that Kelly's defection would have meant a wholesale withdrawal, but the Rentonians word was his bond and the team went from strength to strength until it ran into the Scottish final in its first season, the first of many records. Looking back over the years and knowing the influences at work, one can say with absolute certainty that it was a case of no Kelly, no Keltic - as we know and do not pronounce it today.

1888 EXHIBITION

As it happened, Celts very first venture was a cup tie, though not a Scottish one. The city was then holding its first Exhibition, and as one would expect, football was one of the most successful sidelines of that most successful adventure. Abercorn, now long defunct, had the honour of being Celts' first opponents in a serious engagement.

The League system, with its fixed schedule existed as yet only in the brain of the Birmingham Scot, Mr McGregor and did not come into being until two years later. Haphazard friendlies filled the bill when clubs had no club fixtures to fulfil - national, city or county. So having finished with Abercorn at Kelvingrove, Celtic invited Hibernian to Parkhead and the depleted eastern club came very well out of the affair, the first game played on Celtic territory in the first season of the new club. The previous May meeting with Rangers might be termed an off season or end of season bout.

By 3 goals to 2, Celts won their first home fixture and then went on to defeat Airdrieonians away by 6-0 and Clyde at Barrowfield 5-1. Dumbarton Athletic were then met and beaten 3-1 in the second round of the Exhibition ties and in the following week Celts had a hint of what was coming to them in the first bid for the Scottish cup. Not content with taking part in the Exhibition ties and defeating Dumbarton Athletic on a Tuesday evening, they went over to Cathkin and met with their first defeat; 4-3 to Third Lanark. Thursday found them better at Paisley, where they had the better of Abercorn (4-2) and they wound up their first month by defeating Partick Thistle.

That first month was a very busy one, nine matches played, with three played on consecutive days and one defeat. This was so very like the Celtic we have come to know.

TO STIFLE ARGUMENTS

As no club appears more often in the 'Answers to correspondence' sporting column of the Evening Times than Celtic, it may be profitable to repeat some early results and so stifle many arguments. Rangers were Celts first opponents and first victims in what may be called the off season fixture of May, 1888. Hibs were Celts' first visitors and first victims in the Celtic's first season proper on August 4th, 1888. Third Lanark were Celts' first conquerors at Cathkin on August 22nd - all three being friendly fixtures, Abercorn were the first to meet Celtic in a cup tie of any kind - the Exhibition trophy on August 1st 1888.

There now arrived the great day, the day of days, September 1st on that day Shettleston were drawn to meet Celtic at Parkhead on the first round of the Scottish Cup. There was no doubt as to Shettleston turning up. But what of the home team how many who took park in the nine matches of August would face the starter on the 1st day of September, a day that tied a player to a club for the rest of the season?

Peter Campbell of Renton still had hope that Kelly and McCallum would return to the village club; John McFadyen tried every move as the great day drew near, to entice Groves, McKeown, McLaren, Dunbar, Coleman, and Gallagher back to the Easter Road fold; Tom Maley was badly wanted at Cathkin, a bid made to brother Willie to stray no farther from Cathcart than Crosshill. Ten were bespoke; Dunning alone lacked a suitor.

THE GREAT DAY

This game of catch the ten was no child's play and many a sleepless night did most of the Parkhead "Komitee men" spend while players were making up their minds. Fortunately, one of the ten came to a quick decision. All during the month of August, Kelly was warming to Parkhead without cooling on Renton. He did not want to be the first to leave the old club, but when he found that Andrew Hannah was almost fixed up by Everton and Bob Kelso as good as booked for Newcastle, learned also that there were more to follow, he made no secret of his intention to play against Shettleston and so tie himself down as a Celtic player for the remainder of the season - as it happened, for the full term of his football life.

That did it. With one voice the other players said that what was good enough for Kelly was good enough for them. The entire 11 turned out for Shettleston's benefit and a 5-1 victory followed as a matter of course. It is no exaggeration, then to state that September 1st, 1888 was the red letter day in the history of the Celtic Football Club. Doubts gave way to certainly; Parkhead now had an 11 good enough for any enterprise. The way was paved for countless deeds and records.

Kelly had made the Keltic.

CELTIC HIT THEIR FIRST SNAG - FOURTH ARTICLE, 6th June 1931

Defeated by Cowlairs in Exhibition Cup

"The days after their Scottish Cup victory over Shettleston, Celtic hit their first snag. drawn against Cowlairs in the final round of the Exhibition Cup, they found themselves up against a reinforced Cowlairs - a good team made better by the inclusion of Allan Stewart, (Queens Park), and Bob Kelso, (Newcastle).

It was Hibs and Hearts over again, only on this occasion Kelly was on the losing side by 2-0. Accounts were squared a fortnight later, when Cowlairs went to Parkhead on a Scottish cup-tie venture and were well and soundly beaten by 8 goals to 0. Shettleston again had the bad luck to be drawn in a cup tie against Celtic, this time a Glasgow tie, and 11-2 was the verdict. Still, they fared not so badly, since in the same month and in the same competition Rangers lost to Celtic, at Ibrox too, by 6 goals to 1. Although rather out of place, it may be noted here that the first League match between Celtic and Rangers at Parkhead two years later ended in a 2-2 draw, and the return game at Ibrox in a 2-1 victory for Celtic. Many things have happened since those far off days, but Celtic enthusiasts can claim that in the first friendly, Cup and League encounters between green and white and blue, the former did not come off second best.

Queens Do It

What was beyond Rangers was a comparatively easy thing for Queens Park. The amateurs paid their first visit to old Celtic Park on November 17th and as a result Celtic lost all interest in the Glasgow Cup that season through losing a couple of goals. A week later Clyde made their first acquaintance with the new ground and proved to be very disturbing visitors. The occasion was a Scottish Cup tie, the hero of the day being Chalmers, the Clyde goalkeeper and the result, 1-0 for Clyde. Talk of a one man band! This was a one man show - one against an eleven - as may be gathered from learning that Celts claimed and obtained a replay on the grounds that the pitch was unplayable and slaughtered the self same Clyde eleven in the play off by 9 goals to 2. One has only to mention this dual meeting to an ancient Brigtonian to realise that 43 years are as yesterday to your football enthusiast. That defeat, following on victory rankles more deeply east of the "Umbrella" than the presentation of the same trophy to Dundee at Ibrox 21 years later. (Clyde lost 2-0 to Dundee after a second replay in the 1910 Scottish Cup Final, after two draws).

Well Beaten

What Queens did for Celts in the City cup competition, Third Lanark accomplished in the Scottish. The Celts, now using their third keeper, though not quite half way through their first season. Dolan had given way to Dunning, and then the Johnstone man went to Aston Villa and made way for Johnnie Kelly. The new man was at least the equal of Downie, who held the fort for the Volunteers. Third Lanark were making their third appearance in the Scottish Cup final and the third time was lucky. They won the cup because they were the better cup fighters. Celts, making their first bid for the trophy, were by far the more skilful team, but they lacked the dash and vigour of the winners. Moreover, they shot badly, and were well beaten in the protested and second game by the very best eleven that ever wore Cathkin colours.

With the national and city cups lost beyond recall for that season it might be thought that a bold bid would be made for the Charity trophy. As is well known, no club has done more for charity than the club formed for charitable purposes and when the Celtic officials planned an extended tour in England and Ireland they probably imagined that a victory over Renton would be a pleasant wind up. A week's rest availed nothing after playing Bolton Wanderers, Burnley, Distillery and Belfast United. There was still some "chicken bree" in Peter Campbell's pot, and the tourists met with their heaviest defeat in this, their first season, by 5-2.

First Cup

Beaten in all three cup competitions by the ultimate winners, Celtic were as near as could be to attaining their ambition. They had consolation - of a kind - when they landed their first trophy - little fishes are sweet - and even the lowly North Eastern Cup took some winning. On their way to the final, Celts beat Clydesdale, (5-0), Cowlairs, (5-0), and Thistle, (5-0). Northern were beaten in the final at Barrowfield, (2-0), and Celtic thus secured the first of a long line of winning cup finals.

That first season was a long one. It extended from August 1st to May 25th, and the programme ran to 56 matches. Your modern high paid player would scarcely relish this dish. Fortunately there was such a thing as enthusiasm 40 years ago, and it was a thing unknown for a player to feel indisposed bodily or mentally when asked to turn out four times in the same week, as the Celtic team did twice in their first season. Of the 56 matches played, Celtic won 43, drew 3 and lost 11. The season would up with a well deserved victory over the "Invincibles," Preston North End, and all over, the new club gave promise of becoming what it is today, and has been for that matter, since the day of its origin - a dominant figure in the great game".

FOOTBALL'S NEW LEASE OF LIFE - FIFTH ARTICLE, 13th June 1931

"Without a doubt Celtic's first season gave Scottish football a new and a long lease of life. If not actually dead, the game was in a state of suspended animation. Queens Park were so far above the other city clubs as to make local club contests almost trivial affairs; local interest being very circumscribed indeed.

The clubs that really mattered were Dumbarton, Vale and Renton and professionalism was soon to reduce the trio to the level of Clyde, Cowlairs and Northern. Hearts and Hibs maintained a desultory warfare in the east, but Scottish football all over was not getting much further forward ; rather was it going back.

The advent of the Parkhead club completely altered the situation. Thousands who had never given a thought to the game rallied to the support of the new organisation. This would not have meant so very much had not the newcomers brought out many more thousands who held other ideas. Neither section knew the first thing about the game. All they did know, or wanted to know, was that a so called Irish team was making other teams sit up, so it was up to the public to take notice.

MONEY IN THE CUP

Increased interest meant bigger gates, hence we find Celtic, in their very first season, sharing in the first four figure Scottish final gate. Of course that was a two round affair, but four years later we have Celtic and Queens Park playing to a £1400 gate, which was a long way in front of the final of six years earlier, when Queens also were finalists - and winners - Renton being the other lot, and the gate a paltry £303.

Yes, Celts had opened a new era of prosperity for other clubs, for the game in general and the SFA in particular. Such clubs as Dundee, St Mirren and East Fife would not appeal to a Glasgow crowd in ordinary circumstances, but opposed to Celtic in consecutive Scottish finals, they shared in gates of £3489, £4637 and £3996. As with Scottish finals, so with English internationals. The Celtic club was the first to enlarge its terracing for this fixture, and the outcome was a gate of over £2000 as against the £800 drawn at Ibrox two years before.

In the early days of these international contests, Scottish teams had to travel by night, their only refreshment a cup of tea brewed by Johnnie McDowall's spirit lamp. Today we have five figure gates when Hampden is the venue. The spirit lamp is gone, the spirit also, else why should old internationals players have the poor privilege of a free ticket denied them as happened at Hampden a few weeks ago? One can only say that the SFA is a rich concern and at the same time a very poor affair.

ON A BIG SCALE

Ignorance and enthusiasm were marked features of the early Celtic - and anti Celtic - fraternity. "Who has a better right to throw the ball in than the man who kicked it out?" is matched by the authenticated story of a well to do Celtic supporter. "What do you fellows mean by playing at Hampden, Tynecastle, or Paisley when they have a brand new ground of their own at Parkhead?" Home-and-home had no meaning for an individual who was all take and no give.

As the Celtic club has always been noted for doing things on a big scale, it does not surprise one to find the first committee and other officials ran to over twenty members, an unwieldy and not always harmonious assembly. It required two Patrons, an Honorary President, President, Vice president, Honorary Secretary, Match Secretary, Honorary Treasurer, and 14 of a committee to run the club in its early days.

(NB; the office bearers were in fact part of the 14 man committee).

All officials, bar three, were chosen by open vote of members whose sole qualification was ownership of one founder's share, and here the rank and file were known as the "one pounders". As lease holders or guarantors, three qualified for office without a vote. As the years wore on, dissension and jealousy set in; a small but influential section was most anxious to obtain complete control to the exclusion of the "one pounders".

From Tom and Willie Maley's brother, Alec......

HOW THE FAMOUS CLUB HAD ITS ORIGIN

By Alec Maley in the *Glasgow Eastern Standard* on the 13th May 1933;

"From a fleeting thought, born of deep love and sympathy for the poor and often starving children in the east end of Glasgow, emerged Celtic Football Club, which today stands pre-eminent in Scottish football.

HOW CELTIC ORIGINATED

In this short series a few, only a few, of the outstanding stages of its' history will be touched upon. I have no desire to raise any controversy; only to state what my memory forces me to believe to be the facts. It is right and proper for the credit for the birth of the club should go to Brother Walfrid, a member of the Marist Order, who taught in the east end of the city. Having sad experience of the misery in that district, his heart was torn at conditions which he continually slaved to alleviate.

The wonderful enthusiasm among Glasgow Irishmen which greeted the victory of the Hibernians in the Scottish Cup final in 1887, when they defeated Dumbarton at Hampden by 2 goals to 1, gave him an idea, which he almost immediately dismissed as ridiculous. But it kept recurring in his mind, and finally he broached it to several gentlemen who were zealous members of the St Vincent De Paul Society in St Mary's parish.

TO FEED STARVING BAIRNS

"Look at what the Hibernians have done, why shouldn't we start an Irish club in Glasgow and make enough money to feed those starving children among whom I work?" was his plea and so a start was made. Many

players were sounded, but the response was not encouraging as many of them were chary, (cautious), of identifying themselves with an unknown organisation.

Just when the position appeared to be hopeless a suggestion was made that Tom Maley should be approached. He was at that time playing for Third Lanark - then the Third LRV. It was immediately acted upon and a deputation proceeded to Cathcart to interview the young athlete and his father on the subject. The difficulty was at once surmounted, as a heart welcome was extended and besides enlisting one whose personality was at once a guarantee of integrity and earnest endeavour, the assistance of his younger brother Willie, just beginning to show marked ability in the game, was obtained.

A VISIT THAT IS HISTORY

What that visit meant to the Celtic club, to football in Scotland, I and elsewhere, I leave my readers to judge, as besides getting the inspiration to go ahead the services were enrolled of one who was later to add lustre to the club's name on the playing field and athletic field as a legislator and a controller of it's destiny. I refer to Mr William Maley, the Secretary and Manager who has never been out of office from the club's inception.

Soon the ground at Dalmarnock Street was knocked into shape, what before time eager young fellows were busily training, in the hope of being included in the team. Numerous practice games were held and a constitution was drawn up. Today it makes interesting reading. Eleven gentlemen formed the first committee and the original members paid an annual subscription of 5s. A new member had to hand over an additional 2s, 6d on joining; one black ball in four debarred him.

It was laid down that the club, officially born in December 1887, had its principle object to maintain the fund for providing dinners to poor children at school in the three east end parishes of Glasgow. To this end it devoted £5 per week and it is interesting to know that in 1888-89, over £500 was dispersed in charity in addition to the Dinner Table fund; £400 being given in the following season and £500 in 1890-91.

ONLY SECOND CLASS!

The first official season of the club 1888-89 - opened with an Exhibition cup tie in which Celts were included in the second class competition! Abercorn, Dumbarton Athletic and Partick Thistle were defeated, but Celtic had to bow the knee to Cowlairs, specially strengthened for the occasion, in the final, losing 2-0.

Hibernians were defeated in the opening home game by 3-2; and later on in the Scottish Cup, Shettleston (5-1), Cowlairs (8-0), Albion Rovers (4-1), St Bernard's (4-1), Clyde (0-1), and after a successful protest (9-2), East Stirlingshire (2-1) - The two being scored in the last five minutes prophetic feat! - and Dumbarton (4-1) all fell to the conquering Celtic.

THE "SNOW FINAL"

Then came the "Snow Final," with 3rd LRV at Hampden, both teams protesting before the game, which the Warriors won by 3-0, repeating their victory in the replay by 2-1. By this time the Celtic had commanded considerable interest and their defeat in the cup was hailed with the delight by those who resented, or perhaps I ought to say envied, their meteoric rise. These lads in the white shirts and green collars with cuffs and a green Celtic cross, (their original dress), found themselves up against it, I can tell you. But they had a slight reward in winning the North Eastern cup in their first season, beating Cowlairs by 6-1 at Barrowfield".

By Tom Maley himself.......

STORY OF THE RISE OF THE WORLD FAMED CELTIC FOOTBALL CLUB

By Tom Maley in the *Weekly Mail* on 15th July 1916;

"For several seasons prior to the formation of the world famous Celtic club, through the kindness and co-operation of clubs in the east end of Glasgow and what were then called provincial clubs, matches were arranged and the proceeds were devoted to charitable objects. The work of organising and distributing was controlled by members of a society which devoted its energies entirely to charity and in the prosecution of such work knew neither fee nor sect. One figure in this - shall I call it? - agency stood out in bold relief. He was a member of a religious teaching order known as the Marist Brothers.

This religious community staffed several of the largest schools in Glasgow and they were in close touch with their little charges and were beloved by them. Brother Walfrid was the superior of this body about the time of which I am writing and quite apart from his character, disposition and loveable nature, he had a wonderful organising power. He had to like "Father O'Flynn" whom Signor Folly so popularised, "a wonderful way wid him", and no wonder at all, at all, for he was an Irishman. This good man had only to knock and it was opened.

Clyde, Cowlairs, Northern and Thistle always welcomed him and lent ungrudgingly their services. Renton and Hibernians in like manner came at the old man's invite and then the lay members of society referred to "chipped in", so to speak, and failure was really never known. The men who worked thus together were but novices, but ere long they were to become known in the annals of Scottish football as experts and men of repute.

Many and varied had been the attempts to establish clubs on the lines of the Edinburgh Hibernian in Glasgow. It seemed singular that all efforts failed ere the echoes of their birth had barely died away. Shamrocks, Hibs, etc., sprang into existence only to disappear. When the Hibs gained the blue riband of Scottish football I told how they were entertained by their western brethren. It is of these brethren I write. "Then," said the Hibs secretary and mouth piece to the hosts of the evening, "Go thou and do likewise". To continue in scriptual style "And going they did likewise and the fruits thereof are visible even unto this day".

Through the organising genius, the wonderful persuasive powers and the personality of Brother Walfrid, the Celtic club was established. His men carried out his every wish and idea. They knew and trusted their leader and in the knowledge that he, like them, wanted the club for the most laudable objects - charity - and as a recreation for the toilers and his loved east enders, they persevered. In varying degrees, varying according to their circumstances, but always in one degree - and that the highest - these men wrought and toiled.

A place to play and players and means to obtain exercise. Ah, me! But labour was cheap, and it were appraised at the price these men, good and true, set upon their services. They gave them free. Spade work, real and figurative, did they indulge in. The task of soliciting financial help was placed in the hands of experts and men beyond and above reproach, or the breath of suspicion. Amongst my "relics", I have a copy of the first list of subscribers to the Celtic club. Many subscribers "parted" more out of personal regard and esteem for the promoters and collectors than aught else - indeed, they said so and good naturedly remarked; "Will this club last as long as some of its predecessors?"

But I must exercise restraint lest I be drawn into detailed account and into a theme that to me appeals most strongly and has attachment most dear. I must be brief and trust that my readers have been fortunate enough to have read former writings on the rise of the club, if not by me, by my brother. The place to play was obtained, put in order and equipped with a stand. Players were secured and might I say deferentially and with reservation, put in order and after a sort of probationary spell the Celtic club became members of the Scottish Football Association and affiliated associations, Glasgow and North Eastern and Scottish Second XI Association. Thus they became a living entity in football.

The workers in the task of its creation, even though today they may not be actively associated with it, may with pardonable pride say this giant oak came from our acorn. Ties true there are not may left of the first band of earnest and loyal workers - the great reaper has gathered them in. If I am not mistaken, the last to be garnered by the harvester was Brother Walfrid himself. I have said that many of the men who had been associated with this good man in the earliest stages of the club's formation were at the time unknown, but later became prominent figures in the annals of Scottish football.

Keeping solely to the legislative side of the game, such men as the late Messrs William McKillop, MP, John H McLaughlin, John O'Hara and John Glass were in their several capacities highly valued and esteemed. Of course, as every cupboard has it's skeleton, so in this club there were discontents. It needs such to shape a policy very often. For many seasons from within and without the club had to withstand attacks. Didn't a section of the press wage war on the club? Rather! Didn't a big section of the football public reflect the distorted views and yet that very reflection and its origin put life into moribund and decaying concerns and were from a Celtic point of view, harmless.

On our own happy hunting ground we did have a measure of support and encouragement, but away there from - Ye gods and little fishes didn't we catch it! Old and grizzled veterans could tell of the receptions accorded us at the Exhibitions, (note I use the plural) and at a memorable "Fast Day" match at old Cathkin. Our method and style of play was at the first moulded on lines somewhat original, but was football pure and unadulterated all the time.

I read today comments before and after matches we then were down to play and if I had any uncharitable feelings at all and wished to do an ill turn, I would send them to these commentators to reread! In 9 cases out of 10 they were direct inspiration to brutalising tactics. Within the club the malcontents moved in varying ways, firstly an opposition club which for a time seemed to thrive and then came the crash. Then a keen and close division of committee almost to cleavage and then "siding" by players but as becoming men tutored and lead by leaders such as the majority of the committee owed homage to, the differing to agree and agreeing to differ policy dominated, and with the flotation of the club as a company one may safely conclude or assume that the danger of an internal explosion was most remote, whilst internal attacks were met by a spirit as unflinching and as uncompromising as that shown by the earliest pioneers.

It will hardly be my taste to effect a contrast between the Celtic finalists of the club's first season, 1888-1889 and the Celtic of cup renown, 1913-1914, but this much I will say - that a manager in League football today who could assure himself as possessor of such a side as we fielded on the day of the "blizzard final", a quarter of a century ago could almost certainly command success".

CHAPTER FOUR
SEASON 1889/90

"Celtic's entry into the football arena, together with the club's highly successful first season, had brought into being an army of new enthusiasts".

During the short summer break before the advent of the 1889/90 season, the Celtic Committee had a lot on its mind. We had risen to the top of the game in Scotland within one season but we had to ensure we stayed there and so the search for the best players continued with the acquisition of Johnny Madden, Dumbarton's fearless striker. Equally as important was the ability to fend off any would be agents acting on behalf of English clubs, where professionalism was alive and well since 1885. All was going well, except the wandering Willie Groves had got itchy feet again after only one season at Celtic Park and the former Hibs player signed on the dotted line for Everton. However he then had a change of heart and returned to Celtic in time for the start of the season, no doubt after the Celtic Committee had got wind of it and after being accepted back by the Scottish Committee as an amateur.

At least Tom Maley was going nowhere fast, as the Glasgow Observer on 10th August announced his marriage to Miss Elizabeth Mellon at the Catholic chapel in Pollokshaws on Wednesday 31st July. Both Tom Maley and his bride were teachers, with the Celtic player's profession given as Headmaster at St Mirren's in Paisley and his bride, Elizabeth, teaching at Saint Conval's in Pollokshaws.

The Celtic Match Secretary, Willie Maley was best man and one of the other siblings, Father Charles O'Malley celebrated the nuptial mass. Charles was named after his grandfather who also kept the less anglicised version of the surname.

From a local Pollokshaws paper;

Here's a health to you, Tom! may yourself and your wife
Have a hearty good time through a jolly good life;
May the angel of love spread his wings o'er you two
And Providence bless you in all you may do

"May a dozen young Maleys spring up to delight

The heart of you twain in the midst o' life's flight;

All as suave and as pleasant, as modest and true

As their father before them, then Tom! they will do

Here's a health once again and though we must part

Be assured we will cherish your name at Cathcart

CELTIC WIN FORGOTTEN TOURNAMENT AT IBROX

The "Grand Athletic and Football Carnival," was a competition organised jointly by Rangers and Clydesdale Harriers at the start of the 1889/90 season with matches played on Saturday, 3rd and Tuesday, 6th August at Ibrox. Celtic, Rangers, Renton and Third Lanark were the four teams competing with Celtic opening the competition against Renton in a match lasting 30 minutes each half, before Rangers took on the Thirds. A very sizeable crowd of 8000 attended and the teams gave more than a decent account of themselves. After an hour's play, with the Celts well on top after a slow start, both teams had failed to put the ball between the sticks in a hard fought match and so 20 minutes "extra time" was played. During the first ten minutes, the bhoys scored twice and that was enough to settle the tie.

Shortly after, Rangers and Third Lanark took to the field, with the Clydesdale Harriers introducing some sports fare in between. The Harriers had been granted the use of the training facilities at Rangers' Kinning Park ground and then Ibrox and they would go on to hold joint sports meeting with Rangers at Ibrox. Rangers won the match to set up a final with Celtic three days later, but once again the bhoys were far too good for Rangers, who had played surprisingly well, *"remembering the shadow of a skeleton to which they had dwindled at the end of last season,"* as the *Scottish Sport* described them.

Peter Dowds scored the first goal just before half time in an open game with chances aplenty for both teams. The same man added another in the second half and it was enough to give the bhoys a 2-0 victory with both teams retiring to Ancells restaurant in Glassford Street, for the after match prize giving. Medals were presented to the players of both teams, but there is no record of a trophy being handed over by the Rangers Chairman to Father Cunningham, who replied on behalf of Celtic.

The competition, largely forgotten, is well worth remembering as the first where we played extra time and the first we won at Ibrox, albeit a competition with no trophy.

WHISKY AND FOOTBALL

The demon drink remains a hot topic in Scottish Football over three decades since it was banned from our grounds after the infamous 1980 Scottish Cup Final when Celtic beat Rangers 1-0 after extra time. It was said 'a game of football broke out amongst the rioting'.

If anyone considers alcohol, or the lack of it, is a major topic for discussion today, it compared little to the Glasgow of the 1880s where Temperance Society's flourished in their promotion of total abstinence. The League of the Cross was a Catholic tee-total confraternity who went on to organise many of the original Celtic brake clubs in each parish, the fore-runners of the supporters buses in future years. Many pulpits shook to the core with sermons blasting the evils of the demon drink. To be fair, it was a particular curse which only added to the untold misery and despair felt at the conditions of the slums in the east end, where many of the Irish were huddled together in.

The contradiction for the Celtic Committee was that we were open to criticism from those opposed to the modus operandi of players being given the lease of a public house, which gave them an income, but at the same time the added attraction encouraged supporters of the club to frequent said establishments and partake of the demon drink, rather than attend League of the Cross Halls where snooker, dominoes, drafts and cards were the counter attractions on offer, minus the drink.

No-one needed to be reminded that Celtic were formed in the St Mary's League of the Cross Hall at 67 East Rose Street and an example of this conflict was raised in a letter to the Glasgow Observer on the 31st August 1889;

"Sir, every credit is due to the promoters and founders of the Celtic Football Club. One serious and irretrievable blunder, however, they have made and that is the placing of the greater number of their prominent players in public houses. The evil consequences of this step more than counterbalances any good the founders of the club may have accomplished. Our young men are attracted to the public houses where the players are working and so lured from the paths of sobriety.

All the blame attached to this blunder is not the Committee's. If they could have found positions elsewhere for their men they would have done it and I feel confident that if some of our Catholic merchants who are in a position to assist the Committee, would do the needful, the executive of the club would only be too thankful. At present the players so placed are like destroying angels, of good to nobody but the devil and their employers".

CELTS DRAW THE ESTABLISHMENT TEAM IN THE CUP

Celtic Park, in the previous season had been packed to the gunnels with estimates up to 30,000 for the Corinthians match in a ground, by today's more stringent standards, if fitted with modern terracing, would have held around 10,000. It was about to have even the top limits exceeded as the first round draw of the Scottish Cup was announced and Celtic were paired with Queens Park, the Establishment Team and the biggest and most successful club in Scotland by a country mile. The date for the match at Celtic Park was set for Saturday, 7th September 1889 and the whole of the football world held its breath in anticipation.

At first glance, the chances of this draw happening were extremely slim, with two of the favourites drawn together amongst the 150 teams contesting the 1st round ties, but what made it more likely was that the first three rounds were regional. For example, Hibs drew Hearts in the first rounds of the Scottish Cup every other year until they did away with the regional draw in the early 1890s. In the Glasgow area there were far more teams competing than in Edinburgh therefore it was still a major shock when Celtic drew Queens Park in the 1st round.

The committee were taken aback at the sudden impact we made on the Scottish game and consideration was given towards how best we could enlarge Celtic Park to cope with the demand, whilst balancing the finance required to keep players happy and charitable donations coming.

Meanwhile, Celtic played our first home match of the season on the 31st August in magnificent weather against a strong Dumbarton team, benefiting from their merger with Dumbarton Athletic, who had ceased to exist from the 1st August. The match was keenly fought, typical of an early season match with both teams keen to make their mark. The Sons of the Rock scored first in the fifth minute, but Paddy Gallagher equalised just before half time to finish the scoring at 1-1.

"The ground itself had been enlarged and improved during the recess and it really looked in splendid condition". Celtic Park has undergone considerable alterations since last year. The pitch has been lengthened and this together with other improvements make the field one of the best in the city".

In addition the entrance gates were increased from 7 to 10 so after little more than a year at our new ground, the Celtic Committee were making ongoing improvements to cope with the demand.

GLASGOW HIBERNIAN ARE BORN

As the new season started, our fame was spreading with a new "Celtic" club being formed in Manchester under Councillor O'Neill, Rangers' poor form continued from the previous season as they opened with an 8-2 defeat to Clyde at Barrowfield, Edinburgh Hibernian lost 5-1 at Cowlairs. But more significantly it was the name of Glasgow Hibernian that raised the most eyebrows, as they played their inaugural match, away to Stirling outfit, Kings Park and suffered a 5-3 defeat.

The Glasgow Hibernians' guest players that day were; John Tobin (Hibs), James Coleman (Dumbarton Athletic), Ogle (Hibs), Devine (Dumbarton Athletic), Heenan and Connor (Celtic), Duffy and Campbell (Dumbarton Athletic), George Smith and Phil Clarke (Hibs) and Tippin. Four Hibs players, four Dumbarton Athletic players and surprisingly two Celtic reserves, plus Tippin guested for the Glasgow Hibernian team. The fact that Glasgow Hibs had attracted three members of the Edinburgh Hibernian Scottish Cup winning team to Glasgow raised many eyebrows but strangely enough no allegations of "stealing away" were spoken of.

Amongst the founders of Glasgow Hibernian were James Quillan, the ex Vice President of Celtic, who had been voted out of his position at the AGM in June and Hugh McGuigan, a member of Clyde FC who became their Secretary, as named in the Scottish Sport. In a letter to the Catholic Observer informing them that Mr Vallely, late of Benburb FC, was incorrectly described as a member of the new club, the Secretary at that time gave his name as Owen Delaney.

The Quillanites' immediate response after the Celtic AGM, was to contact Edinburgh

Hibernian and discuss a plan to relocate them to Glasgow, which would give them a greater base of support in which to take on Celtic. Edinburgh Hibernian were in such dire straits that some commentators were forecasting the end, but to the Quillanites, Hibernian's difficulty was their opportunity. To Quillan's surprise, however, Edinburgh Hibernian refused to move to Glasgow and so instead Glasgow Hibernian were born on Tuesday, 6th of August, 1889 at a public meeting in the Lesser Bridgeton Public Hall, and a ground was leased on the south bank of the Clyde, across from Glasgow Green at Oatlands, near the Gorbals. By this time the junior team Glasgow Hibernian had ceased to exist.

The following circular was circulated;

GLASGOW HIBERNIAN FOOTBALL CLUB

"SIR - A meeting of those desirous of supporting the above club will be held in Bridgeton Lesser Hall on Tuesday 6th August at 8pm. Business - To hear report and elect committee. A first class field has been secured".

Signed by a gentleman well known in western athletic and football circles and a member of more than one organisation. (Probably James Quillan).

So just when everything was in place for our second season and we had a massive Scottish Cup tie to look forward to, the Celtic Committee didn't have far to look for our immediate threat, just across the Clyde in fact, where the new Irish team in Glasgow threatened to split the Irish support, until then exclusive to Celtic. Edinburgh Hibernian now had not only Celtic to compete with for the best Irish players, but Glasgow Hibernian too, as was seen in their very first game as they fought over the scraps that Celtic didn't want.

But it was still Glasgow Hibernian who had it all to prove. They had a massive task in following Celtic, who already had a year's start on them and to be a success they would have to put on the pitch a better team than Celtic's. A task that every other team in Britain was struggling to do. To their credit, Hibernian Park was ready by the start of September, situated on Rutherglen Road and the new club, with top athlete Paddy Cannon as coach, were advertising season tickets at 5 shillings each. They were drawn against Thistle from the east end of Glasgow in the Scottish Cup and the mighty Queens Park in the Glasgow Cup and this would be the first real test of their mettle.

It is well worth noting that ironically, Glasgow Hibernian set their season tickets price at the same price as Celtic's the previous season, which was the source of the query at the AGM which saw Quillan ousted from the Celtic Committee and led to the Quillanites walking away and forming Glasgow Hibernian.

On 8th August, the Glasgow Evening News spoke to an anonymous Glasgow Hibernian founder, (probably James Quillan), who, when asked if the club was a secession from Celtic, claimed that the new club had a large amount of help and sympathy behind them in no way identified with Celtic. It was also claimed that support was derived from all classes and sects and that charity would be apportioned indiscriminately when required amongst all sects to the benefit of no single one exclusively.

Significantly, the *Glasgow Evening News* headed their article "*New Nationalist Football Organisation,*" and not new Irish organisation. Was Quillan, knowing that he would struggle to compete for Celtic's affections amongst the Irish community, genuinely trying to attract a wider fan base or was he simply having a dig at Celtic? Was he implying Celtic were too Irish and too Catholic at our foundation and the new club would spread charitable donations further afield? The proof would be in the pudding and certainly his words were never backed up with action of any kind. The evidence shows that the club was run as an Irish club and along similar lines to Celtic.

CELTIC PARK IS LIKE A SHOW GROUND

Celtic Park received a good report card in the Scottish Sport before the Queens Park tie on 7th September 1889, when it was stated;

"This is like a show ground, matters are so lively and yet so solemn. At one time it reminds you of a chapel, at another of Vinegar Hill on the Fair Week. (An annual carnival came to Vinegar Hill, on the site of what is now the Forge Retail Park). Fervent devotions are offered every night by devout members of the cloth that the Celts may win. The ground is in fair order and arrangements are being made to entertain the members of the press. Neighbouring pubs are doing a great trade and the drought is expected to last for a week at least if the Celts are victorious".

This contrasted with the same reporter's visit to Ibrox, where he stated;

"A death like stillness pervades this quarter and on the main entrance there is a notice requesting the members and friends of the club to pray without ceasing for a continued run of success. By way of meeting the straight laced principles of the Abstainers Athletic, the committee have given orders to clear the pavillion of strong drink and for this purpose a smoking concert will be held after the match between North End and Clydesdale Harriers tonight".

Rangers were due to meet the United Abstainers Athletic at Ibrox on the 7th September in the 1st round of the Scottish Cup, therefore it was a wise move to stash away all the hard liquor from the committee room beforehand. Smoking concerts had been introduced in recent years at Rangers after the club was tearing itself apart with personality clashes, in fighting and disharmony.

A RECORD CROWD AS THE CELTS TAKE ON THE ESTABLISHMENT TEAM

And so to the biggest game in our short history, a re-enactment of the Glasgow Cup semi final the previous season, but on a bigger scale in this huge Scottish Cup tie. All the ingredients were there for a huge crowd, possibly even a record gate to beat the £521 taken at the Renton game in May 1889.

The Celtic Committee, known for our business acumen and enterprise were said to know nothing of football when we were first formed but they soon learned and on the eve of our second attempt at the Scottish Cup against the biggest club in the land, they came up with a cunning plan. The defensive positions were giving us a headache with Pat Dowling injured in the previous match against Dumbarton and so the committee decided to once again attempt to sign a player who had been invited along before, Jeremiah Reynolds of

Carfin Shamrock. They would travel to his home address in the Irish town of Carfin in Lanarkshire and use their charm to sell the club to him.

The only problem was that Jerry was a massive favourite with his hometown team and any attempt to woo him could lead to the brave committee men literally being chased out of town. A solution was found and in the dead of night when the Celtic support were dreaming of taking Queens Park's scalp, two committee members, President John Glass and Dan Malloy went knocking apprehensively on Jerry Reynold's door.

Maryhill bhoy and former coal miner, Reynolds, was as tough as they come and the committee men knew they had little time to convince the man standing in the hall in his undergarments that he should quickly get dressed and accompany them to Glasgow to make his debut the next day for Celtic in the Scottish Cup! Whatever they said, it worked and Jerry was ushered to a safe house in Glasgow's east end, just hours before one of the biggest matches of his life. Reynolds had played centre forward for the Hibs team en route to their Scottish Cup triumph in 1887, but he missed the final due to injury.

This wasn't the first "kidnapping" in the Scottish game as they became known and it wouldn't be the last, but for the Celts it was a means to an end. If you couldn't beat them you had to join them. On the day of the match, every prediction was met and more but the Scottish Sport couldn't help but have a dig at the Celtic Committee;

"The phenomenal crowd at Celtic Park and the utter inadequate arrangements for their accommodation and admission ought to exercise the minds of the Celtic Committee, and compel them to provide for future contingencies".

The normal sixpenny admission, but with a shilling extra for the grandstand, (double the usual sixpence extra), had put off very few and some estimates went as far as 30,000 in attendance.

The *Scottish Referee* stated;

"Mighty Moses, what a crowd! In the name of wonder, where did they all come from? Sure the field will never hold the one half of the people, notwithstanding that the gates were opened at 13.45".

When the gates opened there were already 500 fans waiting outside with Celtic Committee men including John Glass, Tom Maley and William McKillop having to man the pay boxes as enough men could not be got for the task as everyone it seemed, wanted to be at the game. The pay boxes had been increased from seven to ten, but still this was not enough as *"the solid battalions poured in off Dalmarnock Street and London Road, and the means of entrance were rendered chock a block".*

The members' gate and also the other two large gates had to be opened at kick off by committee men guarded by policemen, and not as some media would have it, after being stormed by fans. 50 policemen were in attendance but they didn't help matters by turning up late, right on kick off as *"500 wild excited people with their money in their pockets rushed into the ground."*

Even the Queens Park team had to be smuggled into the ground through a back garden, which was confirmed by their captain Walter Arnott in an article on the 7th March 1914 in the *Evening Times*;

"The Celts were drawn in the first round against Queens Park and the tie took place on Celtic's ground, which was then in close proximity to their present field. What excitement that tie created, not only in Glasgow, but throughout Scotland. There was no banking on the Celtic's ground of those days and it was confidently predicted that the field would not hold the crowd and these anticipations were realised.

I remember when we arrived in our brake at the Celts' ground, what a sight we beheld. Crowds clamouring to get in, in a manner never witnessed in connection with a cup tie before. We could not get in by the gates but were taken in through an old garden. There were nearly 30,000 inside the field and what a yell rent the air when the teams appeared. Celts' players were a very speedy lot and they set a racking pace in the early stages of the game. There was more excitement among the spectators in the first 15 minutes of that game than in many a whole final tie.

But the excitement made the crowd sway in a body nearer and nearer the touch lines, until latterly the game had to be stopped until the crowd were put back. Frequently this had to be done; indeed, the spectators at one end of the field were actually standing underneath the goal bar. But it was a fast game that was played by both sides and towards the end of the first half Michael Dunbar and Coleman, between them, got the ball through our goal past Gillespie, but to the mortification of the Celts and their followers the point was disallowed for offside. In the second half there was some clever play shown on both sides and each goal in turn ran several narrow escapes of falling, but the end came without either side scoring".

From Willie Maley in the *Weekly News* on the 30th May 1936;

"Celtic's entry into the football arena, together with the club's highly successful first season, had brought into being an army of new enthusiasts. So on this particular day the strain on the ground's capacity was excessive. As a matter of fact, Celtic Park, now covered with houses, was not sufficient to hold all who wished to view the encounter.

There were ten entrances to the ground. On came an ever increasing stream of people as the hour of kick off drew nigh. I can see the crowds yet surging about the gates, pressing and swaying as admission was sought. In some cases it appeared as if there would be trouble. The authorities had not then attained to the efficient handling of football crowds as is the case now.

Inside the ground the scene was also anything but orderly. As the people pressed in so did they arrange, or disarrange, themselves anywhere and everywhere. When the teams lined up, after long delay, the touch lines were almost hidden by encroaching onlookers. The Queens' players had been held up outside by the swollen crowds at the pay gates. They were able to gain admission only by smuggling along a back passage which led through nearby private gardens".

From the *Scottish Sport*;

"20,000 and over was the total gross of humanity that surged, heaved, cheered, hooted, roared and groaned round the Celtic's enclosure on Saturday. It was a scene, sir, which is riveted in my memory for all time and will afford me happy comparison for years to come, so long as football is charged with the vital, engrossing interest it at present possesses for all and sundry".

As soon as the match kicked off, the fence around the pitch failed to keep the heaving masses back and thousands lined the touch line.

In the circumstances, it was difficult for a game of football to break out but the Celts, with new bhoy Jerry Reynolds making his debut after half a night's sleep, matched the visitors in every department. In fact Mike Dunbar scored the only goal of the game for Celtic in the 25th minute, but the goal was chalked off for offside, despite the opinion of one of the umpires on the day, our very own Tom Maley, that the ball was played through from the foot of the Queens Park player, Gillespie and not from our own Johnny Madden as claimed. The goal should have stood and some fans encroached onto the pitch due to over enthusiasm, but order was soon regained. With up to 30,000 inside the ground and lining the touch lines with only 50 policemen to maintain order, it was a very brave decision by the referee, Mr George Sneddon, President of the East of Scotland Association.

The *Scottish Referee* described the controversy, albeit through the eyes of the slightly partisan headline of CELTIC GOSSIP;

"As fair a goal as ever was scored. That for ye, Mr Sneddon; and a Celt's supporter described a triangle on his frontal apex".

Is this the first reference to Freemasonry in refereeing circles in the Scottish game?

"Sure we are playin' again' thirteen men, said another. Who was offside, Mr Sneddon? asks handsome Tom Maley; tell me the man who was offside? But Mr Sneddon knew not, and was as silent as Janefield. Didn't Gillespie play the ball before Dunbar shot it through? queries Tom Maley again; but the oracle is dumb.

At length he speaks. He has consulted with D. C. Brown, the Queens Park umpire. If you appeal for offside against the centre forward I will give it, Mr Sneddon is reported to have said.

When the ball was kicked off from goal, "let me at him" echoed from thousands of throats, and the barricades were broken down and the touch was lined with a living throng. So excited were they that if they could have ventured further they would have eaten referee Sneddon alive.

The bobbies are on the spot, however and kept the crowd back very well. It's the hardest work they have had for many a day; an' sure aren't they paid well for it, said an economic tax payer"

The poor clergy in attendance were even given advice;

"The clergy might mix with the crowd more instead of taking up their places round the pavillion. This would help to keep order".

Queens Park's side of the debate was given by the equally partisan QUEENS PARK WHISPERS but he stuck to the subject of the huge crowd and had very little to say about Celtic's disallowed goal;

"Referee Mr Sneddon had a very difficult, not to say dangerous duty to perform and on the whole did it well. Of course we could not object in the slightest to the decision of offside which he gave.

And the team were bowled along gaily over the stones with no bones broken, and all sound in wind and limb. Great danger to both, however was met with when they drew up at the Celtic's ground. Surging round the pay boxes the crowd fairly blocked the way. To have forced our way in would have made the players quite unfit for the task before them.

Mr Brown has it, however. "This way, gentlemen," and we paraded through a private house next the gates, through a lovely cabbage garden, then over the garden wall, bags and breeches whole and all. And Tom Roberts murmured "Saved."

Mr Charles Campbell mounted the grand stand and surveyed what he would term the "living body of enthusiastic footballisation". Nervously twitching his fair moustache, he uttered audibly, "This match will never be finished."

The *Scottish Sport* quaintly reported the reaction of the Celtic support to the disallowed goal, as they *"showed their disapprobation in a very pronounced manner"*.

You've got to admire the artistic style of journalism back in the day and I think it's safe to say we can imagine the very pronounced manner of the disapprobation shown, although there's no confirmation "Who's the mason in the top hat?" was the song of choice.

The half time break took longer than expected, ten minutes instead of the normal five and those packed together like sardines no doubt began to wonder what was going on. Obviously discussions had taken place in the Pavillion at half time regarding the safest way to proceed, with fans lined up all the way along the ropes and the pitch being encroached upon. It was alleged an agreement had taken place to continue the match only as a friendly and not a cup tie and this was communicated to the press. Eventually due to further encroachments on the pitch the decision was made and some of the crowd eventually began to leave the ground and the match fizzled out to a goalless draw with the important fact that there were no injuries, or worse to deal with.

From the *Scottish Sport*;

A RECORD CROWD AT CELTIC PARK

"The annals of football may be searched and searched in vain for a parallel to the extraordinary incidents witnessed on Saturday last at Celtic Park, Glasgow where the great cup tie between Queens Park and Celtic was down for decision. The vehicular traffic en route was alarming while thousands of eager pedestrians were to be seen everywhere vainly endeavouring to catch on to some mode of conveyance. The scene which met our gaze on arrival was incredible, the entrances which had been increased by three additions - making ten in all - being literally blocked by an eager, impatient, clamorous and exciting mass of surging humanity. For ten minutes we patiently subjected our anatomy to a pressure which threatened to exterminate life's vital spark and finding it impossible to make further progress we had recourse to the undignified process of climbing over the spiked barricade, an operation fraught with peril, grief and danger to our nether garments.

Half an hour previous to the commencement of the tie the enclosure seemed packed to its utmost holding capacity, while as many more were outside and on the way. The grand stand was uncomfortably crowded and likewise every point of vantage in the vicinity. The graveyard wall was lined two deep and the police were powerless to keep the intruders from disturbing the precincts of the somnolent "City of the Dead". What a contrast! What a study for the philosopher! Deeper and deeper still grew that multitude round the immediate environs of the field of play and there seemed no end to the ever increasing throng. Those who assert that football is on the decline must have been rudely shocked on learning the numbers. Far from this being the case, the interest of the rising generation is being engrossed in a manner wonderful to behold.

When the Queens Park drove up to the ground, as usual on such occasions, in a brake, they found it impossible to gain an entrance and had recourse to enter through a private garden in the immediate vicinity. The crowd at this time must have numbered close on 18,000, swelled to 22,000 ere the proceedings commenced".

A letter to the *Glasgow Evening News* summed up the mood, with the author way ahead of his time, advocating all ticket matches;

DANGER AT FOOTBALL MATCHES

"Sir - I was a spectator at the football match, Celtic v Queens Park. I am afraid that visiting football matches will become a thing of the past if the executive does not in future improve on the method of collecting the money at the gates. There might have been loss of life due to the dreadful crush at the entrance. I suggest that a certain number of tickets be issued for each respective place previous to the match, so that visitors may have an opportunity of seeing the game and the players of playing it without hindrance. The spectators cannot be blamed for keeping back the game through overcrowding, as so many were admitted that there was no room outside the fence and they were compelled to encroach on the field.

I paid for the grandstand, being told that there was room, one shilling and sixpence and I am sure many more did the same thing long after the grandstand was filled to overflowing. Admission to the respective places ought to have been stopped when moderately filled, as Saturday's mode of procedure will, I have no doubt, deter many from again visiting football matches".

I am &c.,
FAIRPLAY

The *Glasgow Evening News* pointed out the dangers of inaction clearly;

"It was nothing short of a miracle that numbers were not knocked down and trodden to death in the frantic rush at Parkhead, before which the gates, strongly supported as they were, went down like match wood. The public authorities, as well as the Association officials, should see to it".

The final word from the *Scottish Sport* was a plea for more elbow space for the press;

"The Celtic and all other clubs similarly situated should really make a serious endeavour to give the members of the press at least elbow room. Surely an unobstructable position might be easily ensured to the members of the Fourth Estate".

CELTIC PARK

After the Queens Park match, the Celtic Committee learned a huge deal about the suitability of Celtic Park in its current state to host the level of attraction that the club desired. The capacity would have to be increased, even more pay boxes added and stronger barricades put in place to keep the fans away from the pitch. The most important result from the match was that thankfully there were no reported injuries or worse. The Celtic Committee were determined not to rest on their laurels but with future disasters in mind, they would do well to look back on this day and remember the saying; "There, but for the grace of god, go I".

Not a lot is known about the outside of the original Celtic Park and its entrances but reports from this game are invaluable at giving us an insight, with three gates mentioned, one smaller for season ticket holders and members at the south west corner and two larger ones. Also the ten pay boxes, which would have been located mostly on Dalmarnock Street. The reference to fans pouring in off Dalmarnock Street and London Road and not for example, the Gallowgate, point towards the location of the pay boxes and also the nearby tram depot off London Road.

As we know, the original ground was bounded by the graveyard on its western boundary so there were no entrances from this side. The northern side of the ground was bounded by houses and back gardens coming from the Gallowgate, with Ivy Cottage, a larger house surrounded by gardens at the north eastern boundary of the original ground.

The main entrance to the ground was on Dalmarnock Street, now Springfield Road. This area too would be the main thoroughfare for entrance into the ground as described. Fans would be able to enter via a pay box on Dalmarnock Street and walk all the way round the inside of the ground or as it was called then, the enclosure. Fans wishing to sit in either the original Pavillion stand on the eastern boundary of the pitch or the stand directly opposite which was added at the start of the 1890 season and bounded the graveyard wall, could pay sixpence extra at gates at the side of the stands.

No details have ever been mentioned of the main entrance at the original Celtic Park, although we know that it would have been basic and not ornamental to tie in with the charitable status of the club. Its exact location is likely to have been in line with the Pavillion, giving staff and players the shortest walk to the dressing rooms from the Dalmarnock Street entrance. Behind the goals at Janefield Street we know there was one entrance, possibly a members gate, which was situated near the corner nearest the current Celtic Park. There would be very little room behind the goals at the Janefield Street end for fans to flock in through entrances there so it would make sense for the majority of the entrances to be on Dalmarnock Street where there was space inside the ground for fans to go to whichever part of the ground they desired.

At the south east corner of Celtic Park, just inside the paling was a smaller, second pitch used for training and fans would be required to walk round this to get to their favourite spot. There is no record of any particular part of the ground being the traditional "Celtic End", but its fair to assume that after entering from Dalmarnock Street, fans would go straight to the nearest goal and stand at the Janefield Street end or walk round to the Janefield cemetery side to get a "side on" view of events, before the second stand was built there in 1890.

There is evidence too, from match reports that Celtic favoured defending the goal on the south side of the ground when we took to the field, meaning that when we ran out from the Pavillion we ran to the left side of the pitch, ironically the end nearest the current Celtic Park. When choosing which way to shoot at the start of the game on occasions when there was no advantage in playing, for example, with the wind or not playing with the sun in your eyes, Celtic more often chose to shoot facing north. When we moved to the current Celtic Park, with the Pavillion on the north west corner of the ground, (the corner of the current North Stand and Jock Stein stand), the players naturally ran out and took up the position defending the nearest goal, which became the Celtic end. This tradition carried on when the Main Stand was built in place of the Grant Stand in 1929 and with it, the dressing rooms were relocated from the Pavillion to the Main Stand. The Celtic team to this day still run out to the left and defend the traditional Celtic End.

The Pavillion stand, nearest to the entrances off Dalmarnock Street cost sixpence extra, which would have been enough to have kept the ordinary fan away from this part of the ground. The wooden fencing, with railway sleepers used as vertical fence posts around the boundary were spiked to deter anyone climbing over so we have a picture of the Janefield and Dalmarnock Streets corner of the ground with three gates. ten pay boxes and a main entrance.

With lessons learned from the Scottish Cup tie, improvements carried on at Celtic Park with terracing placed in front of the Pavillion stand in the first week of October 1889, which increased the capacity by a few hundred more. Plans were also put in place for a press box, the first of its kind in the Scottish game. With the Janefield Street cemetery wall providing the best view for fans who stood two deep upon it at the Queens Park match, the Celtic Committee ensured that the cemetery was patrolled by the local constabulary to ensure no repeat at the next home match against Sunderland. Business as they say, is business.

In another Scottish Cup tie between Third Lanark and Partick Thistle at Cathkin, the home of the former, there was no little excitement either when the Thistle fans invaded the pitch in reaction to a nasty challenge on Proudfoot of the Jags. What started as a trickle ended up as an "excited mob" and the safety of the Third Lanark players became a concern as both teams headed for the Pavillion before the pitch was engulfed, assisted by the twelve, yes twelve, policemen on duty. After twenty minutes the pitch was eventually cleared with the assistance of the Thistle fans who vastly outnumbered those whose over enthusiasm had spilled onto the pitch. In the event Third Lanark, who were a goal up at the time, went on to win 3-2.

Just a couple of miles away in contrast to our full house against Queens Park, a "limited crowd" watched Glasgow Hibernian, in their garish green and purple stripes, white shorts and purple socks, lose 3-1 at home to Thistle in the 1st round of the Scottish Cup.

THE BIG CUP REPLAY

The Celtic Committee were justifiably under the impression that as our Scottish Cup match was played out as a friendly, then the rematch should be played again at Celtic Park. However the powers that be in the Business Committee of the SFA deemed the option of Hampden Park to be the safer choice with the entrance fee raised to a shilling, no doubt to limit many of Celtic's robustly enthusiastic following and so home advantage switched to Queens Park, an advantage they used well. Had the match been replayed at Celtic Park, as it should have been, and the entrance fee doubled, it would have had the same effect on the attendance.

Both teams had protested the first match, based on the encroachment of the spectators, but our protest was also based on the disallowed goal which should have stood. Queen's Park's protest had been made formally to the referee but was withdrawn after the match, whilst

Celtic's had been made after the match which was deemed formally incorrect. Strangely if the replay was also drawn, the rules at the time were that both teams would go into the hat for the draw for the next round.

Viator from the Glasgow Evening News was relieved that he didn't have to return to Celtic Park for the replay after complaining;

"Fond hopes rudely shattered, and my five feet of anatomy almost crushed into a jelly, is the experience I have to record of my visit to the Celtic's ground last Saturday".

Less than half the attendance at the original match turned up with the crowd given as 12,000 and once again the first half was a keenly contested one, with the Celts looking the part in an all green strip. Five minutes into the second half, Hamilton gave Queens Park the opener but with twenty minutes remaining, "Darling" Willie Groves headed home our equaliser;

"The point was received with simply deafening cheers, again and again renewed".

With the excitement reaching a crescendo towards the end of the match, Berry broke Celtic hearts with the winner for the home team with only four minutes remaining. The papers were full of stories after the match claiming that Celtic had protested the match on the grounds that Queens Park had played a professional player but after all the hooting and the holloring had died down, the Celtic Committee revealed it had done nothing of the sort and acknowledged we were beaten fairly and squarely.

The *Scottish Referee* on the 16th September 1889 headlined its match report of the match as "CELT v SAXON." Again this showed an early political connotation to the reporting of matches involving the Irish combination and the Establishment Team as both clubs were known.

Our newly formed Irish rivals, Glasgow Hibernian were already out of the Scottish Cup in the 1st round, so they were determined to put up a better show in the Glasgow Cup but lost 4-0 at home to Queens Park as reality set in. The new ground on Rutherglen Road was still unfinished with the grandstand, pavillion and track still not complete and they were now out of the two main cups in a week.

It was a situation that dealt a serious blow to the new Glasgow Hibernian team.

ALL ROADS LEAD TO CELTIC PARK

Celtic took our mind off our Scottish Cup exit with back to back victories over Sunderland, firstly with a 1-0 win in Sunderland on 21st September, when one of the highlights of the match was the pitch invasion by a dog who managed to put a stop to a Sunderland attack and evaded capture until Mick Dunbar eventually coaxed the four legged friend off the pitch without having to resort to making a clown of himself. We welcomed the Wearsiders to Celtic Park a week later and beat them again, this time without the dog and by 3 goals to 2, despite the away team being promised a bonus of 5 shillings for a win.

In fact, of our five matches immediately after the Scottish Cup defeat, four of them were against English opposition, with the other being a home match against Rangers.

Four of the five matches were at home and all roads continued to lead to Celtic Park with all the top teams down south desperate to play there, an astonishing statistic given the club was still in our embryonic stages, just over a year old.

After Sunderland were beaten home and away, Blackburn Rovers were next to arrive on Thursday October 3rd, Rangers on the Saturday and then came Everton the following week. The significance to historians of the Blackburn Rovers match was that, apart from the 1-0 victory against a team considered to be the best to visit Scotland for a number of years, this was the match at which the first photograph was taken of the Celtic team in the old ground, which remains to this day.

The picture shows the team selection, ready for action in the green and white stripes and with captain James Kelly sitting with the ball at his feet; James McLaughlin, Johnny Madden, Johnny Coleman, Mick McKeown, Jerry Reynolds, Peter Dowds, John Cunningham, Paddy Gallagher, Mick Dunbar, James Kelly and Willie Groves.

It also shows a selection of the Committee and background staff too; William McKillop, Tom Maley, John Glass, Trainer Joe Anderson, John O'Hara, Hugh Darroch, Joseph Francis McGroary and Dan Malloy. One unfamiliar face who is named as J Robertson can now be identified as the match referee. J Robertson was a member of 5th KRV and was a member of the Ayrshire Committee of the Scottish Football Association.

Intriguingly the players and committee men are lined up in front of what could be the front entrance of the original ground, or more likely to be the entrance to the Pavillion inside the ground, with a large window at either side of an ornamental doorway and a path leading up to it.

A huge crowd of 12,000 watched the match, including the Preston North End team who had travelled north to take on Queen's Park, and the attendance was bolstered by tickets which were sold at the parish of St Andrew's recent fundraising bazaar which were originally for the Celtic v Abercorn match. Due to the date of the Queens Park replay, the Abercorn match was cancelled and the Celtic Committee agreed to allow the tickets to be used at the Blackburn match, which was a great bonus for the parish. It was common practice in the early days for the Saint Vincent De Paul Society to sell tickets for a Celtic match and take a percentage of the sales for their own funds. It was an agreement that suited both parties.

Just two days after the Blackburn match, on Saturday 5th October, Rangers came to Celtic Park to play a friendly match, quickly arranged after Clyde and Third Lanark had to replay their cup match, which meant their opponents had a free day and so both agreed to play each other. Rangers' record against Celtic so far read played 2, lost 2, goals for 3, goals against 11, but they managed a 1-1 draw on this occasion after Willie Maley had opened the scoring for the Celts.

All roads led to Celtic Park and a week later, Everton took the gravy train north and became the first English team to beat the Celts on home soil, with a 2-0 victory thanks to two first half goals in front of a crowd of 12,000, although they faced criticism for their over physical play.

Dan Doyle, who was to go on to captain Celtic played for the Toffees that day, in their blue and white quartered top and red belts.

Meanwhile improvements were ongoing at Celtic Park in the build up to the match with the terracing of the area in front of the pavillion which gave accommodation for several hundred more. The committee were also looking at plans to accommodate the press more conveniently.

THE CELTS TAKE ON THE MEDIA

With the Celts more than miffed at our exit from the Scottish Cup and the circumstances surrounding it, in particular, being forced to replay a null and void match at the opponents ground, inaccurate media stories soon fanned the flames. These allegations were met by a sharp response from a Celtic Committee unafraid to take all and sundry on in their search for fair play.

After our defeat to Queens Park in the replay, sections of the media created a story that Celtic would protest Queens Park's win on the grounds that they fielded a professional, namely Tom Robertson. The accusation was absurd as Queens Park were above suspicion in this regard, being strongly anti professional, indeed they remain amateur to this day. The unfounded rumour was picked up by the media and used as a stick to beat Celtic with, barely hiding its real intention of accusing Celtic of professionalism, with one newspaper going as far as to dedicating it's full editorial on a non story.

Worse still, an article from an English journal, the Athletic News, criticising Celtic was given ample space in the Scottish Sport on the 17th September, and went as far as to compare our annual charitable donation of £421 to the sum of £650 James Kelly paid for a public house, insinuating that this money came directly from Celtic. The newspaper's mail bag was certainly heaving the following week as the Celtic Committee and no less than James Kelly himself replied in person.

Tom Maley, always the gentleman, acting on behalf of the club acknowledged that we were beaten fairly on the pitch in the replay and we had no intention of protesting, it had never even been contemplated, never mind received any countenance from the committee.

The letter from the Celtic Committee also rang true in the Scottish Sport on 20th September;

"My first impression was that it was a huge joke, but on perusing your notes I changed my mind considerably. Surely the balance sheet of the Celts proves conclusively that the disbursements were all above board. However, the Athletic News, like many croakers requires a squib, from time to time to suit the palates of its readers".

That was it in a nutshell. One year into our formation and a quote directly from the Celtic Committee sums up an issue which is as prevalent today as it was then. Bad Celtic news, whether true or false, sells newspapers.

Celtic Captain, James Kelly didn't miss his target either in the same issue;

"In your issue of Tuesday there is a long extract from the Athletic News, which you very aptly put down as

"Another English Cackle". In this wonderful production there is a paragraph from which it might be inferred that I am indebted to my club for a start in business!

I am neither anxious to advertise this jargon nor my own private affairs; but in justice to my Scottish friends, club and myself, it is but right that I should let the babblers know that the statements are mere imagination. There is no truth in them whatever. My worldly circumstances, without ever being too rosy, have always been sufficient to enable me to conduct my own affairs without any extraneous support whatever.

Yes I have always been able to "paddle my own canoe," (although not a millionaire), without material help from my friends and I still hope to work my way through life in the future as in the past, and will still play football, (in Scotland), for the love of the game only.

Pardon me, Mr Editor, this unwilling intrusion, but I had to write in justice to all concerned, as the mud throwing propensities of the English scribbler can sometimes go too far".

And so there we have it, a detailed denial by the player and not just a throwaway line. Significantly too this was the end of the matter. If Celtic supporters were leasing public houses to players, (not under the club's name or being actioned by the Celtic Committee), we weren't the only ones but we certainly couldn't afford to spend £650 on the purchase of a pub for a player and this story was nailed as soon as it started.

AN HONOURABLE APOLOGY?

As we all know the chances of a full apology printed in the press is hard to find so when this one was printed on 24th September 1889 in the *Scottish Sport*, taken from the *Athletic News*, it's worth repeating;

An Honourable Apology

"Very few people, writes the editor of the Athletic News, will be sorry to hear that Tom Robertson's amateur status was not questioned by the Celtic Club. Robertson is a working man, who knows how to conduct himself, even when in the company of persons superior in the social scale and is much esteemed on that account by the members of the Queen's Park.

I think the Celtic FC were well advised in not lodging any protest, for at the most it could not have affected the Queen's Park. If there is an amateur club in Scotland - and I think there is - it is Queen's Park and Robertson has made himself a great favourite at Hampden, not only by his play, but by his gentlemanly behaviour. If there is professionalism in Scotland - which very few people would go to the trouble to deny - I honestly believe it is not in the Queen's Park club.

When we were informed last week that the Celtic had decided to protest against Robertson, on the ground of his connection with the Notts club, we were more than a little astonished. We gave the facts as we heard them; but the Celtic not having brought them forward in any way, we feel it is our duty to also withdraw them, for we certainly have no intention of allowing an unproved assertion to remain hanging over Robertson's head".

They had no problem printing the unproven assertion in the first place though, which was only corrected after the intervention of James Kelly and the Celtic Committee. The author of the piece issued an apology, without once apologising, and then cloaked the first two paragraphs in waffle to distract the reader from the real issue at hand. Finally when he got round to the point in the last few sentences he made out that he's done us all a favour. A very weak apology of sorts, certainly not an honourable apology, but an apology all the same. I think.

LOCAL PRIEST PRAISES CELTIC AS HE DEPARTS ST MARY'S

Van Der Heyde is not a surname you would have associated with the parishioners of St Mary's in the Calton when Celtic were born but this Dutchman was a popular priest in the parish of St Mary's for five years and a dear friend of the Celtic Committee. He formed a close association with the club, through his parishioners, until his departure to New Orleans in September 1889 where he required a better climate as he was troubled deeply with a continuous throat infection which affected his work.

The parish couldn't let him go without a send off and so many of his friends and admirers joined him at the Mechanics Institute in Bridgeton on Monday 16th September. It included, as usual, a strong Celtic contingent given as Brother Walfrid, Brother Dorotheus, John Glass, John H McLaughlin, Doctor John Conway, Michael Cairns and Pat Gaffney as well as a party of Celtic players; Willie Maley, Mick Dunbar, Neil McCallum, Jerry Reynolds, Paddy Gallagher, James McLaughlin and Pat Dowling.

After an emotional address, John Glass presented the departing priest with a purse of sovereigns as a token of their respect to their faithful adviser and loving friend. Father Van Der Heyde, in his response, stated it was almost an impossible task to reply to such a generous address. He did however thank Celtic Football Club;

"The increased membership of the League of the Cross, he laid at the door of the Celtic Football Club. (Cheers). A fortnight ago there was published a letter in the Glasgow Observer, a letter from a writer in Butterbiggins Road, Glasgow, stating that the morality of St Mary's parish had not improved since the advent of Celtic FC. He was of a different opinion. At least 200 members per half year joined, not because they had a liking for total abstinence, but because the Celtic FC were in some manner connected to St Mary's. (Cheers)".

During the course of the evening Neil McCallum added to the entertainment with a song and John H McLaughlin assisted ably on the piano. Unfortunately, Father Van Der Hyde's remarks about Celtic fuelled the debate about alcohol and were quickly seized upon by the abstainers. The Glasgow Observer were first to respond to distance themselves from the original accusation that the morality of St Mary's had not improved since the advent of Celtic FC. The newspaper saw this as a criticism that they, in printing the letter, therefore agreed with it and they were quick to dispel this notion.

"Father Van Der Heyde, of Saint Mary's, Glasgow, was, on Monday evening, the recipient of a very handsome presentation and address from the Catholics of east Glasgow, on the occasion of his departure to New Orleans. Father Van Der Heyde, during his five years labours in the east end, had deservedly won the high esteem of his people. We are sorry the diocese loses the services of so zealous and earnest a priest and trust that the ill health which causes his departure may speedily vanish.

With regards to one or two remarks by Father Van Der Heyde on Monday evening, we wish to say something.

A few weeks ago a letter over the signature and address of the writer appeared in our columns decrying the attention and hero worshipping paid to the Celtic FC and asserting that the morality, (in a minor sense), of Saint Mary's had not increased since the advent of the famous Irish combination.

Father Van Der Heyde, in his speech on Monday evening, averted to this letter and in a rather bantering, but still serious fashion censured us for printing it, and continuing, spoke as if we had agreed to the letter with our correspondent and impugned the morality of Saint Mary's. In this, Father Van Der Heyde, we hope unintentionally, done us an injustice. The people mentioned are Catholics and their honour is ours. We are surprised that Father Van Der Heyde should accuse us of maligning them.

As a matter of fact our reverend censor made a serious blunder. When Father Van Der Heyde's experience extends, he will doubtless learn that by universal custom, a newspaper is never held as agreeing with its' correspondents. Our columns are open for the discussion of any matter of public interest, and they are as fully at the disposal of Father Van Der Heyde, or any Champion of Celtic FC, as of the correspondent whose letter we published.

To conclude, Father Van Der Heyde in speaking as he did, placed us in a false position by representing us as agreeing with our correspondent and so occupying a hostile attitude towards the Celtic FC and their enthusiastic admirers, the people of Saint Mary's. We do not care to be misrepresented, even unintentionally and through the best of motives and so we take this opportunity of vindicating ourselves with the parishioners of Saint Mary's, the Celtic Football Club and whoever else it may concern".

It was a strong response but it carried a valid point from the editor as he saw it and made it perfectly clear in the last paragraph that the Glasgow Observer did not occupy any hostile attitude towards Celtic by printing the correspondent's letter. Father Van Der Heyde however, had merely stated the source of the letter, he hadn't alluded to whether the editor agreed with it or not by publishing it. The editor obviously saw this point differently. The debate was out in the open and a further two letters were published, one from each side of the debate and ironically the first to respond was the author of the original letter, Owen McGettigan of Butterbiggins Road, Govanhill under the header;

FATHER VAN DER HEYDE AND THE CELTS.

"In last Saturday's Observer, I saw that Father Van Der Heyde attempted to controvert my statement that football was sapping the morality of the youth of Saint Mary's parish. On Sunday I happened to stroll into Saint Alphonsus church and had the pleasure of hearing Father Maginn take up my side of the question and handle it with his well known ability. Needless to say I agree with my countryman when he stated that football is keeping the people from their religious duties and I heartily echo his words - "Would to God that the Celts had never been started!"

Father Van Der Heyde stated that since the Celts had been started they brought on an average two hundred members every six months to join Saint Mary's League of the Cross. The Celts are now nearly two years in existence, therefore Saint Mary's branch should have eight hundred new members, not including the two hundred old ones who were there before the Celts were born. Has it so many? I question if it has.

Nay more, I question if there are forty total abstainers, (excluding officials), in the whole branch. Any person who stood at the corner of East Rose Street and watched the long procession which takes place between the hours of 8 and 11pm, between the hall and the public house at the corner would question if there were forty staunch tee-tomalleys in it itself. Again, Father Van Der Heyde didn't mention that the whole ambition of the Celts was either to occupy a position behind a public house bar or before it. It is a well known fact that several of their number are looking out to buy public houses and if the Saint Mary's League is not encouraging them, it is not preventing them. As long as they and their committee get bossing the League Hall, so long will the hands of true temperance reformers be tied.

As to their general conduct I will say nothing - except that it is not the sort of conduct which will edify the rising generation. When our youngsters see and hear boors cracking jokes which pollute the cars, never working and still having plenty of money and all their offences condued by those whose duty it is to reprove, I say, sir, it will, to put it mildly, give them some novel religious ideas. Even if charity did benefit by it, I would say "Away with it". But does charity benefit? I doubt it. I am almost certain that for every one pound spent in charity, ten pound goes in another direction.

This letter will no doubt appear to many to be too strong. I don't think it - our youth and through them our future church has to be saved from this insidious evil of intemperance and when one sees it doing the devil's work under the shadow of the League of the Cross I think they would be guilty of a grave dereliction of duty if they did not do their best to put a stop to it.

And so Mr McGettigan showed his true colours with his response. Thankfully Patrick Carroll of Cable Street responded in sniper style to Mr McGettigan's scatter gun approach and put the debate firmly to bed and without any supper;

"Sirs,

Your issue of Saturday last, contained a most unfounded and cowardly attack on the Celtic Football Club and Saint Mary's parishioners generally. Who is Owen McGettigan? Or what authority has he to dictate a line of morality on the Celts or the Catholics of Saint Mary's parish? He says Father Van Der Heyde has not condescended to enlighten him on the subject of how many of the Celts whose ambition it is "To occupy a place behind a public house, bar or before it", to use his own words.

Now it is immaterial whether the reverend gentleman answers that question or not, suffice it to say that there are some even of the first eleven of the Celts whose religion and morals, as well as a strict frequenting of the Sacraments of the church, would compare very favourably indeed with those of Mr McGettigan. But when he says it is a fact that many of the Celts are just now looking out for whisky bars of their own, I say that is a deliberate untruth and I challenge him to prove it. There is one of their number certainly has taken to the spirit line but does that affect the whole of them? Or to go a little further, does it reflect on their character in any way? If so, Mr McGettigan will please say.

As to the branch of the League of the Cross in Saint Mary's, Mr McGettigan has made serious charges against it. Can he prove them? I hope the branch will call on him to do so if he can, as quickly as possible. One assertion of his I know not to be true - that is, with regard to the procession from the Hall to the public house in East Rose Street. Not one member of the League of the Cross goes there for any purpose whatever and I fail to see how Mr McGettigan can say so. As to charity, Mr McGettigan fails to see how they aid it. I will enlighten him a little on the subject. Not long ago the Committee of the Celtic agreed to contribute twenty pound per month to the Poor Childrens Dinner Table, as well as a great many other items Mr

McGettigan knows nothing about. I say, sir, actions like these commend the Celts to our grateful patronage and that we should continue to give them all the support in our power. Mr McGettigan speaks about a future church for us Catholics. I deny that we have any claim to such a church. Our church is not to come; we have it now and always had, but we may have a future generation to guard pure as we are doing today.

Now in conclusion, Mr Editor, I do not hesitate to say that Mr McGettigan's attack on Father Van Der Hyde is contemptible and beneath the notice of right thinking men. The reverend gentlemen is not here now. He is gone away to a foreign land and I am sorry to say, not in the best of health and it is not manly to be speaking of him behind his back."

Mr McGettigan's ludicrous accusations and mock outrage, although extreme to say the least, did represent the feelings of a section of the Temperance movement, if his delivery left a lot to be desired.

His name checking of Father Maginn, "when he happened to stroll into St Alphonsus," from the south side of the city to the east end, was of course very deliberate as Father Maginn was a well respected hard liner in the Temperance movement and a man who shared many platforms with Brother Walfrid in their shared passion, the work of the Catholic Young Men's Society in both parishes. If any man would give succour to Mr McGettigan's views it was Father Maginn and it wasn't the first time the priest gave strong views on the demon drink and any link with football. In 1887, after the Irish National League invited Hibs to Glasgow to celebrate their Scottish Cup win, Father Maginn again asserted his dislike of football and blasted the fact that the celebration would take place during the feast of Lent.

In the end, there were no real winners, as the debate highlighted the polar views amongst many Catholics in the city over a serious issue where the misuse of alcohol had many serious affects. It also made the Glasgow Observer think twice about getting involved in the debate or in any controversy regarding it in connection with Celtic.

CELTIC DONATE TO TEMPLETON'S DISASTER FUND

A terrible disaster at Templeton's Carpet Factory on William Street in the east end at Glasgow Green on the Friday afternoon of 1st November 1889 took the lives of 29 women employed in the weaver's shed of the factory after the facade of a four story building in the course of erection was blown down by high winds, collapsing it onto the adjoining weaver's shed.

140 ladies in total were working at the 40 looms in the shed at the time with 32 injured. Of the 29 victims, the youngest was 14 and the oldest was 25. Celtic Football Club immediately donated £20 to the relief fund and it was discovered that St Mary's had lost five parishioners from their parish, Sacred Heart lost three and St Michael's lost one. Sacred Heart chapel was packed for each funeral and Brother Walfrid led the procession to St Peter's cemetery, Dalbeth, along with parish priests Father McCulla and Father O'Connell.

St Mary's held a large requiem mass for the repose of the souls of its' five victims and there was a large turnout from all the mission parishes in the east end, as they all united in grief. Celtic Secretary, John H McLaughlin, played the organ at the requiem mass.

A very moving memorial stands to this day across London Road from the factory with all the victims' names listed.

Celtic also donated £20 to the Mauricewood Disaster, Penicuik on 5th September which took 63 lives in an underground fire at the mining colliery. Between August and the December 1889, at the monthly Celtic Committee Meetings, the following charitable donations had been sent;

£92 to the Poor Children's Dinner Tables at Saint Mary's, Saint Michael's and Sacred Heart.
£20 to the Penicuik Disaster.
£50 to Saint Andrew's Bazaar.
£20 to Templeton's Disaster.
£6 to Cambuslang Poor Childrens Dinner Table
£6 to Neilston Poor Childrens Dinner Table.
£20 to the Clothing Societies at Saint Mary's, Saint Michael's and Sacred Heart.
£10 to Father Bird, the Catholic prison chaplain at Barlinnie.
£10 to Mother Vincent in aid of procuring work for females leaving prison.
£43 to an Edinburgh Catholic Institution after Celtic played Hibs at Celtic Park on 16th November, 1889.

HIBERNIAN TRAVEL TO CELTIC PARK

On 16th November 1889 the Celts were due to play Hibs in a friendly at Easter Road, but with the events of the last occasion thirteen months earlier still fresh in the minds, the decision was made for Celtic to host the match at Celtic Park instead.

It would be the 15th December 1894 before Celtic would next visit Easter Road, on Scottish Cup duty but even then it was a new Hibernian, with a new constitution and a new ground. Hibs had went out of business in August 1891 and didn't return until February 1893 after their well documented disastrous turn of events as well as some equally bad decision making by the committee. It left them without a ground to play on as the owners of the original Easter Road, the Trinity Hospital Committee, claimed more of their land back to build on and also the neglect of the committee in not joining the Scottish League at its formation in 1890.

The second Easter Road ground was near to the original and Celtic supporters who know the area will be familiar with the route to the away end from the city centre, down Easter Road, before turning right along Bothwell Street and across the narrow bridge which crosses the railway line. The original Easter Road ground was on the land where Bothwell Street stands and the current Easter Road is situated on the other side of the railway line. It was on this land that the Celtic players were vilified by the Hibernian support in October 1888.

Ironically, the land where the current Easter Road ground is located, known then as Drum Park, was also owned by the Trinity Hospital Committee and so the newly formed Hibernian Committee had to plead dumb when in negotiations with their "new" landlord.

Back to Celtic Park on 16th November 1889 and Hibs record against Celtic stood at played 3, lost 3, goals for 6, goals against 11. Things were to get much worse for them. With the funds raised going towards Catholic charities in Edinburgh, both committees were satisfied to bring the game to Celtic Park, where a large crowd was in attendance, although Hibernian had originally wanted the game played in Edinburgh, which Celtic declined.

Celtic started the match with ten men for a short time and went a goal behind to a full strength Hibs team, playing with Sandy McMahon up front, however the Celts were far too strong and goals by Mick Dunbar and two by Johnny Coleman gave the bhoys a commanding lead by half time. The second half was more of the same as Willie Groves netted a fourth, then a fifth, before Willie Maley, then Tom Maley added to Hibs woe.

With ten minutes remaining and darkness descending, the game was brought to a halt with the final score Celtic 7 Hibs 1. This time it was Hibs, who were happy to hear the referee's whistle blow early.

OUR FIRST MAJOR CONTROVERSY AS PLAYERS THREATEN TO LEAVE THE FIELD

Celtic's nemesis, Queens Park, the oft referred to premier club in Scotland, again stood in the way of our first major trophy when the clubs met in the Glasgow Cup final on 14th December at Cathkin, the home of Third Lanark. The Celts had an easy passage to the final after 2nd round opponents Victoria scratched, (withdrew), we then beat the United Abstainers, (real name but were then renamed Crosshill), 5-1 at home before dishing out a 4-1 beating to Cambuslang, again at Celtic Park.

Although the club had risen meteorically since our first game 19 months previously, we were still to get our name on one of the three main trophies; the Scottish Cup, the Glasgow Cup and the Charity Cup. The formation of the League at this stage was still almost a year away. Yes, we had won the North Eastern trophy but it wasn't considered to be one of the big three. Incredibly this was Glasgow Cup holders Queens Park's 20th major final in 22 years since their formation in 1867 and they had lost only three. Blackburn Rovers had beaten them twice in the English FA Cup Final in seasons 1883/84 and 84/85, (Scottish teams were allowed to enter the English FA Cup until 1887 when this practice ceased), and they lost once to Renton in the 1889 Charity Cup Final.

Once again both teams were very balanced going into the match but unfortunately the match was to be remembered for all the wrong reasons.

Firstly because we lost 3-2, but secondly because Queens' second goal was so controversial that the Celts threatened to walk off the pitch in protest. The match was halted for seven minutes after Queens scored to go 2-0 up after 30 minutes with both umpires, McQuarrie, (Partick Thistle), and Gilchrist, (Thistle), concurring that the goal was legitimate despite the goalscorer, Hamilton, illegally challenging James McLaughlin in the Celtic goal. The referee, Mr Tom Park, (Cambuslang FC and also the Vice President of the SFA), awarded the goal on the word of his two umpires and all hell broke loose with a couple of bottles flying from the stand and the Celtic players clearly not happy. There was a suspicion of offside about the goal too and in that case, both umpires if in agreement, could force the referee's hand. However in a case of dangerous play, which this was, Mr Park was wrong to defer to the opinion of the umpires and should have relied on his own judgement.

Until then the match had been a bullish affair with both teams not holding back on the treacherous pitch which wasn't conducive to decent football and the atmosphere in the stands wasn't helped in the 20th minute when Groves thought he'd equalised for the Celts, only to have the goal disallowed for offside.

This was the background to Queen's second goal ten minutes later, a decision that many of the newspapers agreed should not have stood. One Celtic player walked off the pitch in disgust and the rest of the team threatened to follow, but after heated discussions with the referee, the Celtic captain James Kelly decided to play on under protest at the second goal. The sight of the Celtic President John Glass bounding down the stairs of the stand may have had something to do with the players' change of heart too.

Two minutes later the Celts, with a spirit that we were to see many, many times throughout our history, fought back and Johnny Coleman got us back into the match to cut the deficit in half. It was now all Celtic as we swarmed forward around the Queens Park' goal, urged on by our fanatical support and that strong feeling of injustice. Justice was done just as the half time whistle was about to blow, as we almost raised the roof off the new stand at Cathkin with the equaliser, to go in at half time at two goals each.

The half time interval lasted only one minute, but this suited the Celts as we continued to have the upper hand as play raged on, forcing corner after corner. One shot hit the post but we couldn't force the winner and it was Queens Park who finished the strongest and grabbed the winner with a long shot from Stewart near the end of the game which beat James McLaughlin in the Celtic goal. The match was over but it was to be a long time before the controversy died down. Celtic carried through our protest that was made on the field of play after the second goal was allowed, but it was queried by the media on the grounds that it challenged a ruling that was set in stone, that is, the referee's word is final.

Worse was to follow in the Pavillion after the match when James McLaughlin, the Celtic goalkeeper, was attacked by a Queens Park player, before a Catholic priest came to his rescue, and the Queens Park player was apprehended by the long arm of the law. A scuffle broke out but thankfully the warring teams were kept apart.

However the damage was done.

The presentation of the trophy took place at the after match social, as was the norm back then, but Celtic absented themselves from the dinner. Later in the evening before the speeches were made the Celtic President, John Glass, Secretary John O'Hara and Willie Groves, who represented the players, all showed face alongside some members of the committee including Joseph McGroary and John H McLaughlin. The latter responded briefly to the toast to explain that the committee had asked the rest of the players to absent themselves from the evening, so that harmony would prevail and that no disrespect was intended.

It was a generous speech designed to pour cold water on what had been a volatile day but more controversy was to follow when it was discovered that Celtic's protest had already been thrown out after a hastily arranged meeting after the game by the Glasgow FA Committee, who organised the Glasgow Cup competition.

There was doubt over the legality of the meeting and worse was to follow when it was decided to award Queens Park the trophy that evening at the social, despite Celtic's protest and before the Celtic representatives had even arrived at the function. The Celtic Committee followed up our original verbal protest with a written protest based on the brutality of Hamilton, the Queens Park player, whose charge on the Celtic goalkeeper James McLaughlin led to the goal. Interestingly the names of two Queens Park players, Stewart and McAra were given as witnesses and testifiers to Celtic's claim.

A full meeting of the Glasgow Committee was convened on the Wednesday, when representatives of both clubs stated their case. The Chairman opened by alleging that the meeting immediately after the game which had thrown out the protest and decided to award the cup to Queens Park that evening had in fact only met informally. It did NOT meet to throw out the protest, but to seek advice on their next step in the saga and that the decision to award the cup was made only because the protest was based on a fact of play, which was unlikely to be over ruled.

And the band played believe it if you like.

The Queens Park representative spoke strongly, claiming the inclusion of Stewart and McAra as testifiers was "an impudent fabrication," on the part of Celtic, though its hard to imagine why Celtic would put forward two Queens Park players as witnesses unless we had their word on the matter.

He also stated that the time was fitting for a rebuke of the players' actions on the day, obviously referring to those who threatened to walk off the pitch, before he issued the threat that the committee may have to decide whether it wanted Celtic or Queens Park as competitors in future Glasgow Cup competitions. Letters from the referee, Mr Tom Park, were then read out as he was absent due to illness and it was clear where he stood on the matter. He suggested a new bye law to deal with the behaviour of the players.

All of a sudden a meeting held to deal with Celtic's protest based on a brutal charge on the goalkeeper had turned into a witch hunt over the players reaction to that injustice by threatening to walk off the pitch. To no-one's surprise the protest was thrown out.

Feelings were running very high and it was the turn of the Celtic Secretary, John O'Hara, who represented the club on the Glasgow Committee, to have his say.

Referring to the inexplicable behaviour of that committee, he went through their actions since the match ended and picked out the errors of their way in holding an illegal meeting, deciding to present the trophy whilst a protest was pending, then holding another meeting to which they were in attendance, after the decision was already made. Either Saturday's meeting was wrong or the present meeting was wrong. In view of the findings of the Glasgow Committee, John O'Hara stated that he would withdraw from that committee and in fact he was the first and may well be the last Celtic representative on the Glasgow Committee.

A very sorry state of affairs had ended but the Celtic Committee had shown a belief in fighting injustice where they saw it and taking it all the way.

One reporter from the *Glasgow Evening News* backed Celtic's stance;

"The withdrawal of the Celtic is not based at all on the action of the umpires at the match or on the treatment their protest met with at the hands of the association. It is solely founded upon the action of the association in handing over the cup when there was a protest lodged, deciding upon that protest, and then on the Wednesday evening following, calling another meeting for the very same purpose and inviting the Celtic to be present. As Mr O'Hara, their secretary said "Why hold two meetings, why present a cup and then have a meeting to consider a protest against it being presented?

This is where the association made a grievous blunder, and it is upon their stupid action that the Celts withdrew from the body. Saturday evening's meeting was a final one. The point of protest was so clear that it was hardly worth considering, so said the chairman, The course of the committee was clear and they acted upon it and handed over the cup to the Queens Park club. Why hold a second meeting to hold a protest about which there was not a shadow of doubt? There was no need of this second meeting. It was affront to the Celtic to ask them to come forward with a protest and witnesses - a protest which had already been decided, and witnesses who, because of that fact, could not and were not heard in defence of the club's action."

Whilst another from the same paper couldn't hide his delight;

What a funny business that was of the final tie for the Glasgow Cup. The Celtic evidently find a licking hard to digest, and we read that they resorted to the paltry trick of leaving the field because they had a goal disallowed. Everybody must rejoice that the Queens Park have won and that they are still able to pose as the only unbeaten first class team in the kingdom - a magnificent distinction as things go nowadays. Strange that the QP can always give the Celtic the knock in cup ties."

It's great to see that unbiased, impartial reporting on all things Celtic was alive and well in 1889.

1889 ENDS WITH A HEAVY DEFEAT AT CELTIC PARK

Similar to the aftermath of previous defeats, the Celts headed south to take on the mighty Sunderland for the third time in three months and we notched up our third win in a row over the Wearsiders, with a 2-1 victory cheered on by a strong contingent of Sunderland Irish.

However, on 28th December, Celtic played Cowlairs in the quarter final of the Glasgow North Eastern Cup at Celtic Park, but due to the hard ground, the match was played as a friendly and not a cup tie, with both teams and the referee in agreement before the match kicked off.

Thankfully it was a friendly, as the Celts took our heaviest home defeat to date, losing by 6 goals to 1. The first half was competitive with the visitors going in 2-1 up, after a goal from Willie Groves in the 30th minute which beat Tom Duff, in reply to two early goals from Cowlairs, but in the second half the Celts took our foot off the gas in the conditions and the visitors pushed on, scoring four more goals in front of a 10,000 crowd.

The annual Donegal Reunion social event, with Joseph Francis McGroary as their Secretary, was held in Glasgow the night before the match and was largely patronised by Celtic players and Committee alike. Not that this had any effect on the score line. We hope!

Glasgow Hibernian also lost 6-1 in the same round, to Northern, who similar to Cowlairs, were also a Springburn team but unfortunately for them, their result stood.

1890 BEGINS WITH A GREAT VICTORY AT CELTIC PARK

Meanwhile the committee, never slow to learn a trick, had fixed up the return of Everton, complete with future Celts Dan Doyle and Alec Brady, to Celtic Park on New Years Day 1890. It was another mouth watering prospect for the Celtic support and we were rewarded for our enterprise, as 16,000 witnessed the bhoys gain revenge for the previous defeat by winning the match by 3 goals to 2.

Tom Maley opened the scoring in the 25th minute with a "long, low and speedy shot," which was received by deafening cheers from the Celtic supporters. The Celts now hemmed the Toffees in and a second goal was scored, but disallowed for a foul. The bhoys couldn't be stopped and on the half hour, a "clinker" of a shot from Jimmy McLaren came back off the bar and Willie Naughton scored with a volley from the rebound. The Celts were well on top and Tom Maley, *"with a quick spurt on the ball,"* made it 3-0 before half time.

The original Celtic Park was bouncing.

The second half was more equal with Everton playing for their pride and they got themselves back into the match with a bit of good fortune after an own goal from Jerry Reynolds as the ball deflected off him. This gave the visitors more belief and after a "scrimmage," they added a second goal which set up a nervy finish. The Celts however got back on the front foot and tried to force a 4th goal without any success, without ever looking like losing a goal at the other end.

In the match report of the game in the Scottish Sport, the first mention of a Press bench is given, after a typical no nonsense tackle from Jerry Reynolds, it also mentions a fair representation of females at early Celtic matches;

"It caused a grin on the stand and an encouraging shout from a coterie of ladies immediately behind the Press bench. The fair sex in this particular corner seemed particularly interested in the Celtic's display and frequently during the game, my placid countenance underwent sundry changes at the quaintness of their remarks".

From this little snippet we learn something else about the original Celtic Park, in that before the Press Box was built, the press were housed in the corner of the ground on a bench with a table.

PEACE AND GOODWILL TO ALL MEN - EXCEPT GLASGOW HIBERNIAN!

On the last day of 1889, the Scottish Sport published a sensational story headed "Trouble In The Irish Camp," centred on a story by Glasgow Hibernian, who complained that instead of receiving traditional goodwill messages in the form of Christmas cards by their countrymen at Celtic Park, the Glasgow Hibs men had received "greetings," telling them that their names would be scrubbed from the Celtic books!

"It is customary at this season of the year for friends to send out congratulatory greetings one to the other. In order to be keeping with the times, the Celtic Committee have sent out to a number of their members, not the well wishes of the season, but a notification that their names have been erased from the books of the club. That they may have committed any offence against the rules of the club the letter does not state, and where there are so many eminent lawyers connected with the club, it was hardly thought possible that the secretary and committee would be allowed to fall into such an error as to pronounce sentence on any member without first giving them an opportunity of being heard. "Jeddart Law" may do out at Parkhead, but it will scarcely do in Brunswick Street, where the matter will now go for settlement, as all those who have been expelled are members of the Glasgow Hibernian Club.

There is likely to be a lot of matter brought forward that will be highly interesting in the Scottish Association, and to the football world in general, as it is the intention of the expelled members' agent to cite all the players of the Celtic Club past and present. There is also in the possession of one of the expelled members some documentary evidence which will be of interesting character".

One interesting revelation from this sensationalism, was that the members of Celtic who formed Glasgow Hibernian had still renewed their membership of Celtic at the same time, which allowed them to attend AGMs. Was it their intention, not only to start up a rival club, but to cause disharmony and disruption at Celtic AGMs, to our disadvantage and detriment?

The Celtic Committee were well within their rights to ban such members, the only surprise was that it didn't come earlier. It's laughable that the Glasgow Hibernian members should run to the newspapers alleging "no rules had been broken," by the tiniest little action of breaking away and forming a rival club. If that's acting in the best interests of the club, i'd hate to see what undermining it was.

Celtic's reply was in private as the accusers were basically laughed at, days later;

"Trouble in the Irish camp! Celts threatened with legal proceedings! All the players to be cited! That sensational bill heading caused your own "Puffer,"(the author of the piece), endless replies to queries at Celtic Park, where the conduct of the Glasgow Hibernians and their silly threats are being pooh-pooh'd."

Nothing more was heard on the matter but was a deal done behind the scenes? If the former Celtic members had any incriminating evidence that could cause the Celtic Committee any concern, it was our duty to deal with it. This was the first public fall out between both clubs but there's no doubt it would have been sorted out in private and not in the public gaze. Was the trade off a deal that meant Glasgow Hibernian members could resume their membership of Celtic only in the event of them leaving Glasgow Hibernian? In the event Glasgow Hibernian only lasted for little over a year and it was interesting to see the return to Celtic Park of their founder, James Quillan.

The Celtic Committee, wordly wise and at the same time street wise too would be well aware of the old saying; Keep your friends close, keep your enemies closer.

By the end of 1889, all was not well at Glasgow Hibernian after a poor start. On November 30th the club let themselves down badly by failing to turn up for a match in Greenock against Carlton with the spectators already in the ground and having to be reimbursed. In December, they suffered heavy defeats by six goals to one at the hands of Thistle, Cambuslang and Northern in the North Eastern Cup as internal feuds threatened to pull the club apart. Star player George Smith from Hibs didn't need the hassle and left for Nottingham and he was soon followed in the new year by ten more players, with another former Hibee, John Tobin acting as an agent for English clubs.

CELTIC - A REBELLIOUS CLUB

The bad feeling over the Glasgow Cup final lingered into the new year and at the next meeting of the Glasgow Committee in January 1890, Celtic's refusal to send a representative was discussed. It could have been worse as we decided not to withdraw from the Association, which would have meant us pulling out of the Glasgow Cup competition, but the Celtic Committee were too cute to make that mistake. Celtic were written to and asked to withdraw our letter of intent to which no reply had been received. This infuriated some of the Glasgow Association and it was even discussed to expel Celtic from the competition as we were a rebellious club!

The battle was not over, but the rebels were winning.

BROTHER WALFRID CARRIES ON HIS GOOD WORK

The work of Brother Walfrid was all consuming and in January 1890 he was present at a social gathering of the Sacred Heart's Young Men's Literary Society, which he himself had set up. Father McCulla presided and was ably assisted by Brother Walfrid and Brother Leo in an evening of song and toasts. Brother Leo proposed the toast to the Literary Society and Brother Walfrid proposed a toast to the guests as well as responding to the toast to our Mother Society, the Children of Mary.

The evening finished, as was customary at most of these gatherings, with all present upstanding for a hearty rendition of God Save Ireland.

In the same week, Celtic Committee man, David Meikleham gave a lecture on St Kentigern at St Alphonsus Young Men's Guild. It shouldn't be forgotten that Celtic, in our early years, were very much a community club, with founding fathers and committee members very much a part of every day life in the east end of Glasgow, deeply involved in the various religious and political organisations at the time.

FEEL GOOD FACTOR EVIDENT AT CELTIC PARK

On Wednesday, 8th January 1890, Celtic held a social event in Pinkerton's Restaurant in Bridgeton, attended by the committee and the players with the good ladies present too. After a fine meal, Honorary President Doctor John Conway presided and was ably assisted by President John Glass, who proposed a toast to "Our club" before giving a short history of the club.

Tom Maley then took to his feet and representing the players gave worthy praise of John Glass, before presenting him with a suitably inscribed magnificent marble clock and gold badge. The much loved President was, for once, speechless and Treasurer John H McLaughlin continued the speeches with a toast to "The Ladies," with Willie Groves ably replying on their behalf. The dinner tables were then cleared and dancing replaced the speeches until a late hour. In little over two short years the club had risen to a prominence in the game undreamt of and a rip roaring evening celebrating that fact was the least the pioneers of the club deserved.

ALL NOT WELL AT HIBERNIAN PARK

Suddenly the name of Glasgow Hibernian hit the headlines again in February 1890, just six months after their formation, when it was announced that they would host a fundraising competition with a gold cup put up by their coach and former athlete Paddy Cannon, a trophy which he had won in Paris.

A meeting was held on March 7th, in Frasers on Queen St, Glasgow with representatives present from the eight participating clubs invited. It was a clear sign that all was not well at Hibernian Park and far from rivalling Celtic, the new Irish team were struggling to keep their head above water. The rules for the fundraising competition, which they had originally hoped would be competed by the best teams in Scotland and England were set as follows;

1. All ties to be played on a Saturday at Hibernian Park.

2. The gate except in the final to be divided into three equal portions, of which they claimed one portion.

3. The final tie to be subject to the same conditions as the Scottish Cup final.

4. All arrangements were to be made by a committee of the Scottish Association, conjointly with Glasgow Hibernian FC.

5. The finalists were to be presented with very superior badges.

In the event, Renton and Dumbarton were the biggest teams participating and the draw was made as follows; Clyde v Cambuslang, Thistle v Dumbarton, Renton v Cowlairs, and Glasgow Hibernian v Vale of Leven, with the ties played on Saturday, 29th March. The semi finals were played on the 5th April, and a week later, on 12th April, Dumbarton beat Thistle 6-1 in the final. The competition failed to attract any of the bigger teams with the bigger followings and therefore the tournament failed to do what it set out to do, to alleviate Glasgow Hibernian's severe financial plight.

Underlining the point, the tournament marked Glasgow Hibernian's first appearance of 1890 and a fortnight later, in mid April they suffered a big defeat, by seven goals to two at Airdrie as they limped along. They managed to muster a team to play Cowlairs on 3rd May at Hibernian Park where admission prices were slashed to half price to attract a crowd. They also put up a team again Partick Thistle and Royal Albert before the end of the season but all three matches were lost.

Their first season had been nothing short of a disaster, so bad that it would surprise no-one if they failed to appear for the following season.

CELTIC v THE GLASGOW ASSOCIATION

Back to the dispute with the Glasgow Association and in February 1890, it was still dragging on with the Association miffed at what they considered an insult with Celtic withdrawing their representative on the committee. A further letter had arrived from Celtic Park with the Celtic Committee sticking to their guns in seeking justice.

The dithering Glasgow Association were all of a fluster and tried to convince themselves that they were in the right, in holding an informal gathering after the cup final and indeed presenting the trophy despite an ongoing protest. After more deliberation, ie, dithering, it was decided to accept the withdrawal of Celtic's representative. Regarding punishment to be handed out to Celtic, the discussion ranged from writing a letter, to banning us for the rest of the season, but in the end a vote of censure, which meant nothing, was passed and even then, the vote was split by five to four.

Once the dust had settled, the Celtic Committee had made it abundantly clear that we would not stand idly by and accept anything less than a level playing field. Less than two years since our formation, the founders of the club had the confidence to take on and defeat the Glasgow Association Committee and it sent a clear message right through the heart of the Scottish game that we were not to be messed with.

On or off the pitch.

One other legacy of the controversy was that a firm rivalry was to form which pre dated that of the "Old Firm," complete with its religious and political mix. Celtic and Queens Park were now firmly seen as the biggest rivalry in the land, with Rangers not yet capable of becoming the Establishment Team, fit to take on the new Irish upstarts.

In the *Scottish Sport's* match report on the Glasgow Cup Final, it stated;

"It is said the Scotch are clannish, and foregather on all great and even small occasions. It is only necessary to form one of a crowd at such a contest as that of Saturday to become convinced that the Irish are also clannish, but do not take their pleasures and adversities so philosophically as do the natives of North Britain.

The patriotism of the Irish and Scotch was appealed to and I fear the religious element was not absent.

The introduction of religion into sport is to be deprecated on every ground . It is out of place, it is undesirable, it is calculated to lead to fanaticism - and a fanatic is never a reasoning being - and finally, it is wrong. It was where it ought not to have been. How much then of the unpleasantness that characterised the game can be apportioned to race and how much to religion would be difficult to determine".

All very fine words, (except the outrageous accusation that the Irish "do not take their pleasures and adversities so philosophically as do the natives of North Britain"). Sadly, again, those words would have carried more weight if they had been used to target the ongoing sectarian signing policy of Rangers or indeed the lack of Catholic players at Queens Park.

CELTIC PARK AND HIBERNIAN PARK HOST REPRESENTATIVE MATCHES

Celtic Park hosted its first inter association match between Glasgow North Eastern Association and Ayrshire Association on Saturday, 1st February 1890, with the Glasgow team winning 6-2. Meanwhile, the ground of Glasgow Hibernian, despite their on and off field troubles, was chosen to host the Junior international match between Scotland and Ireland two weeks later on 15th February, which the Scots won by no less than 11 goals to nil.

OUR FIRST GOALSCORER NEIL McCALLUM DEPARTS

Neil McCallum, who scored Celtic's first ever goal in the 5-2 rout over Rangers on 28th May, 1888, signed for Blackburn Rovers in the first week of February 1890 after playing his last match at Cowlairs in a 5-0 win in the replayed Glasgow North Eastern Cup 2nd round match, a game in which he scored.

The bold Neil was to return a year later claiming he had signed for the Lancashire club in a moment of madness!

CELTIC - THE GREATEST TEAM ON EARTH

The Celts' stock continued to rise and on a visit to Birmingham to play a return match with Mitchell St George on 22nd February, 1890 at Cape Hill, we were greeted with the headlines;

"Cead Mille Failthe, the first visit to Birmingham of the Greatest Team on Earth, that fine Glasgow combination, the Celtic".

We weren't the greatest team on earth just yet, and we travelled with a weak side minus James McLaughlin, Peter Dowds, Paddy Gallagher and Willie Groves and paid the price going in 3-0 down at half time. Despite rallying in the second half, the game finished 5-2 to the home team. It was an even more painful experience for Celtic Secretary, John O'Hara, who broke his collar bone at Crewe train station, allegedly after some careless shunting by the traincrew. Poor John was laid up in bed for a fortnight before he could make an appearance at Celtic Park.

CELTIC PARK HOSTS THE INTERNATIONAL TRIALS

Celtic Park held the trials for the selection of the Scotland team for the first time on 8th March, 1890 when two representative trial teams played each other with the best players selected for the internationals. Six clubs were represented in the blue team, (named the Probables), and seven clubs were represented in the white team, (named the Improbables), whilst Rangers, were represented in the umpiring, (by John Mellish), such was their standing in the game. Mick McKeown, James Kelly, Jimmy McLaren and Willie Groves represented Celtic, all playing in the Probables team, which was self explanatory.

The "Scottish Seven" was the name given to the organising committee who chose the teams for the international matches against England, Ireland and Wales each year and our very own Tom Maley was the first ever Celt in their number.

CELTIC DEFEND GLASGOW NORTH EASTERN CUP

The North Eastern trophy came round again and the Celts were keen to defend our trophy. Our first round tie was at home to Clydesdale on 7th December and although we had only ten men, Clydesdale turned up with nine and immediately withdrew before the match, which was played as a friendly. Willie Groves scored twice in the first half with one from Mick Dunbar sandwiched in between, as the bhoys went in at half time 3-0 up. During the second half Johnny Coleman added a fourth before Willie Groves added another for his hat trick to finish the scoring at 5-0. The second half was remarkable in that the Celtic goalkeeper, James McLaughlin, didn't touch the ball a single time!

The quarter final draw brought the toughest available as Cowlairs were drawn out the hat as our opponents. With the match on 28th December declared null and void due to the condition of the pitch, the match was replayed at Celtic Park on 18th January in a rainstorm. Despite the conditions a large crowd attended and the bhoys had to face the heavy wind and rain in the first half. Cowlairs took full advantage to take an early lead and the scoring stayed the same as the half time whistle blew despite both teams having chances. In the second half, we took the game to Cowlairs and Tom Duff, not for the first time, was in excellent form in the opposition goal. With the bhoys continually pressing, Willie Groves scored a deserved equaliser with fifteen minutes remaining with a low shot into the right corner, to force another replay.

The date was set for the following Saturday, 25th January, at Gourlay Park in Springburn and although the rain stayed away, the Celts played with a strong wind in the first half and took advantage of it with two early goals by Willie Maley in the seventh minute and Johnny Madden five minutes later in front of the biggest crowd Gourlay Park had seen.

Emphasising the importance of the match, James Kelly of Celtic and McPherson of Cowlairs turned out for their teams and declined the invitation to play in the inter city match between Glasgow and London. Cowlairs started the second half the better team, with a strong wind at their backs but the bhoys, at full strength, added a third after a fantastic piece of passing between Willie Groves and Neil McCallum covering the full length of the pitch, ended with the latter scoring.

"The roar which greeted this seemed to burst the rain cloud which spun across the sky in frantic chase, as if in mimicry of the mortals below".

Willie Groves, after a quiet first half was now in top form and added a fourth after some scintillating dribbling and running with the ball into the wind before slipping it past Duff.

"The slight cheer which broke out as he first became conspicuous swelled with his progress and burst forth as he scored into a roar like that of a hungry lion, which might have been heard miles away".

The description of the last goal of the five, again by Willie Groves, is even better from the on form Scottish Sport hack;

"With the litheness and speed of a panther, he wove his way through forwards, halves and backs with the assistance of Coleman and while his opponents stand to faultlessly claim some infringement, he again defeats the bewildered Duff and the Celts are winners of the tie by five goals to nil".

The semi final draw brought Celtic and fellow easterders, Thistle, from Bridgeton together and in the other tie Rutherglen played Northern, from Springburn. Beechwood Park, off Dalmarnock Road was packed to its capacity despite the attraction of Queens Park playing Vale of Leven in the Scottish Cup Final just a couple of miles down the road at Hampden, as Celtic and Thistle battled it out on 15th February for a place in the final.

Thistle managed to keep things tight in the first half with only a goal from Mick Dunbar separating the teams, but it was a different story in the second half when Celtic reserve player Mick Murray added a second, before Johnny Madden, Johnny Coleman and Willie Groves ended the scoring at 5-0. Another Celtic reserve, goalkeeper Burns played in place of James McLaughlin and despite the one sided scoreline, he contributed some good saves when called into action.

The Celts had warmed up for this game with an eventful match at Tynecastle in a match we lost 1-0, with Hearts gaining revenge for a 7-0 defeat a month earlier. James McLaughlin was missing, having missed the train and he had to be replaced by the Celtic trainer, Joe Anderson, in goals!

Hearts opened the scoring in the first half from a goal that was described as clearly offside, (even the Scotsman admitted it was suspicious), and it took until the second half before the bhoys got into our rhythm. Willie Groves went on one of his mesmerising runs and just as he set himself to shoot inside the box he was hacked to the ground by Adams. A certain goal was denied and not even a foul was given, (penalty kicks were not introduced until 1891). Groves lay stunned before he got to his feet and ran at the perpetrator of the crime and retaliated with a punch, before mayhem ensued with Groves and Adams swapping blows, before the police and Hearts officials broke up the free for all.

When the dust had settled, the referee, who claimed he didn't see the original lunge by the Hearts player, sent Willie Groves off, (you couldn't make it up), but after further heated discussion it was decided that both players should bury the hatchet and allow the match to continue at eleven a side.

Back to the North Eastern Final and on 15th March 1890, Celtic battered it out with Northern at Clyde's Barrowfield ground in Bridgeton, where we won the trophy the year before. One team stood between us and 2 in a row and the Celts were keen to match the reserve team, the Celtic Crusaders, who won the North Eastern Second XI.

Although Northern, with a conveniently strengthened team, put up a brave fight, the Celts took the trophy home to Celtic Park for the second year in a row, thanks to first half goals by Johnny Coleman and Peter Dowds which was enough to give us victory by two goals to nil. It was to be the last time the club took part in the North Eastern Association Cup as we soon outgrew the competition, but it remains the only annual competition we have a 100% success rate in to this day.

The Celtic Crusaders, the name given to our reserve team for our first two seasons, also won the Second XI North Eastern Cup so it was a successful tournament all round for the Celts. The name chosen for the Celtic reserve team was an interesting one, the Crusades being the wars sanctioned by the Catholic church in the middle ages with the aim to restore Christian access to the holy lands around Jerusalem proclaimed by the Pope, no less, in 1095.

CELTIC CELEBRATE SAINT PATRICK'S DAY

The first annual social gathering, or soiree, to celebrate St Patrick's Day by the members and staff of the club took place in Waterloo Rooms on Monday, 17th March 1890, at the corner of Wellington Street and Waterloo Street, near Central station, where the Alhambra theatre once stood. Present along with the full Celtic team, was the recently departed Neil McCallum, who received a mixed reception.

After the tea, Doctor John Conway presided and stated that Celtic had been unique in its object from the very start, the fundamental object of the club being charity. Up until now, the club had spent £1500 on building the ground and every penny had been paid. In the previous year the club had donated £421, 16s, 9d to charity as well as playing charity matches throughout the country of which the funds raised for charity was not recorded but would amount to around £150.

This season already, Celtic had donated between £300 and £400 to charity and we were not finished yet. In the last year we had narrowly missed out on winning the Scottish Cup and this year we nearly won the Glasgow Cup and still had hopes of winning the Charity Cup. Doctor Conway hoped the members and friends of the club would long be spared to meet on St Patrick's Night in the same way they done that evening and a full programme of music followed.

Meanwhile, Brother Walfrid was also present at the soiree the following week at the Bridgeton Institute after Father Thomas McCulla, from Sacred Heart, was transferred to Saint Patrick's parish in his native Ireland.

GLASGOW'S FINEST MARK SAINT PATRICK'S DAY

Saint Paddy's Day in Glasgow in 1890 was the biggest celebration of the year for the massive Irish population of the city, where it was estimated that around 2000 illegal "drinking dens" thrived, otherwise known as Shebeens, from the Irish for illicit whisky, or unlicensed houses.

The timing of the police raids that followed were no coincidence and a wide net was cast around the hardened, as well as the seasonal drinkers alike, who faced fines up to £10, which they could least afford. or six months imprisonment.

PROPOSED SCOTTISH FOOTBALL LEAGUE

On Thursday, 13th March 1890 in Holton's Hotel in Glassford Street, Glasgow, representatives from the following 12 clubs met to discuss the formation of a Scottish Football League; Celtic, Rangers, Cambuslang, Third Lanark, Cowlairs, St Mirren, Abercorn, Hearts, Renton, Dumbarton, Vale of Leven and Saint Bernard's.

It was felt strongly that the League would be beneficial to the game in Scotland as well as to the clubs themselves. The League would be run on an amateur basis in harmony with the well established Scottish Football Association. All in attendance were unanimous in favour of the proposal.

The following motion from Celtic's John H McLaughlin was seconded by Mr Richardson of Hearts and unanimously agreed;

"That a committee be appointed from this meeting to draft the rules and constitution of the proposed League, and submit them to the various clubs determined upon at this meeting; and that these clubs be requested to send representatives with full powers to a meeting to be afterwards convened".

The first committee appointed were as follows; John H McLaughlin, (Celtic), William Wilton, (Rangers), Mr Lawrence, (Dumbarton), Mr Henderson, (Cowlairs), Mr Graham, (Renton), Mr Towns, (St Mirren) and Mr Thomson, (Third Lanark). Mr Lawrence was appointed interim secretary and John H McLaughlin as convenor.

By the end of May the fixture list had been agreed and the following office bearers elected; Chairman; Mr A Lawrence, (Dumbarton), Vice Chairman; Mr George Henderson, (Cowlairs), Secretary; Mr John H McLaughlin, (Celtic) and Treasurer; Mr William Wilton, (Rangers).

CELTS ON TOUR - WE'RE ON THE ROAD AGAIN

The Celts travelled south to face the cream of football on our Easter tour of England and Ireland but with our four internationals playing for Scotland against England, it was a patched up Celtic team that lost 4-0 at Bolton and 3-1 at Everton. At Pikes Lane, Bolton, on Friday, the 4th April, "Good Friday," the Celts were three nil down at half time with our depleted side, but we still continued to play good football, which was appreciated by the large home crowd.

The Athletic News, reporting on our visit to Liverpool stated;

"As a club, the Celtic are only in their infancy, but the fame they have acquired on the football field is sufficient to draw a crowd of mammoth proportions".

Dan Doyle played at full back for Everton in front of a very healthy attendance of 12,000 in the match at Anfield, which was Everton's original ground until they moved to Goodison in 1892 after a fall out with the landlord, who then formed Liverpool FC in the same year. Both teams were level at half time, after Johnny Madden equalised the home team's early opener just before half time, but it was Everton who finished the match stronger with two late goals giving them victory in a match where it was remarked that both goalkeepers had little to do. This was Celtic's second game in two days and it told near the end as we tired.

To put a bit of perspective on this result, Rangers played Everton shortly afterwards and lost 6-2 at Ibrox, giving an aggregate of 3 goals for and 14 goals against in their two encounters with the Liverpool club. Ouch.

OUR FIRST EVER SUBSTITUTION

On the Sunday, the players had a day off and took a steamer across the Mersey to New Brighton on the Wirral, where an enjoyable day of rest was had by one and all. Thankfully the international caps, James Kelly, Mick McKeown, James McLaren and Willie Groves arrived just before midnight on the Sunday, just in time to play the next match at Leamington Road, the home of Blackburn Rovers on Monday, 7th April.

James Kelly, fresh from his appearance in the 1-1 draw between Scotland and England at Hampden wasn't fresh for long, as he had to go off with an ankle injury very early in the match for the first time in his career, an injury that kept him out for two weeks. With no substitutes allowed back in the day, we played on with ten men until Blackburn obliged and allowed Willie Maley to take Kelly's place. This was to be Celtic's first ever substitution.

Blackburn scored first and went in at half time a goal to the good but the bhoys fought back well with Dowds equalising, but we couldn't get the winner our play richly deserved.

We then travelled by train to Fleetwood and from there to Belfast by steam boat for our second trip to Ireland, where we met Distillery on their home ground, the day after we met Blackburn Rovers. Despite fielding another depleted side, in our fourth match in five days, we were four up by half time and won comfortably by 6 goals to 1. No doubt, the tired Celtic party were happy to return home on the Wednesday for a well earned rest.

THE DEATH OF FATHER MAGINN

On Wednesday 9th April 1890, the death of the hugely popular Father Maginn from the parish of St Alphonsus occurred at the young age of only 42

The man from Clonduff, County Down was known as a zealous leader of his flock, strictly adherent to the attitude towards alcohol of the Total Abstinence Society, the Temperance Society and the League of the Cross, branches of which he organised in his parish. He was deeply involved with the committee of the Whitevale Refuge for Catholic children and was a fierce critic of proselytism. A hugely influential parish priest at St Alphonsus since 1874, he also organised a branch of the Catholic Young Men's Society in the parish and although he was not a fan of football, which brought its own distractions that didn't sit well with his strict discipline in terms of religious observance, he was well known to Brother Walfrid through their work with the CYMS. His Celtic connections also included Doctor John Conway, the doctor who attended to the priest in his final days.

Indeed William McKillop, who had been elected onto the Celtic Committee in 1889, was announced as the Honorary Secretary of the Father Maginn Memorial Fund after a large meeting was held on the 13th April to erect a fitting memorial in Saint Peter's cemetery, Dalbeth.

FIRST "OUTSIDERS" GUEST FOR CELTIC

On Saturday, 12th April 1890, Celtic had arranged to play Notts County at Celtic Park but a combination of injuries on our tour of England and Ireland, Willie Groves guesting for Hibs in the Roseberry Cup in Edinburgh and bizarrely Johnny Madden not yet back from the extended Easter visit to Ireland, Celtic requested four guest players from Cowlairs to make up the numbers against Notts County.

Cowlairs obliged in what was common practice in those days and Tom Duff, Kerr and the two McPhersons, James and John, replaced the injured McLaughlin, Kelly, McLaren and also Groves. In total James McLaughlin, James Kelly, James McLaren, Willie Maley, Johnny Coleman, Willie Groves and Johnny Madden were all unavailable and the crowd initially thought the players were missing due to Father Maginn's funeral until the real story came out.

Although both Maley brothers being unable to play, the McPherson brothers played for Celtic and the Oswald brothers played for Notts County. (John McPherson was to go on to sign for Rangers shortly afterwards and remained there for twelve years).

Another noticeable name on the teamsheet was that of the unfortunately named Harry Butler Daft, an outside left who appeared for Notts County on 137 occasions, scoring no less than 58 goals in two stints, including an appearance in the 1891 FA Cup Final for Notts County at the Kennington Oval against Blackburn Rovers, which they lost 3-1. He also won 5 caps for England, including the match against Scotland on 5th April 1890, the game in which James Kelly, Mick McKeown, James McLaren and Willie Groves played for Scotland in the 1-1 draw at Hampden.

Daft by name. Not daft by nature.

Back to the game, which was a reporter's nightmare with Daft through on Duff, thankfully Rafael Scheidt wasn't born yet. Tom Maley scored for Celtic in the first minute before the visitors replied before half time and the match finished 1-1, but it was remembered for the accusation that this was the first match that "outsiders" played for Celtic, as guests for one match. Until then, the modus operandi was to give young players a chance from the likes of Broxburn Shamrock or Carfin Shamrock or one of the many other smaller Irish teams to see what they could do. Anyone from outside this circle, it seems, was deemed as an "outsider" by the media.

On 15th April, the *Scottish Sport* stated;

"It was a new experience for the Celtic to call in the assistance of outsiders to assist them against Notts County. A reference to the report of the game will explain the why and wherefore".

The match report contained the following;

"The ground eleven was in the peculiar position of having in its ranks no fewer than four Cowlairs representatives and this fact is worthy of being placed on record, as rightly or wrongly, the Celtic have been regarded by the public as being a club exclusively creed in the selection of its players for all matches."

"Exclusively creed in the selection of its players for all matches," left no doubt what the press meant by *"outsiders."* They meant that the four players who guested for Celtic against Notts County was the first occasion when a non Catholic played for Celtic. Again, back in the day, this wasn't anything out of the ordinary for an Irish club, but as the club grew and started to challenge the natural flow of things, it was a matter of time before it would be brought up as a stick to beat us with. Other teams, of course, were ignored.

Tom Duff, the Cowlairs goalkeeper, indeed played another four matches guesting for Celtic against Bolton, Wolves and Preston in friendlies before playing too in the Testimonial match against Old Renton. He was said to be the best goalkeeper in Scotland and the word on the street was that he would be signed up for the new season. For whatever reason, this didn't materialise and we signed James Bell from Mauchline instead. Tom Duff was certainly an "interesting" character but more on him later.

In another interesting snippet the same newspaper reported;

"A very interesting event occurred last week in the domestic circle of the esteemed treasurer of the Celtic. It did not prevent John H McLaughlin from turning out at the Notts County match on 12th April".

This would be the birth of John H McLaughlin's son, also named John H McLaughlin, who would also go on to enjoy a career in football, most notably playing for Hamilton Accies in the Scottish Cup Final in 1911 and also the replay against Celtic when we won 2-0 after a 0-0 draw. Young Johnny had started with Strathclyde Juniors before going to Hamilton Accies in 1910 then being transferred to Morton in 1913.

John H McLaughlin, the founding father would have dreamt of his son playing for Celtic one day but it wasn't to be.

CHARITY CUP SEMI FINAL

The Charity Cup was our last chance of major silverware for the season and so it took on extra significance as we faced Third Lanark at Hampden Park on 19th April 1890. Willie Maley played in place of the injured James Kelly who was recovering from his ankle injury against Blackburn Rovers and he was badly missed.

In an even match, the Celts played with the wind in the first half but couldn't make our superiority pay. It was an indifferent performance by the bhoys who didn't really get going as the game headed towards a nil-nil draw but with just six minutes remaining disaster struck and Thirds scored two goals in a minute to give them a surprise 2-0 win and leave the Celts trophyless in the three major cups for the second season in a row. Progress had been astonishing for the new club, but we were frustrated that it hadn't yet translated itself into major silverware.

JOHN HIGNEY, ORIGINAL CELTIC SUBSCRIBER PASSES AWAY

On Monday, 28th April, at a General Meeting of the club, President John Glass told the assembled members the sad news that John Higney, a major backer of the club since our inception had passed away. This was a huge loss as John Higney was one of our most generous financial backers, having donated 20s, the top tier of donations to the original subscription list in January 1888.

HEARTS HOSTILITY TOWARDS CELTIC - AGAIN

With the season finished apart from friendlies, the Celts took on seven matches in the month of May. The first of which was back at Tynecastle, which only three months earlier had resembled more of a boxing match than a football match at one stage. If our goalkeeping situation looked strange on our last visit when James McLaughlin missed the train and forced trainer Joe Anderson to play between the sticks, it was only slightly less peculiar with Willie Maley making his debut in goals, again with McLaughlin out.

Flawed genius, Mick McKeown, had quit the club the previous week after a minor fall out with fellow full back Jerry Reynolds, but he returned for this match and played in James McLaren's place at right half due to injury, despite having played for Glasgow Hibernian during the week. After that match McKeown made it clear he had decided to play for no club at present. John Hendry, who recently left Rangers, was drafted in to guest for the day in McKeown's position, making him the second player to have played for Celtic and Rangers, after Neil McCallum, who had guested in one match for Rangers at Aston Villa. It was thought that following McKeown's indecision, Hendry may be the man to replace him, but this wasn't to be.

To the game itself and similar to the last one at Tynecastle, Hearts took the lead and it remained so at half time. The Celts, similar to the last game came more into the match in the second half and this time our pressure was rewarded with a controversial goal. Back in the day whilst the keeper had the ball in his hands after a save it was legal for him to be "charged" by a player, hence right up until the 50s, once a keeper had the ball in his hands he would kick it out as quick as he could before being charged.

On this occasion, Mick McKeown charged the keeper before he had the chance to kick the ball out, forcing him to go over the line with the ball still in his hands, before he threw the ball up into the air and away from danger. The Hearts umpire gave a corner, whilst the Celtic umpire gave a goal. The referee agreed with the Celtic umpire and uproar ensued from the Hearts support.

The scoring wasn't finished and with the Hearts players resorting to rough house tactics once more, Willie Groves was bundled to the ground by Begbie and they were made to pay as the darling of the Celtic support flighted the ball in for Mick Dunbar to score the winner.

The *Scottish Sport* summed up the Hearts support thus on the 6th May;

"Had any opponents of our national pastime been present at the match between the Celtic and Heart of Midlothian on Saturday, they would have had their adverse convictions strongly fortified by the disgusting scenes that were witnessed in that now very notorious enclosure..... The first half of the game had been only a few minutes old when it was apparent that the vast crowd was animated by the usual hostile feeling towards the Celtic.

A long experience of these of these enthusiasts has satisfied us that nothing, justice being the least likely, will appease them and so it turned out, for until the finish of the game they maintained a course of action against the referee and players which was most disgraceful. Epithets were hurled which some of the users could not spell, and at the conclusion the referee was received with a burst of yelling and hooting, an imitation of which would be beyond the powers of all the mad dogs and cats that could be collected.

Whether the Heart of Midlothian Club is to be blamed personally or not, the fact remains that their ground has been brought into disrepute and they are sure to be the sufferers. It may be urged that the club has no control of its supporters, but without stopping to discuss that matter, the precept of example can be appropriately pointed out for the edification of those who require it".

Today, Hearts fans are ridiculed by the Celtic support as the "minis" or the "diets," pointing towards their penchant for being a smaller version of the original Rangers. Strangely, at a time when relations between Celtic and Rangers were described as very cordial in 1890, Hearts fans "were animated by the usual hostile feeling towards the Celtic."

This feeling of hostility was naturally an extension of the animosity of the Hearts support towards Hibernian in the early days, as not only were Celtic a bigger Irish team than Hibs, our early teams contained a number of their players. Interestingly, it is evident that the traditional animosity felt by sections of the Hearts support towards Celtic, pre-dated that of Rangers' fans hatred towards Celtic by a number of years.

CELTIC THROW DOWN THE GAUNTLET TO THE CREAM OF ENGLAND

With the season coming to a close, the Celtic Committee, with their usual dynamism, arranged a tasty finale for the Celtic support, with no less than Bolton Wanderers, Wolverhampton Wanderers, (their first match in Scotland) and Preston North End vying for the longest name at Celtic Park, as the sign writers around the ground broke into a cold sweat. Bolton, Wolves and Preston, as they will be hereby known, all came, saw, but didn't conquer, similar to every other team from south of the border with the exception of Everton.

Bolton, with seven Scottish players in their team, came nearest on the 10th May when they earned a 2-2 draw, taking advantage of the fact we were missing goalkeeper James McLaughlin, as well as James McLaren, Paddy Gallagher and Johnny Coleman with Tom Duff, Willie Maley, Willie Naughton and Johnny Cunningham taking their place. The teams had met only five weeks previously when the bhoys lost 4-0 at Bolton, when again we were missing four first team players, this time away on international duty. The Celts would rather remember the last visit of Bolton to Celtic Park, almost a year to the day, when we won comfortably, by 5 goals to 1.

On this occasion, both teams played a fast attacking style in front of the large crowd, in an end to end game which thrilled the support. Bolton took the lead unexpectedly, which only made the Celts more determined to push forward and this was rewarded by an equaliser from Mick Dunbar. Before half time, however slackness crept in at the back and Bolton added a second to go in 2-1 up at the break. The second half was much of the same with the Celts enjoying the bulk of the pressure but we were finding Bolton difficult to break down. Finally near the end of the match, Willie Naughton scored a brilliant goal to finish the game level at two goals apiece.

Next up were Wolves on the 17th May, both teams were under strength and it showed, with the game described as average for the most part. Mick Dunbar, Jimmy McLaren and Johnny Coleman were out for the Celts and Brodie, Allen and Mason were absent for the visitors. The only word of note from the first half was Johnny Madden's goal from a free kick which separated the teams but the fans had five more goals to look forward to in the second half.

With the wind at our backs, reserve player Galbraith took his chance to shine, adding a second goal before Willie Groves did what Willie Groves did best to make it three nil, just minutes later. This woke the Wolves from their slumber and they rattled off two goals in quick succession before the Celts finished the scoring at 4 goals to 2. Last, but not least, came the famous Preston North End, five days later and the Invincibles were made to look vulnerable at times, in a fast and furious match which didn't flag. With the match heading for a 0-0 draw, we grabbed the winner in the last few minutes after the visitors went a man down through injury.

Tom Duff and John Hendry again played for the club as we noticeably relaxed our reliance on players from an Irish background guesting for the club, after criticism in the press in April after our match with Notts County. The next step was the signing of a non Catholic player for the season and with both Duff and Hendry being pursued, it seemed that this was now imminent in time for the start of the 1890/91 season, especially with our desperate situation in trying to fill the goalkeeping position.

BROTHER WALFRID IN THE COMMUNITY

On Sunday 11th May, 160 boys and girls made their First Communion at Sacred Heart chapel and were treated to a sumptuous breakfast in the school rooms after morning mass by no less a man than Brother Walfrid!

THE "OLD RENTON" CONTROVERSY

The final game of the season was on 31st May at home to "Old Renton," a team made up from the famous Renton team who not so long ago had been given the legend, "The Champions of the World". It was billed as a testimonial match for former Renton legend, James McCall, but was really a charity match with the other half of the funds raised going to a charity of Celtic's choice, the Little Sisters of the Poor. However alarm bells soon started to ring with the allegation that as many of the former Renton players were now playing as professionals in England, they would be barred from playing against any amateur opposition in Scotland, no matter what guise it was under.

James Kelly and Neil McCallum played for their old team, Renton, (under the name "Old Renton" in the match that finished two goals each but just like the Glasgow Cup final against Queens Park, controversy was to linger for a long time. The issue raised was that Celtic didn't have official permission from the SFA to play the match, as the players playing in England as professionals were debarred from playing under the SFA's jurisdiction in Scotland, even though it was for charitable purposes.

The *Glasgow Evening News* took up Celtic's side on 30th May;

"Tomorrow will see a fixture which, if old renown possesses power to draw, should attract crowds - I mean the meeting between Celtic and Old Renton, in aid jointly of the McCall Testimonial and on the Celtic side, the Little Sisters of the Poor. I cannot for the life of me see why such a bother has been made about the match. The fixture is quite legal so far as I can see. Any combination can play a Scottish club if it chooses and under whatever name it chooses, but it cannot play anyone it chooses.

To play in the Old Renton team, McCall and Kelly should have had permission of the Association but that is all that effects the fixture so far as the laws of the Association are concerned. The objects, or rather the joint objects, are worthy ones - a benefit match today is not by any means an innovation, nor can it be said the precedents are not authoritative".

That was it in a nutshell, however other sections of the media soon took the SFA's side and cranked up the heat on the official body to punish Celtic. The Scottish Sport on the 3rd of June, 1890 summed this up perfectly with sections of an editorial which remains to this day one of the most sensationalist anti Celtic diatribes witnessed.

"We are nearing the brink, and when the topple over comes someone will get hurt. The Celtic, in carrying out their match with Old Renton, have snapped their fingers in the face of the SFA, and if that body only resents the indignity placed upon it, in the way it should, east end charities, in the course of a month or two, will have to look beyond football for support. The action of the Celtic is indefensible, it is in direct contradiction to the wishes of the SFA, as embodied in Mr Park, and contrary to the spirit which animates, or is supposed to animate, amateurism.

The limited but unmistakeable opinions we have expressed on the matter have brought down upon us the wrath of the weak knee'd brigade of critics who prefer to support influential wrong doers to the principals of right. While it is easy to strangle sycophancy of this, the worst description, it is much easier to hold its inconsistency and utter senility up to the light and let the public do the strangling if need be. We have been accused of making a mole hill into a mountain by people who, while bombastically professing to be the most chaste apostles of amateurism, not only endeavour to palliate an act which, while it may not be a direct fracture of the law, is an insolent outrage on the life principles of amateur football.

The Celtic, when they played the match with Old Renton, became law givers and law interpreters and we sincerely hope and trust that they will be made to pay, and pay sweetly too, for their perversity and waywardness. While amateurism has a leg to stand on, we will support it, and neither clubs, principalities, nor powers will shift our allegiance. We care not how soon the crucial point of the struggle may come; we are prepared. To those who are steeping their souls in sin, under the wing of purity, we give a fair warning. We will not begin the battle if we can help it but if we do, we will hit hard and mercilessly, and our blows may fall in places where they are least expected".

As a perfect example of how the media in the 1890s worked similarly as they do today, ie, depending on which way the wind is blowing or more to the point depending on whose ear they were listening to, the Scottish Referee, on the same subject reported;

"The playing of the match "Old Renton" v Celtic has raised considerable diversity of opinion. There are some who maintain that the Celtic club has made itself amenable to the discipline of the Association by taking part in what has been characterised an illegal fixture. But it must be remembered that in the laws of

the Association, there is no rule defining an "illegal" fixture. The subject is never referred to and no penalty can be imposed without the sanction of law".

"The Celtic club have been blamed for playing the match and are said, in defiance of logic and commonsense, to have defied and revolted against the association. If any mistake has been made, it was made by the Renton club proper in approaching the Association at all. It is a pity that this case should be made so much of and that party feeling should be fomented and that the Association should be invited to act ultra vires" (beyond the powers).

"Charity never faileth. Matches on behalf of the best of the graces are now all the rage. In the way of supporting deserving institutions, the Celtic are far ahead of all our clubs and set them a most worthy example. We think it cannot be too well known that a large portion of Saturday's match against Old Renton was handed over to the Association of the Sisters of the Poor. It would be very interesting to know the exact amount the club has either directly or indirectly contributed to the charity's good cause; we imagine if the sum could be ascertained that it would startle us by its magnitude. All round we are pleased to see the readiness with which such clubs like the Celtic lend themselves to aid our charities, and we hope that the influence of the good work may remain with all who in any way contribute to forward such matches".

The reader can make up their own mind which response was measured and in possession of the facts that no by law had been broken and which one was hysterical, more akin to a soap box preacher on Glasgow Green on a Sunday afternoon than a national newspaper.

The *Scottish Sport*, on 6th June, got personal;

"The method of its creation aroused suspicion, but still might be honest even here if the club did not create, by its injudicious action, proves that everything is not right according to the laws of amateurism, as laid down by the SFA. We find a lot of football players, belonging principally to the Hibernian and Renton clubs, every man of Irish extraction, banded together into a club which, at its birth, is one of the most powerful combinations in the kingdom.

All the men change their places of abode and come to Glasgow, where after a short residence, they either become the nominal proprietors of, or are connected with, public houses. We remember well what an outcry was raised when the Blackburn Rovers, or some of their wealthy supporters, started Hugh McIntyre in the Castle Inn. Yet here we have in Glasgow the identical system pursued in the case of the Celtic. We talked then of sham amateurism and raised the cry of "football in danger" but the system extended until the veiled pro became the pure and unadulterated article which now rules the roost in England and is creeping insidiously into Scotland.

These Celts could not have placed in their pubs without someone backing them up. The books of the club, if examined tomorrow, will be found to be correct in every detail. Where then does the money come from for men, the majority of whom, prior to their arrival in Glasgow, were labourers and the minority tradesmen - some apprentices....The Celts have influential supporters who do not hesitate to put their hands in their pockets for the good of the club and the arrangement between the players and their patrons cannot be ascertained".

At this point in the debate it would be pertinent to bring in the Scottish Sport's former publication, the Scottish Umpire, which printed on September 11th 1888 a clear invitation to those with allegations of professionalism against Celtic to show their proof or to forever hold their peace. Now two years after no evidence of wrong doing was ever brought forward, the

Scottish Sport is wheeling out the self same old argument and using it as a stick to beat Celtic, without an iota of proof, which they themselves asked for.

The article is worth repeating from September 11th 1888;

"Much has been asserted of late and more insinuated, regarding the mala fide of the Celtic club which, like a mushroom, has risen to a front position amongst the leading clubs of the country in an incredibly short space of time.

Now we are not in a position to affirm or deny these charges and innuendoes, but we are not so un-English as to cry down a club until the accusers have justified their accusations. Let those who so loudly assert the professionalism of the east end organisation come boldly forward like men and prove their assertions, or be forever silent.

It is mean and contemptible to persistently traduce the Celts and yet shirk the responsibility of producing evidence. The Celts may be all they are accused of, but we at any rate are bound to regard them as innocent until they are proved guilty. If they are guilty and that fact is made abundantly evident after a fair trial, then we will be the first to launch the denunciations of indignant public opinion against them until they renounce or amend their ways.

In the meantime, however, neither the charge, nor the evidence is forthcoming in the proper quarter and in consequence, we are entitled to infer that neither can be tabled. We therefore challenge those who have anything to say vitally affecting the status of the Celts to say it, or cease their envious carping. We venture to think that with some, the Celts' only fault is being strong".

The *Scottish Sport* were then forced into replying to an English journal, to whom the original article was aimed at;

"The Manchester Athletic News, in a recent issue, calls us to task for an apparent inconsistency on our part in saying that it is a matter for investigation how five or six members of the Celtic club became possessed of public houses. The inconsistency appears in the fact that in a previous issue, we invited our contemporary to prove that professionalism exists in Scotland ; that he has so far not been able to do.

We never denied and indeed frequently have stated in these columns, that many doubtful transactions took place between certain clubs and their players. That was fully proved during the course of the investigations by the sub committee on professionalism which examined the books of the clubs some years ago".

It was a very weak retort from the Scottish Sport. The original article was aimed in particular at Celtic, pure and simple. They were asking for enough rope to hang us out to dry and when no proof came forward of any wrong doing at Celtic, the Scottish Sport then did a rehash of the same old story without any evidence to back it up, completely contradicting themselves into the bargain.

Their real intent becomes clear later in the same article;

"It is the few doubtful ones we want to get at. Towards these no mercy ought to be extended. They are wolves in sheep's clothing. In England, professionalism sneaked in the same way and in the end the wolves will devour the sheep. That is all but accomplished south of the border and we hope, by timely tackling the evil, to at once secure immunity for the amateur sheep and the destruction of the prowling and sneaking wolf".

Still, they did not answer their own question. Where was the proof of any wrong doing at Celtic? What they did achieve in the above paragraph was the clarity in their words, making it became abundantly clear that the newspaper was getting personal. If we were a prowling and sneaking wolf, we were only playing in a field with a more experienced pack of wolves.

The same newspaper, despite its ongoing onslaught of Celtic, weren't slow to take advantage of the club's hospitality in the close season when their office football team beat Begg, Kennedy & Harpers, wholesale stationers and printers, by 4 goals to 2 before enjoying the ground, pavillion and baths facilities at Celtic Park.

Incredibly the "Old Renton" controversy carried on throughout the close season and into the start of the new season and John O'Hara, Celtic's Honorary Secretary felt compelled to write to the Secretary of the Scottish Football Association to explain the circumstances of the match;

"Dear Sir

From the reports which have appeared in the press of the meeting of your committee on Tuesday last, and the discussion that then took place, there seems to be a total misunderstanding as to the circumstances under which the match between the Old Renton team and the Celtic was played at the end of last season. Before therefore, your Business Committee take up the discussion of this matter, you might kindly lay the following statement of the facts of the case before them ;

About the beginning of May last, we had arranged a fixture with the Vale of Leven, for the 31st of that month, the whole proceeds of which were to be devoted to various charitable institutions. About the middle of May we were approached by the McCall Testimonial Committee to play a match with the Old Renton team for the benefit of that testimonial. This we refused to do. On being further pressed however, we arranged to play a match with that team on the date we had fixed with the Vale of Leven, and that match on half gate terms, as we calculated that the half of the proceeds of an attractive game such as this would more than equal the entire drawings with the Vale of Leven. This half gate of course, as in the case of the latter, was to be devoted to charity. In passing, I may say that the net amount available for division was £217 odd, our share of which was allocated as follows;

Little Sisters of the Poor £50
Whitevale Refuge for Children £20
Lanark Hospital £30
Lanark Orphanage £10

The other half of the gate drawings we understand was given by the Old Renton team as a donation to the McCall testimonial fund. Now my committee do not consider and never have considered that they were playing a Benefit Match. As far as the Celtic are concerned the match was simply and solely a half gate fixture. Our share of the gate we have accounted for; with what the Old Renton did with there's we have nothing whatever to do. Of course we understand what they intended to do with the money, but we can be no more held responsible for the money going to that Testimonial Fund, than we can be held responsible for an English professional team devoting their share of a gate to the payment of their players.

I observe also that it is stated the match was advertised as the McCall Benefit Match or some other such title. That is not correct. No such misleading title appeared either in bills or advertisements and as a matter of fact, the object of the match and the manner in which the proceeds were to be divided was explained in the athletic press at the time.

In reference to the second point urged against us that we ignored the official ruling of the President, I have simply to say that the report of your meeting is the first authentic intimation my committee have had that any such official ruling was given. In the conversation with the president, Mr Willie Maley understood him to distinctly and emphatically refuse to give either official permission or prohibition to the match and that the opinion he then expressed was simply his own private view of the matter. Naturally therefore we concluded that any negotiations the President had with the Testimonial Committee he would take up the same position and I would respectfully point out that if an official ruling was given it ought to have been officially communicated to us.

As it was, we were under the impression that it was only Mr Park's private opinion had been given and as against that we had the opinion of many gentlemen of high standing in the world of football that the match was perfectly legal, we decided to go on with it, had we known that the match had been officially prohibited we would never have dreamt for a moment of running counter to such a decision. We acted in perfect good faith, in the belief that such a decision had never been given. My Committee disclaim entirely any intention of overriding the rules of the Association or of in any way, either in his personal or official capacity, insulting or slighting Mr Park; and this latter charge we repudiate the more emphatically as Mr Park holds, and has always held, a very high place in our admiration and esteem.

I lay these facts before your Committee in the conviction that they have only to be known to completely exonerate us from accusations that have arisen evidently from ignorance of the correct circumstances of the case.

Yours truly
John O'Hara
Honorary Secretary
19 Moore Street, Glasgow, 22 August 1890"

In a very well written letter, the Celtic Secretary concisely covered all the points and clearly stated the facts. This was another perfect example of the intelligence of the early committee and our ability to take on and win high profile cases.

In the event, the case eventually grinded to a close with the SFA censuring Celtic and suspending indefinitely James Kelly and James McCall. This wasn't good enough for the Celtic Committee and a protest meeting between Celtic, Renton and the SFA was set for the 2nd September. Before then, letters were received at the SFA's office from the protesting parties including James Kelly, who along with James McCall were made the scapegoats of the affair for playing without permission for Old Renton.

Mr J K McDowall
Secretary Scottish Football Association
Glasgow, 2nd September, 1890

Dear Sir

We have been summoned to appear tonight before the Professional and Business Committee of your Association, in regard to the match between Celtic and Old Renton. We are glad to have the opportunity of explaining our position, even before your sub-committee, and while we do so, we feel it is only due to ourselves to assert that the clubs in the Association ought not to have any complaints against either them or their players adjudged upon, and a vote taken without the clubs interested having first been heard, as your committee actually did. While we are prepared and willing to give to the Association the dutiful obedience and respect which we owe it, at the same time we have a right to expect, and do expect, that the legislative body entrusted with executive powers shall observe due regularity of procedure and the principle of justice.

We lodge this protest with your Association simply to preserve our own rights and those of other clubs who may be placed in a similar position, and for the purpose of preserving full liberty of action to ourselves and any other clubs in the Association, who either now or in future may be compelled to reluctantly vindicate their rights.

Yours truly

John Glass (President)
John O'Hara (Honorary Secretary)
John H McLaughlin (Treasurer)
Celtic FC

Renton 2nd September 1890

Dear Sir

We have been summoned tonight to appear before your Professional and Business Committees along with the Celtic. We need not state at length the exceptions we are bound to take like any other club to the action of your committee in practically condemning us unheard. We agree with the Celtic to give you every information and explanation we can, but we also reserve full liberty of action.

Yours truly
James Cameron (Treasurer)
Renton FC

Mr John McDowall
Secretary SFA

Dear Sir

On my return from Ireland this morning I notice from the newspapers that I have been suspended for playing in the Old Rentonian team. I beg to apply to your Association for reinstatement in accordance with the precedents of the Association in dealing with similar cases. I was not present last night because your intimation never reached me, my address in Ireland only being ascertained yesterday, when I received a telegram to come back. Please submit this letter to your Committee and let me know the result.

Yours truly
James Kelly
155 James Street, Bridgeton, Glasgow

The whole affair finally ended with Kelly and McCall's suspension rescinded. A precedent had already been set when Queens Park players assisted Corinthians in Edinburgh on 2nd January and they were no less guilty of professionalism than Kelly or McCall had been in assisting Old Renton against Celtic. What was needed was consistency, no matter who a player represented.

TROUBLE AT THE SIX A SIDE TOURNAMENT AT IBROX

During the close season, clubs often organised six a side tournaments to keep their supporters amused and at the one at Ibrox, Rangers supplied six of the twenty two teams contesting the tournament, unfortunately for them not one got past the 3rd round, which was quite an achievement in itself, especially as Rangers provided the referees for all matches from their own officials. The matches were keenly contested and Celtic beat two of the Rangers representatives, Rangers Swifts and the Light Blues in the first two rounds before meeting Cowlairs in the quarter final, which bizarrely kicked off just before 10pm, and ended in a fight as tempers flared.

Cowlairs won the match by two goals and two points to nil but the Celtic Committee weren't happy. The fall out was long lasting as Celtic lodged a protest before the match against Duff and Kerr, men who had obliged us in guesting for the club before the end of the season. Their crime was taking part in a proclaimed, (an unofficial), meeting in Busby weeks before. It was not like the Celtic Committee and may well have been a factor in Tom Duff not signing for Celtic at the start of the new season, as he was tipped to do. On the other hand, the Celtic Committee may have been reacting to Duff not putting pen to paper for the coming season when they lodged the protest, but what is clear is that there was bad feeling between the club and Tom Duff in the close season and this led to him remaining at Cowlairs for another season.

Significantly, guesting in goals for the Celtic six a side team was Dumbarton's famed international keeper John McLeod. Was he our new target for a position that needed urgent attention? Indeed he assisted us, along with other Dumbarton team-mates at a number of 4 and 5 a side tournaments during the close season with the bhoys winning competitions at the following Sports days; St Mirren, Cambuslang, Camelon, Kirkintilloch and at the National Cycling Union Championships, whilst we were runners up at the Clyde Sports. The Celtic Committee, indefatigable as usual, were keen to keep our name to the fore during the close season.

Of 35 friendly matches played that season, 20 were against Scottish opposition, 14 against English teams and 1 against an Irish team. This contrasted with our first season, where we played 37 friendlies, with 27 against Scottish opposition, 8 against English opposition and 2 against Irish opponents. It showed that our fame was spreading with the top teams in England not only clamouring to attract us to their grounds, they were also desperate to visit Celtic Park.

The following teams had visited Celtic Park; Corinthians, Mitchell St George, Sunderland, Blackburn, Everton (twice), Notts County, Bolton (twice), Wolves and Preston (twice). Out of the twelve matches against the cream of England, only Everton managed a victory.

At the end of the 1889/90 season we had plenty to be cheerful about as the club continued to grow, but we had still to win our first major trophy, losing in the 1st round of the Scottish Cup to Queens Park 2-1, and to the same team in the final of the Glasgow Cup 3-2 and also losing the Charity Cup semi final 2-0 at Third Lanark.

Rome wasn't built in a day and the Celtic Committee, along with the growing Celtic support, had much to look forward to.

THE 1890 ANNUAL GENERAL MEETING

At the 1890 AGM on Tuesday, 24th June at the Mechanics Hall, Calton in front of a large crowd there was no dissention, with the malcontents of the previous year long since departed to form Glasgow Hibernian. Secretary John O'Hara had his report adopted without any fuss before Willie Maley gave a very satisfactory Match Secretary's report stating the club had played 47 matches, won 27, lost 11 and drew 9. Although this record for the year doesn't sound as impressive as the previous season, it reflects the calibre of opposition with 14 matches against the cream of England.

John H McLaughlin then gave the Treasurer's report in which he gave a good insight into the running of the club, stating the gross income was £3700, (all the more remarkable considering we were knocked out of the Scottish Cup in the first round), £1000 was paid to opposing clubs as their portion of the gate money, £558 was spent on match expenses which unfortunately doesn't go into any more detail, £510 had been spent on the ground and £500 was donated to charity. Unfortunately the newspaper report doesn't cover all the ins and outs as it stated a large balance of £302 remained, although it only detailed expenditure for £2568 from the £3700 income.

It's well worth looking at the charity donations as again they give an invaluable insight into the thinking of the early Committee; The Poor Childrens' Dinner Tables received £160, the Little Sisters of the Poor received £50, Lanark Hospital, (which was owned by the Catholic church and ran by the Little Sisters of the Poor), was given £30, Whitevale Refuge (which was a local home for destitute Catholic children) received £20, the Greenhead Disaster Fund received £20 and the Penicuik Mining Disaster Fund received £10, a contribution was given to the Matt Harris Fund in Ireland and £20 to the Discharged Prisoners Fund.

The Greenhead Disaster Fund (Templeton's), was set up in November 1889 after a new extension to the carpet factory blew down whilst under construction onto the adjoining weaver's shed killing 29 female staff. The Penicuik Mining Disaster claimed 63 lives in September 1889 as a result of a fire, Matt Harris was a Fenian from Athlone who passed away in January 1890, a Land Leaguer and a fellow member of the Supreme Council of the Irish Republican Brotherhood alongside Michael Davitt, as well as being a Nationalist MP. His grandfather was executed by the British forces after the Irish Rebellion of 1798. The Discharged Prisoners Fund is self explanatory.

From a quick scan its clear that most donations were given to Catholic charities and the committee were unafraid again to mix football with religion and politics as we can see from the political donations too. The club was not slow either in donating, where it was required, to disaster funds as and when they occurred, no matter who were affected which fits in perfectly for the vision of starting a football club with charitable aims. Significantly, it was noted that Celtic had given more to charity than all the other clubs in Glasgow put together.

The Scottish press were banned from the 1890 AGM but the *Irish Sport* took pity on its sister paper, the *Scottish Sport* on 24th June, 1890;

"If Scottish Sport has been hard in its criticisms of the Celtic FC, its officials evidently still cling fondly to Sport and to our Irish contemporary of that title we are indebted for a report of the Celtic's second annual meeting, which was held in the Mechanics' Hall, on Tuesday evening last. There was a large attendance and Dr John Conway, MRCS, presided. Mr John O'Hara read the secretary's minutes of last meeting, which were adopted. Mr Willie Maley submitted a very satisfactory statement, which showed that during the past season the club played 47 matches, won 27, lost 11 and 9 were drawn. 120 goals were scored and 64 lost. The record was an excellent one and it must be borne in mind in judging the results that it was the leading Scotch clubs that were pitted against the Celts in these matches.

Mr John H McLaughlan submitted the treasurer's reports. From this it appeared that the gross income of the club was £3,700. (Applause). One thousand pounds was paid to other clubs as portion of their gate money. The report drew special attention to the charity donations of the club, which amounted to £500, including the Poor Childrens Dinner Table, £160; Little Sisters of the Poor, £50; Lanark Hospital, £30; Whitevale Refuge, £20; Greenhead Disaster Fund, £20; Penicuik Mining Disaster, £10; and Discharged Prisoners' Fund, £20. Their charities had not been confined to Glasgow and vicinity, but extended to Edinburgh and even Ireland, a contribution going to the Matt Harris Fund. The match expenses had been high, under which head about £558 had been expended; £510 was spent on the club ground. After all had been deducted there remained the large balance of £302 as a legacy to the new committee. (Applause).

Mr Willie Maley and Mr John H McLaughlin were thanked for their excellent reports, after which office-bearers were elected. The Celtic, we may add, has given more in charity than all the other football clubs of Glasgow".

The Scottish Referee on the 30th June, was quick to give credit where credit was certainly due;

"The Celtic is a wonderful club to draw gates and last season it's revenue amounted nearly to £4000. No Scottish club is so generous in giving money to charity and none readier to play in aid of deserving objects. During the past season, no less than £500 was given to various charities."

BROTHER WALFRID MAKES GOOD USE OF THE CLOSE SEASON

Monday, 21st July was the date of the annual excursion for the parishioners of Sacred Heart and the chosen destination for this year was Largs with a local band arranged to accompany the large numbers from the chapel to the train station, along with Brother Walfrid, Father Hughes and Father Bird.

The Sports Committee had arranged a full programme of events to keep everyone amused, comprising of games and dancing on the green to the accompaniment of the band who had came along, before the day was completed with some boating and paddling in the water. An exhausted but delighted party eventually arrived back at Bellgrove station in the early evening.

On Sunday, 3rd August 1890, the parish of St Alphonsus hosted the Annual Conference of the Catholic Young Men's Society in the schoolroom on Greendyke Street and Brother Walfrid and Fr Hughes from the nearby parish of Sacred Heart took the opportunity to start up a branch of the CYMS within their parish to ensure they were represented at the conference.

CHAPTER FIVE
THE 1890/91 SEASON

"Beware of the day,
When the Celts shall meet you in battle array"

A NEW STAND IS ERECTED AT CELTIC PARK

Just over two years after Celtic Park was built, it was necessary for the Celtic Committee to increase its capacity to cope with the demand of the club, still in its infancy. The committee, with their usual enterprise, had their eye on the annual Sports Days which other clubs held during the close season and it was no surprise when we announced the first Celtic Sports, which would take place on the 2nd and 9th of August.

Despite the limited space available upon the six acres of the original Celtic Park, a major upgrade of the ground came during the close season with a stand, 250ft long, erected on the graveyard side of the pitch, on the western boundary of the ground that would rival the Pavillion Stand on the opposite side of the pitch. Pay boxes and entrances were also enlarged to improve access to the ground. The hack who alleged the entrances at Celtic Park were nine inches wide, possibly a rotund gentleman, would have welcomed this news.

The *Scottish Referee*, on 11th August stated;

"The press give a hearty vote of thanks to the Celts for their efforts in the way of providing decent accommodation. Other clubs please take note. The Celts new stand is a very nice looking structure and more over a handy one. All the dining will be done underneath it, the accommodation being quite equal to seat two elevens."

The decent accommodation for the press wasn't described in any detail at the time or even its location, in any of the newspapers, except that it was likened to a "dookit," ie a pigeon loft. This didn't tell us a great deal but finally, 41 years later in Veteran's excellent History of Celtic in the *Evening Times* on 1st August, 1931, he tells us;

"Old Celtic Park saw the last of the Old Renton team, the Champions of the World, in the last game of the 1889/90 season. The new Renton took part in the opening game of the next season, and the gentlemen of the press discovered to their delight that at long last provision had been made for them in the shape of a small wooden erection with a raised platform and an overhead covering".

Before the invention of the "press box", journalists would be sat on a bench at a table just off the pitch in the open air and often crowded out by supporters at a big match, no doubt the victims of a few sharp tongues if their match report wasn't favouring the home team, or they had any "history". Alternatively at smaller grounds, they would simply walk around the touchline with a notepad and pencil, with an assistant whose job it was to hold an umbrella above his head when required.

The press stand, as it became known, was first opened on the 16th August, with our inaugural Scottish League match, at home to Renton. Also very interesting was the accommodation built under the new stand, which allowed the club to host the after match socials between both teams in house, saving considerable expense on local restaurants.

A new cinder race track was built around the pitch to accommodate a hundred yards invitation race, a hundred yards handicap, a half mile and a mile flat race and a two miles steeplechase as well as two or three cycle events were planned.

From the *Scottish Sport* on August 15th;

"Celtic Park - Matters never looked so flourishing at Parkhead as at present. A capacious addition to the stand accommodation on the western side of the ground will further convenience the great masses which patronise this enclosure during the football season. Everywhere traces of the painter's brush are visible. The turf itself has received considerable attention and the ground generally improved".

OUR FIRST CELTIC SPORTS

When the first ever Celtic Sports were finally advertised on 9th July 1890, it was clear that the Committee had pushed the boat out to organise an excellent programme of events. Starting at 14.30 prompt with a football tournament, admission prices were set at threepence for the ground and an extra threepence for either stand on the first Saturday and double that for the final day.

The extensive programme was listed as follows;

1. 100 yards Flat Race Handicap
2. Half mile Flat Race Handicap
3. Two Miles Flat Race Handicap
4. 220 Yards Flat Race Handicap
5. One Mile Flat Race Handicap
6. One Mile Ordinary Bicycle Handicap
7. Two Miles Safety Bicycle Handicap
8. Three Miles Ordinary Bicycle Handicap
9. The Sack Race
10. 100 Yards Invitation Race
11. 120 Yards Hurdle Race
12. Five a side Football

The Celtic Committee used the same method of working for the Celtic Sports as they did with the football team, with efforts made to attract the biggest names in the athletic world from Ireland and England to Celtic Park and the most attractive prizes on show to entice them. Three prizes of the highest quality were given for each race and five tea and coffee services were given to the winners of the football tournament provided by Messrs Johnston and Co, who had them on display in their shop window in Glasgow, thus further advertising the event.

The opening of the Celtic Sports clashed with the first day of the Rangers Sports on the same day, but with their usual determination, the Celtic Committee stuck to their guns and kept to the date announced with Willie Maley acting as Secretary, Tom Maley as Clerk of the Course and John H McLaughlin amongst the prime organisers.

"Build it and they will come," was the motto and once again we were proved to be correct.

The inaugural Celtic Sports were opened on Saturday 2nd August, with Celtic Park packed and enjoying the new experience. The new cinder track received a mixed reaction as it was too sharp at the corners and as yet still unbanked. This forced the cyclists to slow down to a crawl when negotiating corners for fear of ending up in the crowd and the short term solution was for the grass pitch to be utilised at the corners to provide a gradual bend. Unfortunately the terms of the lease hindered the building of a cinder track to any great standard due to the tightness of the ground available.

The Celtic Committee, with their usual wherewithal, quickly announced an improved cinder track would be built in time for the next annual Sports day at Celtic Park. The feedback from the *Glasgow Evening News* was favourable on the 8th August;

"The Celtic's Sports last Saturday had an attendance which was more than gratifying, and it augurs well for tomorrow's gate, when the second and more important meeting takes place."

There was plenty of interest for the large Celtic support on the second day of the Sports, with no less than seven Celts taking part in the five different races on foot including big names such as James Kelly, Willie Maley, Tom Maley and Paddy Gallagher as well as reserves McMorrow, Harkin and Gallagher. None of the Celts were brave enough to take part in any of the bike races but both captain, James Kelly and club member and original subscriber, John Brown joined in the fun in the Sack Race.

The biggest cheers of the day were reserved for James Kelly's win in the 220 yards race and for top athlete Tom Maley, who also ran with the Clydesdale Harriers, when he pipped J Weir of Milngavie at the post to beat an impressive field that included the famous Daniel Delany Bulger from Dublin in the 100 Yards Race. Only five of the fifty one runners ran off more of a handicap than Maley, with Bulger running off scratch and Maley just 3 yards in front of him, which shows just how well respected he was.

Daniel Delany Bulger, (Dan Bulger), brought his own style of starting a race to Scotland for the first time when he crouched down on all fours with his fingers on the marker line ready to uncoil like a spring when the starter's pistol was fired. The rest of the participants stood upright in the usual manner and were left in Bulger's wake. Soon Bulger's approach, thought to be invented in America, swept through the sport but the first day it was seen in Scotland was at Celtic Park on 9th August 1890.

We were first!

The *Glasgow Evening News* on 11th August stated;

"A fitting close to a brilliant athletic season and a magnificent introduction to the coming football season aided the Celtic in their first athletic meeting on Saturday afternoon at Parkhead. Determined to score a success, the energetic and experienced committee left nothing to chance, and in the matter of programme, as well as in the laying out of the grounds, the arrangements were most complete.

Considering the short time at the disposal of the committee, they have done wonders, the track, though a little soft, comparing favourably with that of older clubs. The patrons of the Celts, appreciating fully the efforts the club had made to cater for their amusement, turned out in their thousands, a record being scored in this respect. Both stands were filled to overflowing, whilst the ropes were lined round and round with eager, enthusiastic spectators. A portion of the eastern stand was reserved and here the handsome lot of prizes were on view".

The *Scottish Sport* on 12th August stated;

"The first attempt of this famous and popular football club at holding an athletic meeting was a pronounced success. Some excellent sport was afforded the 6000 spectators who assembled at the spacious ground of the club at Parkhead, the majority of whom were supporters of the Celtic and of Irish nationality. The weather was on its best behaviour, though a high wind was decidedly against fast times except in the 100 yards, the wind blowing down the straight at the backs of the sprinters, who were also assisted by a drop in the track".

To round off the perfect day, Celtic won the 5 a side football tournament as we beat Cambuslang by a goal and one point to a point in the final.

By 1890, questions would have been asked about the suitability of the original ground in regards to its size and the fact we were rapidly outgrowing it. We had signed a five year lease and so breaking it would have meant paying a heavy financial penalty as well as the expense required to locate and erect a new ground. For the time being the original Celtic Park was the only space available and we'd have to make do and improve the capacity where possible, without at the same time stunting the growth of the club.

THE SCOTTISH LEAGUE BEGINS

The Scottish Football League was founded in 1890 to guarantee Scottish clubs a fixture list of competitive matches throughout the season without depending on friendlies to bolster the calendar, which until then had compromised of the three main trophies of the Scottish Cup, the Glasgow Cup and the Charity Cup. Celtic, not surprisingly played a major part in the inception of the League along the lines of the English League, which had been formalised since 1888. Celtic's John H McLaughlin was rewarded by being given a place on the Committee of the new legislative body, the Scottish Football League where he used his great oratory skills to lead the rest of the Committee.

As an aside, John Herbert McLaughlin, as well as being an excellent debater, Treasurer of Celtic and Secretary of the Scottish League, was known to play the organ at St Mary's chapel of a Sunday. One morning whilst at the organ he suddenly realised that he had left the match takings from the day before in his office under the grandstand at the original Celtic Park, instead of taking them home on a Saturday after the match.

Thinking on his feet, he decided to feign injury and hot footed it out of the chapel to hail a cab to nearby Celtic Park as quick as his legs could carry him. Finally on arriving at Celtic Park he discovered the swag bag, complete with hundreds of pounds was still in his office, exactly where he left it. Now feeling a lot better he returned to St Mary's and to his duties on the organ, with the Celtic match takings sitting alongside him and never far from his thoughts.

The first competitors in the original Scottish League were Abercorn, Cambuslang, Celtic, Cowlairs, Dumbarton, Hearts, Rangers, Renton, St Mirren, Third Lanark and Vale of Leven. Of the eleven, only Celtic, Dumbarton, Hearts and St Mirren remain today in their original form. Renton only lasted five weeks in League competition that season after being suspended and their results were nullified after they had played Edinburgh Saints in a friendly match, a team who were in reality Saint Bernards, (from Edinburgh), who had been suspended for allegations of professionalism. Renton sued the SFA and won their case, and were reinstated to the Scottish League at the start of the 1891/92 season.

Significantly Queens Park, then Scotland's Establishment Team, declined to take part and thus began the decline of the club from the prominent place in the Scottish game they kept during the previous two decades to bit part players when professionalism was finally introduced into the game. Queens Park bucked the trend and remained amateur, as they do right up to the present day. Hibernian too hastened their own demise by not turning up to register their participation.

OUR FIRST SCOTTISH LEAGUE GAME

The first Scottish League game was played on August 16th 1890 at the original Celtic Park when fittingly Renton, the originators of the idea to initiate the League, took on Celtic, who were largely responsible for carrying on the suggestion and bringing it to creation. Renton, only two years previously had won the Scottish Cup and had been dubbed the "Champions of the World," after beating the English Cup holders West Bromwich Albion at Hampden, but since then, their star was falling. Neil McCallum, who had to walk home from the second Hampden to Renton after missing the last train in 1888, had joined Celtic along with James Kelly and this occurred during a break up of their great team with others attracted south. The Celts, with our meteoric rise, were tipped to take the new Scottish League by storm and Celtic Park as usual was busy with an enormous crowd, with both stands packed as well as 6000 around the ropes raising the attendance to over 8000.

It was noted in the *Scottish Referee*;

"The game was twenty minutes late in starting owing to the demands of the enterprising photographer".

Unfortunately, as yet, these photographs have never surfaced. Have no doubt, they will.

Celtic were without Johnny Coleman and Mick Dunbar and had to make do with half back Jimmy McLaren in goals, as this position was still not filled and we continued to struggle, throughout our first two years of existence, to attract and keep hold of a decent keeper. Willie Groves and Johnny Madden were played out of position on the left and in the centre of attack and reserve players Willie Naughton and Hugh Gallagher failed to rise to the occasion on the right side. Renton played their old legend Jim McCall, who had played professional in England but in doing so they risked the wrath of the Scottish League.

The game had started badly for the Celts, with Jimmy McLaren hardly taken up his position between the posts when Renton scored in the first minute. Two goals followed within a minute on the half hour mark but the scoreline was harsh on the bhoys as ironically Gow in the Renton goals had been much busier than McLaren, and Gallagher's goal before half time put a slightly fairer reflection on play.

The bhoys continued to press and hit the bar in the second half, but it was the visitors who finished off the scoring ten minutes from the end as we chased the game for a second goal. The final score was flattering to Renton, there had only been two corners in the game, both to Celtic, but how the media rejoiced in this first big shock of the season with the *Scottish Sport* hardly containing their joy with its opener;

"Bravo Renton. Such was the ejaculation heard all over when the result at Celtic Park was made known on Saturday evening last".

In fairness, the Dunbartonshire side were the better team on the day and deserved to win thanks to their quick passing game before Hugh Gallagher scored our historic, first ever League goal.

A week later on 23rd August, the Celts travelled to Tynecastle to take out the frustrations of our home defeat in the first match on Hearts. This was our third visit to Tynecastle, with both previous trips certainly not lacking in controversy and this one wasn't to disappoint either.

Whilst the two previous matches were closely fought affairs, this one was clear cut, as the bhoys struck a rich vein of form, going in at half time three nil up thanks to two goals from Johnny Madden, the first one a screamer which went in off the underside of the bar in the 11th minute, before Willie Groves made it three with a volley before half time. The Celts were forced to play for ten minutes with ten men after Baird reacted to our first goal with a high kick to Peter Dowds' eye which forced him to leave the field with a severe cut and return with a bandage over his head to the loud cheers of the vociferous Celtic support.

Willie Groves scored his second and Celtic's fourth goal and the Hearts players reacted by kicking everything that moved as the bhoys waltzed past them for fun. With half an hour still on the clock the Hearts support flocked to the exits whilst the Celtic support cheered every touch. Just to rub salt in their wounds, Peter Dowds, with a heavy bandage covering one eye, scored a delicious goal with a precision shot from outside the box which dropped right under the bar to finish the scoring at Hearts 0 Celtic 5.

Unfortunately the action didn't end there as a Hearts supporter launched his bowler hat at Tom Maley, who was acting as umpire on the sideline. Maley was unhurt as he picked up the hat and smashed it with his umpire's flag, before fending off his attacker with a rapier lunge to the stomach in self defence!

The *Scottish Referee* on the 25th August, hit out at the rough play of Adams of Hearts near the end of the match, criticising his reprehensible actions and warning him that he brings great discredit to himself as well as to Hearts before delivering this timely piece of advice;

"Why not take a beating like a man?"

Ironically the victory remains our record win at Tynecastle in a League match to this day.

Celtic had a new goalkeeper between the sticks, listed as AN Other on the teamsheet but he was not troubled. AN Other in fact turned out to be *"That old veteran of Mauchline, Jamie Bell,"* (as described by the *Scottish Referee*, despite him only being 24 years old). Our new signing from Ayrshire club Mauchline, was guesting for Hurlford during the tail end of the 1889/90 season and came to our attention after his fine displays in the Kilmarnock Charity Cup, which Hurlford won, beating Annbank 3-2 in the final at Rugby Park on the 30th May, after a replay, and thus depriving their opponents of a treble after they won the Ayrshire Cup and the Ayr Charity Cup.

Bell was also in excellent form in the semi final when he kept a clean sheet, "turning aside every deadly shot that came his way," as Hurlford beat Kilmarnock Athletic 5-0.

Jamie Bell started his career at Mauchline, before earning a move to Dumbarton, but he was unable to shift the likes of James Macaulay or John McLeod, both Scotland caps and ended up returning to Mauchline, where again his form picked up, although the team's fortunes had dipped. Guesting at Hurlford, he was putting himself in the shop window and it certainly worked when he was approached by Celtic in August 1890, to become the first non Catholic signing by the club. Indeed he may have initially come to Celtic's attention on the 12th January 1889, in our Scottish Cup semi final tie with Dumbarton at Fatal Boghead when he was between the sticks for the home team. We may have won 4-1 but we were suitably impressed to ensure that three of the Dumbarton team, Jamie and Jack Bell, no relation, and Johnny Madden ended up at Celtic.

Our next League match at Celtic Park on 30th August 1890 was against Cambuslang and our new goalkeeper, signed for the one season as they were in those days, as opposed to longer term contracts, received a warm welcome from the Celtic support. He had no time to bask in it, however, as we found ourselves a goal down after 10 minutes into his home debut and so the scoring stayed until the start of the second half.

James Kelly and Jimmy McLaren were both out injured and Willie Groves and Paddy Gallagher were forced to play despite carrying a knock and the bhoys reshuffled our pack at half time with utility player Peter Dowds pushed up front from his usual left half back position. He soon repaid our faith with an equaliser as the Celts took command. With seven minutes left on the clock and despite all our possession the match was still all square at a goal apiece, but finally the floodgates opened with five goals in seven minutes, four of which fell to the bhoys. Peter Dowds put the Celts 2-1 up in the 83rd minute before Barney Crossan scored a third and following a frantic burst of goals in the final three minutes, Dowds scored again for his hat trick and Willie Maley made it five with the visitors scoring with the last kick of the ball to complete the scoring at Celtic 5 Cambuslang 2.

Just as we were building up a head of steam, we only played a further two League matches from September to the end of the year. In a heated battle at Cathkin in front of a 10,000 crowd, we lost 2-1 to Third Lanark in a rough house as Jimmy McLaren was kicked up and down the park. The "Ould Giniral," no shrinking violet himself, was able to defend himself and he responded in kind, with our hard men Mick McKeown, Paddy Gallagher and Jerry Reynolds not slow to join in as tempers rose. The referee, who was offering no protection, was described on the day as "slow, partial and blind," and he didn't ingratiate himself to any of the players when he blew for half time with four minutes still left to play. With the players walking off the pitch as he realised his mistake, he decided to add the four minutes on at the end of the game.

The referee, a former Vale of Leven player, was having a nightmare and the Celtic players were so incensed, they threatened to walk off the pitch after disputing Third's late winner, which the bhoys were convinced had not crossed the line. After a prolonged delay, the goal stood and the match was played to a finish. Thankfully there was less controversy in Paisley as we beat Abercorn comfortably by 5 goals to 1. The home team took a shock lead before two goals by Peter Dowds and one by Hugh Gallagher turned the game in our favour by half time, before Peter Dowds scored another two in the second half to make his total for the day a very satisfactory four goals. Incredibly for the next 16 matches, it was cup games and friendlies that took precedence in the embryonic days of the Scottish League.

Having played 5 League matches, won 3 and lost 2, we would have been satisfied that our points total at this time would be 6 points. Not so. Our first match was considered null and void after Renton were suspended from the League. This of course suited us, as our 4-1 defeat was scrubbed from the books, but worse was to follow when the League Committee deducted Celtic four points for playing new signing Jamie Bell against both Hearts and Cambuslang as two weeks notice had not been given beforehand.

The ruling was clear as the League Committee stated; "A player must be registered 14 clear days before playing in a League fixture and must not during that time, play for any club, whether in the League or out of it. He must absolutely refrain from playing. This fact we trust will be patent to all interested, both players and officials and we hope to see no more infringements of this rule".

Therefore in the first four matches of the Scottish League, Celtic Park witnessed a 4-1 defeat in a game that became null and void, the next week we hosted Cowlairs v Vale of Leven after a request from Cowlairs, (their ground was being intersected by a sewer and their new ground at Cowlairs station wouldn't be ready until September), whilst we played away to Hearts winning 5-0 in a game we were to have both points deducted. The following week, we were back at Celtic Park for a 5-2 win over Cambuslang, which again we were to have both points deducted for playing Jamie Bell!

So after 5 League games played, 1 was null and void, in 2 matches our full points total was deducted and after almost a third of the season, with 18 matches played back then, we sat on 2 points after 4 games. It was even worse for Cowlairs, who after 4 games, had won 1 and drawn 1 and were on minus 1 point, after also being deducted 4 points for fielding an ineligible player.

Confused? So is the author!

For two clubs, Celtic and Cowlairs, to have fallen foul of the new League rules, right at the beginning of the first season was argued to be a simple misunderstanding on the reading of the rules, but this didn't gain us any leniency.

MISTER WILLIAM MALEY, CELTIC FC

The *Scottish Referee*, on the 25th August, gave this profile on Willie Maley;

"A great club is the embodiment of a great idea. The Celtic are such a club and Willie Maley was one of the gentleman who put into place and practical shape a plan long cherished for the formation of the club. The wisdom of the originators of the Celtic is seen in the position the club occupies although it has only been two years in existence. The marvellously rapid progress of the club is due undoubtedly to the playing power of the members who compose the team, but it also attributable to the excellent executive, which since the club's inception has guided it's affairs. Mr Maley is one of the best of those.

Too modest to shine on the field where he always seems to be holding himself in reserve, his light burns brightly in the council chamber. The Celtic, like every other club, require advisors and in Mr Maley it has one of the most judicious, one whose opinions are admired for their soundness, heightened by a manner of expression that commands for them increased respect. Mr Maley is not an orator and thinks before he speaks. He looks soft and pliable but that is only a freak of nature, for he is hard - nay, clear headed - and does not wear eyeglasses.

To people in general he is reserved to the border of indifference; among his friends and clubmates he is familiar, yet dignified. Men of Mr Maley's stamp are a distinct gain to the intellectual side of a physical pastime which is bound to benefit by the connection. He was not born with the proverbial silver spoon in his mouth, but he is a gentleman, because he could be nothing else. Our estimate of his character is thus summed up - mild, mannered, manly Maley".

OUR FIRST MAJOR CUP TIE AGAINST RANGERS

Once again the Scottish Cup threw up a very tasty first round tie at Celtic Park with Rangers the visitors. Having gone all the way to the final of the Scottish Cup in our first season, the Celts had now been drawn against one of the form teams of the 168 teams in the hat two seasons in a row and although the takings from the first round the previous season were huge, it failed to make up for the funds and the prestige a good cup run would make. It would be another blow to the finances of the club, still paying for the new stand on the graveyard side, if we were to lose out on the big money from the blue riband cup two seasons in a row.

Although Rangers' record in the Scottish Cup and in all cup competitions throughout their 18 year history was very poor with only one cup win, they were the early form team in the

League along with Dumbarton. So seriously did the Celtic Committee take this game that we postponed a lucrative friendly match at home to Sunderland on the Monday before the match to give the players more time to prepare and recuperate from any injuries. This was unheard of from the enterprising Celtic Committee.

Just like in the Scottish Cup 1st round the season before, the Celtic support thronged to Celtic Park in numbers seldom seen before in Scottish or English football, then the epicentre of the game. Even allowing for the greater capacity at Celtic Park with the stand on the graveyard side built during the summer, the ground was again bursting at the seams with the crowd given at 16,000, with 6000 more locked out an hour before the kick off. The Celts were missing two key men, James Kelly, though suspension, and Jimmy McLaren through injury with Willie Maley and reserve team captain Willie McCallum stepping in to replace them. Patsy Gallagher, as deputy, took James Kelly's place as captain.

Despite the enforced changes, it was Rangers who were forced to defend from the start with the Celts looking the brightest. First Barney Crossan scored from a header *"amidst indescribable enthusiasm"*, then Peter Dowds scored from a free kick, but both goals were disallowed, one on the word of the referee and the other on the appeal of the Rangers players to one of the umpires, Rangers Committee member, Grant.

Things were getting so heated that Tom Maley, acting as umpire, threw his hat away in the excitement and the Celtic Committee man and regular umpire, William McKillop, ran onto the field on a few occasions, letting his enthusiasm get the better of him. In those days the referee would be appointed from the committee of another Scottish team and would be announced during the week in the build up to the game. The umpires would come from each team playing and so Kennedy from Dumbarton FC was the referee with Tom Maley of Celtic and Grant of Rangers running the lines. It just wouldn't work in today's game!

With the Celts in fine form no one could hold us back and five minutes before half time Willie Groves scored a brilliant goal, *"amid scenes of extraordinary enthusiasm"*, with Committee men Tom Maley waving his flag in jubilation and Joseph Shaughnessy raising his hat to salute the fans packed into the Pavillion stand.

Thankfully this time the goal stood. In the second half the battle ebbed and flowed with the Celts starting the better but also relying on new goalkeeper Jamie Bell to make a save or two at the other end. Willie Maley, at half back, played a great game with Peter Dowds and Johnny Madden providing much of the fire power up front as the Celts deservedly went through to the 2nd round of the Scottish Cup where Carfin Shamrock awaited.

OUR RELATIONSHIP WITH RANGERS FROM THE START

No sooner had the cup tie with Rangers finished, than the first air of sectarianism from the direction of Ibrox raised its ugly head around the fixture. A ridiculous rumour circulated that Thomas Wylie, the Rangers defender, was a Catholic and was got at by his co-religionists in the Celtic team and had subsequently lay down in the match. Wylie was dropped for the next Rangers match, which poured fuel on the fire for the conspiracy theorists that was only dampened when it was revealed that Wylie was a member of the choir at Maybole United Presbyterian Church in deepest Ayrshire!

Now is as good a time as any to look at the early relationship between Celtic and Rangers, which soon hardened along religious lines. Celtic from the very start were an Irish Catholic club, a fact we never hid behind. We were formed by an Irish Marist Brother with the backing of the sharpest minds of the Catholic parishes of the east end who formed the first committee. This committee were comprised of men who already had experience of working together in the various Catholic and Irish political groups in the east end and this was one of the reasons why we hit the ground running. The aims of the club were simple, to raise funds for the Poor Childrens Dinner Tables at the three local parishes and the second aim was to provide a beacon of light for the Irish, to give them something to be proud of and call their own.

There is no reason whatsoever for anyone to be ashamed of the background to our birth, in fact it gives us great pride.

Rangers, on the other hand were formed by a group of rowers fifteen years previously, who rowed up the Clyde from the Gareloch and were inspired by the large numbers of youngsters kicking a ball around Glasgow Green in the early 1870s. Originally they formed a rowing club as well as a football club, before the former made way for the more popular sport of football over the next three years. The Scottish Athletic Journal took up the story on 23rd August 1887;

"Soon after a meeting was held and most of the gentlemen being strangers in Glasgow, with a nice eye to the fitness of things, they dubbed themselves "Rangers".

They were inaugurated in March 1872 and played their first match against Callendar in May of that year in a 0-0 draw. Their rise had much more of a gradual effect as they moved ground three times from Flesher's Haugh on Glasgow Green in 1872 to Burnbank, in Kelvinbridge in the west where they spent one season from 1876, to Kinning Park in the south west, where they signed a 10 year lease in February 1877 and then found themselves homeless in February 1887 after the last match was played there between the Ancients and the Moderns, former and current Rangers players with some guests thrown in.

Six months later after playing home matches at Cathkin, they finally settled at the first Ibrox Park, adjacent to the current ground, coincidentally just three months before work started on the first Celtic Park in November 1887. What Rangers' nomadic existence did bring them, however, was a travelling support from each area they had played in, instead of just one area which many clubs had to rely on. Rangers' 'aloofness,' in comparison to Celtic's humility, our humble working class ethics, was evident at the house warming when they opened Ibrox Park in August 1887, when Tom Vallance spoke of their stay at Kinning Park in the *Scottish Athletic Journal*;

"A certain stigma rested on the club owing to their field being in a locality not of the best, while the spectators of the game were not always of the best description, though they were simply such as the locality could afford. I have known very respectable people come to our matches and not renewing their visit, but that has all gone and I am sanguine that in our new sphere we will be able to attract to our matches thousands of respectable spectators".

It was a statement you would never hear from the Celtic Committee who were much more at ease within our own environment, representing a Celtic support, many of whom came from the toughest Irish ghettos of the old Glasgow slums. Was Rangers' aloofness the mother of their sectarianism? The arrogance which later manifested itself with the "We Are The People," attitude, that they were better than anyone else? Of Rangers previous quarters on Glasgow Green, Burnbank off Great Western Road and in Kinning Park, only Glasgow Green was in close proximity to any large Irish population.

It is strange however that Rangers didn't attract even a small percentage of the tens of thousands of Irish who literally crammed into the slums just east of the city centre from High Street to the Calton in particular, within touching distance of Glasgow Green. Neither did one single player come from that community to play for Rangers. Of course there were many teams playing in the public parks in Glasgow Green around the same time as Rangers were throwing down their jackets for goalposts, but surely there was enough Irish to go round?

At the house warming, the Rangers Committee had wined and dined the local dignitaries and the gentlemen of the press to succulent lamb and it paid off handsomely with the "Ibrox Whispers" columns that started up in the Scottish Athletic Journal, to counter the "Hampden Gossip" columns with their stories of Queens Park as Rangers attempted to woo the Scottish media. Needles to say there were never any "Celtic Stories" columns, although of course, there was plenty of Celtic scandal indulged in.

In contrast to this softening of attitudes towards Rangers, before their move to Ibrox when the press were wined and dined, their match secretary, J W Mackay, in particular, was certainly not flavour of the month with the Scottish Athletic Journal after the AGM in June 1887;

"J W Mackay's partisanship for Rangers when officiating as umpire or referee in their matches became notorious and in the end the crowd would not allow him to stand and other clubs actually refused to enter the field with him. All these are incontrovertible facts".

Bad blood remained between the newspaper and Rangers, much of it stemmed, it was thought from Rangers' refusal to purchase advertising space in the newspaper. Rangers' aloofness was evident again at the opening of the original Ibrox Park in August 1887, when the Scottish Athletic Journal opined of the 8-1 defeat by Preston North End, which had to be stopped before the end after the Rangers support invaded the pitch and Preston's star striker John Goodall was attacked;

"What must have been a very pleasing feature of Saturday's proceedings, to the Rangers, was the very large numbers of the better classes that turned out to see the game. It behoves the Rangers to do everything in their power to retain the patronage of these people, who mostly belong to the district and they can only do so by rigidly keeping the rowdier portion of the crowd in order.

It must be remembered that the ground is in the centre of three or four grades of society - Ibrox, Govan, Plantation and the remaining portions of the town. The Rangers will require to do their best to tone down the behaviour of some of these people to a proper sense of decorum and in this job we are sure they may count on the support of the more intelligent portion of the football loving public and of the press".

"We willingly and heartily join in wishing the Rangers a most successful future in their new habitation but without being thought anxious to throw cold water on their feelings, we must candidly say that we do not think the immediate future looms very bright. No one can say that we are wrong in this opinion after Saturday's display and we are certain the Rangers executive are as conscious of the team's inability as we are and by this time doing their best to set things right".

"Rangers made a sorry mess of themselves and the little demonstration at the close was a gentle hint that the people were disgusted with them".

"Preston North End's secretary, Mr William Sudell referred to the unseemly conduct of the crowd and called upon the press to educate the Glasgow public in the matter of manners".

Mr Sudell was being more than generous. The pitch invasion that saw the match cut short as Rangers were losing 8-1 and the attack on the Preston and England star forward John Goodall couldn't be blamed on the Glasgow public. On this occasion, it was a Rangers problem.

Scottish football in the 1870s was primitive and only burst into life with the arrival of Celtic and our men of vision who led the way in not only pushing through the introduction of the Scottish League in 1890, but in introducing professionalism into the Scottish game in 1893. Queens Park were the Establishment Team, the most successful club in Scotland and one that started in similar fashion to Rangers and most other clubs, in that they were a group of men kicking a ball around a park, at grass roots level, appropriately named Queens Park in 1867, before they formed into a football club.

Queens Park were a "gentleman's club," and you would have to look hard to find a Catholic player amongst its ranks. The club didn't have a sectarian policy per se, it was more a reflection of the social standing of Catholics in the city at the time that they were more likely to band together and play for one of the smaller Irish Catholic clubs which numbered up to forty in the country before Celtic's foundation.

The "country clubs" as they were known, such as Renton, Vale of Leven and Dumbarton were more down to earth, with a local connection, and they had no problem in reflecting that with a number of Catholic players. Other Glasgow clubs like Third Lanark and Partick Thistle had no issues signing Catholics but when we look at Rangers the facts are that the first Catholic to sign for Rangers was Tom Dunbar, signed from Celtic in 1891.

The fact that it took Rangers 19 years to get round to signing a Catholic tells us that they were a sectarian club right from the very start. Why then, when Celtic played our first match on May 28th, 1888, were Rangers chosen as the opponents? Rangers were far from big business at the time, with one trophy in 16 years and not even receiving an invite to play in that season's Charity Cup. Rangers were chosen simply because they had a blank day in their fixtures. Strangely relations between the clubs from the very start was reported as "very friendly" with John H McLaughlin from the Celtic Committee even lending a hand, excuse the pun, playing the piano at the Rangers Musical Association on occasion, the "glee club," which had started up in March 1888.

Rangers may not have signed Catholics but the policy didn't extend to the piano players, it seems.

Was it a case of keeping your friends close and your enemies closer in early relations between the clubs? Rangers would have seen Queens Park, as the standard bearers of Scottish football, take on Celtic from the very start and reap the benefits of becoming our biggest rival with the "native Scots" keen to support a team best positioned to take on the new Irish upstarts.

With the introduction of the Scottish League and Queens Park's decision not to take part, Rangers were given the perfect opportunity to become that club. Furthermore with the introduction of professionalism three years later and again with Queens Park remaining amateur, Rangers were handed a massive boost, clearing the field to become Celtic's main rivals. Just as importantly both clubs were from the same city and so when the religious ingredient was added, the relationship was dynamite.

An early example of this manifested itself on the 22nd September, 1894 after a 5-3 win over Rangers in a particularly tousy affair at Celtic Park, when Celtic players complained of sectarian remarks as they were labelled fenians and papists, not by the Rangers support, but by the Rangers players!

Rangers' fortunes had been transformed by the introduction into the Scottish game of Celtic and throughout the 1890s both clubs cemented their rivalry as the top two clubs in the country, with the explosive mixture of religion thrown into the equation. Celtic had an open policy on signings two years after our foundation but Rangers took nineteen years after their foundation to do likewise. The difference was that Celtic's open policy was exactly that and players were signed on merit. Rangers' "open policy" never extended beyond a handful of players until 1989. Tom Dunbar couldn't get a game for Celtic in 1891 and so it was a natural enough move to turn out for Rangers for one season before returning to Celtic, before sectarianism became a major issue.

Robert G Campbell was an interesting character, being a former Celtic player who went on to become a Rangers Director. He signed for Celtic in 1905 from Queens Park but didn't impress and was transferred to Rangers a year later. After his playing days were over, he joined the Rangers Board.

RANGERS DONATE TO THE CATHOLIC POOR BEFORE CELTIC!

In a little known fact, Rangers provided funds for the Catholic poor before Celtic did, when they played in a "Sunlight match," a game played with artificial lighting to the power of 30,000 candles, known as "Braby's sunlight," provided gratis for the occasion by Fred Braby & Co, who built the original Ibrox, and who were desperate to showcase their new invention. The specially arranged match took place on Thursday 8th March 1888, with a 19.30 kick off against the "Scottish Corinthians," a team made up from the infamous 1888 Scotland team who lost 5-0 at home to England, after losing four goals in eleven minutes before half time.

Match adverts in the newspapers stated underneath;

"Proceeds to be donated to the Govan Local Charities."

A practice match had been played on Tuesday, 21st February to test the suitability of the Braby's sunlight, which were deemed second only to the electric light, with four portable lights placed at each corner of the Ibrox pitch. The experiment was deemed a success and with double as many lights, three on each sideline and one behind each goalmouth, enough light could be given to allow players to train outdoors in the winter months and possibly even allow for matches to be played, although this was still a long, long way ahead.

The proceeds from the Rangers v Scottish Corinthians match made interesting reading and were allocated as following;

Dunoon Convalescent Homes; 15 guineas.
Govan and Kinning Park Poor Childrens Dinners; £10.
Coals for the poor of the burgh of Govan; £5.
Poor children as per Father McBrearty of Saint Anthony's, Govan; £4, 5s.

Ooft, as they say on the internet.

Father McBrearty was a hugely popular Catholic priest and a massive figure in the area, well adept at feeding the poor, no matter what the source, and there was no way he would have sat back and allowed a reputable firm in Fred Braby & Co to set up and organise a Sunlite match without his parish receiving a fair share of the proceeds. It seems even Rangers thought better of ignoring him if they wanted a quiet existence in his parish.

OUR FIRST RUN TO GLASGOW CUP GLORY

20th September 1890 was the date of the 1st round tie between Celtic and Battlefield in the Glasgow Cup, the trophy that we were to claim as our first major victory five months later. Twenty four teams took part in the 1st round of the competition that was second only to the Scottish Cup in importance. The full list of those entries are as follows; Celtic, Queens Park, Third Lanark, Cowlairs, Rangers, Partick Thistle, Clyde, Northern, Glasgow Hibernian, Linthouse, Wanderers, Pollokshaws, Maryhill, Carrington, Battlefield, Thistle, Whitefield, Fairfield, Cathcart, Summerston Athletic, Rutherglen, United Abstainers, Pollokshaws Harp and Cambuslang.

Coincidentally the Celtic Second X1 also drew Battlefield in the 1st round of the Scottish Second X1 Cup in the same week and the aggregate score for the two matches was Celtic 17 Battlefield 1, with the first team winning 7-1 and the Reserves winning by a handsome 10-0.

The first team stormed into a 6-0 lead by half time before taking the foot off the gas in the second half watched by Willie Redmond, the Irish Nationalist MP for Wexford and the younger brother of the leader of the Irish Parliamentary Party, John Redmond. Willie Redmond was a close ally of Charles Parnell and also a close colleague of Michael Davitt, Celtic's Patron.

The combined score of 17-1 in the Cup ties was a perfect example of the quality that we were starting to mould in our reserve team, ready to take their chance when handed an opportunity to impress under Reserve coach and local man, James Curtis of nearby Comelypark Place, Gallowgate. One man who did impress was Johnny Campbell, a prolific goalscorer in the Celtic reserve team and he was given his promotion to the first team, making his competitive debut in the Battlefield match at Celtic Park. The rest as they say is history, with Campbell going on to write a chapter for himself in the history of Celtic with his goalscoring exploits.

Although the season was still at an early stage, our bizarre start to the Scottish League meant that we were already leaving ourselves with considerable work to do following the 2-1 defeat at Third Lanark, the match which had been disturbed on occasion when a game of football broke out amongst the rough house tactics of both sets of players. The early committee had recognised that we would be a target for the hammer throwers of the early game and so ensured that in our team we had men who could not only play, but who knew how to handle themselves and seldom took second prizes.

OUR FIRST MAJOR CUP SHOCK - NEARLY!

With the hard work done in the 1st round of the Scottish Cup against Rangers, the Celts could relax and look forward to a relatively easy match in the next round in comparison, with Carfin Shamrock the visitors to Celtic Park. Or so we thought as the first major shock in the club's short history almost unfolded before our eyes.

The *Glasgow Evening News* opined;

"Another capital game should be witnessed at Celtic Park between the Carfin Shamrock and the Celts. The Parkhead combination has ere now been recruited, and well recruited, from the ranks of the shamrock, and this, I take it, should add a little vim to the game tomorrow. The Celts at the moment are in the full tide of success, and if at all well represented should pull through".

It was our third entry into the Scottish Cup and having got to the final in the first year, we had been knocked out in the 1st round by Queens Park on our second attempt and so the Celts were eager to make our mark at the third time of asking.

Make our mark we nearly did, but in the wrong kind of way as we took things far too easy, with some describing the match as "another act of charity by the Celtic". Johnny Madden put the Celts one up and although everyone in the ground expected an avalanche of goals to follow, it wasn't until the 65th minute before the bhoys scored a second, again through Madden. We then took our foot off the gas, seemingly more intent on not embarrassing our friends from Carfin than finishing the game off and we were nearly made to pay as the visitors got a goal back, then to everyone's surprise, they equalised with six minutes remaining to force a replay in Carfin. To the small Irish town of Carfin, this was akin to their heroes actually lifting the cup itself and there was many a toast drank to that evening as they looked forward to welcoming the big Irish team to Carfin.

Two days before we played the replay in Carfin, we squeezed in a match with Sunderland at Celtic Park with the Wearsiders determined to break their duck against the bhoys, our record standing at played 3 and won 3. The Celts had McPherson from Cowlairs once again guesting in place of Jimmy McLaren but it was Sunderland who started strongly and deservedly went a goal up after 20 minutes. The bhoys were struggling to get our passing game together in front of the large 8000 crowd and just before half time we found ourselves two goals down with a mountain to climb if we wanted to keep our 100% record against the men in the red and white stripes.

The bhoys started the second half much livelier, no doubt after a few choice words at the half time interval, and the bhoys "cannonaded the Sunderland citadel," as one match report stated and Johnny Madden scored in the 50th minute, only to see the goal disallowed for offside. We continued to keep up the pressure, but Sunderland too were determined to hold on and hold on they did, until the 80th minute when Madden scored a tremendous effort to get the bhoys back into the game. With Celtic Park buzzing and every man behind the bhoys in green, Madden brought the house down with another goal with five minutes left on the clock to bring us level in a match described as the fastest and finest match seen in Glasgow that season. We continued to press for the winner but it didn't come and although we hadn't competed our 4th win in a row over Sunderland, we remained unbeaten.

The town of Carfin, with its huge Irish population, crammed as best they could into the Byreknowes Park, the Shamrock club's tiny ground, where 6000 were present for the replay as the bhoys dared not underestimate their opponents again.

This seemed to work and we raced into an early two goal lead through Barney Crossan in the third minute and Peter Dowds shortly after. There was no further scoring until Willie Groves got in on the act in the 55th minute to make it three as the bhoys stuck to the task before Breslin scored a consolation goal for the Shamrock to finish the scoring at Carfin Shamrock 1 Celtic 3 in front of a wildly enthusiastic crowd.

"COOKING" THE BOOKS?

As explained elsewhere, in the days before professionalism, it was common practice for players to be given inducements to play for a club, inducements that were often "skimmed off" the official attendance given or filed in the accounts under lost time. In other words payments were legally given to cover hours that players had to take leave from their work to play matches.

Celtic, having already had a few run-ins with the governing body of the SFA, would be well aware that any slip ups would allow that body a chance to hammer the club, therefore the books would have to be in tip top condition ready for inspection. That inspection arrived in September, 1890 when all 45 clubs were asked to hand over their books to the Professional Committee of the SFA within one week. Only two clubs failed to comply, Celtic and Glasgow Hibernian, the latter were in the death throes of extinction, whilst the Celts put forward a very good reason. The Treasurer who held the books had suffered fever in his house and so the books would have to be handed over to the Sanitary Authorities for disinfection before they could possibly be given to the SFA for fear of infection. A doctor's line backed up the story and the books duly arrived a few days later with no issues raised.

One alleged tactic used by the Celtic Committee to entice players was to transfer the certificate of a public house to their name, thus giving the player a full time employment as the nominal proprietor, not involving hard labour. It was one that would also guarantee the custom of the huge Irish support who followed Celtic and who at the same time were not averse to a few refreshments in the company of the landlord who would pour pints during the week and play for their heroes at the weekend.

The average rent of some of the public houses was £80 per annum which compared to the rent of Celtic Park which was £50 per annum. The big conflict lay with the Catholic Church who were disgusted by the contradiction in the club making charitable donations whilst at the same time taking advantage of one of the biggest curses in the area, the supply of the demon drink. Of course if Celtic players were not involved in the licensed trade, it would not disappear overnight and so it was seen as a means to an end, albeit far from being a universally popular one.

James Kelly, the Celtic captain held the license for a public house roughly where the Kent Bar now stands on Springfield Road, near to the original Celtic Park so fans could literally fall out the pub before kick off, cross the road and enter the ground. What a goldmine that was.

Within a few weeks of Michael Dunbar being refused a transfer of license at 429 Gallowgate with the reason given the fact that he already held the license for a pub in Coatbridge and William Groves being refused a license at 22 Taylor St, Townhead, Celtic donated £24, 10s, 8d to the Poor Childrens' Dinner Table fund at the parish of Sacred Heart in Bridgeton, one of the Poor Childrens' Dinner Tables we were set up to fund. The club also made a £20 donation to Father Hughes of Sacred Heart for his efforts in setting up a library for the Catholic patients at Belvidere Hospital.

If Celtic didn't take advantage of well meaning supporters who would lease public houses in players names, would it have stopped those intent on indulging in the demon drink? Of course it wouldn't so in a vicious circle where drink was being consumed, Celtic could at least argue that money was being donated to charity from the profits of the club.

CELTIC - A MODERN FRANKENSTEIN!!

The *Scottish Sport*, reacting to the club's gathering success on the field of play dedicated their editorial on Friday, October 31st 1890 to have an astonishing swipe at Celtic, comparing us to a modern Frankenstein no less, and even referring to a very vague "rumour" that Archbishop Eyre had asked his clergy a cryptic "question" which, they suggested, may be more easier evaded than answered.

Frankenstein was a grotesque monster of a man set up in a scientific experiment gone wrong. It's not recorded if his inventor sued the Scottish Sport for this scandalous comparison to a football club in the east end of Glasgow, founded by a Marist Brother, who donated much of their profits to charitable institutions.

"There are black spots upon the fair economy of football, and one of the most hideous and objectionable of

these is the prostitution of the game to suit the business interest of publicans. We have been told again and again, when we have shown a disposition to look into the business affairs of those who, when they appear in public, it is our duty to criticse, that we are overstepping our ground and that our interference in matters that do not concern us is nothing short of gross impertinence. We like to have people rate us after that fashion, because it is a sure sign that our strictures are having effect.

All are fish that come to our net and while we have not the slightest desire to touch upon the private affairs of those who in a pubic sense come within the sweep of our pen, we cannot allow them to escape criticism when their private affairs interfere with the progress and purity of a sport which we have always tried to maintain in integrity and virtue.

In the light of the proceedings that took place in the Licensing Court the other day, when William Groves, the Celtic centre forward, was refused a transfer licence for a public house situated at 22 Taylor Street, the Parkhead club must now occupy a very anomalous and unenviable position in public opinion. We can compare the club to nothing but a modern Frankenstein; some of its aspects are most fair, others are most repulsive. On the one hand the club dispenses with the lily hand of charity succour to the sick and portion to the poor; on the other hand it watches indifferently, if it does not encourage, its young men throwing themselves recklessly into a business of which every tendency is toward moral ruin.

Of all the clubs in Scotland, the Celtic is perhaps best supplied with publican players and a strange feature of the matter is that these players have only been publicans since they joined the Celtic. We do not mean to insinuate that the Celtic had anything to do with the placing of the men in public houses; where the necessary capital came from to start the men we care not. What we desire to get at is the moral aspect of this football-publican business. This brings us back to the Celtic again. There is no club in the country in which so many interests combine and which is composed of such a great variety of social atoms. One of the club's avowed objects is charity and we have seen from the patronage and interest bestowed upon the club by the Roman Catholic clergy that other and equally commendable purposes actuate, or are supposed to actuate, the members.

It is wrong that a business, such as the publican business, should feed and support itself to the detriment of a fair and honourable sport; it is iniquitous that a club professing charity and many kindred virtues should tolerate, far less countenance, the adoption of the public house trade by its players. The evidence - for and against -submitted at the hearing of Groves' application is a most damaging reflection upon the mental condition of those who can throw aside an honest calling to lure others to drink. The objectors in the Groves case are credited with assuming that because a man is a football player, he must be some sort of blaggard not capable of taking care of a public house. How do our football publicans, smiling graciously from behind their counters, like even the suggestion of such a supposition?

The player-publican, with isolated exceptions is nothing but a decoy and a most miserable morality grabbing decoy at that. We remember many years ago calling upon a player at his place of business - a public house where he was a bar tender. It was a Saturday evening and the place was reeking with the stench of filthy human beings, filthy liquor and equally as filthy tobacco. Our friend, the player, had distinguished himself in the afternoon and in consequence was the object of much attention from those in the bar. There were men in that dirty crowd so mad with drink and enthusiasm that they refused to touch a drop that was not served by the player, who, if he had any human feelings in him must have sickened at the loathsome eulogiums passed upon him as a man and a player. The landlord stood in a corner, his eyes full of glee and his fingers playing the devil's tattoo on his well filled pocket.

This is not an overdrawn picture and the worst of it, is it can be seen in twenty places in Glasgow on any Saturday night you choose. It is to be wondered at then, that a rumour has gone abroad that Archbishop Eyre, the head of the Roman Catholic church in Glasgow, has asked those of this clergy who have supported and patronised the Celtic club a question which , may be more easily evaded than answered? We do not desire that religion should suffer by what we have written on this matter, or what we may write, but we expect that religion, should it so far forget itself as to neglect it's functions, will not, at least, shake hands with the devil and encourage him in his work".

TOM DUFF DISCUSSES TERMS WITH BLACKBURN ROVERS

Meanwhile Tom Duff travelled to Blackburn to discuss signing terms with the Rovers, who were already well served with professional goalkeepers. Duff was the Cowlairs keeper who was guesting for Celtic at the end of the season before the Celtic Committee eventually signed Jamie Bell from Dumbarton in a rushed deal after the season had started. It seems that Duff was confident of his worth as he dictated terms with Blackburn Rovers, asking for a £100 signing on fee and £3 per week and even refusing to play in a trial match to prove his worth. Not surprisingly Blackburn turned down the chance to take him up on his generous offer, but the fact that he refused to accept less favourable terms indicated that he wasn't exactly left penniless by Cowlairs.

This point was of course missed by the press, who were happy enough to devote half a page editorial on the subject of Celtic and player remuneration, but couldn't bring themselves to a line or two to point out the irony in Tom Duff's return from Blackburn empty handed to turn out for Cowlairs, no doubt the club he had always wanted to play for.

OUR FIRST RUN TO GLORY CONTINUES

The 2nd round of the Glasgow Cup again brought the Celts a favourable draw, with a trip to Northern at Hydepark where the Celts were hot favourites to progress. Once again however the underdog put up a brave fight and even took a one goal lead into half time before we came back to win 2-1, thanks to an equaliser from Peter Dowds and a late winner from Willie Groves. Elsewhere, Third Lanark knocked out Queens Park, which was good news for our chances of lifting the trophy.

The quarter final of the Glasgow Cup brought a sterner test, with neighbours Clyde the visitors to Celtic Park. The memory of the protested 1-0 Scottish Cup tie at Celtic Park when Clyde were forced to replay the match, two seasons previous, was still fresh in the mind and no doubt Clyde were intent on revenge.

Intent they may have been but the Celts, minus Willie Groves, were determined to get their hands on the trophy. Clyde started well but were severely hampered when Cullen had to go off injured, leaving them a man short up front. The Celts took advantage of the extra man and Peter Dowds scored the first recorded back heel in a Celtic jersey to open the scoring after half an hour. Johnny Madden added a second before half time to put the bhoys firmly in control and he then notched his second at the start of the second half, before Dowds did likewise and the Celts coasted into the semi final with a 5th added before the final whistle. In the end, the bhoys short passing game at pace outwitted Clyde's old fashioned long ball game.

The *Scottish Referee* on 3rd November gave this witty observation during their match report;

"Several of the clergy patronised their favourites and were as enthusiastic and jubilant at the victory as the every day footballer. One portly clergyman, who sat next to me in the "box" evinced, (revealed), his enthusiasm at the first goal in a rather "striking" or kicking manner, as my favourite corn unfortunately knows today".

The priceless picture conjured up of the portly clergyman letting his enthusiasm get the better of himself by imitating Dowds' first goal with a back heel straight into the unfortunately positioned journalist's corn does not fail to raise a laugh over 125 years later!

Pure, beautiful, inventive back heel by the man of the cloth.

The draw was favourable for us in the other quarter final matches in that it paired Third Lanark with Rangers, which meant that one of the better teams would have to bid farewell to the competition. A 3-3 draw in the first match meant a replay at Ibrox and Rangers continued their horrendous cup record by losing the match. The semi final draw kept Celtic and Third Lanark apart with Celtic paired against Partick Thistle and Third Lanark drawing Cambuslang. Having drawn Queens Park and Rangers in the trophy already, Third Lanark would have been delighted to avoid Celtic.

The 22nd November 1890 was the date and all roads normally would have led to Celtic Park for the big match. Unfortunately the weather wasn't favourable and only 2000 souls braved the heavy wind and rain storms to watch from the uncovered stands and terracing. Playing against the wind and rain, it took us all our time to work the ball up the park, trying to keep the ball on the ground, but it was Partick Thistle who got the first goal. Through sheer determination, the Celts got back into the game with two goals by Barney Crossan before half time and both sets of players were happy to get inside the pavillion at half time to get out of the storm.

The Celtic backroom team were known to have fresh strips prepared for the players in such horrendous conditions and so the Celts were prepared to go back into the storm in the second half with a renewed vigour and fresh strips, with no sign of any abatement to the wind and rain. A cart load of cut hay was laid on the pitch to assist the players' footing on the mud and the match remained a contest until twenty minutes to go when the Thistle keeper had to come off injured. There followed no let up in our play as Johnny Campbell hit two goals and Peter Dowds another as we battled successfully against the elements to win by 5 goals to 1.

Johnny Campbell soon replaced Willie Groves as the darling of the Celtic support, after the latter's itchy feet finally got the better of him and he signed professional terms with West Bromwich Albion. The timing of the signing, after he had been refused a licence for an establishment in Townhead, was no coincidence.

Protests were the norm back in the early days when a club could make it official before, during or after the match. The most common reason was an unplayable pitch, but on this occasion Thistle protested not only on the state of the pitch, but against the inclement Glasgow weather!

Surprisingly, there was already a precedent set when a Third Lanark v Rangers match was replayed but on this occasion the protest was not supported and the date for the final between Celtic and Third Lanark was set for 14th February, after originally being set for December 13th, then changed to 24th January.

The *Scottish Sport* gave a great insight into the mind of their hack, dressed in a tweed suit, hat, boots, collar, cuffs, scarf, gloves, walking stick and carrying a ginger beer flask, who travelled east to Celtic Park in the rainstorm that limited the crowd to a couple of thousand brave souls who were afforded no protection from the relentless downpour;

"As I climbed down, (the office fire escape), with a Parnellesque agility, I thought of Ireland and Home Rule, and instinctively my feet took me in the direction of Celtic Park. Having no desire to be washed out to Parkhead, I got on board a car and we floated along quite gaily and in very quick time too - for a Glasgow tramcar - to Parkhead Toll. The objectionable part of the journey dated from there as I had to wade the rest of the way.

When I got beneath the roof of the press stand I shook myself out of the many folds into which the rain had brought me and took a look around. There were some almost motionless objects massed around the ropes and on the stand. These I took to be human beings and believers in the efficacy of the "water cure". I was in need of some other sort of cure, but though I was among plenty of Irish, what I wanted was not to be found. When the officials were satisfied the game could go on without the aid of life buoys, the players took to the field - or rather as much as would stick to the soles of their boots and they could conveniently carry. I may also remark that although they did not use the life buoys they were pretty lifeless "bhoys" ere it was all over.

The Celts had to play against the wind and rain in the first half and they never got such a washing in all their lives. They started by losing a goal, but when they had sufficient water to suit their tastes they played, as an Irishman elegantly put it "Like the devil in a shebeen on a Sunday". Young Crossan got two nice goals before half time and when they took the other end of the field Campbell slapped on a couple and Dowds closed the account with a fifth. The Thistle were all this time doing their very best but their very best was not nearly good enough.

On such fearful ground, I have never seen such clever forward play as the Celts showed on Saturday. Every man jack of them revelled in the mud like a schoolboy and the backs were not one whit behind those in front. Some people would like us to think that McLaren's retiral from the game is a sad loss to the Celts, but these people only have to see Willie Maley at his best to be for ever shut up. When they are at it, they should take a peak at Mick McKeown. On Saturday, McKeown, in a pair of white pants and an old jersey that was faded almost to the point of goneness, was a sight for gods and men.

To those clubs who are still in the running for the Glasgow Cup and have hopes of reaching the final, I say;

"Beware of the day,
When the Celts shall meet you in battle array"

HIBS EVICTED FROM EASTER ROAD

Hibs' very existence was in doubt when in November 1890, the Trinity Hospital Trust who leased land to Hibs to build their Easter Road ground on, decided to extend their grounds and building work on Easter Road was commenced. The Hibs Committee were well aware that they would have to make provisions for such an outcome but they failed to bid high enough for Logie Green, the old ground of Edinburgh Saint Bernards which was less than two miles north west in the Powderhall area of Edinburgh. Hibs were now facing homelessness, but the committee failed to act quick enough in the circumstance.

St Bernards were the third force in Edinburgh at the time and went on to win the Scottish Cup in 1895 and build New Logie Green, adjacent to the original ground and it became the only ground to host a Scottish Cup Final outside Glasgow on 14th March, 1896 when Hearts beat Hibs 3-1 in front of a crowd of 16, 034.

As an aside, "Darlin" Willie Groves was back playing for his first club, Hibs, in 1896 but couldn't replicate his winner in the 1887 Scottish Cup Final for Hibs against Dumbarton, although he did score their only goal on this occasion. Alex King who scored for Hearts went on to sign for Celtic after no doubt first being noticed by the Celtic Committee when he scored a hat trick against us in a League match at Celtic Park on 14th September, 1895 when Hearts beat Celtic 5-0, a score line which remains our record home defeat, in a competitive match. Strangely just six weeks later we were to record our biggest ever win to date, with a resounding 11-0 win over Dundee on 26th October.

In November, 1890, the future of Hibernian Football Club remained in serious doubt.

DUNDEE HARP "REMODELLED"

Dundee, similar to Glasgow and Edinburgh had a large Irish Catholic contingent, many of whom gave their support to local team Dundee Harp, who were formed in 1879 and who played in the local and regional competitions as well as the Scottish Cup. The most famous story concerning the club was their 35-0 win over Aberdeen Rovers in the 1st round of the Scottish Cup on 12th September 1885, thereby giving them a world record until it was discovered, incredibly on the same day, that Arbroath had beaten another Aberdeen team, Bon Accord 36-0 in the Scottish Cup too. Ironically the referee in the Dundee Harp game originally had the score as 37-0, but the Harp Secretary noted he had only recorded 35 goals and so his score line was recorded.

On 26th November 1890 a meeting of the club was held, presided over by Monsignor Clapperton and with other clergy present, it was decided that the club "would in future be conducted on the same principal as Celtic". A telegram from Celtic was read out wishing the Harp every success in its new management. The Celtic Committee were on very good terms with Dundee Harp and had been very grateful to them for playing in only our second ever game on 9th June 1888 at Celtic Park when Dundee Harp went well out of their way to bring a team to Glasgow in the close season.

There was no suggestion that Dundee Harp were being re-organised along the lines of a feeder club for Celtic but in hindsight, this may well have suited both clubs down to the ground. The choice of players was restricted to Irishmen and players of Irish extraction, which was how the club were previously run throughout their most successful period. Over the next few weeks a new Committee was set up with two Catholic priests, Father Holder and Father Harris, in place as Honorary Presidents and James Diamond, their former Secretary, brought back to his previous role.

The reaction in the *Scottish Sport* was interesting;

"With such a large Irish constituency as that to be found in Dundee, we can imagine no better field for a first class Irish team, and with the influence of the Roman Catholic clergy at its back, its sectarian success can almost be assured".

Again this is an example of a group of Irishmen forming an Irish club and it is seen by the media as a perfectly normal thing to do. However this opinion changed in an editorial in the same newspaper just three days later;

"While we welcome the reconstruction of the Harp, we are sorry that it has been deemed advisable to run the management under the patronage of the church. We do not believe in clubs formed in sectarian lines; it does the cause of religion more harm than good and it brings the charity and humanity of sport into a narrow channel for the outflow of tolerance and the coarse feelings of our everyday life. The Harp, by following the lines of Celtic, are introducing into Dundee and the north of Scotland, a phase of football which we happen to know does not have the sanction of some of the finest and most Catholic minds of the Romish church".

Such a strong outburst, one would think, would be balanced across the board to include clubs with a sectarian signing policy such as Rangers, but sadly, this remained elusive.

Dundee Harp's record in the Scottish Cup was modest in their nine attempts, with two 1st round exits, two 2nd round exits, three 3rd round exits, with a 4th round exit in 1885/86 followed by a 5th round exit the following season, their best attempts. In the Harp's best cup run in season 1886/87, they drew the mighty Dumbarton in the last 16, before withdrawing from the tournament amid a controversy that was to have a serious effect on the club's stability. (More on this shortly). Dumbarton went on to play Hibs in the final, losing 2-1 in the match that was to prove to Brother Walfrid that an Irish team could be successful and at the same time raise funds to feed the poor.

Just two seasons later Celtic made our debut in the same tournament, one of 13 Irish teams amongst the 158 entered to play for Scotland's top prize. The following is the full list of the 26 Irish teams to have played in the Scottish Cup; Celtic, Hibs, Dundee Hibs, Glasgow Hibs, Springburn Hibs, Paisley Hibs, Cambuslang Hibs, Hamilton Hibs, Vale of Leven Hibs, Campsie Hibs, Smithston Hibs, Edina Hibs, Carfin Shamrock. Broxburn Shamrock, Motherwell Shamrock, Whifflet Shamrock, Kirkintilloch Harp, Leith Harp, Dundee Harp, Hamilton Harp, Johnstone Harp, Pollokshaws Harp, Duntocher Harp, Erin Rovers (Perth), Erin Rovers (Bathgate) and St Peter's (Partick).

It's interesting to look at the effect Celtic's formation had on other Irish clubs in Scotland and although the effect on Hibs is well documented, albeit with the acknowledgement that they were already on the decline, Dundee Harp too had seen better days before our arrival. The cause of their downward spiral brought great controversy and it involved their great run to the 5th round of the Scottish Cup in season 1886/87. The last 16 draw gave them a tough tie away to Dumbarton and with no hope of causing an upset, as well as the costs involved in travelling to Dumbarton, the committee decided to scratch, (withdraw). Instead of doing so gracefully however, the committee came up with a plan to offer Dumbarton a £20 guarantee to play a friendly with Dundee Harp in Dundee, which they agreed to do.

All fine and well and above board, but what they didn't do was to notify the supporters and even their own players that the match was being played as a friendly and not a last 16 Scottish Cup tie as the adverts for the game blasted out! As often happens on these occasions when a plan is thought up, whatever can go wrong, will go wrong and Dundee Harp put up an enormous fight on the day to gain a fantastic 2-2 draw and to earn a replay at Dumbarton.

When the replay didn't happen, the plan was rumbled and the locals, as well as the SFA were none too pleased, in fact they were up in arms. Dumbarton were quickly cleared of any wrong doing and the finger of guilt was pointed at the Secretary of Dundee Harp, James Diamond. The Secretary, however, was quick to put his case forward in the *Scottish Athletic Journal*;

"Regarding the football match, Dumbarton v Harp, said to be a 5th round Scottish Cup tie, it being currently reported in Dundee and elsewhere that I was the sole offender in the arrangements for the above match, I hereby beg to offer an explanation so that the public can judge for themselves who was really to blame in the matter.

At a Committee meeting of the Harp FC - the presiding officer - after a considerable amount of talk, it was agreed to scratch in favour of Dumbarton on condition that a friendly game should be played in Dundee instead, with a guarantee of £20 to the visitors should the gate prove a failure. The Dumbarton, having accepted this arrangement, I was authorised to have the bills printed, and on no consideration was I allowed by the Harp's executive to keep the words "5th round Scottish Cup tie" out of those bills.

Having thus carried out my instructions from the Committee, I think the public should put the saddle on the proper horse".

The *Scottish Athletic Journal*, in turn, offered sympathy to the Secretary in the whole sorry affair;

"Mister Diamond has long been the Harp's Secretary and he has had not a little to do in bringing about the great success which has attended the efforts of the club. We are sure that it will not be long before Mister Diamond will be reinstated in the office which he filled so worthily. We fancy the shoe would have fitted better had the Secretary of the second eleven been suspended instead of Mister Diamond. Looking at it in any way, the whole affair brings great discredit to the Harp".

In the following witch hunt, the full Harp committee, including Secretary James Diamond, were forced to stand down. With the support disgusted at being hoodwinked by the committee, Dundee Harp's crowds plummeted to around 1000 and on the next visit of Dumbarton to the city, only 200 turned up for one of the biggest attractions of the season. It's just as well not too many were inconvenienced, as the pitch was covered in thawing ice and the Harp didn't tell the visitors they had brought the usual kick off time of 12.45 forward thirty minutes, so when Dumbarton turned up just before the assumed kick off time, the Harp had already called the match off, refunded the fans and informed them that Dumbarton had failed to turn up!

In the aftermath, nine Harp players were then "ghosted" south, at the behest of agents with bags of gold working for English clubs, who were a great threat to clubs north of the border before professionalism came in. The club then decided to play a mixture of Scots and Irish players as the production line of promising young Irish players on the east coast, not as dependable as it was on the west coast, was drying up. This policy however was to change on the 26th November 1890, at the meeting at which it was decided that the club was "to be conducted on the same principal as Celtic".

Dundee Harp failed to regain a level of success and were suspended by the SFA in 1894 for failure to pay match guarantees to visiting teams. A fortnight later Dundee Hibernian were formed and they changed their name to Dundee Harp in 1896 before going bust a year later. It's worth pointing out that the Dundee Hibernian who were formed in 1909 and changed their name to Dundee United in 1923 had no connection to the Dundee Hibernian who were formed in 1894, after Dundee Harp's demise.

OUR SCOTTISH CUP RUN CONTINUES

Meanwhile the Celts' Scottish Cup run was at the quarter final stage with a tough draw away to Dumbarton, who led the League race. Following our defeat of Rangers and Carfin Shamrock, we faced a trip to Wishaw to play Thistle of that ilk and on paper the biggest trouble we faced was from the train company which delayed our arrival at the packed ground by half an hour. After an even start to the match as both sides sized each other up, Peter Dowds put the Celts one up after 20 minutes and Johnny Madden followed that up with a second to give us a two goal lead by half time. Further goals by Johnny Campbell and Johnny Madden put the bhoys on easy street before Leslie joined in the fun hitting the ball into his own net to give the Celts an unassailable five goal lead. Wishaw Thistle then scored the next two goals at the correct end before the bhoys finished the scoring, 6 goals to 2 in our favour.

A trip to Dundee was next out the hat and a game against Our Boys on the 8th November. West Craigie Park in Dundee was the furthest Celtic had travelled to date in a competitive match and the Dundee Irish, (no doubt with a sizeable number from Dundee Harp), made sure there was plenty of encouragement for the bhoys in green. In fact no Scottish Cup ties were played in Glasgow in the 4th round ties for the first time ever with all three teams remaining, Celtic, Queens Park and Third Lanark all drawn away.

The *Evening Times* gave a flavour of the Celtic support with the story of an Irishman who joined the train at Perth which took the players and fans to Dundee;

"When the Glasgow team reached Perth, a number of enthusiasts came aboard for Dundee. Among them was a lively, garrulous, (excessively talkative!), old Irishman, who loudly proclaimed that, though he had never seen the Celtic play, he had, sly old dog, consistently backed them in all their engagements and had made money thereby. This old boy seemed to know a thing or two, because he wound up a smart bit of personal history by declaring that after seeing with his own eyes the Celtic play today, he would be prepared to die".

As was oft times our wont in similar matches around this time, frustratingly, the Celts were slow starters and found ourselves a goal down early in the game, but we quickly rallied, as was also our wont, and scored three goals in quick succession before half time. Johnny Coleman scored the first, before Barney Crossan scored two goals in as many minutes. Heavy rain fell throughout the game but it had no effect on the bhoys "scientific" play, with shot after shot fired at Our Boys' goal, but the home team did well to keep the score down and so it ended, their boys 1, our bhoys 3. The home team's committee may not have had the greatest imagination when thinking up a name for the team, but Mr McCulloch from Our Boys was a great ally to Celtic and also Hibernian in SFA circles when we looked for a friend in a friendless place.

Our Boys protested the result, due to the weather and the condition of the muddy ground, (their own ground), but they didn't manage to send the protest in time so it wasn't heard. With another large crowd guaranteed for any replay, it was a tactic often used by smaller teams. Dumfries Wanderers' protest to have their Scottish Cup tie replayed against Morton after their 6-4 defeat due to one of the Morton players changing his jersey at half time was surely taking things to the extreme.

A very interesting tie took place in the next round with another away draw, this time at Royal Albert from Larkhall. The town, in those days was populated by mining or the labouring classes and the Celtic players were guaranteed a "warm" welcome when they arrived in the Lanarkshire village on the 12.30 train from Glasgow Central, accompanied by John Glass, John O'Hara, Tom Maley and also James Kelly, who wasn't fit enough to play.

The match was played on 29th November at Raploch Park, Larkhall, just a week after the wind and rainstorms that swept across Celtic Park in our Glasgow Cup semi final against Partick Thistle and so as a precaution the Celtic Committee telegraphed the home team to ascertain the condition of the pitch. "Ground in fair order, come out" was the reply from the Royalists and so the Celtic party made their way to Glasgow Central train station.

On arrival in Larkhall, they discovered that "Ground in fair order, come out" translated as "Hard pitch covered in frost with a thin layer of snow on top, stay in the house and light the fire." Immediately James Kelly pronounced the pitch unplayable for a cup tie but after a lengthy discussion agreed that a friendly, lasting thirty minutes each way could be played instead, with the crowd of 3000 already gathered. In truth, the pitch wasn't even playable for a friendly and both sets of players kept well away from each other, which was a wise decision, as one mistimed tackle in the conditions could lead to injury. In the event the tame bounce match finished with two goals apiece.

The *Scottish Sport's* report on the match contained more detail about the reporter's train journey than the actual match itself and was written in the non politically correct, if highly amusing, verse of the day:

"They, (the train company), very considerably provide entertainment, by the way, in the shape of big clod hopping Irishmen, full of Parnell and bad whisky, who thrust themselves into the seclusion of your cosy "first" and turn your head white with their brogue and blasphemy. On Saturday evening on the way home and at Cambuslang, two of these boys dropped into my compartment in company with a gust of air that

froze the marrow in my spine and a stench of alcohol and narcotic stimulants that melted the frost on the window panes. Of course they talked about Parnell. If their opinions are at all indicative of the mind of the Irish people, then the uncrowned one may as well pass in his checks at once".

As was common place back in the day, the Celtic Committee offered the Royal Albert £30 to play the replay at Celtic Park as they doubted the Larkhall pitch would be ready even in a week's time, given the weather conditions. Royal Albert turned down the opportunity of the cash incentive and a slice of the larger home gate at Celtic Park to maintain home advantage. And so the match was replayed a week later at the same ground, in front of an even larger crowd of 5000 and the Celts once again arrived on the 12.30 train from Glasgow Central and were met at Larkhall station by a three piece Italian band playing the hornpipe, accordion and engaging in dancing which entertained the bhoys immensely.

To the match itself and we were soon coasting after two early goals from Johnny Campbell and Jimmy McLaren, before Campbell scored again just before half time. Back in the day, the players were given one minute for a refreshment at half time before the game restarted and Johnny Madden added a fourth in the second half as the Celts strolled to a 4-0 victory. However with 12 minutes remaining there was a pitch invasion, not a rare occurrence in those days in such cramped grounds, but this one stopped the game and after two attempts to clear the field were unsuccessful by both sets of players along with the full might of the Larkhall police force, (two coppers), the players were led off the pitch before the final portion of the game could be completed.

Royal Albert protested the game, citing that the last 12 minutes were not played. The referee, a Mr McLean then gave his opinion on the reason for the pitch invasion, stating that the home fans had been enraged by a tackle by Jerry Reynolds on Clelland which left the Royal Albert player winded. He clearly stated that "the home supporters refused to leave the field as they wanted the Albert to get another chance". Surely this evidence was clear enough for the SFA Committee not to give the pitch invaders exactly what they wished for? Don't bet on it.

The referee also reported Tom Maley, who was acting as an umpire at the match when he struck Frame, a Royal Albert player, on the right side of the head with his flag after Frame had tripped Johnny Madden. An apology from Tom Maley, immediately after the incident, was accepted by the referee and no further action was taken by the committee after it was stated that Maley had tried to split up Madden and Frame and was struck on the mouth by Frame, before acting in self defence.

Incredibly, the SFA President, Mr Tom Park then stated that the game should be replayed and stated the only decision was the destination of the replayed match. Royal Albert were accused directly by Celtic of pre-arranging the pitch invasion in an effort to get another game they had little chance of winning just to swell their balance books. It was also argued that the home team were responsible for the conduct of the fans, therefore the match should be replayed at Celtic Park.

The feeling was expressed that no set of supporters should be rewarded for invading the pitch in an attempt to have a match replayed but this was countered with the claim that it couldn't be stated for definite which set of fans invaded the pitch! Why would the Celtic support invade the pitch when we were winning 4-0? It made no sense, but in the end the replay was ordered to be replayed, bizarrely at Ibrox Park and on the very next day, with one day's notice of the decision!

Celtic requested in that case, that the proceeds from the match should be donated to charity, but the SFA ruled the decision was outwith their remit and so after three matches, Celtic finally beat Royal Albert 2-0 at Ibrox Park on 13th December, (the date originally set for the Glasgow Cup Final), to go forward to the quarter final of the Scottish Cup where Dumbarton waited patiently.

As can often be the case when teams get too familiar with each other's styles when playing too many times in a short space of time, the match was a dull one which only livened up in the second half when the Celts came to life. We got our reward in the 50th minute when Barney Crossan got on the end of a corner to give the bhoys the lead we deserved, but it wasn't until near the end that the tie was put to bed with Johnny Campbell netting a second to finish the scoring at 2-0 to Celtic with Royal Albert not feeling so flush.

In a footnote to the whole episode, the actions of Royal Albert protesting for a replay were compared to their actions in a similar situation, when they led 1-0 against Carfin Shamrock with five minutes remaining when a pitch invasion occurred after a set to between Frame, again, of Royal Albert and Clifford, who was to go on to play for Celtic. The game was stopped short but on this occasion Royal Albert claimed the tie!

And so to "Fatal" Boghead we travelled by train on the 20th December to a snow covered Dumbarton to play the quarter final of the Scottish Cup. A pitch inspection was made around noon and the decision was announced that if the snow was cleared the match would go ahead. This duly happened and an announcement was then made, but the crowd was limited due to the difficulties in spreading the word at a late stage.

Despite the late notice, many Celtic supporters travelled by train to Dumbarton sporting their shamrock adorned cards in their hat bands with the words "Play Up, Celtic."

When the teams took to the pitch, James Kelly made it known that he deemed the pitch unplayable and lodged a protest. The referee thought the pitch was playable and the game went ahead despite the Dumbarton captain agreeing with Kelly. Just 60 seconds later the Celts were a goal down as we struggled to adapt to the bone hard conditions. Dumbarton were the better team on the day and with Jerry Reynolds taken off injured and the bhoys down to ten men, the home team added two second half goals to avenge the Celts' Scottish Cup semi final defeat of Dumbarton two seasons previous. Some Dumbarton fans ran on the pitch near the end, but fortunately, they were quickly cleared from the field and the match was allowed to finish.

The matter was not over and Celtic followed up on our protest which was made before the match by our captain, James Kelly. No mention was made of the pitch invasion near the end and due to the festive season, the date set for the protest to be heard wasn't until after the New Year.

PRESS LAUNCH ANOTHER ATTACK ON PLAYERS IN THE DRINK TRADE

On the 21st November, the *Scottish Sport* again used its editorial to launch another attack on the perfectly legal case of supporters with contacts in the drink trade, offering a player a nominal proprietorship of a public house. It guaranteed its instant success as it would be heavily patronised by supporters of that club and at the same time, the player would be rewarded for his perfectly legal occupation.

Not surprisingly, the Sport used the example of Willie Groves departure to West Bromwich Albion after being refused the lease of a pub in Townhead.

"Our recent strictures on the player-publican question have not borne much fruit and we are therefore compelled to return to the charge, booted and spurred, as it were. We cannot for the life of us understand why the Association should not undertake this question. It is a deep one, it is true, and its ramifications are not easily compassed, but surely the ruling body is under some obligation to make enquiry into the matter when we remember that this intimate relationship with and close identification of the public house with the football field is ruining the morale of the game and in transforming the fair virtues of a manly sport into hideous and contaminating vices?

In the early days of professionalism in England, it was the habit to blazon forth upon the destructive tendencies of the life of the football pro, principally on account of the fact that the pro had then a double occupation - he was a boniface by night and a player by day. Very few Scotch players now in England occupy public houses, simply because the clubs find it cheaper to pay for their talent through the hand instead of through the till. We could not care to say that the latter is the method adopted by those of our clubs who have men employed in public houses, but, like the canny Highlander of the tale, we have our "thochts". Any suspicions we may have are well founded and are built upon as logical conclusions as one could come to.

Let us instance the case of Groves, late of the Celtic. We introduce the name of the Celtic for no other purpose than that of identifying the player Groves - Groves of the Celtic. Groves has joined "the glorious band of professionals" - why glorious we scarcely understand - but previous to his doing so, he applied for and was refused a license for a public house on the north side of Glasgow. The report of the hearing of the application by the licensing authorities kept a slur upon Groves and the Celtic club which has not yet been removed from the public mind. A question we were inclined to ask at the time was - if Groves could afford to enter upon a speculation which involved a capital of perhaps £500, why did he find it necessary to take the professional shilling the moment that speculation was made impossible to him.

By asking this question we do not mean to convey a hint that the Celtic club was at Groves' back - we give the Celtic credit for more astuteness - but what we believe is that Groves was backed by friends of the club, or perhaps what has come to be known as the "trade", who knew that Groves behind the bar of almost any public house would mean it's entire success".

In its editorial, the *Scottish Sport* had answered its own questions and at the same time, it had ignored some of the facts and over egged the pudding in its speculation over costs involved in setting up a player in the licensing trade. The Scottish Referee had reported, on the 25th August, that a Mr McLennan, acting on behalf of Willie Groves, had applied for the transfer of the license at 29 Taylor Street, (Scottish Sport stated 22 Taylor Street), Townhead from the current occupant, a Mr Murdoch at the Glasgow Licensing Court.

He argued that the player's current status as a prominent footballer at Celtic Football Club should have no bearing on the application, as the public house had already been licensed for five years and the transfer was initiated at the behest of Mr Murdoch after losing the services of his son. Indeed the occupant made the point that far from trafficking the license, he was selling at the same price he had bought, even though he had made spent £50 on alterations.

He made the point too that if Mr Groves was granted the license, his conduct would be under the attention of the police, who were within their rights to bring this to the Court's attention, who could then deprive him of the license for any misdemeanour. Mr McLennan further added that he had a certificate from Mr Joseph Shaughnessy, lawyer, who gave a true testimony of Mr Groves' character. On being questioned whether Mr Shaughnessy was involved with Celtic, Mr McLennan again stated that this should have no effect on the credibility of his certificate. The final question was asked whether the license was wanted for the club rather than the player and this was denied. The article in the Scottish Referee then stated that the license was granted. This was either an error or an appeal was made which Willie Groves lost.

Misfortune followed Groves immediate career in England and after signing for West Bromwich Albion, the English League suspended him for a month pending a hearing, with regards to the fact that he had already signed for Everton and they had not released his papers. Nottingham Forest added to the confusion when they stated that Groves was in Nottingham to sign for them, before West Bromwich Albion managed to get a hold of the player and obtained his signature.

OUR TWO MAIN IRISH RIVALS DISBAND

Little over a year after the arrival of Glasgow Hibernian, formed by James Quillan after being ousted from the Celtic Committee in the AGM in June 1889, they were declared bankrupt in October 1890 after a hugely unsuccessful attempt to rival our very own Irish club. With huge debts from the ground that they had built on Rutherglen Road, south of the Clyde from Glasgow Green, with very limited early success and with players deserting to the English League they had no option to declare themselves bankrupt after only 14 months in business.

The biggest surprise was that they had managed to make a re-appearance at the start of the 1890/91 season at all but they played a 2-2 draw with Armadale before heavy defeats at Airdrie and Hurlford in their opening friendly matches. In the Scottish Cup they drew Kelvinside Athletic away and after a 1-1 draw they knuckled down to win by 5 goals to 1 with former Celtic player Willie Dunning still making an appearance in goals. Wishaw Thistle, were drawn in the next round, but Glasgow Hibs were beaten by 4 goals to 1.

In the Glasgow Cup, they fared no better and after a draw away to Summerston Athletic in the first round, they lost the replay at Hibernian Park. They managed to stumble into October, but after failing to muster a full team for the trip to Dundee to play the Wanderers, they lost the match by 5 goals to 2. Their last ever match was on 18th October against Thistle at Beechwood Park, Bridgeton when they lost 2-0.

The Glasgow Evening News on 20th October stated;

GLASGOW HIBERNIANS CLUB DISSOLVED

REMARKABLE DISCLOSURES PROMISED

"The Glasgow Hibernians Football Club has been dissolved. In connection with the dissolution it is stated that the secretary will probably bring an action against the late treasurer to have his books going over. Should this be done it is alleged that disclosures will be made affecting the amateur status of a prominent club in Glasgow and seriously affecting three prominent players of a third."

In the same month, they were declared bankrupt with the owners in hiding as the final bills for the building of their ground outstanding. The last named Secretary of the club was W Tillows of 12 Mathieson Street in the Gorbals. In the event no disclosures were ever made affecting the amateur status of a prominent Glasgow club nor of three prominent players of a third.

On 6th February 1891 an advert was placed in the newspapers stating;

FOOTBALL FIELD FOR SALE - For Sale, by private tender, the Grand Stand and Pavillion situated on Football Field, Rutherglen Road, belonging to the Glasgow Hibernian Football Club. The Stand is fitted up in first class style and has all the latest improvements and has accommodation for 1000 persons. The ground is well laid off and has good track. Lease of ground may be arranged for. For further particulars apply to Joseph Martin, 97 Buchanan Street, Glasgow.

The Post Office Annual Directory shows this address as Joseph Martin's Solicitors. Were Celtic tempted to make an offer? Interestingly by the December General Meeting, the Celtic Committee were in a position to announce a 10 year lease on the land that was to become the present Celtic Park, so were they aware of the landlord's intentions to increase the rent on the original Celtic Park tenfold by February of 91?

Certainly they would have been watching the situation unfold with interest with Glasgow Hibs disbanding and their ground, Hibernian Park coming up for sale. There is no record of Celtic making any bid to either purchase the stand and pavillion and move them to either Celtic Park, old or new and there is certainly no record of any discussion to relocate Celtic Park a couple of miles south across the Clyde to Hibernian Park. Option 1 was a possibility but option 2 certainly wouldn't have been considered.

In December 1890, Edinburgh Hibernian were forced to disband following their eviction from Easter Road the previous month. After the Trinity Hospital Trust had made their intention known that the lease would come to an end to allow the charity to build on the ground and after Hibs' offer to St Bernard's for their ground at Logie Green was turned down, the Hibs Committee decided to put the club out of business, hopefully temporarily until they got their house in order. There were no other pitches suitable in their area and they didn't welcome the ignominy that went with the team having to return to playing football on a public pitch.

In truth, Hibs had been on the decline since they won the Scottish Cup in February 1887 with players departing for richer pickings down south. It cannot be denied that the formation of Celtic cut off the supply of young Irish players to the east and they had to rely on the much smaller Irish market in Edinburgh for up and coming talent. However our emergence was only one of a number of serious issues ongoing at Hibernian at the time and they were masters of their own downfall.

BROTHER WALFRID AND HUGH DARROCH ATTEND CEREMONY AT SAINT MUNGO'S SCHOOL

Brother Walfrid and Celtic's Treasurer Hugh Darroch attended the annual prize winning ceremony at Saint Mungo's in the last week of December despite the very inclement weather in the city which prevented Archbishop Eyre's attendance.

Brother Walfrid had taken up his first teaching role at St Mungo's in 1869 and Hugh Darroch was a former pupil and so they were always more than happy to return to see the remarkable progress made at the school, which one speaker remarked was on a par with, if not surpassing any other schools he had worked with in London and Dublin.

NEW YEAR MATCH 1891

To add spice to the Scottish Cup protest and no doubt a few thousand to the home gate, League leaders Dumbarton arrived at Celtic Park for the Holiday fixture friendly on New Years Day with a 12.30 kick off, just under two weeks later.

For the friendly, Sandy McMahon, who would go on to become a Celtic legend, guested for Celtic as well as Jimmy McGhee, after their own club, Edinburgh Hibernian had went out of business a couple of months previous. The ground was indeed packed with an estimated attendance of between 12,000 and 15,000 paying to watch a highly entertaining 1-1 draw. Willie Maley opened the scoring in the 20th minute, heading the ball home from a corner, but Dumbarton equalised shortly afterwards. The visitors were then reduced to ten men after an injury to defender, Duncan Stewart, who was examined by Celtic's Doctor Scanlan and the away team deserved credit for withstanding the frantic Celtic pressure in the last ten minutes as we tried in vain to snatch the winner.

The SFA held their meeting a week later at their headquarters in Waterloo Street and discussed Celtic's protest of the cup tie at Dumbarton. Mr Dunn of Cambuslang FC, who refereed the match, stated that on the day of the match, he attended Boghead at 11am at the request of the Celtic secretary John O'Hara to carry out an early pitch inspection. He deemed the pitch unplayable due to a covering of snow and requested that the snow be cleared. When this was carried out he stated that he made a further inspection and announced the pitch playable. It was confirmed that the captains of both teams had protested before the match at the decision to play the match.

A vote was then taken which split the committee right down the middle at six votes each. Crucially, one member, a Mr Wilson had to leave the meeting before the vote was taken and it was thought that he would have sided with Celtic. However, on the casting vote of the Chairman the protest was dismissed and the Celts were out the cup. Dumbarton were through to the semi final but they were heavily criticised for withdrawing their protest only after they went three goals up.

Every other pitch in the Glasgow area had been deemed unplayable the same day but the decision was made and there was no further grounds for protest. It only made the Celtic Committee even more determined to get their hands on silverware.

CELTIC CONNECTION AS THE CATHOLIC LITERARY ASSOCIATION IS FOUNDED

Another example of Celtic in the community was evident as the Glasgow and West of Scotland Catholic Literary Association, to give it it's full name, was founded in early 1891 after an inaugural meeting was held in the old Mitchell Library in Ingram Street, Glasgow. Our founding fathers were never far away from such gatherings and present from Celtic FC were Doctor John Conway, Joseph Shaughnessy, Stephen J Henry, Joseph Francis McGroary, John McDonald and John McCreadie. The agreed object of the Association was to promote Catholic interests through discussion at their weekly meetings.

THE CELTS WITHDRAW FROM THE CUP

With the growth of the club in only its third season still on the up, a decision was made by the committee to "scratch", that is to withdraw from the match against Northern in the North Eastern Cup, which as the name suggests was for teams in the north and east of Glasgow.

There was no ill feeling at the decision and Celtic Park was awarded the final between Northern and Clyde on the 4th April in a match that was memorable for the number of sending offs, three in total with two from Northern and one from Clyde in a match Clyde went on to win 3-2. The competition had been good to us with Celtic winning the trophy in the two seasons we competed in it, with a 6-1 victory over Cowlairs on 11th May 1889 at Barrowfield, followed up by a 2-0 victory over Northern on 15th March 1890 at the same ground.

GRAND THEATRICAL FOOTBALL MATCH AT CELTIC PARK

On Wednesday, 27th January at 2pm, a grand theatrical football match, complete with full pantomine costume, took place at Celtic Park between the Grand and the Royal threatre companies. Amongst the costumes on show were ballet dancers, policemen and clowns, (not much change from a normal Saturday match), but also in attendance were Londoners, Miss Billy "Minnie" Barlow and Miss Flo Bilton, two of the music hall's biggest stars of the day, gracing Celtic Park with their presence.

THE CELTS WIN THE GLASGOW CUP

From the *Scottish Referee*;

"If ever a club deserved to have their name inscribed on a trophy worthy of the name, that club is the Celtic".

LOVE'S GOLDEN DREAM

Arrah! Bould Celts, you've gained the day
By honest, sterlin', hardy play
Be jabers now, the Glasgow Cup
The QP must deliver up

Erin Go Bragh, each son will shine
And dance a jig in merry style
The Warriors thought our bhoys near dead
But no! We live still in Parkhead

Ach! Phat d'ye say? "Our time has come"
Av course, me bhoy, Celts always run
The foeman. Ever they're watching
And when they die, they do it scratching

Last year we got a sad rebut
The boot's now on the other "fut"
It won't fit well, for 32
Is the measure of a Celtic shoe

Good bye, old Third, sweet is revenge
But not with malice, not one tinge
We feel 'gainst you. Till next we meet
Adieu old Third, "Revenge is sweet"

Poetry again summed up the joy of the Celtic support after the long awaited date with destiny of 14th February 1891 ended with success as Celtic and Third Lanark contested the final as they did two years previously when they broke the attendance record for the Scottish Cup Final when the Celts on that occasion lost out after a replay.

Neither side had ever won the Glasgow Cup although Thirds had won the Charity Cup the previous year and the Scottish Cup of course, the year before.

10,000 crammed into Hampden Park for the 12.30 kick off with the majority said to have hailed from Erin's Isle or were of Irish descent. The Celtic team that won our first major trophy was ; Jamie Bell in goals, Jerry Reynolds, (who married the week before), and Mick McKeown as the two full backs, Paddy Gallagher, James Kelly and Willie Maley the three half backs and Johnny Madden, Jimmy Boyle, Peter Dowds, Johnny Campbell and Mick Dunbar the five man attack.

This was the typical set up in those days with the Celts playing the usual 2-3-5, a two man defence operating as full backs with the half backs given the responsibility of defensive duties too. The five man attack was made up of two wingers, two inside backs and a centre forward.

The weather conditions were good on the day if a little windy, but nothing that could threaten the match going ahead and the Celts played against the wind in the first half but kept our passing game short for better accuracy. We were soon rewarded when a nice shot from Johnny Campbell in the 20th minute hit the post and rebounded off the Third's keeper Lochhead and crossed over the line. Campbell had made a name for himself in the reserves with his goalscoring exploits and with Willie Groves now departed down south, Johnny was making his mark in the first team too.

The scores stayed the same until half time and the Celtic support were in confident mood as we took to the field shooting this time with the wind. Thirds however changed their tactics back to their favoured close control dribbling game which gave them greater possession against the effects of the wind.

Tom Maley had delivered a few words of inspiration at half time saying;
"It's very near us boys. Keep at it with a will and the day is ours".

The Celts soon stepped up a gear and it was Peter Dowds who got the all important second goal in the 55th minute from James Kelly's corner, amidst wild scenes of enthusiasm. Celtic were hemming Thirds in and Johnny Campbell soon got his second and Celtic's third to put the game beyond doubt, Johnny Madden scored a fourth which was controversially chalked off before Campbell scored directly from a free kick to cap a fantastic Celtic performance to finish the scoring at Celtic 4 Third Lanark 0.

The after match social at the Alexandria Hotel on Bath Street was a very harmonious event with Third Lanark taking their defeat well, as the better team on the day had clearly won. John Glass responded to the toast in modest fashion but took the opportunity to remind everyone of his prediction two years previous on the occasion of the after match social when Thirds beat Celtic in the Scottish Cup Final, that he was sure that in the near future, *"the boot would be on the other fut."*

Crowds followed the team to Bath Street and remained there with "Hurry Up Celts" and "Good Old Celts" written on card and placed in their hats. This was well before the days of team colours and about ninety years short of replica strips on display but the fans certainly made their presence known with their horns and constant singing and dancing well into the night. One reporter from the *Scottish Sport* left Bath Street to pop into Mick Dunbar's licensed premises on the Gallowgate to give the news which was already being celebrated, before making his way to St Mary's Hall, 67 East Rose Street, where the club was born.

There he described the scene.

"Billiards etc were at a standstill. One man who had been at the game was giving a graphic account of the day. Many of the older men there knew nothing whatsoever of short passes, dribbles, shots etc, all they knew, all they wanted to know was that their pets had won and didn't they carry their heads high when the recitor of the narrative concluded by saying "And bhoys, that's how the best team that ever played football won the cup".

Back in the day the trophy wasn't presented at the game or even at the after match social.

Celtic had to wait another two weeks before being presented with the cup at a smoking concert attended by most of the participating teams at Moirs Restaurant, West Nile Street on the Wednesday evening of 25th February. Celtic President John Glass again responded to the toast before taking the trophy home with him to adorn his sideboard. Celtic Park in those days did not have a trophy room and so the agreement was that a different member of the committee would take a turn in taking a trophy to their own home for safe keeping! Some of the most famous trophies in the Scottish game were to adorn many a sideboard in the Gallowgate in the coming years.

The *Glasgow Evening News* summed up the feel good factor at Celtic Park;

"Few will deny that the Celts deserve the Glasgow Cup. They have fought long and well, not only for it, but for the greater cup as well. Their game against the Third was one of the best the club has ever played and not only by their beautiful football but by the manner they behaved on the field they have raised themselves considerably in the eyes of the public, who already are backing them for the Charity Cup as well.

Previous to the final with the Third, the Celts executive were sorely troubled concerning some of their players; now, as Mr Glass would say, the boot is on the other foot, and the Third are going through a similar experience. The Celts are now a happy family, and they wish all the clubs to be the same. The Glasgow Cup will be presented to them on Wednesday night".

Just a week later on Saturday 21st February, the Scottish Cup Second X1 trophy was won by a record score as the young Celts came back from a goal down to beat Saint Mirren 13-1, with 9 of our goals coming in the second half at Thistle's ground, Beechwood Park in Bridgeton, in front of a record crowd for a reserve match. James Curtis's sideboard must have been straining that night.

It had been an incredible run by the reserve team with a total of 58 goals scored to 7 conceded in our seven matches including the final as follows ; a 10-0 win over Battlefield, a 9-0 win over Northern, a 12-1 win over St Johnstone, a 6-0 win over Royal Albert, a 4-3 win over Morton, a 4-2 win over Hearts and a 13-1 win over Saint Mirren in the final.

BACK TO LEAGUE BUSINESS

With the Glasgow Cup and the Scottish Second X1 Cups both safely tucked away we could now turn our attention to the League and pulling ourselves up the table. Nearing the end of February, we had still only played 6 League matches and sat on 4 points, 13 points behind Dumbarton albeit with 3 matches less played.

Our League match on the 3rd January at home to Cowlairs was, incredibly, our first in the competition since the 25th October when we had beaten Abercorn 5-1, and on this occasion the scoreline was the exact same, after we followed our customary gift of giving the away team a goal of a start in the first half, this time right on the 45th minute. A header by James Boyle, followed up by another header from Tom Maley put the Celts in control, before Johnny Campbell, Tom Maley, again and Johnny Coleman, all scored past Tom Duff in the Cowlairs goal, to make the second half more comfortable. Cowlairs had just arrived back from down south on the morning of the game after their English tour and they visibly tired before the end of the match, with the bhoys not slow in taking advantage.

The fixture pile up hadn't been helped by the thrice played Scottish Cup tie with Royal Albert and also our "League" win over St Mirren on 27th December, which had to be played as a friendly due to the hard condition of the pitch. The Celts won by 4 goals to 2 in a match remembered for James Kelly's goal. Unfortunately, it was into his own net, as he tried to run the ball back to keeper Jamie Bell, but instead ran the ball into his own goals.

When the League match was finally played on the 7th February, "within the Celtic's snug and tidy enclosure," as the Scottish Referee described it, we led by three goals to nil at half time, thanks to goals by Johnny Campbell in the 15th minute, Peter Dowds with a high shot into the west corner after a pass from Johnny Madden and the latter himself scored the third after a scrimmage inside the Saints box. The game was fast and furious and James Kelly controlled the middle of the park with his renowned bursts of determination which carried the ball from defence to attack, possibly akin to Roy Aitken's charges in the 1980s, with a little more subtlety. James Boyle played well too and although his career at Celtic Park didn't set the heather on fire, he was to make his name at Woolwich Arsenal, where he captained the Gunners in a game against Celtic in 1897.

In between, we showed our inconsistency away to Vale of Leven on 24th January, on a day when we were forced to play with ten men after Mick McKeown missed his train. A bad day just got worse despite the Celts opening the scoring as the home team scored two in the next five minutes to go in at half time 2-1 up, before scoring a third late on with the Celts pressing for an equaliser.

All of this meant as we prepared for our visit to League leaders, Dumbarton on the 21st February, we sat in second bottom place, 13 points behind the home team, albeit with two games in hand. Dumbarton were the form team in the country, despite losing the Scottish Cup Final to Hearts in a major upset. The Celts would need to take our cup form into League battle as there was not much between the teams despite the points difference.

On the day, the home team scored the only goal of the first half and added a second early in the second period, before the Celts started to play and stormed back into the game to score twice. The first came from a stramash in the Dumbarton goalmouth following a corner that caused confusion before being headed through and the second came from a lovely shot from Mick Dunbar after an exhilarating attack. It was a well deserved draw and gave the Celts great belief as we came back from two goals down at the home of the table toppers. With the four points deducted at the start of the season, our League position was a false one and one that we were determined to remedy.

Four League matches followed in as many weeks for the first time, resulting in a home victory over Hearts by one goal to nil, scored by Peter Dowds, who rose to beat the Hearts keeper to a cross from Johnny Madden in the second half of a very even match, (although some newspapers give the goal to rising star Johnny Campbell).

The reporter from the *Scottish Referee* attended the match and stated;

"The cheery tones of Secretary O'Hara calling upon his men set me all a quivering to see the battle begin. Not that I was cold, mind you, for the Celts are a hospitable lot and a drop of the poteen was just the thing to warm up the cockles of an old fellow's soul on such a raw day".

Hearts came under attack for playing a weakened side but they were let off lightly after stating that one player had missed his train and two others were given their own choice of either playing for Hearts that day or attending the first Scotland trials. In the event both players decided to play in the trials so the club couldn't stand in their way. This allowed the Celts to overtake St Mirren in the League table and draw level with Hearts and Vale of Leven, both sides having played more matches. Abercorn and Cowlairs took up the bottom two positions as we sat in joint 5th position, with a keen eye on climbing the table.

A visit to Whitefield Park in Cambuslang was next on the fixture list to the team sitting in third place, three points ahead of the Celts with two matches more played. The League was so tight that only three points separated the five teams sitting between 3rd and 7th place, so a victory would put us with touching distance of third place, with two points for a win back in the day.

James Kelly retained his place in the Celtic team in preference to attending the Scotland trials at Tynecastle and in doing so denied himself the chance to captain Scotland in the Home Internationals. But he couldn't stand in the way of Cambuslang's good League form as they went two goals up by half time, before the bhoys responded through Johnny Madden in the second half. The home team, however, were not to be denied and they scored a third before the end to underline Celtic's inconsistent form in the inaugural League season as we remained in 6th place of 10 teams at the halfway stage. James Kelly must have wished he had attended the Scotland trials, as he had to come off injured at Whitefield Park, only the second time he had failed to finish a match he started, the first one being at Blackburn Rovers.

The next two matches were at home, first to bottom of the table Cowlairs and then to second placed Rangers, who were in a two horse race with favourites Dumbarton for the first title. Thankfully there were no surprises at the Cowlairs match and the bhoys raced into a two goal lead in the first five minutes, with both goals scored by Peter Dowds. Frank Dolan, the brother of Michael Dolan who played in Celtic's first ever match enjoyed a rare appearance taking over from the injured James Kelly with a performance that was described as cool, capable and showing good judgement.

Tom Duff was again in goals for Cowlairs and he must have feared another hammering after such a good start by the bhoys. But try as we might we couldn't get the goals our play deserved and the match finished Celtic 2 Cowlairs 0, lifting us to 4th position, 3 points behind Cambuslang with a game in hand.

The Celtic Committee were not over enamoured with the restrictions the new League was putting on the club. Admittedly it provided some excellent matches but it also provided some less than glamorous affairs too, with some crowds given as anywhere between 2000 and 3000, as was the case at a recent match with St Mirren. The enterprising committee would, no doubt, prefer to fill the fixture list with invites to top English teams as we'd done in the past and earned top dollar from.

Whilst we were out the League race, we could still have a say in who took the trophy between Dumbarton and Rangers, both of whom had to travel to Celtic Park. We also had to face Rangers at Ibrox. One quaint novelty about football in the early days was that opposition teams were welcomed at away grounds with a round of applause, but stranger still the referee too was welcomed in a similar fashion. Whether he was accorded the same hospitality at the end of the game was a different matter.

CELTS TIE THE KNOT

James Kelly and Jerry Reynolds both got married, (not to each other), within a couple of weeks, in late January and early February when captain James Kelly married the daughter of Francis McErlean, the Belfast man who was also Celtic's Vice President. Meanwhile Jerry Reynolds was married on Tuesday 10th February. Both of which bore gifts from Celtic FC, £15 to captain Kelly and £10 to Reynolds.

CELTIC PARK AWARDED THE INTER CITY MATCH AGAINST LONDON

Celtic Park's fame spread when it was awarded the prestigious inter city match between Glasgow and London on the 21st February 1891. It was recognition of the part the ground had played in Celtic's success and the east end was buzzing with excitement at the thought of the arrival of some of the finest players in London on their doorstep. The Glasgow team was already selected and James Kelly and Mick McKeown were to be honoured to represent Glasgow at their home ground.

Unfortunately the London Association postponed the match, citing a difficulty in raising a team that could commit to travelling the distance to Glasgow, after invites had been sent. They asked that future Inter City matches between the two should be played in London on an annual basis with a guarantee of up to £100 and a half share of the gate given to Scotland.

English football around that time was dominated by northern clubs and so it seemed for London in 1891, that Glasgow was a road too far.

CELTIC CELEBRATE SAINT PATRICK'S DAY

The club celebrated St Patrick's Day at committee member William McKillop's house on Monteith Row, beside Glasgow Green, as the shamrock was toasted and drowned in drink to a merry tune, late into the evening. Michael Dolan got the biggest cheer with his comical rendition of "The Boys That Were Reared on Potatoes," whilst Tom Maley gave a recital in verse of his favourite poetry and the rest of the bhoys sang to their heart's content.

CELTIC AND SCOTLAND CAPS

It was interesting to note in an article in the Scottish Sport in March 1891 on the amount of players each club had selected for the annual Scotland v England matches down the years from the first tie in 1872 in which Scotland had enjoyed remarkable success with 11 won, 3 lost and 5 drawn. Queens Park not surprisingly had the highest representation with 39 different players having received 98 caps, in second place was Vale of Leven, with 12 players having received 28 caps, then Dumbarton with 9 players having received 21 caps, Third Lanark with 8 players having received 10 caps, Rangers with 6 players having received 10 caps, Renton with 4 players having received 7 caps, then Celtic with 4 players having received 6 caps, albeit in our short three years existence.

THE FIRST LEAGUE MATCH BETWEEN CELTIC AND RANGERS

Rangers arrived at Celtic Park on Saturday, 21st March 1891 for the first ever League match between the clubs, having never beaten Celtic at home, away or at a neutral venue. Celtic were missing captain James Kelly and Mick Dunbar, who were injured, but they were ably replaced by James McGhee and Sandy McMahon, who had joined up at Celtic Park after Hibs had disbanded.

The match started at a frantic pace and Rangers opened the scoring in the 20th minute, in front of an enormous crowd of 12,000, before Peter Dowds equalised before half time, "amid tremendous acclamation," as the Celts piled on the pressure. Rangers were glad to hear the half time whistle but it was the away team who started the second half better, however in a breakaway Peter Dowds scored his and Celtic's second, with a shot from sixteen yards to put the Celts ahead as the bhoys surged back on top.

Rangers however were determined to keep the pressure on Dumbarton at the top of the League and with only eight minutes remaining they equalised to set up a pulsating finish. Both teams piled forward looking for the winner but it was to no avail, despite close things at both ends and the final whistle blew with the score 2-2, which was said to be a fair reflection of the play.

The *Scottish Referee* wished both teams all the best, not with tips on how to improve their play, but with the following;

"Forward the Light Brigade to victory; and Celts, remember the Wolfe Tone of Ould Ireland and the glorious "Sunburst" of the Emerald Isle".

OUR EASTER TOUR OF ENGLAND

Of the 11 matches since the start of the year, the Celts had played 8 League games, 2 friendlies and the Glasgow Cup Final so it was time for an Easter break and a return to some high profile glamour matches with the Celts collecting a tidy guarantee at each venue naturally. Bolton Wanderers, Ardwick, Blackburn Rovers and Sheffield Wednesday were the opposition and with a reputation to protect even this early in the club's development it's certain that the quote "Celtic don't play friendlies" was as well suited then as it was commonplace a century later.

The Celts travelled by train to our base in Manchester on the Thursday and the time was passed by the usual speeches and discussions by the orators of the party, Mick McKeown and Mike Dunbar, who kept everyone entertained. A cheer was asked for at the tiny Ayrshire village of Cronberry enroute, an area which Mick McKeown was familiar with as nearby Lugar Boswell were his first football team. On the next day, Good Friday, the bhoys made the train journey from Manchester to Bolton to take on the famous Wanderers and enroute during the speeches to pass the time, Cronberry was again mentioned in jest and the stationmaster, who was travelling on board the same train joined in the fun, as he quipped;

"I knows nowt about Cronberry, but I can tell thee summat of raspberries," best read in a strong Paddy McGuinness, Bolton accent.

On arrival at Bolton, the Celtic party stumbled across the union of Carters and Lorrymen's industrial action which brought a large procesion through the town with much of it at a standstill. Despite this, our second annual Good Friday match at Pike's Lane, Bolton was attended by a decent crowd and a very impressive Bolton side raced into a two goal lead by half time with the strong wind at their backs. Jimmy McGhee opened the scoring in the 18th minute, unfortunately into his own goals and the home team made it 2-0 fifteen minutes later.

The Celts rallied in the second half and taking advantage of the high winds we got a goal back after a few minutes and followed this up with an equaliser with fifteen minutes left on the clock. We were now well on top and pressing to clinch a famous comeback. With the bhoys camped around the Bolton goals, the winner finally arrived, or so we thought, but it was disallowed, despite the Bolton goalkeeper turning and carrying the ball over his line after making a save.

On arrival back at Manchester, the Celts enjoyed a smoking concert, complete with song and dance, the latter provided by Mick McKeown as he performed a ballet dance, hopefully not the Nutcracker, that brought the house down. A day later, on the Saturday, whilst Scotland and Ireland played at Celtic Park, we beat Ardwick 7-2 in Manchester, the highlight of an easy match being a hat trick by Peter Dowds. The home team were captained by a David Weir, hopefully not the same elder statesman who went on to play for Rangers between 2007 and 2012. Ardwick, who beat Newton Heath 1-0 to win the Manchester Cup in 1891, were then admitted as founder members to the English League, Division 2 and after financial difficulties, they were reformed as Manchester City in 1894. Newton Heath changed their name to Manchester United in 1902 and a famous rivalry was born.

Celtic President John Glass and William McKillop joined the Celtic party in Manchester in the small hours of Sunday morning having acted as mine host to the Scotland and Ireland teams at Celtic Park and they were given a hearty reception. On the Sunday we enjoyed a day off and St Chad's Catholic chapel was visited for morning mass before the rest of the day was taken up by a sight seeing tour of Manchester, including a trip to Belle Vue Zoological Gardens, otherwise known as Manchester Zoo, where the bhoys mingled with the parrots, elephants, kangaroos, lions, bears, rhinoceroses and hippopotami, (rhinos and hippos to me and you). If this wasn't your thing, there was also a large amusement park and botanical gardens to pass the time of day.

On the Monday we visited the English Cup holders Blackburn Rovers at Ewood Park, which was the scene of the England v Scotland match the following Monday. Rovers had relocated from their original ground at Leamington Road during the previous summer and despite another disallowed goal, the Celts won 2-0 with two second half goals, one from a header following a corner and the second goal came near the end. The Rovers had struck the bar three times in the first half with the wind at their backs which thankfully they failed to take advantage of.

We ended our English tour at Olive Grove, where we played Sheffield Wednesday the following day in front of 7000 spectators, with our fourth match in five days. The home team opened the scoring before Peter Dowds equalised before half time. Paddy Gallagher gave us the lead in the second half as we pressed and an own goal in the last few minutes made the final score, Sheffield Wednesday 1 Celtic 3. The tour had started with an own goal, supplied by our own Jimmy McGhee at Bolton and had ended with an own goal, supplied by Harry Brandon of the Wednesday. All told, it was a very successful tour with three wins, a draw and no defeats, scoring 14 and conceding only 5 against some of the finest teams in England on their home turf, which underlined once again that we were a force to be reckoned with.

On the way home the Celts fulfilled a promise to Brother Walfrid to visit Saint Joseph's College in Dumfries, ran by the Marist Brothers. The annual College Sports Day finished on the Wednesday and who better than Celtic to close the meeting with a light hearted match against the College team, bolstered by some ex students and refereed by William McKillop. Jamie Bell, Jerry Reynolds and Mick McKeown swapped jerseys at half time and played for the College team and after 90 minutes of good fun the match ended in an entertaining 3-3 draw.

The college band led both teams on and off the field and an after match dinner was arranged in the College Refectory with speakers from both Celtic and St Joseph's giving thanks for such a memorable day. Surprisingly James Quillan's name is given as one of those in attendance as well as many of the Celtic Committee who had travelled especially for the event. Even more surprisingly, his name was to crop up in future Celtic AGM's therefore it appears that after his defection and the founding of Glasgow Hibernian in 1889, he was allowed back into the fold after their disbanding.

Brother Walfrid would certainly have attended the Sports Day at St Joseph's that day. Did he travel from Glasgow with James Quillan to smooth things over with the Celtic Committee?

CELTIC PARK AWARDED OUR FIRST INTERNATIONAL MATCH

The only international match ever played at the original Celtic Park took place on Saturday, March 28th 1891, appropriately between Scotland and Ireland. The home internationals with Ireland and Wales were seen as less glamorous than the big match against England and so it was commonplace to field a second string in these matches. The choice of Celtic Park for the Irish international was no coincidence with Celtic's Irish support turning up in large numbers to fill the SFA's coffers for what would normally be a modest attendance. The Celtic Committee would get a large slice of the cake too, naturally.

When the teams were announced, the only Scot who wasn't earning his first cap was Gillespie of Queens Park. Jimmy McLaren was the only Celt picked in the Scotland team but he had to pull out due to a family member's illness. Jack Reynolds, however, who was to sign for Celtic in 1897, played for Ireland and was a massive favourite with the home crowd who outnumbered the Scots. Strangely Reynolds went on to play for England and indeed played and scored against Scotland at New Celtic Park before he signed for Celtic.

The *Scottish Referee* stated;

"We have never heard such encouragement given to a "foreign" team as that bestowed on the Shamrock's representatives on Saturday".

The game was won 2-1 by Scotland on a pitch affected by the snow, frost, thaw and rain which gave it the consistency of glue, with Ireland, who were wearing the ancient colour of blue, unlucky not to get a draw by all accounts. The bhoys in blue had started the better team against a weak Scottish side but the home team settled down after opening the scoring after five minutes against the run of play. The floodgates that usually opened in this fixture remained closed however and a closely fought game was played out with the Irish team surprising everyone by giving as good as they got. On the hour mark Scotland went two goals up but still the Irish team fought on and scored a deserved goal for their efforts near the end with a mud raker which defied a whole crowd of players in the box.

Try as they might, they couldn't force a surprise equaliser and the Irish were beaten, but certainly not disgraced, by the Scots who grafted as hard as the Irish throughout. After the match both teams were entertained at the Bank Restaurant on Queen St. The attendance was a record for the Scotland v Ireland international and thus began a long tradition of the Irish team playing Scotland at Celtic Park. The SFA were more than happy with their £185 cut of the takings and the Celtic Committee equally happy with their share which comprised of the takings from both stands.

AGENTS BEWARE THE JOHNSTONE VIGILANTE COMMITTEE!

In the days when amateurism ruled, the policy of signing a player would often descend into so much farce that it resembled a scene out of a cowboy film. One example was Everton's efforts to sign our very own Peter Dowds in February 1891. The residents of the peaceful village of Howwood in Renfrewshire had never seen anything like it as they partook of their Sunday afternoon stroll in the park. A well known agent, acting on behalf of Everton, was spotted in the area and word soon spread that Dowds was his intended target.

Back in the day, an English agent would simply turn up at a player's residence, wave a professional contract in front of his face, promise him the ends of the earth and bundle him into the back of a taxi to the nearest train station for the trip back across the border. No discussions took place between the clubs at any level and no transfer fee was required to be given to the amateur club. On this occasion, the agent underestimated the value of the word on the street and the Johnstone vigilantes soon took chase, forcing the agent's car into a hedgerow and ordering the trembling agent to flee, without his prize asset.

The *Scottish Sport* warned;

"A Vigilante Committee has been formed in the district and woe betide the gent who tries to woo Dowds from his team".

On another occasion, no less than Fred Dewhurst, Preston North End's star player sent

CELTIC – PARK.
1887 – 92.

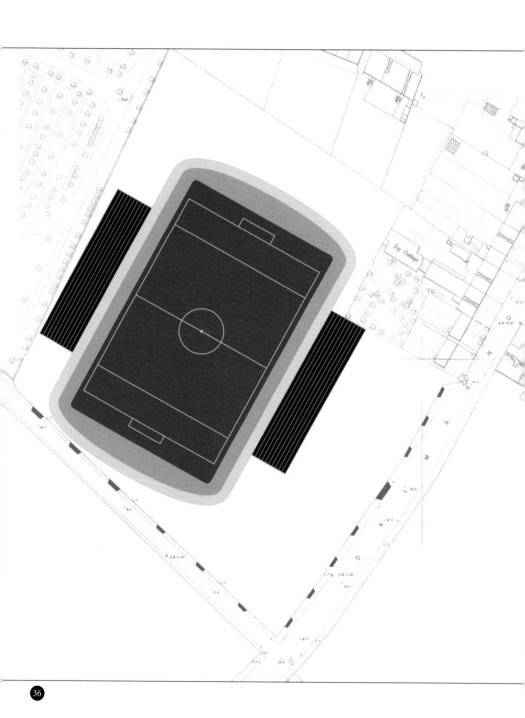

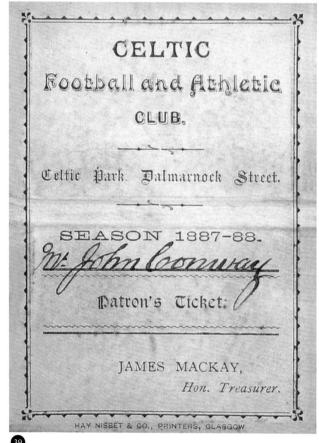

Opening of Celtic Football and Athletic Park,
Dalmarnock Street, Parkhead.
Grand Opening Match—Exhibition Day, May 8

HIBERNIANS
VERSUS
COWLAIRS
Kick-off at 6 p.m. prompt.   Admission 6d., Ladies Free.
Grand Stand Sixpence extra each person.
The Park is two minutes' walk from the Parkhead and
London Road Tramcar and Railway Stations.

CELTIC
Football and Athletic
CLUB.

Celtic Park. Dalmarnock Street.

SEASON 1887-88.

Mr John Conway

Patron's Ticket:

JAMES MACKAY,
Hon. Treasurer.

HAY NISBET & CO., PRINTERS, GLASGOW.

J. KELLY, Renton F.C.

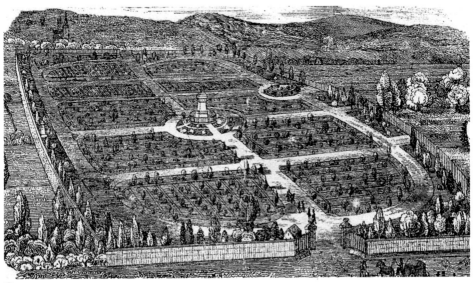

GLASGOW CUP TIE—Saturday, 27th October

RANGERS

VERSUS

CELTIC

IBROX PARK, Copeland Road   Kick-off at 3.15 p.m.
Admission Sixpence. Ladies Free. Grand Stand
Sixpence extra each person.

47

SCOTTISH CUP TIE — Saturday, 3rd Nov.

CELTIC v. ST. BERNARDS.

POWDERHALL, EDINBURGH.

The Committee have made arrangements with N.B.R. Company to run a Special Train to Edinburgh, on Saturday, 3rd November, 1888. Train leaves Bellgrove 1.30 p.m., and Parkhead 1.35, returning from Edinburgh (Waverley) at 7.30 p.m. prompt. Return Tickets, 2s. 6d., available by this Train only. Tickets may be had (8 to 9 p.m.) from Tuesday till Friday at the League of the Cross Hall, St Mary's, 67 East Rose Street, St. Michael's, Great Eastern Road, and Sacred Heart, Howard Street, or from any member of the Committee.

48

GRAND CHARITY FOOTBALL MATCHES.

CELTIC
v.
MITCHELL'S ST. GEORGE'S (Birmingham).
CELTIC PARK, PARKHEAD.
Monday, December 31st; Kick off 2 P.M.
ADMISSION, SIXPENCE. | STAND, SIXPENCE.
Members and Ticket-Holders are Requested to pay.

CELTIC
v.
CORINTHIANS,
CELTIC PARK, Parkhead.
Thursday, January 3rd, 1889; Kick off 1 P.M.
ADMISSION, SIXPENCE. | STAND, SIXPENCE.
Members and Ticket-holders are Requested to pay.

49

SCOTTISH FOOTBALL ASSOCIATION.

PROTESTED FINAL TIE.
SATURDAY FIRST, 9th FEBRUARY, 1889.

3rd LANARK

VERSUS

CELTIC

HAMPDEN PARK, CROSSHILL.   Kick-off
at 3.30 prompt.
Admission One Shilling. Ladies Free.   Grand
Stands One Shilling extra.

50

THE CELTS.

W DUNNING

P. GALLOCHER

McKEWON

M. MILLEN

JAS. KELLY

J. McLAREN

McCALLUM

W. GROVES

J. COLEMAN

M. DUNBAR

T. MALLEY

54

55

56

57

58

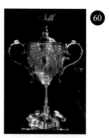

SCOTTISH FOOTBALL ASSOCIATION.

INTERNATIONAL MATCH.

SATURDAY, 28TH MARCH.
SCOTLAND
V.
IRELAND,
CELTIC PARK, PARKHEAD.
Kick-off at 4 P.M.
Admission, 6d.; Ladies Free.
Grand Stands, 6d extra each Person.

68

69

Cullen; Reynolds and Doyle; W. Maley, Kelly and Dowds; M'Callum, Brady, Madden, M'Mahon and Campbell. Inset. Mr John Glass and Mr T. E. Maley.

70

CELTIC TEAM
which won Scottish Cup for first time,
1891-92.

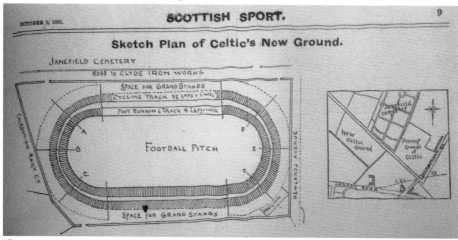

Dowds a telegram asking him to meet him at a Glasgow hotel. Unfortunately the telegram was intercepted by Tom Maley who responded, "Peter can't come, but I will!" Dewhurst took the hint and never bothered Dowds again. Other agents fared even worse than Everton's, with Kilmarnock supporters on one occasion, when discovering an agent attempting to make good his escape with one of their players, decided to tar and feather him as an example!

It would surprise no one to hear that the Celtic Committee were particularly adroit at seeing off agents intent on kidnapping our players. Fast forward to the close season of 1892 for the best example.

THE RACE FOR THE FIRST LEAGUE TITLE - THE CELTS STILL HAVE A SAY

By mid April, the two teams at the top of the first Scottish League were neck and neck, with the Sons of the Rock level with Rangers but with one game less played. The problem was their game in hand was at Celtic Park where Celtic very seldom lost. Although our League form had been erratic, our record against the two teams at the top was good, the problem was the points dropped against the teams nearer the bottom of the table so with a home match with Dumbarton and an away match with Rangers to play, we still had a large say on who would win the title.

Our biggest problem was again, inconsistency, as proven by our trip to the Buddies' first ground at Westmarch, Paisley to take on St Mirren the week before and returned pointless after a 1-0 defeat. A win would have maintained our progress as we would have leapfrogged Hearts in 4th place, but instead we sat a place behind in 5th, marooned in mid table, with Cambuslang in 3rd place a distant seven points away with two matches more played. We needed to go on a decent run in the League to attain, at best, 3rd spot, but we also had our pride and a large say in the destination of the title to think about as table toppers Dumbarton arrived at Celtic Park on League duty. Our downfall was our results against the lesser teams so taking on Dumbarton was just what we needed to get the best out of the players who always rose to the challenge.

This was the fourth match between Celtic and Dumbarton this season, with the New Year friendly at Celtic Park ending in a 1-1 draw, the League meeting at Boghead also finished in a draw at 2-2 and of course Dumbarton ending our interest in the Scottish Cup with a quarter final defeat at Dumbarton by three goals to nil. Both teams had protested due to the condition of the pitch caused by the heavy snowfall, but Dumbarton then withdrew their protest after they won the match, which caused ill feeling.

In the first half the Celts were back to our best, outplaying the visitors and our efforts were rewarded in the 25th minute when Sandy McMahon intercepted a slack pass at the back by a Dumbarton defender to throw off Boyle's attentions and toe poke the ball between the sticks, the ball striking Kerr on its way in. The match opened up and both sides had their chances to score on a number of occasions but both goalkeepers were on top form. The nearest to another goal came from Bell of Dumbarton in the second half when he put the ball through the sticks following a corner, but the goal was disallowed due to offside, without hesitation from the referee. The away team were so incensed by the decision that they considered walking off the pitch, before changing their minds. The game finished 1-0 to Celtic, and the visitors decided to protest the match, which was ironic after their actions after the Scottish Cup game, but the SFA Committee dismissed the protest unanimously.

The Celts had used our height and weight advantage to outmuscle Dumbarton, which was a new departure and added a new string to our bow, if and when required.

Dumbarton then lost their match to Rangers at Ibrox by 4 goals to 2, which went towards avenging the 5-1 hammering Dumbarton had given to Rangers at Boghead earlier in the season. With only two matches remaining the advantage fell to Rangers who were now two points ahead. Their only problem was that their next game was against, you guessed it, Celtic at Ibrox.

THE CELTS WEAR BLACK ARMBANDS IN HONOUR OF DECEASED PRIEST

Father Thomas Cunningham, the parish priest at Saint Bride's in Cambuslang had been a very popular figure around Celtic Park alongside his brother, Father Charles Cunningham from Saint Mirin's in Paisley. And so it was with great sadness that the news was received at Celtic Park on the afternoon of Tuesday, 7th April 1891 of the death of the 37 year old priest, taken long before his time.

John Glass, William McKillop, Tom and Willie Maley represented Celtic at his funeral and as a mark of respect the flags flew at half mast at our next home match, the 1-0 win over League leaders Dumbarton on April 11th as the players wore black crepe on their arms for the Glaswegian, Father Tom, as he was affectionately known.

CELTIC COMMITTEE PROPOSE CHANGES TO SFA CONSTITUTION

Before the final SFA meeting of the season on 10th April, the Celtic Committee again showed our mettle by giving the appropriate notice of our proposals to alter or amend a number of changes to the constitution, all of which were read out. Learning from the debacle at Boghead in the Scottish Cup when Dumbarton withdrew their protest after they won the game, the Celtic Committee proposed the following;

"A protest lodged by one club cannot be withdrawn without the consent of the other club. Should the latter refuse to allow the withdrawal and lodge intimation as above, it shall then be considered and decided on in the usual way".

Also referring to the thrice played tie with Royal Albert, the Celtic Committee proposed the following;

"In the first four rounds of the competition in any match which results in a draw, an extra half hour shall be played".

The Celtic Committee were learning quickly on our feet and proposing amendments to rules as we gained experience, no doubt with the following old adage in mind; Fool me once, shame on you; fool me twice, shame on me.

Ironically, the Celtic Committee, who had arranged three games through the summer month of June, 1888 as we capitalised on our momentum after the opening of Celtic Park and our own first game, then proposed to the SFA Committee that no matches should be allowed to be played during June and July, except the 4 and 5 a side matches which we favoured during the close season;

"No matches shall be played between May 31st and August 1st of each year without the consent of the Committee. This does not apply to competitions, limited to five or less players on each side".

Ironically one of the first clubs having to look for that permission would be Celtic, in order to play the final match of our Treble winning season the following year!

ENGLAND'S FINEST TRAVEL TO CELTIC PARK

Before the Celts could turn our thoughts to the League match at Ibrox, Blackburn Rovers, Bolton Wanderers and Preston North End all made their way to Celtic Park to take us on. In an extraordinary match with Blackburn Rovers on the 13th April, two days after our game with Dumbarton, the match finished at five goals apiece, with five scored in each half. The Celts led 3-2 at half time, but lost the second half by the same scoreline in a thrilling match we should have won. Jerry Reynolds turned up late, forcing us to start with ten men, but in a match with ten goals there was more than one defender posted missing at different stages.

The Celtic Committee had agreed with Blackburn Rovers before the Good Friday meeting at Ewood Park, that the home team would take all the takings so when the bumper crowd of 12,000 turned up and £343 was drawn at the gates, it was deemed a wise decision, especially as 7000 had attended the match in Blackburn.

The same agreement was also reached with Bolton Wanderers and again Celtic benefited when 10,000 turned up to watch the match five days later as opposed to the 4000 who watched the teams in Bolton. Charlie Kelly replaced Jamie Bell in goals and Sandy McMahon, enjoying his legendary partnership with Johnny Campbell on the left, scored both goals as the Celts won the match 2-0, with the first coming just after half time from a thunderous shot and the second coming near the end of the match after more good play with Campbell. Strangely, the Celts had three goals disallowed and stranger still was the decision to do without the five minute half time break and to stop the match ten minutes early to allow Bolton, (with their seven Scots players, two Welshmen and two Englishmen), twenty five minutes to get from Celtic Park after the 16.00 kick off to catch the 17.50 train home from Glasgow Central!

Around 125 years later anyone trying to catch a train from Glasgow Central at 16.50 after a 15.00 kick off, wouldn't be able to do it in a helicopter!

Preston North End became the third part of the English triumvirate, (all three teams were in the top 6 in the English League), to visit Celtic Park on the 21st April and they too were sent home empty handed with two goals from Sandy McMahon and two from Peter Dowds giving us a 4-0 win. McMahon scored the first with a splendid low shot two minutes after kick off and the scores were the same at half time with the Celts well on top. In the second half it was all Celtic as Preston tired quickly and three more goals were rattled in with Dowds grabbing his first of two goals within a few minutes of the start with the ball deflecting in off Ross in the Preston defence. McMahon then got his second, with a shot like a canon, to end the scoring at Celtic 4 The Invincibles 0.

Two former Celts were in the Preston side and both were interesting characters. Barney Crossan, who would return to Celtic in 1895 and was drafted in to play on the 28th November, 1896, on the infamous day when Peter Meehan, John Divers and Barney Battles went on strike due to press criticism. He was again drafted in on the 9th January, 1897, this time having to play in his work trousers, after we only had seven men in the infamous Scottish Cup exit at Arthurlie. The other former Celt was Hugh Gallagher, formerly of Carfin Shamrock, who had scored our first League goal eight months earlier.

Jamie Bell was again replaced in the Celtic goal by Charlie Kelly, but the Celtic Committee were quick to state that Bell was injured and not dropped after losing five goals to Blackburn. Charlie Kelly's two former teams had both disbanded, Glasgow Hibernian and Edinburgh Hibernian so he wasn't exactly the lucky mascot for the team. To his credit he kept a clean sheet against two of England's finest. "Proud Preston," sitting two points behind Everton at the top of the English League were saved any more punishment when the match was bizarrely brought to a premature end with 15 minutes to go, even though the visitors didn't have a train to catch. Preston had played Leith Hibernian the day before the Celtic game and were beaten by 3 goals to 1 in Edinburgh which caused huge shockwaves in the east of Scotland. It's no wonder they wanted to return south as quick as possible to lick their wounds.

In four matches at Celtic Park in ten days, over £1000 was taken at the gates with only a half gate to be paid out to Preston, a third gate to be paid to Dumbarton and appearance monies too. The rest went into Celtic's coffers and it was no wonder that we were described as the *"novelty purveyors to the millions,"* such was the attractive opposition we laid on and the crowds that turned up to see us taking on all comers. The committee did not forget the reason why we were founded and a donation of £60 was made to the Poor Childrens Dinner Tables fund, over and above our normal commitments.

OUR FIRST EVER LEAGUE MATCH AT IBROX

Before we could think of our first League match at Ibrox, we faced Third Lanark at home, then Cowlairs away with a renewed confidence having sent the cream of England back home to think again, once again.

Continuing the story of the season, the Thirds match ended in disappointment which brought the bhoys straight back down to earth, despite a good performance that deserved more than the 1-1 draw after we had scored first in the fifteenth minute from a free kick 16 yards from goal. Thirds responded with an equaliser just before half time and despite excellent play by Sandy McMahon and Johnny Campbell on the left, we simply couldn't break down the Thirds' defence.

Next up was a trip to Cowlairs, our fourth last League match of the season and if we were going to capture 3rd spot we would have to win them all. It was a patched up Celtic eleven that took to the rain soaked pitch at Cowlairs for this midweek fixture with Jamie Bell, James Kelly, Paddy Gallagher, Willie Maley and Johnny Madden all unable to play. John Cunningham, formerly of Edinburgh Hibernian and James Kyle from Benburb made their debuts for the Celts and Michael Dolan, veteran of our very first match in 1888, took Bell's place in goals with Tom Dunbar drafted in from the reserves for a rare appearance, playing alongside his brother Mick.

Given such a makeshift side, even though we were playing the team at the foot of the table, there was no gaurantees we would bond and play our normal game but these fears were blown away by half time as Mick Dunbar scored two goals to give us a 2-0 lead, the first with a swift low shot in the 20th minute and the second just before half time following a free kick. We turned on the style in the second half, with our superior passing game in full flow and added three more goals to finish the scoring at 5-0 to give Cowlairs their first defeat at their new ground, Springvale Park, in Springburn. Tom Duff, once again, would have been sick of the sight of us.

With Dumbarton completing their League campaign of 18 matches with a win at St Mirren that put them 2 points ahead of Rangers, the Ibrox club knew exactly what they had to do, they had to gain 3 points from their final two matches, at home to Celtic and Third Lanark, if they were to be crowned champions. Fortunately for Rangers, goal difference did not come into it as they were well behind Dumbarton, so with Third Lanark lurking in the bottom of the table and not thought to have a chance at Ibrox in the last game of the season, the pre match talk was all about a draw being good enough for Rangers at home to Celtic to clinch the title a week later.

The Celts though, weren't travelling to Ibrox as bit part players on the 2nd of May, we were central to the play, with a full strength team with the exception of Tom Dunbar replacing Mick McKeown who had to visit his dangerously ill sister in Dalmellington, Ayrshire. After starting on the front foot the bhoys took a thoroughly deserved lead on the half hour thanks to a goal from Peter Dowds. The lead didn't last long however as Rangers equalised before half time.

Worse was to follow when Mick Dunbar was forced to leave the field with an injury and the Celts had to play the second half with ten men. Playing with the wind however, the Celts were the better team and when McCreadie of Rangers had to come off injured with thirty minutes remaining, both teams were balanced at ten men each. The draw would do the home team but the Celts just kept on pressing and with 15 minutes remaining, we got our reward as Johnny Madden fired home the winner to send the home fans into despair and the away fans into ecstasy. It was a totally deserved 2-1 victory for Celtic and one that meant Rangers had to beat Third Lanark just to share the first League title. Celtic's record against both Dumbarton and Rangers on League duty was won one and drawn one against both teams, to remain unbeaten.

CELTS AIM TO FINISH FIRST LEAGUE CAMPAIGN ON A HIGH

Following the League win at Ibrox, the Celts had two home matches to fulfil against Vale of Leven on Tuesday, 5th May and Abercorn the following Tuesday. To capture 3rd spot we needed no less than two victories and the first resulted in a resounding one at that, 9-1 against Vale of Leven, which became the record League victory, albeit in only the first ever season, but it also underlined our inconsistency during the campaign as we had lost 3-1 at Vale of Leven earlier in the season.

The bhoys were flying, completely outplaying the Vale, who had Docherty in goals to thank for not getting a bigger mauling. By half time the score stood at 3-0 and the Celts didn't let up in the second half with a further six, to the Vale's one solitary reply. For the record the goals were scored by Sandy McMahon (3), Johnny Campbell (2), Jimmy McGhee (2) and Peter Dowds (2). Our final match of the League season against Abercorn was next and to ensure third place in the League, we had to win. The visitors had nothing to play for as they sat in 7th place, a very creditable achievement for the Paisley team, who sat one place above their fellow Buddies, St Mirren, in the League table.

Having lost to Celtic already in the season, 5-1 at home, this Abercorn side were intent on keeping the score down and they put up a stubborn defence which kept the game goalless with thirty minutes remaining. Thankfully the ever dangerous Sandy McMahon got the breakthrough before Jimmy McGhee added another to give the bhoys a 2-0 victory and 3rd spot in the League.

Ironically we only found our League consistency in the last six matches, winning five and drawing one. Rangers beat Third Lanark in their final match of the season to draw level with Dumbarton at the top and although goal difference, goal average and results head to head were all in favour of Dumbarton, the ruling at the time meant a play off between the two. When this match was drawn 2-2, it was decided to share the first title.

Celtic finished 8 points behind both teams, having had 4 points deducted for playing Jamie Bell in our second and third matches of the season despite the player not having two weeks clearance since his last game for his former club. If we hadn't messed up, and the blame must fall with the Celtic Committee for the administrative error and the sluggishness in finding a goalkeeper, a task we had the whole close season to accomplish, we would have had 25 points. It still wasn't enough, but the point is that we wouldn't have had the severe blow to our momentum at the start of the season which certainly affected our mindset during the campaign.

We shared the best defensive record with Dumbarton over the 18 League matches, with 21 conceded, whilst we were behind both Dumbarton and Rangers in the goalscoring charts, our 48 goals to their 61 and 58 respectively. Celtic were the only team who managed to play a game against Dumbarton without losing a goal, (in our 1-0 victory), and only on one occasion did we play the ninety minutes without scoring a goal, (in our 1-0 defeat at St Mirren).

Celtic and ironically Cowlairs were the only teams to pick up a point at Boghead, Dumbarton, who scored 35 goals in their nine home matches with 8 conceded, averaging almost a 4-1 win per game. The Celts home form was good, with 7 wins and 2 draws against Rangers and Third Lanark, with 26 goals scored and 8 conceded. It was our away record which was to cost us dear with 4 wins, 4 defeats and a draw, with defeats at Vale of Leven, St Mirren, Cambuslang and Third Lanark all the more galling considering we drew at Dumbarton and won at Ibrox.

LOWEST ATTENDANCES AT THE ORIGINAL CELTIC PARK

The last two home matches of the season are noted too for the attendance figures given for both midweek matches against teams at the bottom end of the League, when most fans would be working. 2000 attended the Vale of Leven match, a figure that had been recorded at other matches too, in particular in bad weather and 1500 attended the Abercorn match. These attendances should be taken in the context of the times when 10,000 was seen as a large crowd and run of the mill League matches against unattractive opposition could attract a crowd of three or four thousand.

Therefore the crowd of 1500 for the match against Abercorn on Tuesday, 12th April 1891 could be seen as the lowest for a competitive match at the original ground.

The lowest crowd for a friendly match at the original Celtic Park was in our first season when Airdrie were the visitors on both occasions and the attendance was given as 1000. On Saturday, 29th September 1888 we won 4-1 after thrashing the Lanarkshire team 6-0 in Airdrie six weeks previous and on Saturday, 26th January 1889, a similar attendance turned up to watch a game of two 35 minute halves which ended 1-1.

THE CHARITY CUP

The stuffy old men in charge of Scottish football, were wary of the power of the new kids on the block at the Scottish Football League and this disdain soon manifested itself at the end of the first League season with the arrangements for the annual Charity Cup competition the battleground. The Glasgow Merchants Charity Cup was an annual knock out tournament by invitation only to teams in and around Glasgow, although no exact criteria was ever confirmed, and matches were played at the end of each season. Since its inception in 1877, Queens Park had won it on 7 occasions, Renton on 4 occasions, with Vale of Leven, Third Lanark and Rangers each winning it once.

The trophy was donated by the Glasgow merchants and all funds, as it says on the tin, went to charity. The Charity Committee was made up of five members of the SFA Committee and two Glasgow merchants and therein lay the problem. The dispute in 1891 rose over the difficulty in arranging fixtures in the month of April, which led to a dispute between the clubs, who had already watched their fixture list extend over 34 dates throughout the season, and the Glasgow Charity Cup Committee who refused to alter set dates for fixtures to be played and instead deemed, heavy handedly, that any club who refused to play on the designated date would be replaced. The upshot of the fall out was that Celtic, Rangers and Third Lanark decided not to compete in that year's competition to enable them to complete their League fixtures.

Charity was the big loser as the only other team with the box office appeal and a large enough support who remained in the competition was Queens Park. In the event, Airdrieonians, Partick Thistle and Northern were invited to play in place of Celtic, Rangers and Third Lanark, which did little to whet the paying spectator's appetite. In the semi finals on 11th and 18th April, Northern beat Airdrie 3-1 and Queens Park beat Partick Thistle 2-1 respectively. Queens Park then went on to beat Northern 9-1 in the final on 2nd May after the first match on 25th April was drawn 1-1, (the replay was oft times a ploy to get another big pay day). All of these dates were already taken up on the fixture list, with Celtic for example playing three League matches and a match with Bolton so therein lay the SFL's problem in allowing its top Glasgow clubs to take part.

The whole point of the tournament was to raise money for charity but on this occasion, not surprisingly, only £150 was raised, which fell well below the usual takings. Something had to be done to make up the shortfall and make good a bad situation which didn't reflect well on anyone. A hastily named League Charity Competition was agreed for the one year only and was set up with Celtic, Third Lanark, Rangers and Dumbarton the four participants with the season extended specifically to allow the matches to take place. Ironically the committee formed under the name of the League Charity Committee, with Tom Maley as Secretary, had to go to the SFA for permission to play these matches in May and June.

The *Glasgow Evening News* described Maley as;

"Diligent in business and fervent in spirit, and has lent himself most willingly to crown the season with charity's golden chapel".

Inviting Scottish Cup winners, Hearts, to the original competition had originally been discussed as it could only increase the attraction and therefore the charity donations. Unfortunately Hearts were unable to fit the competition into their season and so Celtic were drawn against Third Lanark to be played at Ibrox on Saturday 23rd May with Rangers playing Dumbarton at Celtic Park the week before on the 16th May.

Dumbarton took care of Rangers by one goal to nil in a rough house at Celtic Park, complete with a sending off for both teams in the "Charity" match, in the build up to their play off tie for the League title five days later at Cathkin, home of Third Lanark. Instead of concentrating on the poor fare on the pitch, some of the press bizarrely speculated on the non appearance of members of the Celtic Committee at the match. It was noted in the *Scottish Referee* on the 18th May;

"Councillor John Ure Primrose, (of Rangers), sat in the press stand as also did Joseph Shaughnessy whilst on the pavillion stand could be seen many football heroes, who in bygone days have thrilled the crowd with enthusiasm by doing deeds in the football arena".

The Celts made easy work of Third Lanark by 8 goals to 1, but due to a protest by Third Lanark regarding the condition of the pitch after heavy rainfall, the game was only played as a friendly, with the replay ordered to be played at Celtic Park. Not for the first time in this kind of ruling there was a difference of opinion, with Tom Maley claiming he had spoken to the Third Lanark representative before the game and offered to play the game as a friendly which the Thirds declined. Then at half time, whilst the Celts were two goals to the good, it was alleged that Third Lanark had changed their minds and that the referee had already made it known before the match that a friendly would be played instead of the cup tie.

Third Lanark's side of the story was that Tom Maley did indeed offer to play the game as a friendly, which they declined before the match, but that after Celtic had scored the first goal, the referee told the Third Lanark representative that the match would be played as a friendly, which the Thirds naturally agreed to. When asked, the referee claimed he had told Tom Maley this. Whether the Thirds had changed their mind about playing the game as a friendly after going two goals down or the referee had changed his mind after Celtic went one goal up, the Celtic players were naturally incensed and a heated debate took place whether they should play the second half or not. Thankfully the wiser heads prevailed and the argument of the doves, that they should carry on due to the charitable nature of the competition outweighed that of the hawks, that they were the victims of an injustice.

The Celts had raced into a 3-1 lead by half time thanks to goals by Peter Dowds and two from Sandy McMahon and they turned their frustrations into positive energy by not letting up in the conditions in the second half, notching another five goals, with two goals from Johnny Campbell, another from Peter Dowds, one from Jimmy McGhee and one from Sandy McMahon, giving him his hat trick.

The League Charity Committee met on the Tuesday and decided that the Celtic v Third Lanark tie should be replayed and as Ibrox was unavailable due to the Scottish Cycling Union Sports which were being held at the ground, the tie would be played at Celtic Park on Saturday, 30th May.

The Celts almost repeated the score line a week later after storming into a four goal lead by half time, obviously still fuelled by the feeling of injustice they harboured from the first game a week previously. Peter Dowds opened the scoring after ten minutes with a goal that was greeted with great enthusiasm before Jimmy McGhee scored from a spectacular overhead kick. Not to be outdone, Dowds scored another in the 25th minute and Sandy McMahon chested the ball over the line, from a cross by Johnny Madden to put the Celtic firmly in control with little over a quarter of the tie played. The Celts were enjoying the lovely May sun in front of a big crowd and in the second half we notched two more goals from Dowds and McMahon before the Thirds grabbed a consolation goal to end the match at Celtic 6 Third Lanark 1.

Incidentally the Celtic team popped into Bells, the photographers on their way to Ibrox for the first game and had their photograph taken with the Glasgow Cup. As yet this photograph has not been seen, but time will tell.

The Celts now had a golden chance to add the Charity Cup to the Glasgow Cup but we had to face Dumbarton, our conquerors in the Scottish Cup. Even the title of the competition couldn't be agreed on with the SFL referring to it as the League Charity Cup and the SFA referring to it as the Supplementary Charity Cup. The original date had been put back a week at our request so it wasn't until Wednesday, 10th June that the teams took to the field at Cathkin Park in front of a very healthy crowd of 8000.

Despite Celtic being installed as the favourites due to our late season form, the ten day break from our last match did us no favours and we were stale, chasing the game, with Dumbarton the better team on the day.

The *Scottish Sport* match report on the 12th June described the match thus;

"Against Parkhead's headlong brilliancy was pitted Dumbarton's dourness,"

However it was Dumbarton's dourness that put paid to Celtic's brilliance, which was sadly lacking on a day we were stuck in a close season mindset. 12,000 packed into Cathkin Park on a sultry June evening with the Celtic support out in full force joined by an enthusiastic gathering of Dumbarton fans. Dumbarton's opener came in the 20th minute and although the bhoys responded by going on the front foot for a while, we created few chances and deserved to go in at half time a goal down. In the second half we continued to struggle a yard off the pace and Dumbarton scored a second in the 50th minute and a third followed with ten minutes to go as the Celts were well beaten on the day.

From the *Scottish Referee* on 15th June;

"Now Erin's son laid low
Yet not by fatal blow
Up men and forward go
Determined still
Erin! stands ebb and flow
On with a will"

After all was said and done the money raised for charity was £820, when added to the original amount of £150 gave a much more respectable figure of £970 raised for charity. Given that one of the ties was played in heavy rain, (our first match with Third Lanark) and that the final was played on a Wednesday night, the takings, although down on the previous four years, were applauded. In the spirit of the competition, the four participants had agreed to save on expenses by contributing £10 each to buy the medals for the winners which cost £25 and the medals for the runners up which cost £15.

The SFL and the SFA had locked horns for the first time, but it was the SFL who flexed their muscle the strongest and forced the competition to be arranged around their fixture list at the end of future seasons. What it did show too was the oft times complex side of Scottish football, whereby the two main organisers of the game in Scotland couldn't organise a charity competition without politics getting in the way.

THE CELTS EXTEND OUR HAND OF FRIENDSHIP

Before the season had finished, the Celts agreed to play Renton and Cowlairs at Celtic Park, both for different reasons, but both reflected the nature of Celtic that has remained true to this day, a club who are not slow to extend the hand of friendship to assist a club or a player in their hour of need.

The first was against Renton on 9th May at Celtic Park. The crack Dunbartonshire club had been dealt with abhorrently by the SFA at the start of the season and were suspended from all football, including the Scottish League after only four matches of the season following the henious crime of playing a friendly match against a team called Edinburgh Saints, who were in reality St Bernards, a team who had been suspended allegedly due to the dreaded word "professionalism".

Renton successfully sued the SFA and were reinstated into the League in time for the start of the 1891/92 season. The Celtic Committee immediately arranged to welcome them back to Scottish football by inviting them to Celtic Park for a match. Councillor Angus Campbell triumphantly led the Renton team out onto the pitch, a team savaged by the decision of the SFA, and no less than 10,000 spectators gave the visitors a fantastic Celtic welcome with resounding cheers bellowing around the ground.

125 years later, the Celtic support still carry on this tradition, showing support for the underdog, wherever he may be. This was the first example and not the last of an opposition team being welcomed to Celtic Park just as warmly as we welcome our own.

The match itself, which was billed as a "Grand Welcome Match", gave an understrength Renton the chance to get some match practice and was played in the true spirit of the game. For the record the bhoys opened the scoring in the 30th minute when Peter Dowds passed to Sandy McMahon and the bold one did the rest with a lightning shot. Abraham from Renton equalised before half time and the goal was welcomed as warmly as Sandy McMahon's counter was, such was the generosity of the Celtic support. Five minutes after the break, Sandy McMahon notched the second with a header, to restore our lead and the bhoys were happy to keep the foot off the gas. The nearest thing to another goal was when Peter Dowds struck the crossbar with a shot but a good day was ended with a 2-1 win and both teams heartily cheered off the pitch.

On Wednesday 27th May, the Celts played Cowlairs in a benefit match for Phil Clarke, the ex Hibs player who we had tried, unsuccessfully, to capture as one of our very first signings, but he had still played for Celtic on a number of occasions. Phil was now suffering badly from ill health and his career was over. Members were encouraged to pay at the gate instead of using their season tickets as the Celtic Committee, as usual, were not slow in showing our charitable side. The match finished Celtic 2 Cowlairs 1.

THE 1891 ANNUAL GENERAL MEETING

The AGM took place on the 16th June at the Mechanics Hall, Canning Street, Calton. Although matters on the pitch and off it financially were well in order, there was a motion on the agenda that went straight to the very heart of the club's foundation, our very raison d'etre as it were, and it was proposed by no less a man than Doctor John Conway, our much respected first Honorary President.

John O'Hara's report as Secretary was very well received with the club having played 49 matches and won 34, lost 8 and drawn 7, with goals scored 148 against 63 conceded. The Glasgow Cup had been won, we were beaten finalists in the Charity Cup, beaten quarter finalists in the Scottish Cup and in the League we were 3rd. Our Reserve team had played 36 matches and won 30, with 6 drawn and no defeats, with half of these matches against first elevens and most of them away from home. They had won the Second XI Scottish Cup and the Second XI

North Eastern Cup and they would also have won the Second XI Glasgow Cup, had one been competed for. Incredibly they had scored 169 goals and conceded only 25.

The Treasurer's report was equally as impressive. Income totalled £4427, 11s & 2d which included £302, 15s & 2d carried over from the previous year. An interesting insight is given into the popularity of the club's fixtures with friendly matches bringing in more than League fixtures; £1400 was brought in from 13 friendlies, £1140 by 14 cup ties and £1100 brought in by the new League fixtures.

Expenditure was given as;

£1031, 3s & 8d paid out to visiting clubs as their share of the gate
£545 & 14s had been donated to charity
£847, 8s & 1d was paid out in match expenses
£147, 4s & 5d was paid in trainer's wages and trainer's expenses
£546, 15s & 9d was paid out in rent, taxes, repairs, cost of new stand, two ponies and a harness
£689, 12s & 6d was paid out in travelling expenses and lost time of the first team and the reserves, with the reserve team accounting for £325, 11s & 4d of that total

The cash balance carried forward was £275, 9s & 9d.

Two things stood out regarding the expenditure column. The first was that we were paying a trainer's wages and also "lost time" to both the first team and the reserves. Lost time was the phrase commonly used to cover reimbursements to players who had to take time off work to play for the club. Remember the players were all officially still amateurs so were not on a professional wage. Covering expenses and reasonable "lost time" was expected by the club, but did the sight of that expenditure outgrowing the donations given to charity unsettle some of the committee?

Unlike James Quillan at the 1889 AGM, the motion proposed by Doctor John Conway went straight to the point and regarded paid officials.

"The action of the committee in creating paid officials, without consulting the general body of the club was incompetent and should be annulled."

The motion was seconded by John H McLaughlin, ironically the man who was to lead the charge for the club to become a Limited Company throughout the next six years until he finally got his wish in 1897, but on this day he was in the strange position of being labelled a so called "malcontent". Doctor Conway criticised the actions of the committee for paying men who at the last General Meeting were elected to do the job for nothing. He made the point that there were plenty of gentlemen before him who would willingly take over the duties for the love of the club and the object for which it was formed and so long as such could be got, he opposed paying anybody.

John H McLaughlin, in agreeing, stated that the appointment of the paid officials, (detailed in the list of expenditure as Secretary John O'Hara and Second XI Secretary James Curtis at a cost of £43, 10s), had actually doubled the cost of sundry matters instead of saving the club money and therefore the appointments had not been a success.

The member who originally proposed the appointment of paid officials was John Brown, the Vice Chairman of the Thomas Moore branch of the Irish National Foresters based in Cumberland St, Glasgow and he raised a direct negative which was seconded by Joseph Nelis and supported by that man again, James Quillan, who had now turned up at an AGM, (obviously having been allowed to renew his membership). Ironically two years after walking out of an AGM to create a rival club, after falling out with the committee, he was now back and supporting a counter motion that backed the committee. In the original proposer's view, paid officials were necessary as it was better to have one person who could conduct the secretarial business of the club rather than rely on a number of committee men at extra cost with the ensuing pressures on their time.

Once the debate had settled a vote was taken and those in favour of Doctor Conway's motion numbered 74, those against 102. Although defeated, the vote was a close one, with the Doctor only 15 short of a majority. Canvassing by both sides would have been undertaken in advance of the meeting to gauge support and its possible that the Doctor believed he did have enough support to go ahead with the motion and was only defeated on the night, after the members numbering almost 200 listened to the debate.

Certainly his point was valid, that is, a decision made by the committee to create paid officials should have went to the general body which could only have happened at the AGM. Ironically the number of votes he was short of a majority, fifteen, was the same number of bodies on the Committee who made the decision to create paid officials without consulting the general body so in effect the vote had split the membership of the club right down the middle.

Doctor Conway knew that in raising his concerns at an AGM, in which he was due for re-election, he stood the risk of failing to be re-elected if his motion was not passed and this is exactly what happened. Both Stephen J Henry, (who had just had a motion defeated to include the word "cycling" into the title of the club due to no seconder coming forward), and Joseph Michael Nelis were nominated.

Both Nelis and Henry had been with the club from the very start and they now put down the challenge to Doctor Conway, who had been our Honorary President since the club's inception. Nelis had of course seconded the direct negative to Conway's motion and in doing so he was making it known that he stood directly against the Honorary President, with the election next on the agenda. Having been on the winning side of the motion, it followed then that he won the election, although on this occasion it was by a large majority.

Doctor Conway then lost again in a vote against John Glass for the Presidency of the club, in honesty, a fight he was never going to win. In the following reshuffle William McKillop replaced Frank McErlean in the Vice President's chair, Tom Maley was appointed as Treasurer replacing John H McLaughlin, who narrowly defeated John McFadyen to be appointed into the post of Secretary after John O'Hara stepped down following excellent work since our foundation. So in one of life's ironies, John H McLaughlin who had seconded the motion to annul the appointment of paid officials, was now elected into the post of you guessed it, paid official.

The popular half back Willie Maley was unanimously re elected as Match Secretary.

The first work of the new Committee was to agree a £20 donation to the Evicted Tenants Fund in Ireland, which they duly did. The meeting had lasted from quarter past eight in the evening until quarter past two in the morning, a full six hours in which it was reported that;

"The anti officialites, as the opposition in the Celtic Committee had been called, had been cleared out."

However it failed to live up to the newspaper billing with prophesies of rowdyism.

Indeed it was reported that;

"The Celtic FC, besides being masters of organisation, know how to conduct the business of their meeting in the orthodox manner, and themselves in a proper manner."

In a strange sign of the times, the new Secretary, John H McLaughlin, attended the Rangers "smoking concert" a week later at Ancells, in Glassford Street, where he accompanied the Rangers Musical Association, (glee club), on the piano.

Changed days indeed.

The AGM of 1891 is now regarded as the first battle for the soul of the club, between the charitable and the business sides of the club and it is a debate that still rumbles on between some Celtic supporters to this day.

By agreeing to create paid officials, the membership were stepping away from the wholly charitable aims espoused only four years earlier but at the same time they announced at the AGM that charitable donations had risen by over 20% on the previous year. Our balance at the AGM totalled £821, 3s and 9d before donations to charity of £545, 14s so in effect we donated two thirds of our profits to charity.

It was not a matter of one or the other, was it more a sign of the times that to succeed we had to pay the piper? Or was it the beginning of the end for the club's soul as the business side came more to the front in a battle that was to last another six years with only one outcome? Certainly once the floodgates opened there was no plugging the gaps with professionalism not far away, a move that was to change the course of Scottish football history for ever.

Interestingly, the *Glasgow Observer*, (who often printed words of thanks from different Catholic organisations for donations received from Celtic FC), seemed more than happy with the Celtic Committee in May 1891 stating;

"The Celtic management are about the smartest any team going possesses. They have the knack of spotting an opportune thing".

The Scottish Sport on 23rd June however put a different spin on things and possibly hit the nail on the head;

"It has been better known than an open secret for some time that the committee of the Celtic, who have just demitted office, were not exactly of one mind on several matters not quite unconnected with the club's management and general policy. As a matter of fact, it was split into two distinct and opposite parties, both of whom were

suspicious and distrustful of each other. Such a state of affairs, although not probably visible to the casual eye, was utterly inimical to the best interests of the club. Had it been allowed to continue, it is not going too far in the direction of mere speculative prophecy to assert that it would have finally culminated in a serious breach, which might have been disastrous to the club and would probably also have been in time, regretted by both sections. We were however, pleased to see that by the constitutional intervention of the membership, at their annual meeting last Tuesday evening, such a serious contingency has been avoided.

It would be incorrect to assert that the difficulty of the position has been obviated by the total defeat of one of the parties; for while there has been a decided triumph for what may be called the ministerial party - and it would have been most serious if a perceptible want of confidence had been shown by the membership towards them - still the triumph has not been all along the line. And indeed, it is perhaps as well that the semblance of a compromise has been left. We trust that the matters of disagreement having been adjudicated upon and settled by the only tribunal which could properly pronounce upon them - the annual meeting - the distracting friction will now be entirely removed and the new committee go into a new season with the energy and harmony which alone can guarantee success. Let old differences be buried and renewed enthusiasm take their place and we have no fear of the future of the popular club".

28 nominees were put forward for the 9 vacant posts on the committee and depending on what newspaper you read, after the elections the following were successful; Arthur Murphy, Joseph Shaughnessy, David Meikleham, James Curtis, Stephen J Henry, John McQuade, James Kelly, G Bradley and D McIntyre. Of these, Murphy, Henry, McQuade, Bradley and McIntyre were elected for the first time. The Scottish Sport and Referee differ in their accounts, with the Sport referring to Bradley and McIntyre being elected, whilst the Referee has neither, and has John A McCreadie instead. A year later at the 1892 AGM, neither of the three names were re-elected onto the committee.

What is clear that in just two years, since the Quillanites had been routed at the 1889 AGM, we were again in the middle of a split which threatened the stability of the club in which good men were lost to the club. In fact after the 1889 AGM, when we all started to sing from the same hymn sheet again, only six survived the 1891 AGM: John Glass, Willie Maley, William McKillop, John H McLaughlin, Joseph Shaughnessy and James Curtis. Albeit John O'Hara had stepped down, Dan Malloy had emigrated to America and we suffered the tragic losses of Hugh Darroch and Michael Cairns, but Doctor John Conway in particular was a very sad loss to the club just four years after he had played a pivotal role in founding the club with his speech on 12th February 1887 at St Mary's Hall as we feted Hibernian on their Scottish Cup victory. The wounds were never healed with our first Honourable President and tragically he died just three years later, in 1894 at the young age of 35.

The battle lines had been drawn and although the business side had struck the first blow, this would be a long war that would last another six years before reaching its conclusion, the biggest loser being the charitable aims of the club at its inception.

A closer look at the charitable donations during the season released at the AGM, gives an invaluable insight into the thinking of the club's founding fathers. Similar to the previous year almost all donations went to Catholic charities, and one of the biggest donations was made to the Irish Prisoners Aid Fund. Once again another example of how at our inception, football, politics and religion were central to the mix.

St Mary's Poor Childrens Dinner Tables Fund; £119, 15s, 8d
Sacred Heart Poor Childrens Dinner Tables Fund; £67, 9s, 4d
St Michael's Poor Childrens Dinner Tables Fund; £33
Dalbeth Convent; £45
Belvedere Hospital Catholic Library; £20
Mrs Healy donation; £1
Prisoners Aid Fund; £25, 15s
E Haining donation; £3, 3s
Owen Hughes; £5, 5s
St Josephs Conference, St Vincent De Paul Society; £3, 10s
Benburb FC donations; £10
Re J McDonald, Dunoon donation; £7, 7s
Rev Bernard Tracy; £10
Rev I De Mauleanero donation; £7, 7s
Rev JJ Foley, Balfron; £7, 7s
Little Sisters of the Poor; £35
Whitevale Refuge for Children; £50
Lanark Orphanage; £25
Lanark Hospital; £45
Clothing Society at St Mary's; £14, 17s, 4d
Clothing Society at Sacred Heart; £6, 2s, 8d
Clothing Society at St Michael's; £3
Clothing Society at St Alphonsus; £5

Marriage presents were also given to captain James Kelly and Jerry Reynolds, as mentioned, £15 and £10 respectively.

Celtic were now at the forefront of Scottish football, leading the way on and off the pitch. Our balance sheet of income and expenditure was larger than Third Lanark, Queens Park and double that of Rangers, who came in a distant fourth.

Minutes of the meeting from the *Glasgow Evening News* on 17th June and the Scottish Referee on the 22nd;

"The third annual meeting of the Celtic Club, which has been longed for by some and dreaded by other members of the club, came off on Tuesday night in the Mechanics' Hall, Canning Street, Calton, and although the meeting was confined to members only, in obedience to the demand of my editor, I ventured forth to the meeting to hear what I could of the proceedings, which were expected by everybody to be of a stormy nature. I arrived at the hall a little before eight o'clock, and found it packed with a respectable but excited audience, who were much taken up with discussion amongst themselves that they did not observe me sliding under the table at the entrance and seating myself at the side of the platform to watch and hear.

Sharp at 8 o'clock, Mr John Glass, the President, took the chair and called upon the Secretary, Mr John O'Hara, to move the minutes of the previous meeting, which was unanimously adopted. The Secretary then submitted his report, which stated that the club had just passed through the most successful year in their history, having beaten every club of any importance in England and Scotland, the list including victories over the Scotch and English Cup holders. Besides being third in the League, (though they had beaten the joint champions in the League contest), the club were possessors of the Glasgow Cup; and the reserve team, which had not been beaten during the season, were holders of the Scottish and North Eastern trophies, and had established a record during the season which was not likely to be broken for some time to come.

The summary of the first eleven matches were - Played 49, won 31, lost 8, drawn 7, scored 148 goals, and lost 63. Reserves played 36, won 30, lost 0, drawn 6, goals scored 187, lost 32. These preliminaries having been concluded, the agenda paper was taken up, and Doctor Conway rose to propose that "The action of the committee in creating paid offices and appointing paid officials without consulting the general body of the club, was incompetent, and should be annulled."

The Doctor went on to criticise the action of the committee, who, he said, were creating a bad precedent in paying men who at the general meeting were elected to do the work for nothing, for if the principle was not to put a stop to now it was hard to say where the thing would end. He maintained that there were plenty of gentlemen before him who could and would take over such duties for love of the club, and the object for which it was formed, and so long as such could be got he would oppose paying anybody. Mr John H McLaughlin seconded the motion, and in a very lengthy speech, in which he was repeatedly interrupted, he went on to show that the official had not been a success, for the expenses of sundry matters had been almost doubled since the officials appointment, although the office was created for the purpose of saving money to the club. Mr John Brown, as the original proposer of the official, moved the previous question and gave as his reasons for doing so that the club had lost money by having to send members of committees to do business which an official could perform at a little cost to the club.

Besides, he often heard men say they had not time to do this or do that, whereas with an official, the thing had only to be mooted, and it was done at once, Mr Joseph M Nelis, in a few remarks, seconded the previous question. After some further discussion, in which much heat was engendered, Mr Thomas Flood, in his speech which was certainly the tit-bit of the meeting, condemned the manner in which both sides had carried on the controversy. Coming into the meeting, he, along with other members, was handed two lists of names asking his vote for them, as he was not a supporter of any party, he decided to vote for the men on both sides who, he thought, would work for the interest of the club.

He severely condemned the action of the committee in appointing not only one official, but two officials without calling a general meeting of the members; but, on the other hand, he was of opinion that an official was necessary to the proper conducting of the clubs affairs. He believed every member of the old committee was thoroughly honest and trustworthy, still he thought it advisable in a case such as theirs, were upwards of £4000 passed through the hands of a few individuals in nine months, that men should be at the head of affairs who had the interest of the club at heart before anything else. He moved that - "We hereby agree to the appointment of one salaried official to look after the club's affairs, but we regret that a general meeting of the club was not called earlier for the settlement of this affair." Mr John A Macreadie rose to second this motion, but the Chairman decided that as it was the past action of the committee that was under consideration he could not accept the rider.

On a division being taken, there voted for Dr Conway's motion 74, and Mr Brown's amendment 102, the figures being received with much demonstration by the officialites. The Treasurer's statement was then submitted, which showed the income to be £4427, 11s, 2d and the expenditure £4152, 1s, 6d, leaving a balance of £275, 9s, 9d in the hands of the Treasurer. Mr Richard Ford demanded that the Treasurer, (Mr John H McLaughlin), should read the report, but the feeling of the meeting was against the idea, and the report was unanimously adopted. A number of amendments to the rules were proposed, none of which were carried, with the exception of one moved by Mr Joseph Shaughnessy, and seconded by Mr Thomas Flood, that a general meeting be held every six months, at which a statement of affairs be submitted. This was agreed to unanimously. At this period of the meeting the excitement had considerably toned down, and the members were getting into a better humour with one another, so after some minor matters had been disposed of the meeting braced itself for the election of office bearers.

Dr Conway, Honorary President, was unseated in favour of Mr Joseph M Nelis; Mr John Glass, President, was elected in opposition to Dr Conway, also proposed; Mr William McKillop was elected Vice President over the head of Mr Francis McErlean, unseated; Mr Tom E Maley was elected Treasurer instead of Mr John H McLaughlan, who was shifted to the position of Secretary in room of Mr John O'Hara, the much abused official, who gave the meeting some idea of the unenviable nature of the post and who declined to have it at any money; and Mr William Maley was unanimously re-elected Match Secretary. The election of nine of a committee took a couple of hours, there were so many nominations and to add to the delay someone took away the ballot papers and new ones had to be provided. During the counting of the votes about a dozen songs were contributed to the members of the club and players and these had the effect of making everyone be on good terms.

Ultimately it was found that the "officialites" had carried the day and that Messrs, Arthur Murphy, James Kelly, Joseph Shaughnessy, David Miekleham, James Curtis, John McQuade, Stephen J Henry and John A McCreadie were elected. Mr John H McLaughlan was chosen as League representative, Mr Tom E Maley representative to Glasgow Association, Mr James Curtis 2nd X1, Scottish Association and Mr Patrick Gallagher captain of the team for next season. The meeting, after awarding a vote of thanks to the chairman broke up at 3am, most of the members waiting til the finish".

The minutes from the *Scottish Sport* on 19th June;

"The Mechanics Hall, Bridgeton, was the scene of the annual meeting of the Glasgow Cupholders. A very large turnout of members were present when, at about 8.15, President Glass, with his colleagues in office, made their appearance on the platform. The business was opened by Mr John O'Hara reading minutes of last general meeting, These were unanimously adopted. Thereafter Mr O'Hara read his secretarial report for season just concluded. This report - a very excellent production indeed - dealt with the success of the club's efforts, especially the prowess of the individuals of the first and reserve teams, and also referred to the divided state of committee. This report was very favourably received and accepted by the meeting. An objection was raised by Mr John McLaughlin regarding membership and minuted matter, but was summarily dealt with.

Prior to the Treasurer's report being read, the motion on agenda paper in name of Dr Conway was put to the meeting by the Doctor, who in his speech supporting the same occasionally left the point at issue, and had to be called to order by the Chairman. The motion was in the following terms:-

"The action of the committee in creating paid officials, without consulting the general body of the club, was incompetent, and should be annulled". Mr John H McLaughlin seconded the motion and in a very lengthy statement endeavoured to prove that the official, instead of being a preventive of expense, actually increased expenditure. The speech was frequently interrupted with cries of "Question" etc, and from this it was evident that many of the "facts" were according to some minds mere "creation of figures". A direct negative was moved in a very brief, concise, and clear manner by one of the pillars of the club and seconded by Mr Joseph M Nelis and supported by Mr James Quillan. Mr Thomas Flood, in a rather clever, though long speech, endeavoured to move another resolution, which was of course ruled out of order. Mr Tom Maley then appealed to the Chairman to take a vote, as he was of the opinion that for a specific purpose the debate was being prolonged. Acting on the appeal, the Chairman asked Dr Conway, the mover of the motion, to close the debate, and a division was then taken. For Dr Conway's motion, 74; against, 102. Thus the first encounter ended favourably to the officials. The Treasurer's report was then adopted.

The various amendments to rules, as appearing on agenda paper, were then taken up. For want of a seconder Mr Stephen J Henry's proposal to include cycling in the title and description of the club was lost. Mr John H McLaughlin proposed that the Match Secretary be hence forth known as the Assistant Secretary, but it was negatived; and his other proposal to delete Rule 10 was similarly disposed of. Amendements by Dr Scanlan and Mr James McKay were also defeated. Mr Joseph Shaughnessy was more successful in his amendment, it being passed by a very large majority - in fact unanimously. His amendment was that a half yearly general meeting should be held. Half time was now called; indeed, by the hurried exit of several of the members, it was "half" time literally and figuratively.

On coming into the meeting, (at the outset at half time), members were presented with a small handbill soliciting support for certain gentlemen named, and asking that support on the strength of a leaflet issued a day or two prior to the meeting. Others possessed a small card, (MS). These papers were now carefully scrutinised; here and there tickets were at work doing all in there power for their favourite. The first office to fill was that of Honorary President, a position held by Dr Conway since the origin of the club. For this position Mr Joseph Nelis was nominated, as was also Mr Stephen J Henry. On a vote being taken Mr Nelis was declared to have been elected by a large majority. Mr Francis McErlean was ousted from the Vice-Chair, (held by him for the last two years), by Mr William McKillop.

Mr Tom Maley easily received appointment as Treasurer (lately held by John H McLaughlin). As Secretary, Mr J H McLaughlin was appointed after a close vote, his opponent being Mr. John McFadyen. The popular left-half back, (Willie Maley), was unanimously re-elected Match Secretary. For positions on committee, 28 names were submitted for the 9 vacancies. During enumeration of votes an excellent concert was extemporised. Mick McKeown opened the proceedings, which were never allowed to flag by efforts of Messrs Sandy McMahon, Paddy Gallagher, Jimmy Boyle, Frank and Mick Dolan, Mick Dunbar and Johnny Coleman as representing the players, and Messrs John A M'Creadie, J.A. Bradley, Joseph Shaugnessy and James Cairns as the non-playing element. It was now well past the wee sma' oor ayont the twal," yet the members seemed to be quite as earnest and as zealous as when the meeting opened. The Chairman, on taking the results of the ballot, did not keep the members very long in suspense.

The following were declared to have been duly elected members of the committee;- Messrs *Arthur Murphy, *G Bradley, Joseph Shaughnessy, David Meikleham, James Curtis, *Stephen J Henry, *John McQuade, James

Kelly and *D McIntyre, of which those marked thus* are new members. Messrs John H McLaughlin and Tom Maley were representatives to the League and Glasgow Football Association respectively. On the motion of Mr McGinn, seconded and supported by Messrs Arthur Murphy and Joseph Shaughnessy, it was agreed to give a donation of £20 to the fund for relief of evicted tenants in Ireland, The general meeting sent a recommendation to the committee that Paddy Gallagher be appointed captain for the ensuing season, and a suggestion made by Mr John A McCreadie regarding "smoking concert" was also transmitted, Two a.m. was now reached, and after according a very hearty vote of thanks to the chairman, the meeting dispersed at the early hour of 2.15am.

Prolonged though the meeting was there was a complete absence of what even the most pessimistically inclined individual could carp at. The Chairman gave full scope for debate, provided of course, that the elementary principles were not encroached on, viz.- irrelevant matter or personal allusion. One or two attempts were made to adjourn, but these miserably failed. The last effort was the removal of "ballot papers," (officially stamped). The substitution necessary under these circumstances of course delayed matters considerably, though a member suggested that ballot papers could be sent per post to members and returned similarly, a suggestion that was received with anything but satisfaction.

Dame Rumour has not in any way lost her prestige, she - poor old soul! - prophesised all sorts of things in connection with the meeting - rows, scenes, ejections, and what not, and all, were conspicuous by their absence. Former meetings, though not so protracted have been more exciting and interesting. One would fancy on reading the day bill of a contemporary, that the meeting was something akin to Committee Room, Number 15, and that Celtic and rowdyism were synonymous. The contrary is the case and had a member of the press been really present, judgement could have been formed that the Celtic FC, besides being masters of organisation, know how to conduct the business of their meeting in the orthodox manner and themselves in a proper manner".

THE RETURN OF THE PRODIGAL SON

One name that cannot be ignored at the AGM of 1891 is James Quillan. The successful businessman who owned a cooperage on Janefield Street right behind the Celtic end at the new Celtic Park was now back in the fold with the new Celtic Committee whilst at the same time he was defending an action taken against him and members of the defunct Glasgow Hibernian by Thomas McDougall for payment of the work done in the erection of the barricade around their ground, Hibernian Park.

Proving membership of the club was difficult as no regular rules or records were kept by the club and so it showed with the case of James Quillan's membership. However it was judged that he was a promoter of the club and gave credit to the sum of £10 and so Sheriff Erskine Murray found against him to that amount.

Was James Quillan in the right place at the right time regarding the split in the committee in the build up to the 1891 AGM? Certainly he was confident enough not only to turn up at the AGM but to second a direct negative to the motion. He may not have been welcomed without the split in the committee but as often happens during an argument, strange bedfellows appear and there was no stranger a circumstance than James Quillan's re-appearance.

THE DEATH OF CANON HANNAN

The death of Edward Joseph Hannan on Wednesday, 24th June 1891 from pneumonia which followed a severe bout of influenza at the age of 55 cast a dark spell over the Catholics of Edinburgh but also touched the hearts of many more throughout the country. The priest from Ballingarry in County Limerick had served faithfully at only one parish, St Patrick's in Edinburgh, since he was ordained on 13th May 1860, with the exception of a short six week familiarisation at St Mary's, where he took up his first position on 17th August 1861. It's fair to say however, that within a short while, his influence spread far from his adopted city.

Co founder of Hibernian in 1875, Canon Hannan was the club's first manager until his death in 1891 and the religious bond he shared with Brother Walfrid could have played a part in Hibs' decision to stop off at St Mary's Hall in the Calton on 12th February 1887 to celebrate their Scottish Cup win with the Glasgow Irishmen. Canon Hannan's Hibernian were central to the main ingredients coming together at our foundation, he showed Brother Walfrid that football could raise funds for charitable needs and he also showed his fellow Irishman that an Irish team could reach the very top in the game and be successful. Crucially in doing this, he helped put all the main ingredients together in the one place at the one time, St Mary's Hall, when the Glasgow Irish realised that they could do likewise.

Hibernian fans revere the memory of Canon Hannan and it should always be remembered that the Celtic family have a great deal to be thankful for too in memory of this great Irishman.

THE SEARCH FOR A NEW CELTIC PARK

Although we were now well into the close season, one eye was already on the second Celtic Sports which would take place on Saturday 1st and 8th of August. Improvements had already taken place on the running/cycle track in May when it was widened and banked and by the middle of June the new cinder track was completed.

Although there was no mention of it at the June AGM, during the summer of 1891 the Committee learned that the landlord, Alexander Waddell, had decided to raise the rent on the land where Celtic Park stood from £50 per annum to a whopping £450, a decision that gave the committee little option but to look elsewhere for the promised land.

In honesty the men who ran Celtic would have been well aware that in three short seasons we had outgrown the cramped boundaries of the original ground which was bound on the west by the graveyard and on the east and south by Dalmarnock Street and Janefield Street. On the northern boundary lay houses so there was no room for expansion. Even the improvements on the cinder track came at the expense of the football pitch which had to be narrowed to allow for the widening and banking.

By summer 1891, the Committee knew that with the five year lease expiring in November 1892, they must act quickly to get the issue resolved. The landlord's decision to increase the rent tenfold was certainly the catalyst to look elsewhere but I have no doubt whatsoever that even if the rent had stayed the same it only delayed the inevitable, which was the club's relocation from the Holy Grail, the original Celtic Park, to a larger ground. If anything the landlord did us a favour by focussing minds on the future of the club, with the decision best made sooner rather than later.

In Willie Maley's book, *"The Story of the Celtic,"* published in 1939 he states that other sites were looked at too;

"At one time it was thought to go out to Possilpark or Springburn, but as the Cowlairs had sort of official rights to the northern district the idea was abandoned. When one sees the extension of the city, Possilpark would have been a great spot for the Celts, where with very cheap ground in those days a wonderful enclosure might have been there now as the Celtic stadium".

The *Scottish Referee* on 20th July 1891 stated;

"Regarding their new field - which is all but settled upon, the lease I believe only requiring to be signed - I had a look at the park and it does not present a very inviting appearance. It will require a deal of levelling up and the expense of erecting hoarding, making a new track, fixing stands etc, will make a big hole in the club's exchequer. But the hardy Celts doubtless, will survive the trouble, and once more will rise as of yore, smiling and triumphant. The proprietor of their current ground is inexorable and the Celts think he has other than monetary reasons for wishing them away".

The last sentence here is very interesting. "Inexorable" is a very strong word to describe the proprietor and his determination to oust the club from his land. It translates as unstoppable, unavoidable, immovable, unyielding, inflexible, uncompromising. It leaves no doubt that there was no room for negotiation whatsoever and he wanted us out. "The Celts think he has other than monetary reasons for wishing them away," points towards the proprietor increasing the rent nine fold knowing that there was no way Celtic would pay it. It was a paper exercise with the intention to get rid and wasn't a starting point in the negotiations and the word "inexorable" underlines his attitude.

What other reasons, apart from money, which the newspaper alluded to, would he have? Certainly there was no great rivals for the land, it had lay empty before our arrival and indeed it lay empty after our departure for more than a decade when the land was finally sold and council houses built on the land in the new century. Sadly, reasons based on race and religion couldn't be ruled out for our eviction from the first ground.

The Celtic Committee didn't let the grass grow under their feet, (excuse the pun) and in the same week, the *Scottish Sport* stated;

"The Celtic FC are expected to fix their new habitation this week".

On the 27th July, the *Scottish Referee* stated;

"Celtic, I am informed, have signed a long lease for their new field and operations have already been started to put the place in ship shape. The Celts do not require to leave their present enclosure for some little time yet, and they intend when they do leave to have their new abode ready to step into, so that no hitch may occur in bringing off fixtures".

On the 4th August, the *Scottish Sport* stated;

"Celtic Park was looking well on Saturday. There is more grass on it at present than we have seen for some considerable time. A close season evidently benefits grounds as well as players. The press box has been enlarged and enclosed, an improvement which will be best appreciated by the fastidious knights of the pencil".

This shows that although we were intent on remaining at the original ground for only one more season, improvements were still made to it with regards to the running/cycling track and the press box.

The search for the location of a bigger ground would ideally lay within the east end of Glasgow and importantly too in the heartland of the parishes of St Mary's, St Michaels or Sacred Heart as it was there that we now had a sense of belonging, we had made that area our own with its large Irish population nearby and thankfully we didn't have to look far. Diagonally south west of the original site and on the other side of Janefield Street, lay a disused brick yard, complete with a 40 foot deep quarry hole, half filled with water. It couldn't have been in a worse state of disrepair but the founding fathers could see beyond that, for it had the two things we needed more than most; size and location. The committee knew that if there was one lesson to be learned from the original Celtic Park, it was the need for expansion and room for growth, not just for the coming years as Celtic took Scottish football by storm, but for the future decades, if not centuries and so they were proven correct.

The one thing we did not lack was support and with many of the Irish in the east end experienced in the building trades, we were never short of hard graft.

THE KELLYS, THE WHITES & THE GRANTS

Ironically almost exactly a century later, with the findings of the Taylor report on January 1990, Celtic Park was required to be all seated by August 1994, and so the Board was busy carrying out a similar search. The difference in a century was that in 1891, the Celtic Committee was comprised of some of the sharpest minds in the game, way ahead of their time and at the cutting edge of the revolution that shook Scottish football free of the stuffy old middle class men who ran it previously.

In 1990, the Celtic Board was comprised of the Kellys, the Whites and the Grants, amongst others, who had ran the club into heavy debt and were under severe pressure from the fans to deliver on the pitch and now off it too. They were well behind the times and the only revolution they would see, was the one led by the fans, which ousted them. Their ancestors had served the club with various degrees of distinction but this was well beyond a group of men whose expertise was in self preservation.

James Kelly had started the Kelly dynasty at the club, almost from our inception as he was our first captain who then went on to serve on the committee before the club went public in 1897, when shares were first allotted and he became a member of the Board which he served for 35 years up until his death in 1932, including 5 years as Chairman between 1909 and 1914. When James died, he was replaced on the Board by his son Robert who served on the Board until 1971 when he died, including 24 years as Chairman from 1947 to 1971. When Robert died he was replaced by his nephew Kevin Kelly who remained on the Board from 1971 until 1994 when he was ousted, having served almost 3 years as Chairman from October 1991 to February 1994. Kevin's cousin Michael Kelly, also joined the Board in 1990 but quickly became a hate figure and was also ousted in 1994.

Thomas White started the White dynasty in 1906 when founding father John Glass left him his shares on his death. Tom White was the Chairman of the Irish Nationalist newspaper the Glasgow Star & Examiner, which was founded by the Irish National League as a competitor to the more conservative Catholic Observer. John Glass was on the committee of the Home Government branch of the INL in Glasgow, who were responsible for the decision and he saw Tom White as his protégé. White served on the Celtic Board until his death in 1947, an incredible 41 years including 33 as Chairman from 1914 to 1947. Incredibly Colonel John Shaughnessy is the longest serving Celtic Board member, beating White by a few months. Tom White's son Desmond joined the Board in 1947, after originally taking up Willie Maley's secretarial duties in 1939 shortly before he left the Manager's post. Desmond White remained on the Celtic Board until his death in 1985, serving 14 years as Chairman from 1971 to 1985. His shares and place on the Board were then taken up by his son, Christopher White in 1982, who was thought to be more interested in rowing than in football and he lasted until 1994 when he too was ousted.

James Grant began the Grant dynasty after serving on the Celtic Board from 1897 when he was elected onto the first Board after acquiring shares when the club went public. Grant was from Toomebridge in Ireland and invested heavily in Celtic from our original share issue. He was to build the Grant Stand in 1899 which was the original stand on the main stand side and he remained on the Celtic Board until his death in 1914. His shares were then held by Celtic Director and fellow Irishman Thomas Colgan who had married James Grant's daughter in 1906. On the death of Thomas Colgan in 1946, the Colgan/Grant block of shares passed down to his daughter Mary Colgan, (James Grant's grand daughter), who was based in Toomebridge, and she instantly became the third largest shareholder behind the Kellys and the Whites.

The Kelly, White and Grant triumvirate or family dynasty were reaching their maximum grip on the club's shareholding and it took almost 50 years to wrestle control from them. In 1956, Mary Colgan died and a large part of the shares went to her uncle Neil Grant and her aunt Felicia Grant, who both remained unmarried. Neil passed away in the early 60s and once again a lady in Ireland, Felicia Grant, held major sway in the Celtic shareholding, making her the largest shareholder with almost 20% of the total.

On her death in 1973 in Belfast, half of the shares were distributed to family in Ireland, America and Canada and the other half went to her nephew James Grant in Scotland who then passed them onto Tom Grant, who was James Grant's great grandson. Tom Grant became the first member of the family to serve on the Board in 1985, since James Grant in 1914 and he lasted until he was amongst the members of the old Board ousted in the Revolution of 1994.

THE SEARCH FOR THE NEW CELTIC PARK REACHES A CLIMAX

On the 11th August 1891 the *Scottish Sport* stated;

"The Celtic, we understand are at present in hopes of securing seven acres of presently waste ground lying immediately to the southwest of their present field, which they will quit in another year.

The position of the proposed site is a little nearer the city than the present one, which will not, we should say, be regarded in the light of an objection by footballers in general. Although it is little better than a free coup at present, it is all the same ample in size and therefore capable of being transformed, with the expenditure of money and trouble into one of the finest enclosures in the country.

Considering the expense which the removal is likely to entail upon the club, the Committee will doubtless make sure that this time they are sufficiently secured against early disturbance. We believe the Committee, in laying out their new ground, are determined to lead the way in efficient track accommodation. They have fully experienced the necessity for greater cycling facilities and are determined to supply it.

We shall not be surprised if they lay down two tracks, a three laps one exclusively reserved for cycling and a quarter mile inside one for foot racing. If they adhere to that proposal, we do not hesitate to prophesise that their ground will be a favourite haunt of the humming wheel, which is bound to increase greatly in public favour and finally become the summer sport of the people."

On the same date, the same newspaper stated;

"The Celtic, when they obtain their new ground, contemplate laying two cinder tracks, one of four laps for foot racing and a second reserved exclusively for cycles, which will be three and a half laps to the mile, with 4 foot of banking at the bends. This may stimulate the authorities at Hampden and Ibrox to do the same. Until cyclists have a track for themselves they need not expect to approach English times".

CHAPTER SIX

THE 1891/92 SEASON

Now once again your colours bright
Triumphant, carry through the fight
Do honour to the green and white
And bravely win the cup!

During the busy summer months of 1891, work was going ahead at Celtic Park on three fronts;

1. The improvement of the first team with three massive signings in Dan Doyle and Alec Brady from Everton and Neil McCallum's return from Notts Forest, after the introduction of the "Amnesty," whereby any amateur Scottish players who signed a professional contract in England were allowed to return home to play "amateur"

2. The improvements on the cinder track to ensure the success of the second Celtic Sports on 1st and 8th August.

3. Securing the ground where the second and current Celtic Park was to be built on.

On the 1st June 1891, the Scottish Referee reported;

"The track in Celtic Park has undergone great improvement. The ugly corners, to the detriment however of the football pitch have been widened and banked. In view of the Sports, great attention is now bestowed on the track."

Meanwhile over at the original Ibrox Park, the committee were fighting over the shade of green that the goalposts and railings had been painted. Taking up an idea from Trent Bridge Cricket Ground, they had agreed to paint the structures in a pale pea green, but this wasn't communicated well to the painter and decorator who brought along his finest pot of emerald green paint.

Such was the fuss caused by the sight of Ibrox resplendent in emerald green that the rumour soon spread that Celtic were recanting to Ibrox and Rangers were being "papped oot," to borrow a Glasgow vernacular. A certain painter was last seen dashing along Paisley Road West and working long into the night to correct his erroneous ways.

THE SECOND ANNUAL CELTIC SPORTS

On 14th July 1891 adverts were placed for the 2nd Annual Celtic Sports at the original ground and yet again, the Celtic Committee surpassed themselves, attracting some of the biggest names in the athletics world from Scotland, England and Ireland. The Sports were ran over the first two Saturdays of August, which was to become the tradition and started at 14.30 sharp. Admission prices were set at sixpence, with sixpence extra for both stands.

The list of events was impressive with Irish Nationalist MP for North Mayo, Daniel Crilly presenting the prizes;

1. 100 yards Handicap.
2. 440 yards Handicap.
3. 880 yards Handicap.
4. One mile Handicap.
5. Two miles Handicap.
6. Four Miles Invitation Flat Race.
7. 120 Yards Hurdle Handicap.
8. 100 Yards Invitation.
9. One Mile Bicycle Handicap.
10. Two Miles Bicycle Handicap.
11. Three Miles Bicycle Handicap.
13. 220 Yards Handicap.
14. 300 Yards Handicap.
15. The Boys Race.
16. Dribbling Race confined to players.
17. Five a Side Football Tournament.

5000 were in attendance on the first day of the Sports, (the Preliminaries), which was a very respectable turn out especially as the Rangers Sports were being held on the same day, although at a different time. The highlight of the day for the crowd, who stayed inside the ground for up to five hours, was the One Mile and Four Mile races in which England's top three runners, Salford Harriers' William Morton, Edward "Will" Parry and James Kibblewhite took part. In a close race, Kibblewhite, (in dark colours), pipped team mate Parry, (in maroon), to the post in the One Mile, with Morton narrowly beating Parry to the tape in the Four Mile, after all three were together in the finishing straight in front of the Pavillion stand's deafening cheers, as the standites, *"rose at them and greeted the finish of the 4 miles invitation race with tumultuous cheers".*

The Maley brothers had a contact in Manchester, John Allison, of Ardwick FC and the Salford Harriers who would be of great assistance in bringing some of the biggest names in athletics to the Celtic Sports. John Allison had a masseuse business in Manchester and Willie Maley would send injured players to him as he was known as the best in the business. John Allison would go on to serve on the Manchester City Board and also became a Celtic shareholder in 1897.

A cursory glance at the names of some of the athletes back in the day reflects the era and also the changing times with Fred Bacon, Alf Shrubb, Willie Snook, Sid Frost, Bobby Bridge and Charlie Daft giving a working class feel to the game, portraying men who took part initially for the fun and the fame rather than the fortune. Claude Leggatt, the Long Jump champion, would earn his keep in advertising alone today, no doubt with a catchphrase to boot, (excuse the pun).

Celtic players Peter Dowds, James Kelly, Tom Maley and Paddy Gallagher each won the heats of the 100 yards Handicap sprint before Peter Dowds easily won the final, beating Tom Maley and Paddy Gallagher, although he did get a 10 yards start. In the 250 yards Handicap James Kelly, (6 yards start), beat Tom Maley, Peter Dowds, (25 yards start), and Paddy Gallagher.

Three interesting spectators in the Pavillion Stand at the Sports Day were Dan Doyle and Alec Brady of Everton and Neil McCallum of Notts Forest, all three of whom were on the verge of signing for Celtic. Neil McCallum was even cajoled into playing for the Celtic Number 3 five a side team and scored a goal.

The second day of the Celtic Sports continued to attract the biggest names and the highest attendances, despite the heavy rain which made the ground heavy. Tom Dickenson, the Quarter Mile champion of Ireland, arrived as a guest of the club and Celtic players Tom and Willie Maley, (no slouches on a running track), as well as Peter Dowds, Paddy Gallagher, James Kelly and Pat McMorrow again took part.

Former St Mungo's pupil and fans' favourite Robert Anton Vogts, Bobby for short, was the top attraction in the cycle races and he didn't let anyone down, winning the Two and Three Mile races though he was shut out in the One Mile. Although the tight corners at the original Celtic Park, despite considerable improvements, did not lend itself to cycle racing, it was Vogt's daring style at the bends which won him the day.

In the 5 a side competition, the Celts had fielded five of the ten teams due to a disappointing take up and so it was no surprise when the Celtic Number 1, consisting of Duff, (guesting from Cowlairs), John McLeod, (guesting from Dumbarton), James Kelly, Sandy McMahon and Johnny Madden beat Kilmarnock Athletic 1-0 in the final with McMahon scoring the winner to claim the handsome musical boxes as first prize. The runners up received silver watches and third place received oak and silver inkstands. The Celtic 5's had kept their hand in as usual during the close season by taking part in various competitions including the opening of the Dundee athletic grounds at Carolina Port and they were delighted to take home the first prize "tombstone" clocks, beating Renton in the final, with the runners up returning to Dunbartonshire with biscuit boxes, a prize that would come in handy for the Celtic Board of later years.

Sandy McMahon also won the Dribbling Race, beating Johnny Madden in the final after Peter Dowds, James Kelly, Johnny Campbell and Collins had won their heats too. Pat McMorrow won the One Mile Handicap race, beating Quate of Ayr Utd, so the Celts were well represented in the medals and our large support was well entertained for their sixpence.

The Celtic Committee were out in full force to ensure the success of the Sports with Joseph Nelis and David Meikleham acting as judges, John Glass as referee and Willie Maley as secretary, fresh from his summer holiday in the Isle of Man. William McKillop and John H McLaughlin were the clerks of the course and John A McCreadie, Bradley, McIntyre, John McQuade, Stephen J Henry, James Curtis, John O'Hara and Joseph Shaughnessy acted as stewards. The track had been improved and everything in the committee's power had been done within the limited confines, for the competitor's enjoyment.

The *Scottish Referee* summed up the work of the committee perfectly;

"The Celtic are blessed with an indefatigable, painstaking and energetic executive, who never lose an opportunity of catering, with extraordinary enterprise, for the patronage of the public. Notably has this enterprise been conspicuous on several occasions, especially in being first to arrange a "Welcome Home" match with Renton, immediately that once famous club was reinstated, and then again we have another instance of it in bringing to Parkhead, a trio of England's best long distance pedestrians".

The *Glasgow Observer* added to the feel good factor;

"The Celtic Sports last Saturday was one of the finest meetings of the season".

A HUGE CELTIC CROSS IS ERECTED

St Peter's cemetery, Dalbeth just a mile along London Road, east of Celtic Park is recognised for many things, but it is now known, thanks to the work of the Celtic Graves Society, as the final resting place of over thirty former Celtic players, management and Founding Fathers. It's a treasure trove of Celtic history and a tour of the cemetery, courtesy of the Celtic Graves Society, including the 8 foot Celtic Cross erected by the group to mark Celtic's 125th anniversary is highly recommended.

On that tour you will not fail to see the 18 foot tall Celtic Cross erected in honour of Father Maginn from the parish of Saint Alphonsus in the Calton. When the hugely popular 42 year old priest died on 9th April 1890, his parishioners and those of the surrounding areas were so stunned that they started a subscription for a suitable memorial at his grave, raising the incredible sum of £270, mostly by the parishioners of St Alphonsus, but it was noted that subscribers came from the rich and poor alike. The fact that many parishioners struggled to put food on the table in 1890 reflects the esteem they had for the deceased priest for such a magnificent sum to be raised.

Shortly over a year later a ceremony was held at the packed graveside to unveil the massive Celtic Cross, which dominates the skyline to this day. William McKillop and Joseph McGroary represented Celtic FC, with apologies received from both Brother Walfrid and Brother Ezekiel of St Mungo's.

THE FIRST EVER PENALTY KICK

The close season of 1891 had brought some changes to Scottish football as the International Conference held in Glasgow in June agreed with the proposal for the invention of the penalty kick and the new pitch markings of a 6 yard and a 12 yard line. Strangely the goalkeeper was allowed to advance up to 6 yards from his line when facing a penalty.

The first ever penalty kick was awarded to Airdrie at Broomfield and on Tuesday 4th August 1891, the first penalties were awarded for and against Celtic in a friendly at Cappielow against Morton in the opening match of the 1891/92 season. Referee J McCallum of Dykebar awarded a penalty to Morton and Dick beat Duff, the new Celtic keeper with a swift low shot. Celtic were then awarded a penalty, and Neil McCallum, Celtic's first ever goalscorer on May 28th, 1888 stepped up to take our first ever spot kick. Unfortunately the Morton keeper, McLellan, stayed on his feet as McCallum shot right down the middle and the ball landed firmly in the keeper's arms to defy the Celts in a lively match which we won by 5 goals to 2, after coming back from 2-1 down.

Tom Duff, Celtic's new keeper had finally signed on the dotted line at Celtic Park after Cowlairs, who finished bottom of the League in the inaugural season, failed to be re-elected and couldn't secure a place in either the Alliance or the Federation Leagues. They were replaced in the top division by Leith Athletic, and Renton were re-instated, with Clyde also elected to join the League as the numbers rose from 10 to 12 teams participating. Jamie Bell returned to Hurlford, dropping down a League and he didn't get off to the best start, losing five goals on his debut as his team lost 5-4 against Pollokshaws. Ironically he was voted one of the best players on the pitch with Hurlford 4-2 up with 15 minutes remaining before losing three goals, one in the last minute.

In another change, the role of the umpire was significantly reduced and they were renamed "linesmen", limited to ruling on whether the ball was still in play and who would be awarded the goal kick, shy or corner. The referee was now the sole and final arbiter of the laws of the game!

Thankfully for Celtic, a proposal for away teams to get a half share of the gate instead of a third was defeated. During season 1890/91 Celtic received £117, 16s, 2d from other clubs as a third share of the attendance, when in most away games we would have the support of at least half of the crowd. In return we gave out £256, 16s, 2d, more than double what we got from away games, despite the fact that away fans attending Celtic Park were in a small minority.

THE FIRST HUGE IMPORTS FROM ENGLAND

Dan Doyle and Alec Brady caused a huge stir when they made their debuts for Celtic away to Cowlairs on Monday, 10th August, in a friendly match won 6-3 by the Celts, despite going in at half time 3-1 down.

The *Scottish Sport* on 14th August 1891 summed up the mood perfectly;

"I can't remember when I saw so much jubilation among the Celtic officials as was evidenced on Monday night. On entering the Cowlairs' enclosure, Mr John O'Hara buttonholed me and there was a mischievous twinkle in his eye as he quietly whispered - "I'm sorry you're too late for the names of the team, but perhaps you can distinguish the men for yourself".

There was something in his manner which I did not quite comprehend, but glancing over his shoulder in the direction of the players, I was astonished to behold the Everton cracks, Doyle and Brady, in the Celtic ranks. I felt inclined to shout Hurroo! and in the excitement I almost extinguished the light of day from Mr John H McLaughlin's left optic with a lighted "Caporal". The latter tried hard not to grin, but there was an itching around the corners of his mouth which betrayed his ill concealed attempt to puff on complacently.

Mr James Curtis wrung my hand, he was too full of emotion to give utterance to the great joy he was experiencing. A voice, (mocking), behind him ejaculated, "Everton, Mr Molyneux, Athletic News", and then the individual dropped down in a fit of spasmodic coughing. He came around alright, but for a full hour and a half that party could do nothing but grin - and such a grinning!

"You never know what a day may bring forth", I said," or a night either", some other fellow chimed in. Then at intervals between the play I was told something about a drive in which the names Doyle and Brady occurred". Can't you get a stop press edition?", "Wire to Mark Lane!", "Send a message of consolation to Mr Molyneux!" and other similar suggestions were literally poured into my ears while a running fire of good humoured banter prevailed all around.

I could not help ruminating on Everton, and contrasting the situation there when the gloomy tidings was made known at Anfield Road. The Celts have triumphed in this matter, and Scotchmen are delighted that English clubs are being left in the lurch and that some measure of retribution is being meted out to them. Bravo Celts!"

The Celts were striking a blow and sending out a message to English clubs loud and clear that the one way tide of Scottish players departing for the greener grass, (and professionalism), of England could work both ways. Professionalism wasn't introduced into the Scottish game until 1893 and so English agents would simply jump on a train north and dangle a contract in front of their target and escape on the next train south complete with their new signing, or "kidnapping". How this could work in reverse and a professional player under contract at Everton could be enticed to leave and sign for an amateur club such as Celtic in 1891 was the cause of much consternation with the confines of "shamateurism" once more being questioned.

The Celtic Committee, frustrated by these confines and well aware that approaches were being made to their top players had followed through with their plan, allegedly, whereby a player, with the assistance of Celtic supporters within the licensing trade would be offered a lease on a public house, in Doyle's case in his adopted Bellshill. The bar would then become an overnight success with a Celtic player acting as mine host and the player could coin in up to £5 a week from it with little cost to the club apart from "lost time" to the player to make up for shifts he would miss when playing for Celtic and also the annual lease. This at a time when Everton were offering £3 a week. The organising of this cunning plan was arranged through a generous supporter and there was no paper trail to the club. In fact the club were doing nothing wrong, they were simply doing what others did.

Sections of the media on both sides of the border were not amused and so the rumour mill and the mud slinging began. The *Glasgow Evening News* threw the first stone, in a gossip column named "Cuttings From English Athletic Papers";

"There is good authority for saying Doyle's terms for staying with the Celtic were that he should be put up in a first class public house, and that all the in going charges, including fixture and stock, should be paid for. It is easy to see what this would "tot" up to, and when an estimate of "expenses" is made we shall soon realise what whitewashed amateurism means."

It was classic rumour mill hysteria, with a story on this occasion originating from Everton alleging what was supposed to have been said in front of witnesses and presented as fact without any evidence to back it up. Once the rumour was started, the coup de grace was then completed with hysterical reaction to one's own allegation. If this was Everton's only evidence, they were in bother, because even with sworn statements it was a case of one man's word against another.

In the same article, the newspaper followed up;

"So Daniel Doyle has again shown us what a mean spirited professional footballer is capable of doing, and the Celts have now two brilliant specimens in Doyle and McCallum. I have heard of the elasticity of the professional football player's conscience, but I should imagine Doyle and McCallum are about the worst examples we could find; and I should not think their reception on any English ground would be very cordial".

If you can't beat them, as they say, join them. The problem in this case was that Dan Doyle was no shrinking violet and he had already committed himself to Everton for the season and was under contract, indeed he had been paid up front for two thirds of his £3 per week wages over the next two seasons. Little wonder that Everton were up in arms, but their issue was with the player, not Celtic. The Three Amigos of Cadete, Di Canio and Van Hooijdonk, over a century later had nothing on this legend who knew exactly what he wanted, and what he was worth.

Everton threatened to take the matter to a court of law and tried to get English clubs to refuse to play Celtic if we fielded Doyle and Brady. This was never going to work because the fixtures for Celtic's tour of England and also English clubs coming to Celtic Park were already set in stone and if any club tried to force changes to the opposition's team or refuse to play, then the full might of the law would come down on their head. In any case, this was a disagreement between Everton and two of their former players, with of course the involvement of Celtic. It had nothing to do with the English or Scottish Football Associations, certainly the English FA had no jurisdiction over the Scottish game in any way, shape or form so their hands were tied and their scaremongering was exactly that.

The English FA were perfectly happy to sit back and watch as English agents kidnapped Scottish players with impunity. The Celts were striking a blow, not just for our own club, but for Scottish football in general in signing the two best players from the biggest team in England and we would not be moved.

In the end Everton's case was brought before the General Meeting of the SFA and the whole thing fizzled out in less than 15 minutes without Doyle, Brady or the Celtic Committee even being called to speak. Everton produced no proof of professionalism against Celtic and were only going on a verbal communication when Doyle had spoken of the public house with a guarantee of £5 a week wages forthcoming from him joining Celtic. Doyle had used this as a leverage to get more money out of Everton as he believed that he was being paid less than team mates who weren't worth as much as him to the club.

A letter was then read out from John H McLaughlin, the Honorary Secretary of Celtic, complaining about the legislation raised by the English FA whereby English clubs could not play Scottish clubs if the team included any players who had been reinstated under the recent amnesty agreed by the SFA. By "reinstated", McLaughlin meant that Scottish amateurs who had signed professional contracts down south and had therefore barred themselves from playing in Scotland, were allowed to return to Scotland to play as amateurs under the new amnesty. The situation didn't raise its ugly head again after the Blackburn match, who incidentally, had recently signed full back Mick McKeown from Celtic.

CELTIC v MINERVA DRAMATIC TEAM

Both Celtic Park, new and old, have witnessed its fair share of drama down the years with characters aplenty but it's doubtful if it ever witnessed a match involving Celtic, as full of character as it did on Monday, 24th August, when the Minerva Dramatic Club, complete in fancy dress took on the Celtic first team in a charity match.

Seven months earlier Celtic Park hosted a similar character match between the Royal and the Grand theatre companies but this was the first time the Celtic team were roped into proceedings.

Clowns, fat pantomime policemen and dudes in pantaloons may have been commonplace in the 20th century at Celtic Park but not in 1891, when they lined up in full comical costume, against Celtic's finest at the strangest curtain raiser ever witnessed. So popular was the event that it became somewhat a tradition in following years. Unfortunately heavy rain limited the attendance to a few hundred and the teams were given as follows;

CELTIC

Jerry Reynolds, (dressed as Dugald Cratur), Dan Doyle, (dressed as a bull fighter), Willie Maley, (dressed as a jester), Mick Dunbar, (dressed as the Pirate King), Sandy McMahon, (dressed as a Broth of a Bhoy), Johnny Campbell, (dressed as an old Canadian), Johnny Madden, (dressed as Mexican Joe), and Johnny Coleman, (dressed as Pantaloon).

MINERVA DRAMATIC CLUB

The opposition contained an old wife, a highlandman, an Irish comedian, Jack Tar, a mongrel dog, the devil and a dairymaid. The referee even took part in the fun too and he was dressed up as Sam the Freezer, although he was probably more mobile than some of the refs seen at Celtic Park down the years. Full backs Jerry Reynolds and Dan Doyle, sorry Dugald Cratur and Toreador, played up front with the forward line playing in defence. The result of the game was never revealed, if anyone was even counting, but what is certain is that a good time was had by one and all!

Maybe this kind of charity match should make a comeback one day?

OUR SECOND LEAGUE SEASON STARTS

Back to serious business and our second League season started where it all began a year earlier, at Tynecastle, (with the previous year's opener with Renton declared null and void), as we embarked on our final season at the original Celtic Park with the intention of going out with a bang. The Celts arrived late, which delayed the kick off for almost half an hour, which in turn increased the anger levels of the already irate home support at the prospect of facing the bhoys in green. The biggest ever crowd to watch a football match in Edinburgh was in attendance with estimates given at around the 10,000 mark with a good contingent following the bhoys in green with former Hibs player Jimmy McGhee, in particular, given a good reception.

This poses an interesting question of the Edinburgh Hibernian support during the 18 months when their team was out of action between 1891 and 1893. Did a section, in their own team's absence, take to supporting Celtic? Back in the day before the advent of the brake clubs, travelling to "far flung" destinations like Edinburgh posed many difficulties, especially for the masses who could ill afford the entrance fee never mind the travelling expenses from Glasgow.

Did sections of the Hibs support turn up at matches between Hearts and Celtic at nearby Tynecastle to actively support the Irish team or was their intentions to antagonise their former rivals Hearts? Why would Jimmy McGhee, who had stayed with Hibs right up until they disbanded, be given such a good reception? Was it from a section of Hibs supporters, backing Celtic? In the event, Celtic underestimated the Hearts team, having won the opening match of the previous season 5-0, and we paid for this over confidence with a surprise 3-1 defeat. The first goal came just before half time and the Celts had only ourselves to blame as we took our five minute half time break from the traditional Tynecastle rough house.

Often on days like this when things don't go well, we all need someone to blame and Tom Duff obliged in the scapegoat department as he failed to hold a shot to gift Hearts a two goal lead. The home team had broke away on a counter attack and with the Celtic defence in offensive positions, the extraordinary sight of the whole Hearts forward line bearing down on Duff became apparent. Instead of passing the ball around the forward line and into the net past the vastly outnumbered custodian, the Hearts player shot and easily scored, without the need to involve his other four attackers. A few minutes later it was three and finally the bhoys woke themselves up and showered the Hearts goal with shot after shot, but our only consolation came in the last minute with a goal by Johnny Madden, too little and too late.

Rangers were the first visitors to Celtic Park on League duty on Saturday, 22nd August 1891, a team who had yet to beat us. Ever. A crowd of 12,000 took up every space available, this description pointing towards the true capacity of the original ground as they watched Dan Doyle and Alec Brady make their debuts at Celtic Park. Indeed they went home happy after three second half goals finally broke the stubborn Rangers defence who had defied the bhoys time and time again as we "besieged the Rangers citadel". Rangers defender James McIntyre had to make himself scarce to the Pavillion for a new pair of long shorts after he tore his first pair when heading the ball, but it was the entire Rangers team who were desperately trying to hide their embarrassment as Sandy McMahon and Johnny Madden scored two goals in a minute before Johnny Campbell headed a third to complete the scoring at Celtic 3 Rangers 0.

The Celts were eager to start our League campaign better than we did in the previous season and games against Clyde, Renton and Abercorn gave us the chance to go on a decent League run. The Celts struck form, beating Clyde 7-2 at Barrowfield, Renton 3-0 at Celtic Park before beating Abercorn 5-2 in Paisley. Including the Rangers match we had made up for our opening day defeat at Tynecastle in style by winning our next four on the bounce and scoring eighteen goals into the bargain with the loss of only four. We sat in second place in the League behind the early pace setters Hearts, with Rangers, in contrast in third bottom place after losing three of their four opening matches.

At Barrowfield, the bhoys got their shooting boots on with Neil McCallum opening the scoring after ten minutes when the keeper bundled his shot over the line and Sandy McMahon scored two in as many minutes, the first with a quick low shot and the second with a header just before half time to put the bhoys into a comfortable position. Ten minutes into the second half however the match was back in the balance when Clyde scored from a free kick, fully 30 yards out, before they added a second shortly after. The Celts responded in style and Sandy McMahon scored his third and Celtic's fourth just five minutes later. The bhoys were in top form swarming around the Clyde goals and it was no surprise when McMahon scored his fourth goal in a row to make it 5-2, before Neil McCallum scored a sixth and Alec Brady a seventh to make the final score Clyde 2 Celtic 7, as the whole Celtic front rank "kept dancing around the Clyde keeper". On this form, no team in the country could live with us and so it proved.

The heavy rain at the home match against Renton had not affected the attendance but it was noted in the Scottish Referee, on 7th September;

"It is unfortunate that their numerous patrons have perforce to submit themselves to the inevitable when the rain comes down. However all grumbling will cease when the club enters their new enclosure, and the prospective covered stand will prove a boon and a blessing."

The wind and rain couldn't stop the bhoys fine run of form and this time it was Johnny Campbell who took the chance to shine, scoring a hat trick, with two first half goals followed up by a third, three minutes into the second half. The only surprise was that there was no more scoring as both sides had chances in an open game. The name of James McLaughlin, Celtic's goalkeeper before Jamie Bell was back in the newspapers as he became a registered referee and a top class one at that by all accounts.

The match against Abercorn on 12th September 1891 was noteworthy in that the goalkeepers were brothers. Tom Duff was in goals for Celtic and his older brother Andrew stood between the sticks for Abercorn. Indeed, although he lost five goals, Andrew was deemed the best player on the pitch. For the record, another set of brothers played that day, but it wasn't the Maleys, it was the Cuthbertsons of Abercorn.

To the match itself, and only five minutes were on the clock and the bhoys were two up thanks to goals from Sandy McMahon and Neil McCallum. Abercorn pulled one back but the Celts were then awarded only our second ever penalty kick and a chance to restore our two goal lead.

Neil McCallum had missed our first ever penalty and this time it was the turn of Dan Doyle to step up, but his shot too was saved. Our first two penalties ever were both saved but eventually three minutes before half time Sandy McMahon got the third to make it 3-1, but incredibly the dogged home team went straight up the park to pull it back to a one goal deficit again. The Celts finally got our act together in the second half and two more goals, by Neil McCallum and Johnny Madden with fifteen minutes remaining, put a more realistic reflection on the scoring.

Celtic enjoyed a great support at the match with the Paisley Irish turning out in big numbers, *"every good and true Irishman in Paisley and district was out to cheer on the bould bhoys,"* along with those from the East End of Glasgow who had travelled by way of the "Fitba Specials," the trains which on this occasion started at Bellgrove station at 3.10 pm, calling at Gallowgate, Main Street and Pollokshields stations before arriving at Paisley Gilmour Street in time for the match at Underwood at 4pm. The cost for the return ticket was 6d, which could be purchased from Celtic Committee members at the different stations rather than at the railway booking offices!

Talk about organisation, the Celtic Committee had thought of everything, right down to organising the train tickets for away matches. The game of football today has many superstars who are idolised by the fans, but back in 1891 the popular Celtic defender Jerry Reynolds nonchalantly shook off all the attention as he made his way through Paisley Gilmour Street train station to catch the fitba special up the road, with the Paisley femme fatales stampeding in his direction whilst shrieking his name, "Jerry, Jerry, Jerry," in one of the earliest examples of hero worship.

A fortnight later on the 26th September, another home League match was affected by heavy rain, this time with Dumbarton the visitors, but yet again it didn't put off the Celtic support, with fully 12,000 in attendance. The thunderstorm in the first half turned so heavy that the referee had to halt the match before eventually restarting, but it was the Celts who took best to the conditions as two second half goals, the first from a low hard shot from Johnny Campbell and the second in the last minute from a Sandy McMahon header to give the bhoys a 2-0 victory. Poor Dumbarton had to play the whole game in their drenched strips, whilst the bhoys came out for the second half in dry, faded green jerseys.

This was to be the match where Tom Duff's rheumatism was badly affected by the inclement weather and he found himself out of the team for the rest of the year, with the exception of a couple of matches out of fourteen.

As the *Scottish Referee* stated on 12th October regarding the match at Partick Thistle;

"The reason why Duff was not playing is that he had an attack of rheumatics since the Dumbarton match".

After five matches, the League was starting to take shape with Celtic in second place, a point behind Hearts with Dumbarton in third place on the same points as Celtic. At the other end of the table a poor Rangers team sat third from bottom, with two wins and three defeats to their name. The Scottish Referee, reporting on the Dumbarton match on the 28th September, gave another insight into the so called press stand, which wasn't really a stand at all;

"Artificial thunder was produced on the top of the press stand when Campbell scored. Thanks to the kindly interference of Tom Maley it ceased. But the rain proceeded".

Celtic supporters had taken to playfully thumping the roof of the dookit which housed the press and only ceased to entertain themselves at the behest of Tom Maley. This must have been quite a common occurrence and worthy of great wind up value to the wags amongst the support.

RIVALS STRUCK OFF SFA MEMBERSHIP

At the SFA meeting on Tuesday, 18th August 1891, Glasgow Hibernian and Edinburgh Hibernian were among the list of eighteen teams struck off the SFA membership list for non payment of subscriptions.

LET THE PEOPLE SING THEIR STORIES AND THEIR SONGS

We've already read from reports that the early Celtic support had a fervour and devotion akin to a support who were following "more than a football club", and this is similarity remains to this day, however early examples of the songs we used to sing are few and far between.

The *Scottish Referee* gives one example from the Celtic v Dumbarton match at Celtic Park on Saturday, 26th September and it's no surprise that a classic Irish folk song of the day was taken up by the Celtic support.

"Come Back To Erin," a classic Irish ballad, it was noted, *"was the favourite hum on Saturday".* Mavourneen is Irish Gaelic for "my beloved" and the full lyrics are as follows;

Come back to Erin, Mavourneen, Mavourneen,
Come back, Aroon, to the land of my birth;
Come with the shamrocks and spring-time, Mavourneen,
And its Killarney shall ring with our mirth.
Sure, when we lent you to beautiful England,
Little we thought of the lone winter days.
Little we thought of the hush of the star shine
Over the mountains, the bluffs and the brays.

Chorus;

Come back to Erin, Mavourneen, Mavourneen,
Come back again to the land of my birth;
Come back to Erin, Mavourneen, Mavourneen,
And its Killarney shall ring with our mirth.

Over the green sea, Mavourneen, Mavourneen,

Long shone the white sail that bore thee away,

Riding the white waves that fair summer morn in',

Just like a Mayflower afloat on the bay.

Oh! but my heart sank when clouds came between us.

Like a gray curtain the rain falling down,

Hid from my sad eyes the path o'er the ocean.

Far, far away where my Colleen had flown.

Chorus.

Oh! may the angels, O wakin' and sleepin',

Watch o'er my bird in the land far away!

And it's my prayer will consign to their keepin'

Care o' my jewel by night and by day,

When by the fireside I watch the bright embers,

Then all my heart flies to England And thee,

Cravin' to know if my darlin' remembers.

Or if her thoughts may be crossin' to me.

Chorus.

NEW GRAND STAND AT CATHKIN PARK

Thanks to the new lease of life given to the Scottish game since Celtic's formation, the fortunes of Third Lanark, amongst others were on the up. So much so that at the start of the 1891/92 season they were confident enough to erect a new covered stand which had a framework of iron and steel, the first in the land.

The stand was 250 foot long comprising of one central section 50 foot long with two side sections, both 100 foot long jutting forward slightly to command a better view of the pitch. The front row was raised over 7 foot from the ground to overlook any fans in front, similar to Celtic's Pavillion, and it had ten rows of seating, all covered by a corrugated iron roof. Four separate pay boxes, one at each end and two nearer the centre, each with stairways were all within the body of the stand. The under framing of the stand, including all girders and columns which came into contact with the ground was constructed of rolled iron set into heavy concrete foundations which gave a large space under the stand for future requirements. A Press Room was built with room for twelve reporters at the north end of the stand nearest the pavillion, with telephone and telegraphic rooms underneath.

The capacity was 2000 seated comfortably with twelve poles blocking the view for some and the Third's Committee ingeniously came up with the idea of putting a flag on top of each with one letter spelling out Third Lanark. The total cost was £1000. This was the state of the art grandstand in 1891 which was the standard that we would have to aspire to and beat at New Celtic Park.

THE FIRST FOUNDING FATHER PASSES AWAY

Hugh Darroch, one of the founding fathers of the club at our inception and a man who had served as the first Treasurer for the initial two years sadly passed away at the young age of 32 due to cancer in September 1891.

From the *Scottish Referee* on September 14th 1891, some beautiful words;

"By the lamented death of this gentleman, the Celtic club has lost one of it's earliest and most enthusiastic supporters. When the formation of the club was first mooted Mr Darroch threw himself heart and soul into the idea. To his energy, and that of several other gentlemen in the east end of Glasgow, the club owes its marvellous success and it is largely due to their self denying labours that it has attained the honourable position it holds in the world of football.

Appointed first Treasurer of the club, Mr Darroch enjoyed the fullest confidence, not only of his brother directors, but of the entire body of the membership. This, though not latterly in office he retained until death, severed the link that bound the Celtic and he together.

It cannot destroy however that feeling of respect the members entertain for him as a man, whilst the sad event has served to heighten him in the regard and estimation of the poor and needy, who found him ever a friend to succour and help them. With all who mourn Mr Darroch's loss - relatives, friends and fellow members of the Celtic - we join in feeling of tenderest sympathy, especially for the family circle bereft of it's crown and head. The poignancy of their grief will be sweetly chastened by the memory of the worthy life of him whose lose they mourn and like the soft murmur of the vesper bell at even tide, their quivering lips may whisper "Requiescat in Pace".

The flags flew at half mast at Celtic Park as the funeral cortege passed by consisting of 12 carriages en route to the old part of St Peter's cemetery, Dalbeth on London Road. The coffin was covered in beautiful wreaths, with the largest coming from Celtic, and the club were very well represented with the full committee and most of the players in attendance.

BROTHER WALFRID DEFENDS EVENING CLASSES

A letter printed in the *Glasgow Observer* in September 1891 from a Mr Colvin, a member of St Alphonsus Young Men's Guild started a debate after he encouraged Catholics of the city to avail themselves of every opportunity to advance themselves through education and in particular to participate in greater numbers at the evening classes held at many schools in Glasgow.

He added that many young Catholics could be seen at football matches, at ballrooms or at billiard halls, but he could count on two hands the numbers attending evening classes, which, he argued lasted only one hour and could be attended two or three times weekly. He hit out too at youth who preferred to attend debating clubs as the city already had too many orators and time would be better spent learning at evening classes.

One thing that is guaranteed about a controversial letter to a newspaper, is that there will be no shortage of correspondents eager to point out the error of the author's ways and so it was on this occasion as the debate livened up with points scored on both sides. The first blow was struck by a keen member of a debating society who hit out at Mr Colvin's assumption that Glasgow's youth only attended football matches, ballrooms or billiard halls and he went on to propose that Mr Colvin himself would benefit from enrolling as a member at the recently established Catholic Literacy Society.

Ouch.

Mr Colvin got the final word in when he quoted no less a man than Brother Walfrid, who had informed him that since his letter was published, the subject had been thoroughly discussed at a meeting of the youth of Sacred Heart the previous Sunday, with the outcome of that meeting being that no less than ten young men joined the advanced evening classes held at nearby schools.

Touché.

OUR FIRST DEFENCE OF THE GLASGOW CUP

Our defence of the Glasgow Cup began when the 1st round draw gave us a trip to lowly Kelvinside Athletic as we attempted to retain our first major trophy. Cashing in on the draw, Kelvinside agreed to play the match at Celtic Park and take a share of the larger gate, but finances aside, this was the draw they dreaded, playing an on form Celtic who had been scoring goals for fun against some of the best teams in the country.

The trophy had been started up in 1888 and Celtic were the third winners of the cup that was deemed as secondary only to the Scottish Cup. Cambuslang beat Rangers 3-1 in the first final and Queens Park won in the next two seasons, beating Partick Thistle 8-0 in the 1888/89 season and Celtic in the 1889/90 season by 3-2, the winning goal almost being the precursor for a walk off by the Celtic players in protest, only to be held back by John Glass as he came bounding and leaping out of the Cathkin stand.

With the Celts on fire, Kelvinside were in line for a hammering and so it turned out as the bhoys won the match 11-1, but the visitors had decided to "scratch," that is withdraw, having took the trouble to turn up and take home their share of the takings and the record shows the match was played as a friendly. No team in Scotland could stand in our way as we went on a magnificent unbeaten run of 20 matches in all competitions including friendlies from the 22nd August to New Years Day 1892 and the infamous friendly match with Dumbarton.

The next round took us to Partick Thistle's original ground at Inchview in Whiteinch where there were cars and "Clutha Steamers" to the ground every few minutes. None of your fitba specials to this game, a short trip doon the water was the order of the day. Coincidentally the last time we had played Thistle was in the semi final of the Glasgow Cup the previous season which we won 5-1. Thistle put up a better fight this time, but a goal from Sandy

McMahon in the 12th minute gave us a 1-0 lead at half time, before Johnny Campbell and Alec Brady added to the scoring in the second half in front of 4000 spectators to finish the match at Partick Thistle 0 Celtic 3.

Northern were beaten 3-2 in the quarter final at Celtic Park after the original 6-0 match was replayed following a protest by the visitors before the match, due to heavy fog. If the first game was a formality against the Alliance club, (Second Division), the replayed match was anything but. In fact Northern took a shock 2-0 lead, with the opener coming in ten minutes and the second before half time. In between, Tom Maley did a Charlie Tully and scored directly from a corner, but, like Tully's effort, it was disallowed.

The bhoys started the second half with a renewed confidence and Alec Brady scored in the first minute and thereafter the Celts simply bombarded the Northern goal, (strangely enough as we shot into the northern goal facing the Gallowgate). Finally we found our shooting boots and the match was tied at 2-2 with a goal from Neil McCallum, but it wasn't until the 75th minute that we scored a deserved winner. Northern remained dangerous on the counter attack and the Celts were greatly relieved when the final whistle went.

The semi final draw was kind to the Celts as Linthouse, from sunny Govan, were drawn as our opponents at Celtic Park. The Govan team were huge outsiders to stand in the way of our third Glasgow Cup final in successive seasons and so it proved with the Celts racking up 9 goals to Linthouse's 2. By half time the score stood at 7-2, which is the highest amount of goals witnessed in 45 minutes at the original Celtic Park. Celtic strolled to a three-nil lead before the mid table Alliance team struck back with two goals of their own. This only made the bhoys angry and we notched up four goals in quick succession before half time. Luckily for Linthouse, there was only two more goals added in the second half. For the record, the goals were scored as follows; four from Sandy McMahon, three from Johnny Madden and a goal each by Neil McCallum and Alec Brady.

In the other tie Clyde beat Queens Park 3-2 to earn another crack at Celtic on 12th December at Third Lanark's ground Cathkin, although their previous meeting that season on the 29th August in the League at Barrowfield resulted in a 7-2 victory for the bhoys. It was a fall from grace and a sign of the times for the defeated semi finalists, Queens Park, who had defeated Rangers 3-0 in the quarter final. The Celts were on fire in our final season at the original Celtic Park.

Clyde's build up to the final didn't go smoothly as they suffered a humiliating 8-0 defeat to Hearts in the Scottish Cup and the writing was firmly on the wall. The Celts build up wasn't as straightforward as it should have been the previous week when we turned up 20 minutes late for our League match at Leith Athletic and made hard work of the match. Fortunately for the Celts, with the match all square at two goals each with fifteen minutes left to play, the referee brought the game to a halt due to darkness.

THE GLASGOW CUP FINAL - HERE WE GO TO TWO IN A ROW?

On the day of the Glasgow Cup final on the 12th December, not surprisingly a freezing cold one, the underdogs of Clyde started off the better team and threw everything at us, but our defence remained solid. It took twenty minutes for the Celts to settle into the match and adapt to the conditions but when we did, we soon took the lead through Neil McCallum and then added a second through Alec Brady before half time. The talk at half time was about how many the Celts would win by, but Clyde were not finished yet and three minutes into the second half they got themselves back into the game to reduce Celtic's lead to one goal as snow started to fall heavily. Clyde then threw everything at us but the Celtic defence could not be broken. Finally with 25 minutes left on the clock, Sandy McMahon increased our advantage to two goals once again to the delight of the Celtic support as reported in the Scottish Sport on 15th December;

"Judging by the wild yells with which this success was hailed, the Parkhead contingent gave vent to the delight which this relief to their pent up feelings afforded them, in a manner characteristic of Irishmen".

The stuffing was now knocked out of Clyde with the snow beating down heavily in their faces and the bhoys took full control of the game. Alec Brady added a fourth a minute later, before Johnny Madden added two more with a Johnny Campbell goal sandwiched in between to finish off the scoring at 7 goals to 1, giving the Celts our first trophy of the season and our second Glasgow Cup in a row. In fact we had now won the Glasgow Cup twice in the calendar year of 1891 due to the previous season's final being put back from its original date in December 1890 to February 1891.

Back in the day the trophy was not presented immediately after the game and was held back until the after match function that evening, complete with speeches from both clubs, which was all very civilised. This changed after our controversial defeat to Queens Park in 1889 when the Glasgow Cup was presented to the victors at the after match soiree even though Celtic had protested the outcome of the match. Surely a trophy cannot be presented to a team before a protest could be investigated, the Celtic Committee had argued. In conceding the point however the Glasgow Association then changed the ruling so that the trophy would not be presented at the after match function, even if there was no protest. A case of throwing the baby out with the bath water indeed.

The Alexandra Hotel in Bath Street often held the after match function and in attendance, as well as both teams and committees, were the Glasgow Association Committee and representatives from each participating club. The Chairman welcomed all, before inviting a selection of those present to start the ball rolling with a song. It was a bit like a New Year's party at someone's house with everyone doing their favourite party piece. It just wouldn't work in today's game.

Then came the speeches. First off was the President of the Glasgow Association who commented on the match itself before proposing the first toast of the evening to the finalists. Tom Maley, representing Celtic replied to the toast in his usual generous and humbling manner.

From the *Scottish Sport* on 15th December;

"It affords me very great pleasure indeed in having the honour to reply on behalf of the Celtic - honour in virtue of the Celtic again being the Glasgow Cup holders and pleasure because of the high eulogium Mr Geake has passed on both Clyde and Celtic.

The play, I consider was not represented by 7 goals to 1 and scarcely indicates the game. It may seem strange for me to say this, but I can recognise merit when I see it and I hope I get credit for it. I am glad we are in the position of cup holders. I am sorry for the Clyde, but at the same time I have a much greater regard for our club. We have fought our way to the front under great difficulties. Let them fight on too! Their day is coming I feel sure and when it does we will be the first to congratulate them".

John Collins on behalf of Clyde then responded, before the night was finished off, again with a song. The first part of the treble was in our hands in our final season in our original ground.

THE FIRST TOUR ... OF AMERICA?

It's incredible to even contemplate that in 1891 the talk on the street was of Celtic touring America and Canada. Only three years after our formation, word of our fame had spread from the home countries to the thousands of Scots and Irish ex pats across the pond, however the game in the "New World" was still in its infancy and could in no way support or finance a trip, literally into the unknown, which could have had disastrous financial consequences.

The Canadian national team were at the time touring Britain but it was one thing a North American team travelling to such a hotbed of support for the game and another thing still for a home based club team to travel to America. The manager of the Canadian team was wheeled out in an Irish newspaper to give his opinion and he gave a very good insight into the state of the game in North America at the time. According to Mr J R Ellis, the best time for the trip would be May and June, (close season), with the first match in New York to start the tour on a high and the next in Philadelphia. From there Pawtucket in Rhode Island State should be visited and then a match arranged in Fall River against the Rovers and possibly the Olympics and East Ends as well.

Crossing the border to Canada, Ottawa, then Toronto would be visited where a select from the four or five teams playing there could be opposed. Berlin Rangers or Seaforth could be next or a game against the Canadian national team. Crossing back to America, two or three games could be arranged in Detroit and Chicago where the Thistle were the best of the teams playing there. The last match of the tour could be back at Fall River, with the biggest gate, against the American national team. In all, ten matches could be played in five weeks but crucially breaking even was far from guaranteed.

Indeed the final point was proven when it took a further forty years for the Celts to tour North America for the first time, taking with them the Scottish Cup in 1931. At least for James Kelly, Willie and Tom Maley they finally got to see the great US of A on Celtic duty, albeit after a hefty wait. Ironically too, many of the cities we visited to play matches, were the same destinations suggested forty years previous with Philadelphia and New York at the start of the tour followed by Fall River and Pawtucket in Rhode Island State, and then Chicago and Toronto.

To break even in 1891 the club would need guarantees of £75 from 12 matches, just to cover the cost of the return journey on the steamboat and hotel accommodation for ten weeks in cities which craved baseball, not football. Thankfully, better was thought of the idea and it never reached further than first base, excuse the pun.

THE ENGLISH CUP HOLDERS COME CALLING - WOULD DOYLE PLAY?

The Autumn Holiday fixture was a big date on the calendar when Celtic would take advantage of a blank day from League matches by taking on the cream of England and so the English Cup holders Blackburn Rovers were invited to Celtic Park. Mick McKeown, who had left Celtic in the summer, was now playing for Blackburn although he was still a firm favourite with the Celtic crowd, despite his "idiosyncrasies".

Although his place at full back had been filled by the mighty Dan Doyle, this was the first visit of the season to Celtic Park by an English club, the significance of this was that the English FA had ruled that any English team who played against a professional playing for a club other than the one he was registered with would face a suspension.

Celtic gave Blackburn the benefit of the doubt and left out Dan Doyle, Alec Brady and Neil McCallum with the game only a few days away. We were then further weakened by injuries to Tom Duff, Willie Maley, Sandy McMahon and Paddy Gallagher. However reserves such as Charlie Kelly, Johnny Cunningham, Hannah, Devlin and Coleman took their chance to shine and Devlin, indeed, scored on his debut to equalise after Rovers went a goal up. Johnny Madden put the bhoys 2-1 up in the second half, but Blackburn fought back to equalise before Madden again notched the winner in a five goal thriller, watched in the stands by the Rangers and Everton teams who had played earlier at Ibrox with the visitors winning 4-1. Not only were Celtic one of the top teams in Britain, but our "reserve" team weren't far behind it seems.

The *Glasgow Evening News* described Celtic's play against the English cup holders;

"In the second half the passing and manipulation of the home team was superb and left the opposing backs and halves standing bewildered".

THE FIRST SKETCH PLAN OF THE NEW CELTIC PARK

At the start of October, the Celtic Committee released the first sketch plan of our new ground, which was bounded by the Caledonian railway line on the west, by Janefield Street on the north and by Newlands Avenue on the east, (named after Lord Newlands, who was the landlord of New Celtic Park). The space on the south side of the current main stand right down to London Road was not included in the original 10 year lease in 1891, and was only bought in 1929 with the building of the new Main Stand, which became the new main entrance at Celtic Park on Kerrydale Street. Between 1929 and 2014 this space was used as a car park until the building of the highly impressive Celtic Way.

The sketch showed two new tracks, the outer one to be used as a cycle track, banked at each bend and was 3.5 laps to the mile. The inner track was for foot running and was 4 laps to the mile. The Celtic Committee were making it clear we had big plans for the new ground which would include the best cycling and running tracks of the day, to enable us to attract the biggest names to the annual Sports. We would also be in a position to lease the ground out for other organisations to host their Sports Days at Celtic Park.

North and south of the pitch there was space for a stand on each side and the terracing behind both goals followed the oval shape of the tracks which gave Celtic Park its original shape. The original oval shape of the ground was due to the popularity of cycling and running and the need to incorporate both tracks in the new ground.

Interestingly, the original Pavillion in the sketched plan was sited in the south east corner of the ground, rather than in the north west corner where it was eventually located. Why was it planned to be housed in the south east corner of the ground? Why was it changed to the north west corner? What we do know is that the planned grand stand, the Grant Stand, on the south side of the field didn't come to fruition until 1899 as it was felt that the ground on the south side of the pitch would need time to settle as that was the location, near the south east corner where the original 40 foot quarry hole had been filled. This meant that the stand on the north side would be the first one built and the beating heart of the new ground would be on that side. It made sense then to build the Pavillion beside the new stand, although it could still have been built on the east side of the stand, rather than on the west side.

The building of the Pavillion on the north west corner of the ground, which housed the changing rooms was the reason behind the west side of the terracing becoming traditionally known as "The Celtic End". The simple reason for this was that the Celtic players in training and also at matches would run out of the Pavillion and take up their positions on the nearest side of the pitch. In matches over the years this meant defending the Celtic end.

OUR NEW LANDLORD WAS AN INTERESTING CHARACTER

James Henry Cecil Hozier was born in Tannochside, Uddingston in 1851 and was educated at Eton and Balliol College, Oxford before taking up his first job at the Foreign Office in 1874, aged 23. Two years later he became the Diplomatic Secretary to the Conservative Lord Salisbury, then Private Secretary between 1878 to 1880 to the then Secretary of State for Foreign Affairs. Five years later when Lord Salisbury became British Prime Minister, Hozier was appointed as his Foreign Secretary and Private Secretary. It was all very far flung from the coup in the east end of Glasgow that was soon to be known as Paradise.

In the same year, James Hozier sat for the South Lanarkshire seat for the Conservative Party but was beaten. A year later he offered to make way to another Unionist when the seat became available so as not to split the unionist vote and also to thwart Gladstone and the Liberal Party's Home Rule ambitions. This offer was declined so he sat and won the seat himself, by 18 votes over the Liberal candidate, and it was a seat he kept until 1906.

In 1892, just after leasing land to the Celtic Committee for the building of Celtic Park, he could have become the Under Secretary for Scotland, but instead decided to "stick to South Lanarkshire, as long as South Lanarkshire stuck to him". James Hozier became Lord Newlands on the death of his father in 1906 but the title died with him in 1929 as he was childless. Hozier's grandfather on his mother's side was a John O'Hara, not the Celtic Secretary, but his cousin did become Clementine Churchill, wife of Winston Churchill.

But i'll leave the best bit until last, the man who we bought the holy ground from and where Celtic Park stands forever, James Henry Cecil Hozier, was the Grand Master Mason of Scotland from 1899 to 1903.

THE LEAGUE RACE CONTINUES

On the 3rd October 1891, the Celts travelled to Paisley to take on St Mirren for the first time this season but we didn't get things all our own way by any stretch of the imagination. In fact the Saints were the better team for much of the game as they reshuffled their forward line to good effect against our depleted side missing Tom Duff, Willie Maley, Peter Dowds and Sandy McMahon. Tom Maley and Johnny Coleman were brought back into the team and played up front, Alec Brady was moved from the front line to half back and Charlie Kelly once again replaced Tom Duff in goals.

Our normal passing game, "scientific play," as it was termed, brought two first half goals by Neil McCallum which should have settled the bhoys down but it didn't. The first goal came from a smart pass from Johnny Madden and as the St Mirren keeper slipped on the wet grass, McCallum was left with the simple task of passing the ball into the empty net as he put the Celts one up. The second came from a corner just before half time when McCallum slipped the ball between the unfortunate keeper's legs. In the second half, against a resurgent Saints team, we had to replace the science with force after they pegged a goal back, but our two man defence of Jerry Reynolds and Dan Doyle kept up the shutters, Doyle in particular played a brilliant game, to ensure no more goals as we took the two points home, by all accounts a very fortunate two points, with the final score, St Mirren 1 Celtic 2.

With injuries biting hard going into the winter, the Celtic Committee were fortunate in that we had a decent back up of players in the very decent Celtic reserve team, managed by James Curtis. Back in the day, eleven players would be selected, with substitutions not allowed and to complicate matters, the reserve team would play at the same time with the location depending on the whereabouts of the first team's match. For example, as Celtic played St Mirren at Westmarch in Paisley, both second elevens would be playing at Celtic Park. Cup competitions were different as the draws were completely separate, with the first team, naturally, given preference over the use of Celtic Park.

If a first team player was injured before the match, or had failed to turn up for whatever reason, a mad dash would be made for a reserve team player to get to the ground as soon as possible and come on late. On occasion an injured player would still play, just to make up the numbers as no more than nuisance value. The Celtic reserve team in 1891 was; Charlie Kelly, Collins,

Tom Dunbar, Willie McCallum, (captain), Frank Dolan, Johnny Cunningham, James Boyle, Johnny Coleman, McGeechan and Joe Foran. Frank Dolan's brother Michael played in our very first match in May 1888 and often still played as goalkeeper in place of former Hibs player Charlie Kelly.

The Scottish Cup holders and early pace setters Hearts arrived at Celtic Park on League duty two weeks later amidst tremendous excitement which brought out the biggest League crowd to date. 16,000 crammed into Celtic Park with 800 Hearts fans travelling on the fitba specials from Edinburgh. Amongst their number was Sir Lewis McIver, a Liberal Unionist politician who tried to ingratiate himself with the mainly Protestant Hearts support with the looming General Election in April 1892 in which he was up for election in the nearby Edinburgh South ward. Ironically he fell 431 votes short of the Liberal politician and was unsuccessful.

This was a crucial match as the Celts were keen to avenge our defeat in the first match of the season at Tynecastle as we sat four points behind Hearts at the top of the League with three games in hand.

The stage was set for a classic, but heavy rain on the morning of the game left the pitch less than perfect for Celtic's fast moving passing game. However it was the Celts who took to the conditions better than our opponents and we fully deserved our opener in the 10th minute after Johnny Campbell shot, then Dan Doyle hit a powerful drive that the keeper could only parry and Sandy McMahon was in the right place, at the right time to head the ball home. We went in at half time a goal to the good, although it could and should have been more. Hearts started the second half with more of a purpose, but after only four minutes the Celts scored a second after the Hearts keeper saved a shot from Sandy McMahon but the rebound fell to Johnny Madden who simply walked the ball into the goals with the keeper out of position.

Ten minutes late Sandy McMahon made it 3-0 with a header and the Celts seemed more intent to play to the gallery, allowing Hearts back into the game. With our foot off the pedal, Hearts scored a consolation goal with a fierce drive, but the Celts avenged their 3-1 defeat on the first game of the season in kind. The visitors from the east had brought a sizeable support with them, but they couldn't muster a song between them thanks to the under par performance of their team who were outplayed on the day. So quiet were they in fact that doubt was expressed whether the fitba specials from the east had ever arrived at all.

On the 24th October, Vale of Leven were the visitors to Celtic Park and nobody gave the Dunbartonshire team a chance as they sat isolated firmly at the bottom of the League with 9 defeats and 1 draw from 10 matches played. The biggest surprise was that it took Celtic twenty minutes to open the scoring with Alec Brady obliging and Johnny Madden adding a second five minutes later with a tap in after Brady's shot was saved. With the bhoys playing with the Vale, there were no more goals in the first half but Sandy McMahon soon added a third with a header at the start of the second spell. Johnny Madden added a fourth before the Vale finally got one back. In a totally one sided match Madden scored two more to give him a total of four goals as the score ended Celtic 6 Vale of Leven 1.

Remarkably it would be just over two months before our next League match was played, as our match on 14th November against Cambuslang was postponed due to the Glasgow v Edinburgh Inter City match being played at Celtic Park and the League match with Leith in Edinburgh on 5th December was postponed due to darkness setting in after the Celtic team arrived late. Every other date was taken up by Glasgow Cup and Scottish Cup games, which was a good problem to have of course, as it meant we were still in both competitions.

By the end of October, our record this season stood up to every other team in Britain, with the exception of Nottingham Forest. Having played 15 matches, we had won 13, drew 1 and lost 1. We had also scored 65 goals in the first three months of the season, which made us the highest scorers, and we conceded only 19.

CELTIC PARK AND THE CELTIC SUPPORT

The *Scottish Referee* on 19th October described the Celtic support against Hearts and the fortress that Celtic Park was becoming;

"The vastness of the crowd, fully 16,000, appeared to overawe the visitors, who throughout never seemed to shake off the feeling that they were not playing at home. It is perfectly clear that the venue of a match has a good deal to do with the result. The Celts by their appearance must have more than pleased their friends. There was no mistaking the spirit in which they entered on the contest. On their present form, and at Parkhead, it is doubtful if there is a combination anywhere which could beat them".

Also in the same paper on the same day;

"Bedad, and did ye ever see such a crowd of the bhoys? Every one of them real patriots, too; Celts to the tip of their finger nails. And it did your heart good to see the way they behaved, too. Gentlemen couldn't have conducted themselves better. It was a job getting to the ground. Sure if I was pitched off one car, I was chucked out of a dozen, but I took it all in good part, bless you; for wasn't I going to see the finest football match as was ever played?

Mighty narrow doors you enter by, though. Worse crush than the first night at a pantomine; but then wasn't I going to see the Celtic lick them Hearts? And wouldn't I just stand no end of crushing and inconvenience to see that beautiful sight? What a lot of purty girls were there too - one or two real sweet charmers in front of the stand, and the way they laughed and clapped their little hands when our bhoys were walking through them Hearts!

It was a fine sight and I would have given a lot to have been beside the little dears. If there is one thing more than another that appeals to my heart, it's the sight of a pretty face - and a drop of the cratur.

We were all bursting with suppressed excitement waiting on the teams coming out. When they finally made their appearance, we stretched our lungs a bit in real Irish fashion. We welcomed the visitors cordial like, though we knew that the bhoys were going to lick them.

What a row it was when the game began! Every one of us seemed to be bent on shouting himself hoarse in the first ten minutes of the game. Every little kick and pass was applauded to the echo and when Sandy McMahon headed the first goal, we - well, we did shout and dance and shake each other by the hand, we did".

The above is a fantastic description of the Celtic support that has transcended time and caught the raw emotion that only a support with a special attachment to the club, can have. We're not just a city team like thousands the world over. To quote Tommy Burns;

"When you pull on that jersey you're not just playing for a football club, you're playing for a people and a cause."

The Celtic support at the foundation of the club were a people and a cause who were discriminated against because of their race and their religion in a hostile environment. They had no choice but to huddle together in the Irish "quarters" of the city in the poorest slums the city had to offer. To them, Celtic were far more than a football club, Celtic Park was their beacon of light shining brightly amongst the poverty and fear. When they attended a Celtic match they could be themselves, they could express themselves and they could take pride in their race without fear of attack. Celtic Park was their haven. The Celtic support, as well as the players and the Founding Fathers, built Celtic from nothing.

We are Celtic. Players will come and players will go, but one thing is absolutely certain; the Celtic support goes on forever.

CELTIC OUTGROWING OUR FACILITIES

Off the pitch there was another reminder that Celtic had outgrown the confines of Celtic Park when a barricade that separated the fans from the track and the pitch gave way under the size of the crowd and fans took up the extra space on the track. Thankfully there were no reported injuries.

The *Scottish Sport* reported on the 16th October 1891;

"The pressure of the immense crowd was so great that the enclosing barricade gave way. The extra accommodation afforded on the track can easily liquidate the repairs. A few clubs wouldn't object to a broken barricade every week - from the same cause".

The new press box, sometimes referred to as the press stand, but described as a "dookit", had been enlarged and enclosed in the close season but was not big enough to hold the numbers present for the match of the day. The press would have to like it or lump it as there would be no further improvements until the new ground was built.

From the *Scottish Sport*;

"The Celtic press box requires extension, if Saturday's experience goes for anything. It was inconveniently crushed - and not by reporters - some of whom were in danger of losing their tempers over the jam. By the by, might not an easier means of ingress and egress be adopted. On field days the knights of the pencil have literally to fight their way into their dookit".

At the Blackburn Rovers match a couple of weeks previously, the reporter at the match gave an insight into the location of the press box at the original Celtic Park with the following;

"In squeezing my corporeal, (bodily), frame through the pavillionites to the press dookit, I encountered one or two of the Celtic Committee."

From this we can deduct that the press stand was next to the main Pavillion stand and to gain access from Dalmarnock Street, reporters would have to walk along the front of the Pavillion, where some of the committee would be hanging about. The press "dookit," a raised platform with a cover, stood at either side of the Pavillion and the best bet would have been the north side, as they had to walk past the Pavillion to access it but also the fact that in both sketches of the original Celtic Park, both taken at the south west corner of the ground, there is no press stand seen. Was it hidden, north of the Pavillion Stand or was the artist drawing his sketch from within the press stand, where better than a raised platform with a roof over your head to draw a sketch during a match? The allocated seating for the press, it appears, would on occasion be taken up by supporters therefore it seems there was no checks put in place to ensure only the press were sitting in the press seats.

One other downside of the press stand was the racket made by the Celtic support when we scored as we banged our firsts on its wooden roof, no doubt taking great satisfaction in the deed. The "dookits" would certainly have been cramped and calls by the press to have them enlarged or extended were very likely to have been based on merit. The problem was the lack of space in the original ground. A "dookit" is a Glasgow word to describe a pigeon loft, or could be used to describe an enclosed space with no windows or doors, but it's very possible too that a wee bit of exaggeration was being used by the pressmen, who were oft times adept at that particular skill.

WORK BEGINS TO BUILD NEW CELTIC PARK

The first spadeful, heralding the commencement of work on the current Celtic Park began in earnest on Monday 19th October 1891, according to the Scottish Sport on the 27th October;

"Operations have commenced upon what will be known hereafter as New Celtic Park. The first spadeful was lifted last Monday week. It is expected that the new grounds will be ready in time for the club sports next season. The contractor will however require to work hard to accomplish that".

From the *Glasgow Evening News* on Friday 23rd October;

"The first sod of the Celtic new ground was cut yesterday by Mr James Mackie, who performed the ceremony in the usual fashion. The committee of the club attended and Mr John Glass, it is said, will preserve the cutting in a glass case".

RANGERS RESPOND

It would be naive to think that the work of the Celtic Committee in building New Celtic Park, the biggest and best football and athletics ground in the country, would not have focussed the minds of the other Glasgow clubs in particular. We have already seen that Third Lanark built a new "state of the art" stand at Cathkin, but what about Rangers who had one eye firmly on hosting the 1892 Scotland v England match?

Rangers had moved to the original Ibrox Park in August 1887, after their lease had expired on their Kinning Park ground in February of that year. They flew the Scotland flag above the west end of their main stand and the cost of building the ground in 1887, complete with running track was £1300. Just four years later, despite their on field problems and a lack of success, Rangers held a special General Meeting on Wednesday, 21st October and agreed to go ahead with the building of a second covered stand on the south side of the pitch which would extend their seated capacity by 3000, and would rise above the terracing already on that side of the ground and would come at a cost of around £1200.

This came despite one club member interrupting the discussion to state that Rangers needed a team more than they needed a grandstand! Fast forward 90 years when the second Ibrox Park was rebuilt to include three new all seated stands and the joke doing the rounds then was that they had built the stands the wrong way round.

They were facing the pitch.

Ouch.

As if to underline their problems on the pitch in 1891, Rangers then lost 5-1 at home to Clyde in their next League match, with the "Ould Giniral", former Celt, Jimmy McLaren the star of the show for Clyde.

THE FIRST GLASGOW/EDINBURGH INTER CITY MATCH AT CELTIC PARK

Celtic Park was chosen to host the Inter City match between Glasgow and Edinburgh, (sometimes known as Glasgow v East of Scotland), on Saturday, 14th November 1891 and Celtic were represented by Dan Doyle, (captain), Alec Brady and Peter Dowds in a match that ended in a 2-2 draw. This was only the third time Glasgow had hosted the match out of eleven meetings but the unbeaten record was kept with one win and two draws. Sandy McMahon withdrew from the match on health grounds, after being invited to play. He didn't fancy being kicked up and down the pitch by the Hearts hammer throwers in the Edinburgh side!

THE FIRST TRANSFER BETWEEN CELTIC AND RANGERS

Tom Dunbar, full back of the Celtic reserve team became the first player to transfer between Celtic and Rangers at the start of November 1891. Tom was unable to oust Dan Doyle, Alec Brady or Jerry Reynolds from their place in the Celtic defence and the chances of him doing so sometime soon were nil. Rangers on the other hand were struggling in the bottom half of the League and Dunbar was possibly miffed that after Mick McKeown had left Celtic for Blackburn Rovers, he wasn't given a chance to hold down a place at full back. Ironically Tom Dunbar played against Mick McKeown in Celtic's 3-2 win over Blackburn Rovers on 1st October and played a blinder. Unfortunately he went straight back into the reserve team and possibly these reasons were on his mind when he approached Rangers.

The new signing was pushed straight into the Rangers team against non League Queens Park in the quarter final of the Glasgow Cup, but his inclusion couldn't stop another defeat for his new team, by three goals to nil, watched by Colonel Bill Cody from Buffalo Bill's Wild West cowboy tour which was showing in Duke Street, Glasgow.

CELTIC: THE EARLY YEARS

Cowboy outfit beaten by amateurs, watched by Buffalo Bill. The irony was lost on no-one.

All the Glasgow League teams now had a former Celtic player in their ranks with Tom Dunbar at Rangers, Barney Crossan at Third Lanark and Jimmy McLaren at Clyde. Jimmy McGhee also left Celtic to join Abercorn in Paisley, but he could only play in cup ties having already played for Celtic in a League match this season.

Tom Dunbar was the brother of Mick Dunbar, one of the original Celtic team who played on the 28th May, 1888 and who was then signed from Hibs. Mick Dunbar became a massive favourite at Celtic Park, and served on the Celtic Committee after his playing days were over and also on the Celtic Board until his death in 1921.

Tom Dunbar, after his stint at Ibrox, re signed for Celtic and became one of the original shareholders named in the list of subscribers in 1897.

There's a good question for a pub quiz...

What former Rangers player bought shares in the original Celtic shares issue in 1897?

The question may also be raised about Rangers sectarian signing policy which debarred Catholics from employment in the Rangers team. There were a handful of Catholics who signed for Rangers from 1891, and certainly they were well aware that Tom Dunbar was a Catholic at the time of his signing. In fact it was Dunbar who initiated the contact and Rangers possibly felt they were in no position to turn down an approach from a decent player who could cure their ills, even if he was a Catholic. To be fair to Tom Dunbar, the evils of sectarianism had not totally cast its shadow over Rangers at the time he played for them, his only wish was to fulfil his ambition to make it as a football player, something he wouldn't get a chance to do in the Celtic reserves.

Interestingly, Tom Dunbar married the daughter of Peter Glass, who was the brother of John Glass, the first Celtic President.

MICK McKEOWN SUFFERS A NASTY INJURY

Former Celtic full back, Mick McKeown, received a nasty gash on his leg, which kept him out of the Blackburn Rovers side for six weeks, after horseplay in the Ewood Park dressing room following training.

After climbing up on the wash stand, with one foot in the basin and the other on the framework, suddenly the basin gave way under his weight, and as he fell the sharp edges of the basin caused a large gash in his left leg, just at the knee. Fortunately medical staff were on hand to stitch the wound and he was conveyed to hospital to rue the day he took on a wash basin and came off second best.

EVERTON VERSUS DAN DOYLE 2

Just as the dust had settled on the Dan Doyle case, it emerged that Everton had decided to commence legal proceedings against Dan Doyle for the wages he had been given by Everton on a two year contact in advance totalling £111 and also for breach of contract. Joseph Shaughnessy, lawyer and Celtic founding father defended Doyle.

In the end, the sheriff decreed that Doyle should pay back £69 to settle the action which had been agreed by the new Celt as he had signed in May and so by his calculations, £42 was due to him in wages up until the month of August, when he joined Celtic. Everton contested this 14 weeks of service Doyle claimed to have given them as he had joined their club during the close season. The sheriff requested further proof regarding the £42 but in the end both parties settled amicably out of court and the matter was finally closed.

FOOTBALL AND CHARITY

"Football and Charity," ran one of the headlines in the editorial of the Glasgow Observer on 21st November 1891 in praise of Celtic's charitable ethos;

"The Celtic Football Club has had, since its inauguration, many an eulogy, but none greater than that bestowed on it by the Reverend Doctor Redman, who preached in Edinburgh on Sunday last, in aid of the Lanark Hospital. The Celtic had extended to this most deserving institution a portion of its surplus and earned thereby from Reverend Doctor Redman the apostrophe; "All honour to them for this Catholic spirit co existing with the manliness of their athleticism".

The Hospital, we may add, is in great need of funds and as its claims on the Catholics of Scotland are strong as its needs are urgent, we trust many of our readers will be moved to spare from their abundance a donation in aid of so good a work. Sister Clare Redman, The Hospital, Lanark, will acknowledge and gladly forward collecting cards to such as may be disposed to write for them".

In the same month, the Scottish Sport carried articles about Celtic donating £20 to Father Hughes at Sacred Heart in his efforts to set up a library in the City Fever Hospital within his parish. The Celtic Committee also sent our usual £20 monthly donation for the maintenance of the Poor Childrens Dinner Tables in the three parishes of the east end.

OUR SCOTTISH CUP RUN BEGINS

The Celts were drawn away to St Mirren in the first round of the Scottish Cup and we offered to play the game at Celtic Park, which often occurred when the home team would rather cash in financially than gamble on a better chance of causing an upset. It didn't happen this time and the Celts travelled to Westmarch, the Saints' first ground, on 28th November. By half time the Saints must have wished they agreed to the switch as they were well beaten in front of a crowd of around 4000, with the Celtic support in a clear majority on a day when Queens Park were also in Paisley at the same time on cup duty against Abercorn.

The heavy rain and wind made it difficult to play any kind of football but it was the Saints who surprised everyone by taking the lead in the 15th minute with their first attack after the Celts had bombarded the home goal time after time. The bhoys responded quickly and before the Saints knew what had hit them, they were 4-1 down by half time. The first goal came from Johnny Madden and was followed in the 30th minute by an own goal with the ball fortunately bouncing off McFarlane, the Saints' defender. Willie Maley and Sandy McMahon added a third and a fourth in the five minutes leading up to half time and the tie was finished as a contest. The home team rallied in the second half and pulled one goal back but it was the Celts who went marching on after a 4-2 victory.

Kilmarnock Athletic, (not to be confused with local rivals Kilmarnock), were drawn away to Celtic in the next round on the 19th December and despite having beaten Bridge of Allan in the last round 7-2, they weren't given a chance of causing an upset in what was a massive step up in class for the club from the Federation League. Their chances were tough enough, without scoring two own goals to give the Celts a 2-0 lead at half time but fortunately enough for them, the Celts were happy to keep our foot off the pedal in the second half and we were content to see a long range shot from Peter Dowds finish the scoring at Celtic 3 Kilmarnock Athletic 0.

In the quarter final draw we were paired with Cowlairs at Celtic Park. Due to the severe frost, the game was put back to 23rd January, which meant that we hadn't played a match of any description for almost three weeks. Thankfully this didn't show and the match finally went ahead on a pitch covered in mud, sand and sawdust, not a cocktail conducive to the beautiful game. Making short work of the conditions, we were three goals up by half time, shooting into the goals at the Janefield Street end. Johnny Madden got the Celts off to a great start with a beauty in the 5th minute, before Sandy McMahon scored a second in the 38th minute and another was added before half time.

The Celts kept up the pressure in the second half and Alec Brady got a fourth goal before Neil McCallum and Johnny Madden were forced to come off injured as we finished the last 20 minutes with nine men. Cowlairs scored with the last kick of the ball and the game finished 4-1 as the Celts marched into the semi final. Rangers, Queens Park and Renton joined us in the semi final draw and the Celts drew Rangers at Celtic Park, having already beaten them in both matches played that season, 2-0 and 3-0 at home. This was Rangers' first appearance in the semi final of the Scottish Cup in eight years and Celtic's second appearance in four years.

THE FIRST HALF YEARLY GENERAL MEETING

At the proposal of Joseph Shaughnessy at the AGM in June 1891, it had been agreed that the club would also hold a half yearly meeting in December and so this became the first and was held in the Caledonian Halls on London Road, Bridgeton on the Tuesday evening of December 8th.

From the *Glasgow Observer*;

CELTIC FOOTBALL CLUB

BI-ANNUAL MEETING

"The Celtic Football Club held a half-yearly meeting in the Caledonian Halls, London Road, Glasgow on Tuesday evening. There was a large attendance of members, and Mr John Glass, President, occupied the chair. Mr John H McLaughlin, Secretary, submitted the report for the half-year. This document, which was an

elaborate one, stated that the club had now got together a team which, in the opinion of good judges, was the best in England, Ireland, or Scotland. The 1st team had played 22 matches, won 18, drawn 3, and lost only one, which, was the best record of any first class club in the United Kingdom. Amongst the defeated clubs were the Heart of Midlothian, Rangers, Blackburn Rovers, and Dumbarton. They were now getting into the finals of the Cup ties, and there was no doubt the team would do their utmost to bring fresh laurels to the club. While the team were busy on the battlefield the committee had been no less energetic in the council chamber.

Being an Irish club, it was but natural that they should have a greedy landlord, and they had one who was working to take a high place amongst, rack-renters in Ireland. In the old country these gentlemen were satisfied with doubling, or at the worst trebling it, but the bright genius who boasted the possession of the Celtic Park wanted nine times the present rent for a new lease, and instead of £50 per year, he wished to increase the annual rent to £450. The committee could recognise a hint when they got it, and as this one appeared pretty strong, they decided to shift, and had now secured a ten year lease of a splendid field close to the present ground. Everything would be done to make the new enclosure the best football park in Scotland, and they had every reason to believe that it would be ready for the opening on the occasion of the annual sports next year. The park, when completed, would accommodate from 30,000 to 40,000 people. The report concluded with a fitting reference to the late Mr Hugh Darroch, formerly Treasurer of the club.

Mr Thomas Flood moved the adoption of the report. It not only reflected credit on the members of the team and their Glasgow followers, but it would be welcomed by their countrymen all over Great Britain, who took a deep interest in the working of the Celtic Club. Irishmen in Scotland, in past years, had been made little of, because they had very few of their number in business or in positions of responsibility in the country, but they had lately demonstrated that not only in commercial life could they be successful, but they had proved the possession on their part of an amount of pluck and perseverance by the manner in which they had risen to the top of the ladder in the football world. The Celtic team was the pride of the Irish race in England, Ireland, and Scotland, and he hoped and trusted that the members of the team would stick together and add fresh victories to their record, and still further enhance the name of the Celtic Club.

Mr Stephen Henry seconded the motion. They had in the splendid report submitted by their Secretary, Mr McLaughlin, a proof of the ability of Irishmen to manage any concern in which they took an interest. They had in their team and club membership men who were fit to compete favourably with those of any similar institution in the country, and in the cup ties and other engagements which the club had before them he had no fear but that the interest of the club, the fair fame of their nationality, and the exposition of genuine football would be the first consideration of those players who had in the past represented the club with such splendid success. The motion was carried unanimously".

It was a harmonious meeting with great pride taken in the performance of the team on the pitch, but off it too by the committee who had tied up a 10 year lease of the ground on which the current ground is now built. 1891 was a groundbreaking year for the club. We were now established as one of the best teams in Britain, if not THE best team and we had now secured a ground large enough to ensure our progress continued at pace.

The General Meetings, as always, gave a direct insight into the thinking of the men who ran the club and it remained abundantly clear that we were extremely proud of our roots as an Irish club. We hid it under no bushel, we made no apologies for it, indeed we screamed our pride in it from the rooftops and the words of John H McLaughlin, Thomas Flood and Stephen J Henry extol the virtues of that pride at the club's General Meeting. John H McLaughlin's clever comparison between the Celtic Park landlord and the rack-renters in Ireland struck a note as it was a very familiar one. Many of the members present at the meeting would have had first hand experience of the landlord system used in Ireland, whereby a Scots or English landlord could double the price of the rent or more and even evict the tenants into the street almost at a whim.

THE BATTLE BETWEEN CELTIC AND RANGERS BEGINS - OFF THE FIELD

John H McLaughlin, in his report at the General Meeting, gave the first insight into the capacity of the New Celtic Park, when he stated it would accommodate from 30,000 to 40,000. He also stated that everything would be done to make the new enclosure the best football park in Scotland. This would not go unnoticed at Ibrox and they set about a programme of improvements and extensions that would take the capacity of their ground to over 40,000.

Make no mistake whatsoever, the rivalry between Celtic and Rangers started not in the latter part of the decade with both teams vying for trophies on the park. The rivalry began with the building of both grounds within nine months of each other and with the ultimate goal the hosting of the biggest match in football, the international match between Scotland and England, which would in turn attract prestige and no little profit that would be ploughed back into the ground to ensure it was the biggest and best and able to maintain the forward momentum of the club and our mushroom like growth.

THE FIRST USE OF GOAL NETS

Meanwhile at the original Celtic Park, it was agreed that goal nets would be used on a trial basis, starting with the League match against St Mirren at Celtic Park on the 26th December. The Celts won 2-1 after Johnny Campbell opened the scoring in the 10th minute, but the visitors levelled 10 minutes later. James Kelly was then forced to come off due to injury and the Celts played the rest of the game with ten men. At half time the supporters moved round to congregate behind the goal we were shooting into and although the new goal nets had only been used twice, they got a close up view when Alec Brady finished the scoring with 15 minutes to go, 2-1 in Celtic's favour.

That's another good question for a pub quiz.

Question: Who was the first Celtic player to put the ball in the back of the net?

Answer: Neil McCallum on the 28th May 1888 in the 5-2 win over Rangers?

No. It was Johnny Campbell on the 26th August 1891 in the 2-1 win over St Mirren.

PROGRESS CONTINUES AT NEW CELTIC PARK

On Friday, 18th December the *Glasgow Evening News* reported;

"The Celtic's new ground is being gradually put into ship shape order, the workmen being busily employed upon it daily".

The *Scottish Sport* reported on the same date;

"The new ground of Celtic FC goes on apace. It is now enclosed with a substantial barricade of corrugated metal and very soon turf will be laid on the playing pitch. Laying out of tracks is engaging attention and mixtures for same are being carefully concocted and analysed".

This report signified tremendous progress in levelling out the ground in just under eight weeks as the spadework had started on 19th October. The playing surface was now level and ready for the laying of turf. This showed that in under two months, the first phase of levelling the "free coup" was complete and the next phase of laying out the running and cycling tracks had begun. Testing was being carried out on the newest methods to ensure both tracks were made to the highest standards and of the best quality available.

The new corrugated fence boundary ensured that we had something worth protecting so the workmen and volunteers could work in peace with the massive task in hand. At the same time Rangers enlarged their terracing on the west and north west sides of the first Ibrox Park but were still pondering the decision to build the new covered stand on the south side of the pitch, where they had acquired additional ground, which they claimed made Ibrox the largest football enclosure in Scotland.

Not for long, mused the Celtic Committee.

CELTIC'S FIRST THRASHING

The Celts had a busy programme of friendlies lined up over the New Year with matches against Dumbarton at home on New Year's Day, Third Lanark at Cathkin the day after and Rangers on January 4th, back at Celtic Park.

With three games in four days, the Celts replaced the injured James Kelly for the Dumbarton game with Cherry from Clyde guesting. The holiday fixtures were always popular and none more so than the New Years Day game when fans would first foot Celtic Park and meet up with friends and family at the same time. On this occasion 15,000 turned up for a friendly.

The *Scottish Sport* on January 5th set the scene;

"Full and running over was the New Year's gate at Celtic Park. You had to undergo a 10 minute crush before you cleared the pay gates and then even standing room was at a premium. The gate alone was £450 and both stands were packed".

"Some of the select had to resort to strategy to get inside. We know of a party who got through a kitchen and ever so many garden gates".

"The only place on the whole ground that was not crowded was the generally crowded press box".

The party who had to clamber through a kitchen and over garden gates to access Celtic Park must have read the match report from the match with Queens Park two years previous when the visiting team had to do likewise. Although Celtic Park was bound on the south and east by a main road and on the west by a cemetery, the ground north of Celtic Park was populated with houses and in the north east boundary sat Ivy Cottage, a spacious house with large gardens. This would have been the access point mentioned for a select few who could not gain access by normal means.

Both teams were neck and neck at the top of the table and on the one occasion they had met this season, Celtic beat Dumbarton 2-0 at Celtic Park in a League match, therefore a close game was expected in this friendly. Many of those present may have been full of the festive spirit, literally, but they didn't expect the Celtic team to be full of good will at best or even under the influence too as some performances suggested.

With the ground crammed full in anticipation of a good match, behind the scenes the Dumbarton team were protesting at the choice of referee, a Mr RF Harrison, President of the Ayrshire Association. Incredibly they stated uncategorically that if another referee wasn't found, they wouldn't play the match and to make their point, some players even started to put their own clothes back on. Sickened by this attitude in a friendly match from the visitors and with no reason given for the complaint apart from a dislike for the referee, the Celtic Committee had no choice but to find another referee and promptly too. As it turned out Mr J Marshall was in attendance at the invitation of Dumbarton and also Mr James Robertson too, both of whom were experienced referees. The latter obliged and thankfully the match proceeded as advertised. Or not as the case turned out.

Major Burke, of Buffalo Bill's Wild West show kicked the game off in splendid style but its a pity he couldn't play in goals. By half time the Celtic support would have been forgiven for thinking there was room for only one cowboy in goals and he was already in position. Having started off the better team, with John McLeod, the Dumbarton keeper saving well from Johnny Madden, Sandy McMahon and Neil McCallum, things started to go wrong in the 20th minute, when the Sons of the Rock scored two goals in as many minutes, the second of which is described in the Lennox Herald on the 6th January as;

"A long shot, almost from the corner flag, a soft shot - which Duff might easily have saved."

The Celts broke up the other end, determined to get back into the game to no avail and just five minutes later it was three, with the Scottish Sport summing up the last line of defence thus;

"Duff's goalkeeping was very indifferent".

Heads went down in the Celtic team and on the 40th minute another goal was added, then another just before the half time whistle blew. Incredibly we were 5-0 down at home by half time and the performance of Celtic goalkeeper Tom Duff was raising 15,000 pairs of eyebrows. The whole ground was mystified at the performance of the normally reliable goalkeeper, but the facts were that of the five goals lost, four were saveable.

The *Scottish Sport* on the 5th January made the following observations;

"They (Dumbarton), did not come into too close quarters with the backs, but hit upon the happy, and as it turned out, profitable expedient of shooting from the open ground between the two lines of the home defence.

By this they made another favourable discovery; they found that Duff was very much off, and that they had only to knock loud enough to have the door quickly opened. From that moment they never ceased to knock".

"The first goal was put in with a long saveable shot after twenty minutes play, and a second of the same sort sailed through a minute afterwards. The first four goals were all put on in the same easy fashion. With custodians changed, the score at the interval might have been transferred to the other side of the ledger."

A damning indictment it was on the goalkeeping performance of Tom Duff, but you can't be five goals down at half time without apportioning some of the blame on the rest of the Celtic team too, particularly the defence. The forwards weren't as sharp as they normally were either and had missed a fair few chances. As the first paragraph above alludes to, Dumbarton shot on sight, with the knowledge that all was not right with the goalkeeper's ability to save the easiest shot. The biggest surprise was that it took them 20 minutes to realise this. Surely too Duff's team mates would have urged a change in that department, if not the Celtic Committee who would have been incandescent with rage at half time at the humiliation they were watching unfold before their very eyes. However before the days of substitutions, the goalkeeper could not simply be replaced. He could have been moved upfield with an outfield player taking his place in goals but we were already carrying an injured player in Peter Dowds.

The other alternative was to take Duff off completely and play with ten men. Surely he must have received the attention of the club doctor at half time in the pavillion, as well as the trainer, who had responsibility for ensuring the team were prepared and were in tip top condition? If Duff was suffering from the effects of rheumatism he should never have played. If he was under the influence of alcohol over the festive period that was affecting his performance, he should have been taken off without hesitation as soon as it was noticed.

The second half wasn't much better with Peter Dowds eventually having to come off injured with twenty minutes remaining and the Celts were forced to carry on with ten men. Dumbarton added two more goals, on occasion simply waltzing past our half backs, before they scored another just before the final whistle. Ironically, after Dowds went off, this was our best part of the game as we finished as we started, as the better team.

The only problem was the 8 goals we lost in between.

The *Scottish Sport* continued;

"Only for half an hour was the game a runaway affair. For the other hour it was not an altogether unequal fight, and strange to say the Celts both started and finished best. The Celts never approached their usual standard of play, even when they had full possession of the ball".

"The Celts were fairly out their stride and never really recovered it. Their general movement, after the first brief burst, was slow and clumsy. They assisted their opponents as much as themselves with their ill judged

passing. If they cast the larger share of the blame upon Duff, they do not make a Jonah of him. He it was who chiefly gave them away, although it must not be concluded that he was the only failure. In fact, it is a question whether there was even a moderate success in the entire team".

The Dumbarton team, on the contrary, were well up for the game, even with two reserve players they had to play from the start;

"There was not a vestige of holiday about Dumbarton. Every man - subs included - were lion hearted and deer limbed".

The *Scottish Sport* carried on with the finger pointing in the aftermath of the defeat;

"The opinion was freely expressed that if goalkeepers were reversed the result would have been very different. Undoubtedly it would. It was McLeod's fine saving in the first quarter and Duff's dreadful losing all through, that chiefly contributed to the new record. Duff for the day spelled his name D-U-F-F-E-R. It will take a lot of his best saving to recover the reputation lost".

At the after dinner speeches under the west stand, referring to the scoreline, the *Scottish Sport* reported;

"It was rather tall to be generally received as a correct measure of the respective teams. It has a smell of liquor about it; but of course the Dumbarton are not responsible for that".

The newspaper had chosen its words carefully and a rumour was born. The "tall" scoreline was completely unexpected between the top two clubs in Scotland and so the finger pointing exercise had to begin. It wasn't just an off day, it was more than that, given our record of success, this result was totally extraordinary and there is no doubt the Celtic support would have been scratching our heads wondering how it could have happened. The *Scottish Sport* is clearly suggesting the consumption of alcohol on the Celtic team's part to the titillation of the conspiracy theories of the day, but nowhere is there any mention of Duff's rheumatism. The movement of the outfield players too has already been described as slow and clumsy but this is far from conclusive. The match kicked off at 2pm on New Years Day so anyone stupid enough to have enjoyed some festive spirit at the bells would certainly have been under the influence during the match.

The *Scottish Referee*, much less sensational than their rival, the *Scottish Sport* said;

"Celtic did not for some reason or other play their usual effective and brilliant game, for there was a lack of that quickness, alertness and confidence on the ball, which as a rule characterises the tactics of the Parkhead men, while it is the opinion of more than one capable judge, that had goalkeepers been reversed a different result would have been seen".

Summing up some of the other performances in the *Lennox Herald*;

"Jerry Reynolds played hard all through but found a tough opponent in Bell. Dan Doyle lacked his usual freshness. The play of Cherry, (guesting in place of James Kelly), was extremely disappointing, he was having a miserable game. Peter Dowds did not play in his usual effective fashion and found more than his match. Sandy McMahon and Johnny Campbell's combination was repeatedly broken up".

Incredibly this had been our first defeat since the opening game of the season in August. It was not only our biggest ever defeat, it was the biggest ever defeat recorded in first class football at the time, thankfully as it was a friendly, it wasn't recorded as our worst ever defeat in a competitive match. This "honour" goes to the infamous 8-0 defeat we suffered at the hands of Motherwell at Fir Park in a "meaningless" final League match after the title had been lost and it happened just days after we had won the Scottish Cup final in 1937, beating Aberdeen 2-1 with the same team. Goalkeeper Joe Kennaway came off injured at half time and had to be replaced by inside forward Willie Buchan in goals and Jock Morrison in defence was forced to retire injured, which didn't help.

The upshot of the first match of 1892 was that Tom Duff never played another game for Celtic. When signed in the summer from Cowlairs, he was judged to be the best keeper in Scotland. Now his surname had became an adjective; a byword for something duff, ie, not very good and a description that lasts to this day, a bit like a "Sebo", the chant that still goes up at Celtic Park after a sitter is missed, in honour of the infamous Rangers player.

The suggestion that Duff had played under the influence of alcohol, as well as some of his team mates was never proven and the added complication of his rheumatics needs further investigation. On the 26th September, in the home match with Dumbarton, Duff suffered from rheumatism compounded by the non stop torrential rain at that game. He missed the next eleven matches before returning for the Glasgow Cup Final on 12th December against Clyde. In his absence, Charlie Kelly and Michael Dolan had done an average job, conceding 15 goals as we scored 43, in an unbeaten run with nine victories and two draws. Only three clean sheets were kept and the Celtic Committee knew that whilst Kelly and Dolan were decent stopgaps, Duff was the better keeper of the three. In the first six matches of Duff's absence we lost five goals, but in the next five matches we lost ten goals, two in each game which was a fact that unnerved the Celtic Committee with the upcoming Glasgow Cup final against Clyde.

Duff was brought back in for the final and played the next two matches against Kilmarnock Athletic in the Scottish Cup on the 19th December and St Mirren a week later in the League, both at Celtic Park before the Dumbarton match, which was to be his last. In the Kilmarnock Athletic match, it was stated in the Scottish Sport;

"Duff is not yet quite recovered and on Saturday guarded the Celts goals, not in uniform, but well muffled up".

Whether rheumatism, alcohol or a mixture of both played a part in his downfall will never be known for definite but he was definitely not a well man since September and should not have been selected to play in the Dumbarton match unless 100% fit. Duff's Celtic career was over and he was replaced by Joe Cullen, the Benburb keeper who agreed that very night to guest for the club and make his debut the next day, before signing on the dotted line. It was a huge step up for an inexperienced junior player to be plunged straight in at the deep end with Celtic's heavy fixture list in the second half of the season, but Joe grabbed his chance. He became known for his coolness and courage and he went on to become a firm favourite and enjoyed a distinguished Celtic career over the next five seasons before joining Spurs. Sadly Joe died at the young age of 35 in 1905 from pneumonia.

What this episode proved was the ruthlessness of the Celtic Committee, not afraid to make a decision when a decision had to be made. They were hurting after the mauling from Dumbarton in front of our own fans and someone had to pay. That man was Tom Duff.

Even the *Glasgow Observer* struggled to sum up the match with their typical pro Celtic spin;

"The Celtic FC had an enormous gate on Friday last, when they met the Dumbarton on their own pitch at Parkhead. The play of the Celts was a deep disappointment to their supporters, who were in the majority, immensely, if one might judge by the paucity of the applause which greeted the success of the opposing club, a greeting different indeed, to the mighty shout which rends the air when the Celtic score a point.

The pavillion and stand were crowded with notabilities. Major Burke, of the Wild West, kicked off in lieu of Mr Healy, who telegraphed his inability to attend".

Tim Healy was a County Cork man and the elected Irish Nationalist politician for North Longford. The gate was mentioned, as well as the opposing teams, the lack of applause and even the list of celebrities, everything in fact but the score line! Ironically Dumbarton were third choice opponents for the New Year match, our first choice was Notts Forest and failing them, Sunderland.

So it could have been worse!

CELTIC AND THE GLASGOW OBSERVER

Now would be as good a time as any to explore the history of the *Glasgow Observer*, styled "The Catholic Organ for Scotland," and its connection to Celtic. The newspaper was acquired in 1887 by Charles Diamond, from Maghera in County Derry, an outspoken and often controversial character, just two years after the first issue on 18th April 1885. The newspaper was an instant hit with the Catholic population of Scotland and a letter in its third issue on 2nd May 1885 from the Belfast Morning News best summed up its popularity;

"We have received a copy of the first number of the Glasgow Observer - an organ started to specially represent the Irish National and Catholic interests of Scotland. There are nearly half a million Catholic Irish in Scotland and the starting of an organ to specially represent them shows their growing influence, power and organisation.

The Glasgow Observer will support the Irish popular party. It will support Home Rule for Scotland. It will advocate a thorough reform of the land system and it will uphold the rights of the working men. It appears to devote special attention to Catholic educational subjects. The paper is an 8 page sheet very creditably brought out and from the first number we augur for it a successful career. Our contemporary states that nothing can be further from its intentions than to run counter to the many journals which are daily and weekly flowing into Scotland; but it points out quite truly that these are quite unable to devote that amount of space and attention to purely local subjects which it would be its special function to do.

We think there is abundant room for such an organ, if properly conducted and we heartily wish it success, all the more so as we understand its editorial management is in the capable hands of a gentleman who was long connected with this journal".

The Glasgow Observer was to go on to form a very close relationship with Celtic with future columnist "Man In The Know," only unmasked as Irishman Charles Quin on his death on the 27th May, 1933, aged 66, from an attack of cerebral hemorrhage in his home town of Pomeroy. Tom Maley, who was thought to be Charles Quin's original contact at Celtic, along with Celtic Board member John Shaughnessy and also Arthur Murphy were part of a large contingent from Glasgow who attended his funeral.

Charles Quin qualified as a teacher and taught at St John's school in Glasgow after studying at Hammersmith College in London, however he changed profession in 1893 when he joined the staff at the Glasgow Observer as a journalist and rose to the position of News Editor. He will be best remembered for his reporting of Celtic Football Club, as Charles Diamond reflects on the great work of his true friend and colleague in the *Glasgow Observer*;

"Readers of our sports pages must have formed a strong affection for the "Man In The Know", who week after week described sympathetically and often with brilliance the doings of the Celtic Football Club. The "Man In The Know" was really CQ, who identified himself with the Celtic from its earliest days when it began as a philanthropic sports organisation to raise funds for various Catholic charities, an ideal from which in later years it has fallen away.

But even when it became a purely commercialised undertaking out for dividends, the Man In The Know had a keen eye for the merits of the Club and of individual players.

He always gave praise where possible and turned a more or less blind eye to faults and defects whether in individuals in control or in individual players. He had indeed a great share in making the name and fame of the Celtic, and in far off lands his articles sounding the virtues of his favourite club were eagerly sought for week by week.

The appreciation of the followers of the club was manifested in many ways, and no want of it in any other quarter could diminish the affection which the "Man In The Know" felt for the famous football combination. He had the soul of a poet, the mind of a philosopher, and better than all, the heart of a child and a sense of humour unfailing and without acidity".

Man In The Know's first article was on 3rd March 1897, at a pivotal time for the club when we became a Limited Company ran by a Board of Directors, but his most memorable match reports came from two Celtic v Rangers matches, the first describing the Celtic support during our 2-0 victory at Ibrox on 1st January 1921, with both our goals coming from Joe Cassidy;

THE BRAKE CLUBS' PROCESSION

By far the most interesting feature of Saturday's great annual carnival at Ibrox was the procession of Celtic brake clubs, flag wagging, trumpet blowing and joyously celebrating on the homeward journey. The inspiring spectacle of the packed terracing - a mountain of massed humanity - and the thrilling incidents in the game itself have only a secondary place in my memory as compared with the amazing pageant which traversed Paisley Road as the shades of eve were falling fast.

All the world now knows that the segregation of the rival crowd worked like magic. The blue and green brakeists never saw each other. They approached and quitted the field by different routes and they occupied opposite ends of the ground. Also they were supposed to leave all symbolic paraphernalia outside the field and so the bugles, ricketties and whistles were silent for the day. The instrumentalists were idle and the great game was played to a vocal accompaniment only.

I saw one man with a revolver and another with a hatchet. What they meant to do with these weapons I cannot guess. Possibly they came over from Belfast. Anyhow there was never a ripple to disturb the oily placidity of the day's proceedings. Players and spectators alike were on their best behaviour. Some of the brakeists eluded the official edict by taking their flags off the poles and stowing them in their pockets. They were there all right and were duly produced when the goals were scored. At the finish I saw one individual drape himself in a huge green and white flag, as with a shawl, while his jubilant comrades sang "Wrap the Green Flag Round me Boys". If this practice is persisted in I foresee that the day is at hand when spectators will be searched before being allowed to pass the turnstiles".

!!!

A JOYOUS PAGEANT

There has been considerable outcry lately regarding the behaviour of certain brake clubs, especially when visiting away fields.

"These complaints do not apply to the Celtic brake-clubs, whose members, reasonable sentient human beings, are models of decorum and possess official testimonials to their blameless behaviour. They are out merely to enjoy themselves in their own way without infringing the law or interfering with any body. They are fond of singing, and to this no-one can reasonably object. On Saturday, the boys sang to their heart's content. They gave us so many rousing choruses. "Hail Glorious St. Patrick", "God Save Ireland", "Slievenamon" "The Soldier's Song" and a ditty of their own to the tune of "There Is A Happy Land," and introducing the names of favourite Celtic players.

These and the inevitable "Keep the Green Flag Flying," whiled away the time of waiting and brightened the afternoon at intervals. When Cassidy's goal made victory sure, it was fine to hear the massed thousands at the western end of the Ibrox oval chanting thunderously "On Erin's Green Valleys".

But, as I have remarked, the greatest scene of all was the homeward procession of the scores of beflagged brakes loaded with enthusiasts, delirious with the heavy vintage of victory. The most amazing and amusing ingenuity had been displayed in suitably inscribing the score on the sides of the various charabancs.

No two brakes showed quite the same wording. The humorists got in much fine work and absolutely vetoed the simple legend - "Celtic 2 Rangers 0". Cassidy figured large with the chalked inscriptions. We had "Cassidy 2 Undefeated Rangers 0," and "Cassidy 2 Henderson 0", a personal thrust at the much boomed Rangers centre. Then we had the semi political allusions - "Rebels 2 Black and Tans 0" and "Sinn Fein 2 League of Nations 0", the latter a sly allusion to the cosmopolitan character of the blue team.

Every brake apparently had a travelling opera company aboard and the beloved green and white was shown everywhere - on tall hats, tin hats, knitted caps and mufflers, mascots, sweaters etc. There was at least one horse drawn brake, the four beautiful horses gaily caparisoned in the club colours. Of course the flags, bugles, ricketties etc, forbidden in the park, got full show on the homeward journey. It was a delight to see the boys so thoroughly enjoying themselves. It was their turn and they made full use of it. Good luck to them and to the team which gave them ample cause for rejoicing".

"There is a Happy Land", was a hymn sung in praise of the Sacred Heart, adapted by the Celtic support in the 1920s with the lyrics changed where required, to pay homage to the favourite players' of the day.

There is a happy land, far, far away,
Where saints in glory stand, bright, bright as day;
Oh, how they sweetly sing, worthy is our Saviour King,
Loud let His praises ring, praise, praise for aye.

Come to that happy land, come, come away;
Why will you doubting stand, why still delay?
Oh, we shall happy be, when from sin and sorrow free,
Lord, we shall live with Thee, blest, blest for aye.

Bright, in that happy land, beams every eye;
Kept by a Father's hand, love cannot die;
Oh, then to glory run; be a crown and kingdom won;
And, bright, above the sun, we reign for aye.

What say we bring this song back in memory of the 1920s brake clubs, with lyrics adapted to today's stars? The tune was used as the soundtrack to the opening scene in the 2005 movie "The Proposition", which received positive reviews and starred Guy Pearce, Ray Winstone, Emily Watson and John Hurt, and was set in the Australian outback, ironically in the 1880s.

In the second match report from our 1-0 defeat at Celtic Park on 25th October 1924;

HALLMARKED HOOLIGANS

"Those of the spectators at Celtic Park on Saturday, who, previously had never heard the Orange war songs "Kick the Pope," and "Boyne Water," are now thoroughly versed in these refined and reasonable expositions of Williamite culture. Rangers have probably one of the biggest club followings in Britain and the number doubtless contains many respectable, fair minded and well conducted people. But there are others.

On the terracing at the Dalmarnock end on Saturday, there was congregated a gang, thousands strong, including the dregs and scourings of filthy slumdom, unwashed yahoos, jailbirds, nighthawks, won't works, burro-barnacles and pavement pirates, all, or nearly all, in the scarecrow stage of verminous trampdom. This ragged army of insanitary pests was lavishly provided with orange and blue remnants and these were flaunted in challenge as the football tide flowed this way or that. Practically without cessation for ninety minutes or more, the vagabond scum kept up a strident howl of the "Boyne Water" chorus. Nothing so designedly provoking, so maliciously insulting, or so bestially ignorant has ever been witnessed, even in the wildest exhibitions of Glasgow Orange bigotry.

The yelping whippets in the adjoining field seemed in comparison to be sweet voiced, reposeful philosophers. Blatantly filthy language of the lowest criminal type assailed the shocked ears of decent onlookers. There was no getting away from it, chanted, as it was, by thousands of voices in bedlamite yells. All this plainly and painfully audible in the press box, yet not one word of protest or condemnation has appeared in the Glasgow newspapers, all of whom had their men at the game.

The stentorian use of filthy language is a crime against the law of the land. Policemen lined the track and listened to the hooligan uproar ; yet nothing was done to stop it. The scandal was renewed with increased violence in London Road after the match. Is it possible that the blue mob can do just anything and get away with it? Prompt official steps were taken to suppress and prosecute the green brake clubs who dared to sing "The Dear Little Shamrock" in Paisley Road. Yet thousands of foul mouthed and blasphemous Orange ruffians are free to run amok over the east end of Glasgow. How do you account for it?"

In the previous encounter in the Glasgow Cup final, just three weeks earlier between the two teams, again at Celtic Park and in front of 80,000, Man In The Know was on the ball;

"Inside an impressive and memorable spectacle was on view. The Celtic crowd massed at the pavillion bend, the central point being occupied by a band of youths wearing green and white headgear and proudly displaying bannerettes of green, white and gold. They sang their Irish choruses lustily. In answer to this challenge, the Rangers crowd at the Dalmarnock end waved kerchiefs of orange and blue and chanted their football ditties thunderously. Just before the teams appeared, an enthralling drama was enacted at the Rangers end. Right in the middle of the blue bannerettes, the Free State tricolour suddenly appeared. It seemed sheer madness for anyone thus to invite certain destruction. But, as it was explained to me in the press box, it was either a captured flag or a bought one and had been brought there for a purpose.

What that purpose was, we quickly understood. A tall fellow climbed on one of the crush barriers and waved aloft the flag of green, white and gold. Then, when every eye was riveted upon him, he slowly and vengefully tore the emblem into shreds, rolled the fragments into a ball, scornfully spat on it and then flung it to the winds. All this, to a deafening obligado of shrieks, howls, curses and threats that turned the place into an ear splitting pandemonium".

Sadly, for Man In The Know he was ploughing a lonely field and the more things changed, the more they stayed the same as Rangers abhorrent sectarianism was going to get far worse before it ever got better.

THE CELTS FIGHT BACK

The Celts had to pick ourselves up from the Dumbarton debacle promptly and we had the chance just twenty four hours later at Third Lanark with the Celtic support desperate to bury the memory of this disaster. James Kelly and Peter Dowds were still injured so two half backs were drafted in from Broxburn Shamrock, O'Byrne and McCann. The first half was even with both Broxburn players taking their chance to shine and we also had another significant change to the team from the day before, with Joe Cullen from Benburb replacing Tom Duff at very short notice.

With the New Year hangovers finally wearing off, the Celts were lively but fell behind after half an hour. Showing a determination that was lacking the day before, we rolled up our sleeves and got straight back into the game with Johnny Campbell scoring the equaliser before half time.

The Celtic support turned up in big numbers at Cathkin to back our team and they were rewarded with a spirited second half performance that brought two more goals, both for the bhoys as Sandy McMahon scored the second in the 55th minute and Neil McCallum added a third, ten minutes later, to finish the scoring at Third Lanark 1 Celtic 3. It was critical for us to bounce back from such a disastrous result as the hawks in the press were already circling above Celtic Park with premature news of our season's demise. Football throws up some very strange results to this day but there was none stranger than Dumbarton's 7-1 defeat to Hearts at Tynecastle on the same day, just a day after they had beaten us 8-0, bizarrely a turn around of 14 goals in 24 hours for the Sons of the Rock.

Two days later, Rangers arrived at Celtic Park, bizarrely on a horse drawn brake with a German band playing and the team singing along, an unusual spectacle indeed. They were compared unkindly to a Sequah show, a travelling showman who arrived in town on a painted wagon, complete with a brass band and incubents dressed up as cowboys and indians playing for the crowd. Some say he was an entrepreneur, others say he was a quack. Maybe the comparison to Rangers oompah band wasn't so ridiculous. What the Great Sequah did claim was that he could cure rheumatism and the main part of the show involved inviting sufferers onto the stage where he would use his god given powers, known as Sequah's Oils, to cure their ills.

By sheer coincidence copious amounts of Sequah's Oils would be readily available for sale to the captive audience. (Please note other rheumatism oil products are also available). In a footnote to the story, its a pity he didn't ride into town before the New Year's match with Dumbarton to cure Tom Duff's ailment.

If the Rangers Oompah Band was the earliest recorded mind games, it didn't work. The Celtic Committee kept Joe Cullen in goal and also kept faith in the Broxburn Shamrock half back pairing of O'Byrne and McCann, who once again distinguished themselves. Johnny Madden opened the scoring in the 20th minute but we were then reduced to ten men after Alec Brady was forced to come off with a head knock. Instead of defending our lead until half time, the bhoys went out for a second and it came just before the interval with a goal from Tom Dunbar in his first match for Rangers against his former club Celtic. Unfortunately for Tom, he was wearing the blue of Rangers and he put the ball through his own net to give the bhoys a 2-0 lead at half time.

Can you imagine the uproar if that happened now?

To add to Rangers woes, Mitchell limped off injured from the bone hard pitch at the stroke of half time and at the start of the second half, Alec Brady made his return, with his head swathed in bandages. There was to be no more scoring and Joe Cullen, keeping his place in goals, did everything that was asked of him, his coolness and courage shining through.

We were back on form, focussed and at the start of another undefeated run of 13 matches, where we would win 8 in a row and score 28 goals in the next 5 matches and only concede 5, as we blew away the ghost of the first match of the year. During the months of January, February and March we only played three League matches, one per month due to the freezing weather, indeed during the months of February and March we only played a total of five matches which would have repurcussions with a fixture pile up at the end of the season.

After our 4-0 victory at Cambuslang on the 30th January, the League race was now at the halfway stage for us with eleven games gone and we were handily placed behind Dumbarton and Hearts who had played more games. Our record was very good and we had ten wins and one defeat, but Dumbarton were the team to beat, sitting at the top of the table eight points ahead of us, with no less than five games more played. The 4-0 victory at Cambuslang may too have been the match that convinced the Celtic Committee to sign Joe Cullen for the rest of the season for although the scoreline was flattering, it didn't tell the story of the first half. Cambuslang, despite their lowly League position in second bottom place, had a go at the Celts from the kick off and deserved to go in one or two goals up at the interval, but instead it was Sandy McMahon and Johnny Campbell who notched two goals on the stroke of half time to put the bhoys two up.

The home team had given their all in the first half only to be defied by Cullen but they were spent in the second half as the bhoys ran them ragged. Alec Brady added a third in the 75th minute and the bhoys notched another goal near the end to finish the scoring at 4-0.

Our next League match brought Third Lanark to Celtic Park on the 27th February. The first half was a very open affair with both sides enjoying their share of chances, but it was Sandy McMahon who put the bhoys ahead in the 30th minute after a cross by Neil McCallum. The Thirds came straight back and were rewarded with an equaliser following a "wild scrimmage," but before the half time whistle was blown, Johnny Campbell had restored our lead with a splendid goal. The bhoys upped their game in the second half and although it was still an open contest, with the Thirds throwing caution to the wind, it was the superior play of the Celts that brought three more goals from Johnny Coleman with a low shot into the corner of the net, Sandy McMahon with a header and finally Johnny Campbell to finish the game at Celtic 5 Third Lanark 1.

Having played 12 matches, we were in third spot, one point behind Hearts with three games in hand and six points behind leaders Dumbarton, with four games in hand.

As an aside, an insight into the make up of pantomine goers in Glasgow in 1892 was given in the *Evening Times*, (it was a quiet news day), when it was claimed that during the performance of Bo-Peep, cards were held up from the stage in the colours of Celtic, Rangers and Queens Park. When the cards in the colours of Rangers or Queens Park were held up, it was said that the applause almost brought the house down. When the cards went up in Celtic colours there was a great booing and hissing, which it reported, *"must be very irritating to the Irishmen present"*.

The working class Celtic support may not have rushed out to watch a pantomine in plush surroundings of an evening, but they certainly knew how to fill their ground better than Rangers or Queens Park.

RANGERS PLAY CUP TIE AT CELTIC PARK

Dumbarton Rangers played Annbank in the semi final of the Scottish Second XI Cup at Celtic Park on Saturday 9th January. Dumbarton Rangers had already beaten Celtic and Rangers reserve teams enroute to the semi final and they would be forgiven for thinking their name was on the cup. In the event, the cup tie was not for the purists on a bone hard pitch covered in snow. Dumbarton Rangers raced into a two goal lead but the Ayrshire team came back in the last five minutes to score twice and force a replay.

Celtic were given a day off as we had six players representing the Glasgow team against Sheffield in the Inter City match at Hampden in which Glasgow won 4-2. The Celtic contingent were Jerry Reynolds, Dan Doyle, Willie Maley, James Kelly, Johnny Madden and Sandy McMahon.

THE GLASGOW CATHOLIC CHARITY BALL

Wednesday, 27th January 1892 was a big date in the social circles of Glasgow Catholics as the annual function was held in St Andrew's Hall. Not surprisingly, the Celtic Committee were in attendance in large numbers with their better halves as the dancing lasted from 8pm to 3am. Timothy J Walls was a well known organiser of huge social functions in the city and he was elected as Secretary of the organising committee as well as fellow Celt, William McKillop, who was Treasurer.

Other committee men included Joseph Shaughnessy, John McCreadie, James Quillan, Stephen J Henry, John H McLaughlin, John McKillop, Tom Colgan, John McQuade and John O'Hara as well as players James Kelly and Paddy Gallagher.

CELTIC v RANGERS - SCOTTISH CUP SEMI FINAL 1892

The 6th February 1892 was the date for the last Scottish Cup tie ever played at the original Celtic Park and it would be a repeat of our opening game in May 28th, 1888 between Celtic and Rangers. Celtic would have settled for a repeat of the score line that day, 5-2, and incredibly with five minutes of the match remaining, that is exactly how the scores stood.

The Celts scored three goals in ten first half minutes and stormed into a resounding 4-0 lead at half time. The opener came from Johnny Cunningham in the 15th minute with a beauty, before Sandy McMahon, Alec Brady and Neil McCallum put the game beyond doubt in the first half. The visitors tried to get back into the game but Alec Brady meandered through the Rangers defence and added a fifth soon after the break to underline the difference in class between the teams. Rangers didn't give up just yet and they got a goal back as the rain lashed down making underfoot conditions far from ideal for a game of football.

The pitch had been rolled and sawdust spread before kick off but Rangers got through the mud to add a second and then a third with five minutes remaining as the Celts took our foot off the gas and almost paid for it. Eight goals in a Celtic v Rangers match remains the record in a competitive match to this day, though it has been equalled on a number of occasions since, with the highlights being the 5-3 win at Celtic Park in the League just three years later in September

1894, the unforgettable 7-1 win in the League Cup Final in October 1957 and the 6-2 win as Martin O'Neill announced a new era at Celtic Park in August 2000. There were also 4-4 draws in February 1957 in the Scottish Cup at Celtic Park and in a League match at Ibrox in March 1986.

The 1892 match however remains the only time seven goals have been scored in the one end at a Celtic/Rangers match.

As an example of the brevity of some match reports back in the day concerning the importance of a Celtic v Rangers Scottish Cup semi final, the following is given from the *Dundee Courier*;

"The Glasgow Irishmen had the advantage of playing on their own ground and in the first half they almost ran round the Rangers, the score at the end of the first 45 standing; Celtic 4, Rangers nil. However in the second period the light blues spurred up and for the remainder of the match had the game. After Celtic scored the fifth, through good luck, Rangers put on 3. Final standings Celtic 5, Rangers 3".

There you are, what else do you want to know?

Our old friend, Viator, from the *Glasgow Evening News* had something nice to say about Celtic in the pre match build up and it deserves repeating;

"The Celtic look upon the match as a foregone conclusion, (this was denied by the Celtic Committee), for they have defeated the Rangers this season already, and they do not see what is to hinder them doing so again.

I bespeak a large crowd for the Celts have a following who stand by the green and white stripes through thick and thin."

AN UPDATE ON NEW CELTIC PARK

From the *Scottish Referee*;

"Gratifying progress is being made with the Celtic's new field. It is still in an unreclaimed condition, but soon there will be order where chaos now reigns. It will be one of the most complete fields of the kind in Britain, although it will be rather expensive to keep up. But the Celts are quite alive to that and other responsibilities. They are ambitious, and it is this very ambition that gives one the impression that the enterprise, no matter how large, will be carried out with success.

A gang of about thirty men has been regularly employed at the Celtic's new field until stopped a couple of days ago by the frost. The field is gradually being put into ship shape and when completed will be one of the handsomest enclosures in the city. A new pavillion will be erected, but the old stands will be removed from Celtic Park and re-erected on the new field".

The final sentence revealed the good housekeeping of the Celtic Committee in taking both stands at the original ground with us to New Celtic Park. Despite the heavy expenditure on New Celtic Park, it was noted that the committee still remained true to our pledge at the birth of the club to donate £5 every week to the running of the Poor Childrens Dinner Tables in the east end of Glasgow.

THE PROPOSED TOUR OF AMERICA RUMBLES ON

In their lead editorial on the 13th February, the Glasgow Observer turned their attention to the discussion on Celtic's proposed tour of America in 1893, warning of the last time a team of Irish athletes did so;

THE CELTIC FOOTBALL CLUB

"The Celts, it is said, contemplate a visit to the United States in 1893. Those responsible for the management of the club know their own business no doubt, but we take the liberty of telling them a little story about the last team of Irish athletes who went to America amid a great flourish of trumpets. The tour was a dead failure and at last a crisis came. A big hotel bill was unpaid and the members of the team could go no further until this was satisfied".

A SHORT HISTORY OF CELTIC BY THE GLASGOW OBSERVER

In the same issue, on the 13th February 1892, the *Glasgow Observer* published a large advert with the wording;

CELTIC FOOTBALL CLUB
(Finalists in the Scottish Cup Ties)

GRAND PRESENTATION PLATE

With next issue, Saturday 20th February, the day on which the Final Tie is to be played, we shall present gratis with every copy of this paper, a magnificent lithographed portrait group, comprising players and officials of this renowned Irish Athletic combination, whose prowess on the football field has placed them in the first rank of athletes. The whole eleven players, as well as the officials are Catholic Irishmen and the picture will form a souvenir which every Irishman may possess with pleasure and pride. The plate will be printed on superfine paper, suitable for framing and will be given away, gratis, to every purchaser next week. Order at once from your newsagent.

Paper and picture..... One penny.

The following week, along with the free lithographed plate of the team and officials, came the following short history of the club;

"The club was formed in the summer of 1888, the meeting at which it was decided to start the Club being held in St Mary's Hall, Glasgow. It was attended by representatives of St Mary's, St Michael's and Sacred Heart parishes. There were also several Catholic gentlemen outside these parishes, well known in athletic circles, amongst them being the brothers Maley, who from the start were enthusiastic in their desire to have a first class football club in the west. In this desire they were heartily supported by Messrs John Glass and John O'Hara and to these gentlemen much of the credit of the establishment of the club is due.

The Hibernians of Edinburgh, a club which in its day played a brilliant part in the national pastime, once being the winners of the Scottish Cup, where at that time in a backward state and the players seeing a splendid prospect opened up to them by the establishment of a club in the west, threw in their lot with the new organisation. The best of these having been duly installed in the team, the additions secured from Renton, Third Lanark and other clubs soon brought the public to witness the abilities displayed by the combination.

The first season in which they played in the cup ties they made several records. They beat the four Dunbartonshire clubs in their first season. They ran into the semi final of the Glasgow Cup competition and got into the final of the Scottish Cup, being knocked out of the competition by two goals to one, the Third Lanark being the winners of the trophy. The following year found them finalists in the Glasgow Cup ties and last season they were third on the League list and winners of the Glasgow Cup. The present season has however been the most brilliant in their eventful history. In the League competition they have so far lost the fewest number of points of any team in the competition. They have won the Glasgow Cup for the second time in succession and are finalists for the national trophy.

During the present season they have won every match played with the exception of two, one of which was with the Heart of Midlothian in a League fixture in Edinburgh and then against Dumbarton at Parkhead on New Year's Day. At present there is not a team in the country with so good a record and this fact speaks volumes for the pluck and science which these hardy lads have put into the game.

Every member of the present team is an Irish Catholic, Irish either by birth or descent. Joseph Cullen, the goalkeeper who is the latest addition to the Celtic ranks, comes from the Benburb, an Irish junior team and he last year represented Scotland in the International with Ireland and would likely have again got capped this year had he remained in the junior ranks. Jeremiah Reynolds, right back, belongs to Maryhill, where he played in his early days, afterwards migrating to Carfin Shamrock from which club he blossomed into a "Celt". Daniel Doyle, the left back, hailed from Airdrie and played first as a senior in the Broxburn, from which he joined the Edinburgh Hibernians, and afterwards played several seasons in England, his last club being the Everton of Liverpool.

William Maley, the right half back, and one of the founders of the club, played for a long time in the Third Lanark, also in Cathcart. He has this season represented Scotland against Canada and gave a splendid account of himself on the occasion. James Kelly, the captain of the team, and its centre half back, is the best man in his position in Scotland. He originally played for Renton, his native village and is one of the "Champions of the world". He played for Scotland against England in 1888, 1889 and 1890 and is sure to get his cap this year. Peter Dowds, left half, comes from Johnstone, and played in the Harp there until 3 years ago when he joined the Celtic reserve. His superior abilities, however, soon won him a place in the first eleven, where he is at present recognised as one of the best left halves in the country.

Cornelius McCallum, outside right forward whose parents belonged to Tyrone was born in Renton and like his mate Kelly, was one of the world's champions. He joined the Celts the same season as did Kelly and has, with the exception of a short stay in England, constantly played in the Celtic team. He has had an Irish international cap, (for Scotland), and is presently value for an English one. Alexander Brady, inside right, is also a Renton youth, who has spent some time in England. He returned to Glasgow along with his club mate Doyle at the end of last season and being reinstated under the Amnesty, threw in his lot with the Parkhead team. His younger brother is a present a shining light in the Renton.

John Madden, centre forward, is at present the finest centre Scotland possesses. He is a native of Dumbarton and played in that team up until two seasons ago when he joined the white and green stripes at Parkhead. Alexander McMahon is an old Hibernian player, whose abilities were never recognised when in Edinburgh, but who, since he joined the Celtic club is pronounced the finest forward at present in the county. He presently plays inside left and is certain of his cap against England in April next. He has already played in an international match against Canada this season. John Campbell, one of the Benburb youths, belongs to Springburn. He is a splendid support to McMahon on the left wing and is one of the best shots for goal in the country".

THE SECOND FOUNDING FATHER PASSES AWAY

Michael Cairns became the second founding father to be taken from us at an early age. The writer, (lawyer), passed away on Thursday, 18th February 1892 at his home at Apsley Place, Glasgow at the young age of 35.

His invaluable work as a lawyer helped guide the club through many shark infested stormy waters and he was a great friend of Doctor John Conway, the man who no doubt encouraged his involvement with the club from our inception. Indeed it was Doctor John Conway who attended to the ailing young man throughout his illness. Tragically Doctor Conway passed away just two years after his friend in 1894, aged only 35 and both men are buried together in the Conway family plot, in St Peter's cemetery, Dalbeth, just a mile along London Road from their beloved Celtic Park, as Michael Cairns' parents and relatives had predeceased him.

The *Scottish Referee* on 22nd February 1892;

"General surprise and regret has been occasioned by the death of this worthy gentleman, which took place at his residence, Apsley Place, Glasgow on Thursday last. Mr Cairns took a very prominent part in the management of the Celtic club and besides was an ardent lover of football.

He served his apprenticeship to the legal profession in the office of Messrs Murdoch and Stewart, Glasgow. On leaving their office he became assistant to Mr A R Ferguson, writer, Neilston, agent for the Clydesdale Bank. He was also agent for the Neilston branch of the West Renfrewshire Liberal Association. Three years ago he began business on his own account in Glasgow and his wide circle of friends enabled him to form a growing and prosperous business. His advice was always sound and therefore respected and he had every prospect before him of enjoying a successful professional career.

Death unfortunately has suddenly ended this and deprived many of a true friend and general favourite. Genial and kindly of disposition, Mr Cairns will be missed in the business and social spheres in which he moved. He was but 34 years of age, a fact that lends poignancy to the great grief experienced by his relatives and friends".

THE BIG FREEZE OF 1892 STRIKES AGAIN

With the date set for the Scottish Cup final on 12th March, the Celts were as keen to get as many games in as possible during the month of February and so on 13th February, the Celts fixed up a friendly with Battlefield from Glasgow's south side, but by the end of the match the visitors wished they hadn't bothered, with five goals in each half to no response giving the Celts a resounding 10-0 victory. For the record the goals were scored by Johnny Madden, (hat trick, one a penalty), Alec Brady, (also a hat trick), Johnny Campbell with two goals and Sandy McMahon with one goal before the match reporter gave up and didn't mention who scored the last goal.

Incidentally, our 9th goal, scored by Johnny Madden, was our third ever penalty and our first ever successful one, Neil McCallum and Dan Doyle having missed the previous two. In three games during February, the Celts put 20 goals past Rangers, Battlefield and Third Lanark and this put us in a very confident mood for the biggest game of the season on 12th March against Queens Park in the final of the Scottish Cup at Ibrox.

Whilst Battlefield had obliged with the record scoring friendly match, the Celts also wanted their home match against Cambuslang to be played on 20th February as both teams had no fixture. The only problem was that Cambuslang had their annual soiree on the Friday night. They too had been keen to play a bounce match with Battlefield but they were ordered the day before the match that they must play Celtic in a League match, as we still had a few matches outstanding. Long before the days of the internet and mobile phones it was left to the Celtic Committee to spread the word as best they could and every spare space in the area was plastered with a hoarding advertising the game.

Just as luck would have it, Jack Frost took over on the morning of the game and the work had to start again, with every advertising board plastered with the word POSTPONED.

How Glasgow Wanderers wished their visit to Celtic Park to oblige us in a friendly match a week before the cup final on 5th March had been postponed too, for with the Celts fielding half a team of reserves, we still managed to score 13 goals to no reply. Glasgow Wanderers were on a hiding to nothing in agreeing to the match but it gave some of the first team valuable match practice before the biggest match of their lives, and so the Celts were eternally grateful.

THE BATTLE BETWEEN CELTIC AND RANGERS CONTINUES - OFF THE FIELD

Whilst Celtic were building New Celtic Park from scratch, Rangers were busy responding by building a new stand at Ibrox, increasing their terracing, improving their track and widening the lane at the Copland Road end to allow more convenient entrance to the ground. They were rewarded by hosting the Scottish Cup Final on 12th March and were also best placed to be awarded the Scotland versus England match in April. This without a shadow of a doubt began the battle for supremacy between the two clubs. On the pitch the Celts were ahead of their rivals and therefore no real rivalry existed. Rangers simply weren't at the races.

However the choice of finalists in 1892 was very convenient for Rangers, as a Celtic versus Queens Park final could not be played at either Celtic Park or the first Hampden Park at Crosshill where Queens Park played, as it would give either team home advantage. The only other possibility was Third Lanark's ground at Cathkin Park, just north of the current Hampden Park, but they had neither the support nor the finance to commit to the kind of expense Rangers were spending on their ground, thought to be to the tune of £2000.

CELTS PREPARE FOR THE CUP FINAL

Future Celtic teams would prepare for big matches by spending a few days at Seamill on the Ayrshire coast, but two days before one of the biggest matches in our short history, some of the Celtic first team took part in a bizarre practice match at Celtic Park between a little known team called the Brandon and a 22 made up of Celtic players and Mexican cowboys, (yes you read that correctly), with the Brandon winning by 10 goals to 3.

"Red Indian", in the *Scottish Referee* on March 14th quipped;

"The excuse the cowboys make for their big defeat is that they can't play football properly unless they are on horseback. The excuse the Celts make is that they never could play a winning game against black and white jerseys, but if they can't play a better game than they did against our cowboys, I can get a team of eleven squaws to knock everlasting snakes out of them".

No doubt charity was the big winner.

THE SCOTTISH CUP FINAL 1892 - OUR DATE WITH DESTINY

With Queens Park electing not to play in the Scottish League, both clubs hadn't met for two seasons and in fact Celtic had never beaten Queens Park, our best showing was the draw at Celtic Park in the first round of the Scottish Cup in 1889. Intriguingly this was billed as a League versus Non League final.

The week before the match the "Trials" took place at Cathkin Park which comprised of two matches played between two chosen teams made up of 44 players invited from which the best would be selected for the Scotland v England match in the next month. It was on the same day, the 5th March, when Celtic played the bounce match against the team at the bottom of the Federation League, Glasgow Wanderers at Celtic Park, so the players who hadn't been invited to the Trials got some game time too.

The Celts were at full strength for the final, whilst Queens Park were missing their mainstay, Walter Arnott in defence. Only Willie Maley, James Kelly and Neil McCallum remained from the team of 1889 who had last reached the Scottish Cup final. Opinions were divided in the build up to the game, as this was Queens Park's 10th Scottish Cup Final of the 19 contested and they had won every one. The new kids on the block however were intent on blowing away the stuffy old men and we were backed by a whole new generation of fans, who until our emergence had been lost to the game.

The original date for the Scottish Cup final was set for 20th February but because of the big freeze and heavy snow, the game was put back to 12th March, however the cold weather remained a threat, even then. As it was, in the five weeks since the Scottish Cup semi final, we had only played one competitive match due to the inclement weather and that was our 5-1 League win over Third Lanark on 27th February.

The *Glasgow Evening News* on the 12th March gave this summary of Celtic;

THE CELTIC

"Founded in the season 1887/88, the team composed of all the talents rushed at once to the front. Primarily formed to advance the cause of charity in the east end, the club has served nobly the purpose of its promoters. No other organisation has devoted more of its spare cash to the interests of the poor and needy.

Like the famous Ministry, the team did not justify the promise their acknowledged powers as players of the game warranted. It was most creditable to them, however, that they reached the position they fill today. In 1889 when they met the Third Lanark, they were defeated after two matches by 2 goals to 1. That final is not yet forgotten, for it established a record as to numbers and money collected.

It is a great compliment to the Celts that they are likely today to break the record of 1889 at Ibrox. This season the club, with a renovated team, which includes several returned prodigals, have maintained their reputation; they have only experienced two defeats - namely, from Dumbarton and Hearts. In the ties not nearly so much has been asked of them as the Queens, for the Rangers are the only first-class team they have ousted from the competition, and that after a very close finish, the club against the Queens has fared second best in three out of the four previous matches played.

These defeats they say were due to inexperience, and with a better balanced eleven than ever they have had, they expect today to retrieve their lost laurels, and break the Queens record of never having lost a Scottish final tie."

In our first appearance in the Scottish Cup final in 1889, it was the snow that forced a replay and it seemed a repeat could be on the cards on this occasion too. Snow had started to fall on the Tuesday before the game and by the Friday, when the pitch was inspected twice, an inch and a half of snow was lying on the Ibrox grass. Underneath the snow it was felt the pitch was playable, a thaw had set in and a further inspection was set for 9am on the morning of the game when the snow could be cleared if required.

Required it was too as two inches of snow now covered the pitch seven hours before the advertised kick off time. The Govan Cleansing Department was contacted and they saved the day, bringing fifty men and a covering of hayseed and sand to ensure the pitch was cleared by 12 noon when the gates opened. The popularity of the fixture was indeed the biggest danger to the game going ahead as Ibrox quickly filled up when the gates were opened four hours before the 4pm kick off. Building work went on right up until the morning of the game and by 2.30pm the ground was full. By 3pm it was filled beyond bursting point and the order was finally given to close the gates, with thousands more locked outside and the rooftops of nearby tenements on Ibrox Terrace full to bursting.

If the 1889 Scottish Cup final broke all attendance records with our first appearance, then this was to blow them all away. The admission fee of one shilling to the terracing and an extra shilling to the stand put off no-one, even though it was double the sixpence charged into Celtic Park. Rangers' new stand on the south side of the ground was opened in time for the match, although the roof was not yet erected, nor the ornamental work completed. There's no doubt that many tables went without food in the East End of Glasgow that week but it would be worth it to be there when our bhoys won the cup.

Outside the ground the Celtic brake clubs, with their bugles blowing and their banners waving, announced their arrival as the procession went on for miles. The fitba special train services were organised to carry thousands from St Enoch's in Glasgow city centre to Ibrox station and also from Springburn, calling at Bellgrove and the Gallowgate, departing every few minutes between 2pm and 3pm. Extra buses left from Argyle Street and Jamaica Street and even Clutha, (Latin for Clyde), steamer boats sailed from Stockwell Bridge to Highland Lane in Govan. 100 Celtic fans even sailed over from Ireland for the match!

Inside the ground a large banner was unfurled in front of the Pavillion with the legend painted in bold green;

"Good old Celtic. Hurry Up!"

The "blue riband" of Scottish football was at stake, the handsome trophy manufactured by the Buchanan Street jeweller George Edwards & Sons, with the central panel representing a picture from the first International match which appeared in the Daily Graphic. The Celts' preparation was well organised as usual and the team had lunch at the Bridge Street Hotel before travelling to Ibrox in four seater cars. Nothing had been left to chance and with the official party was a shoemaker, probably arranged by John O'Hara or David Meikleham, who would advise on the best form of footwear with either studs or bars used dependant on the conditions underfoot.

Well over 40,000 were inside the ground as James Kelly led the Celts onto the pitch at ten minutes to four, with Queens Park following five minutes later. The crowd far outweighed the record for a Scottish game and just four years into our existence there was no doubt who enjoyed the biggest support in the land on such an occasion.

There was little space available for the fans to go and as the ground filled from the back of the terracing, so the fans at the front were forced to scale the barricades and encroach on the pitch looking for a place on the opposite terracing. The policemen on duty were drastically outnumbered and it was only when those on the terraces and stands repelled the invaders by pelting them with snowballs from all directions that order was restored. The feeling amongst the Celtic support was at fever pitch on the verge of our greatest ever victory but behind the scenes the decision was being made, with the approval of both teams, that the match could not proceed as a cup tie and would be played as a friendly.

This decision would not be unpopular with the Treasurers of both clubs as it would mean another pay day at the replay. Rangers would benefit too from the takings from the stand and the SFA would get their cut twice too.

In those days it was the norm for a match to be played as a friendly in such conditions as it could lead to unrest if the match was postponed with the crowd already assembled. Similarly the decision would not be relayed to the fans for fear of a backlash. In the "Snow Cup Final" of 1889, between Celtic and Third Lanark the fans took the hint that it wasn't a competitive match when the players took to the field and pelted each other with snowballs. In any event, 150 policemen were on duty at the match to ensure order, including four on horseback.

The decision on this occasion to play the game as a friendly was the correct one as play was often stopped during the first half due to pitch invasions as the fans crowded around the touchlines. The problem was that with both teams still eager to entertain their huge supports, it was the second half when the game slowed down, before the fans were aware that they were watching a friendly and not a cup final.

For almost an hour the match was evenly balanced on the treacherous surface where surprisingly both teams managed to play some good football. Queens Park started the better but the Celts grew into the game as it wore on. James Kelly from the half back position almost scored a beauty when he stormed forward past a couple of defenders before firing home an unstoppable shot which sailed inches over the bar. Queens Park had refused Celtic's proposal to use goal nets and this could have caused a major controversy if the shot was inches lower and disputed.

The Celtic President, John Glass, ran the line on one side, whilst Richard Browne of Queens Park ran the other in the days before neutral linesman. Indeed John Glass was so wrapped up in the game that on one occasion he forgot himself and ran the full length of the pitch to remonstrate with the referee, Mr Sneddon, President of the SFA!

Chances were few and far between, but it was the Celts who took the lead in the 58th minute after a shot from Johnny Madden was saved and Johnny Campbell followed up to score the rebound. Queens Park raced straight up the pitch from kick off and scored what they thought was an equaliser but it was deemed offside as the Celts held on. Both teams had chances to score in an entertaining finish to the game but the Celts won the game, if not the cup. We would have to do it all again on the 9th April, again at Ibrox, with the admission fees controversially doubled to limit the attendance, before common sense prevailed and entrance was set once more at one shilling.

THE CENTRE SOD IS LAID AT NEW CELTIC PARK BY MICHAEL DAVITT

On Saturday, 19th March 1892, Celtic returned to League duty with a home match against Clyde. The fixture with our neighbours was a popular one, but even more so as this was just after St Patrick's Day and the Celtic Committee had invited Michael Davitt along to kick off the match. More importantly he was to attend the pre-match ceremony at New Celtic Park to lay the piece of Donegal turf on the centre spot, using a specially made silver spade gifted to him by the club.

The ceremony was fitting in so many ways. First of all we were marking the centre of the pitch with Irish turf in a symbolic gesture of our Irishness. We were holding the ceremony at the nearest match to St Patrick's Day and we were inviting our Patron and Irish Nationalist Michael Davitt to carry it out.

The symbolism was clear.

One scribe, signing himself off as D. A. Johnson captured the moment thus;

On an alien soil, like yourselves I am here
I'll take root and flourish, of that never fear
And though i'll be crossed sore and oft by your foes
You'll find me as hardy as thistle or rose
If model you need, on your pitch you have it
Let your play honour me, and my friend, Michael Davitt

The scribe was rumoured to be "an East End Headmaster" by Willie Maley in a Celtic Handbook. Could it have been Brother Walfrid himself, Brother Dorotheus, or even Tom Maley who all fitted the bill? Maley would have been the likeliest and was certainly a fan of quoting poetry. After being welcomed to the original Celtic Park shortly after 3pm, with a banner flying from the member's entrance to the Pavillion proclaiming "Cead Mile Failthe To Davitt", (A Hundred Thousand Welcomes), Michael Davitt was driven in a carriage the short distance along Janefield Street to New Celtic Park with Doctor Tanner, (MP for Mid Cork), John Ferguson, (political ally of Davitt and leader of the Irish National League in Scotland), Celtic's Chairman; John Glass, Vice President; William McKillop, Secretary; John H McLaughlin, Treasurer; Tom Maley, Honorary President; Joseph Nelis, Match Secretary; Willie Maley and Doctor Scanlon.

Also in attendance at the ceremony were Hugh Murphy, Joseph Shaughnessy, John McKillop, David Fortune, Stephen J Henry, John McCreadie, James Quillan, Arthur Murphy, J Montague as well as the rest of the Celtic Committee and most of the players and also John McGuire representing Benburb FC and B McGuire and John Graham from Clyde FC amongst others.

From the *Evening Times* on 18th July 1931;

"An address of welcome was presented by two little boys dressed in Robert Emmet costumes and in these days of the movies, it may be of interest to learn that one of the little chaps became the father of Eddie Quillan, the American screen favourite of today. A photograph of the presentation to Davitt was taken and a carefully preserved copy will be presented to the young comedian when he pays his promised visit to Glasgow this summer".

In a fascinating story, 8 year old Joseph Quillan, the son of founding father James Quillan was one of the boys to read out the welcome to Michael Davitt. After the death of James Quillan in 1901, seven months after he filed for bankruptcy after losing a court case for slander against him by his brother in law and being liable for costs, Joseph Quillan emigrated to Pennsylvania, USA. He went on to become an actor and in 1907, his son Eddie Quillan was born and followed in his father's footsteps, making it big in Hollywood and starring in over ten films including Mutiny On The Bounty in 1935 and also appearing in the popular TV show "Little House on the Prairie," in a career that lasted until 1987, three years before his death.

Joseph Nelis, the club's Honorary President introduced Michael Davitt, who then laid the "foundation sod" of fresh Donegal turf that arrived that morning, complete with a splendid bunch of shamrocks growing in the centre, on the pitch at New Celtic Park.

Michael Davitt stated that;

"He was delighted to have the honour of laying the centre sod of the new park which belonged to the Celtic club. He could assure them that the prowess of the Celts was well known and appreciated by their countrymen beyond the sea, who were proud to witness the successful efforts of an Irish team in Scotland. He hoped they would have much prosperity on their new ground and that no Saxon would be able to cross the sod of Irish turf now laid without sustaining defeat".

Joseph Nelis then closed the ceremony by requesting cheers for Michael Davitt, before they took the short trip back to the original Celtic Park to watch the Celtic v Clyde League match.

Michael Davitt kicked the match off to huge cheers from the home crowd and before long Doctor Tanner raced 40 yards onto the pitch to come to the aid of a Clyde player who was injured, beating the Clyde trainer to his own man. Unfortunately that was the sum total of the action as the Celts failed to repeat our 7-2 League win earlier in the season or our 7-1 victory in the Glasgow Cup final. In fact we failed to score at all and the match finished goalless.

Michael Davitt had to leave near the end of the game to attend a large rally in the City Halls in Glasgow but he returned to attend the ceremony at Pinkerton's restaurant in Bridgeton, the players' favourite after match haunt near Celtic Park, and was greeted enthusiastically after supper, as he accepted the Glasgow Cup trophy on behalf of the club. He spoke modestly of Celtic's victory, who were in his words, *"A credit to their country and an honour to Scotland"*. He expressed his delight at the splendid play shown by the players on both sides and he trusted that Celtic would still pursue their successful career, and in further competitions if any trophies were won, it would be won fairly and squarely. He stated he never felt more sick of politics that he did that afternoon when he had to leave the splendid exhibition of football being given by Celtic and Clyde, his first football match in twenty years, to attend a political meeting.

Incidentally, at the St Patrick's Day demonstration/rally held by Michael Davitt in the City Halls, a selection of Irish airs were played on the grand organ by none other than Celtic Secretary John H McLaughlin. Sharing the same platform was a large representation from Celtic, including Founding Fathers, office bearers, committee men and players, some under their other guise as members of the various political and religious groups in the city; John Glass, William McKillop, Willie Maley, Hugh Murphy, Stephen J Henry, John C MacDonald, Dominic McCreadie, John McCreadie, Doctor Scanlon, James Quigley, Joseph Cullen and Michael Dunbar.

Later in the evening, after the supper and presentation of the Glasgow Cup, the committee and the players invited Michael Davitt to a side room before John Glass presented him with a gold badge, similar to the Glasgow Cup badges given to the winners, and asked him to accept;

"As proof of their very great esteem for him as an Irish patriot. There was no man deserved such respect as a man who spent his life in his own country's cause and there are few who would deny that Mr Davitt had been particularly earnest in that direction."

Michael Davitt on accepting, stated that;

"He would wear it and cherish it as a gift from a body of Irishmen who formed in the opinion of their opponents of that afternoon, the premier club of Scotland. He was not surprised at the progress of his countrymen in the football circles of Scotland, for in every form of athletic exercise Irishmen at all time took foremost place. Whether at walking, running, jumping or rowing, Ireland was well represented and why not at football?"

John H McLaughlin and William McKillop then said a few words before the evening's entertainment was brought to a close. Michael Davitt was then taken to William McKillop's house, on Monteith Row near to Glasgow Green, where he was a guest during his stay. The following day, Michael Davitt addressed a meeting of the Home Government branch of the Irish National League at their hall on Watson Street and amongst the members present were many of the Celtic contingent he had met the day before including John Glass, Stephen J Henry, Doctor Scanlon, Arthur Murphy and of course, William McKillop himself.

Incidentally at the Celtic versus Clyde match both sets of supporters showed their charitable side with donations given to the striking Bridgeton Weavers totalling £25, which was £16 more than was raised at every other ground in Scotland put together.

BUILDING WORK CONTINUES ... AT IBROX PARK

Whilst progress was continuing apace at the New Celtic Park, major building works at the first Ibrox resulted in the capacity increasing to 39,730 which broke down as follows; 6000 in the three stands, 8,350 standing room in front of the South Stand, 15,230 standing room at the west end of the ground and 10,150 standing room in the east end of the ground. Terracing for a further 5,090 was in the course of construction which would give a capacity of 44,820.

The commitment to building a ground so large at a time when a crowd of 10,000 was seen as a large turn out, was a direct response to Celtic's ongoing work to build New Celtic Park with a capacity up to 40,000. Of that there can be no doubt, but what it did underline to the Celtic Committee was that the popularity of the game was moving on at a hectic pace and they would have to keep up to survive. Old Celtic Park had served its purpose well but the timing of the landlord's decree that the rent would be increased was the perfect kick start needed to propel us onwards and upwards.

The question could be asked why did Brother Walfrid and the committee not make the second ground our home in 1888 and thus save the expenditure of the relocation?

The answer is simple. At the very beginning, the club was formed with the most humble ambitions possible, simply to feed the poor children on our doorsteps. We had to find the most convenient plot of land available that was low maintenance, which already had the basic requirements of a grass pitch and room for a stand, terracing and entrances. Old Celtic Park was perfect for these aims as there was no guarantee that this project would be a success. The last thing Brother Walfrid wanted was to found a club with charitable aims, only for it to flounder under heavy debts that could have been used to feed the needy.

New Celtic Park required too much work and was too big for our requirements in 1888. Four years later we had grown to fit it.

THE FOUNDATION SOD IS STOLEN

Less than three weeks after the first sod of Donegal turf was laid in the centre circle of the New Celtic Park by Michael Davitt, it was stolen by persons unknown. Whether it was a thieving bigot who was an enemy of the club, of which there were many, or whether it was a souvenir hunter of the Celtic persuasion we will never know, but the incident was soon recorded in prose as follows with the author in little doubt;

The curses o' Cromwell blast the hand that stole the sod that Michael cut
May all his praties turn to sand, the lyin, crawlin, thievin scut
That precious mite of Irish soil, with verdant shamrocks overgrown
Was token of a glorious toil, more fitting far than fretted stone
Again I say may heaven blight that envious pilfering soulless knave
May sunshine ever be like night - may that sod flourish o'er his grave.

By curious coincidence the day the sod was laid at the new ground, our game against Clyde at the old ground was our first and only goalless match ever played at the original Celtic Park. The nearest to a 0-0 match was the first round of the Scottish Cup on 7th September 1889 against Queens Park when no goals were scored, but the match didn't finish due to the amount of fans inside the ground causing the pitch incursions that followed.

The point dropped was our first dropped since the opening match of the season in August and we followed it up by another shock draw at Vale of Leven on 2nd April, with four goals shared. Scotland played England at Ibrox on the same day which meant that we were without three very important players in Dan Doyle, James Kelly and Sandy McMahon. In a disastrous match in front of 21,000, when the new stand was finally covered, Scotland went a goal down after 35 seconds and were four nil down after 20 minutes, before they gained a semblance of respectability with a second half performance that was rewarded with one goal back from John Bell in the 80th minute.

Our trip to bottom of the League side, Vale of Leven, should have meant a guaranteed two points but we made life difficult for ourselves. Neil McCallum scored the opener with a relatively weak shot, but the home team went straight up the pitch and equalised. If this wasn't bad enough, to the surprise of even the home supporters, the Vale scored again before half time. Neil McCallum got his and Celtic's second, finishing off a lovely run from the right, but try as we might the home team held on for a hugely surprising draw.

We now required to win our four matches in hand to be equal with Dumbarton. Having played only three matches in February, including the bounce match against Battlefield, and three in March, including the bounce match against Glasgow Wanderers, due to the big freeze we were now forced to play seven matches in April and six in May in the quest for the three cups and the League title.

Of course, we still managed to squeeze in a lucrative midweek friendly, in the build up to the Scottish Cup Final when Nottingham Forest visited Celtic Park in the Bank Holiday match on Monday, 4th April and we played it safe by including four guest players; the McCall brothers from Renton, Ellis from Mossend Swifts and Taylor from Hearts. Dan Doyle and Alec Brady once again were not allowed to play against English opposition, however the bold Dan took the opportunity to act as linesman and was seen waving his flag furiously on more than one occasion, no doubt kicking every ball from the side line.

It was a lively match and McCall got the only counter of the first half in the 27th minute with a smart goal, which was a fair reflection of the play. Ten minutes into the second half, Sandy McMahon scored a second, following up after the keeper had saved his original marvellous shot. In the 80th minute, Forest got one back, but Sandy McMahon immediately restored our two goal lead and we took advantage of the visitors going down to ten men due to an injury when, in the last minute, we brought an exciting match to a close with a fourth goal to make it Celtic 4, Notts Forest 1.

THE SCOTTISH CUP COMING HOME TO REST IN CELTIC PARK?

PLAY UP, BOULD CELTS

Now once more bhoys, the end draws nigh
For Scotland's cup, the final tie
Once more we raise the battle cry
Play up bould Celts, play up!

Now once again your colours bright
Triumphant, carry through the fight
Do honour to the green and white
And bravely win the cup!

9th April 1892, the date of the cup final replay soon arrived and with it the chance to became one of the greatest days in the short history of the club, a day when we could announce our arrival on the scene, not as a team with potential, but as the best team in the land.

The *Glasgow Evening News* on Saturday, 9th April gave this summary of Celtic;

"The Celtic club was formed in December 1887, and since its formation has contributed largely to charitable institutions, to which end it devotes £5 per week. According to the club's report over £500 was donated in 1888-89, £400 in 1889-90, and £500 in 1891, exclusive of the sums raised by the charity competitions and benefit matches played by the club. The Celts presently hold the handsome Glasgow Cup, having defeated Clyde in the final tie thereof. In playing ability, the Celtic occupies a high position in the football world, attained by genuine, sterling play. Never yet have they had the high honour of possessing the national trophy, and today they mean to fight tooth and nail to accomplish that object. They, too, like their redoubtable rivals, are placed at some disadvantage today through the absence of Madden. Dowds will play centre, and Gallagher will accept Dowd's place".

Johnny Madden was out injured since the first final and had to be replaced. There were a number of options but no one who could directly take the place of Madden. Peter Dowds, the versatile half back, had played up front before and had a decent scoring record and so he was pushed forward in Madden's absence and the warhorse Paddy Gallagher was played in Dowds' position as half back. Queens Park in turn were missing their two defensive stalwarts, Arnott and the unfortunately named Smellie.

The attendance at the replayed Cup Final was less than the original match where estimates were around the 40,000 mark. With money very tight, the attendance at the replay was given as around 25,000. Interestingly, the make up of both sets of supporters was alluded to with the Celtic support on the terracing and the Queens Park supporters in the stands.

"Classes and masses" said someone when the Queens scored, the hat throwing, stick waving etc, being largely indulged in by the stands. When the Celts scored, the "shilling a time" spoke.

Unlike at the original match, the weather held up although the strong winds were to play a major part in the game. With both sets of supporters housed comfortably and 200 policemen on duty, at least there would be no need for the incursions witnessed at the first match. John Glass again acted as linesman on one side, whilst Richard Browne from Queens Park ran the other line with the President of the SFA, Mr George Sneddon in charge as referee.

Queens Park played with the strong wind in the first half and made their advantage count when Waddell opened the scoring in the 20th minute with a long range effort which alluded everyone. With both their defenders out injured it was doubtful if this would be enough to stop the Celts in the second half from firing on all cylinders with the wind at our backs. The Queens,' instead of holding out and defending their lead, decided to try and press on for a second goal that would win the cup but this plan backfired as they were hemmed back time after time.

Four minutes into the second half, a gentle overhead shot from the right by Johnny Campbell gave the Celts the equaliser and two minutes later the same player scored the goal of the match after some wonderful combination play with McMahon as the Celts swarmed around the Queens' goal. The score stood the same until the 70th minute when Sandy McMahon got the third from a great individual run and some Queens' fans headed home. Seven minutes later James Kelly scored the fourth from a free kick which took a deflection on its way in and McMahon got the fifth with a header in the last minute.

Our bhoys had won the cup and the following names are etched on the first chapter of the history of the club as the first players to bring the Scottish Cup back to Celtic Park;

Joseph Cullen, Jerry Reynolds and Dan Doyle, James Kelly, Willie Maley, Paddy Gallagher, Alec Brady, Peter Dowds, Neil McCallum, Sandy McMahon and Johnny Campbell. Johnny Madden played his part in the first game and would have been in the replay if he wasn't injured.

The Celts had never been beaten at Ibrox and this was to continue. The score line, a decisive 5-1 victory and it was to be 80 years before a team would score more than five goals again in a Scottish Cup final, when Celtic beat Hibs 6-1 on 6th May, 1972.

With the second part of the Treble in safe hands, John Glass was quoted after the match as saying it was the happiest moment in his life. It was the culmination of five years of work and devotion from the committee, the players and the Celtic support and bhoy did we celebrate.

The reaction to our victory is recorded in the *Scottish Sport*;

"The news of the victory, when it reached the various Celtic centres in Glasgow, was received with vociferous cheering. Bands were called out and paraded the streets; music was at a discount. "Ta - ra - ra - boom - de - ay" was the score with any amount of drumming in it. Even the youngsters seemed inspired, for there was a rush on tin whistles and oyster tins that boded well for the trades, but ill for the residents".

The *Scottish Referee* on 11th April described the scene;

"There was much jubilation on the part of the Irish population of Edinburgh and Leith when it became known that Celtic had won the Scottish Cup".

"Coatbridge was en fete on Saturday over the victory of the Celtic. In the second half, when it was intimated that the Celts had scored three goals in ten minutes, you might have heard the cheers at Ibrox. Had the Celtic team been immersed in the whisky that was drunk to their health, the Parkhead lot would have been non est"

When the intimation came that 'our team' had won in such a handsome manner almost everybody who could muster a cheer and a grin at once put them in evidence. Even the women lent a hand, and helped in no small measure to make the rejoicings hearty. But it was when 'the boys came marching home again' from the aristocratic Ibrox that the fun began in earnest . . . As the evening wore on, the whole East End put on an air of alleged gaiety and a colour of deep carnation that would have given an unenlightened stranger the severe knock of astonishment.

Bands! You ought to have seen them. They perambulated the whole district until well on in the evening, and with the aid of a liberal use of party music helped to make things hum along merrily. Of course this caused a risk of a ruction with [King] Billy's men. But what of that? Truly the East End was a perfect turmoil until the very early hours of the Sunday, and many of the crowd won't be able to get over the rejoicing racket for days to come."

On accepting the trophy, John Glass said;

"The club had wrought long and hard for it. Four years ago we had played the Third Lanark in the Final and lost, but now the Celts had reached the summit of our fame. I would have great pleasure in being the custodian of the Cup for a year, if not longer".

After the presentation at the Alexandria Hotel, the Scottish Cup was driven away in a four wheeler accompanied by John Glass and Tom Maley and watched by a large cheering crowd. On arrival at St Mary's Hall the scene was described thus;

"What a scene when St Mary's Hall was reached, the cheering and handshaking defies description. From far and near the crowd came to look on that which has long been the goal of their ambition, and I question very much if that Hall ever held the same number of people as it did on Saturday. One enterprising ice cream vendor had a transparent picture of the team set out tastefully in his window, together with the result".

From Willie Maley in the *Daily Mail* in 1915;

"The second game was an eye-opener for the Queens' supporters as our lot walked away with the 'goods' winning by 5 to 1. Both sides showed changes, Dowds playing centre for us vice Madden, injured, and Sellars playing back for Queen's, vice the redoubtable Walter Arnott. Our lot stamped themselves that day as the champions of Scotland without a doubt, and their football was delightful to watch.

What a happy lot we were that night when the Cup was taken up to Saint Mary's Halls by John Glass of happy memory. Poor Glass, he looked as if his chief end in life had been attained, and there was not a happier man in the universe than he that night. In his speech in replying for the club he reminded his bearers of his prophecy when we were beaten by the Third in 1889, and told them he knew then we would do it yet. Cups won nowadays like the Scottish carry with them bonuses of very substantial size; but, I may tell those interested, that the bonus for that cup was a new suit of clothes for each man.

I had then attained one of the greatest honours of a footballer's career in winning my Scottish Cup badge . . . Our three-leaved-shamrock success of that year (Scottish Cup, Glasgow Cup, Charity Cup) had not been touched by any other club since the inception of the competitions, and so we started our record-making career of cup-winning."

From the *Glasgow Observer* by "MPH" on 12th April 1892;

"The glad news far and near proclaim
To Ireland flash it o'er the sea
That Erin's exiled sons have gained
A great and glorious victory;
The football trophy valued most
From Maidenkirk to Orkney's shore
From Scotland's foremost football teams
An Irish team has snatched one more

All honour to the dauntless Celts!
Their fame is ours, I ween;
May victory ever smile upon
The boys who wear the green!

In many a clime in bygone days
Was Irish prowess oft displayed;
In every field of peaceful thought
Has Irish genius conquests made;
Nor has the brave old race decayed
Of late they proved on Ibrox Park
That even on the football field
As elsewhere they can make their mark

Then glory to the dauntless Celts!
Their fame is ours, I ween;
May victory ever smile upon
The boys who wear the green!

When learning's lamp had flickered low
From Sicily to Baltic's wave
In hundreds Erin's sons went forth
To teach the nations, souls to save;
Nor has the race's spirit died
Last Saturday they stood arrayed
On Ibrox Park on serried ranks
To teach how football should be played

All honour, say we to the Celts!
Their fame is ours, i ween;
May victory ever smile upon
The boys who wear the green!"

From the *Scottish Referee* on 15th April, by "JA";

Ho! comrades, come listen and i'll tell you of the game
Fought for the much prized Scottish Cup betwixt two clubs of fame;
The Queens Park and the Celtic met on bonnie Ibrox ground
Two better clubs in Scotland are nowhere to be found

The "bould ould Celts," by Kelly led, first stepped upon the field
The Queens soon came with Robertson, determined not to yield;
With wind and sun against him, young Dowds kicked off the ball
And twenty minutes after, the Celtic had a fall.

One goal to nil 'gainst Parkhead bhoys brought rapture to the Queens
Who in the first half played their best against the bould ould greens;
Twas Waddell with a long, low kick who sent the leather through
A hearty cheer rose from the crowd as twixt the posts if flew.

Undaunted by the Queens success, the Celts came first again
And soon they showed the good old Queens that short would be their reign
Three minutes after starting brave Campbell scored a goal;
Two minutes more he scored again within the right hand pole

Baird tried his best to save them, but never had a chance;
The "bould ould Celts" supporters began to scream and dance
McMahon scored another with twenty minutes gone
Young Maley still another and the game stood four to one

Twas all up with the Queens Park now, they tried their best to score;
A minute ere the whistle blew McMahon scored one more
Five goals to one! Poor, poor Queens Park; the bhoys have proved too strong;
Three cheers for bould ould Celtic, and may all live long.

Controversy was never far away, especially in victory for the club, and *The Bailie*, a weekly publication wasn't slow to start a rumour;

"I understand that the trophy captured on Saturday week by the Celtic Football Club, now adorns the altar at a Roman Catholic chapel in the east end of the city. O! Old knights used to hang up the spoils of war in their churches and chapels. Other times, other trophies."

The story was picked up by the tabloids who ran with it without checking the facts or getting a quote from Celtic. Surely not, says you. The denial from Celtic was swift and the story was firmly put to bed.

21 years later, in Tom Maley's long running articles in the Glasgow Observer, some light was shed on the story in his reminiscences;

"What a happy party we were that night. John Glass, as the players left the field, with outstretched hands and words of greeting, helping their entry to the dressing rooms. To the present Chairman, (then captain), he turned and said after all the effusions were over "Man, Jimmy but i'm proud of ye. This is worth all our trouble".

Aye it was a great night and when at an hour when little boys are supposed to be fast asleep, the Cup was taken to the sleeping room of an Institution not a hundred miles from Parkhead, the effect was electrical. No alarm bell, no automatic wakener ever stirred up slumbers as did that Cup held below the lowered light of an ordinary gas bracket.

What a cheering these boys gave and how earnestly and sincerely they, with boyish enthusiasm, said "Good old Celts! Only those favoured to hear can realise or understand".

The description Tom Maley gives points, not to St Mary's chapel as the destination of the trophy, but to Whitevale Refuge for Catholic children at 21 Whitevale Street, which stood on the site currently occupied by the present St Anne's chapel, near Duke Street and less than a mile from Celtic Park. The institution was founded by Archbishop Eyre of Glasgow, (Celtic's Patron), and was opened on 2nd February, 1887. It was ran by the Sisters of Charity and its aims were to offer a temporary shelter to children whose destitute circumstances endangered their faith or morals, through proselytism.

The *Glasgow Evening News* on Tuesday, 12th April joined in the satire with a cartoon sketch depicting Glasgow born Bennett Burleigh, the Scottish Labour politician standing for the Tradeston seat being asked;

"Would Mister Burleigh, if returned to parliament, include Celtic Park as part of Ireland in the Home Rule Bill?"

"Certainly, by all means," was his retort!

It didn't help his campaign as he finished third behind the Liberal Unionist and the Liberal candidates with around 10% of the vote.

But the final word on our historic first Scottish Cup was left to an Irishman, who summed up the joy of every Celtic fan on seeing a sign after the game saying;

"Keep to the right," the bold Barney exclaimed; *"Kape to the right? I will reel right, left and centre going home this night, or my name is not Barney Mulligan!"*

CELTIC PARK HOSTS JUNIOR SEMI FINAL AND FINAL

Celtic Park hosted the Glasgow Junior Association Cup final between Vale of Clyde and Jordanhill on 9th April, 1892 and on the 30th May it also hosted the Evening News Charity Cup semi final between Vale of Clyde and Dean Park from Govan, which Vale of Clyde won 2-0.

CELTIC OPEN ANOTHER PARKHEAD GROUND

On Monday 31st May 1892, Celtic sent our reserve team to nearby Helenslea Park to open the ground of Parkhead FC, Glasgow's oldest junior club. A very respectable 1500 spectators enjoyed the occasion as the Celts ran out 6-1 winners, with Dan McArthur in goals for Celtic against his old junior team.

THE LEAGUE RACE REACHES A CLIMAX

With the Scottish Cup and the Glasgow Cup safely residing on the sideboards at the homes of John Glass and Joseph Shaughnessy respectively, before the days when we had a trophy cabinet at Celtic Park, the focus now turned back to the League race with Celtic having eight matches to play in the final six weeks of the season. Ironically it was Celtic who had put forward the motion to the SFA General Meeting that no matches should be played during June and July and this should be officially considered close season but with the Charity Cup ties looming as well as our League commitments, the effects of the big freeze in February and March were now in danger of seriously hampering our march to glory with a backlog of fixtures.

We now faced seven League matches in a row in four weeks between 16th April and 14th May. Ground had been lost to Dumbarton with the surprise draws against Clyde and Vale of Leven and there was no room at the top for any more slip ups. Cambuslang came to Celtic Park in the first of those seven League encounters as the cup holders were welcomed onto the pitch with a deafening roar, which was described in the *Scottish Sport* on 19th April thus;

"They certainly couldn't complain of the reception they received when they emerged from the Pavillion, as it was hearty in the extreme".

With the exception of Johnny Cunningham replacing Alec Brady in attack, it was the same Celtic team who had put green and white ribbons on the cup. Celtic Park and its inhabitants were bursting with pride and it showed on the faces of every man, woman and child who had came to applaud the efforts of a club who had risen in just over four short years to the pinnacle of the Scottish game.

In such an atmosphere nothing could go wrong, but once again that fatal flaw of starting slowly, going a goal behind to a weaker team and then having to break them down raised its ugly head. The visitors opened the scoring in the 25th minute, (around the time many of the early match reports used to describe every opening goal), probably meaning it happened sometime around the middle of the first half. Cambuslang certainly weren't overawed by the occasion and they defended stoically against everything we threw at them in the first half.

Dan Doyle, as he often did, led the battle cry in the Pavillion, encouraging his team mates onto greater things and it soon had an effect. Five minutes into the second half, Peter Dowds scored the equaliser after incessant pressure from the bhoys, which we kept up and were rewarded again fifteen minutes later with a "fizzle" of a shot, from Sandy McMahon. The Celts were well on top with Cambuslang hemmed in for almost the entire second half, but there was always the fear in these type of matches that they would break out and score against the run of play, but this was exactly what didn't happen as Neil McCallum gave us some breathing space with 15 minutes remaining to finish the scoring at Celtic 3 Cambuslang 1.

Just two days later, the replayed match at Leith Athletic was next on the fixture card after the original match in Edinburgh had been stopped short due to darkness drawing in after the Celts had turned up late with the score level. How the Celts wished we were level near the end of this game as we chased our tails after Leith took a shock two goal lead in the first half. A future Celt was responsible for the second goal, James Blessington, who had his shot deflected into the net by the unfortunate Jerry Reynolds.

Blessington was to sign for Celtic just four months later and its no doubt this match helped bring the attention of the Celtic Committee to his door as he gave Dan Doyle a torrid time. This time we didn't manage to turn the game around and despite clawing one goal back in the second half, when Sandy McMahon headed home from a James Kelly corner, to loud cheers from the large Celtic contingent, our forward play was, at times, too elaborate when a straight pass was the best option. The bhoys made herculean efforts to save the day as the Leith citadel was besieged, as they say, but the whistle went on another shock result, "amid scenes that defied description in Leith."

A large crowd, numbering 8000 had gathered to see the cup holders, no doubt bolstered by a number of former Hibernian supporters on their home patch but incredibly, the day had started off badly when the Celts again turned up late in Leith and the match was held up for fifteen minutes to await the arrival of our team. Leith and Hearts were the furthest flung teams from Celtic Park but the far east of Scotland wasn't exactly on the other side of the world and there was no excuse for turning up late again with a perfectly good train service, (debatable), in operation between the two major cities. Of the other nine opponents in the League, three were from Dunbartonshire; Vale of Leven, Renton and Dumbarton, two were in Paisley; St Mirren and Abercorn and other four were in or just outside Glasgow; Third Lanark, Clyde, Cambuslang and Rangers.

We were left to rue the day we turned up late in Leith. "Sleepless in Seattle", this wasn't, but "Late In Leith" was to define our League challenge in 1892.

One deflated fan expressed his despair in an ode to the *Scottish Referee*;

ERIN GO HOWL!

Ochone! Whirrasthrue! Are yez really deflated bhoys?
Down on yer marrow bone ivery man!
Repent av the sins that yez all have been guilty av
Throth, tis mesilf that most wish yez bad scran!
Phwat in the name of Owld Nick waz yes afther bhoys?
Cudnt yes play at Owld Reekie's back dure
The game that yez played wid the Queens down at Ibrox
Rowlin the spalpeens all ower the flure?

Is there niver a word av a lie in the story bhoys?
Is it thrue that Leith bate yez by two goals to wan?
Sowl, tiz mesilf that is clane broken hearted, thin
Begorra, to believe it is more nor i can!
Say tis a lie an i'll niver desert yez bhoys!
Say tis a lie an rejoice my sad sowl!
Devil a wan av yez dairs aiven spake av av it
Bad case to yez all, may yes die av the cowl!

To think that twas only a thrifle av days ago
Yez kep wan an all av us shoutin leck mad
Hurrooin an leppin becaze yez had won the Cup
Dhrinkin your health hilths all in jugfuls, bedad!
Sorra the wan av yez now can howld up his head
Och, yez are polthroons right thro, wan an all
Ireland, my counthry, the glory's departed now
Were clane bare wance more, sure, at kickin the ball!

With Dumbarton next up in the two horse race, a win at "Fatal Boghead" was a necessity if we were to draw level on points at the top. As usual the Celts had a massive support with us in Dumbarton, with 500 travelling on the fitba specials and the Dunbartonshire Irish turning out in big numbers to cheer on the Celts. Unfortunately, Johnny Madden was still out injured and remained so until the last few games of the season, Willie Maley too was out with an inflamed throat and the experienced Paddy Gallagher came in along with the inexperienced Johnny Cunningham in their place.

Similarly to the cup final, a strong wind had a major impact on the game with the Celts winning the toss and playing with the wind in the first half. Dumbarton's goal was bombarded for the full 45 minutes but the Dumbarton and Scotland custodian John McLeod played a blinder and kept his goal safe.

We were up against it in the second half, playing against the wind in a must win game but try as we might we couldn't get the goal our play deserved, the nearest to a goal came when Sandy McMahon hit the post with a fine shot. Then with only ten minutes left, Miller scored the only goal of the game for Dumbarton and the Celts returned after the post match meal eight points behind the hosts, although we had two games in hand and still five matches left to play. The better team on the day had lost, but the Celts kept our head held high as President John Glass asked for three cheers for Dumbarton, which were returned in kind to the Celts.

Wins in our final five matches over Abercorn, Renton, Rangers, Leith and Third Lanark were vital if we were to keep the pressure up on Dumbarton and we needed the Sons of the Rock to lose two out of their three matches against Clyde, Rangers and Abercorn.

The 30th April was a big date on the calendar with the Celts at home to Abercorn and Dumbarton away to Clyde. Surprisingly Clyde won at a canter by 4 goals to 1 to open the door back up to the bhoys in green. Meanwhile over at Celtic Park, one goal was all that we had to show in the first half for the visit of Abercorn, with some of our finishing met with howls of frustration by the Celtic support. This was a weak Abercorn team, minus four of their best players but lo and behold, Abercorn equalised with their first attack of the second half. Thankfully before frustrations rose further, Sandy McMahon regained our lead before Johnny Campbell scored a third as the match finished, Celtic 3 Abercorn 1.

With two games left for Dumbarton, provided we won our two games in hand, the deficit was down to two points and all of a sudden, the pressure was on the Sons of the Rock. Their next match was at home to Rangers on Wednesday 4th May, the night before we played Renton just a few miles away in the Dunbartonshire village. Dumbarton beat also rans Rangers 4-1, however the game was declared null and void because the official referee hadn't turned up, (would you believe), and the match was ordered to be replayed. Dumbarton won again, this time by 6-0.

The pressure was back on us for our trip to Renton but the Celts responded well and made light work of the day by returning home four goals to the good with no goals conceded as we played magnificently with some of the best passing from the forwards seen in a long time in the district, in our second of three matches in seven days. Renton's task wasn't made any easier when Joe Lyndsay had to retire near the end of the match with a broken bone in his shoulder after a challenge from Dan Doyle but the bhoys were well worth our convincing victory.

For Alec Brady, it was the second big engagement in his home town within three days, as he married his sweetheart on Tuesday 3rd May. Two days later we travelled to Ibrox to face Rangers with a depleted first team suffering from the hectic schedule of matches and no time to recover from knocks. In total, James Kelly, Peter Dowds, Johnny Madden and not surprisingly Alec Brady were all missing with James "Fish" Kyle, and Paddy Gallagher drafted into the middle of the park while Johnny Cunningham and fellow reserve player "Sparrow" Flannigan, making his debut up front.

The reasons behind the nicknames weren't given, but the thought of Sparrow heading for Ibrox brings memories of an old song in the Jungle, whereby one pondered what one would do if one had the wings of a sparrow and the rear end of a crow, if one flew over Ibrox tomorrow, what one would do to those below.

I digress.

On the same day, 7th May, Dumbarton's last match of the season was away to Abercorn in Paisley. To keep the race going, we needed to win at Ibrox and we needed Dumbarton to lose at Abercorn, which would enable us to draw level at the top, if we won our last two outstanding matches against Leith Athletic and Third Lanark. This would then force a play off between Celtic and Dumbarton for the Title.

There was an added complication too. Hearts sat two points behind Dumbarton on the final day and they were away to Third Lanark. If they won and Dumbarton lost, they too could be in a play off. If Dumbarton lost and BOTH Celtic and Hearts won, there would have been three teams in joint position at the top of the table, which would have given the Scottish League a major headache! If goal difference or goal average had been in play Dumbarton would have been first, Celtic second and Hearts third, but if head to heads had been introduced at the time we would have been first.

Fortunately for the Scottish League none of these results were to transpire. Unfortunately Abercorn were forced to field a very weakened team with sickness in the camp, but it's doubtful that they could have beat Dumbarton with their strongest eleven available anyway. In the event they did themselves proud, holding the Sons of the Rock to a nervy 1-1 draw. As it turned out, with so many enforced changes on our visit to Ibrox, the bhoys struggled to gel and after losing a goal in the opening minutes, it took us an hour to get level when Johnny Campbell equalised. Sandy McMahon was forced to come off for twenty minutes in the second half which also contributed to a somewhat disjointed performance on a disappointing day.

Final score; Rangers 1 Celtic 1.

Therefore, it was a good day for Dumbarton, despite their 1-1 draw in Paisley as third placed Hearts also slipped up, after winning seven of their eight last matches, they lost 3-2 at Third Lanark, which left the Sons of the Rock six points clear of Celtic, although we had two games in hand and three points clear of Hearts. The League race was over and Dumbarton were worthy winners, but the Celts had important business a week later when Leith Athletic came to Celtic Park and we had revenge on our mind.

THE LAST LEAGUE MATCH AT THE ORIGINAL CELTIC PARK

Saturday 14th May 1892 was the date that the original Celtic Park hosted its last ever League match, in the penultimate match of the 1891/92 season against Leith Athletic.

The visitors had put a serious dampener on our League aspirations with a shock 2-1 win just a month earlier, but the Celts were keen to end our League campaign at Celtic Park on a high. A large crowd was in attendance with many discussing the composition of the Celtic team, such was the length of our injury list. As the team ran out the Pavillion it became clear that some big players were indeed missing with Willie Maley, Peter Dowds, Sandy McMahon and Johnny Madden all out. Thankfully we had Paddy Gallagher replacing Maley, Hugh Clifford replaced the departed Dowds and Joseph Foran and "Sparrow" Flannigan came in from the reserves in place of McMahon and Madden. Amongst the strangest reasons given for a player to be unavailable to play was in the case of Willie Maley, who had to remain at work due to the busy time of year at his Outfitters shop on the Gallowgate, which still stand to this day.

Peter Dowds on the other hand had a very good reason and had already played his last game at the original ground as he was lured south to Aston Villa before the season ended, being replaced by Hugh Clifford from Stoke. It was a sign of the times as English agents thronged to Celtic Park keen to take away our best players, who were amongst the finest in the game.

Similar to the very first ever match at Celtic Park, Neil McCallum scored the opener, this time with an overhead kick after 25 minutes and Joseph Foran added a second just before half time. There ended the scoring as the Celts took our foot off the gas in the second half and coasted back to winning ways.

Our final League match was at Cathkin on 24th May and the match was only a few minutes old when Johnny Campbell put us ahead. Hugh Clifford had impressed on his debut and so he kept his place in a strong Celtic team. Neil McCallum added a second after latching onto a pass from Alec Brady before Johnny Campbell scored his second and Celtic's third with fifteen minutes remaining. The final goal of our League season went to Third Lanark with four minutes left on the clock but it made no difference to the outcome. The bhoys leapfrogged Hearts into second place, finishing two points behind Dumbarton. Rangers finished in 5th place, a distant thirteen points behind Dumbarton.

Of 22 matches played in the 12 team League, we won 16, drew 3 and lost 3, scoring 62 and conceding 21. Unusually we were only the third top goalscorers, behind both Dumbarton and Hearts but our goals against column was easily the best in the League. Of 11 home matches, we won 10 at Fortress Celtic Park, with only Clyde avoiding defeat with a 0-0 draw. Every other team who visited Celtic Park on League duty had lost two goals or upwards and only St Mirren managed to get away with a one goal defeat. Our weakness was our away form, especially at grounds where we were expected to win. From 11 matches, we won 6, drew 2 and lost 3. Defeats at Tynecastle and Boghead were half expected but the 2-1 defeat at Leith Athletic, as well as the 2-2 draw at Vale of Leven, were the difference between winning and losing the League.

Clyde were involved in the two highest scoring matches, both at Shawfield, when they lost 10-3 to Hearts and won 10-3 against Vale of Leven. Leith also took 10 off the hapless Vale of Leven, winning 10-0, and Third Lanark beat them 9-2 as the poor Vale team picked up only 5 points, with 5 draws from 11 home matches and no points any away matches, losing a total of 99 goals.

PROFESSIONALISM RAISED AT THE SFA AGM

Celtic's Secretary, John H McLaughlin, the finest orator and debater within the SFA chambers, took the opportunity at the Annual General Meeting to raise once again the question of the introduction of professionalism in the Scottish game, citing candidly that under the current state of affairs the true amateur had less liberty than the thinly veiled professional and indeed not only were clubs paying their players, they were also paying themselves. The introduction of professionalism would halt the departure of home players to the English game and place all parties on an honest footing.

Known for his classic put down remarks and one liners, John H McLaughlin's best of the day were;

"You might as well attempt to stop the flow of Niagara with a kitchen chair as to endeavour to stem the tide of professionalism", and *"Dogs don't like butter because they can't get it!"* referring to those who don't want professionalism as they couldn't afford to play players.

He moved the following motion on behalf of Celtic;

"Players shall be either amateur or professional. Any players receiving remuneration or consideration of any sort, above his actual hotel and travelling expenses, and more than one day's wage in any week for lost time, shall be considered to be a professional. A day's wage shall not exceed 5s, but players must not be paid for more than the actual time lost. The Association might hinder the adoption of professionalism meantime, but it was bound to come, and they might as well put a kitchen chair to stop the flow of Niagara as to try and stop professionalism. He knew of a dozen clubs who were professional."

Tom Maley seconded the motion.

In the event, a vote was cast with 78 in favour of professionalism and 104 in favour of amateurism. It was a defeat but a close one. Professionalism was looming nearer and the kitchen chair in the Niagara was looking close to collapse. The introduction of professionalism was only a matter of time.

HIBERNIAN PARK LEASED OUT

The forgotten site of the doomed Glasgow Hibernian ground, Hibernian Park again crept into the news before the end of the season when it was leased by the Clydeside Amateur Rowing Club. A strange decision for a rowing club to lease a football ground but the location of the ground on the south side of the Clyde at Oatlands was probably the biggest clue. It was thought also the club wanted to make use of the running track to attract a wider athletic audience.

SECOND ELEVEN CUP FINAL AT CELTIC PARK

The popularity of Celtic Park, even in its final throes, was seen with the hosting of the Benburb v Oakvale Junior Cup final on May 11th 1892. Benburb were fellow "wearers of the green," and there was no guessing who the Celtic support would have been backing.

CELTIC ANNUAL GENERAL MEETING 1892

Celtic AGMs of the early 1890s followed the same modus operandi in that once the date was announced, the media speculated on its level of notoriety and they would then be obliged to report that disagreements were dealt with without the predicted fuss. And so it was to the Mechanics Hall in Canning Street, Calton on Tuesday, 17th May when the membership were circulated with an invite to attend. The date was earlier than usual, but a large number of members, around 200 in total, were in attendance.

The omnipresent John Glass was in the Chair and the reports from Secretary John H McLaughlin and Treasurer Tom Maley were adopted unanimously, with one interesting point of note the fact that a Business Committee would replace the Ground, Finance and Match Committees. This was in an effort to cut down on the number of different Committee meetings, which stood at 107 for the previous year, over two per week. It was a major draw on the Committee's time and gave a good insight into the huge workload of the men who made up the early Celtic Committee.

Given the attention to detail that defined the early Committee this was debated in full with Joseph Shaughnessy in favour of the status quo as it gave more members the chance to play an active role in the club. John H McLaughlin's proposal was for a seven man sub committee to be appointed by the General Committee, instead of the three sub committees at present who were elected by the membership. The seven man committee would be made up of the President, Secretary, Treasurer and four elected Committee members.

John H McLaughlin's proposal of one sub committee instead of three was adopted but Joseph McGroary's proposal that the sub committee should be elected at the General Meetings annually instead of by the smaller body of the General Committee was adopted too. The fact that there were always numerous applications for the annual elections for the committee shows the level of hands on support we had from the community who were willing to give up so much of their time for no financial reward whatsoever. They simply wanted to play their part in the building of our club and every one of their names, whether elected onto the committee or not, should be remembered.

Despite the heavy outlay on the new ground at £1398, 11s 3d, expenditure and income for the season reported a profit of £20, 9s with £4468, 11s accrued against £4448, 2s spent.

As an aside, this compared well with the second, third and fourth biggest clubs in Glasgow, ie, Queens Park, Rangers and Third Lanark for season 1891/92 as follows;

Gate receipts;
Celtic; £4093, 12s, 9d.
Queens Park; £3768, 2s, 8d.
Rangers; £3678, 19s, 5d.
Third Lanark; £1348, 7s, 6d.

Team's expenses - Fares, entertainment, insurance, uniforms etc;

Queens Park; £1125, 12s, 2d.
Rangers; £1122, 12s, 10.5d.
Celtic; £752, 16s, 3d.
Third Lanark; £702, 18s, 9d.

Outlay on ground;
Rangers; £1635, 17s, 3.5d.
Celtic; £1398, 11s, 3d.
Third Lanark; £951, 14s, 2d.
Queens Park; £737, 14s, 11d.

Rent, wages & gate expenses ;
Celtic; £562, 13s, 9d.
Rangers; £449, 14s, 1.5d.
Queens Park; £391, 7s, 5d.
Third Lanark; £226, 18s, 3d.

The outlay on grounds is very interesting. It shows all four Glasgow clubs spending huge amounts, with Rangers actually spending more on extending the capacity of the first Ibrox, (where they would remain for only another seven years), than Celtic did on relocating. Albeit this was just the initial outlay on the new Celtic Park and in answer to a question at the AGM, John Glass stated it would take at least another £2000 to put the new ground into the shape they would like it.

Back to the AGM and some detail of our expenditures were given as follows;

Percentage of gate receipts to visiting teams was £949 and this was down from the £1031 paid the previous season. Charitable donations were £217, 10s, which was down from £545 the previous season and was very disappointing. Of that total, £140 was donated to the Poor Childrens Dinner Tables, £50 to the Evicted Tenants Fund in Ireland and £10 towards a memorial to Father Tom Cunningham from Cambuslang.

John H McLaughlin, in our defence regretted that the cost of the new ground had taken a heavy toll on the club's usual charitable donations and he was further saddened to say that during the next year they would have to refuse many claims that they would otherwise have found favour with. He could only hope that in future years they would be able to more than make up for the present circumstances.

The Annual General Meeting gives us is an insight into the source of the name "Paradise", which has been unofficially given to the ground. During John H McLaughlin's Secretarial report, using his customary flowery language, he is reported in the *Scottish Referee* thus;

"When they last met, he took the liberty to liken their new enclosure to a sahara - a wilderness whose agricultural product consisted of half bricks and broken bottles, and ornamented with a huge abyss on the one side that might serve as a crater to Mount Vesuvius. He had hoped to be able to announce that that desert had now become a Garden of Eden, but unfortunately one side was still being utilised as a gigantic free coup".

He could promise them however, that when finished, their new ground would be one of the finest football grounds in Britain.

One member replied;

"Will the players dream of Paradise when flitting on its sward," and the name stuck with the media taking up the phrase "From the graveyard to Paradise."

The graveyard referred to was obviously the one on the other side of Janefield Street, which bounded the original ground. Referring to the running and cycle tracks at the new ground, John H McLaughlin encouraged this to be utilised to its fullest so that the Celtic name should be feared and respected in athletic sports as well as in football. He added;

"They should remember that while only 11 players could play in the football arena, hundreds could struggle in the various other forms of sport for the supremacy of their race".

The record for the season to date was given as 43 matches played, 33 won, 4 lost and 6 drawn with 156 goals scored and 58 conceded which was the best season yet for the club with the team described as the best that has ever carried the Celtic colours. Three more matches were played after the AGM with all three won, by an aggregate of 8 goals to 2 making the record for the season 46 played, 36 won, 4 lost and 6 drawn with 164 goals for and 60 against.

During the election of the office bearers, Archbishop Eyre and Michael Davitt were again chosen as Patrons unopposed, John Glass was re-elected unanimously as President, Joseph Shaughnessy as Honorary President in the place of Joseph Nelis who retired from the position, Tom Maley as Vice President in the place of the retiring William McKillop, John H McLaughlin as Secretary on the proviso that he would be given an assistant, James McKay as Treasurer and James Curtis replaced Willie Maley as Match Secretary after Maley refused the offer.

Nineteen names were nominated for nine vacancies on the Committee and the following were elected; Willie Maley, James Kelly, James Cairns, John McQuade, John O'Hara, Arthur Murphy, Stephen Joseph Henry, James Moore and Tim Walls.

Goalkeeper Joe Cullen was given a special mention after a great season in which he was elevated from junior football at Benburb, to winning his first medal with Celtic since making his debut on the 2nd January at less than a day's notice. He was congratulated too in not being "elevated upwards" after surviving the explosion at Messrs Higginbotham's Mills near Glasgow Green which killed three employees just a few weeks after the Scottish Cup final.

Entertainment in the way of song was given by players Joe Cullen and Sandy McMahon as the votes were taken and the meeting, a harmonious one, was finally closed at 11.30 pm.

The minutes from the *Scottish Sport* on 20th May 1892;

THE CELTS ANNUAL MEETING

"General meetings have become notorious latterly for the length of time they occupy, the smount of vituperation indulged in and the small amount of reform accomplished. Contrary to anticipation, the Celtic

annual general meeting did not gain the notoriety that was freely predicted. The sederunt, (session), was of normal length, vituperative language was at a discount and reform was certainly achieved by reason of the improvements in present existing rules.

The meeting was largely attended. The chair was occupied by the perpetual president, Mr John Glass. The usual congratulatory outbursts over, Secretary John H McLaughlin submitted his report - a lengthy and interesting document. The meeting was unanimous in its adoption of it. Treasurer Tom Maley next introduced his budget. Questions were invited; a few asked; satisfactorily answered and then a unanimous approval followed. The agenda paper was next dealt with. The most important change brought about was the substitution of a Business Committee for the Business, Finance, and Match Committees. The meeting also resolved to institute a challenge cup for schools. Thus far had the meeting preserved its unanimity. Election of office bearers was the next item on the card. Still no change in the gratifying tone. His Grace, Archbishop Eyre and Mr Michael Davitt were chosen as Patrons; Mr Joseph Shaughnessy was elected as Honorary President; John Glass, President; Tom E Maley, Vice President; John H McLaughlin, Secretary; James Mackay, Treasurer and James Curtis, Match Secretary.

The monotony was relieved, however, on the election of committee. Nineteen gentlemen were nominated for nine seats. During the lull - necessary for counting the votes - harmony was indulged in. Messrs Joe Cullen, Sandy McMahon and J Hennigan entertained the membership until the poll was declared as follows:- Messrs Willie Maley, James Kelly, James Cairns, John McQuade, John O'Hara, Arthur Murphy, Stephen J Henry, James Moore and Timothy Walls. Messrs Willie Maley and John H McLaughlin were appointed to act as representatives on the Glasgow Football Association and League, whilst Mr James Curtis was selected for Second Eleven Association. Messrs Thomas Flood and John McFadyen were selected as auditors and a vote of thanks to Chairman concluded the business.

GLEENINGS FROM THE CELTIC MEETING;

A record attendance. Close on 200 members were present.

Unlike former years, election literature was absent.

The team was well represented.

Mr McLaughlin's report contains some very catchy phrases.

He deplored the necessity of presenting his report so soon, thus depriving him of the privilege of proclaiming the club as triple cup holders. What say you, Dumbarton?

The tit bit of the season was undoubtedly the dual defeat of the QP.

The present team is dubbed "The best that has ever carried the Celtic colours". Comparison challenged with any team of the past or present.

Record for the past season - 43 matches played, 33 won, 4 lost, 6 drawn; 156 goals, against 58. What price Pearsons weekly prize with above record?

Failure to secure first League championship attributed to unfortunate accidents.

107 meetings of committee. Just cause for matrimonial squabbles.

"The committee have by their exertions converted a desert whose agricultural was half bricks into a Garden of Eden." This little figure of speech cut rather a comical aspect when someone wanted information as to the whereabouts of an agriculture producing desert.

Another member wished to know the product of the Garden of Eden.

Will the players dream of Paradise when flitting on its sward?

And will Gerry be a real live angel? Such where the general queries.

Every faculty will be afforded for all branches of sport.

The demise of Mr Cairns and Mr Darroch was touchingly referred to.

Treasurer Maley's report did not admit of rhapsodies of speech.

Figures have a peculiar elegance of their own. Income, £4468, 10s;

Expenditure, £4468, 6s; balance £20, 4s.

New ground has cost up to date £1200.

Charities have been benefited to the extent of £230 in cash, whilst indirectly the Reserves have been instrumental in giving at least another £50 by their services.

The proportion of gate drawings paid to visiting teams amounted to nearly £950.

Only one item on the balance sheet was questioned, viz, refreshments.

Satisfactory explanation was given to the queriest.

Joe Cullen was the recipient of many congratulations on his narrow escape from being "elevated" at Higginbottoms explosion.

Eleven o'clock - well - ten minutes to - saw a change in the numerical strength of the meeting, but only for ten minutes, and then refreshed, the membership tackled the election of committee.

Willie Maley and James Kelly were equal at the head of the list. The meeting broke up at 23.30 and was without doubt the most harmonious meeting that has ever yet been held by Celtic FC."

From the *Scottish Referee* on 20th May;

CELTIC FOOTBALL CLUB

ANNUAL GENERAL MEETING

"There is probably no club in the Scottish Football Association whose annual meeting gives rise to so much anticipation and speculation among the members as the Celts, and the meeting held in the Mechanics Hall, Canning Street, Calton, last Tuesday evening, was in point of attendance of members and general enthusiasm equal to any of the annual meetings yet held by the club.

At the hour for starting, 8pm, the hall was filled and prompt to time, President John Glass commenced the proceedings by having the minutes of the half yearly meeting read and adopted. Mr John H McLaughlin, Honorary Secretary, then read the fourth annual report, in the course of which he stated that the Celtic Club had, during the past year, upheld traditions of former seasons, and had even surpassed them. He was sorry that the report could not have been delayed for a couple of weeks, when he anticipated being in the proud position of claiming not only the title of Glasgow and Scottish Cup holders, but of Charity Cup holders as well. (Cheers). Whether they succeeded in securing that triple crown or not, however, they were fully entitled to congratulate themselves on the results of the season so far.

When they took into consideration the amount of hard work that their players had to go through, the number of them who, at one time or another, had been incapacitated through injuries and the quality of the opponents they have had to meet and beat, they might fairly, and without disparagement to those gentlemen who had represented the club on the field in former years, award the present team the palm as being the best that ever carried the colours of the club (Applause). He would go further, and that without boasting, and challenge comparison between the Celts team of 1891-92 and any other team that ever played the game (Loud applause).

During the season, up until the end of April, the First Eleven had played 43 matches, of which 33 were won, 4 lost and 6 drawn. They had scored 166 goals and lost 58 goals. The Reserves had played 30 matches, won 25, lost 2 and drawn 3, scoring 130 goals and losing 50 goals. He, (Mr McLaughlin), thought these very satisfactory records, and in future years, when perhaps, cast down by some unexpected defeat, it would be at least a little balm to their wounded feelings to look back on that little item, which told them that on April 9th 1892, they beat the Queens Park in the final for the Scottish Cup by 5 goals to 1. (Applause). He would fain linger on that tempting "tit bit" in their history and he regretted that he had to pass it over with such brief reference.

There was another competition in which they had been engaged, but which had not terminated - for them - in as satisfactory a manner as they would have liked. He referred to the League competition. Dumbarton club had attained the first place and they, (the Celts), had the prospect of being second on the list. He was exceedingly sorry to say that they had failed - and failed only through a series of unfortunate accidents - to secure the honour of being League champions for the season. But when they remembered that their team had played almost twice as many matches during the season as their victorious opponents, he thought that Dumbarton had not much pull over them after all. (Hear, hear). He thought that considering all the circumstances that the fact of the Celts being the possessors of the two most important cups in Scotland should make them feel very well satisfied with themselves.

Mr McLaughlin then went on to refer to the attendances of the committee at the various meetings. A glance at their record would show that they had, during the year, put in a fair amount of work, having held a total of 107 meetings of committee. Were he inclined to talk about records, he would say that for regularity in attendance they could give most clubs a start and a beating in that matter. It was becoming painfully evident that the devotion of some of their married committee to their club duties would someday bring them into matrimonial squabbles with their outraged spouses.

One of the most important parts of the committee's work during the year had been the laying out of the new ground. When they last met he took the liberty of likening their new enclosure to a sahara - a wilderness whose agricultural produce consisted chiefly of half bricks and broken bottles, and ornamented with a huge abyss on the one side that might serve as a crater for Mount Vesuvius. He had hoped to be able to announce that that desert had now become a Garden of Eden, but unfortunately one side was still being utilised as a gigantic free coup (Laughter). He could promise them, however, that when completed their new park would be really one of the finest *football grounds in Britain, and they would be shortly able to welcome them to a home such as was not possessed by any other club in the country.*

He regretted to say that their new park, having swallowed up a large measure of their income, had prevented them this season giving to charity as much as formerly, and it was the more lamentable to think that during next year they would also have to refuse many claims that they would otherwise have received favourable consideration. They could however only hope that in future years they would be able to more than make up for what they were lacking at present.

It seemed to be forgotten that the club, while a football club, was also an athletic club as well; and while the Celt had always done well at football, he could boast that he had excelled also in any other part of sport he cared to take part in. (Hear, hear). On their new field the club had provided facilities for the various forms of athletic exercises. They wished the Celts of Glasgow to take advantage of these; they desired that the Celtic name should be feared and respected in athletic sports as well as in football. The matter lay in the hands of the members themselves, and if they had any friends who could ride a cycle or perform any athletic exercises better than the average, the committee would heartily welcome them to their new ground, and would guarantee them every encouragement and help. (Applause).

They had to remember that while only eleven players could play in the football arena, hundreds could struggle in the various other forms of sport for the supremacy of their race. Mr McLaughlin having touchingly referred to the death of Mr Michael Cairns, a prominent member of the club, concluded by trusting that at next annual meeting they would be able to enjoy an even more rosy retrospect than he had been able to put before them that evening. (Cheers).

Mr M McGinn moved the adoption of the report. It reflected credit on Mr McLaughlin, and was certainly the most masterly effort that had yet been performed by any of their secretaries. Dr Joseph Scanlan seconded. It was just such a report as they might expect from a man like Mr McLaughlin, whose qualities had been not only discovered by the Celtic Club, but who had commanded recognition from outside bodies as well. (Applause) Mr Joseph Michael Nelis supported the motion which was unanimously adopted. Mr Tom E Maley then read the financial statement which showed that the income during the year had been £4468, 11s and the expenditure £4448, 2s, leaving a balance on hand of £20, 9s. Among the items of expenditure were marriage presents of £10 each to Messrs Alec Brady and Peter Dowds, members of the team. £217, 10s was given towards various charitable and other purposes, including Poor Children's Dinner Table £140, Evicted Tenants Fund, £50; Memorial to the late Father Cunningham, £10; and Memorial wreaths for Messrs Hugh Darroch and Mr Michael Cairns, (Celtic), and James Dunlop (St Mirren FC). On the motion of Mr James Moore, the report was unanimously adopted as being highly satisfactory.

Alteration on rules being the next business, Mr McLaughlin moved that the Honorary President in future have no seat on the general committee by virtue of his office, as the position should be an honorary one in every sense of the term and this was defeated by a large majority, an amendment, moved by Mr Arthur Murphy, that the rule remain as at present, being carried. Mr McLaughlin next moved that instead of electing a sub committee to look after finance, one for ground, and one for match business, that one sub committee only be appointed by the general committee, consisting of the President, Secretary and Treasurer, and four members of committee, who shall give a full report to the general committee at their monthly meeting. He had now experienced committee work and he could not see any reason for the existence of three separate sub committees, when one could manage the affairs much better. They were only in one another's way at present as a number of them were on each of the three and consequently the meetings of each could not be going on at the same time. Mr Tom E Maley seconded. He held it was most desirable that the work of the club should be concentrated into as few hands as possible, as it would then be all the more satisfactorily done. It was nonsensical to have members of one committee waiting on the other committee being done with their meeting before they could get a sufficient number to go on with the other meeting.

Mr Joseph Shaughnessy moved that the rule as at present be adhered to. He did not think it would be advisable to place the management of the club in the hands of seven members of committee. The rule at present kept the members of the general committee in touch with the active business of the club and gave them a greater interest in it. They had got along very well last year and all appeared to work well together. Mr Charles Stewart seconded. Mr McGinn thought that the number of the sub committee should be eleven. The general rule provided for eleven and he thought they should be acted up to. Mr Thomas Flood proposed that the sub committees should be limited to five each and that their work should be reviewed by the General Committee every month. The Chairman, however, ruled that this was a new proposal and could not be accepted as 14 days notice had not been given. A long discussion on this point ensued, Messrs Joseph Francis McGroary, Charles Stewart, Bernard McCreadie, James McCreadie, Mick Dunbar, Paddy Gallagher, John McFadden, Dr Scanlan, Peter Glass, Joseph Shaughnessy, Timothy Walls, Richard Ford, Tom Maley, William McKillop and several other members taking part.

Ultimately Mr McLaughlin's motion was adopted by a large majority. Mr McGroary moved that the four members of this sub committee be elected separately at the general meeting of the members annually. Mr Stewart seconded. Mr Mick Dunbar moved they be elected by the General Committee. Mr McQueen, in seconding, said that this proposal looked like passing a vote of no confidence in the committee after electing them. Mr McGroary said that there were some of the committee not elected by the general meeting and he thought they should not have the power to appoint any sub committee. On a vote being taken it was decided that the general committee elect their sub committee.

On the motion of Mr Arthur Murphy it was decided that in future a member could be admitted to the club on the majority of the committee supporting his admission - open voting in all cases to be the rule. Mr Jerry Reynolds seconded this proposition, Mr John H McLaughlin moved that a challenge cup competition be instituted by the club for schoolchildren, his object being, he said, to make children take an interest in playing the game, and by this means he had no doubt the Celtic club would afterwards benefit, as they would by and by have a larger number of recruits to draw upon who would be capable of doing valuable service to the club. (Applause).

The motion was unanimously and heartily agreed to. In reply to Mr Richard Ford, Mr John Glass said that it would take at least £2000 more to put the new ground into the shape that they would like it. The election of office bearers was next taken up. His Grace, Archbishop Eyre and Mr Michael Davitt were re elected Patrons. Mr Joseph M Nelis retired from the position of Honorary President, and Mr Joseph Shaughnessy was elected to the post, Mr McLaughlin being proposed but declined to stand. Mr John Glass was unanimously and enthusiastically re elected President for another year. On the motion of Mr William McKillop, the retiring Vice President, Mr Tom Maley was chosen for that position. For Secretary, Mr John H McLaughlin was re elected, that gentleman taking the office on the understanding that he would have an assistant. On the motion of Mr Tom Maley, Mr James McKay was chosen Treasurer in room of Mr Maley, who had been elevated to Vice President.

Mr Willie Maley refused the renewed honour of being Match Secretary and Mr James Curtis was appointed in his place. after a keen competition, Messrs Tim Walls, James Kelly, Willie Maley, Arthur Murphy, Stephen John

Henry, John O'Hara, John McQuade, James Moore, and James Cairns were appointed members of committee and Messrs John McFadden and Thomas Flood auditors for the coming year. Mr Tom E Maley, was re elected representative to the Glasgow Association, Mr James Curtis representative to the Scottish 2nd XI Association, Mr John H McLaughlin to the League, and Mr John Glass to the Charity committee. During the counting of the votes a number of capital songs were rendered by Messrs Joe Cullen, Sandy McMahon, J Hennigan and others. The meeting was a most harmonious one throughout and came to a close shortly before twelve o' clock".

THE CHARITY CUP

With the League lost by two points to Dumbarton on the final day, our attention turned to the third cup available to us, the Charity Cup which was to be contested by Celtic, Dumbarton, Rangers and Queens Park. As the name suggests, the clubs gave up their time for free with all funds raised at the gate donated to charity. Clubs were specially invited to contest and not surprisingly Celtic featured every year thanks to our huge support but we were yet to grace the final.

The Celts drew the toughest tie against Dumbarton, with Rangers playing Queens Park in the other match. The clever money in the early years of this competition was on a drawn match as this would increase the funds available to charity and right on cue, Queens Park drew with Rangers and the match was replayed at Ibrox.

Also at Ibrox on Saturday 21st May, the Celts faced Dumbarton but the fixture pile up was taking its toll, with up to eight injuries to contend with. On the day, a huge crowd of around 10,000 turned up swelling the Charity Cup coffers by £310, compared to the £170 drawn at the Rangers v Queens Park match. Dumbarton played with the wind in the first half but it was the Celts who started better, keen to avenge our defeat in the crucial League match. McCallum scored from a long range effort in the 6th minute but the goal was disallowed, then Dumbarton suffered the same fate in the 34th minute when a goal from Taylor was disallowed. To this day no one knows the reason why both goals didn't count.

Four minutes before half time, Dumbarton went ahead and both sides were happy to draw breath as the half time whistle blew in the strong wind with the game turning into a rough house with no tackles shirked. The advantage of the wind was on the Celts side in the second half but it wasn't until the 63rd minute that we drew level when McMahon headed home the equaliser. McLeod in the Dumbarton goal was tested again and again as the Celts piled forward with Johnny Madden playing his first game back after long term injury and against his old team. The pressure paid off from corners from Johnny Campbell, when Sandy McMahon headed home his and Celtic's second before McDonald, the Dumbarton defender, deflected the ball into his own goal for Celtic's third goal in a whirlwind ten minute spell, to finish the scoring at Celtic 3 Dumbarton 1.

In the other tie at Ibrox on Monday 23rd May, Rangers again drew with Queens Park and extra time of 30 minutes was started, however after 10 minutes the game was brought to a halt due to insufficient light. It was decided that a third match would be played on Saturday 28th May at Celtic Park, with the final then played out the following Wednesday.

The problem with this date was that it now extended the season into the 1st of June which couldn't be helped but it also clashed with Celtic's close season tour of Ireland.

In the event, the Celtic Committee were left with no choice but to cancel the Irish tour and concentrate on winning the Treble.

Ironically for Celtic Park, its last few weeks of existence was amongst the busiest it had seen in its short history and the Fleming Cup Final was played there on Monday 23rd May between Caledonia Swifts and Stonefield with the former winning by 6 goals to 1. Not surprisingly with the amount of games, the pitch was a quagmire and indeed Stonefield protested, based on the state of the pitch at the end of the game, but the pitch had been the same for both teams and the protest was thrown out.

Five days later Celtic Park hosted the Charity Cup second replay between Queens Park and Rangers and this time the result was decisive with Rangers winning by seven goals to one, to reach the Charity Cup final for the first time in nine years. Charity was a big winner too with £470 taken at the three matches it took to decide the tie.

In one of those quirks of fate it would be Rangers who would play the last competitive match at Celtic Park against Celtic, just the same way it all started four years earlier. The venue had only been chosen due to Ibrox being unavailable as the Clydesdale Harriers had been given the use of the running track for a Sports meeting on the allocated date. Queens Park too had stated Hampden was not available after the end of April.

Meanwhile, the Celts kept our eye in with a friendly against 5th Kirkcudbrightshire Rifle Volunteers, (or 5th KRV for short, thankfully), at Palmerston, Dumfries and we enjoyed a good limber up with an 8-1 win. John Glass and Joseph Shaughnessy accompanied the team and the pupils of St Joseph's College in Dumfries were also present in large numbers, maintaining the link between that fine Marist establishment and Celtic, fostered by Brother Walfrid. Indeed it is in those Marist grounds in Dumfries where our founding father spent his last days and where he lies at rest.

Jock Stein, right up until the 1970s kept up the Celtic tradition of taking the Scottish Cup to the college where the Marists taught to show it off to the pupils every time we won it. How fitting would it be if we regained that humble Celtic tradition?

ONLY RANGERS CAN STOP OUR FIRST EVER TREBLE

Celtic's chance to cap a remarkable season with our first Treble arrived on Wednesday, 1st June 1892, a Treble that no other club in Scotland had ever achieved. The Charity Cup had been contested since 1877 and Queens Park were the most successful with 7 wins from the first 9 competitions, broken up only by a solitary success by Rangers and one by Vale of Leven. Renton then went on to win the trophy 4 years in a row, before Third Lanark picked up their first win before Renton regained the trophy in 1891 and were the present holders.

Rangers were our opponents in this year's Charity Cup final at Celtic Park and the Celts were at full strength, with Paddy Gallagher instead of Hugh Clifford chosen to replace the departed Peter Dowds. The decision was no doubt based on the conditions, which were not ideal following the heavy rain that fell and formed puddles on the pitch. This would be a game for rolled up sleeves rather than our normal quick passing game.

Both teams slugged it out, giving as good as they got in the first half but neither was able to force an advantage. The second half was different as the game came to life and the Celts went on the front foot, knowing that the Treble was within our grasp. Johnny Campbell only took ten minutes to open the scoring with a neat header from a cross by Sandy McMahon after some good play with Neil McCallum and the bhoys took great confidence from the goal and piled the pressure on the Rangers defence, which included Tom Dunbar. A second goal was scored, but it was ruled offside as we tried to finish the game off, and it wasn't until the 85th minute when Johnny Madden popped up with another header that the Celtic support could relax in the knowledge the Treble was finally won!

So delighted was Ned McGinn, Celtic supporter and club member that he sent a telegram to Pope Leo XIII giving him the good news that the bhoys had won the Treble!

And so the final competitive Celtic match was played at Celtic Park and it ended as it had all begun, with a win over Rangers, but better than that, it announced to the world of football that in less than five years, in the lifetime of Celtic Park, Celtic had risen to the very top of the game and had fulfilled our two main objectives;

"The main object is to supply the east end conferences of the St Vincent de Paul Society, with funds for the maintenance of the "Dinner tables" of our needy children in the missions of St Mary's, Sacred Heart and St Michael's".

And secondly to provide a beacon of light to the impoverished Irish and to give them something to be proud of which was alluded to in the General Meeting in December 1891, from the quotes of Thomas Flood and Stephen J Henry.

Honorary President Joseph Nelis accepted the trophy on behalf of Celtic at the City Chambers from Baillie Paton, as the Lord Provost was unavailable, and with the sideboards of John Glass and Joseph Shaughnessy, already creaking under the weight of the Scottish Cup and the Glasgow Cup, it was left to Mr Nelis's sideboard to take the weight of the Charity Cup.

In accepting the trophy, Joseph Nelis's words rang true;

"It was appropriate that the Charity Cup should have been won by Celtic, for the club was formed for the purpose of helping charitable institutions, in fact it was our very raison d'etre. The Celtic had been very fortunate in charitable, as well as football respects, for they had been able to carry on the noble work of the Free Children's Dinner Tables, (maintained at it's sole expense), in three of the districts of the east end, (Parkhead, Calton and Bridgeton).

Out of the funds of the club there had been expended £1,300 for charitable objects during the last three years. The Celts also held the Glasgow Cup and the Scottish Cup and none of these cups had been won without having been played hard for. Their countrymen both at home and abroad were proud of the performance of the Celts and he hoped the club would do us well during the forthcoming season".

The total raised from the Charity ties was just over £1173, of which the two games Celtic were involved in raised £311 against Dumbarton and £380 against Rangers. The three matches between Queens Park and Rangers raised £168, £74 and £232. As a result £1000 was donated to charity, but the story didn't end there as it was raised by the weekly Catholic Observer, that only £80 had been donated to Catholic charities.

"The allocation of funds from the Charity Football matches gives to the Poor Childrens Dinner Table £15, Society of Saint Vincent De Paul £15, Little Sisters of the Poor £15, Whitevale Refuge £15, Lanark Hospital £20. In all it will be seen that Catholic charities receive £80. The sum is unfairly small.

We number admittedly one fifth of the population, and most people will grant that one fifth of the gates was contributed by Catholic followers of the Celts and Catholic football enthusiasts generally. Of course, the infirmaries receive rather large dividends of the total and there are general in their scope, but as £1000 was received, we cannot pretend to be satisfied with less than a tenth of that sum".

The story was naturally met with mock outrage in the mainstream media for daring to raise questions over creed, but there is no doubt that the article in the Observer fired a shot across the bows of those who dared ignore the impact Celtic had made and served as a reminder that Catholic charities, just like any other, shouldn't be overlooked. Especially now that Celtic had risen to such prominence in such a short time.

OUR RECORD SCORES AT OLD CELTIC PARK

Celtic 5 Rangers 2 on May 28th 1888 in our first ever match.

Celtic 8 Cowlairs 0 on September 22nd 1888 in the Scottish Cup, 2nd round.

Celtic 11 Shettleston 2 on October 6th 1888 in the Glasgow Cup, 2nd round.

Celtic 9 Clyde 2 on December 8th 1888 in the Scottish Cup 3rd round.

Celtic 7 Mitchell St George 1 on December 31st 1888 in a friendly.

Celtic 6 Corinthians 2 on January 3rd 1889 in a friendly.

Celtic 5 Hibernian 4 on March 9th 1889 in a friendly.

Celtic 7 Hibs 1 on November 16th 1889 in a friendly.

Celtic 7 Hearts 0 on January 4th 1890 in a friendly.

Celtic 7 Battlefield 1 on September 20th 1890 in the Glasgow Cup, 1st round.

Celtic 9 Vale of Leven 1 on May 5th 1891 in the League.

Celtic 6 Third Lanark 1 on May 30th 1891 in the League Charity Cup semi final.

Celtic 11 Kelvinside Athletic 1 on September 19th 1891 Glasgow Cup, 1st round.

Celtic 6 Vale of Leven 1 on October 24th 1891 in the League.

Celtic 9 Linthouse 2 on November 21st 1891 in the Glasgow Cup semi final.

Celtic 5 Rangers 3 on February 6th 1892 in the Scottish Cup, semi final.

Celtic 10 Battlefield 0 on February 13th 1892 in a friendly.

Celtic 13 Glasgow Wanderers 0 on March 5th 1892 in a friendly.

RECORD DRAWS

Celtic 4 Abercorn 4 on March 2nd 1889 in a friendly.

Celtic 5 Blackburn Rovers 5 on April 13th 1891 in a friendly.

THE SUN GOES DOWN ON THE ORIGINAL CELTIC PARK

Two more matches were to be played at Celtic Park whilst both stands were taken down and rebuilt as the Janefield Street stand at New Celtic Park. The first was the Glasgow Second Eleven Cup final between Cambuslang and Clyde on Friday 17th June after the first two matches were drawn.

Four days later the *Scottish Sport* reported;

"Old Celtic Park is looking rather bare since the west stand has been removed. Bit by bit the barricade is being removed, gratuitously in many cases".

Clearly not one bit of wood would be wasted from a ground that was only four years old and the resemblance between the steep steps of the Pavillion, the number of rows and the space in front for the extra seating at the Janefield Street stand at New Celtic Park is uncanny. Indeed the early pictures of that stand at New Celtic Park are basically the old Pavillion and west stands at Celtic Park with a corrugated iron roof over them and extra seating placed in front.

And so the very last game of football played by Celtic at Old Celtic Park took place on Saturday 16th July, 1892 between Celtic and Clyde, fittingly in a fundraiser to raise much needed finance for the Evicted Tenants fund in Ireland, a political cause and a just one. The irony of Celtic's eviction was lost on no-one and both teams were warmly received on entering the pitch. The match was played on a pitch surrounded only by terracing and no stands and ended in a 1-1 draw in front of 3000 spectators. Tom Dunbar returned from his one season jaunt at Ibrox and in doing so became the first Celtic player to have been signed from Rangers. Sawyers opened the scoring in the first half for Clyde but the Celts threw everything at the visitors in a fast and furious second half and it was Johnny Madden who scored the equaliser with a splendid low shot which was received by a tremendous burst of cheering. The bhoys continued to press but couldn't beak down the plucky Clyde defence and so Johnny Madden's goal was the last one ever scored at the Old Celtic Park.

In total, Celtic played 98 matches at the old ground, winning 73, drawing 18 and losing only 8. Of the eight matches lost, seven were friendlies. The only competitive match Celtic lost at the original Celtic Park in the League, Scottish Cup, Glasgow Cup, Charity Cup or North Eastern Cup was on the 17th November 1888 when we lost 2-0 at home to Queens Park in the Glasgow Cup. The next defeat at home in a competitive match came in the last home game of the 1892/93 season after we had clinched the League title, when we lost 5-2 to Third Lanark on 18th May, 1893 at New Celtic Park.

The cream of England all queued up to arrange a friendly at Old Celtic Park and our list of suitors in four seasons was long; Mitchell Saint George, Corinthians, Bolton Wanderers three times, Preston North End three times, Sunderland twice, Blackburn Rovers twice, Everton twice, Notts County, Wolverhampton Wanderers and Notts Forest. Of the 17 matches against English opposition, only 1 game was lost, against Everton, 2-0 on 12th October 1889. 12 were won and 4 drawn.

ENGLISH AGENTS ATTEMPT TO LURE CELTIC STARS

Unfortunately the cream of England also queued up with a big bag of gold in an attempt to entice our best players south under professionalism.

Jerry Reynolds tells the story that after training one day he popped into a tobacconists on London Road with Sandy McMahon and Neil McCallum waiting outside, but when he came out the shop both men had disappeared to Nottingham! McMahon and McCallum had pre arranged the meeting and both were "kidnapped" by Nottingham Forest and hidden outside the city for fear of the Celtic Committee tracking them down and returning them home before he had played his all important first game.

Sandy McMahon himself takes up the story in the *Scottish Sport* on 26th August, 1892;

"Last Thursday morning Messrs John Glass and Mick Dunbar left Glasgow and arrived at Sheffield in the afternoon. Johnny Madden, who was there, was advised beforehand of their coming and met them at the station. The deputation put off very little time in that town and left their friends there under the impression that they, (Glass and company), were going on to London in pursuit of me. A wire was sent from Sheffield to London as follows: "Take McMahon off at once to Nottingham; Glass and Dunbar on his track."

They did not go to London - had indeed, no intention of going. They spent that night and the next in Nottingham. Parties had been arranged with to wire to Glasgow the moment they had seen me. The Celtic got to know on Saturday last, while the match was being played at Parkhead, (first match at New Celtic Park, Celtic 4 Renton 3), that I had returned to Nottingham and two of the committee were despatched on Saturday afternoon en route for Nottingham. I had arranged to go to church on the Sunday but the Nottingham Committee, evidently smelling a rat, induced me to go for a drive instead.

On Monday morning last, while walking with Barbour, (late of Renton, now of Nottingham Forest) and Neil McCallum, I met my brother and a member of the Celtic Committee, (David Meikleham). The latter put the question straight to me, "Did I intend to remain in Nottingham?" Ere I could reply, McCallum exclaimed "Yes, he is not going back to Glasgow and neither am I". The member of the committee replied at once, "It will be time enough for you, McCallum, to come back when you are asked."

I said, "I'm for Glasgow anyway and I am very glad to see you." My brother hailed a cab at once and when we had got seated McCallum shouted to the driver, "Now look here, you don't drive these fellows; they are from the Celtic Committee and they are taking away McMahon. If you do drive them it may be the worst for yourself." On hearing this the driver refused to take us and we got out of the vehicle.

We took to our heels and ran a considerable distance followed by McCallum. We hired a "shandrydan", (a rickety two wheel cart), at a neighbouring hostelry and drove off into the country to give McCallum the slip and when about fourteen miles from Nottingham, struck a wayside station. We couldn't get a train to anywhere within an hour and a half and as we suspected that some of the Nottingham men might be on the prowl, we continued our drive, arriving eventually at Manchester from a village, the name of which I don't remember. Here we stayed until Tuesday morning. Before entering Manchester station I sent a friend who was with me to scout and he returned with the intelligence that Radford, Nottingham's Secretary and five members of the club were on the station platform. We left Manchester that forenoon and arrived on the same evening at Glasgow".

Regarding the letter sent to John Glass and signed by Neil McCallum and Sandy McMahon, *"We beg to inform you that we have left the Celtic club and have signed for Nottingham Forest on a legal agreement. We have left to improve our position,"*

McMahon had this to say in his defence;

"About the letter, I wrote it to the dictation of the Nottingham Secretary and signed it on the spur of the moment without the least intention of ever remaining at Nottingham. I enjoyed my little trip very well and the Nottingham people were very kind to me, showed me the sights of their city and by all the means in their power tried to impress me with the superiority of Nottingham as a resort for football players; but I'm home and I've come to stay".

And so we have the incredible story, in the player's own words, describing the efforts of the Celtic Committee to recapture players lured south by agents from English clubs, in the days before professionalism was brought in north of the border and players could be "kidnapped." Worst still, it was done without any need for a transfer fee and the original club's only hope was to recapture their player before he had played his first match for his new club, whether or not a contract had been already signed.

The level of planning and organisation involved in recapturing a player was articulate to the finest detail and required a level of espionage not normally associated with a football committee. In short, the Celtic Committee were advised by a Catholic priest of the location of Johnny Madden and Alec Brady and both men were contacted, with Madden confirming his intentions to return. John Glass and Mick Dunbar set off on a pre arranged meeting on Thursday, 18th August to recapture Madden at the train station and this was achieved with the minimum of fuss.

Glass and Dunbar then made it known that they were travelling to London to seek out McCallum and McMahon, (who were holed up in hiding), knowing that word would reach Nottingham Forest, but this was a ruse and instead both Celtic men headed to Nottingham instead. Both Celtic Committee men stayed in Nottingham on the Thursday and Friday awaiting the players' return via train, but this didn't happen and they had to return to Glasgow on the Saturday morning without McMahon and McCallum, who they would have played that day in our first match of the season at New Celtic Park.

Word got to the Celtic Committee on the Saturday that after their departure from Nottingham, McMahon arrived in the city with his escorts from Nottingham Forest. The Nottingham Forest Committee would have been well aware that the Celtic party would have to leave first thing on the Saturday to return home for our first match of the season. What they didn't know was that Celtic Committee man David Meikleham and also Sandy McMahon's brother were despatched to Nottingham in their place on the Saturday afternoon with the brief to return north with both players.

Whilst the Nottingham Forest escorts were still on their toes on the Sunday, talking McMahon out of attending mass in case the priest or someone else in the parish notified the Celtic Committee, they dropped their guard on the Monday and whilst McMahon was out walking, the Celtic men pounced. Meikleham and McMahon's brother, after confirming that Sandy wanted to return, first of all bundled him into a taxi before being "papped oot," and then ingeniously made good their escape from Nottingham on a rickety old two wheeled cart!

The Nottingham Forest Committee should have known better, as this was their second attempt to capture McMahon. On the first occasion, their dastardly deed was foiled by the player's landlord, who intercepted a telegram from the agent, (Peter Allan, from Dundee who was working on behalf of Nottingham Forest), to the player arranging to meet him near Celtic Park. The telegram was handed over to John Glass who arranged a welcoming party at the pre arranged location to send the agent home alone, tarred and feathered and with a flee in his ear, but to his good fortune he didn't turn up.

Johnny Madden and Alec Brady were also targeted by Sheffield Wednesday, decimating our five man forward line of Madden, Brady, McCallum, McMahon and Campbell. What the English team didn't count on was the Catholic priest in the area tipping the Celtic Committee off about the players hide out and movements and John Glass and Michael Dunbar, (as described above by Sandy McMahon), were despatched south. With Glass using his natural gift of being able to talk the birds down from the trees, Madden agreed to return, although Brady remained.

The agent for Sheffield Wednesday lamented;

"I would be the last to introduce any element of theology, but i may say you had to be to be specially careful if you ever ventured to do any spying on the ground of a club which was run under the auspices of Roman Catholics. They always seemed to have bands of supporters who are especially alert and eager".

BROTHER WALFRID TO TAKE HIS LEAVE

Ominously, a small snippet of information, hidden in a column at the bottom of the page in the *Glasgow Observer*, a week before the Celtic AGM on Tuesday 16th May was to have a dramatic effect on Celtic in particular throughout the 1890s and beyond;

"His Grace, the Archbishop paid a visit to the Sacred Heart Schools, Bridgeton on Tuesday last - Brother Walfrid of the Marist Community in Glasgow visited the headquarters at Dumfries".

It's likely that the significance of this was that Brother Walfrid was being informed, a week before the Celtic AGM, that the Marist Brothers were transferring him to London. It was kept quiet and wasn't in the minutes of the meeting which would be perfectly natural as any announcement would have to come from the Marist Brothers and not from Celtic Football Club.

Indeed it's likely that Celtic's warm up match in Dumfries against 5th KRV, the week before the Charity Cup Final and attended by the pupils of St Joseph's College who were taught by the Marist Brothers, was a final treat arranged to mark Brother Walfrid's farewell.

Fittingly St Mungo's Academy, where Brother Walfrid first taught, held their annual sports day at the original Celtic Park on Friday 3rd and Saturday 4th June, just a few days after the Treble was clinched. The Marist Brothers had arranged a long and varied programme with prizes included in running, hurdling, cycling and even a blindfold race which was ran in a downpour which brought no little hilarity to the proceedings. The next day the weather was much more favourable with the varied programme again providing good competition, especially in the football tournament, as well as considerable amusement in the Sack Race, the Egg Race, the Three Legged Race, the Hop, Step and Jump Race, the Standing Long Jump as well as the Long Kick and the High Kick.

A thoroughly enjoyable couple of days was had by the pupils, as well as the Marist Brothers, who arranged it all and when it came to an end, Brother Walfrid must surely have taken a few moments to himself to look around the old ground, still almost reverberating to the children's laughter as well as the cheering Celtic supporters at many of the huge matches played there since December 1887, four and a half short years since he leased the barren space to build a football ground for a people and a cause.

It was with a very heavy heart, but with everlasting pride that the much loved and respected Brother Walfrid left the original Celtic Park that day.

FIRST HAND ACCOUNTS - BY THOSE WHO WERE THERE

THE CELTIC CLUB

By Granuaile in the *Scottish Football Annual 1892*;

"The success of the Hibs in winning the Cup had been well received in Glasgow and suitably acknowledged in the east end, where the Hibs had performed frequently for the noble cause of charity. The idea of forming a team to play for the specific purpose of charity dawned on a few, was circulated, and as a result a committee of enquiry was instituted. The result of the enquiry was very satisfactory and one fine morning the football world was made aware of the birth of a new club, weak, 'twas true, at its birth, but subsequently it grew and thrived mightily.

About this time there was a superfluity, (the term is used restrictedly), of Hibs, Harps and so forth and the public mind was not disturbed by the announcement of the advent of the new organisation. The committee of the new scheme were in no way embarrassed by this preservation of equanimity on the part of the public. Steadily their work of organisation went on. Ground - in the shape of a free coup - was secured and put into a decent condition, the necessary funds being very easily obtained. A stand next made its appearance.

This systematic and business-like process awakened the lethargy into which the public had fallen over the new Irish club. Rumours began to circulate as to the composition of the team and quite a flutter was created in the inner circles of many clubs. The first players of note who associated themselves with the club were the brothers Maley and Phil Clarke. Johnny Coleman, Mick Dunbar and Paddy Gallagher soon followed and then at no late stage the complete organisation, which gave the public full value for their cash, made their debut.

The opening of Celtic Park was not performed by the Celtic, at least, "official Celtic". The Hibs and Cowlairs performed this necessary ceremony in the germinal stage of the club's history. The opening match, officially, fell to the lot of the Rangers and the keynote of success which was struck on that occasion has been well sustained, (very well sustained - so the Light Blues fancy). The Celtic team on that occasion was a peculiar one - a strange mixture. The Dundee Harp, then a power up north, were tackled soon after; also Mossend Swifts and then the Clyde. In this latter match defeat was sustained.

The season proper now dawned on the Celtic. Their appearance in the various competitions gave rise to much speculation. The Exhibition ties had enabled them to place good teams on the field, somewhat varied, 'tis true, and singularly enough by a somewhat "various" team they were defeated in the final of the competition, viz, Cowlairs, who with a much strengthened team, effected the downfall of the Celts. The competition just referred to was indeed a very troublesome one for the Celts and it is a matter of regret that their players were not well received by a portion of the crowd.

It is on record that the then President, (and still the President), passed a remark concerning the conduct of the spectators when his team complained to him of the treatment they had received ;

"Let them scoff and jeer; the Celts will yet force them to acknowledge merit" - a prophecy which has had its fulfilment.

The earlier stages of the Scottish ties saw them pitted against their whilom, (past), conquers - Cowlairs. Celtic Park was crowded to its utmost to witness the tie. Public curiosity was aroused. Defeat was to be atoned for or again inflicted. Cowlairs had whipped up a strong team. Robert Kelso had arrived from Newcastle to assist them in the struggle. The Celtic team was Willie Dunning, Paddy Gallagher, Mick McKeown, Willie Maley, James Kelly, Jimmy McLaren, Neil McCallum, Johnny Coleman, Willie Groves, Mick Dunbar and Tom Maley. The latter player had been highly successful at athletic meetings and was not expected to play, Connor being the substitute. However at the last moment he turned up to witness the contest; but instead of acting like an onlooker, he played along with Dunbar.

The game was a good one and for fully half an hour the Cowlairs kept the Celts out; but latterly the Celts asserted themselves and won by the tall score of 8 goals to 0. Here was a "wiping out" with a vengeance. This very sensational opening in the competition gave "the youngsters" a hallmark. In the prognostication thus early made, the Celtic were in the forefront. That there was reason for it was shown by their appearance in the final tie. The last barrier prior to reaching that stage was the famous "Sons of the Rock." The game was played on Boghead ground and after as grand a display of football as one would wish to see, the green and white emerged victorious by 4-1.

The memorable "snow" final which followed is an event in the history of the club. Through snow that was inches deep on the ground, against a hurricane of wind and in the teeth of a blinding snow storm, did the 3rd LRV and the Celtic contest the issue. The game had been pre-arranged as a "friendly", neither team caring to risk their chance. The Thirds were returned winners by 3-0. The following Saturday the game was replayed, and after a keen struggle in which the Celts had none the best of luck, the game was adjudged to be the Thirds by 2 goals to 1. This was rather a damper to the hopes of not a few followers. The team had prior to this encountered the famous Corinthian band and administered to them the greatest defeat they as a team had received.

In the Glasgow Cup competition, the Queens Park, rather unexpectedly overthrew the Celtic by 2 goals to nil. The goalkeeping in the game in question was certainly not a feature. The record for the season was a good one. Only some 12 or 13 players were at the disposal of the committee and taking into consideration the number of matches played, 56, of which 42 were won, 3 drawn and 11 lost; scoring 199 goals against 85 - every credit is due to the men who made it. Their play was the theme of admiration, pretty and fascinating - so much so that on a tour in Lancashire, the local papers burst into ecstasies over the skill and science exhibited.

The seond season opened auspiciously. The team were made a little stronger in defence. In the early round, Queens Park were opposed; and after a game which, in the opinion of many, was converted from a win into a draw by an error of judgement, the Celts were beaten on replaying at Hampden and thus ousted from the national ties. Nowise disappointed, the field of action was widened. Sunderland - a team *of talents - Blackburn Rovers and other leading organisations appeared on the Celtic ground and made amends for the disappointment felt by the followers of the team. Of all the English combinations that appeared on Celtic Park, one and only one can boast a win - Everton and at what a price? The reputation they made was not worth enjoying.*

The Glasgow ties afforded some little satisfaction and in this competition, the Queens Park and Celtic met in the final. The disagreeable incidents of that game are scarcely worth recalling. Again fate denied the Celts a cup. An English tour - fairly successful - with a visit to Ireland and then the sequence thereof - dismissal from the Charity cup competition. after a miserable game, closed the season, the record for which was; Played 47 matches, won 27, lost 11, drawn 9; whilst 120 goals were scored against 64. Scarcely so good as the previous year.

Last season, the formation of a League gave the fixtures under that heading a tinge of excitement. That national and city ties, together with League fixtures, so monopolised the dates that the North Eastern Cup, which had been held by the Celts for two seasons, had to be given up. The first League match was a reverse for the Celts, Renton winning by 4 goals to 1. On this occasion, the "Giniral," as an old and tried half back was and is called, appeared as goalkeeper. That reverse, together with a deduction for playing an ineligible player, was the means of keeping the Celts pretty low on the League list for a time.

In the Cup competition, they steadily fought ahead, but where they had previously conquered they fell, Dumbarton beating them by 3 goals to 0. In justice to the team which played it should be said that the state of the ground was such that they could run no risk and protested, together with Dumbarton, against playing a tie. After the match, Dumbarton withdrew their protest and the Association upheld the game as a tie and accordingly, the Celts were again out of the running.

The Glasgow Cup next concentrated their energy. The final was reached, and their opponents were their old friends of the "blizzard final". Fired with the thoughts of the previous final and spurred on with the resolution to win a final, the Celtic played hard and brilliantly and won the day, 4 goals to 0 being the result. The scene at the finish of that match was a great one and the "bhoys" met with a grand reception.

Following this success, an English tour was undertaken and the reputation of Scottish football wonderfully increased thereby. Ardwick, Bolton Wanderers, Blackburn Rovers and Sheffield Wednesday were encountered, with the following results; Ardwick, 7-2 in favour of Celts; Wanderers, a draw, 2 goals each, whilst Celts had two disallowed; Blackburn Rovers, 2 goals to 0 in favour of Celts; and Sheffield Wednesday, also a win by 3 goals to 1. This result had never been achieved by a Scotch team on tour and it did a great deal to restore some of the lost prestige of Scottish football.

The close of the season was rendered interesting by the brilliant play of the Celts, who smote lustily all they came across. The Supplementary League Charities, however, saw them bow to their keen rivals, Dumbarton, by 3 goals to 0. Certainly on this occasion, the Celts were not fit. They had played far and away too many matches, whilst their opponents were fresh. The record for the season was: 49 matches played, 34 won, 8 lost, 7 drawn; whilst 148 goals were scored against 62.

And now to the present - the most successful season in the club's history. It is useless to refer to all the deeds of greatness performed this season. They are fresh in the minds of all. The unique record speaks for itself :-Three cups, second in the League championship and with a record not approached by any club of standing in the three kingdoms. Renton claimed for themselves the title, "Champions of the world". If they deserved the appellation, surely the Celts do. Their form has been consistent, their play always brilliant and effective, and many who previously jeered at them are now most laudatory in their expressions. Their victories have been popular over the length and breadth of the land; the team is known and familiarly talked of. The village tenor sings their prowess; the youthful artist depicts them in brilliant colours, (the great left wing in particular being represented as winding through a maze of multi coloured opponents), whilst the grey haired patriarch rests ill at ease until he hears the final result of some important fixture. That such is the case is deservedly so.

The bond of charity is a wide one and the large and continuous support given to charity by the Celts has endeared them to all. Since the formation of the club, something like £1500 or £1600 has been given to charity in cash alone, whilst the services rendered by the team have been of equivalent value, at least for £500 more. The primal object of its formation was charity. Many a poor little ill-fed and ill-clad waif has had a new lease of life given to it by the funds derived from the source of revenue afforded by the Celts.

The hand of the marauder has, on the whole, dealt moderately with the team since its inception. There is a bond existing between the players which is hard to sever and which is the keynote of success. Of those who listened to the "wiles", only a few are away; the remainder have returned.

This season marks a new and blots an old epoch. The club leaves, or rather is evicted from, their pitch. Determined to keep pace with the times, they have obtained the lease of a hole! And a free coup. This they have, by an immense outlay, converted into a magnificent playing pitch, bordered with two tracks. The ground is adjacent to the present, but it is in every way superior. It is in final stage of completion.

In the earlier life of the club - indeed at the present day - if sensationalism be aimed at, the Celtic is supposed to form a splendid target. The annual meetings of the club were always to be lively scenes, etc; but somehow or another these events were carried out with more respect for the power of the chair than even the parent body exhibited. Long may this state continue the club has still the benefit of its early advisers and the majority of it "good old has beens", and with such at the helm there is no fear for its future success. The players and committee are at one; each studies the other and with such reciprocity has the Celtic gained the pinnacle and with continuance of such will they will remain there.

Good old Celts! Such is the cry that greets them, such is the only expression that many an ardent follower can give to his feeling, wrapped up as they are entirely in the "bhoys". It is ejaculated with heartiness and sincerity. From across the seas has the phrase been cabled, and an echo has been heard from the eastern climes, whilst the sunny south re-echoes it. Men who have never seen the Celts - who are absolutely ignorant of football - join in the cry. Thus is the Celtic known and respected. May they long be so; and *may that admiration for them be as unbounded, that love as sincere and as deeply routed, as it is in GRANUAILE."*

"The new ground is specious and must feel like heaven, when compared to the old. The spirits of the graveyard will no longer have a free view of the Celtic. That stand has been moved from the old to the new".

From *The Celtic Handbook in 1933/34* by Willie Maley;

"The years have stretched out to forty five since the real inception of our club, and another five years will bring us to the Jubilee year of the Club which was early on spoken of as a mushroom growth, fated to rise and flourish for a short time and then fade into its previous nothingness. What an answer has the team and management of our great club given to the weak-kneed ones of the old days and much more important to the bigots of 1888 to 1890 when our very existence was threatened by the "unbiased" sports of these days".

An old song of 1889 used to say;

"Keep up the pressure, Good Old Celts, keep piling on the goals
You know exactly how to put the ball between the poles
So let your foes do what they will and let them sneer and snub
They'll do no harm, not even alarm, the Good Old Celtic Club"

A TRUE CELTIC TALE

"Pride of place must always be given to Celtic's first season, not by reason of its being the first year, but because of the circumstances of its formation and the unique circumstances which it created. It is correct to say that the men who set the machinery in motion were absolute novices so far as football knowledge etc., was concerned, and it's equally correct to say that from the formation of the Association and the inception of the cup competition even to the present day, no club has ever made such a sensational debut and continued in the limelight as did and does the Celtic. "Knowing" novices were those early Celts. They enlisted men who knew and played the game, and, most desirable asset, amongst such men one who could create a team spirit. First sensation of he new team was the defeat of Cowlairs by 8-0.

"No defence in the kingdom could have stopped the Celtic forwards - Neil McCallum, Johnny Coleman, Willie Groves, Mick Dunbar, Tom Maley." So wrote a leading critic of 1888. And a crowded snow clad Hampden saw a first season club contesting for the final tie of the Scottish Cup. Twice was the tie played. Ask any of the surviving Celtic trio to tell their story of the result which was officially given; 2-1 against Celts. Read the summary of results for 1888-89 and know better why the first season deserves pride of place. Played 56; Won 42, Lost 3 and Drawn 11. Scored 199 goals; Lost 85!

One of the most appealing seasons in the club's career is that of 1891-92. Look at the picture it holds up. All three cups won, a good second in the League competition, and the opening of a new ground. An epoch marking year surely. The old trouble - landlord - brought about a change of field, and it was in keeping with it, that a seeming impossible site was converted into a splendid enclosure. A case of leaving the graveyard to enter Paradise. A happy title did that pressman strike. The lessons learnt and the experience gained on the old monument to the loyalty and fidelity of the pioneers of the club - did they not give of their labour to construct it - were not lost.

The splendid pedestrian and cycling tracks which surrounded the playing area on which champions from the world over showed their paces added another title; "The home of sport." It was an auspicious occasion and great day when the late Michael Davitt laid the centre sod, (fresh from Donegal), with a handsome silver spade presented him by the club. The ceremony was witnessed by a goodly crowd.

The souvenir seeker or vandal carried off that Donegal sod, its shamrocks never bloomed, but what befell the one who removed the sod no man knoweth; he had to carry the weight of the poet's wrath and curse. The ceremonial over, the party watched a League match between Celtic and Clyde. Incidentally, Celtic had beaten Clyde most decisively in the Glasgow Cup Final three months previously by 7-1. Of the League match, Davitt said, "That if he had to see many such he would forswear politics for football, so much had it impressed him. He accepted the Glasgow Cup too, from Arthur Geake, (Queens Park), the President of the Glasgow Football Association, for Celtic and from the Celts he received a medal similar to that which the players had received.

Superior to misfortunes and the clubs opposed, once more as finalists in the Scottish Cup, Celtic appear. Unbeaten in Scottish Cup finals and record holders of the cup were their opponents, Queens Park. Morale as well as ability had to be beaten down if the cup was to be won. Handsomely the team did that. The first game saw Celtic win by a single goal. The game was played under almost impossible conditions at Ibrox. The field a veritable quagmire, the crowd encroaching on it so much so that at intervals play had to be suspended. Like Queen's, Celts held that a final tie warranted better and fairer conditions. The replay ended in a more decisive victory for Celts, 5-0, being the score in their favour.

The defensive work of Dan Doyle, Jimmy Kelly and Willie Maley in the final match was a revelation, whilst in the van the famous left wing of Campbell and McMahon played ducks and drakes with the weakened Queen's defence. What a pity talkies and movies were not the vogue in those days some forty years ago. The scene at the presentation ceremony at the Alexandria would have been a big show. For those who remain it is easily visualised, easy of recall. Confessing, as he received the cup, that grand old Celt, John Glass, in a voice choked with emotion, said;

"Gentlemen, this is one of the proudest and happiest moments of my life".

If cheers meant anything, then there were others who so felt, and the many telegrams which came later from all parts of the world carried like sentiment. And later, when the cup arrived at the wee old hall in East Rose Street, another joyous scene was there. The players and officials were as enthusiastically welcomed as the cup. No doubt some of my readers will recall that great night and the happy party gathered, who when the hour of departure had come, set off with the "God bless you," of Brother Walfrid ringing in their ears.

What of the Charity Cup? Would we win it? Not that we couldn't, oh dear, no!

Drawn against Dumbarton, who had discounted our chances in the League by reason of a very lucky win over us at Boghead, our first match was certainly a spicy one. It lived up to that for about fifty minutes and then it was Celts on the high road to the final. For some time our opponents could not emerge, then at last Rangers took the field against us. Not all the enthusiasm of our following had been used up. A clear cut win and well deserved, though easily won, (2-0), brought home the cup to its proper resting place, as Honorary President Joseph Nelis remarked when getting it, and to substantiate his words, four successive years thereafter it was won. Is it a happy augury? Chairman Tom White has been heard to say, "It's time that we were getting the Charity Cup again".

To the "spoke" in our League wheel at Boghead I have referred. I might also add that by reason of playing two cripples at Leith, two points went west, for at the match, and standing by, were two fit and experienced men who could and ought to have been played. Two Toms at that, Dunbar and Maley. That cost us the flag, but later when flag as well as cups were won we had no regrets. Some season was 1891-92, and let me not forget our Sports, the best ever seen in these parts, conducted and carried through by Willie Maley in a way none could surpass. Our team's record read: Played 43; Won 33; Lost 6; Drawn 4; Goals for 156; Against 58!

Not unfairly have I selected 1891-92 as one of our best seasons. For those who lived through those great days it will prove refreshing to have it recounted and the supporter of today must feel some pride that the pages of this club's history hold such great records and, not the least by any means, our players will find in perusing the short summary of their predecessors an incentive to live up to the best traditions of the club, and, in a few words, "Go and do likewise".

From the *1937/38 Celtic Handbook*, Willie Maley, in his final years as Celtic Manager, gets emotional as he realises his life time at Celtic Park is nearing an end;

"It was in September 1887, that the Celtic enthusiasts of that period - composed of football followers of the Edinburgh Hibs, (who won the Scottish Cup that year), resident in the parishes of St Mary's, St Andrews and Sacred Heart - made up their minds that it was time Glasgow had an Irish club. They held some meetings, from which the "weaker hearts" were quickly eliminated, and a start was made in the formation of the Celtic club. It was January 1888, before matters took a distinct shape and with a very enthusiastic committee, the formation of the new ground went ahead, and it was duly opened on 8th May 1888, by Cowlairs v Hibs.

From that date, the good ship Celtic took the high seas of football, and in spite of many storms, both inside and outside, they have weathered all the lot, and today the same old ship still rides the sea, but in a grander and finer form than in its early days.

Now after the formation of practically three grounds, (as the present ground was completely rebuilt in 1929), the club holds a position second to none in the football world, and its teams, over the fifty years of the club's existence, has made football history all over the world where the game is played. The records of its teams down the years are written in scarlet letters on the pages of football, and there is no one who loves the name of Celtic who cannot point with pride to what Irish enthusiasm and energy has done for the sake of Scottish football and for the name of the Celtic club.

The fame of the club is worldwide, and wherever they have travelled, they have left behind them memories of football played as it out to be played. If the "old hands" who formed this great club of ours could but come back to see what their pioneer work has done for their beloved Celtic, how proud they would be.

I remember on an occasion when, at a dinner after a "Final Tie" in which Celtic had lost, an ill mannered lot of listeners could not restrain their glee at the Celtic downfall, and voiced tham in no uncertain voice. John Glass, then our President, in returning thanks for his side in the vote of sympathy then moved, referred to the bunch of biased interupters. He said; "Celtic would weather this defeat like all good sportsmen, and I prophesy that those who come here today to jeer, will by the powers of the Celtic, come in time to cheer". That prophecy has come true long ago, and today our club needs no "claque" of followers to boost their abilities.

The "Celtic game" which came into being in 1888 when we beat Cowlairs by 8 goals to 0 in a Scottish Cup tie, is still with us, and the close passing game, for ever to be associated with Celtic teams, has won us cups and fame wherever we have played. The year just passed has been one of great worry, as i have said, and I think that it will be granted that to me especially this has been true.

When I "took the shilling" for Celtic in September 1887, i was 19 and a half years old, and I played for them at the age of 20, and in the fifty years that have passed since then, I have spent my life literally for the club, which has grown so dear to me. I have seen the great ones of the old days, both officials and players, pass on in the way of all things human, and still my enthusiasm has stood the test of the years, and the sight of the "green and white" jersey is as sweet to me today as when I first wore it in 1888. What stories have been told of these long years, and what pride and happiness have they not brought us all, with very few of the "dark days" in between, (for which I say "Thank God," with all my heart).

It has been said; "There's a sweet little cherub that sits up aloft looking after the life of Poor Jack, (the sailor)." I am one of those who think and know that there has been in all these years a guiding hand over us, and, when things looked darkest, it came forth to sweep away the clouds and bring us the "blue heavens" of success again.

In the same *Celtic Handbook*, by "An Outsider"

MY VIEWS OF THE RISE AND PROGRESS OF THE CELTIC

"My admiration for the Celtic club occasions many of my friends considerable surprise, even amazement, in view of the fact that I have nothing in common with what is understood to be the sympathies of that body. On the other hand, I make no secret of my contempt for the opinions of those who seek to introduce extraneous matters into sport, believing that the latter is a thing apart from religion and everything else, in short, a common ground on which all should meet on level terms.

From conversations I have had with several who recall the birth of Celtic, I am convinced that its reception was not notable for any particular warmth by those who, like my own critics, were inclined to look at it through party coloured glasses. The amusing part of the business is that this very antagonism assisted materially in building up and strengthening the structure which, after half a century of storm and stress, stands as a living memorial of sound, businesslike and dignified management.

It is to the everlasting credit of the Celtic club that the original object of its birth has never been forgotten - this was to provide food for the poorer children in the East End of Glasgow. Indeed, the first constitution, which I have been privileged to inspect, provided that a certain sum be given annually for this purpose, and that has been rigidly adhered to - the amount of money given away every year to charitable objects would surprise those, as it did me when I was told, who have no conception of the philanthropy of the club.

I think there is something admirable about a club which so faithfully fulfils the promises made fifty years ago; the directors do not regard this as anything but a duty - another reason why I am an admirer. Celtic's contribution to football is not confined to the many brilliant exponents of the game who have sported the Green and White - it goes deeper than that".

BROTHER WALFRID'S LEGACY

The *Glasgow Observer*, in only its 12th issue on 4th July 1885, had given us the first mention of Brother Walfrid and his colleague Brother Christopher in highlighting their work, after up to 1000 children from the parish of Sacred Heart celebrated their First Holy Communion at 9.30 mass, followed by a substantial breakfast in the girl's school room. Mr Connell of the organising committee, in his speech thanked, amongst many others, *"the indefatigable Brother Walfrid,"* before the day was brought to a conclusion by the children's vote of thanks to Brother Walfrid for the treat provided that day.

Brother Walfrid's story is the early story of Celtic. To the deep disappointment of Glasgow's East End where he was much loved in Catholic circles, the news was made official in the Glasgow Observer on 6th August that he was being transferred from his post of Brother Superior at St Joseph's Marist headquarters to London's East End amid a number of relocations within the Marist Order. Worst still, the transfers were taking place before we played our first match at New Celtic Park.

"His numerous friends in the city will hear with sorrow of the departure of Brother Walfrid from amongst them. For nearly thirty years he has laboured increasingly for the education of Catholic children. He conducted the schools of the Sacred Heart with singular success. He also assisted in founding in this parish, a branch of the Young Men's Society, by whose members he is held in great respect.

On Wednesday night this Society met under the presidency of their spiritual director, Father Bird, and presented a farewell address to the good brother. The address, which was couched in the most affectionate language, expressed the deep sorrow of the members at parting with such a trusted friend, and wished him every success in his new duties. The Brother, in reply, thanked the members and exhorted them to continue in the course they had hitherto pursued, to frequent the Sacraments, and obey the injunctions of the spiritual director. In a few days, Brother Walfrid will leave for London, where his order have a large establishment. He leaves Glasgow with the hearty good wishes of all who knew him".

The parishioners of Sacred Heart, where he had worked since the opening of the parish in 1873, also arranged to present Brother Walfrid with a testimonial commensurate with his services to the parish, adding that;

"There is not the slightest doubt that the movement will be successful."

Celtic FC also announced in the half year General Meeting in December, that they would do likewise and set up a committee charged with agreeing and working towards a fitting testimonial. The heartfelt sorrow that engulfed the Catholic community in the east end of Glasgow was mirrored by the feelings amongst the Celtic support at the loss of our founding father, our guiding light, but why was this happening now and why a transfer to London which cut off his involvement with Celtic?

The *Glasgow Observer* on 6th August 1892 contains the answers;

"Last week the pupils attending several of our largest Catholic Boys' Schools, under the charge of the Marist Brothers, were both taking leave of old tried friends, who were starting to other fields of labour and making the acquaintance of "new Brothers". We do not remember hearing such sober talk among our young folks about the Brothers and their whereabouts for an age. We ourselves had so closely allied each Brother with the school in which he was teaching, that we could not dream any change possible.

Brother Walfrid and the Sacred Heart school were one and the same thing; so were St Mary's and Brother Dorotheus; St Alphonsus and Brother Ezekiel. These good Brothers, if we remember rightly, have been on an average about twenty years in Glasgow, most of which time was spent by them at the above schools.

Brother Walfrid's arrival in the city dates back some twenty eight years. As already mentioned in a former issue of this paper, he goes as Superior to one of the Marist Brothers most important houses in Britain, that of Regent Square, London. He leaves behind him in Glasgow a host of the warmest friends. Brother Dorotheus takes his place as Superior of the monastery in Charlotte Street, and headmaster of St Alphonsus School, Greenside. Thanks to his untiring energy, St Mary's School, where for the past sixteen years he has unostentatiously, day by day, gathered his ever increasing multitude of boys, can now boast of being the largest Catholic boys' school north of the Tweed. His former duties now devolve upon Brother Thomas, who we learn, went through his apprenticeship in the school, and after spending a year in one of the Marist Brothers' training colleges on the continent, returned as assistant to St Mary's. We wish him God speed in his arduous task.

St Alphonsus School, to which Brother Dorotheus has been appointed by his superiors, was the place where one received the genial welcome of another Brother who has been changed - Brother Ezekiel. If we are not mistaken, he entered upon his duties about 1880 and for the past twelve years was the soul of that important and successful school. He was especially noted for the interest he took in the boys after their leaving school; hence the Vesper choir, composed not of mere children, but of young men whom he had kept together from their boyhood; hence also, the Junior Guild of the Sacred Heart, the members of which, Sunday after Sunday, he so zealously instructed and encouraged to qualify themselves to swell the ranks of the Young Men's Guild.

Brother Ezekiel has been promoted to the position of Superior of St Mungo's Academy, Townhead, and under his care we are not inclined to entertain any doubts concerning that Institution's future prosperity. He taught at the Academy three or four years before taking charge of St Alphonsus. As notified in our last week's issue Brother Andrew has been appointed to replace Brother Walfrid at the Sacred Heart, Bridgeton. Brother Christopher, late Superior at St Mungo's, is removed to St Joseph's College, Dumfries to recruit his health, somewhat shattered by severe work in connection with the science classes at the Academy. He meanwhile will devote any spare energy to the preparation of students for various university examinations. We also learn with pleasure that Brother Martin, whom we knew formally at St Mungo's Academy, is to form part of the staff of that establishment during the coming year".

And so we learn that the reshuffle which transferred Brother Walfrid to London was a major one, involving many of the most experienced Marist Brothers in the city and in this reorganisation, Brother Walfrid's promotion was a huge one, going from the Headmaster of Sacred Heart in Bridgeton and also Brother Superior, based at Charlotte Street, the Marist headquarters in Glasgow, to his new position of Brother Superior at one of the Marist communities' most important houses in the whole of Britain, that of Regent Square, in bustling London.

In summarising, Brother Walfrid was replaced at Sacred Heart by Brother Andrew, who was transferred from London to take up the role and he was replaced as Brother Superior at Charlotte St where the Marist Brothers in the city resided, by his Assistant Superior, and great friend, Brother Dorotheus.

37 year old Henry Currie, (Brother Dorotheus), as well as becoming the Brother Superior was transferred from St Mary's School, where he was headmaster, to St Alphonsus, where he retained the same position. His position at St Mary's was taken up by his Assistant and younger brother, James Currie, (Brother Thomas), just a fortnight short of his 29th birthday. In the St Mary's school log book, Brother Dorotheus, couldn't hide his disappointment when he made the news official on Monday the 8th August, two days after the Catholic Observer broke the news about Brother Walfrid's departure;

"I regret exceedingly to have to notify my departure from this school".

Brother Ezekiel was transferred from St Alphonsus, where he was headmaster, to the position of Brother Superior at St Mungo's Academy, replacing Brother Christopher who was transferred to St Joseph's College, Dumfries to recuperate after ill health brought on by his workload. As part of the shake up, Brother Martin, formerly of St Mungo's Academy, would also return to the Academy in the coming year. Interestingly, the article dates Brother Walfrid's arrival in Glasgow some twenty eight years, back to 1864. From "Life Before Celtic," we have learned that his first teaching post was at St Mungo's in 1869, therefore the years between 1864 and 1869 would have been his novitiate in Beauchamps, northern France.

Fittingly the last word on the subject for now, comes from the Glasgow Observer on 13th August 1892 in the simple, underwhelming fashion that the beloved Brother Walfrid would have appreciated;

"Brother Walfrid, before leaving for London, was the recipient of a presentation from the Celtic Football Club".

Brother Walfrid's departure was to have a pivotal effect on the immediate future of the club over the next half decade in particular when we faced the battle for the club's soul. If Brother Walfrid had remained in Glasgow would we have followed the route we took, culminating in the decision to turn the club into a limited liability company in 1897 or would we have continued to strive forward as a club with charitable donations remaining the club's raison d'etre?

What impact would Brother Walfrid's influence have had on the debate and equally how long could we have continued with mounting debts as a primarily charitable organisation? Without a shadow of a doubt Brother Walfrid would have ensured the transition would have been as smooth as possible and he would have made certain that charity always remained at the heart of Celtic Football Club.

Although he never got to see a match at the current Celtic Park before his departure, Johnny Campbell noted that he was the first person on the platform to welcome the Celtic players in the Scotland team to London in 1893 for the match against England at Richmond. Indeed he bounded onto the train on the platform to waken the Celts up, such was his excitement at seeing them!

Brother Walfrid was to return to Glasgow in 1897 and 1908 on visits and on his first visit he attended a function in his honour at Sacred Heart and he finally got to attend Celtic Park during the Celtic Sports. In May 1911, Celtic made their most extensive European tour to date, playing 9 games in 6 countries, winning 7 and drawing 2. On the return journey, they stopped off in London and visited Brother Walfrid. Tom Maley accompanied the Celts on tour and thankfully he was there to record Brother Walfrid's words;

"Well, well. Time has brought changes. Outside ourselves there are few left of the old brigade. I know none of these present players but they are under the old colours and quartered in the dear old quarters and that suffices. It's good to see you all so well and I feel younger with the meeting. Goodbye, God bless you."

James Kelly, Willie and Tom Maley were the only Celts in the party from the early years but Brother Walfrid made it clear that although time had moved on, as long as the club was playing in the same colours and in the same ground that was good enough for him. The Founder of the club was now in his 71st year but it is evident that the meeting was not only the highlight of the tour for Kelly and the Maley's, it benefited Brother Walfrid too as he mentioned when he signed off in his customary manner with *"God bless you."*

Just four years later, on 17th April, 1915, Willie Maley spoke for every Celtic supporter at the Celtic AGM with the following statement;

"The death of our old friend, Brother Walfrid, robs us of the last of the leading founders of the Celtic club. This grand old man was in our club's early days a model of unceasing effort and energy and much of our club's early success was due to him.

I could tell you a tale of how the dauntless Celt tackled a certain editor, whose anti Celtic writings were his strongest feature, but a few interviews and straight talk soon convinced the scribe that he was dealing with a club that had come to stay and would stand no nonsense and I am pleased to say after years found for us in the erring, one a real Celtic friend.

Brother Walfrid's work for us, by reason of his vocation, was really a labour of love and until his death he was as keen as ever to hear how his "boys," as he termed the team, were doing. He must have spent a considerable period near the blarney stone in his young days, as his persuasive powers, once experienced, could never be forgotten".

Commenting on the passing of Brother Mark, one of Brother Walfrid's charges, the *Glasgow Observer* on 12th January, 1921 lamented;

FAMOUS MARISTS

"The recent death of Reverend Brother Mark, the headmaster of Saint Alphonsus Boys School, Glasgow recalls the fact that in his early days he was a junior in the Marist House in Charlotte Street. About that time, Brother Walfrid or slightly later, the head of the house was the late Brother Walfrid, one of the ablest and certainly one of the most popular Marists that Glasgow so far has known. Brother Walfrid was headmaster of the Sacred Heart schools, Bridgeton and was in all parochial matters a most useful henchman to Father Noonan, the founder of the parish.

To Brother Walfrid, more than to any other individual, was due the foundation of the Celtic Football Club, which first took being with the main purpose of providing funds for the Poor Childrens Dinner Table in the Catholic schools of the East End of Glasgow. Brother Walfrid, like Brother Mark, was a Sligo man and although the boys he trained in the Sacred Heart schools, Bridgeton are now the grandfathers of the congregation, his name and memory are deservedly held in unfading benediction."

Almost a century later, Brother Walfrid's name and memory remain deservedly held in unfading benediction and whilst there is a breath left in the Celtic support, that will stay the same, for eternity. Brother Walfrid was a man of the people and he, in turn, left us Celtic, the people's club.

WELCOME TO PARADISE

The Celtic's New Ground from the *Scottish Sport* on Friday 22nd July 1892

A GIGANTIC UNDERTAKING

"We had the pleasure and privilege of being shown over New Celtic Park one evening last week by John H McLaughlin. To those who are familiar with the spot where the club will in future be located, the magnitude of the undertaking will best be conceived. An old brickfield, half filled with water to the depth of forty feet or more is the last place on earth where one would expect any organisation to construct a modern athletic enclosure complete in every respect. Yet with that enterprise and practical application which has all along been characteristic of Celtic Football Club officials, the herculean task was undertaken with the least possible delay,

and, astonishing to relate, the result is the construction of one of the best, if not actually the finest ground in the kingdom. When we take into consideration Hampden and Ibrox Parks, with their well equipped grounds, and in a lesser degree Cathkin, we make bold to say that, with the latest addition, Glasgow can lay claim to be the first city in Britain so far as its athletic grounds are concerned.

A faint idea of the enormous difficulties with which the contractors of New Celtic Park had to contend may be gathered from the fact that almost the entire soil is foreign. The lowest estimate that could be obtained to cover up the great hole was 78,000 carts of earth. At the time of our first visit, (Thursday week), this extraordinary computation had been exceeded by 22,000 carts, and there was still a gap outside the rail, on the south east side, to fill up, something like 45 yards long, the last of the quarter mile hole. When it is further borne in mind that the club officials had practically to rely on their own efforts during the progress of the laying out of the ground in all its intricate detail, the wonder is how it was all managed. Yet there it stands today, the playing pitch looking as if the turf had existed there for many years.

The pitch has been carefully laid, and has been framed all round. The grass on it has been already cut three times. Water has been introduced into it at both ends, behind the goalposts, for the double purpose of watering the ground itself, and likewise both tracks. The ground is perfectly level, and once the three ton roller has made a few journeys over its surface, it will to appearances be quite like a bowling green. It is in playing condition meantime, and the opening match will see it tested publicly. We may say that the five a side competition on August 9th will be the first occasion on which the ground will be used, (this was postponed), and the annual sports on August 13th, for which a most elaborate programme has been arranged, will also take place there.

Everything is being pushed forward with that end in view, and the contractors are bound by agreement to have everything finished. From a spectator's point of view, New Celtic Park will satisfy the most exacting. Outside the playing pitch are the two tracks, and beyond the outer one the usual barrier has been carried right round. Some idea of the circumference may be gathered from the fact that it takes 1500 spectators to line it round and round. The spectators on the lowest level are raised six feet above the level of the playing pitch. There are tiers, three feet apart, with a gradual rise of twelve feet, so that everybody can see, and that comfortably. In this respect there is a decided improvement on both Ibrox and Hampden Parks. It has been a matter of progressive education with the public, so far as athletic grounds are concerned, and the improvements at other grounds have been accepted by the Celtic officials in the direction of further development, and that with highly satisfactory results.

A glance at the following little map will show exactly the locale of the new ground. anybody who was at old Celtic Park, (we only know one man who hasn't, and he happens to be a rugby light!), will have no difficulties in finding his way to the new home of the Scottish cupholders, a club which has endeared itself in the hearts of thousands everywhere.

Unlike Cathkin and Ibrox, there will be no ornamentation in the construction of the grand stands. "We have been followed the example of Queens Park FC," said Mr McLaughlin, "believing as we do, after mature deliberation, that a plain, substantial accommodating structure meets the demands of the public, in taking into further consideration the enormous profits on corrugated iron, a wooden structure is what is best for a football club". Finance is always a primary consideration, and the Celtic, while taking this step have spared neither time nor money in making their ground realise expectations.

The grand stands are two in number. One is erected on the north side on a parallel with Janefield Street. It commences 15ft, east of the Pavillion, and will be carried along 320ft, or 70ft longer than that of the Rangers

FC, which is the largest we have in Scotland. There will be 15 tiers of seats in it, or two more than at Rangers, giving accommodation for 1000 persons more. The entrances will be from the back. The stand on the other side is likewise, of wood. It is only partially erected, the contractors awaiting the filling up of the soil to permit of its being finished. (This was a trestle stand with terracing which initially took up only the western part of the pitch).

The Pavillion is likewise of wood, with a neat ornamental frontage. It rises to a height of 30ft, and is supported in front and centre by two rows of iron girders - four in each - one row in front, and the other in the interior. The interior consists of separate apartments for visiting and home teams, with separate doors, also separate lavatories, hot and cold baths - etc. There is also a club office with an entrance from behind. The portion immediately in front of the office with entrance at is utilised for a stairway leading to the hall above. Here visiting teams will be entertained and victualled on the premises. This arrangement has much to commend it, in as much as it enables all the players engaged in a match to participate in the after-meeting. Like other clubs, the Celtic were often at a disadvantage in this respect, frequently more than the half of the team being absent owing to the distance that had to be travelled to their usual place of entertainment. It will be a saving, not only of time, but, we believe of money also, which in itself as we have said, is always a consideration. Exclusive of painting, plumbing, slating, etc., the bare cost of the construction of the Pavillion is £500. Its appearance is enhanced by a balcony about 12ft above the floor level. The Pavillion will be reserved only for players and officials, an order which we believe will be rigorously enforced.

The press box is to be situated in the centre of the north stand, with a private entrance, and proper steps will be taken to ensure that it is reserved for members of the "fourth estate" exclusively.

The cycling track presents a rather singular yet withal pretty appearance. The top dressing is a material resembling a Sedona tyre, and its introduction was purely the result of an accident - a discovery which has already saved the club officials an immense amount of trouble and annoyance. If the material retains its solidity, its introduction in the construction of new tracks is a certainty. We were astonished when Mr McLaughlin told us that the completed portion had only been laid within a week. It was as hard as adamantine, and a wheel going over it would make little or no impression. The track originally was meant to be 3 and a half laps to the mile, but, we believe this has been exceeded.

The banking at the corners has been carefully looked after, special attention being directed towards making it the best in Scotland. It has a gradual rise from the inner edge, and is banked up to fully 4ft. Comparing it with Hampden and Ibrox tracks, the banking exceeds that of the former by 2ft, and the latter by 1 and a half foot. It is anticipated that our best strikers will be able to attain some marvellous performances upon it, in width it is 20ft all round, and 20ft in the finishing straight. The banking is carried well into the straights and riders will be able to negotiate them with the greatest freedom and safety. We tremble now for our Scotch records while the surface has been carefully looked after, due attention has been paid to the foundation, which is laid with bricks, every one of them being placed.

The width of the track is 20ft in the centre, with a gradual increase til the straight, (24ft), is entered. It is only to be expected that the surface will not quite be up to perfection at the start, but we make bold to say that the persons who will be most gratified and astonished with the track are the men mostly interested, viz, our Vogts, Lacailles, McLarens, Torrances, Campbells, etc, etc. Next season it will receive a much finer top dressing which will further perfect it. On the authority of a gentleman who has extensive experience of cycle tracks in England and Scotland, we are informed that it is the best track outside London. He considers the design and formation perfect, and once *the surface is improved slightly, and the dressing and drainage what it should be, the track will be simply perfect. as perfection is at the present day known. The track will be reserved exclusively for cycling. It is protected by a barricade all round. The inner track is for flat racing, and is divided from the cycling track by a patch of turf 2ft broad. It is 4 laps to the mile. It is a bit soft meantime, but that can only be expected. Its surface is different material from the cycle track, best mill-ground ashes being used for top dressing.*

We again visited the ground on Wednesday last, and were further delighted with the imposing appearance of what we believe rivals Ibrox Park, so far as accommodation is concerned. The whole is enclosed by corrugated iron. Mr McKay, the new Treasurer of the club has been superintending its construction since the undertaking was commenced on October 23rd, 1891. The last of the old ground erections were demolished on Wednesday - a sufficient indication that all will be right for the opening. In conclusion, we have to congratulate the Celtic club, and especially its officials, on the complete success of their gigantic venture. We wish them every measure of prosperity in their new home."

As Celtic Legend Neil Lennon said on the final day of the 2010/11 season;

"This isn't the end, this is just the beginning".